WEDGE

FROM PEARL HARBOR TO 9/11
HOW THE SECRET WAR BETWEEN THE FBI AND CIA
HAS ENDANGERED NATIONAL SECURITY

MARK RIEBLING

A TOUCHSTONE BOOK
Published by Simon & Schuster
NEW YORK   LONDON   TORONTO   SYDNEY   SINGAPORE

TOUCHSTONE
Rockefeller Center
1230 Avenue of the Americas
New York, NY 10020

First Touchstone Edition 2002

TOUCHSTONE and colophon are registered trademarks
of Simon & Schuster, Inc.

For information regarding special discounts for bulk purchases,
please contact Simon & Schuster Special Sales at
1-800-456-6798 or business@simonandschuster.com

Manufactured in the United States of America

1   3   5   7   9   10   8   6   4   2

The Library of Congress has catalogued the Alfred A. Knopf edition as follows:
Riebling, Mark.
Wedge: the secret war between the FBI and CIA / by Mark Riebling.
p.   cm.
Includes index.
1. Intelligence service—United States.   2. United States. Central Intelligence Agency.
3. United States. Federal Bureau of Investigation.   I. Title.
JK468.16R56   1994
327.12'0973—dc20   93-43703   CIP
ISBN 978-0-7432-4599-9

Grateful acknowledgment is made to the following for permission to reprint previously published material:

ATHENEUM PUBLISHERS: Excerpts from *The Night Watch* by David Atlee Phillips, copyright © 1977 by David Atlee Phillips. Reprinted by permission of Atheneum Publishers.

CURTIS BROWN LTD.: Excerpts from *My Silent War* by Kim Philby (Ballantine Books), copyright © 1983 by Kim Philby. Reprinted by permission of Curtis Brown Ltd.

WILLIAM COLBY: Excerpts from *Honorable Men: My Life in the CIA* by William Colby (Simon & Schuster, Inc., 1978). Reprinted by permission of the author.

HARPERCOLLINS PUBLISHERS, INC.: Excerpts from *Facing Reality* by Cord Meyer, Jr. (Harper & Row, 1980), copyright © 1980 by Cord Meyer. Reprinted by permission of HarperCollins Publishers.

INTERNATIONAL CREATIVE MANAGEMENT, INC.: Excerpts from *The Bureau: My Thirty Years in Hoover's FBI* by William Sullivan (W. W. Norton & Co., Inc.), copyright © 1979 by William Sullivan. Reprinted by permission of International Creative Management, Inc.

THE NEW YORK TIMES COMPANY: Excerpt from "FBI Is Said to Have Cut Direct Liaison with CIA" by Robert M. Smith, copyright © 1971 by The New York Times Company. Reprinted by permission of The New York Times Company.

RANDOM HOUSE, INC.: Excerpts from *The FBI-KGB War: A Special Agent's Story* by Robert J. Lamphere and Tom Shactman, copyright © 1986 by Robert J. Lamphere. Reprinted by permission of Random House, Inc.

TIMES BOOKS: Excerpts from *The Ends of Power* by H. R. Haldeman with Joseph DiMona, copyright © 1978 by H. R. Haldeman and Joseph DiMona. Reprinted by permission of Times Books, a division of Random House, Inc.

To Jessica Cohen

CONTENTS

Contents

WEDGE

FOR SPECIAL
SERVICES

ON MAY 25, 1941, Commander Ian Fleming entered the United States on a secret mission. He took a taxi from LaGuardia Field to Rockefeller Center, in midtown Manhattan, where he got out with his boss, Rear Admiral John H. Godfrey, the director of British naval intelligence. Flags of a hundred nations fringed the plaza's International Building, as if to advertise the many spy services within: America's Federal Bureau of Investigation on the 44th floor; the Japanese consulate on 35; and on 36, behind a door marked "Rough Diamonds, Ltd.," the British Secret Service. When Fleming later began writing novels, he would have his fictional James Bond shoot a Japanese cipher clerk here—hinting that this was based on the author's own killing of a Japanese agent, by "accidentally" crashing a construction sandbag through a window. As far as history can establish, however, Fleming's real purpose in America was at once more prosaic and more profound. In the words of a Most Secret British document, he was to help Godfrey "report on United States intelligence organizations," and "to coordinate them with those at the disposal of the United Kingdom." In practice, that would mean pushing for an American central-intelligence agency, and helping choose its chief.

The task fell mostly to Fleming, for the admiral had to handle such matters as the hunt for the German battleship *Bismarck*, and in any case it was Fleming's job, as an assistant, to read files and command facts. He began working closely on the project with station chief William Stephenson, a Canadian millionaire-inventor and former amateur lightweight boxing champion, cable address Intrepid. Stephenson's secret duties, performed under a cover as passport-control officer, included recruiting agents like actor-playwright Noël Coward to report on fascist sympathizers, and hiring Italian crime families to sweep the New York docks for Nazi spies. Another of Stephenson's tasks was to liaise with the Americans, and he had been urging them to create their own spy service while there still was time.

The problem assumed a new urgency on the day after Fleming arrived. Worried by Japanese aggressiveness in the Far East, President Franklin Roosevelt declared a full "state of emergency." On the eve of her inevitable entry into the worst war in world history, it was pathetic and dangerous that the United States had no brain trust to analyze foreign affairs, no espionage service to practice the darker arts of clandestine collection, no counterspy component to keep her secrets safe. America was not exactly a secret-intelligence virgin—General Washington had been helped by Nathan Hale and hurt by Benedict Arnold, and Pinkerton's detectives had caught Confederate spies for Abraham Lincoln—but the country still had no central intelligence.

Instead, Fleming learned, feuding U.S. intelligence chiefs had a jurisdictional "twilight-zone" problem. Two years earlier, Roosevelt had decreed that the FBI would handle spy work in the Western Hemisphere, while military and naval intelligence would cover the rest of the world. Although these "Big Three" were ordered to pool their efforts, that was easier demanded than done. If, for instance, the Navy was running a double agent in Hawaii, and he came to the continental U.S., must he then be handed over to the FBI? Naturally the Bureau thought so, and naturally the Navy thought not. When Roosevelt convened a Cabinet meeting on these matters in April 1941, all parties admitted that "a certain amount of twilight zone was inevitable," but the president did not see why it couldn't be overcome. In Britain, he observed, such matters were handled by "a gentleman known as Mr. X, whose identity was kept a complete secret." Why shouldn't America have its own Mr. X? The Big Three agreed that it would help to have a single coordinator; who that man should be, they would leave to the president.

The president had then turned to Winston Churchill. FDR did not especially like the prime minister or his alcoholically bombastic "curtain raising of history," but America needed British experience and advice. Admiral Godfrey and his young attaché had thus been invited to visit.

After sitting for a few days with Stephenson at Rockefeller Center—drinking gin and smoking Turkish cigarettes, digesting case histories and reviewing P-files (personality dossiers)—Fleming began to grasp that there was really one main obstacle to the centralization of American intelligence. So in early June, the British team boarded a train to Washington, to confront him.

• • •

As FLEMING RODE SOUTH on the Palmetto Express, anticipating a meeting with one of the world's most famous and admired men, he turned over in his mind what he had gleaned from Stephenson's big, baize-bound P-file on John Edgar Hoover. Stephenson had built a psychological profile, and the FBI director's personal life and background were emphasized, according to Stephenson's papers, because they were "regarded as fundamental to any understanding in London of a relationship that does not always run smoothly."

By conventional standards, Hoover was not an especially attractive person. He was short, and had been rejected on sight by his high school football coach. His squarish face was accentuated by a jutting jaw and a pug nose; the overall effect was of a bulldog. A childhood stutter had earned him the derisive nickname "Speed," until he conquered it, like the Greek orator Demosthenes, by secluding himself and practicing speeches. As with many who could not rely on natural gifts, he developed other ways of making himself liked. He was a collector of good jokes and anecdotes, a social drinker of Jack Daniel's, and when his friends had children, he ordered the FBI's Crime Lab to imprint their tiny toes on gold coins. But Hoover had also developed a general inwardness, a social self-reliance, a pride in his own privacy. He never married, did not date, and rarely accepted invitations to parties; when he did, he always brought along Clyde Tolson, his best friend and chief deputy. He didn't talk politics or philosophy, never voted, never put up a Christmas tree. He was undeniably intelligent, but not intellectual, and seemed to have assimilated a typically bourgeois view on matters of the mind, valuing education yet scorning ideas. There was a definite provincialism to his outlook; he had never left the United States, and "never trusted any foreigners," as his own men knew—not exactly a selling point for a prospective coordinator of foreign intelligence. His personal life centered on a fine city home crammed full of antiques, a perfectly tended garden, and two cairn terriers. Otherwise he cared for little but his work. "Hoover is a man of singleness of purpose," Stephenson's file had said, "and his purpose is the welfare of the Federal Bureau of Investigation."

His family had worked in Washington's bureaucracy since the Civil War, and Hoover, born on New Year's Day 1895, seemed to have inherited a special gene, or genius, for government work. He began at twenty-one, as an indexer at the Library of Congress, while going to night law school at George Washington University. Three years later, in 1919, he became a clerk in the Justice Department's General Intelligence Division; after five years of working Sundays, he was heading the department's Bureau of Investigation. The Bureau had existed since 1908, but had become a corrupt political police under the Harding administration; Hoover's defining innovation was to make it "clean." A strict code of conduct was imposed, and enforced less by punishment than by the sheer force of Hoover's personality. He also did his best to make the Bureau competent, substituting lawyers and accountants for patronage hacks, and promoting solely on merit. At the time, he was not yet thirty years old, but he knew what he wanted to do, and did it well. As Stephenson's file noted, Hoover's job was "both his pride and his vanity."

The truth of that assessment hit Fleming full force as he entered FBI headquarters at 9th Street and Pennsylvania Avenue, in downtown Washington. White tiles shone everywhere; workmen were repainting, cleaning, polishing. The British visitors trooped down a maze of corridors, past long rooms filled with chittering typewriters, against a stream of special agents in gray flannel suits and snap-brim hats. The whole place had the busy humming feeling of a bureaucracy actually at work. A receptionist took their names and showed them to a waiting room adorned with trophies of the FBI's famous cases, from Bolshevik bombings to the hunt for bank robbers like John Dillinger. Though it was an obvious attempt at image management, Fleming could not help being impressed. He knew the Bureau's successes were due partly to technological factors, such as tommy guns and fingerprinting, but even more to lessons Hoover had learned at the Library of Congress. Through so simple an innovation as comprehensive cross-referencing, both bureaucracy and criminal science had entered the information age.

So, too, had popular folklore and public relations. Hoover was not going to hide his bureaucracy under a bushel basket, and he had early learned the value of mass media, using radio and motion pictures to project the shining ideal of the government agent. In 1935 James Cagney, who had glamorized gangsters in *Scarface* and *Public Enemy*, reversed the aesthetic by playing a special agent in *G-Men*; from that moment, in the public imagination, Hoover's government agents were demigods. American myth had previously provided only individual heroes: solitary trappers (Daniel Boone), lone-gunslinger sheriffs (Wyatt Earp), crazy-ass all-purpose misfits (Buffalo Bill). There had been no collective order of virtue, no legion of honor, until Hoover's American Knights. Like King Arthur's men, Hoover's heroes were thought to be chaste, incorruptible, invincible, and they went around the country doing good deeds. As real knights had done in medieval times, Hoover's men literally kept roads safe for travelers and protected the country's treasure in its vaults. The FBI had almost a holy aura about it, and Hoover was showered on holidays with flowers, food, and candy. "If we didn't have Mr. Hoover and the FBI," one citizen wrote the editor of *Life* magazine, "I would like to know how you and I would exist."

In 1936, at the height of his popularity, Hoover had been given authority to track down foreign spies in the United States. After three years of good work in that field, President Roosevelt had cut him a full third of the U.S. intelligence pie—the whole Western Hemisphere. Now, in 1941, Hoover's undiminished popularity and power made him an attractive candidate for director of central intelligence. And his Bureau was definitely well fitted, in some key respects, to be the spy service Fleming foresaw.

The FBI was a virtual trap for facts. From almost two hundred field offices, more than two thousand special agents teletyped all new data daily to headquarters in Washington, where an army of clerks indexed it for easy retrieval. In the terminology of a later era, the FBI might be viewed as a giant computer made of human beings. That suited strategic intelligence, the construction of a big picture from an updatable universe of bits, as well as counterintelligence (CI), the thwarting of enemy spies. Both depended on accurate records, for one never knew in advance which bits of data might burn the enemy's agents or plans.

To get those bits, the Bureau had planted secret agents of its own. For the past few months, Hoover had been sending operatives of his Special Intelligence Service (SIS) into Latin America under cover as soap salesmen, stockbrokers, and journalists. The game could get dangerous, but SIS agents had been tutored in jujitsu, and were drilled in hip shooting and night firing with the pistol, shotgun, machine gun, and .30'06, .351, and Remington 81 rifles. More important, for purposes of secret intelligence, they were as "secure" a unit as any in the world, being well disciplined, highly motivated, and "clean" to a fault; none was likely to have the kind of character weaknesses that could lead to entrapment or blackmail by foreign powers. They were learning on the job and making some mistakes, but could be expected to improve, Fleming noted—provided they got proper tutoring from British experts.

That was perhaps the most important requirement, a willingness to work with London. For the past year, Stephenson had been trying to effect what his files termed "the closest possible marriage between the FBI and British Intelligence." Serious courtship had occurred in Bermuda, where mail sacks from the Pan Am Clipper were secretly taken to the basement of a pink hotel, there to be "chamferred" for secret writing by Nazi agents. Some take from that operation had been provided to SIS, which was now tangling covertly with at least four spy rings in the New York area. A member of one ring, William Sebold, had even been turned into a double agent; the FBI had installed Sebold in an office with a hidden camera and microphone, yielding legal evidence against the entire Nazi network, and had also set up for him a radio transmitter on Long Island, for the relay of misleading material to Berlin.

But Fleming knew that the very cases celebrated in the trophy displays, and other factors that made Hoover both popular and feared, did not necessarily make him a good spy chief. Indeed, Stephenson had recently been getting cold feet about the bride he had been wooing. The problems were built into the strengths.

FBI agents compiled a mound of data, for instance, but Hoover's policy discouraged them from analyzing it. A law enforcement officer's main duty was accurate collection of information—"just the facts"—and every memo disseminated outside the Bureau carried the caveat: "this document contains neither recommendations nor conclusions of the FBI." Putting the Bureau in charge of American spying might lead to a lot of prosecutor's briefs but very little strategic intelligence, since there would be no way to filter signals from noise.

Even if analysis were to become FBI policy, moreover, Fleming believed that the Bureau's criminal investigators should be flanked with teams of experts from different backgrounds. FBI agents were good sniffer-dogs, but they were not especially promising material for a brain-trust. Most struck Fleming as Irish-Catholic Texans from second-rate law schools, which not only invited British snobbery, but made it difficult to find plausible covers in places like Peru, where some SIS agents went around pronouncing *gracias* as "grassy-ass."

Hoover's dominant personality, so often a plus, also made him enemies. Secretary of War Henry Stimson thought him "a good deal of a prima donna," military intelligence chief Sherman Miles found him "very childish, petulant," and Stephenson believed the U.S. spy service "needed as its chief a man less rigid and sensitive to potential rivals."

Finally, intelligence work required a system of discipline less strict than Hoover's, one that did not crush creativity or imagination. Realizing that "impressions made by Special Agents on the public have a great deal to do with developing cooperation on the part of the public," the FBI had imposed a strict administrative code that extended even to a man's appearance and personal life. Agents had to wear dark suits, white shirts, and snap-brim hats; cut their hair two inches above the collar in back, and comb it *just so* on top so that there would be "no pointy heads"; they must keep a handkerchief in the right front pocket so no heroically firm handshake would be marred by "wet palms." Coffee was not allowed at desks, unmarried agents were not allowed to spend the night at girlfriends' apartments, and no FBI man must ever be drunk. The resulting white-knight mystique did ensure public cooperation, to the point where the flashing of an agent's gold badge was often enough to make an arrest, and a gun was almost superfluous. Most agents therefore tolerated such petty tyrannies, just as similar rules were endured by college football players or Marines, which many FBI men had once been, or by Catholics, which most FBI men still were. There was some logic to Hoover's tyranny; adherence to a common code solidified the FBI "team spirit," the sense of membership in a "family." Fear of The Boss did not sap this spirit, but rather made it possible. There was no "democracy" or "individuality" under Hoover, any more than there was a under a football coach like Knute Rockne, or a general like Pershing, or the Pope; if you were going to go up against Notre Dame, or the Nazis, or the Devil, without discipline enforced by fear of your coach, or your commanding officer, or the wrath of God, you weren't going to win. Still, strict enforcement of such regulations did create a certain climate of fear, and some of the brighter agents had quit because, as one put it, "I always had the feeling that someone was looking over my shoulder, checking up on what I was doing and how I was doing it. In fact, some of the FBI discipline verged on thought control."

Some reeducation had been attempted with Hoover's spy chief, Percy "Bud" Foxworth, who had gone to London in February for a crash-tutorial in spying. But his ten-week report card showed little progress. Fleming believed, as he would soon write in a secret memo to London, that the FBI spies were a "small and uncoordinated force," mostly "amateurs without special training," who "have no special means of communication," and seldom any clearer brief than "to go and have a look." FBI agents had been taught to look, but not to *see*; they thought only about arresting spies, and Stephenson struggled to keep them watching the Sebold ring instead of busting it up. Nor, alas, was much energy devoted to divining enemy plans. " 'Intelligence' in the United States generally means 'Security and Counter-espionage,' " Fleming would report. "The concept of 'Offensive Intelligence' is not well understood."

What Fleming meant by "offensive" had to include Stephenson's mischief on the docks. Britain was fighting for its very existence, and His Majesty's Secret Service was not going to let a few Yankee laws sink vital convoys in the North Atlantic. But neither was the FBI going to stand by idly while American laws were disobeyed, and Stephenson had warned Fleming that a "flap" was brewing over the recent murder of a suspected Nazi spy.

Still, Hoover seemed to be very much an antifascist. He had shown considerable courage in working secretly with British intelligence, given that the liaison might create an international crisis if exposed. Maybe, then, there still was hope.

Godfrey and Fleming were led through a large conference room, past a ceremonial desk, and into a small, plain, almost Spartan private office beyond. The furniture was old, and a small desk was piled high with papers and files. There sat forty-six-year-old J. Edgar Hoover. He struck Fleming as "a chunky enigmatic man with slow eyes and a trap of a mouth." But he received them graciously, and listened with close attention as the admiral urged him to help create a new intelligence system. Godfrey gently ticked down a list of British "wishes": an improved program to prevent naval sabotage, a special branch for the debriefing of war prisoners, a means to ensure the security of ciphers, a capacity to provide topographical target maps, a more thoroughly trained network of spies, a brain center to analyze intelligence, and, most important, a single coordinator to eliminate the twilight zones.

When Godfrey was finished, Hoover "expressed himself firmly but politely as being uninterested in our mission." Instead he complained, as Fleming had feared, about the British murder of a Nazi spy in New York. The Bureau had learned that a certain British sailor was telling U-boats where to intercept convoys, and Foxworth had shared that lead with Stephenson. Soon afterward, another FBI man had said to Stephenson, "Someone ought to give the treacherous son of a bitch the chop." Stephenson had chopped his own hand against his desk and said, "I already have." The special agent thought he was joking, but the sailor was found dead in a basement. Fleming had already heard Stephenson's side of the story, and felt the act was justified: "There was overwhelming evidence against the seaman. Killing him quickly perhaps saved hundreds of sailors' lives and precious supplies." But Hoover was having none of that. His willingness to work with the British, though inspired by genuine patriotism, would be conditioned above all by the interests of his Bureau. He would accept pilfered mail from Bermuda, but not dead men in Manhattan.

The admiral promised to relay Hoover's protests to Churchill, who was known to have great influence over Stephenson, but Hoover was not placated. As Fleming later noted, the FBI director's toes were "covered with corns," and the meeting ended sooner than the British expected. With the air of doing a favor, Hoover had his guests guided through the world-famous Crime Laboratory and down to the basement shooting range. Fleming was awed by "the shattering roar of the Thompsons in the big dark cellar," but he and the admiral left Hoover's headquarters reconvinced that intelligence and police work could not be made to mix.

Still, there was another option.

• • •

FLEMING FELT A TWINGE of excitement as the admiral lifted the brass knocker at William Donovan's Georgetown home, an old brick beauty. Fifty-one years later, it would host a victory party for a president-elect whom some called a draft evader, but for now it housed one of the most decorated men in American military history. Donovan answered the door himself, hugged the admiral, and shook Fleming's hand. He was husky, blue-eyed and silver-haired, fifty-seven years old, a millionaire lawyer, in an expensive suit sloppily worn. There was something in him of the overgrown leprechaun, and as he led his guests into a room of books and comfort, Fleming was already under the spell of Wild Bill.

No one knew where the nickname came from; they only knew that it fit. Some said it came from the Irish side of the tracks in Buffalo, where Donovan had grown up; some from Columbia University, where he had been a mediocre law student and star quarterback; others from the dark forests of the Argonne, where he led charges against German machine-gun nests in 1917. Still others said it derived from his stint as an assistant attorney general, during which Donovan had raided his own social club for violating Prohibition. The adjective also fit Donovan's crazy travel schedule, which was a principal reason the British were interested in him.

Roosevelt called him "My secret legs." An international law practice gave Donovan "businessman's cover," an excuse to travel the world on unofficial fact-finding missions for the wheelchair-bound president; he had gone into fascist-occupied Ethiopia in the 1930s, when no one else could get in, bringing back a complete report on Mussolini's troops, and had performed similar missions in a dozen other countries. By July 1940, he had been quietly moving around London, to determine whether His Majesty's subjects would survive the Battle of Britain. After he returned to Washington and urged FDR to loan Churchill some warships, British support for Wild Bill became practically a point of honor. Churchill had put Donovan in touch with Admiral Godfrey, who found him a worthy student in late-night tutorials on secret intelligence. Since then, Stephenson had befriended Donovan and convinced him of the need for a secret service. In fact, just before the Fleming-Godfrey mission, Stephenson had cabled London: "I have been attempting to maneuver Donovan into the job of coordinating all United States intelligence."

Donovan was sympathetic to British problems with the FBI. Although he himself had a decent working relationship with Hoover—when Donovan referred to him potential informants in Germany's U.S. underground in 1940, Hoover reciprocated by offering valuable contacts in the Far East—the two men also had a history of tangles tracing back to Donovan's days as assistant attorney general. In 1924, Donovan had reviewed Hoover's statutory authority for tracking communists and found it lacking. When Hoover uncharacteristically buried a Donovan request for justification, Donovan had to hound him into a "paper confession" about the illegality of his subversives index. There followed conflicts over Donovan's "borrowing" of agents for what Hoover considered improper purposes, mutual resentment over each other's perceived ambition, differences between Donovan's loose administrative style and Hoover's detail-mindedness. They made a stark study in contrasts, the dashing millionaire jock and the homely, hermitic bureaucrat, and Fleming could see why they clashed. The essential difference of temperament was perhaps shown best by their respective activities during the defining event of the age, the Great War. While Donovan had been in Europe bayoneting Germans, Hoover had stayed behind a desk at Justice, organizing index files. Donovan had become a hero, but Hoover remained a clerk. No matter how famous and powerful Hoover became, no one ever thought of calling him "Wild Edgar."

But while it was easy to romanticize Donovan, he did have his flaws, as the admiral had warned Fleming. Wild Bill tended to be an enthusiast, to think too broadly, to start projects and not follow through. He was not a "fact man," and for that reason was not considered an outstanding trial attorney. He could also be careless in matters of security. Five months earlier, Fleming himself had sent the potential intelligence chief, on the admiral's behalf, transcripts of German propaganda broadcasts ridiculing "Colonel Donovan" for losing secret papers at a nightclub in Sofia, Bulgaria.

The main problem with Donovan, though, was that he kept saying that he didn't really want the job of U.S. spy chief. He would do what he could to help form a new American secret service, and promised the British duo every facility in Washington; he was even putting them up at his house. But what he really wanted was to be a general with troops. The immediate task, Fleming informed London, was to "persuade" Donovan "to increase his personal interest in intelligence."

As appeals to his patriotism only pushed him toward the battlefield, the British team tried to engage him intellectually. Donovan was a soldier-jock with a curious mind; he not only seemed to have stepped from Plutarch's tales of ancient heroes, but had actually read, dog-eared, and underlined them. He confessed he would like someday to write a world history of spying, and as the admiral and Fleming supplied him with memoranda on subjects like the "security of intelligence sources [and] Cyphers," they could see him becoming excited, as a boy might be about building an airplane model. He asked them for their ideas, and they obliged with "details as to how U.S. intelligence could be improved in the common cause." Fleming closeted himself in a back room for two days, and produced longhand a sample charter and supporting notes. Above all, Fleming urged, America must centralize intelligence to gauge enemy intent. To that end, Donovan should infiltrate into the Axis nations, on neutral passports, officers with "trained powers of observation, analysis, and evaluation." These agents "should be under the protection of a strong government department," yet "should not be controlled by the FBI, which has no conception of offensive intelligence and is incapable of a strategic mentality."

Donovan was intrigued, and thereby hooked. He wrote a secret proposal for the president, sometimes following Fleming's words closely, but also adding ideas of his own. "Information is useless unless it is intelligently directed to the strategic purpose," Donovan wrote. "We have scattered through the various departments of our government, documents and memoranda concerning ... the Axis, which, if gathered together and studied in detail by carefully trained minds ... would yield valuable and often decisive results." But even though facing the "imminent peril" of "total war," the United States was "lacking in effective services for analyzing, comprehending, and appraising" information "relative to the intention of potential enemies."

Donovan sent his letter to the president on June 10; the move was part of a carefully timed gambit, and coincided with a British intelligence mission, that very evening, to the White House. Fleming himself did not get to see the president, but the admiral obtained an invitation to dinner with the Roosevelts, and told Donovan and Fleming about it when he got back, late that night. FDR had not actually been present for the meal, and the admiral had instead been lobbying Mrs. Roosevelt and two aides when the president suddenly wheeled himself in. He was in a puckish mood, and would brook no matters of state; everyone was ushered into the drawing room, where they watched a movie on snake worship in Laos. Afterward, Godfrey gained a private hour in the Oval Office, during which, as Fleming duly reported to London, the Donovan plan was "discussed with the President direct, and Colonel Donovan's qualifications as Coordinator of Intelligence were advocated to Mr. Roosevelt."

The president was an easy sell. He was getting so much information from so many departments, he admitted, that it would be good to have some kind of filtering, gatekeeping, sense-making mechanism. The next day, on June 11, he asked his appointments secretary to set up a long lunch with Donovan. Given the president's schedule, however, this meeting could not be arranged until a week later, on June 18—and during that interim there developed an intense bureaucratic counterattack.

Donovan had done his best to avoid this fight. The proposed agency, he had assured Roosevelt in his letter of June 10, would "neither displace nor encroach upon the FBI, Army, and Navy Intelligence, or any other department of the government." On June 11, after hearing from the admiral that he was probably "in," Donovan had even telephoned Bureau Assistant Director Edward Tamm, professing that his unit would "not in any way interfere with what the FBI was doing." But Tamm told him coldly that as far as Hoover was concerned, "a Controller was neither necessary nor desirable at this time," and soon the Big Three closed ranks against Donovan. "If there's a loose football on the field," G-2 (military intelligence) chief Sherman Miles warned his colleagues, "Wild Bill will pick it up and run with it." Only a month before, the Big Three had agreed that a coordinator was necessary, but now they reversed themselves: such an office would be "calamitous," "too cumbersome," "a positive detriment to . . . swift and secret action." The only area in which a coordinator might help was counterespionage, since foreign spies were constantly crossing turf lines, and even here the Big Three claimed to have "reduced [the] twilight zone as far as it is possible to do so."

But Roosevelt's mind was made up. Wild Bill went to the White House at 12:30 p.m. on June 18 and, as Fleming recorded, "was offered by the President and accepted the post of 'Coordinator of Intelligence [COI].' " Fleming cabled the news to Rockefeller Center, and Stephenson wired Churchill: "You can imagine how relieved I am after months of battle and jockeying in Washington that our man is in position."

There was, however, a hitch. Counterespionage—the one area, Hoover and the other chiefs had already agreed, where conflict was inevitable, and a coordinator needed—remained, under Roosevelt's rules, the single area in which jurisdiction was split. A wedge was to be driven between foreign and domestic spy-catching. Donovan's central-intelligence agency would work against enemy spies overseas; Hoover's FBI would continue to handle them at home. It would later become an article of faith, even among intelligence professionals, that this schism was effected because Roosevelt wanted to protect Americans' civil rights, which the president feared might be threatened by a superagency. In fact, the division was made for bureaucratic, not constitutional reasons. It was made to placate J. Edgar Hoover. It was necessary to divide counterespionage geographically, the White House announced, so that COI would not "supersede or duplicate . . . the Federal Bureau of Investigation."

This was, of course, a highly arbitrary way to carve out national-security duties. Why shouldn't American spy-hunters be allowed to follow spies' tracks continuously, wherever they led? "The jurisdiction was divided at the water's edge," complained Richard Helms, who later became one of Donovan's successors as U.S. spy chief. "When you are dealing with something that has both foreign and domestic aspects to it, the line has to be wavy. There is no other way to do it that I know of. It is like cutting a man down the middle."

To keep the two halves of the man from walking in opposite directions, Fleming knew, would be virtually impossible. A less severe division between internal security (MI5) and foreign intelligence (MI6) had been causing its own share of friction in London, and Fleming himself would soon help handle, in Lisbon, one special project that was widening the MI5-MI6 wedge. If such disputes were to be minimized in the U.S., there would have to be close liaison between Donovan and Hoover, who did not like each other. Indeed, Hoover's previous pro-forma helpfulness had begun to change once Donovan seemed likely to become FDR's official legs; already he had rallied the Big Three against COI, which he reportedly called "Roosevelt's Folly."

Sensing that Hoover's resistance would only stiffen, Fleming went out of his way to suggest a palliative strategy. Lest COI be "still born," he counseled Donovan on June 27, it was crucial to "enlist the full help of the FBI . . . by cajolery or other means." This would require good "liaison officers," but things could be taken beyond that. Why not, Fleming wondered, seek billeting in Hoover's headquarters at Justice? His building was "secure, and [had] central communications," and putting COI so close at hand might mollify J. Edgar. Likewise, counterespionage, where Bureau collaboration would be crucial, could be conducted by "a nominee of Mr. Hoover." The important thing was to make an overture of peace.

Wild Bill gave it a try. That very day, he solicited an appointment with the FBI director, but Hoover was not available to see him. Rebuffed but resolute, Donovan spoke instead with Assistant Director Tamm, saying he wanted "to allay any fears." His new unit, Donovan said, was merely to be "a laundry" through which the material of other agencies would be "ironed out and distributed." He said he had not sought the COI job and did not want it, but, now that he had it, he wanted his people to visit the Bureau and emulate its administrative expertise. He even proposed an "advisory group," which he hoped the Bureau would join.

Tamm said he would consult "the boss," and Fleming took that as evidence the Americans were "taking steps to put their own house in order." If Donovan assumed his coordinating duties "with vigour and speed," Fleming recorded as his mission finished in July, there was no reason why U.S. intelligence should not become "an extremely valuable offensive weapon." As if in promise of that, Donovan had given him, as a parting gift, a .38 Police Positive revolver, inscribed: "For Special Services."

WEDGE

Fleming carried the gun with him as he caught the Clipper to Lisbon, proud of his role in helping the Americans create a central intelligence agency. He had no idea, at the time, just how utterly his visit had failed to eliminate the American twilight-zone problem. Nor had Fleming any inkling, as he left New York, that he was about to meet the man who would become his real-life model for James Bond, and whose case was about to be passed into the Hoover-Donovan twilight zone, where it would be bungled in a way that brought America into the war.

BOOK ONE

THE WAR
AGAINST
WILD BILL

CHAPTER ONE

THE TRICYCLE
TRUST

AT 2:30 P.M. ON TUESDAY, August 12, 1941, a secret agent entered
the United States with information that Japan was planning to bomb
Pearl Harbor. Tan, hatless, twenty-nine years old, he disembarked from
a Boeing 314 Flying Boat, the Pan-American Clipper from Lisbon, and
lolled across LaGuardia Field. Deep Slavic lines ran from the wings of his
nostrils to the corners of his lips. His straw-brown hair was brushed
straight back, parted on the right, and receding at the temples, giving the
face a heart-shaped look. His passport declared him to be Dusan M.
Popov, a native of Yugoslavia. Only a few days earlier, in the Lisbon
suburb of Estoril, he had been shadowed by Ian Fleming; many years
later, he would recognize some of his own adventures in Fleming's first
novel, *Casino Royale*.

After an hour in Immigration, Popov obtained a six-month visa and
caught a cab to Manhattan. He checked in at the Waldorf Astoria Hotel,
showered, ate a room-service sandwich, and inventoried his gear. It all
seemed in order. There was $58,000 in small bills, provided by the Ger-
mans, plus $12,000 he'd made by staking the German money in Lisbon;
four telegrams, individually folded in five-by-seven-inch sheets of thick
white paper; a codebook for secret radio transmissions to Berlin, disguised
as a hardbound popular novel; the torn half of a business card, to present
to a contact who would give him a radio; and one vial of white crystals,
soluble in two ounces of distilled water, to make invisible ink. Satisfied,
and anxious to see the city, Popov locked his suitcases and pushed them
into the closet, marking their exact positions, by his own account, "with
faint pencil lines and a single hair secured by saliva."

He walked out of the Waldorf and down Park Avenue, then crosstown at 42nd Street, to Broadway. Nowhere in the world, he thought, was there a feeling of so much sex and money and light. Passing an automobile showroom, he admired a maroon Buick Phaeton with red leather upholstery and a black sliding sunroof. Ten minutes later, he had bought the car and been guaranteed delivery, registration included, the following day. When he returned to his room at the Waldorf, he was high on the promise of American efficiency, and conscious that he mustn't let it affect performance of his mission.

Routinely he unlocked the closet and stooped to check his suitcases. Someone had disturbed them; they were no longer aligned with the tiny hashmarks, and the hair was missing. Had a hotel valet tried some petty theft? Nothing was missing. Hitler's Abwehr? He doubted they would have assigned anyone to check on him. The FBI? That was probably it. Calling it part of the game, he went to bed early, to be ready for what he assumed would be an early-morning meeting with his new handlers.

Five days passed, but no one called. Popov opened a checking account, took delivery of his car, and sat on his bed by the telephone. So much for American efficiency.

Not until August 18 did he get the call. Not until the day after that, in a hotel room near Pennsylvania Station, was he finally meeting with Assistant Director Foxworth of the FBI.

They talked for three hours. Popov, who went by the nickname "Dusko," explained that he had originally been recruited by German intelligence, the Abwehr, to operate in London, but hated the Nazis for overrunning his homeland, and for the past year had really been working for the British under the code-name "Tricycle" to deceive Berlin. The British had learned the basics of such deception from the Soviets, who in the 1920s had created an "anticommunist" spy network, the Trust. Since the Trust attracted genuine anticommunists but was infiltrated by informants, it posed no threat to the regime, yet it did serve as a convenient conduit for false information. British intelligence had been badly burned by the Trust—its "Ace of Spies," Sidney Reilly, had been sucked into its operations, compromised on a mission to Moscow, and was never seen again—but the lesson had been learned and was being employed against a new enemy. The British had created their own "Trust" of German agents, and so controlled virtually all Abwehr spies in Britain. To preserve German confidence in Popov, MI6 not only arranged for him to pass carefully screened secrets but concocted life histories of spies he had allegedly recruited. By summer 1941 the Germans believed Popov to head a whole network of agents, and had given him $60,000 to pay those nonexistent sources.

He had received that sum in Lisbon, but there had been a hitch. He was supposed to hand the cash to MI6, but was stuck with it until his next scheduled contact. That would not happen, however, until MI6 settled a dispute with MI5, who felt they should have been told earlier about the case. Ian Fleming's Naval Intelligence status had made him a good neutral party to watch Popov until the matter was resolved, and Fleming had followed the double agent through a smoky Estoril casino. As Popov later told it, Fleming watched from the fringes while Popov cleaned out the local braggart, a Lithuanian count. At one juncture Popov counted $50,000 onto the green felt, but the Lithuanian didn't have enough cash to match that bet and went home humiliated. Afterward Fleming went over to Popov, bought drinks, and introduced himself. He was impressed not simply because Popov had shown nerve but because he had in the process increased the operating funds available to British intelligence.

Since Popov had seemingly been so successful in England, the Germans had now sent him to the United States to rebuild the Sebold spy ring, which had been decimated by mass FBI arrests two months before. Popov told Foxworth he would contact five or six persons on an Abwehr list, but instead of trying to recruit them for the Nazis, he would secretly try to "turn" them to work for the United States. He was also supposed to supply answers to an espionage questionnaire concerning Pearl Harbor's defenses, provided by his superiors in Berlin at the behest of their Japanese allies. With FBI help, however, Popov would furnish false responses, to misdirect any pending Japanese attack.

Foxworth asked to see the questionnaire. Popov reached into his briefcase and unwrapped four telegrams. "They contain a new and very ingenious method of communication," he explained, angling one of them under a lamp. Each telegram hid a dot containing microtext queries about U.S. Pacific defenses.

Foxworth seemed amazed. Whole pages on the dot of an "i"? If that was true, it was something new and sensational. He would send it for analysis to the Bureau's lab, on the next train to Washington.

Popov hoped that the microdots would indeed be developed and disseminated quickly. It would also take time to select false "feed" intelligence and relay it to Berlin, to mislead the Axis in case of any pending attack.

Foxworth nodded sympathetically—but told Popov they'd have to wait "to get specific instructions from Mr. Hoover."

Popov wondered at the delay. Already a whole week had been lost. Weren't there other U.S. agencies involved? In England, authorities had formed a special double-agent committee, composed of representatives of all the various intelligence services—naval, military, internal security— to deduce Axis war plans from the kinds of questions posed. There was some inevitable rivalry between internal security and foreign intelligence, between MI5 and MI6, but that was all the more reason to be sure that everything was coordinated, because running double agents, like assembling strategic intelligence, was a tremendous undertaking that required interagency cooperation.

"I know," Popov would later quote Foxworth as saying. "That's the trouble. Theoretically, the FBI is concerned only with counterespionage in the United States. Believe me, Mr. Hoover is doing a marvelous job of that, but he is limiting his intelligence activities to that alone. I'm not sure he is eager to allow other services to mix in our work."

AS IT HAPPENED, one other agency needed desperately to mix in the FBI's work, or at least to share in its product. At nine-thirty every workday morning, a secret team of scholars met at the Library of Congress, in Washington, D.C., in a room dominated by a strategic map of the world. Their top priority, according to meeting minutes, was to obtain "a general picture of the situation in regard to Japan." Formally called the Board of Analysts, though also known as the "College of Cardinals" or the "Bad Eyes Brigade," they worked for William Donovan's COI.

Overseeing COI's Far East efforts was Kenneth Landon, a philosophy professor on leave from Earlham College. When he reported for his first day of work and swung open the door of his office, it hit somebody.

"Good morning, sir," said a tall young man in a seersucker suit. "My father sent me over to see whether I can help out."

It was Captain James Roosevelt, the president's son; everyone called him Jimmy. His job, he told Landon, was politely to pressure other intelligence agencies into turning over "all information bearing on national security," as his father's edict required. By charter, COI could not investigate enemy espionage in the United States, and Donovan had yet to establish his own collection channels overseas; he had dispatched a lone secret agent to the East, but the man had not reported back. Detection of Axis war plans would thus depend on getting information from other agencies. Just how badly Landon would need such outside input was clear when he was given access to a locked four-drawer cabinet labeled "Southeast Asia Intelligence." Three drawers held nothing; the last, a sealed docket stamped "Top Secret," contained two magazine articles recently clipped by COI, both of them written by Landon.

So, on August 19, as Foxworth was interviewing Popov in New York, Landon dispatched liaison officer Roosevelt to FBI headquarters to ask for information on the Far East. Although Hoover now promised to do "anything and everything possible to assist and cooperate with" Donovan, as COI files recorded, Jimmy Roosevelt was skeptical. Despite Donovan's June 27 overtures to Tamm, Hoover had refused to appoint an adviser to COI, declined to help set up a good paper flow, and failed to recommend a candidate for counterintelligence chief.

But Roosevelt let those issues lie, and pressed one other matter. On the day before, he said, COI had set up an Oral Intelligence Unit in New York City, for the debriefing of foreigners who arrived by Pan Am Clipper. Since the FBI was already doing that, and since it would take place domestically, COI would naturally reserve its debriefings to persons referred by the Bureau—but it was vital to have those referrals. Hoover did not disagree, but asked that Donovan send over a memo detailing the nature of COI's "foreign-intelligence" interest in such domestic debriefings.

The next morning, Jimmy Roosevelt went to his In box and read the memo Donovan had prepared for Hoover. Noting that "much useful information might be obtained from covering the arrival of Pan American Airways passengers," especially regarding "questions bearing on military information," Donovan asked to be made part of the process. "In doing this, however, I don't want in any way to interfere with what you may be doing. Therefore, before attempting anything along this line, I wanted to take it up with you."

On the surface, it was a reasonable enough request. But Roosevelt knew enough about interagency politics, and the geographical division between COI and FBI, to realize that coverage at American ports was an area of potential dispute. Pan Am's New York gangways brought foreign travelers, but were they a foreign or a domestic concern? The answer, of course, was both. He just hoped J. Edgar would see it that way.

ON SEPTEMBER 17, five weeks after Popov's arrival by Pan Am Clipper, FBI headquarters sent Rockefeller Center a translation of the microdot questionnaire. As Foxworth read it, he could discern what seemed a clear Axis military interest in Pearl Harbor. Popov was supposed to determine:

1. Exact details and sketch of the situation of the State Wharf and the power installations, workshops, petrol installations, situation of Dry Dock No. 1 and the new dry dock which is being built.
2. Details about the submarine station (plan of situation). What land installations are in existence?
3. Where is the station for mine search formations? How far has the dredge work progressed at the entrance and in the east and southeast lock? Depths of water?

4. Number of anchorages?
5. Is there a floating dock in Pearl Harbor or is the transfer of such a dock to this place intended?
Special task—Reports about torpedo protection nets newly introduced in the British and U.S.A. navy. How far are they already in existence in the merchant and naval fleet?

This was not the first time Foxworth had seen evidence of German curiosity about Pearl Harbor. Five months earlier, after a known German agent, Ulrich von der Osten, had been run over by an automobile in Times Square, FBI agents had searched his room at the Taft Hotel and discovered a detailed report on defenses at Pearl and nearby Hickham Field. Written in cursive on ocean-liner stationery, the report referred to maps and photographs "of interest . . . to our yellow allies," which had apparently been sent to Berlin. But now Popov was asking for some of the same information. Was the Abwehr merely testing him, by asking questions to which it already knew the answers? If so, couldn't this mean that the Germans had lost confidence in him?

Foxworth himself had reasons to sour on Popov. On September 1, without consulting his handlers, the double agent had moved into a penthouse apartment on the twenty-second floor of a brand-new building at 530 Park Avenue, at the corner of 61st Street. Foxworth sent some agents to inspect the place, and it was pretty damned nice—high above the noise of the city, lots of sunlight, and Popov had even hired a Chinese servant. At that rate, Foxworth had to wonder how long the Abwehr's cash was going to last.

Then there was the "playboy problem." The Bureau kept a close surveillance on Popov's penthouse, and it did not go unnoticed that he conquered the French starlet Simone Simone one morning, and in the afternoon seduced her mother. The man was simply a swordsman. Because he made a habit of bedding two women at once the story went around that this was how he earned the cryptonym "Tricycle." He was also driving around with a married woman, an English fashion model who was supposed to be flying to Reno for a divorce. That last put the brass in a sticky position, because the Bureau was charged with enforcing the Mann Act, which made it a crime for men to transport women across state lines for immoral purposes. When confronted about his life-style, Popov countered that he should be judged by his work, by the "results."

As it happened, "the results" presented the biggest problem of all. After nearly three months in America, Popov had failed to contact a single Nazi spy. His secret-ink letters to Abwehr mail drops went unanswered. He claimed he didn't really expect to hear from the Germans until he'd secured an operator for his radio station, but Foxworth wondered whether Popov wasn't simply an opportunist who'd been used up. The British had just given him over—and when the British services gave you anything, you had to look at it closely. The whole Donovan business had finally proved that the British, helpful as they sometimes were, could not be fully trusted.

But the case must go on anyway. The existence of von der Osten's data and Popov's questionnaire would conduce to a double-agent game. Knowing some of what Berlin already knew, the Bureau could tailor its lies to that prior base of truth. In November, Foxworth therefore sent Popov to Brazil, to give his torn half of a business card to an Abwehr contact who would arrange for Popov to pick up a radio transmitter, which Foxworth would then use to pass lies about Pearl Harbor's defenses. To make those lies credible, Foxworth turned to Naval Intelligence, giving them Popov's questions on September 25 and asking for false answers, "the reliability of which the Germans would not be able to check on." If all went well, Popov might be sending false data to Berlin by January 1942.

Foxworth meanwhile wondered whether he should pass the Pearl Harbor queries to Donovan. That would be a simple matter, for Foxworth's assistant, Arthur Thurston, was in contact several times weekly with Donovan's New York office. But Foxworth sensed that the Popov queries were not merely routine Pan Am passenger intelligence, such as COI kept asking about. He also knew that Hoover had no great affection for the coordinator of information. Foxworth would do no special favors for COI, then, without an okay from the boss.

BY MID-SEPTEMBER 1941, Donovan was becoming frustrated. The bureaucratic reality of his work was considerably less enticing than he had been led to expect by Ian Fleming and British intelligence. He could barely get enough furniture for his offices, let alone information for his officers. He had recruited foreign-area analysts from universities like Michigan and Yale, but when they showed up he could only house them in buildings vacated by the Public Health Service, down by the breezeless Potomac River. Medical researchers left behind some animals in cages, and, naturally, office jokes arose over "whether to put the monkeys on the payroll—if there was ever going to be a payroll." News of the working conditions somehow reached Berlin, which ridiculed Donovan's new unit as "50 professors, 20 monkeys, 10 goats, 12 guinea pigs, and a staff of Jewish scribblers." But no one laughed when an infected monkey bit a secretary, and neither she nor the other women would go near the building until a solution was arranged. So Donovan's employees arrived at work one morning in early fall to see smoke coming from an incinerator chimney, while their director chatted on the steps outside with Jimmy Roosevelt. Under such conditions, with the stink of frying rhesus fur and no intelligence, it seemed absurd to even attempt a "strategic picture" of Japanese intent.

But assembling just such a picture was the first and primary task assigned by the president, and Donovan did not want to disappoint. So on September 15, when he finally got an answer to his August 20 letter about Pan Am passengers, Donovan was cheered by Hoover's pledge "to instruct my Special Agents to obtain any information that you desire from the incoming passengers, and see that this information is promptly relayed to you." But as September turned to October, the FBI seemed to be sending only trivia, such as the report of a rice riot in Yokkaichi, "during which many were hurt." Donovan's carefully phrased thanks—"We will want to make use of this in a study we are now making of the Pacific situation"—served as a tactful reminder that he was interested in seeing anything the Bureau might possess about Japanese war plans. He nudged Hoover again on December 2, when they attended a luncheon with representatives of G-2 and ONI about possible Pacific threats. The next day, Hoover sent over intelligence from a missionary who had just returned from Japan, which revealed nothing about Tokyo's intentions.

Far more helpful was news that same morning from Donovan's lone secret agent in the East. In three months undercover as a correspondent for the Chicago *Daily News*, Edgar Ansel Mowrer had tried to find patterns of travel by Japanese "businessmen"—spies—who might be casing Pacific targets. From Saigon, Hanoi, Djakarta, Singapore, Bangkok, Rangoon, and Hong Kong, Mowrer had found his way to the Philippines, where sources reported a Japanese war fleet sailing west. Mowrer suggested that the Japanese were going to "do something soon." Information obtained from the War and Navy Departments by Jimmy Roosevelt confirmed that a Japanese flotilla was massing for action, and Donovan's Far East analyst, Landon, also foresaw a Pacific offensive. A recent U.S. oil embargo had raised tensions with Tokyo, and the replacement in October of moderate Prime Minister Prince Fumimaro Konoe by militant General Hideki Tojo, who declared that "the essence of freedom is to live and die for the state," seemed to confirm a new Japanese aggressiveness. Donovan began telling his deputies that the U.S. would somehow be drawn into the war "before the end of the year." By December 4, FDR had explicitly ordered him to examine U.S. Pacific defenses against possible Japanese raids.

In a final attempt to figure out what was happening, COI officer Ferdinand E. Mayer approached Saburo Kurusu, a special Japanese envoy who had been dispatched to Washington. Squeezing through a hostile crowd

outside the Japanese Embassy on Massachusetts Avenue, Mayer visited
Kurusu at 11:00 a.m. on the morning of Saturday, December 6. The two
had met during diplomatic service in Peru in the 1930s, but Kurusu was
not his typical self; even in the embassy's drawing room, he kept turning
his head to see if anyone was approaching. There was extreme danger,
Kurusu said, of war with the United States; "hotheads could upset the
applecart at any time."

Mayer's mission seemed to confirm Donovan's darkest suspicions. The
key question now was not whether or even so much *when* the Japanese
flotilla would attack, but *where*.

POPOV'S PEARL HARBOR questionnaire might have been of some value
to COI analysts trying to puzzle out Japanese plans. The Germans had no
forces whatsoever in the Pacific, so it was likely they were doing a favor
for their Japanese allies. Perhaps, then, Popov's questions might hold clues
to Tokyo's intent. It might have occurred to an intelligence analyst that
the Japanese were interested in Pearl Harbor's torpedo defenses because
they were considering bombing Pearl Harbor with torpedoes.

But the FBI did not employ intelligence analysts. If other agencies
wanted to analyze Bureau-supplied information, that was fine with the
Bureau, and in October a paraphrase of the entire questionnaire had been
passed to Naval Intelligence. Yet that was only for purposes of deception,
without sourcing or context, with no particular urgency attached to the
request. Consequently, no deceptive data had yet been transmitted by
Popov, who on December 7 was still in South America, arranging for
delivery of his transmitter. Nor was ONI, in any case, the agency charged
with putting together "a general picture of the situation in regard to
Japan." That was the job of the Far East Division at Donovan's COI.

In hindsight, it would seem obvious that the Bureau should have shared
Popov's questions with the fledgling central-intelligence agency. But Hoover had reasons for not wanting to give Donovan sensitive information,
and some of them were good ones.

As early as June 27, when Donovan consulted Tamm, Hoover had
sensed that Wild Bill's overture was at least partly an attempt to soften
the Bureau's position. It didn't take much knowledge of Donovan's character to disbelieve his protestations that COI would be doing only memo-
laundering, but that laundry function alone was a threat, since it meant
that Hoover would be reporting to the president *through* Donovan, which
amounted really to reporting *to* Donovan, at least on intelligence matters.
Donovan's true intentions, moreover, blew back to Hoover through the
FBI director's many gossip channels in government. At the end of July, a

source reported that "Donovan is taking it very easy in the new position; that he plans to continue to do so for about a month, after which he will let it be known that he is the man behind the scenes." To snuff out any bureaucratic opposition in the delicate early days, it seemed, Wild Bill was putting on a mild front.

If that was his plan, it didn't work. An informant relayed rumors that soon a special someone-else "would be appointed to take the place of Donovan . . . as coordinator of intelligence activities." The source, according to a Bureau summary, had heard that "many Senators and others on the Hill . . . are particularly opposed to Donovan, they believing he is a publicity-seeker and will use this position merely to build himself up. [Source] stated that strangely enough this opposition comes mostly from the isolationists he is acquainted with, and, also strangely enough, this group favors Mr. Hoover for such a position." From the White House, too, there were rumors that "the President would be very receptive to a suggestion that Mr. Hoover take over COI . . . as he felt that the operation of COI had been a miserable failure . . . and a waste of money." Given that Hoover still had a shot at being director of central intelligence, he certainly wouldn't go out of his way to consolidate Donovan's position.

Nor was Hoover going to jump through hoops for Jimmy Roosevelt just because he was the president's son. The boy was insufferably spoiled and arrogant, and would drop by without notice, then not return calls. It apparently did not occur to him that he had no right to inconvenience others, or exploit his father's position; he seemed to feel the normal rules didn't apply to presidential families. By December, Hoover had discreetly taken the "Jimmy problem" to one of the president's assistants. According to an FBI memo, "Certain faux pas committed by James Roosevelt in the Donovan office and the problem of having him removed to another agency were discussed."

While Jimmy Roosevelt was busy mucking things up, another irritant emerged: the contents of a Bureau file on Donovan. In the November 21 issue of *Collier's* magazine, a columnist asked an FBI source whether the Bureau was sending Donovan all intelligence having a bearing on national security. The answer: "Donovan knows everything we know, except what we know about Donovan." Although Hoover wrote Wild Bill to assure him that "the Bureau does not possess any information concerning you," the Bureau had, in fact, been keeping a file on Donovan since 1924, when he reported the theft of a motorcar, and it was being updated even as Hoover denied its existence. In this file was a 1936 report that Donovan was collecting "anti–G-men material" and conspiring "to have the Director fired" if Republicans ever returned to power. Scraps collected throughout the fall of 1941 included the fact that "from time to time news stories have made reference to Colonel Donovan being a logical successor to the present Director of the Federal Bureau of Investigation."

Such allegations could be written off as typical products of the capital's rumor mill, but other reports indicated that Donovan was a poor administrator who did not really have his unit under control. One informant, who went to COI's offices to discuss secret matters, reported to Hoover that "The undisciplined atmosphere . . . sort of playing and not working and of 'boondoggling' struck me when I observed the secretaries in the anterooms. . . . In spite of the fact that the talk was to have been confidential, people kept coming in and going out of the room and [one of Donovan's men] dropped in and put his feet on the desk." Donovan had hired Hawaiian Pineapple Company President Atherton Richards, regarded as a brilliant executive, to be his right-hand man for administration, but Donovan himself was "totally unfit temperamentally to administer any such agency," as one source told Hoover.

Perhaps most damningly, Donovan's personal behavior suggested that COI was an unsafe repository for secrets. Wild Bill's loss of secret papers in a Sofia nightclub was only one of the serious security breaches. Donovan's own chief of research and analysis, Stanley Lovell, recalled that the COI chief "drove his security officers, Weston Howland and Archibald Van Buren, to the brink of despair. . . . [He] would talk about the most secret affairs at a cocktail party or a dinner, according to our chief of security, and be furious if he were criticized for it." Some tidbits in FBI files even suggested that Donovan might be vulnerable to blackmail by hostile powers. When a suspected Mussolini agent was arrested in July 1941 for impersonating a U.S. government employee, the man's attorney "claimed he had something on Col. Donovan," and that if Donovan refused to get his client off, they "would make a public matter of him."

Hoover had immediately notified Donovan of that threat, and it is unclear what resolution was ever effected, but the Bureau began to link Donovan with other presumedly fascist elements. For instance, Donovan had become "a very good friend of" Count John Perdicari, the U.S. representative of an Italian tobacco firm, who was "believed to be a German spy." Perdicari seemed to know a good deal about Donovan's various trips to Europe, and "Donovan was believed to have been asked to use his influence in obtaining a visa for Count de Perdicari to return to Italy." FBI documents also noted that "Donovan's name has been associated with German activities," including the Friends of New Germany, an organization run by an "active Nazi propagandist," located "on the same floor as the German Consul at 17 Battery Place." Donovan had even reportedly made some attempts to contact the anti-Semitic publisher of the *American Gentile*, and was listed as a reference by a suspected Nazi sympathizer who held "key positions in both industry and government in California."

No substantive proof was ever uncovered of wrongdoing by Donovan in his relations with suspected fascist agents. In fact, the Bureau was probably only uncovering Donovan's efforts to recruit agents with good fascist "credentials" for secret work in Europe. But hearing that Donovan was "a very good friend of . . . a German spy" could hardly have encouraged Hoover to share the "take" from anti-German agents such as Dusko Popov. Even if the Bureau had analyzed Tricycle's Pearl Harbor questionnaire as strategic intelligence, Hoover's rational concern for operational security—or, from another perspective, the efficiency of his witch-hunts —would probably have kept Popov's queries from Donovan. "With the distrust of Donovan's outfit that existed because of his lax security, Hoover wouldn't have passed him anything that was truly sensitive," ventured FBI agent Lawrence F. McWilliams, who reviewed Bureau documents of the period. "I don't think *anybody* in their right mind would have passed him a damn thing."

So Hoover didn't. As Donovan's files recorded, COI was "consistently . . . denied the privilege of taking part in these [Pan Am passenger] interrogations, even though incoming passengers and crews have information which is of primary interest to this agency." Nor was the Pearl Harbor questionnaire ever furnished to COI. The full, original text remained in Hoover's files on Sunday, December 7, 1941.

Hoover, it must be noted, was not the only one to hold back on Donovan. Security concerns had caused Army Chief of Staff George C. Marshall to deny COI access to intercepted Japanese cable traffic, known as "Magic," which might have provided clues to Tokyo's intentions. Perhaps it was such security worries—coupled with jurisdictional delicacies, and an active desire to see America enter the war—that had also kept the British, despite their backing of Donovan, from sharing Popov, or his Pearl Harbor intelligence, with COI.

But whereas Donovan was soon able to engineer cooperative arrangements with the U.S. military, as well as with the British, a truce with Hoover would always elude him. Instead of shocking the rivals out of petty bureaucratic bickering, America's formal entrance into the war only exacerbated the conflicts that came from cutting a man down the middle. Though created to placate the FBI director, this geographical division of counterintelligence duties would only excite Hoover's ire over the next years and decades, when Donovan, and a half-dozen CIA directors, repeatedly and necessarily breached it.

CHAPTER TWO

NO-MAN'S-LAND

IT WAS JUST BEFORE midnight on December 7 when Donovan was ushered in to see the president. The Oval Office was dark, and Roosevelt sat alone in a pool of light cast by his desk lamp. He was tired and pale. "They caught our ships like lame ducks," he told Donovan. "Lame ducks, Bill! They caught our planes on the ground! It's a good thing you got me started on this intelligence agency." Donovan did not know about Tricycle's questionnaire, and therefore could not have mentioned it, but he did complain that the military, the FBI, and everyone else had been holding back. To obviate such interagency problems, he asked for a presidential order authorizing him to collate "strategic information" in the Americas.

Armed with that order, issued two days later, Donovan began building a network of agents in the Western Hemisphere, which previously had been Hoover's private preserve. He also started assembling, in earnest, a colorful and talented yet deeply flawed roster of personnel—making Donovan's unit both the most celebrated and romanticized outfit in the war, from the public point of view, and one of the most overrated and incompetent, to Hoover and the FBI. In the months after Pearl Harbor, these personnel differences were admixed with questions of turf. The resulting patterns of conflict would run deeper, and last longer, than any personal hostility between Hoover and Donovan, and would be carried over, with the foreign-domestic dichotomy, at the official creation of CIA.*

HOOVER'S HEROES WOULD never have found themselves working, like so many of Wild Bill's, down behind Washington, D.C.'s old Heurich Brewery. As described by one who knew: "That corner of Washington is drab and down-at-heel. A rambling brick brewery, its copper roof green with age, a row of dilapidated warehouses, a skating rink. Nearby some colliers are tied up in the Potomac, and a coal-yard clatters dustily. A line of colored tenements climbs the weed-grown grubby hill away from the

---

*Since Central Intelligence officers have commonly referred to their Agency simply as "CIA" rather than "*the* CIA," while the Bureau is usually known by its agents as "the FBI," that idiosyncrasy is reflected herein.

river, and at its top, presiding over the scene, are the ugly twin cylinders of the city gas works. . . . No one gave a second glance at the brashly familiar brewery, sprawled like an amiable bum." Donovan's position confined him to the squat dullness of the Administration Building or "Kremlin," but as his organization expanded, most of his men worked in places like the brewery, or in unmarked wallboard-and-wood "temporary" structures on the Mall. The isolation, anonymity, and low-budget grubbiness, of course, were all part of the secret-boys-only-after-school treehouse charm. Hiding out from your wife down at the brewery or over in the "tempos," you could roll up your sleeves, drink bad coffee, and think of crazy ways to save the world.

That was the Donovan spirit. Where Hoover was a prudent bureaucrat who discouraged creativity, Donovan was an idea man. He was also a man of action—*ideas into action*, that was the soul of COI. "Some of his ideas were a little crazy," recalled one of his men, "but he had awfully interesting ideas, and usually he'd send 'em off to someone on the staff, and just expect them to go ahead and do it." Do it! Act! Wild Bill was like the football coach who went up to you on the sidelines, spanked you on the ass, and yelled in the earhole of your helmet: "Just get out there and hit someone!" The shabby chaos of COI's offices seemed to encourage brainstorming. One famous undertaking was spawned by an unsolicited letter to the president from a Mr. Adams of Irwin, Pennsylvania, asserting that the Japanese were deathly frightened of bats and suggesting that America consider the opportunities for "frightening, demoralizing, and exciting the prejudices of the people of the Japanese empire" by a "surprise attack" in which Japan would be bombed with live specimens. The president passed Adams' letter to Wild Bill with a note asserting that "this man is *not* a nut." Donovan promptly commissioned the curator of mammals at the American Museum of Natural History to work with the Army Air Corps; bats were strapped into catapults and flung, and their trajectories noted on clipboards, but the project was terminated when it was discovered that bats would freeze to death at forty thousand feet. Also, though no one had bothered to check Adams' assertion at the time, it turned out that the Japanese did not fear bats.

Minor facts like that were always falling through the cracks. Unlike Hoover, the master administrator, Donovan was forgetful, disorganized, disdainful of detail; he ran COI, it was said, like a country editor. He may have wanted to manage his outfit as efficiently as Hoover did the FBI, but it simply was not in him to be a bureaucrat. He hated red tape and loved to break through it. Organizational outlines were fuzzy, standard operating procedures were unknown, and discipline was lax; Colonel Donovan's own wrinkled Army uniform was not regulation-issue.

Even if chains of command had been properly structured, many operatives were so far removed from headquarters, and so infrequently in
touch, that it wouldn't have made much difference. One exasperated
officer told the Bureau that "on numerous occasions ... he had wired
Col. Donovan for instructions, but had not received any." Hearing about
that, FBI agents like Lawrence F. McWilliams would be aghast: "In the
Bureau, if you were in the field and didn't get back to headquarters in
the morning, you were fired by the afternoon."

Of course, Donovan men would point out, that was just the problem:
"The Bureau people were scared to death of Hoover. They could hardly
breathe without knowing if it was in line with policy." How far that was
from the liberal, cerebral climate under Donovan. His analysts were encouraged to question, to criticize; "yes-men" were reprimanded. He was
heard to say, "I'd rather have a young lieutenant with guts enough to
disobey an order than a colonel too regimented to think and act for
himself." That such an ideal as "free thought" would be consciously cultivated was partly a function of the fact that many of Donovan's men came
from the highest levels of American literary life (author and playwright
Robert Sherwood, poet Archibald MacLeish, critic Malcolm Cowley); it
was also a precondition for the harmonious coexistence of members in a
motley group. If FBI men were "Identikit," or "all cracked from the same
mold," Donovan's "crazy outfit," as Navy Secretary Frank Knox called it,
resisted easy characterization. The cast included people like the French
chef Julia Child, Hollywood director John Ford, baseball catcher Moe
Berg, fashion designer Count Oleg Cassini, and former G-man Melvin
Purvis, famous as the man who shot Dillinger; and there was the well-
connected homosexual leftist Carmel Offie, who used his edgy charm to
collect the wives of influential men. "We attracted the most extraordinary
group of people," the typical Donovan retiree would proudly say. "It was
really fantastic, around the world, what turned up. Our people were not
at all as parochial as Hoover's."

That was how it looked through one end of the telescope. For his part,
Hoover was heard to deride Donovan's disciples as "a group of arrogant
amateurs" encroaching on his own terrain, or, more usually, as "Ivy
League dilettantes." A great many COI men did indeed come out of the
Ivy League, especially Yale, and there was a certain tension in the general
difference of social class between personnel. After June 1942, when Donovan's COI became the Office of Strategic Services (OSS), his enemies, like
Hoover, would sometimes call it "Oh So Stupid," but "Oh So Social" was
the name that stuck. That moniker, like the stereotype of the Bureau
being "Foreign Born Irish," was both apt and misleading; Donovan was a
social climber, not a socialite, and he did not deliberately surround himself

with Ivy Leaguers, or "old boys," so that he could pal around with "men of his own class." He wanted experts to analyze foreign affairs, talented writers to craft subtle propaganda, operatives who knew a few languages and could find their way around Europe. It just so happened that the best qualified people came from the country's better schools.

Besides, if Donovan's organization was home to bluebloods, it also had its share of black sheep. One idealistic young COI man posted overseas found the quality of his colleagues "appallingly low"; as the organization expanded with the war and absorbed military personnel, it became a "convenient dumping ground for useless career officers," not to mention a means of draft evasion for "playboy bankers and stupid sons of wealthy and politically important families." Also, a secret intelligence service in time of war needed "special services" from safecrackers, footpads, and confidence men, and so Donovan provided a sort of "foreign legion" for many with silty reputations. This did little to detract from the COI-OSS mystique, which itself turned on the idea that even men of fine reputation, far from home, could find themselves doing bad things for a good cause.

But the incorporation of known criminals into sensitive government work, where they could hope for both immunity from future prosecution and clemency for transgressions past, did not please the country's top law-enforcement official. The arrogant naïveté of Donovan's staffers only worsened the situation. When Hoover blocked a special visa which Wild Bill had requested for a new employee, Donovan's assistant Ernest Cuneo tried to go over Hoover's head, protesting to Attorney General Francis Biddle that the individual in question had merely made "a few youthful mistakes." Biddle checked with Hoover, then summoned Cuneo and humiliated him in the presence of the FBI Director. "A few youthful mistakes?" Biddle queried. "Tell him, Edgar!" Hoover informed Cuneo that Donovan's recruit had two convictions for manslaughter and two for first-degree murder.

More commonly, however, the Bureau disapproved of Donovan personnel who had past histories of "German activities," as Hoover had noted before Pearl Harbor, or a pattern of association with "Communist elements," as became more usual in the months after. But Donovan's men found that communists and former fascists could make highly motivated recruits against a fascist enemy, and regarded Hoover's resistance as just one more manifestation of FBI pettiness. COI's Malcolm Cowley, attacked by Hoover as a "subversive," went to see an official at Justice. "I made the obvious remark that most of the FBI investigators seemed pretty stupid. 'Of course,' he said. 'You don't expect us to get *bright* law-school graduates, do you, for $65 a week?' I learned something about the sociology of the FBI. Its investigators, who have to have law-school training, are for the most part either Southerners or Catholics"—as if it somehow mattered very much that the FBI was not made up of members of the Eastern liberal establishment, as if that difference in social class somehow explained everything.

Cowley's characterization was a smear job. It was certainly true, as Fleming had noted in 1941, that the Bureau did not employ many Ivy Leaguers; FBI agent Robert Lamphere would recall that "On the first day of New Agents class, an instructor asked if anyone in the class was from Harvard, and the one who admitted it was singled out as if he were a different breed. It was sort of in fun but not entirely." But Cowley's implication that "the bastards are too bourgeois to understand us" only obscured the fact that known communists *were* allowed to work for OSS, as long as they were effective against the Axis—and that this offered great chances for penetration by Soviet spies. Indeed, the Soviets would manage to place at least seven agents in Donovan's organization. In most cases, Hoover warned Donovan about these people, and Donovan kept them anyway. "I have no authority over Donovan," Hoover lamented to Tamm, "and of course he doesn't check with me before he acts."

Neither did British Security Coordinator Stephenson, and Hoover's ire only increased as a number of Stephenson's agents were absorbed into COI. Stephenson's relations with the Bureau had been increasingly rocky in the eight months since Donovan had been made Coordinator. It was generally felt that Hoover had never forgiven the British role as "midwife," and now as nursemaid, to Donovan's brainchild. Nor was Hoover pleased by Stephenson's habit of doing things in New York without asking permission, and in March 1942 Senator Kenneth McKellar, a Hoover ally, introduced a bill that would force Stephenson to list all his agents and detail their doings, or else be kicked out of the country. To get around that requirement, Stephenson simply gave over many assets to Donovan. That did not solve the problem, but only transferred it to COI, especially since some of Stephenson's assets were "tainted," in the sense that Hoover already was on to them.

So it was with the case of one Yale graduate and communist sympathizer, who joined COI that very month. He would become, according to Hoover's agents, "the source of a lot of headaches" for the FBI and, according to COI veterans, the pretext for an attempt by Hoover to "strangle this unwanted newcomer [COI] at birth."

A few days after Pearl Harbor, a fat man with a red beard hurried past the ice rink at New York City's Rockefeller Plaza and entered the International Building, guarded by its two-story bronze sculpture of Atlas holding up the world. He almost took the elevator to the 35th floor, as he had done so often in past months when calling at the office of Rough Diamonds, Ltd. This time, however, he went one floor higher and found his way down the corridor to Room 3663, the newly opened local branch of COI.

Allen Dulles shook his hand. Dulles had thinning brown hair, thick gold-rimmed glasses, and a striking white mustache that made him look as if he had recently sipped a glass of milk. He already knew something of the man seated before him, this left-leaning homosexual who was considered, even by his backers, "a delicate case," and by his attackers, "a fraud, a liar, and an insecure man." He knew that this American citizen had been working as a British agent for fourteen months, that he now wanted to serve his own country, and that his name was Donald Downes.

Downes was an "old boy" questing for a new life. He'd come out of Phillips Exeter and Yale ('26), where he had roomed with James Gould Cozzens, the novelist-to-be, who kept pet snakes under the bed and made Downes a lifelong ophidaphobic. There followed fourteen years during which Downes found little meaning in the working world. He coached boys' athletics at Cheshire Academy, a few miles from Yale, until April 1940, when, roused by anti-Nazi pamphlets, he sought work in which he could use his "ideals as weapons." Family contacts put him in touch with British intelligence, and William Stephenson had hired him to see if Nazi money was behind isolationist activism in the United States. Through infiltrators, and a subcontracted burglary of Nazi Bund offices, he had found some financing of neutralist organizations in Cleveland and Boston, but no systematic control of major groups like America First. Downes had been at his typewriter reporting these conclusions on December 7 when he heard about Pearl Harbor.

Now, he told Dulles, he was willing to turn over his files to Donovan's group, whether the British wanted him to or not. He was willing to be trained, to relocate, to pay his own expenses. He just wanted to be part of the game.

Dulles mulled. He was wary about even having this man in his office, since Downes readily admitted that his work for the British had "put the FBI on my tail." Still, Downes was an operator with some field experience, a commodity that COI now desperately needed but found in short supply. Downes seemed perhaps too enthusiastic, maybe a bit unbalanced, but these were heady days; the country was at war. Dulles promised that he would consult Donovan and be in touch.

Downes' gung-ho attitude and good British references apparently won over Donovan, for Downes was soon shipped off to a secret base where COI's secret warriors were being trained, the legendary "Camp X." The compound was hidden on an old Canadian farm at Oshawa, near Toronto. Under the guidance of a major from the Shanghai police, Downes took a two-week crash course in the basics of surveillance and countersurveillance, lock-picking, mail-opening, parachuting, demolitions, night movement, stealth, forgery, firearms. There were also the techniques of "silent killing": improvisations like the rolling of newspaper into a sharp point, for the puncturing of a victim's throat; a rock in a sock, which could smash a skull; quick pulls at the corners of a man's mouth, which would supposedly tear his cheeks "like blotting paper."

On returning from Camp X Downes reported to Q Building, one of COI's wooden "tempos," where Donovan's chief assistant, James R. Murphy, gave him his first mission. The U.S. was planning an assault on Nazi-held North Africa, to be known as Operation Torch, and for this campaign it was important to know whether key neutral nations—Turkey, Portugal, Vichy France, and Spain—would side with Hitler, or with the Allies, or stay neutral. "We want to be able to read their cables," Murphy said. "You will be given a completely free hand, technical advice and aid from the British, and whatever sums of money are needed subject to our approval, that is Allen Dulles' and mine. You can count on us for all help and aid possible, unless you are caught. Then, we agree, we have never heard of you."

DOWNES UNDERSTOOD THE NEED for such precautions, for he would be poaching on Hoover's turf. After Donovan's conference with FDR at midnight on December 7, COI had been officially charged with coordinating intelligence in the Western Hemisphere, but Hoover protested that he should not yield control over SIS just because the Japanese had bombed Pearl Harbor. A harried Roosevelt ordered his feuding bureaucrats "to straighten out this whole program among yourselves." The matter had finally been settled at an interagency conference on January 6, 1942, when State and G-2, themselves worried about losing autonomy to a coordinator, sided with the FBI. Donovan's only consolation was that he could "on special occasions" send agents into Latin America—though only "with a specific mission (not under cover)," and only upon the personal approval of the Bureau. Those same proscriptions were to apply to COI operations anywhere in the Western Hemisphere.

But Downes regarded such "arbitrary geographical limitations" as unworkable, and decided to ignore them as he operated against the embassies. Early in 1942, he infiltrated the Vichy embassy in Washington by arranging the sexual compromise of a female worker, and obtained proof that Vichy was violating economic agreements. Next he penetrated the

Portuguese mission, by promising a college education to the janitor's son, but no proof of Axis sympathy was procured. He then targeted the Turkish consulate, without success, but by March he was concentrating on fascist but neutral Spain, the true key to lighting Torch. If Generalissimo Franco kept Spain neutral—if the Germans could not mass troops at the Pillars of Hercules—the Mediterranean would remain open, and the Allies could land at Morocco. But Franco and Hitler were friendly, and there seemed every possibility that Spain might instead side with the Nazis. It was therefore crucial that Spanish ciphers be obtained, and cable traffic scrutinized for clues to Franco's intentions.

To ASSEMBLE A BURGLARY team, Downes slipped into Mexico City and began stalking the coffeehouses, basements, and back alleys where the anti-Franco underground moved and met. He selected two agents for the embassy job and recruited others to be commandos in North Africa. While in Mexico, however, Downes also checked up on one of Donovan's secret networks—consisting, according to COI files, of "about 20 civilian agents operating throughout Mexico," especially at "strategic points along the Gulf of California," where they were "prepared to give any information relative to suspicious ship movements." Those sources had originally been handled by Naval Intelligence, according to Donovan's records, "because of the apparent inability of FBI to effectively handle" coverage of Japanese subversion. Hoover had reluctantly accepted ONI's role, and the agents' reports had been forwarded to the Bureau until mid-December 1941, when ONI's unique Latin American chief, a hairless hunchback named Wallace Beta Phillips, officially transferred to COI. Phillips' agents began reporting to Donovan on such matters as mysterious planes taxiing down secret landing fields along Mexico's Pacific Coast, where a clutch of Japanese businessmen had moved from California just before Pearl Harbor.

Donovan regarded the network as valuable, but his staffers were nervous about it, and even before Downes' mission had sensed that it was in danger of compromise by the FBI. "Inasmuch as the Presidential Directive has forbidden COI to operate in the Western Hemisphere, we are at the present time carrying on an activity in Mexico in violation of that directive," Donovan was cautioned by a deputy on February 19. "A recent letter received by Mr. Phillips definitely suggests that FBI is at least aware of our arrangements in Mexico, and it may bring the matter up at any moment."

By April, the Bureau had indeed brought the matter up. Apparently

Downes had made contact with some of Phillips' seaport watchers, and was watched, in turn, by the FBI. "I have been advised through Mexican sources that there is presently operating in Mexico one Donald Downs [sic], who is representing himself as a representative of your organization in Mexico," Hoover wrote Donovan on April 2. "I assume, of course, that Downs has no connection with your organization since the Bureau has received no notification of his employment by you or of the fact that he is operating officially in Mexico. Appropriate steps are, therefore, being taken to bring about a termination of this man's representation."

Donovan replied, untruthfully, that he did not employ Downes. Hoover wasn't fooled, and, along with Undersecretary of State Sumner Welles, complained to FDR that Donovan had "some ninety agents operating in Mexico . . . in violation of the President's instructions." As punishment, it was urged that Roosevelt have "the Donovan organization dissolved."

That bureaucratic offensive hit Donovan at a hard time, for he was convalescing in a New York hospital after an auto accident had aggravated an old war wound, causing a blood clot to break loose and lodge in his lung. Roosevelt did not mention Downes or the alleged ninety agents when he conveyed get-well wishes to Donovan later that month, but Donovan heard of the Hoover-Welles conspiracy from Navy Secretary Knox, and through a haze of sedation defended himself to the president, dictating to a bedside stenographer that he would soon "go into the field again," but was "angry and indignant" because "by now the well worn lie has been retailed to you that I had or have some ninety representatives . . . in Latin America. . . . I assure you that your real concern must be with those who bring such stories to you about men who are trying to serve you loyally, because this tale is a dirty and contemptible lie."

Fortunately for Donovan, his protestations were believed by Roosevelt, who pressed the accusers for evidence. Welles claimed that the original figure of ninety agents had come from "an official high in Colonel Donovan's office," but could produce only an account of Downes' mission to Mexico City, and the names of four Donovan employees. "The FBI has other records," Welles lamely added, "which will take more time to dig up."

There the danger died, but Donovan, back at his desk by early May, ordered an internal review of the entire situation. A State Department contact informed him that the affair of "the famous ninety humpty-dumpties" had developed out of Wallace Phillips' network. Phillips, who had since transferred to London, insisted by cable that Hoover had initially approved the transfer of Naval Intelligence spotters to COI but had then created the ninety-agents myth "for reasons of his own." Phillips appended the opinion of his British colleagues that "Hoover, who apparently spread [a] rumor about the British having 3,000 agents in the U.S., would certainly not hesitate to spread a similar rumor about any other service."

THE DOWNES "rumor" had been true, however, and Donovan's denial only upped the stakes, as did the June 13 transformation of COI into the Office of Strategic Services (OSS). To integrate its work into the Allied effort, Donovan's organization was resettled under the Joint Chiefs of Staff. That meant a pro-forma loss of autonomy, but also entailed some bureaucratic protection. Hoover thus predictably opposed creation of OSS; he warned Assistant Secretary of State Adolf Berle "that Donovan would attempt to take over the legitimate functions of the FBI, particularly those relating to SIS." Berle insisted that Hoover needn't worry, especially since Berle himself, a Hoover ally, was on the Joint Committee supervising OSS. But Hoover was not so sure, and Wild Bill sensed correctly that the FBI director would be waiting for the slightest pretext to accuse OSS of breaking faith. Donovan warned Downes that the whole embassy operation was "very much against the law, and if you get caught we're in terrible trouble."

Downes insisted he would deny everything if caught and wait for Donovan to "spin him out," but privately he had some cause for concern. He had taken precautions against all imaginable contingencies but one— "betrayal by someone high enough in the American Government to know what we were doing." His two antifascist agents, back from Camp X, thought their apartments in Washington had been searched, and felt that on a few occasions they had been followed. Downes assured them it was "only the FBI checking on strangely behaving individuals in Washington," but a friend at the Justice Department had warned that Hoover suspected OSS of "penetrating" embassies and was "annoyed." Foreign embassies on American soil might be, at best, a jurisdictional "no man's land," but Downes knew that "the no-man's-land between the FBI and OSS was dangerous territory."

The operation proceeded, however. Downes infiltrated an agent into the Spanish Embassy as a secretary, recruited a New York City safecracker, and set up an elaborate infrared-photo lab. All was ready by the last week in June, when Downes' agent deliberately damaged the dial on a vault where the codes were stored. The embassy called the safe company, which agreed to help "the war effort" by sending over Downes' safecracker, who thus obtained the combination and a key to the vault's inner door. At ten o'clock on the evening of June 29, with the embassy staff occupied till late at a Maryland roadhouse, the burglars entered the building. At exactly 11:15, the team returned to their safehouse, where machinery was put to work on the coding tape. By 1:10, they had taken over thirty-four hundred photographs. The developing and printing was finished just as a hot dawn broke over Washington. The burglars re-entered the embassy and replaced the tape. Downes stuffed the "product" into an old suitcase and caught the prebreakfast plane to New York, where a delighted Allen Dulles examined it over breakfast. For at least a month, until the roll was changed on the Spanish machine, OSS could decipher their telegrams.

But the operation would have to be repeated every time the Spanish put in a new roll. All went easily again in July, August, and September. Then, on October 21, the team was followed by an FBI car. They tried to lose it, and thought they had. At eleven o'clock they were inside the embassy, in front of the safe, beginning to open it, when they heard sirens. As FBI agents converged on the front entrance, the burglars scrambled out a side exit into a service alley, hopped a high fence, and by that narrow margin avoided arrest by the FBI.

When Donovan and Murphy heard about the episode, around dawn, they were deeply disturbed. The team had made off with the cipher data, but the Bureau obviously knew a lot about what OSS had been doing. They had awakened the whole street, and would owe the Spaniards some explanation. What if the FBI now said something to the Spanish that led them to suspect that the burglary had targeted their code systems? That would certainly lead to a cipher change, with possibly dire implications for the invasion of North Africa. The special agent who led the attack on Donovan's team insisted he had talked with no Spanish official, but OSS could only wait to see whether their source had been compromised.

Meanwhile, on the day after the burglary, Hoover sent Donovan a thinly veiled reminder that Downes' embassy doings were fully known. He demanded to know "the location of any representatives," allegedly so that the Bureau might "verify any impersonation complaints." No such complaints had been made, but that was hardly the point. Hoover had Wild Bill against the rail, and was attempting a blatant power play that would allow him to monitor OSS personnel.

Looking for ammunition in case the battle escalated, Donovan's staff began reviewing the history of their relations with the FBI. Though no new liaison man had been formally appointed since Jimmy Roosevelt's January commission into the Navy, a number of promising domestic counterespionage leads had been turned over to the Bureau. In New York City, Donovan's men had tipped Bud Foxworth to a Manhattan machinist "whose brother is a member of the Gestapo"; identified the daughter of a Mrs. Walter Hidden as Goering's mistress; discovered that Nazi propaganda was distributed at "Hanna's Service Station"; and implicated as Nazi spies a German-American mechanic in Mount Vernon, New York, a ski instructor at Williams College, and a Dr. Ancieto Montero, "supposedly expert on tropical diseases." But what had the Bureau done in turn for OSS? The FBI did provide some incidental intelligence, but much of it was believed of doubtful value. When Hoover sent over maps depicting "penetration of the totalitarian [Axis] countries in Latin America," Donovan wrote back to thank him—"These are very interesting"—but an OSS analyst haughtily scrawled: "These charts are too general to give any important impression of the actual distribution of Axis activities. They are typical of the work of non-geographers, and represent an unfortunate waste of time and money. We can do much better."

On the eve of landings in North Africa, moreover, Hoover's men had come dangerously close to exposing key Allied cipher operations. A depressed Donovan was heard to say that "the Abwehr gets better treatment from the FBI than we do."

THE DOWNES AFFAIR was "resolved" in November 1942, when Donovan agreed to turn the embassy operation over to Hoover, and promised that any future "infiltration of installations" would be cleared with the Bureau in advance. "It [penetrating embassies] very properly was the Bureau's business, not OSS business," OSS's legal counsel Lawrence Houston would later admit. But Downes, ordered to entrust his crew to "a Mr. Brown" at the FBI, was less sanguine about the deal. "The personnel, almost to a man (and woman), came back later to protest. Instead of being treated as patriotic people making war for their country, Mr. Hoover's Mr. Brown treated them as so many stool-pigeons, as inferior people who had sunk to the depths of being police spies and informers—the classical cop attitude toward the underworld weakling whom they use to trap gangsters."

By the time he heard those complaints, however, Downes was already preoccupied with other projects. The Spanish cipher system had not been blown by the Bureau, after all; Spanish neutrality had been ascertained, and on November 8 the Allies landed easily at Casablanca and the coast near Algiers. Downes then volunteered to vault into the North African fray with his Spanish-communist commandos, to help protect Allied supply lines from profascist guerrillas, and on November 17 he left the United States by plane for a dusty, romantic reach of world that must surely be beyond the compass of Hoover's FBI.

It was not. Downes himself, when arguing that OSS operations could not be held back by "arbitrary geographical limitations," had conceded that, likewise, "the FBI . . . must be allowed to follow its investigations, no matter to what part of the globe they may lead." He had never expected Hoover to hold him to those words, but special agents were already being posted outside the Western Hemisphere as "legal attachés" at selected embassies. Unlike Hoover's SIS agents, the "legats" were to have no "operational" duties, and were to clear any investigations with Donovan. Unofficially, the legats sometimes had little patience for such delimitations, as Downes was to discover in the case of a Nazi sympathizer named Charles Bedeaux.

An expatriate American industrialist in Algiers, Bedeaux dreamed of building a pipeline to pump palm oil across the Sahara, from Oman to Dakar, and thence to a fat-starved Germany. Trapped by the Allied landings, Bedeaux was arrested for treason on tips from Guy and Jacques Calvert, two OSS spies in the Vichy Sécurité Militaire. Downes, in Morocco, knew that Bedeaux had friends in Washington, and guessed there would be some political pressure for his release, so he ordered Guy Calvert to photograph financial records proving Bedeaux's collaboration. Sure enough, a few weeks later, the originals disappeared. Two FBI agents then arrived to take Bedeaux—and "any relevant documents"—back to the United States.

Downes flew to Algiers. After coaching Guy on how to handle the G-men, he hid in the fitting room of a dress shop owned by the brothers Calvert, where he could overhear the FBI's interrogation of Guy. The agents knew Guy had made photostats of the papers, and warned him: "Technically we could arrest you. . . . The papers are rightly ours. It is entirely our jurisdiction." Calvert protested his ignorance. There was mumbling between the FBI men. "Probably OSS. We'll never get them back. . . . Let's go."

Their voices faded. Downes later heard that Bedeaux, under the protection of Hoover's men, had committed suicide by taking poison while changing planes in Florida.

A year later, as an OSS detachment moved north with the Allied offensive, Downes met up with Donovan in Italy, and heard that his boss was also still having problems with Hoover. Downes took him out in a PT-boat to watch Naples burning, rimmed with orange, belching columns of black, and Mount Vesuvius smoking gently in the distance. Donovan stood in the prow, steel helmet shading a face stern and set with anger.

"It's hell on the front back in Washington, too," he told Downes. "I have to compromise every day. The FBI's gunning for us every time we have a new idea."

Donovan's newest idea—actually, it had come to him from the British—was the creation of a special OSS division to handle double agents and deception. But Hoover's Bureau was also running doubles, or trying to. The result was a "deception gap," and it was already imperiling Allied plans for the invasion of Normandy.

CHAPTER THREE

DOUBLE CROSS

AGENT TRICYCLE HAD SPENT December 7, 1941, getting a sunta 1. To arrange for receipt of a radio transmitter, he had left New York Ci₍y by Pan Am Clipper on November 14, making Rio de Janeiro by the 18th, and giving the torn half of his business card to "Alfredo," the Abwehr's top agent in Latin America. Alfredo had agreed to send a transmitter to Quebec, where Popov could pick it up. Popov was returning to America aboard the luxury cruiser S.S. *Uruguay*, which was just pulling out of Port of Spain, Trinidad, when the captain told the passengers about Pearl Harbor. Popov would recall feeling a pulse of pride. Despite his problems with the Bureau, he knew that American officials had possessed his Pearl Harbor questionnaire since August 19, which was almost five months' warning. He was confident, he later said, that the United States had scored a great victory—and bitter when he learned the truth.

As Popov arrived at Manhattan on December 15, 1941, FBI agents were ferried out in a tugboat and boarded the ship before it entered the harbor. Popov would record that he grilled the agents about their failure to use his Pearl Harbor intelligence; Bureau records have been censored on "national-security" grounds exactly at the point where such recriminations should have been documented. But when Popov told the agents that his Brazilian handler had given him more microdot queries, the Bureau's reaction was plainly more electric than it had been in August, before America was at war. "This is vitally important," Hoover scrawled on the case summary. "Get copy of 'dots' so I may see them." By year's end, the FBI was finally playing Tricycle as a double agent, using him to disinform the Germans—an undertaking crucial to any eventual U.S. invasion of the Continent. But the Bureau's approach to this deception game would only further alienate Popov and his British sponsors, causing a dramatic expansion of Donovan's empire.

Popov told the agents that the new dots were concealed in "butterfly trays"—souvenir serving platters with beautiful dead specimens preserved under clear enamel. Like most of the returning tourists on the *Uruguay*, Popov had brought home a few of the trays, and immediately after the boat docked, agents seized all of them on board. A Bureau technician removed the backs, studied the paper stuffing used to put pressure on the butterflies, and peered patiently through a hundred-power microscope. Dots were found in the wing of a butterfly in one of Popov's trays, but none of the others yielded any. Thorough examination could not be done without removing each wing and cutting into the frames, but the attorney general refused a special FBI request to impound permanently the property of U.S. citizens.

Still, Popov's dots contained suggestive intelligence questionnaires. "In the U.S.A. a cartridge powder is manufactured which is practically smokeless and with a weak muzzle flash," one query noted. "Further details requested, color of the muzzle flash, color of the smoke. If possible the constituents of the powder." Another dot held a seven-page list of interrogatories about U.S. atomic-bomb research—how the U.S. processed uranium ore, "to what degree of purity, the quantity they processed, and the amount they had in stock." By answering these and other questions plausibly but incorrectly, the U.S. might deceive Hitler's High Command about the state of U.S. weaponry and tactics. The FBI consulted G-2 for "feed" material, and in January 1942, after Popov's radio set was transshipped to him from Brazil via Quebec, phony data were bleeped in code to Berlin.

But though the messages purportedly came from Popov, the FBI did not let him know what they said. According to one British intelligence officer who handled his case, Tricycle "was not even taken to see the radio station which had been built for him, with the result that he was in danger of being caught out by a snap question from a genuine German agent in America or by a request to send a message at short notice. Soon the Germans were complaining that his reports lacked 'meat,' and they began to suspect . . . that [Popov] was working under [Allied] control."

What had happened was that the FBI cut Tricycle out of his own operation, because they suspected that he might still be working for Berlin. If Popov was legitimate, the Bureau reasoned, and had really been sent to America by the Nazis to build a network, Berlin should have put him in touch with other agents. But after six months in-country, Popov "had not uncovered the identities of any [German] espionage agents in the United States," as one FBI skeptic noted, and he had "been given the names of no contacts in this country by the Germans at Lisbon or Rio de Janeiro." Were the Germans on to him? Was he playing a double game? SIS agent Sam Papich was assigned to keep a close watch on Popov, and microphones were again planted in his apartment. A year after his arrival in America, the FBI officially dumped Tricycle back to MI5, on the grounds that he was a "liar" and was "too expensive to justify his retention."

He returned to London and became the ward of the "XX" or "Double-Cross" Committee, a British interagency group that aimed to mislead the Reich about Allied war plans. With the storming of Italy in September 1943, the ring began to close around Hitler's Reich, and the Allies started planning Operation Overlord, the invasion of France. The Double-Cross Committee used Popov to tell the Nazi High Command that American troops would slash at the pastoral region of Pas de Calais, not the cliffs of Normandy.

But the predominantly American makeup of the invasion force created definite difficulties for the Double-Cross team. Though General Dwight Eisenhower had been sufficiently impressed by North African deceptions to authorize the manufacture of standardized, portable, prefabricated decoy equipment, G-2 initially showed little interest in strategic deception, and even less skill. During summer 1943, in Operation Cockade, the U.S. Army had aimed to relieve the Russian and Mediterranean fronts by pinning enemy forces in northwestern France; troops were maneuvered, misleading information was planted on agents, the coast was bombarded—but the Nazis never reinforced the region, and in fact some troops were actually moved from it. Because the fictional Cockade assault was "wildly out of proportion to the real forces available," as a G-2 report later concluded, the enemy analyzed Cockade as merely "a large-scale exercise from which he had nothing to fear." Obviously, if the Americans were to help the cause rather than hamper it, the British would have to design a suitable American "Double-Cross" capacity within the U.S. intelligence community, just as they had worked to create a coordinator of information in 1941.

COULD HOOVER'S FBI do the job? Despite the mangling of the Tricycle game, even Double-Cross critics like Montgomery Hyde had to admit that "as the war progressed, increasing numbers of [FBI] double agents were put into operation in the Western Hemisphere," mostly on British initiative, but nonetheless able to deceive the Germans about such matters as Allied ship movements. By 1943, it seemed, the lessons of earlier failures had been learned; the Bureau was effectively running Walter Koehler, a Dutch veteran of German World War I intelligence, doubled by the British, and sent by the Germans to rebuild the Sebold network where Tricycle had failed. Through Koehler, the FBI was sending the Germans radio messages which "undoubtedly played a useful part in the general scheme of enemy deception," according to Hyde, who also credited Hoover because he undertook to plant false data on the German Embassy in Washington. One such bum steer was the claim that, if Hitler used poison gas against Britain, Churchill would retaliate with "secret weapons," including "some kind of glass balls containing chemicals producing such terrific heat that they cannot be extinguished by any known means."

The "new" Hoover even shared some Koehler data with OSS. In December 1942, he relayed to Donovan extremely sensitive intelligence "obtained from a German espionage agent [Koehler] who has recently landed in the Western Hemisphere," including the identities of Nazi agents in the European Theater. Among these was "von Werthern," a native of German colonial Africa who was "reported to be very clever." Operating out of Brussels, von Werthern employed four men for special service along the French coast, "equipped with 14-watt radio sets," who "in the event of an invasion . . . were to remain behind the lines and communicate information to Germany." All four agents also moonlighted for a Vichy-collaborationist assassination squad known as "Todt" (Death), which sought to liquidate OSS agents and DeGaullist partisans. The identities of such stay-behinds were especially prized because, as an official British government account later noted, they had " 'submerged' themselves in their communities over a period of four years and [had] civilian occupations," making them "difficult to uncover." One of the Todt agents, known as "Ritter," would soon be of special interest to OSS, because he was stationed precisely at the dummy invasion site, Calais. If allowed to spy freely, Ritter could conceivably compromise the whole D-Day deception; if doubled by OSS, he would be in a unique position to deceive Berlin about Allied invasion plans; if killed, he would at least tell no tales. The FBI's Koehler tips, then, could be immensely valuable to OSS soldier-spies like William C. Colby, who parachuted behind the lines to neutralize the pro-Nazi networks.

But if Hoover had begun to live down his reputation as a policeman, he also proved more than capable of returning to his crime-busting ways. As an official British Government history noted, "the FBI continued to regard double agents primarily as instruments for catching other spies." When the Abwehr sent Popov more money in 1942, the Bureau had tried to draw the courier into a trap, which could have indicated to the Germans that Tricycle was under Allied influence or suspicion. After Popov had showed SIS his new microdots, Hoover had ordered: "See that no more butterfly trays are allowed to enter U.S. at any port"—which could have told the Nazis their technique had been compromised, and caused them to adopt a new one, which the FBI could not monitor. Similarly, when the Bureau was let in on British analysis of deciphered German signals, Hoover passed the information to Brazilian police, who rounded up fifty-seven suspected German spies; the British feared that the Germans might deduce that their codes were compromised, and change them. A British intelligence official would later lament: "The trouble at this stage was that Americans handled some information with reckless disregard for consequences. By trumpeting successes, they tipped off the enemy."

In an attempt to restrain Hoover's enthusiasm for prosecutions, the Double-Crossers lobbied Washington for creation of a "joint interservices committee." The result was an Anglo-American board, the Joint Security Control, based in Washington, set up in January 1943. But the JSC "did not produce any meeting of the minds between the FBI and the British authorities on the subject of deception," as one British authority ruefully recalled.

Unhappy with the FBI, the British turned to OSS. Donovan's outfit had the jurisdictional right to operate in Europe, where most deceptions would be targeted and maintained, and Donovan himself was on better terms with British intelligence than Hoover. Perhaps most crucially, the British found Donovan's officers much more "our type," especially since the contingent of Americans arriving in London for counterintelligence tutelage after April 1943 consisted largely of hard-drinking, Anglophilic literary critics and historians from Yale. The guru of the group was poetry professor Norman Holmes Pearson, who struck the British as "hail-fellow-well-met, and have you heard the latest one about the girl in the train?" Pearson could also be serious and smart enough, when it counted, and was suitably humble about the fact that he and his American academics were, in essence, going back to school. With the trust and cooperation of their transatlantic cousins, Pearson's trainees became the core of a new counterintelligence component, effected by quiet British pressure on Donovan and formalized on June 15, 1943. Appropriately enough, the American brainchild of Britain's XX Committee was christened "X-2."

THE NEW UNIT was overseen in Washington by Donovan's most trusted deputy, his former law clerk James R. Murphy, who had come to Washington in the summer of 1941, as he said, "to keep the knives out of [Donovan's] back," and was now charged with sticking them into the backs of the enemy. That was to be done by literally destroying the effectiveness of German intelligence, by both offensive and defensive means. Defensively, X-2 would protect against hostile penetration and deception; offensively, it would penetrate and deceive. It would be both sword and shield.

But both offensive and defensive functions had to be closely coordinated with the FBI, which kept its monopoly on operations in the Americas. X-2 documents of the period acknowledged, for instance, the importance of "FBI relations" for "the interchange of biographical data on individuals who are known to be or are suspected of working for the enemy, including pertinent and timely information on enemy agents moving back and forth between Eastern and Western Hemisphere." Detection of enemy spies, and their possible recruitment into the D-Day deception game, depended on the exchange of such information.

Murphy therefore created a special section to handle FBI liaison. Effective December 1943, the section was headed by Horace Peters, a thirty-five-year-old Baltimore lawyer who had gone to Choate and Yale before working on watch lists and secret-writing cases for OSS. Peters began staying nights to review cables for material of potential interest to the FBI, and the Bureau reciprocated by sharing with Peters a mountain of pursuable leads. Mail openings in Bermuda revealed that a Colombian had been hired by the Nazis to spy on U.S. aeronautical production, and that the Vienna-born representative of a Swiss gun company had come to the U.S. to promote the manufacture and sale of 20mm cannon, but was associating with suspicious "pro-Nazi" persons. Thanks to FBI cooperation, such individuals could be used by X-2 to mislead Hitler about Allied invasion plans. The Bureau also serviced more exotic OSS requirements, such as the June 1944 request for pornographic pictures of Japanese women. Believing that "the Japs are sending obscene photographs of American girls through India and other such countries, in an effort to create the impression of lax morals on the part of Americans," OSS was "desirous of disseminating similar material with reference to Japanese girls," and wanted to know if the FBI had such items in its files. The Bureau discovered "35 or 40 photographs of this nature" in the Obscene File of its Crime Laboratory, and Hoover gave his handwritten "O.K." for OSS to access the dirty pictures. Murphy could not have been completely insincere when he sent Hoover a special note "to express appreciation for the cooperation the Federal Bureau of Investigation has extended to the X-2 Branch of OSS during our first year of operation."

But despite the best efforts of Peters, there were problems. A key German operation was the smuggling of diamonds and platinum from the jungle mines of Brazil, via Lisbon, to Berlin; the Allies became aware of the traffic when the captain of a Brazilian ship discovered eight hundred grams of platinum and fifty grams of commercial diamonds in the false bottom of a Portuguese doctor's stethoscope case. Interrogated by Portuguese police, the doctor confessed that many jewelers in Rio de Janeiro were working for the Nazis. The latest methods of concealment included false bottoms to boxes, double soles to socks, and "hollow soles and heels to footwear." FBI agents had begun infiltrating the courier system and planting useless materials in place of strategic goods, while OSS toughs worked Lisbon's docks. But Murphy's deputy Thomas W. Dunn concluded in February 1944 that there was "no fixed policy regarding OSS participation in efforts against smuggling." Dunn consulted U.S. blockade-enforcement officials to see if X-2 coverage could be expanded into Hoover's hemisphere, but was turned down flat: the Bureau was already doing a much better job than OSS, Dunn was told. When Dunn asked for a copy of one especially valued FBI smuggling report, "so that we might study its method," he was told OSS did not have a "legitimate need" for the information. Murphy never got the chance to remodel X-2's reporting along the lines of the FBI. A British-proposed conference to coordinate diamond efforts never materialized, and smugglers slipped between jurisdictions for the duration of the war.

In other cases, such as that of a man who was being cuckolded by young John F. Kennedy, Murphy would ask for help and get none at all. Shortly before Pearl Harbor, Hungarian-born film director Paul Fejos had set up something called the Viking Fund in New York, ostensibly to finance explorations in search of lost Inca cities in the Peruvian jungle. Murphy suspected such missions might be a cover for gathering intelligence for an Axis invasion of South America, or even for refueling German U-boats, especially given the unique characteristics of Fejos' expeditionary yacht. Bought from Howard Hughes and donated to Fejos by Swedish gun manufacturer Axel Wenner-Gren, a known Nazi spy, it was the largest private boat in the world, featuring sophisticated radio gear and a battery of machine guns and rifles. Hoover meanwhile worried that Fejos' wife, Danish journalist Inga Arvad, might be a German agent, and knew she had been intimate in 1941–42 with Ensign Kennedy, then assigned to Naval Intelligence. Fearing that Arvad might be trying to compromise Kennedy into revealing secrets—he was at the time handling naval intercepts for ONI—the Bureau had tapped the couple's phones and bugged their rooms, which produced the terse note by a G-man in the surveillance log: "sounds of sexual intercourse." Hoover's investigation was still open in December 1944, when Murphy requested data on Fejos and the Viking Fund, only to find them "the subjects of a current investigation" by the FBI, who "for this reason . . . are unable to give us any information and request we do nothing in the matter."

FBI anti-Nazi projects even threatened Donovan's hegemony in Europe, where the Bureau reportedly plotted to kill the Führer. John Nichols, the son of Hoover's close aide Louis Nichols, would later allege that "Mr. Hoover, my father, and a third man whose name I don't know developed a plan to go behind German lines and assassinate Hitler. They actually presented this plan to the White House, and it got bucked to the State Department, and they got taken to task by Secretary of State Hull. What they had in mind was a three-man assassination team, and my father talked as though he and Mr. Hoover somehow hoped to take part themselves. My understanding is that this was no joke—they really did hope something would come of it."

Nothing came of the Hitler plot, if there ever was one, but in 1943–44 the Bureau did begin increasing its work in the European theater, especially in Portugal. In June 1943, Murphy learned that agent Paul Darrow had arrived in Lisbon under cover as a flight radio operator on the Pan Am Clipper. Murphy regarded that occurrence as "most unsatisfactory and mysterious," and got the local chargé d'affaires to broker harshly a punitive arrangement under which FBI representatives could be stationed in Lisbon: "1. They are to conduct no positive, active FBI work in Lisbon; 2. Use no funds; 3. Set up no organization; 4. Engage only in Liaison work; 5. If their presence does not work out to [our] satisfaction, they are to leave that area."

The settlement was about as lenient as the Treaty of Versailles, and as workable. The Bureau necessarily engaged in "positive, active" work—it had never been explained how they might restrict themselves to "negative, inactive work"—and its agents continued poking into OSS affairs overseas. One investigation embarrassed OSS by uncovering that fifteen hundred rolls of 35mm film, purchased by Donovan staffers from Eastman Kodak in the summer of 1942, had appeared on the black market in Lisbon. Another probe established that OSS financial attaché J. Ray Olivera was close to "a known German agent," Jacques Wolfgang. Though Olivera had been quietly dismissed, X-2 resented "the unusual nature of the questions asked by the Bureau," feeling it could take care of its own.

There also developed a general feeling that loud, open-faced FBI agents did not really know how to move through the secret gardens of intelligence work, and that their presence might actually imperil D-Day deceptions. In October 1943, for instance, OSS Lisbon urgently cabled Peters with news that, "According to information given to a number of persons by the head man in Lisbon of the U.S. Federal Bureau of Investigation, Allied plans called for invasion in the vicinity of Trieste, after the surrender of the Italians, and the landing by United States forces would be made there during September, while invasion of the Netherlands and the north of France would be accomplished by English and French troops."

Such open discussion of purported Allied war plans by an FBI agent could be read two ways, and both were bad. If the Bureau was trying to misinform the Nazis, they were doing it without coordinating with X-2's efforts in that same sphere; their misinformation might be at odds with Murphy's own delicately crafted fictions, and that might cause the Nazis to suspect deception. If, on the other hand, the FBI man was simply engaging in loose talk about what he believed were the Allies' real intentions, that was a breach of security even less forgivable. "With your permission," Peters immediately wrote Murphy, "I would like to make this the basis of a verbal complaint to [FBI] (1) as a violation of the jurisdictional agreement, (2) indiscreetness on the part of the FBI which endangers and undermines the activities of the OSS in that area."

THE COMPLAINT was made, and indiscretions lessened, but more potential deception-gaffes were created in the moonlit midnight of August 9, 1943, when two Nazi spies disembarked from a German trawler off São João da Barra, Brazil, paddled ashore in a rubber raft, buried radio gear in a sandpit, and were promptly arrested by local police. One of the agents, Marcus Baarn, was supposed to have settled in Rio to monitor ship departures; the other, Wilhelm Kopff, was to have set up a transmitter and safehouse network. The Bureau immediately began exploring "the possibilities of utilizing [the captured spies] as double agents," as Hoover reported to Assistant Secretary of State Berle. If they could initially be made to "contact Germany in accordance with their prearranged schedules," and if news of their arrest could be kept from the Abwehr, they could be used to disinform Berlin.

Though Baarn proved too unstable to be of value, the FBI got right to work with Kopff. The captured agent assisted in the coding of radio messages, but was not allowed to touch the transmission key, lest he manage to get off a warning signal to his masters. Though aware that the danger of detection was great under these circumstances—every radio operator had a unique tapping style—a stand-in studied and practiced Kopff's touch, and the FBI felt the Germans would be fooled. But on Halloween, Kopff somehow managed to get the tapper to precede a message with the diagraph "NR13," which according to Kopff's codebook would have indicated "danger." The Germans showed no further interest in Kopff, and in January 1944 the FBI shut down the game.

Once the case was "bad," however, Hoover apparently felt it could be shared with OSS. Naval and Military Intelligence had been kept current by special courier since August 16, but Donovan did not receive documentation until January 1944. Consequently, there was yet again a very real danger that information conveyed to the Nazis by the FBI in one part of the world would contradict that fed by OSS in another.

That situation was particularly vexing to the British XX Committee, which had the unenviable job of trying to coordinate double-agent operations between two rival American agencies. "Difficulties arose from interdepartmental competition, not to mention jealousies," recalled Double-

Crosser Montgomery Hyde. "The FBI employed double agents (usually in conjunction with BSC). Donovan's OSS employed more. Naturally each agency kept its operations secret from the other, with the result that the FBI would sometimes suspect and investigate an agent who turned out to be under the control of OSS."

To address the FBI-OSS difficulty, the Double-Cross Committee sent over a paper emphasizing need for total consistency in deception, and William Stephenson pressed the issue at a White House conference with FDR and Hoover. "The lie must be consistent, both with the truth, as the enemy knows it, and with all other lies that have been told him," the British kept saying. "The enemy's efforts to estimate our capabilities and intentions are continuous—and so must be our deception." That was why it was imperative that double-agent games "be coordinated and directed from a central point."

It had been hoped that the JSC could coordinate things, but American counterintelligence was still cut down the middle, and there remained a troubling "deception gap." Coupled with a general German suspiciousness about agent reports which might now be caused by the Bureau's blowing Kopff and Baarn, that dissociation could mean that D-Day would be a disaster. At worst, it could mean that the Nazis would catch on to the game and read deception messages "backward," as if through a mirror, to deduce the Allies' true plans. It could mean that hundreds of thousands of American soldiers, instead of achieving tactical surprise, would be slaughtered on the beaches of Normandy.

Just how perilously close the plan came to exposure would become clear only afterward, when it was learned that Hitler had suspected the truth—that Calais was the feint and Normandy the target—but had uncharacteristically given in to his staff. Who could say which piece of anomalous data from a poorly coordinated double-agent game might have caused Hitler's advisers to side with him, or encouraged the Führer himself to back his hunch? An official Army postmortem acknowledged darkly that, despite the good result, the great deception had proceeded under "the complete independence of each service—and definitely suffered thereby."

FORTUNATELY FOR THE ALLIES, the sheer scale of the D-Day game—double agents, notional radio traffic, dummy landing craft displayed in harbors—overwhelmed the interagency gaps. On June 6, 1944, the Germans were totally taken in. Hitler's high command was paralyzed by the existence of the "real" army, which they believed would invade any day at Pas de Calais, and unheedful of the Normandy landings, which they believed a diversion. When Donovan went ashore at Normandy, Allied strength was so superior that he was almost disappointed.

Recently promoted to major general, Donovan had been trying to get in on the landing, but Eisenhower wouldn't let him. He had to content himself with watching from an offshore cruiser, and not until the third day did Donovan and his London station chief, David Bruce, get their boots wet in the surf. By then the Germans had been swept back, but Donovan said, "Well, we've got to go in and do something." He "borrowed" a general's command car, and drove with Bruce into an area where the Germans were still firing from the bushes. The old war hero desperately wanted to be shot at, to shoot back—to win one more medal, or perhaps to simply die a soldier's death—but the fire from the bushes was soon suppressed, and Donovan went back to his boat.

For OSS detachments working with the Allied Expeditionary Force, however, there remained much to do by way of mopping up. Murphy was ordered to form a pool of case officers for doubling captured enemy agents on the Western front, ideally "for the establishment and maintenance of cover and deception channels." This activity was concentrated in Rome and, after Charles de Gaulle led his Free French down the Champs Elysées on August 26, 1944, in Paris, where Murphy predicted that the enemy was "laying plans for post-hostility intelligence operations." Because the "transfer of enemy funds for intelligence purposes" would be integral to any such underground, a watch list of pro-Nazi French was passed to the FBI.

That was an easy matter, for the Bureau had moved into Paris, but also a prickly one, because the Bureau was beginning to make trouble. Hoover wanted custody, for instance, of the I. G. Farben Company's Paris director, notorious for trading with the Nazis, who was being held by X-2. Donovan refused to turn him over until so ordered by Eisenhower. In early January 1945, X-2 Paris cabled Murphy about three additional FBI men on their way to France, where they were supposedly to "observe Communist activities in Europe." The cable warned of a definite extension of FBI duties abroad, but saw no chance of reining in such "renegade Americans" unless steps were initiated in Washington.

Donovan demurred, for at the time he was tangled up with Hoover over relations between U.S. and French intelligence. He had befriended André Dewavrin, de Gaulle's intelligence chief, and in September 1944 invited him to the United States to receive the Distinguished Service Cross. General Eisenhower would have approved Donovan's pro-forma request had not Hoover objected that Dewavrin was behind 1942's "Duke Street Murder," the killing in a London basement of a suspected German spy.

Eisenhower sided with Hoover; Dewavrin was miffed. Donovan tried a flanking maneuver, telling Secretary of State Cordell Hull it was "necessary for us to lay short and long range plans with [Dewavrin] and to cement for the future intelligence relationships which we have effectively developed over past months." Hull acceded, on the condition that there be no publicity, and Dewavrin came to the U.S. with his staff. But Hoover struck again, warning Attorney General Francis Biddle "that Colonel De Wavrin [*sic*] is in the United States to organize and set in operation a secret intelligence organization in behalf of the French Government . . . Foreign powers must not be permitted to become established on American soil and should be discouraged whenever possible from taking root any place in this Hemisphere . . . particularly when dealing with [a] government which is provisional in character and within which strange and ruthless forces are at work."

Biddle conveyed Hoover's concerns to Roosevelt, and Dewavrin's reception in the U.S. was chilly. Offended, the French spy chief blamed Donovan, who had been formally charged with arranging the visit. Returning to his "strange and ruthless" homeland, Dewavrin promptly ordered OSS out of Paris. Donovan fought the order, and was able to keep a ghost staff, but Franco-American intelligence relations would never fully recover from the insult to Dewavrin. Sixteen years later, a Soviet KGB defector would tell U.S. debriefers the Russians knew of that tension and exploited it; the postwar French spy service, SDECE, was regarded as the weakest link and point of penetration into the Western alliance, since its officers were so uniformly anti-American.

Given the general tension over FBI work in Europe, Murphy was in no mood to hear, in March 1945, that Hoover wanted to add still more agents in Paris, where they would "function strictly in a liaison capacity as do the Special Agents assigned to the other American establishments at London, Lisbon and Madrid." Exasperated, Murphy listed X-2's objections in a blistering memo to Donovan.

1). This is simply an extension of the program Mr. Hoover has been undertaking for a long time to establish an intelligence network in Europe, which I feel must be considered in that light.
2). Mr. Hoover does not stick to facts when he says that the agents to be attached to the Embassy in Paris "will function strictly in a liaison capacity as do the Special Agents assigned to the other American establishments at London, Lisbon and Madrid." The agents at those places do not confine themselves to liaison activities.
3). I am interested in Mr. Hoover's statement that "hardly an espionage case arises in the United States that does not have some phase of its activity located in France which necessitates inquiry if we are properly

to complete the matter." *We have always made that same statement both in SI and CE work leading into South America but apparently Mr. Hoover feels that the argument applies only to FBI.*

4). The FBI already has three representatives in Paris, not attached to the Embassy. In many respects they duplicate the work of X-2.

5). I recommend that we oppose any further appointments of FBI men to Embassy positions in Europe until our own relationships are clarified, at which time it may be entirely appropriate to have FBI men, but to have them keep strictly within their proper bounds. We have watched them encroach in London, Lisbon, Madrid and in Italy. These things, together with their announced intention and desire to get into the foreign field after the war, are beginning to present a problem upon which OSS should take a firm position.

Murphy was a prophet. The problem of FBI expansionism would preoccupy Donovan over the coming year, and already the rival organizations were competing for leverage in the restructuring of U.S. intelligence that would surely come with postwar peace. The outcome of this struggle would be of no small import as America moved from defeating her present enemies, the Japanese and the Nazis, to containing her erstwhile allies, the Soviets.

CHAPTER FOUR

AMERICAN GESTAPO?

ON DECEMBER 7, 1941, FBI agent William Sullivan had been wearing earphones and was monitoring a meeting of Milwaukee communists, picked up by a hidden FBI microphone, when the gathering learned that Pearl Harbor had been bombed. Sullivan would later recall that the communists whooped with jubilation, calming only when their leader, Josephine Nordstrand, pronounced solemnly: "This is the greatest opportunity we've ever had. At last we're in. The Japs did what we weren't able to do, get America into the war. Now our job is to penetrate all the patriotic organizations. By doing that, we're going to gain the respectability we've never had."

Nordstrand's prediction was soon fulfilled. Communists were accepted in war-relief organizations, in the regular Army, and of course in OSS.

Respectability increased even more after 1943, when Stalin dissolved the Communist International (Comintern), which convinced many that the communists had given up their goal of world conquest. In fact, control of fronts and foreign communist parties was simply transferred to the International Department of the Central Committee of the Soviet Communist Party, but Westerners did not know this then. There was some awareness of subversion, but few saw the Soviets as an espionage threat. The U.S-Soviet alliance seemed so vital to the vanquishing of Hitler that, when American officials were warned of communist spies by informants like Whittaker Chambers, or Soviet-intelligence defectors like Walter Krivitsky, the possibility was discounted or ignored.

As the war drew to a close, General George Patton wanted to push past Berlin to Moscow, but Americans were tired of international conflict, and hoped the Soviets were, too. Eisenhower's chief of staff, Walter Bedell Smith, attended a Soviet-American friendship dinner at the Waldorf Astoria, exchanged toasts with a Soviet diplomat educated at the University of Michigan, and came away believing the Russians might not be so bad. Even if they returned to their old ways after the war, which appeared unlikely, the successful crusade in Western Europe, and the awesome superiority soon demonstrated with the detonation of two atomic bombs, seemed to show that America was invincible. *Life* magazine editorialized about "The American Century," and one OSS man would remember that "The mood was one of a problem definitely solved, and of power."

Donovan's men had picked up ominous hints of Soviet intentions in early 1944—Yugoslavia was being practically overrun by Stalin's operatives, and communist guerrillas in northern Italy were not being disbanded, as the Soviets had promised—but there was little willingness in Washington to hear what such OSS agents had to say. The clandestine operator's perspective was completely different from that of the desk analyst, who knew communism only intellectually. Field operators were face to face with the Soviets, saw them trying to entice, coerce, or blackmail White Russians to return to the Soviet Union, knew the ruthlessness that accompanied their actions, the almost inhuman disregard for what was going to happen to people they were putting on railroad cars to Siberia. But there was no way that that kind of knowledge could be captured in typescript for someone in Washington, who read reports and looked at maps, and saw only oppressed peasants trying to shuck the yoke of imperialism in faraway lands.

By fall 1944, however, a lurking sense of unease about possible Soviet designs on Europe, coupled with a consensus that there must be no more Pearl Harbors, had begun to spur discussion about the postwar need for a permanent U.S. intelligence system. The debate assumed great urgency around Christmas, when the Nazis counterattacked with total surprise and nearly routed the Allies in the dark forests of the Ardennes. Donovan's area experts had predicted the attack, to be known as the Battle of the Bulge, but military intelligence had disagreed, and the joint chiefs could not pass the president any coherent assessment. No one wanted such a state of affairs to continue once Hitler was vanquished, when America would have to contend with Stalin. Everyone, even Donovan and Hoover, agreed that intelligence collection and analysis had to be centralized. The rub came over how.

ON HALLOWEEN 1944, FDR requested Donovan to draw up a proposal "for an intelligence service for the postwar period, which would be in over-all supervision of all agencies of the Gov't. as to intelligence matters." Three weeks later, Donovan recommended creating a Central Intelligence Agency, or "CIA," to coordinate and collect intelligence. CIA would also have the rather vague authority to perform "other functions and duties relating to intelligence as the President from time to time may direct." But his new CIA, Donovan insisted, "would not conflict with or limit necessary intelligence functions" performed by "other agencies."

Those other agencies were not so sure. A copy of the proposal had come into Hoover's hands by late December 1944, and he promptly ordered his assistants to catalogue "its objectionable features as well as errors of omission." These negatives were presented by FBI Assistant Director Edward Tamm at "a series of conferences with gentlemen not too friendly with OSS," as one of Donovan's deputies told him. OSS tried to get minutes of the meetings, but could report to Donovan only that "such harsh things were said, apparently about you by Tamm, that it was decided that no one outside the committee should have them."

Tamm had in fact collected considerable evidence of Donovan's failings. Though Wild Bill's partisans later claimed OSS was "perhaps the most modern and efficient secret intelligence agency the world has ever known," Bureau files recorded that 85 percent of Donovan's reports were "re-hashes of British intelligence," and that the British themselves were disenchanted with their former favorite. During a Donovan trip to London in early 1945, the FBI's London legat reported that "General Donovan . . . did not desire to see 'any damned British.' I do not know the reason for his attitude . . . but apparently there is some friction between him and the British Intelligence Service." That friction was certainly not unwelcome news to Hoover, considering that it had been Tory interventionism which had put Donovan in power. Donovan had also alienated other important backers, such as Navy Secretary Frank Knox; an FBI informant reported that Donovan was "a constant cause of embarrassment" to Knox, "due to the fact that Donovan used the Secretary's name all over Washington, with all sorts of people, with respect to subject matters the Secretary has no knowledge of. . . . The less that Donovan is seen around the Secretary's office, the happier everybody is, as he has such an apparently unstable personality that there is no way of predicting what he will ask for or do next." An FBI War Department source summed up the anti-OSS mood by saying: "Donovan's past sins are catching up with him."

Sensing Donovan's weakness, Hoover moved boldly to push a plan of his own. Rumors of an FBI proposal were swirling at least as early as November 1944, and by December Hoover had sent one to Attorney General Biddle. Hoover conceded that OSS had met the wartime need for "an evaluation and analysis unit," but contended that peace required a group "established, controlled and operating at the security level and by professional security-minded and trained people"—a clear gibe at Donovan's notoriously lax security procedures. The Bureau allowed that "there should be a worldwide intelligence organization," but conceived of it as essentially a confederation of existing components—with the exception of the OSS, which would be abolished. Donovan's stations in Europe and the Far East would be taken over by Hoover, who would retain his own networks in Latin America. The prized OSS "evaluation and analysis" function would not be turned over to a separate agency, but centralized through interagency pow-wows "not dominated by any one group."

Tamm presented Hoover's plan to the military's Joint Intelligence Committee on December 22, outlining the Bureau's SIS work in Latin America and suggesting that it become the backbone of a postwar foreign-espionage service. Tamm's audience was disposed to accept his message; General George V. Strong of G-2 interrupted several times to compare his experiences with OSS and the FBI, each time belittling Donovan's efforts. When one Donovan defender observed that his evaluation-and-analysis unit was a good one, Tamm pointed out that the majority of the people in that unit were from private industry, and that it would be "practically impossible to keep people of this caliber on the salary that would be paid them as Government employees in the postwar period."

Donovan was meanwhile trying to drum up anti-Bureau sentiment among his own set of minor Washington kingmakers, and in fact had been fighting the very idea of a Hoover plan even before it came into being. In October 1944, Donovan emissaries to the Bureau of the Budget were pre-emptively bad-mouthing the idea that postwar spying should be "tied up with and under the control of a 'domestic police' outfit such as [the] FBI, or any . . . FBI dominated operation." OSS Deputy Director for Intelligence John Magruder expressed his concern to Julius C. Holmes, assistant secretary of state for administration, "that a national crime detective agency such as the FBI was branching out into international intelligence activities," which was "not only opposed to our ideas of the conduct of government but incidentally was very vulnerable politically in the United States." During this sounding-out phase, Donovan avoided confronting Hoover openly; he did not want to open fire before all his cannons were rolled into place, and even refused to sign letters to Hoover, ghosted by Murphy, which seemed unduly hostile in tone. Yet even as Donovan moved quietly to spike the FBI plan, his enemies upped the ante by taking the whole dispute public in a very nasty way.

On the morning of February 9, 1945, Donovan picked up the Washington *Times-Herald* from his Georgetown doorstep to read the front-page headline: "Donovan Proposes Super Spy System for Postwar New Deal. Would Take over FBI." Someone had leaked the complete text of Donovan's CIA plan, which reporter Walter Trohan warned would "pry into the lives of citizens at home," "supersede all existing Federal police and intelligence units," siphon "secret funds for spy work along the lines of bribing and luxury living described in the novels of E. Phillips Oppenheim," and "employ the FBI on some tasks and charge the G-men not to report to J. Edgar Hoover."

Donovan telephoned Colonel Ole Doering, his executive assistant. In a soft voice, he said, "Ole, I want you to find out who did this and report to me."

Doering drove over to "the Kremlin" and traced dissemination of the five known copies of Donovan's CIA plan. By nine o'clock that morning, when Donovan arrived at work, Doering had the answer. He said that J. Edgar Hoover had "personally handed the memorandum to Trohan." It would be said by Donovan's people that their boss had "marked" copies of the memo with tiny textual differences, and that the unique alterations in Hoover's copy turned up in Trohan's article. A Top Secret CIA internal history would note flatly in 1972 that "J. Edgar Hoover, Director of the Federal Bureau of Investigation, is believed to have been responsible for this breach of security, his purpose having been to prevent the creation of a central intelligence agency based on the OSS." Declassified Bureau files would later confirm only that as of March 12, 1945, Hoover's personal copy of the Donovan plan was missing: "An extensive search was conducted by the Records Section in the effort to locate the copy designated for the Director. This search was made with negative results."

In Congress, the leak created immediate and bipartisan protest against Donovan's proposal. That very day, Senator Edwin F. Johnson (D-Colorado) declared that he did not "want any superduper Gestapo"; Representative Clare Hoffman (R-Michigan), denounced the plan as "another New

Deal move right along the Hitler line." President Roosevelt telephoned Donovan late in the afternoon and said regretfully that, in the current climate, there was no way to go on with the plan. They would have to "shove the entire thing under the rug for as long as the shock waves reverberate."

Two months passed. The Allied armies vaulted across the Ruhr, into Germany's wrecked industrial heart. Donovan traveled to Paris and checked into a suite at the Ritz hotel formerly favored by Hermann Goering. He would see that OSS had its role to play in Europe after the inevitable armistice, and when he returned to Washington, he would revive his plan. Roosevelt had asked him only the previous week to reconvene the chiefs of the various intelligence agencies to discuss the matter, and on April 6 Donovan had submitted a revised proposal. The OSS director faded to sleep on the night of April 12, feeling that his peacetime dream for a CIA seemed assured, that he had nothing to worry about as long as President Roosevelt supported him.

The next morning, Donovan was shaving when a young aide banged at the door. There was an urgent OSS message from Washington. President Roosevelt had suffered a massive cerebral hemorrhage while sitting for a portrait and had died. Donovan spent the rest of the day on the edge of his bed, deeply depressed. When someone asked him, "What will happen now to OSS?," Wild Bill said, "I'm afraid it's the end."

HARRY TRUMAN GAVE Donovan hell. That was Truman's way with everyone, but the habit was exaggerated in Wild Bill's case because, as James Murphy would recall, "Truman didn't like Donovan and Donovan didn't like Truman. Period." William Colby considered it common knowledge that his boss and the new president didn't get on, but postulated less personal reasons. "Truman considered him an empire-builder. And let's face it, Truman was a Democrat, and Donovan was a Republican. And you know, if Donovan came home with a brilliant record, he could become a real candidate. So I think the worry was in Truman's mind that he could become a political threat."

Truman's mind was also poisoned by Harold Smith, director of the Bureau of the Budget. A young man who belonged to no political clique, Smith was essentially an "outsider" like Truman, and so could be unswervingly loyal to him. It was to Smith that Truman turned for counsel on the future of American intelligence—or, rather, it was Smith who compelled the president's attention in late April 1945 to a "tug of war" between the various agencies competing for postwar primacy.

Smith's bias was bared when he selected, for Truman's first briefing on the problem, not a panel of service chiefs or a roomful of experts, but the man who happened to be J. Edgar Hoover's immediate boss. On the very day FDR died, Hoover had briefed Attorney General Biddle on "the weakness in and objections to the plan as proposed by General Donovan," and on May 1 Biddle conveyed the Bureau's anxieties directly to the new president. Biddle noted that the FBI was "working highly satisfactorily" in South America, and urged that, "following the war, intelligence coverage should be arranged, but that it should not be the Donovan plan."

Donovan had meanwhile been trying to see the new president, but did not succeed until May 14, when Truman consented to sit with him for fifteen minutes. It was the only private meeting they would ever have, and it was a disaster. As Donovan recalled, Truman said: "The OSS belongs to a nation at war. It can have no place in an America at peace. I am completely opposed to international spying on the part of the United States. It is un-American." Donovan begged to differ, but Truman was icily quiet. Donovan showed him a memo by Roosevelt, dated a week before his death, which asked that Donovan convene various agencies to discuss implementation of the CIA plan; Truman ignored it. When Donovan left, it seemed pretty clear to him that OSS would be dissolved with the surrender of Japan, and that his proposed CIA would not be created, unless Truman could be dissuaded from thinking of it as an "American Gestapo."

Donovan determined to do that by improving the public image of OSS. Taking a cue from Hoover's own genius, Donovan engineered a massive public-relations campaign. A number of journalists who had been recruited into OSS were ordered to interview the most heroic among their colleagues and churn out "now it can be told" adventures. A Madison Avenue advertising man was brought in to oversee the whole enterprise, and a massive blitz upon the American imagination was secretly scheduled for summer's end. "Capital Ax Falling on Priceless Secret Spy System!" cried the Chicago *Daily News* just after Labor Day, and so the barrage began. Where Hoover's campaign had drawn heavily on conservative, isolationist, small-government, anti-FDR newspapers, Donovan relied on organs of exactly the opposite stripe. *The New York Times* praised Donovan's postwar plan, and the Washington *Post* publicized the dubious figure of "4000 stranded fliers rescued by [an] OSS underground railway." Comic books showed dashing OSS operatives in derring-do adventures behind enemy lines. OSS parachutists like Tom Braden, who returned from their secret war expecting to hear the usual jibes about "Oh So Social," suddenly found themselves figures of glamour. The hyperbole was shamelessly purple: OSS was "an organization as revolutionary in our military life as the atomic bomb," and was "perhaps the most modern and efficient secret intelligence agency the world has ever known." Moral of the stories: "Only a permanent central bureau of intelligence—based on the lessons that these men of the OSS have taught us, free from politics and interdepartmental jealousies [!], alert as a seismograph to every global tremor—can insure our future security."

But Donovan overkilled the issue. OSS officer Corey Ford, who played a large role in hyping the agency, later conceded that Donovan's opponents "seized the opportunity to charge that Wild Bill was indulging in vainglorious publicity." When Hoover saw an article stating that Donovan "gave us for the first time in American history a really coordinated intelligence service," he scrawled: "He [the journalist] must be on Donovan's payroll," and that was the general reaction. Columnist Drew Pearson warned readers not to believe the tall tales of daring, which had come to the public's notice only because "little Gremlins in Donovan's entourage were playing with matches." The PR campaign riled Truman, and Smith's attitude only hardened as he realized that public pressure might foreclose options for dealing with Donovan as he and the president saw fit.

Donovan's last hope for victory was a strategic retreat. "I wish to return to civilian life," he wrote Smith. "Therefore, considering the disposition to be made of the assets of OSS, I speak as a private citizen concerned only with the security of his country." This might have made him seem a bit more noble, but Donovan's deputies feared that his withdrawal was a "fatal concession," since the dream of CIA was denied its principal architect and advocate. On or about September 13, Truman ordered OSS abolished.

The only problem was, no one had the heart or courage to tell Wild Bill. The president refused to do it, and Smith fished around for a week without finding any takers. Finally, a week later, he ghosted a letter for Truman. Effective October, Donovan's prized Research and Analysis Unit would be awarded to the State Department, and his foreign operations, including X-2, transferred to the Army. Though the coming diaspora was explained in clinical detail, Donovan was told to regard that not as an end, but as "the beginning of the development of a coordinated system of foreign intelligence." The death of his own creation was hardly what Donovan had fought to attain, but he was supposed to take consolation in the fact that "the peacetime intelligence services of the Government are being erected on the facilities and resources mobilized through the Office of Strategic Services during the war." The letter was a cold, dishonest piece of work, carried over to Donovan by Smith's assistant Donald Stone. Donovan took the news, Stone later said, "with a kind of stoic grace," giving no outward indication of the personal hurt he must have felt about the way in which he was informed.

Stone never told him, and Donovan never knew, that at the same time his termination letter had been put for signature on the president's desk, Smith had also placed there a plan for a new foreign spy service. This was the plan for a "peacetime" organization which the letter to Donovan said would be his true legacy, "erected on the facilities and resources" of OSS— the outcome which, the letter proclaimed, he should take credit for, and view with pride.

It was the FBI plan.

J. EDGAR HOOVER'S long-standing hostility to communism lent a certain credibility to the idea that he was the one to lead American intelligence against the new threat. Though posthumous attacks on his reputation, and his own anti-intellectualism, would all but obscure his role in twentieth century American intellectual history, Hoover was the philosophical god-father of American anticommunism, contributing two key points to its doctrine when writing up his legal brief against Bolshevism as a twenty-four-year-old clerk in 1919. One, *ideas mattered*, and certain violent actions would necessarily result from Lenin's theories. Two, there was a *conspiracy*; the international movement was supported and guided by Moscow. Know-ing communism from its earliest days, he never moderated his views during World War II. "Of course we have to kill the Nazis," he would say, "but you mark my words, a year later—two years later—we're going to be fighting the Communists. They're a great ally today, we have paper for Russia drives, we have this, that, and the next thing, but they're going to be our next enemy. We won't have peace."

By September 20, 1945, when his proposal was put on the president's desk, those who had been listening to Hoover had reason to believe he was right. There was open disagreement among the war's victors over the spoils; the Soviets clearly had their own ideas about what U.S. newspapers were politely calling "the question of freedom in Eastern Europe," and had yet to lift the military government in North Korea, which they occu-pied. Mao Tse-tung's communists were suddenly so strong in China that the nationalist government of Chiang Kai-shek had to accept them as equals in a coalition government, which history taught could only go the way of Alexander Kerensky's partnership with the Bolsheviks in 1918. In late August, an American woman had confessed to being a courier for Soviet spies within a dozen departments of the federal government. On September 5, Igor Gouzenko, a cipher clerk at the Soviet Embassy in Ottawa, Canada, defected and described Soviet plots to steal atomic se-crets. It was in this darkening atmosphere that Truman, having disbanded OSS, immediately cast about for some new means to counter the Soviets.

The proposal that landed on the president's desk on September 20, though rewritten by Smith, nevertheless retained the most salient features of Hoover's plan. Centralization was needed, but not "extreme centralization" or "the creation of a single super-intelligence organization not connected with any of the departments," as under the Donovan plan. Rather, coordination could be accomplished by confederating extant components through interagency pow-wows or, at most, a "small" central staff. Collection of foreign intelligence could be done through the Department of State, which had no assets of its own, but could draw, conveniently enough, upon FBI legations attached to its embassies.

Whatever their true qualifications for foreign service, no one could doubt the anticommunism of the Bureau, and loyalty concerns alone recommended it over former OSS personnel now at Army and State. In the new postwar order, Donovan's policy of tolerating communists suddenly seemed a stupid thing, and cast doubt upon any work done by ex-OSS personnel reconstituted in the Army's new Strategic Services Unit (SSU). The situation was so bad that no one could deny it anymore, as Donovan had done. When SSU obtained information on the armaments of Soviet warships, Naval Intelligence refused to accept it, saying SSU, with its former Donovan officers, was so "riddled with communists" that the material was "probably a deception."

Cleaning out the stables therefore became the first priority of SSU's chief. Colonel William Quinn was Regular Army, respected by OSS veterans as "a tough, open-faced man who radiated a bustling confidence"—a worthy torch-holder, pronounced Allen Dulles, of "the Donovan spirit," but trying to exorcise the Donovan ghosts.

"I took a helluva beating," Quinn would later say. "The FBI did not want a central intelligence agency. They kept pounding about breaking the SSU up, and give the assets to the Navy, and so forth. . . . The theme was, Quinn is clean, but he harbored Communists. And that the OSS suffered because of the looseness of its nature; it even had criminals, lock pickers, and counterfeiters. Which we did. . . . We had this general exodus, and an awful lot of principals were deserting their agents. We were trying to stem the tide of this disintegration of intelligence collection."

So in early October 1945, Quinn went to see Hoover.

"Mr. Hoover, I'm just an Army man," Quinn would recall saying. "I'm not used to all this intrigue and stuff like that. But I hear all these rumors that the place is loaded with communists. You know what everybody in this town is saying about my unit. I would like you to vet every one of my twenty-five hundred principals—both criminally and subversively. Will you help me?"

Hoover leaned back in his chair. "Colonel, this is beautiful," he said, and seemed to mean it. "It's unbelievably refreshing to me. The Donovan days are over. You know, I fought him in South America primarily, and wherever in the world. A hard-headed Irishman. And to have you as his successor come to me for help is just taking all the steam out of my hatred."

After their meeting, Hoover assigned an FBI liaison officer, John Doherty, to work with SSU's Jason R. Paige, Jr., at the old OSS buildings where SSU was quartered. That amounted to "a real penetration," Quinn said, "but he was very nice about it." Doherty said the FBI already had records of seven communists in OSS who had been kept by Donovan over Hoover's protests. One had already left the organization; Quinn had the other six fired. The Bureau began vetting fingerprints, photographs, backgrounds of others. Five weeks later, Hoover was back in touch.

"Colonel Quinn," he said, "I have some good news and maybe a little bad. You are not riddled with Commies, that's the good news. You do have a girl working in logistics who has been dating what we call a fellow traveler who is a very close friend of one of the diplomats in the Soviet embassy." The girl was let go. When Quinn took a satchel of Soviet Baltic Fleet plans to ONI, they were accepted. SSU was back in the club. Quinn didn't care what anyone said about Hoover—all this had gone on while Truman was pondering the proposal that would expand the Bureau's foreign intelligence role, and it was hardly in Hoover's interest to strengthen a rival agency, but that was what he had done. "I never forgot his patriotism," Quinn would say with emotion almost a half-century later. "He helped me when I asked for the help."

Truman was less inclined to ask for J. Edgar Hoover's assistance, however. Since April 1945, the president had contacted the FBI director only "very sparingly," according to Hoover's assistant Cartha "Deke" DeLoach. Truman did not have to worry, as he did with Donovan, about Hoover's political ambitions or loyalty; Hoover had no party affiliation, and no real politics but to serve whoever was over him and to defend his Bureau and his country against apparent enemies. Like Wild Bill, though, J. Edgar was a living legend, and that did not make him especially welcome in the post-FDR White House. The FBI director's eminence might make it politically impossible to dismiss him, but Truman would be wary about enhancing his power. As early as May 1945, the president had fretted about the FBI's "postwar proportions." He told Smith he had been "doing some thinking" about an *information* service for international relations, rather than any *investigating* group. Though he was not dead against a Bureau-based intelligence service, he wished Smith to ponder the wisdom, "from the standpoint of good neighbor relations, about our having the FBI in South America." What was more, Truman indicated that he had some knowledge of the work the Bureau did at home, and that he apparently did not approve of some of it. Smith, though secretly a Hoover backer, was enough of a yes-man to agree that it "was not altogether appropriate to be spending Federal funds merely to satisfy curiosity concerning the sex life of Washington bureaucrats and members of Congress." Truman put more of a point on it by adding that he did not want to put Hoover in charge of a "Gestapo."

Perhaps it was only fair that Hoover should be haunted by the charges that he had apparently used, via Walter Trohan, to destroy Donovan's plan, but there was more to it than the transfer of a journalist's smears. There were Hoover's domestic snoopings for Roosevelt, which included the monitoring of his political opponents and chronicling the extramarital adventures of First Lady Eleanor; there was the tincture of illegal surveillance which Donovan had pinned on Hoover back in 1924, when the director had been forced to admit that his "subversives index" was technically against the law. Hoover had given American anticommunism its basic tenets, but he had also contributed the extralegal ethos that would become its Achilles' heel.

There were also complaints about the overall quality of the Bureau's spy work. William Sullivan encountered a diplomat in Mexico City who said, "You know, you should stop having your men send in material from Nicaragua because we have better material sent in by our own men. Further, much of your material is inaccurate." Undersecretary of State Julius Holmes felt that SIS agents in South America had "consistently showed the results of their training for criminal detection, and the pursuit of an individual, rather than the obtaining of information." And policy specialists, led by George Kennan, grumbled that Hoover's "cop mentality" had poked out America's secret eyes in Moscow before they had even been allowed to open.

The incident in question had begun after Donovan had returned from a Christmas 1944 visit to Russia and proposed exchanging intelligence representatives with the Soviets. Donovan's contingent would be stationed in the Russian capital, and Stalin's NKVD officers would be registered in Washington. The stated purpose was coordination of anti-Nazi operations, but it was also hoped that American agents would stay in Moscow after the war. As Ambassador W. Averell Harriman pointed out, the American embassy had "unsuccessfully attempted for the last two and a half years to penetrate sources of Soviet information and to get on a basis of mutual confidence and exchange. Here, for the first time, we [will] have penetrated one intelligence branch of the Soviet government and, if pursued, I am satisfied this will be opening the door to far greater intimacy in other branches." Of course, such an exchange would also increase Soviet spy resources in the United States. But the Soviets already had agents in-country, and at least the new ones would be identified when they came over. Having *some* agents on their turf, as opposed to none, would definitely create a more equal situation.

Hoover, who would have to watch any new Soviets in the U.S., couldn't have disagreed more. In February 1945, he alerted Harry Hopkins, FDR's close adviser, to "a highly dangerous and most undesirable procedure to establish in the United States a unit of the Russian Secret Service, which has admittedly for its purpose the penetration into the official secrets of various government agencies." The history of the NKVD in Great Britain and other countries showed clearly that the Soviets were after Western secrets. Why, then, should the Soviet spy agency be allowed to function in the United States "without any appropriate restraint upon its activities"?

Hopkins referred the matter to the Joint Chiefs of Staff, who decided that Donovan should be given a chance to defend his plan. Since Wild Bill himself was out of the country, OSS Colonel John H. F. Haskell made the case. After hearing Haskell out, a JCS planning committee found "no reason" for disapproving the exchange. But Hoover went around the planners to the attorney general and the Navy's Admiral William Leahy, and together they persuaded the president to table the plan. As Hoover proudly scribbled on an FBI memo recounting the episode: "I personally protested to Pres. Roosevelt about the plan (It was one of Bill Donovan's brain children) and the President took my side."

By late 1945, however, Truman desperately needed to gauge Stalin's intentions, and so sought the very Moscow presence Hoover had happily torpedoed. Disenchanted with Hoover's narrow stance on the Moscow issue, disliking him personally, and disinclined to create an FBI "Gestapo," Truman rejected any expansion of SIS, as called for under the September 20 plan. Instead, he urged Budget Director Smith to cut FBI personnel to prewar levels, and cast about for "an entirely different solution."

What that might be, the president could not say. Perhaps even he did not know, for in late September he took the strange step of telephoning Donovan, who was then returning to the practice of antitrust law in New York. In this conversation, Donovan had argued against any Hoover-directed organization and recommended Quinn for SSU director; Truman had followed his advice. Donovan had also lobbied successfully to place a young OSS-SSU lawyer, Lawrence R. Houston, on yet another committee considering plans for the centralization of intelligence. By year's end Houston was shuttling between committee meetings in Washington and private strategy-breakfasts with Donovan at New York's Metropolitan Club, and it was Houston, more than anyone else, who successfully bucked Hoover and saved Wild Bill's dream of a CIA.

Pressured by the president to come up with a workable plan, and disarmed by Houston's youth and easy charm where they had distrusted the ambitious Donovan, the service chiefs gave in. They were heartened by Houston's insistence that the new unit would (a) have no separate field-collection assets, and (b) would rely only on Quinn's personnel, which the military controlled. As for the Bureau, the new authority would have no police or law-enforcement powers, and no duties whatsoever within the United States; Hoover could even keep his agents in Latin America. It was the kind of artful compromise of which Donovan had been constitutionally incapable.

Hoover fought it still. As his old allies, the military chiefs, deserted the anti–Central Intelligence coalition, Hoover reversed himself and got behind the idea of a single, stand-alone foreign-intelligence authority—but proposed that it be the Bureau. Forwarded to Truman on October 22 by Attorney General Tom Clark, Hoover's revised "Plan for U.S. Secret Worldwide Intelligence Coverage" made two intriguing arguments.

The first was that "it is not possible to separate the gathering of intelligence from police functions, in view of the numerous criminal statutes, such as those relating to espionage and sabotage, which must be enforced by police action though directly relating to intelligence." In other words, since spies were criminals, spy-catching could not be divorced from police work, as it would be under the Houston-Donovan plan.

Second, whereas the Central Intelligence proposal would divide intelligence coverage along geographical lines, Hoover objected that this was unfeasible—in essence, because it would be like cutting a man down the middle. "Foreign and domestic intelligence are inseparable and constitute one field of operation," Hoover warned. "The German-American Bund and the Italian Fascist organization in the United States originated and were directed from abroad. The communist movement originated in Russia but operates in the United States. To follow these organizations access must be had to their origin and headquarters in foreign countries as well as to their activities in the United States. Every major espionage service has operated on a worldwide basis except that of Britain, which has had a separate organization for domestic and foreign intelligence. But Britain is in the process at present of consolidating the two services based on their experiences through the war period. In order to cope with the activities of various subversive agents in the United States with speed and dispatch, it is entirely evident that their activities must be followed throughout the various countries by one intelligence agency of the United States government. Valuable time, as well as efficiency and effectiveness, is lost if one agency covers their activities in Europe, another in Latin America, and another in the United States."

Wise words, but they never had a chance. By mid-November, an inter-agency board had accepted the Donovan-Houston idea that intelligence should be divorced from police power—otherwise, there might be a Gestapo. Again, the FBI chief was checked by the very charge he had used to derail Donovan's proposal.

Truman was meanwhile growing impatient. He began yelling at his advisers: "I want someone to tell me what's going on around the world! Damn it, there are people coming in from all over the place, different agencies, different interests, telling me different things." The president had been following a congressional inquiry into the failure to be warned on December 7, 1941, and lamented to his young aide, Clark Clifford: "If we had some central repository for information, and somebody to look at it and fit all the pieces together, there never would have been a Pearl Harbor." In the first week of 1946, haunted by fears that Stalin might launch a Pearl Harbor–type attack on Paris or Berlin, Truman ordered his interagency intelligence board to implement a refined version of Donovan's Central Intelligence plan.

Hearing of Truman's order, Hoover went to the White House and argued against it. The Bureau was operating smoothly overseas, it would be easier to expand it than to start a new organization, and anyhow it was impossible to divide foreign and domestic intelligence work. But he was turned down flat, and when he persisted in arguing the point, the president said, "You're getting out of bounds."

So it came to pass that on January 24, 1946, Truman gave a reception at the White House, presented guests with black cloaks and paper daggers, and announced the creation of a new intelligence service. Under a National Intelligence Authority (NIA), made up of the secretaries of State, War, and Navy and the chief of staff to the president, there would be a Central Intelligence Group (CIG). It would "collect, coordinate, and analyze" all foreign intelligence for the president, but would have no "police, subpoena, law-enforcement powers, or internal security functions." In all but a few important respects, it was the agency envisioned in Donovan's plan.

Alas, one of those respects was that CIG was merely a centrally confederated intelligence *Group*, as opposed to the autonomous *Agency* Donovan had wanted, and that was a distinction with some difference. Houston had got agreement on most of the language that had been in Donovan's original proposal, but the consensus had come with a price. Winning over the military chiefs had required chopping at the authority of the new agency until it was a bodyless head. Former Donovan officers in SSU became the active arm of CIG, but technically the personnel and money were contributed by Army, Navy, and State. Real control belonged not to the director of central intelligence, but to those who pulled the purse strings, the military members of the NIA. "The authority over the money was very doubtful," as Houston later admitted, and CIG's new director was certainly not the man to claim it.

Wanting a trustworthy nobody—somebody he and the NIA could easily dominate—Truman appointed as America's first official director of central intelligence Sidney W. Souers. A Missouri businessman and Truman campaign contributor, Souers had served briefly in Naval Intelligence after running the Piggly Wiggly grocery chain. He projected little personal authority, and had little real authority except his high-sounding title. He also had little interest in the job. He had agreed to take it only for six months, until Truman could find somebody better. Not long after he was appointed, SSU European-operations man Tom Braden went to see the new director in his office. "So, what do you want to do?" Braden asked him. Souers looked up from behind Donovan's old desk and chuckled sadly. "I want to go home."

Souers was only too eager to make concessions to the Bureau. The FBI director was made a member of CIG's Intelligence Advisory Board, and was even allowed to seat a man on Souers' planning staff; these moves gave the Bureau genuine beachheads in Central Intelligence. Hoover soon quit the board when he realized his ideas weren't welcomed, and after his man on the planning staff was bested by military members, the order came down in blue ink: "Get out of this thing now. It will not work." But Souers made other overtures to Hoover. As the DCI surveyed his unhappy domain, it seemed to him only logical that the old OSS remnant, X-2, should be handed over to the Bureau. After all, that would eliminate coordination problems and, finally, unite both foreign and domestic counterintelligence in a single organization.

Sensing their possible transfer to the Bureau, X-2 personnel inveighed against it. One senior officer protested to his bosses that "a separation of foreign counter intelligence from foreign positive [SI] intelligence operations would be disastrous to the latter and hampering to the former. . . . Any diversity of agency interests would militate against the success of a coordination which is essential. It is no exaggeration to say that if the X-2 function were to be divorced from positive intelligence work, the SI [foreign-intelligence] office would be forced to establish its own X-2 operations. Out of such an unfortunate situation would arise additional governmental duplication and the possibility of a dangerous conflict of American counterintelligence services. Either represents a consummation to be abhorred."

Souers, never a man to push an issue, quickly backed down. X-2 would stay in CIG. But Souers still thought Hoover could do a good job in the foreign spy field. Indeed, at lunch one day, he even asked Hoover whether he would be interested in absorbing CIG itself, en masse, when he, Souers, retired.

Hoover played coy. He was a shrewd enough bureaucrat to keep his Bureau out of anything in which he wouldn't have total control, let alone no control, as in CIG. The National Intelligence Authority, which was supposed to exercise control, could hardly agree with itself, and CIG's field components were operating without any relation to each other, like the independent joints of a poorly worked marionette. One of CIG's most promising covert-action specialists, Frank Wisner, quit in a paroxysm of rage after he hired and trained two hundred agents to bicycle into East Germany and report on the Russian occupation, but couldn't get approval to buy them bicycles. Two-thirds of CIG's ex-OSS officers followed Wisner and returned to private life; Wild Bill's old assets were being lost, it was said, "like shit through a goose." Donovan began giving speeches, denouncing the warped incarnation of his Central Intelligence dream as "a good debating society but a poor administering instrument." Finally, just before he stepped down in June 1946, Souers got up the nerve to ask the NIA for a Central Intelligence budget of his own, but he was refused.

FORTUNATELY FOR CIG, and much to the chagrin of Hoover, Souers' successor was a man who loved a fight. A fearless test pilot before the war, commander of the Ninth Air Force, which had covered France for D-Day, and most recently intelligence chief for the War Department, Lieutenant General Hoyt Vandenberg was one of World War II's "fly-boys," a handsomely dimpled hotshot who seemed born to wear a white scarf and brown leather jacket. He also had a reputation as a "chopper of dead wood," and after replacing Souers on June 10, he proposed a dramatic expansion of Central Intelligence, which would entail a brazen takeover of J. Edgar Hoover's turf.

It happened in a curious way. To help chop the "dead wood," Vandenberg had brought in a staff of Pentagon colonels, and those who witnessed the blitz would recall with awe how they *simply took over* from any who "did not measure up." The new team closeted themselves in a back room and, without consulting anyone, drew up plans for a self-sufficient CIG. There was a wasteful duplication of effort where the president wanted coordination, and, if necessary, they would coordinate the other intelligence agencies right out of existence.

Some bystanders wondered whether Donovan had been coaching the new director, and certainly Vandenberg's proposal would redefine Central

Intelligence in a way that was positively Donovanesque. To discharge its "vital responsibilities," CIG "should not be required to rely upon evaluated intelligence from the various departments." Rather, "funds, personnel, and facilities" formerly belonging to OSS and currently being run by State, Navy, and War should be "integrated into the Central Intelligence Group." Such expansionism initially caused turmoil within the National Intelligence Authority, but Vandenberg's colonels had some influence on their military colleagues, and it was also clear that Truman was behind Vandenberg and wanted change. On July 6, the plan was approved. CIG still lacked its own budget, but the strings were loosened, and Central Intelligence was given a right to conduct "all organized Federal espionage and counterespionage abroad." That language entitled CIG to reclaim former OSS officers in the Army's SSU, which was to be renamed the Office of Special Operations (OSO).

Vandenberg thought it also entitled CIG to do certain things domestically, like debrief businessmen who traveled overseas. Hoover consented to that, but at a price. CIG-FBI interface on domestic and other matters should be accomplished through one officer, not two; otherwise, there would be only more "confusion, duplication of effort and intolerable conditions to the detriment of the national well-being." Since most contacts would occur domestically, the liaison officer should be a G-man. Vandenberg reluctantly consented, and for the next fifty years, the position of liaison officer would be held exclusively by agents of the FBI.

Hoover had little time to savor his victory, however, for in summer 1946 CIG tried to absorb the Bureau's operations in Latin America. This was the bureaucratic equivalent of a declaration of war. Donovan had trespassed in Mexico, but no one had ever questioned the Bureau's right to run its own collection and counterespionage operations south of the Rio Grande—let alone tried to steal them outright. And what a prize those Latin American networks would be. "That was a damn good setup, all the way down there," SIS man Sam Papich would later say. They had undercover operations, microphone surveillances, the works. And now it would all be taken away?

"Hoover fought it quite hard," Lawrence Houston would recall. But Vandenberg walked right into it, determined to personally present his case to Hoover. As director of central intelligence, he could not do his job if the FBI director was doing the same work. One was likely to expose the other. Either Vandenberg or Hoover should withdraw from the field. Since the National Intelligence Authority had decided that CIG should do all foreign intelligence, the FBI should give way. Logic, however, could not soothe a ruptured pride, and William Sullivan would remember that after Truman sided with Vandenberg, Hoover sent "a stream of admirals, generals, congressmen, and senators to the White House to try to change Truman's mind." But it was a losing fight, because it was obvious where, in the overall intelligence structure, Latin American coverage should go. Had not Hoover himself argued, only eight months before, that enemy agents "must be followed throughout the various countries by one intelligence agency of the United States government"? That "valuable time, as well as efficiency and effectiveness, is lost if one agency covers their activities in Europe, another in Latin America"? The FBI director was irate, but Truman wouldn't budge, and the Bureau was ordered to shut down SIS.

Hoover complied with a vengeance. He removed all personnel, equipment, and records from the Dominican Republic and Costa Rica by mid-August 1946, and soon thereafter from Haiti, El Salvador, Honduras, and Brazil. Central Intelligence protested that there would be nothing left to take over when its officers arrived on the scene. "Hoover pursued a scorched earth policy," recalled Richard Helms, who then worked in CIG's OSO. "He cleaned out all the files, wouldn't allow his agents to talk to the new CIA people about sources. We got nothing worth having. He just cleaned the place out and went home in a sulk." A hurried NIA meeting on August 7 produced a letter to the attorney general, asking him to keep Bureau personnel in place until CIG could assume control. Hoover slowed his withdrawals, but insisted that CIG should not employ ex-SIS agents.

He lost on that one, too. There was a secret war going on with the Soviets, and it was no time to tear down and rebuild a functioning structure just for the sake of bureaucratic pettiness. The new Western Hemisphere Division of Central Intelligence thus assumed a special character, having been almost entirely "made by the FBI."

The decision was left up to individual officers, of course—no one had to join CIG who didn't want to—and a few agents, like Sam Papich, did stay with the Bureau. "My life was the Bureau, plain and simple," Papich would say. "The fellowship and the camaraderie, and whatnot. And I met some of the characters in Central Intelligence—this changed in later years, but at the time I didn't like them at all. They just weren't my type; I thought some of them were probably communists. I didn't know what the hell Vandenberg would do with me, anyway. It wasn't very difficult for me to decide."

But many other G-men did cross over. Their adventures abroad had already attracted them to foreign-intelligence work, and there were opportunities to better themselves financially by "going over." Later it was whispered that a lot of ex-Bureau people had joined CIG partly for the purpose of "penetrating" it and were secretly reporting back through channels to Hoover. It was an unprovable charge, which FBI agents would quickly dismiss, but which CIG officers were rather more inclined to contemplate.

After all, could that kind of behavior be beyond a man who had ordered his Latin American stations to burn their files rather than turn them over to Central Intelligence? The NIA might have mandated that Hoover keep his personnel in place for Vandenberg, but nothing had been said about all that priceless information. The first CIG officer posted to Central America arrived to find only a row of empty safes and a pair of rubber gloves in what had been an SIS darkroom. CIG officials complained to newspaper reporters that their men "arrived in the morning to find the FBI files burned and the FBI agents booked for departure that afternoon." The excuse given was that the Bureau could not be sure whether Central Intelligence was properly "security-conscious."

Was it envy, or was it prudence? Sam Papich, the last SIS man in all of South America, thought Hoover's worries were well founded. "I was glad to be going back to the States, but I worried about the security of people we had been running as agents. I asked some of those people: 'Do you want to be turned over to another outfit?' No way! They were scared." Papich was especially concerned about the fate of a recruitment he himself had made, a European—"the greatest ever, you could write a book on him." As far as the agent was concerned, his work for Papich was a contribution to the war effort; he wasn't a snitch, he was an agent, and insisted on being treated like one; and that's how Papich treated him. But who were these people coming in to claim him, and what would they do with him? The agent didn't know, nor did Papich, nor did Hoover. Therefore the FBI did not turn over everything, and people on the other side of it got mad. Eventually Papich was able to transfer the agent to an ex-FBI man and old friend, but such trust and continuity was not always there, and in general Papich would remember that period of time as "crummy and cold." He added: "To turn over everything we had built— it broke my heart."

The situation did settle down, and perhaps Hoover took some consolation in the fact that he was allowed to keep offices in Mexico City, Ottawa, London, Paris, and Rome. Hoover promised Vandenberg that the legal attachés who remained at those offices had been instructed to handle only the "international aspects" of domestic cases, and that they had been specifically told not to go "operational" or run informants. According to Sullivan, however, Hoover secretly instructed the Mexico City office to be operational, to run informants, to develop foreign intelligence—"to operate completely in violation of our charter." The FBI and CIG would each investigate communism in Mexico, "and the American taxpayer would pay for the duplication."

Still, though Hoover had fought it at the time, Papich believed that his boss was probably consoled afterward by a sort of "loser's relief." From what he knew and what he later learned, Papich didn't think the director, who had never been outside the country himself, was ever really comfortable with the Bureau's foreign work. Proud, maybe, of what had been done against the Nazis in Brazil and elsewhere during the war, but not fully confident. The Bureau could not verify the overseas overtime filed by unsupervised agents, and it was not easy to keep track of unvouchered funds used by SIS men undercover. Controls were in place, but Papich didn't think such rigid procedures would have been practical after the war, certainly not against an enemy as subtle and sinister as the Soviets. Hoover had resisted the SIS takeover as best he could, simply because that was the kind of man he was; it was not within him to give up turf easily. But once he was beaten, Papich never heard him complain.

Nevertheless, the men of Central Intelligence were convinced that Hoover would bear them an eternal grudge for the Latin American coup. In a matter of months, a whole chunk of Hoover's turf had just been chopped off, and it would have been against human nature, let alone Hoover's, for him to have not known some lingering bitterness. It became an article of faith among the Central Intelligence crowd that "J. Edgar Hoover didn't like losing the responsibility," that "he resented the fact that he was obliged to give up his operations in Latin America to the Agency after World War Two." Young CIG officers posted to Latin America were told by superiors that "J. Edgar is never going to forgive us for taking over his territory." Valid or not, that perception would eventually become as important, as powerful, and as damaging as any fact.

ON JUNE 13, 1946, three days after Vandenberg became director of central intelligence, Lawrence Houston had informed him that in a few months, CIG would be technically illegal. In the same spirit of anti-FDR backlash that would lead to the no-third-term rule, Congress had stipulated that no agency set up by the Executive Branch could survive for more than one year without congressional approval. Vandenberg soon put Houston to work on draft legislation, and Houston came up with a charter that was pretty much Donovan's plan for a CIA. Truman's new counsel, Clark Clifford, then brought into the process a group of generals who were working on a reorganizational bill of their own. It was agreed that CIA could piggyback on the behemoth military establishment, and the Agency was formally proposed when Truman sent the National Security Act to Congress on February 27, 1947.

But Hoover had his allies on the Hill. Congressman Fred E. Busbey (R-Illinois) said he worried about Central Intelligence "going into the records and books of the FBI," and Congressman Walter H. Judd (R-Minnesota) introduced an amendment that would prevent CIA "from being allowed to go in and inspect J. Edgar Hoover's activities and work." Otherwise, the Agency might find out "who their agents are, what and where their nets are, how they operate, and thus destroy their effectiveness." The Judd Amendment was carried, but Republicans on the House Un-American Activities Committee still believed the bill did not go far enough to protect the Bureau. Vandenberg began to wonder whether the whole issue of protecting the Bureau was manufactured by Hoover's defenders simply to stall the legislation and spur its sponsors to cutting out the troublesome CIA provision.

If that was the plan, it was doomed to failure. Pressure on Congress to pass a high-sounding National Security Act intensified as Stalin declared that the Soviet Union was commencing a program of massive rearmament. George Kennan declared that until and unless America could meet the Soviets with a strong military posture and covert political or guerrilla actions, "There is really no action we can take in Eastern Europe but to state our case." Donovan found an appreciative audience when he argued, in a *Life* magazine piece, that America desperately needed "central intelligence appropriate to our position as the world's greatest power," and though Hoover wrote on a Bureau summary of the article, "My, my, Col. [*sic*] Bill knows all the answers but few of the facts," the FBI could do little to stop the "Donovan idea" except, through congressmen like Judd, to state its case. After fruitless attempts at filibuster by Hoover's allies, the National Security Act was passed, and on September 18, 1947, CIA was born.

The FBI's defenders had succeeded, however, in limiting the new agency's powers. When it came to matters that touched on Hoover's jurisdiction, Central Intelligence authority had been sharply pruned by two provisos designed to protect the Bureau.

First, the FBI was not obligated to share anything with CIA except data "essential to national security"—and this only "upon the written request of the Director of Central Intelligence." This language, added by Judd, was resented by CIA men like Ray Cline as "a concession to J. Edgar Hoover's independence and fanatic protection of his files." Why should the Bureau, alone among other intelligence agencies, require a written request? And why should Hoover be the sole arbiter of what he should have to share? How workable would such a process be? If another Dusko

Popov came over and was being run by the FBI, would his information be withheld unless requested in writing, and unless Hoover deemed it "essential to the national security"? If he were not obligated in the first place to inform CIA on matters of mutual concern, how would CIA even know about Tricycle's existence, and how would it even know to ask, specifically, for his information? Based on past experiences, could Hoover really be trusted to furnish Tricycle's information by servicing general requests, such as Donovan's October 1941 plea for intelligence on "the Pacific situation"?

Second, CIA's charter stipulated that "the Agency shall have no police, subpoena, law-enforcement powers, or other internal-security functions." Houston added that language, he would later say, because the FBI asked him to. No one at CIA really wanted powers of subpoena and arrest, but the "internal security" prohibition was problematic. Did it mean that CIA could not coordinate or collect foreign intelligence in the U.S.? Could CIA officers debrief a Dusko Popov in New York? And if a CIA overseas employee or agent came to the United States representing a foreign government, CIA lawyer Scott Breckinridge would find himself wondering, "How should he be handled? He remained a foreign intelligence source, peculiarly within CIA's jurisdictional authorization. Yet he could present a security problem, especially if assigned to the diplomatic installation of an unfriendly nation."

These kinds of problems would have to be handled by ad hoc "arrangements between the FBI and CIA," presumably to be worked out by Bureau liaison officers. But as Breckinridge observed, there were "no established ground rules." Nor could there be: the "internal security" clause was really another attempt to cut the man down the middle, to delineate between domestic and foreign counterespionage, which could only mean the creation of new twilight zones.

There was, however, an "out." The director of central intelligence had been granted certain executive powers. At his sole discretion, he could take any actions he deemed necessary "for protecting intelligence sources and methods from unauthorized disclosure." This clause provided a pair of operational baggy pants, in which husky ambition had room to move around. CIA also had the right "to perform such other functions and duties related to intelligence affecting the national security as the National Security Council may from time to time direct." That was Donovan language, verbatim from his 1944 proposal to Roosevelt, and, depending on what the council authorized, it would give the Agency great scope.

But if the executive powers granted CIA's director gave him a certain flexibility, the elastic nature of the legislative language allowed actions which in themselves could create more problems for FBI-CIA relations than they would solve. Looking back on it years later, Breckinridge called the "other functions" provision a "banana-peel clause," and that assessment could just as easily stand for the whole foreign-domestic division, for the lot of fuzzy executive privileges which allowed its breach, even for the National Security Act itself. But that characterization and insight would not come until forty years later, when the shawl of secrecy had been yanked away to reveal the bruises—assassination plots, a divisive "molehunt," surveillance of antiwar dissidents. Only then would it be evident how badly and how often CIA, the FBI, and the country had slipped and fallen.

BOOK TWO

AMERICA'S
JAMES BOND

CHAPTER FIVE

SHAKEDOWN CRUISE

IF ART IMITATES LIFE, and life imitates art, it may be added that life sometimes imitates paperback thrillers. By the 1950s, when Ian Fleming wove into his books both Dusko Popov's daring and the theme of FBI-CIA competition, there had long been a curious cross-pollination between fiction and espionage. Many former intelligence officers had become novelists—John Buchan, Somerset Maugham, Rudyard Kipling, T. E. Lawrence, Graham Greene, John le Carré, and Fleming being among the best known—but novelists had also exerted their influence on clandestine work. One of the founders of British intelligence was also the father of the modern English novel, Daniel Defoe. The German spy scare dreamed up by hack mystery writer William Tuffnell Le Queux in *Spies of the Kaiser: Plotting the Downfall of England* (1909) had led to a British government inquiry, and to the June 1910 creation of the modern British Secret Intelligence Service, later known as SIS or MI6. The term "mole," used to denote a penetration agent in a novel by le Carré, eventually became slang among real intelligence officers. And the creator of James Bond had advised Donovan on the creation of OSS, little imagining that emulation of his aesthetic ideal—the attempt by certain intelligence officers to be America's Dusko Popov, its James Bond—would become one cause of serious friction between the FBI and CIA.

Most professional intelligence officers, of course, would deny that spy novels bear much resemblance to their work. They read them, they enjoy them, but they do not believe them. "The spy heroes of the novelists rarely exist in real life," Allen Dulles would say. "Most spy romances and thrillers are written for audiences who wish to be entertained rather than educated in the business of intelligence." CIA officer Lyman Kirkpatrick later lamented that "The James Bond syndrome, with its emphasis on cloak and dagger adventures, fast cars, and faster women, hasn't helped the CIA image. Most people now look on intelligence as all espionage and action, and fail to realize that the bulk of the work is painstaking assembly of information." One of Kirkpatrick's colleagues, David Atlee Phillips, believed that "Truth would be better served if the symbolic cloak and dagger of the espionage business were replaced by six 3 × 5 cards and a typewriter."

Such objections were no doubt valid, but could also be somewhat disingenuous. The glamorization of real-life intelligence along the lines of spy fiction had actually begun with the 1945 publicity campaign by OSS, which announced that "Behind the abrupt capitulation of the entire German Army in Italy lies a story of machinations as fantastic as a mystery-thriller by E. Phillips Oppenheim." As CIA director after 1953, Allen Dulles encouraged spy novelists, sometimes even providing writers like Helen MacInnes with plots, in hopes of enhancing the image of CIA; "the mystique was there in the 1950s," Agency analyst Ray Cline would recall, because "Allen Dulles loved it, helped create it, and in many ways embodied it." Indeed, Dulles himself was reportedly so intrigued by the idea of a radio homing device, which Bond installed in Auric Goldfinger's car, that he ordered CIA's laboratories to see if they could come up with one. (They couldn't: in cities there was too much interference with the signal.) Some CIA officers, especially cerebral counterintelligence types, avoided spy novels on principle, but many others—including CIA directors Dulles, Helms, and later Robert Gates—felt them a rewarding diversion. Nobody inside CIA believed the books uniformly realistic in the literal sense; like any other career, intelligence had its share of drudgery, and few officers, even in an operations directorate, ever saw physical action. But Fleming's novels were not without their contexts of plausibility. If the life of an infantryman could be characterized as an eternity of boredom punctuated by brief moments of sheer terror, the life of an intelligence officer, too, had its excitements and diversions. There *were* surveillances and secret codes, burglaries and bugs, defections and discoveries, betrayals and escapes, and rarely, but sometimes, kidnappings and murders. But even those were only concordances at the literal level, and said nothing of the deeper truths—emotional, moral, philosophical—which explained the appeal of spy novels to the very men who dismissed them, or, especially in the case of Fleming, the subtle but profound influence of those books on the world they purported to describe.

In January 1952, when Fleming began writing *Casino Royale*, there was no doubting that the Soviet Union was an evil empire, no honest way of denying what Fleming called "their brutality, their carelessness of human

life, and their guile." Stalin was still in power; the communists had fought
UN troops to a standoff in Korea; Berlin had been kept alive only by
airlift; Soviet spies had stolen secrets of the atom bomb; during the war
there really had been a Soviet assassination agency called SMERSH, a
contraction of the Russian phrase *smert shpinom*—"death to spies." It was
realistic, and resonant, to depict the USSR in an aura of grand-scale crime:
conspiring to subvert democracy, break Western morale, disrupt the international balance of power. If the heroes and villains in spy novels were
stylized, a clear distinction between "them and us" was nonetheless deeply
felt by Fleming and his admirers at CIA. Men like Richard Helms thus
hated the later pessimistic novels by John le Carré, which, if more literary
and "realistic" at the literal level, nevertheless rang philosophically false.
Le Carré felt that East and West were equally evil; what was more, his
players suffered from the bureaucratic malaise of mass man in an information society, and were pawns of huge organizations whose work held little
relevance for the realm of human values. Fleming, by contrast, reified
the quite real belief of CIA officers in the importance of their duties, and
the power of an individual to shape world events. True, the age of atomic
secrets had made technological advantage seem more important than
battlefield bravery or even industrial might; scientific knowledge was not
only power, it was *world power*; it was destiny. But that meant that solitary
acts of courage or treason, in the struggle for secret information, could
now be final and apocalyptic—more important to the course of history,
not less. As Fleming put it, "The atomic age has created the most deadly
saboteur in the history of the world—the little man with the heavy suitcase."

Believing that one man could really make a difference, Fleming and
his fans at CIA would never have thought, as had George Kennan, that
there was "no real action" the West could take against the Soviets except
to state our case. James Bond would state our case with a Walther PPK
pistol. Bond's creator had been profoundly affected by the wartime cult
of action, the mystique of Camp X and Wild Bill. In later years, he hinted
that some of Bond's adventures had been based on his own, and would
proudly show the .38 Police Positive Colt revolver that had been presented
him by Donovan in July 1941 with the inscription "For Special Services."
He used his considerable imagination to craft a moral-aesthetic ideal, an
icon for the secret war against the Soviets—an old boy from Eton and
Cambridge, a man of independent means, a gentleman licensed to kill.

Here was the spiritual core of the James Bond novels, of the CIA code
that was its real-life parallel, and of much Cold War controversy between
CIA and FBI: the idea of extralegal virtue. The conception was not without its precedents. In spy fiction, it could be found in Fleming's favorite

writer, Buchan, whose Richard Hannay was a hero convinced of the rightness of his cause, working in exotic locations against a ticking clock, and often with the local police authorities chasing him, since the interests of a Secret Service in wartime took priority over any country's public laws. In American spy fact, the tradition began on December 7, 1941. FBI intelligence man William Sullivan later explained: "When a soldier in the battlefield shot down an enemy he did not ask himself is this legal or lawful, is it ethical? It was what he was expected to do as a soldier. We did what we were expected to do. It became a part of our thinking, a part of our personality. We never freed ourselves from that psychology that we were indoctrinated with, right after Pearl Harbor, you see." Said one OSS veteran: "I broke every law of God and man, but I never did anything for personal gain. I was out to win a war for my country, and you can't fight a lawful war. . . . Where do you want [us] to get information? From churches?"

Donovan himself had plotted the assassination of foreign political leaders, such as Vichy North Africa Commissioner Jean Darlan, and those of his men who remained in CIA became an order of black knights, committed at once to dirty tricks and to honor. Most of the Agency's covert operators believed deeply that intelligence work was "something different," somehow falling outside the normal realm of the law, but that good men could work in this moral twilight without becoming evil. There was nothing wrong with wiretaps, mail-opening, "black-bag" jobs; there was nothing wrong with stealing from thieves, lying to liars, killing those who killed. CIA's code of valor required the betrayal of one trust, that of legality, to uphold another, that of national security. In its own way, it was civil disobedience, like tax protest or the struggle to end segregation. Its "higher-law" rationalizations were those of Henry Thoreau or Martin Luther King; only the goals were different, and the secrecy. It was a strategy kept, when possible, from the president or his Cabinet, who retained a "plausible deniability," yet gave their implicit sanction and blessing.

But this Cold War code grew and operated against the grain of J. Edgar Hoover's basic task, the enforcement of the very laws that CIA would try to break. As CIA expanded dramatically in the early postwar years, and again during the Korean War period, the strains came over CIA's constant "testing" of all rules and boundaries, the pushing of jurisdictional limits which seemed arbitrary, but which happened to be laws. The conflicts were latent at first, but they sharpened in the mid-1950s, as CIA began to open the mail of U.S. citizens, and to violate the sovereign airspace of other nations. During this era, certain interagency developments were paralleled in minor if intriguing ways by certain aspects of Fleming's thrillers, but by the early 1960s secret life would consciously imitate Fleming's art. As CIA's extralegal ethos reached its logical ultimate—assassination—the Bureau would clash with the man who would be presented to an American president as "our James Bond." He was a former FBI agent who'd gone over to the Agency, and he had caused trouble between the two organizations fifteen years before his "license to kill" brought matters to a comic climax, and a tragic resolution.

WILLIAM KING HARVEY, as even his friends had to admit, "was one hell of a case." He had big heavy shoulders and a chest like a horse, goggling eyes like a fish, a face that was all puffed out and ruddy-purple like a turkey-cock; he waddled like a duck, with his arms swinging almost like an ape, and talked in a voice like a frog. He was so fat he had CIA's permission on medical grounds to fly first-class, because he simply could not fit into coach seats. He drank three martinis at lunch, and Jack Daniel's the rest of the time. He was the only CIA man who always wore a pistol to work; on field assignments, he would tuck an emergency .38 into the back of his underwear band, where it would be enclosed by his big fat butt. He was heard to say that he had been to bed with a woman every day of his life since he was twelve, and not everyone disbelieved him. He had been a legend in the Agency since the day he joined, and some people liked him, some did not, but everyone knew who he was. Some thought him, at best, a buffoon; once, when he fell asleep in CIA's Frankfurt Station, with his jacket open to show a polished pistol-grip, someone scribbled out a sign and placed it on his heaving bulk: "Fattest gun in the West." There was no question that this imposing, colorful character, with his taste for guns, drink, and women, looked and sometimes acted more like W. C. Fields than 007. Yet there was a creative hardness to him, a tough suppleness of purpose. He had the patience of a door-knocking street cop, and a way of answering questions no one else had even thought to ask. For a while, especially in the early years, he was one of the few men in U.S. intelligence who really knew much about Soviet spies.

If he was to have a controversial and important career in CIA, Harvey brought with him a mixed record of successes and bungles past. Born during World War I to a well-off attorney in an Indianapolis suburb, Harvey was a good student at Indiana University Law School but an early failure in local Democratic politics, being a poor public speaker and not at all the gregarious-popular type. He put little effort into his subsequent practice as an attorney in Maysville, Kentucky, his pretty wife's part of the world, and was a bored man of twenty-four in December 1940, when he joined the FBI.

By summer 1941, Harvey had been working counterespionage with Sam Papich and others under Bud Foxworth in New York, helping run Nazi spy William Sebold as a double agent until Hoover had Sebold's ring arrested. Harvey helped neutralize the Nazis in New York during the rest of the war, not always happy with the way Washington wanted him to wind down double-agent cases for publicity, but by fall 1945 he was operating out of FBI headquarters on a three-man desk devoted to Soviet counterespionage. There he took charge of the case of the "blond spy queen," as the tabloids later called Vassar graduate Elizabeth Bentley, whose "good New England conscience" had drawn her into a Soviet espionage network, and then had driven her, in November 1945, into the arms of the FBI.

Harvey traveled to Manhattan to hear her story—she had been a courier in a Washington, D.C., ring—and relayed it to Hoover, who was so galvanized by Bentley's allegations that he immediately fired off a Top Secret report to President Truman. Of the fifty-one suspects eventually investigated by the FBI on the basis of Bentley's information, Harvey concluded that at least twelve government employees were definitely "Soviet espionage agents." The shortlist included Assistant Treasury Secretary Harry Dexter White, Truman's administrative assistant Lauchlan Currie, and Alger Hiss, an assistant to the secretary of state.

But the greatest single concentration of Soviet spies, Bentley said, was in OSS. She tipped the FBI to at least six alleged penetrations of Donovan's outfit, including Julius C. Joseph, at the Japanese desk, and Duncan Lee, a confidential legal assistant to Donovan. Bentley said Lee was her first and best contact in OSS, being "cognizant of most of the material directed to Gen. Donovan's attention." According to Bentley, however, Lee had been frightened by Donovan's 1944 proposal for an OSS-NKVD exchange, and was happy when Hoover nixed it, for "he had visions of this group visiting him at his home and thanking him for his cooperation." These were, indeed, not always the most professional of spies. Bentley related how, having been told to either burn certain documents or flush them, Joseph "crammed a mass of flaming documents into the toilet, with the result that the seat was set on fire. His puzzled landlord, surveying the damage, finally walked out of the apartment muttering to himself, 'I don't see how that could possibly have happened.'" But what the Bentley ring lacked in tradecraft it made up in access, thanks partly to the lax security of Donovan's organization. There was no question, Harvey wrote Hoover, that the Soviets had succeeded in placing "a large number of undoubted Soviet agents in positions where they would have access to considerable information of value." In blue ink at the bottom of the page, Hoover jotted: "Most significant."

But despite Hoover's appreciation of his work, the FBI as an institution would not provide the kind of counterstrategy its premier spy-catcher wanted. Harvey recommended "reactivating the Informant Gregory," as Bentley was code-named, "as an operating Soviet agent and utilizing her . . . as a double agent," and tried to get her to "discreetly renew her contacts." Although the operation failed, that did not mean it could not work in other cases—if only Hoover would agree to keep things hushed. He would not. The FBI director insisted on alerting the White House and departmental officials to Bentley's main accusations about penetration of OSS and other agencies. That approach undoubtedly damaged the reputation of William Donovan, and helped SSU chief William Quinn weed out implicated OSS personnel, but it also tipped off the suspects, who had a chance to cease any questionable activities and destroy evidence. If spies could not be doubled and could not be prosecuted, what the hell could Harvey do? He could only watch as the suspects transferred from government to higher-paying positions at places like the Carnegie Endowment for International Peace, immune to the consequences of their actions, smugly deflecting as "red-baiting" any inquiries into their evil work. It was all Harvey could do to assemble a skeleton crew to handle the expanding caseload, and even then he had to breach Bureau procedure to do it. Hoover's policy was to post agents at the "Seat of Government" only on the basis of "administrative ability," but Harvey needed men with counterespionage expertise, not managerial or fiduciary acumen, and only by bureaucratic duplicity did he arrange the fall 1947 transfers of New York anti-Soviet specialists Emory Gregg and Robert Lamphere. His new recruits soon shared his exasperation. Lamphere found Hoover's approach to the Bentley serials "massive and clumsy," counterproductive not only because it scared suspects into covering their tracks, but because "all cases were created equal," and precious resources were squandered on worthless cases while other leads, which seemed more logical, were not pursued. "We believed the FBI had to become more aggressive in counterintelligence against the Soviets," Lamphere recalled, "or we would lose the war with the KGB."

But Hoover would not be moved, and by midsummer 1947 Harvey had fallen into a deep funk. His wife, Libby, confided to Bureau friends that her husband always seemed to be "moody, . . . despondent and discouraged about his work." At a stag party on July 11, in the Virginia suburbs, his colleague Mickey Ladd noticed that "Harvey had been quiet while some of the other men had been quite exuberant." It was after midnight and raining hard when the somber Harvey left his laughing friends and began the drive toward his home in Georgetown. The next morning, his wife awoke to discover that he had never come home.

Worried that he might have been shot to death on some assignment, she called headquarters to see what they knew. Nobody was aware of anything until shortly after ten o'clock, when the missing man suddenly appeared in the driveway of his home. Harvey told his wife, and the Bureau, that he had crossed the Potomac River by the Arlington Memorial Bridge and hung a left at the Lincoln Memorial, then proceeded north on 23rd Street in a downpour so heavy he could hardly see. In a residential section of Rock Creek Park, not too far from Director Hoover's house, he splashed through a huge puddle of water at the same time as another car going in the opposite direction, and the engine in Harvey's car stopped. He coasted to the curb, but was unable to get his car started. He intended to wait for the engine block to drain, but fell asleep and didn't wake up until about 10 a.m., when he was able to start the car and drive home. Harvey was adamant that he had not been drunk, that he'd had only two cans of beer, and the other special agents at the party backed him up; "there was no indication," an FBI memo recorded, "that Harvey was drinking any more or less than anyone else."

But Hoover would hear no excuses. It was against Bureau regulations to be unreachable by Headquarters at any time, not to mention asleep at the side of the road, and it was decided to transfer Harvey to Indianapolis on general assignment. Shunting an agent off to his home town was widely known as a polite way of urging him to retire, and Harvey resigned "with the deepest regret."

A few weeks later, he was working for CIA. The new agency desperately needed someone with his knowledge of Soviet espionage, and Harvey was put in charge of Section C (counterintelligence) within the Office of Special Operations. "That was too bad," Robert Lamphere said, "because his drive and intelligence were the FBI's loss." But for Harvey, the switch was almost too good to be true. Freed finally from Hoover's narrow proceduralism, he could hope for a new career adequate to his merit, a freer hand against the Soviets, and, perhaps, the means of revenge.

As HE GOT TO KNOW the facilities and personnel at CIA, Harvey realized he had found his true milieu. He was really too much of an individualist to have ever felt totally comfortable in the FBI. He'd had difficulties staying within the weight requirements, and had resented the climate of fear that discouraged people from trying their best. Anybody who tried his best was going to make mistakes—and Hoover didn't tolerate mistakes. Harvey much preferred the atmosphere at the new agency, which seemed to have been built on one of Donovan's mottos, "The perfect is the enemy of the good." CIA officers weren't doing everything by committees, by consensus, and Harvey wasn't overly concerned that somebody was going to look over his shoulder or keep him from doing something. If he came in with a stupid, wild idea for an operation, 99 percent of the time it was going to get shot down, but it wasn't shot down in a mean or stifling way. The response was, *Come up with a better idea*. He was encouraged to think and innovate and imagine—activities which were not the way to get ahead in Hoover's meticulously regimented FBI.

Harvey also found, much to his delight, that drinking at lunch was accepted at CIA, even expected, whereas it had been a risky proposition at Hoover's FBI. Probably this was a result of so many CIA men having been in World War II, during which one relieved the stress of the constant threat of death by getting drunk whenever possible. Some had entered the services at seventeen, a wild, impressionable age, perfect for acquiring vices. Others had gone into OSS or CIA straight from college, with house-party weekends, football Saturdays, and all that sort of thing. Often, too, drinking was just part of the job. Intelligence officers would sit around and discuss cases over drinks, and that was where they got a lot of their information. Of course, there were fellows you could say were drunks. Sometimes Harvey himself would work his way into a third martini, or, after work, put down a pint of Jack Daniel's, which seemed like a lot for someone with a gun.

But there was no doubting Harvey's mind. In terms of philosophy, he had what CIA men admired as the "wider view," complemented by a monumental memory. Richard Helms, a young comer in CIA's Office of Special Operations (OSO), sat down with him one afternoon to talk about the Bentley case, and was amazed that Harvey didn't use any notes, just sat there and went through the whole thing, down to the place and hour of certain meetings. It was quite a tour de force, and Helms had to wonder why Hoover had ever let him get away. He must have had a good record at the Bureau overall, but maybe he had done something they didn't like, and certainly he had his share of troubles with the Bureau after joining CIA.

THE FOCUS OF THOSE troubles was often Deke DeLoach, who in 1948 replaced John Doherty as FBI's liaison officer to the Agency. DeLoach was tall and hulking, with the gentle-friendly face of a basset hound, and a voice that was softly deep and smooth. He had a lot of contact with Sheffield Edwards, director of CIA's Office of Security, whom he thought a nice guy. Eventually Edwards became his main point of contact, his informal "opposite number," especially because he didn't much take to some others at the Agency.

There was just something about those CIA types, an arrogance in the way they devoted no effort to impress him. DeLoach always wore a suit and appeared as professional as possible, but CIA officers didn't seem to care how they looked in their ratty tweed jackets with elbow patches, their shirts that needed to be ironed and eyeglasses that needed to be wiped, their chino pants with little brown spots where hot matches or burning tobacco had dropped. You had to be rich just to think of presenting yourself like that. DeLoach assumed just from the airy way they held forth that most had come out of the Ivy League. They would peer up at him from overstuffed brown leather chairs and not rise when he entered, and rearrange their two-gold-pen Schaeffer desk sets while he was talking. Sometimes they could be disdainfully pompous, like professors impatient with wrong answers, and a good many of them had indeed been professors. It was maddening, because DeLoach didn't think that there was much real difference between the intellect of the groups—a Special Agent wasn't *dumb*, he had to have a law or accounting or four-year college degree, and some had done newspaper or cryptanalysis work. The difference was not in the minds, but in the mind-sets: CIA men tended to be a bit haughty and slack, like fellows at a think-tank, while G-men were humble and disciplined, as befitted American Knights.

Sometimes that difference could be eased by meeting outside work hours, and by drinking, and before long DeLoach was attending various events in CIA officers' Georgetown homes. Most of them could be nice when they wanted to, or when they wanted something done. But no matter how hard DeLoach tried—and in truth, he did not try all that hard—he never really was able to get on with Bill Harvey.

Even though Harvey had been forced out, DeLoach knew it rankled the FBI director that Harvey had joined the rival agency. For Harvey's "defection" symbolized a larger problem: CIA was just beginning, and consequently, as DeLoach would say, it was on "a shakedown cruise." Harvey's former helper Lamphere would echo the sentiment: "CIA was very new and, I believe, trying to find itself, resulting in strong resentment." The new Agency was luring prospective special agents, like Yale senior William F. Buckley, Jr., whom the Bureau tried to recruit, and was wooing experienced FBI personnel. DeLoach knew quite a number of FBI agents who had left the Bureau and joined CIA, mostly in the Office of Security, and that could sometimes be a bond, or at least a source of small talk, but it could also be a source of tension. FBI man Sam Papich summed up the director's attitude: "If Hoover had an agent who had been with the Bureau some years, with a good record and whatnot, and all of a sudden he goes to another agency—even if he's forced out—he's left the family. Why? What's wrong here? What a jerk! I think Hoover reacted that way. You were supposed to stay with the family."

So it was with Harvey. Lamphere lunched with him sometimes, but was careful not to let the FBI director know about it. "To Hoover, going from the Bureau to the CIA was almost as bad as going over to the Soviets," Lamphere recalled. "Harvey was definitely on Hoover's list."

DeLoach knew all about Harvey's "disciplinary problems," but also figured he had been unhappy with his FBI existence and that his "broader view" was better suited to CIA. Harvey seemed to be happier, and was friendly at times, but also quite hostile and jealous of his operations. DeLoach would be in Harvey's office, and Harvey would get a phone call and say, "I can't talk much now because there's an FBI man here."

Of course, Hoover was jealous, too. Despite the belief of some agents that he was happy to be out of Latin America, DeLoach felt that the boss "was somewhat upset over the fact that the FBI had been removed from the Western Hemisphere, and as a result, there was some feeling that CIA was infringing upon jurisdiction." That fear proved well founded, according to DeLoach, "on a number of occasions when Harvey attempted to initiate operations in the United States. It was necessary at times to bring Harvey's attention to the fact that clearances must be obtained from the FBI prior to initiating such operations so as not to upset FBI investigations."

Harvey, for his part, was frustrated by disagreements with the Bureau on how to deal with intelligence CIA gathered. That was especially true with regard to defectors, who could supply information that might lead either to prosecutable espionage cases, or to agents who could be doubled back against the Soviets—but rarely to both. Harvey and others at CIA therefore had a natural conflict of interest in sharing any prize catch with the FBI.

"CIA was critical of the FBI for moving on cases and making arrests instead of playing the cases along," Lamphere said. "They took a longer view of counterintelligence coverage. To a degree the FBI thought CIA was in the 'outer atmosphere' somewhere, too far from practical reality. Personally in this area I think the FBI was right, as whenever we tried to play a case for any length of time things went bad, and we were in the U.S. where you can't torture someone as is done in foreign countries."

Sometimes the problem was that no one could decide just whose catch a defector was. In 1949 a former Soviet intelligence officer, said to be Ivan Anisimov, was claimed by both organizations. CIA got to him first, and he was not shared with the FBI. After his initial debriefing by Harvey's staff, CIA watched Anisimov and occasionally contacted him, to keep the association alive. He also came to the attention of the Bureau, which placed him under surveillance, then attempted to take him into custody in a Washington restaurant. CIA personnel rushed to Anisimov's defense, and there ensued an unseemly tussle—a fistfight—between the men of CIA and FBI. No one was seriously hurt, and Anisimov escaped with his CIA protectors, but news of the incident hit the press, and the Washington *Post*'s Herblock even did a cartoon about it. Hoover reprimanded the special agents involved, and Houston went to see the FBI director to make the case for compromise. He found Hoover coolly formal, "not at all a good old fellow," and no explicit ground rules for the handling or sharing of defectors were produced.

BY SUMMER 1948, the FBI-CIA feud had become so bitter that after reading of it in *The New York Times*, Republican presidential candidate Thomas Dewey made it an issue in his campaign. *Times* national security correspondent Hanson Baldwin had chastised both organizations for their "lack of teamwork," and related accusations that FBI agents in Latin America had "burned files" rather than turn them over to the insufficiently "security-conscious" CIA. Baldwin also got after the FBI for refusing to perform loyalty checks for the Agency, reportedly forcing CIA to hire its own security people at considerable expense. Things had become so unworkable, Baldwin reported, that a special commission had been formed to study "not only the Central Intelligence Agency, but also the inter-relationship of this agency with the intelligence activities of the FBI." Baldwin did not tell his readers that he was himself a member of this commission, whose membership was kept secret. The commission's findings, and those of a National Security Council (NSC) study, would lead to a protracted squabble over CIA's domestic duties which eventually involved Hoover's old nemesis.

WILLIAM DONOVAN HAD HOPED fervently that his long-standing advocacy of centralized intelligence might yet persuade Truman to put him in charge of CIA, or at least let him handpick some of its top staff. In January 1947, the FBI's Liaison Section advised Hoover that Donovan was "sponsoring" his OSS associate Allen Dulles "to become executive director of CIG," and warned that, "should Dulles receive the job, he would undoubtedly be a 'Charley McCarthy' for Donovan." But when Vandenberg was bucked up to vice-chief of staff of a newly independent Air Force in May 1947, neither Donovan nor Dulles had been invited in.

Truman had chosen instead Roscoe Henry Hillenkoetter, a fifty-year-old commander of Naval Intelligence. Wounded at Pearl Harbor and recently promoted to admiral, the "amiable Dutchman" was nevertheless considered "a lackluster leader" by Donovan's old hands. "Hilly," as he was soon known, was like Piggly-Wiggly Souers, but worse—slower, duller, less decisive, unwilling to confront the FBI. When the congressional commission queried him about FBI-CIA conflict, Hillenkoetter insisted that interagency relations were now "close," no longer "strained" as they had once been. He was not believed, but without leadership from CIA, the commission could do little more than confirm the existence of the problem it had been set to solve.

The commission's feeble findings were almost immediately eclipsed by the January 1949 report of a Presidential Intelligence Survey Group headed by Allen Dulles, who concluded that CIA should be allowed to coordinate domestic counterintelligence. When Hoover heard about Dulles' recommendation, he countered that coordination of domestic spy-catching should be accomplished through a new Interdepartmental Committee on Internal Security (ICIS), to be chaired by a member of the FBI, and from which CIA should be excluded. Lamphere would recall the ICIS as "a committee being chaired by J. Edgar Hoover which I think to a degree was aimed at keeping CIA in its place. I think this was the low point."

The NSC tried to placate Hoover by offering him a permanent place on the Intelligence Advisory Committee (IAC), an interagency coordinating group chaired by the director of CIA, where the Bureau might contribute to crisis estimates and the planning of secret operations. Hoover refused to attend the IAC, however; CIA officials believed this was because, as one in-house historian ventured, "he would have to sit below the DCI." The NSC gave up trying to budge Hoover, and the FBI's monopoly on domestic security was preserved.

But private citizen Donovan, incorrectly sensing an opening, soon went on the attack. Still hoping to get back into the government, Donovan did all he could to remain in the public eye by trying to co-opt "hot" trends and issues, and in the late 1940s he turned to alarmist demagoguery about communist subversion. "There isn't going to be any shooting war for a long time, because the Reds are winning what they want without shooting," Donovan alleged in one press release. "They've taken nine countries in Europe. They've revived the Nazi State and they have the atom bomb. They've taken China. The Road to Malay and Singapore is wide open. When they march again India will be all but isolated and so will we. If they keep going the way they are, we won't be able to fight a war. The newest weapons are falling before the oldest of them all—subversion. It is time to stop wondering if we will win the next war and find out why we are losing the one we're in."

Donovan's sudden conversion to right-wing reactionary rang somewhat hollow, given his wartime tolerance of communists in secret work, and his critics were quick to point this out. Even before the war's end, concerned citizens had been warning HUAC that OSS "considerations of war-time expediency have endangered our safety." Now columnists attacked him for being a character witness for writer Garson Kanin, "a Communist plotter who stowed away in the State Dept. under false representations." But such assaults on Donovan only caused him to overcorrect. He was a man with something to prove, and he went about proving it, not by confessing the error of his previous policy, but by attacking the competence of the FBI.

On January 9, 1948, Donovan called on Louis Budenz, a special investigator for the Immigration and Naturalization Service (INS) in New York, to discuss "the subversives problem." Donovan began by shooting the question to Budenz: "Don't you think the individual Communist cases could be connected and don't you think you could connect them?" Budenz, taken aback, said he thought he could, but Donovan did not seem impressed. Budenz wondered if he had understood what Donovan meant by "connecting cases together." Donovan elaborated: there was too much "police work" and "detective work" on communism, and not enough "intelligence analysis," which alone could tell the government in advance what communists were going to do. Budenz got the impression that Donovan wanted to establish a kind of domestic OSS to penetrate the Communist Party. Wild Bill seemed to lose interest in the discussion, however, after Budenz more or less defended the FBI. Donovan left saying he hoped to discuss the matter with Budenz again soon, but did not make an appointment.

Hoover found out about the meeting with Budenz, and ordered his subordinates to compose a memo to the attorney general to "completely discredit the statements made by Donovan." The letter merely recapitulated Donovan's views—as if that alone were enough to discredit them—and closed with Hoover's "psychologization": "General Donovan's well known hostility to the Federal Bureau of Investigation is certainly in part due to our exposure of Communist infiltration of the Office of Strategic Services."

Frustrated in his attempts to cut himself a piece of the U.S. anticommunist franchise, Donovan tried increasingly desperate schemes. One was a hokey private spy organization, the American Institute of International Information (AIII), which was to "offer for sale to government agencies, libraries, educational institutions, newspapers and any others who might desire, the fullest information available on a specific subject." The institute expected to obtain its data from ex-OSS personnel in State, War, and Navy, and Central Intelligence, and to Hoover it must have seemed a perfect example of the way Donovan "used his high position during the war to play personal politics calculated to have post-war benefits," as one Bureau informant alleged. It was also a scheme that was bound to fail, and FBI files presented AIII, which soon folded, as proof that "to say the least [Donovan's] judgement is open to question." But Donovan apparently never gave up on the idea of a privatized intelligence network, and it was perhaps with help from just such an enterprise that CIA's covert-action capacity, and much friction with the FBI, was born.

DONOVAN CERTAINLY KNEW how to turn international law into a cover for ad-hoc espionage—that was just what he had been doing for FDR before the war—and in that sense it was only logical that he should return to his old ways once cut loose from government service. Two days after OSS was disbanded in September 1945, he had become partners with former British Security Coordinator William Stephenson in a Panamanian-registered venture called the World Commerce Corporation, which soon placed former OSS or MI6 officers as representatives in forty-seven countries. According to its prospectus, the corporation trafficked in "botanical drugs in bulk, waxes, gums, seeds, spices, and oils"—just the sort of business that Stephenson's friend Ian Fleming later attributed to a fictional firm called Universal Export, which provided commercial cover for James Bond. According to one Donovan associate, the old OSS chief actually kept a secret office in Manhattan, which he made the nexus of a mercenary intelligence system, and appointed a sharp young Armenian exile to maintain contact with secret agents around the world. The uptown office would disseminate reports to Donovan, who returned them after underlining points for the staff to pursue in depth; the marked passages were reportedly typed onto index cards and stored in secret drawers.

Declassified documents in Donovan's FBI file, when collated with other facts, suggest strongly that Donovan was indeed up to more than moving spices and oils. In August 1947, he warned Defense Secretary James Forrestal that "Our French friends" were in need of assistance if they were to continue "making a fight" against communist influence, and raised "the possibility of dealing with this matter independent of government action." Nine months later, in May 1948, a CIA officer confidentially advised DeLoach that "various remnants of OSS personnel who had previously operated in and around Paris, France, were operating in that same locality on a private commercial basis under the leadership of their former director, William Donovan . . . [and] that Donovan had made a trip to Paris for the purpose of surveying and inspecting the activities of the group."

Donovan did, in fact, travel to Paris in 1948, when a number of ex–OSS officers also happened to be there. OSS-London officer Milton Katz was in town as counsel to the Marshall Plan. Donovan's former Far Eastern operative E. Howard Hunt was attached to the Marshall group. Also in Paris for six months during 1948, ostensibly to help American investors rebuild Europe's shattered industries, was an ex-OSS officer who worked for Donovan's law firm, William Casey. Much later, when he became CIA director, Casey would tutor Oliver North in the construction of a Panama-registered, private anticommunist network eerily akin to Donovan's.

Similarly engaged in secret work for Donovan was another former OSS operative who worked for his law firm and eventually became CIA director, William Colby. He did not show up in Paris, but in 1949 he traveled with Donovan to Norway, where for some reason the private citizens were briefed by a Norwegian intelligence officer, as Colby would admit, on "efforts to run down a mysterious supply of uranium that had been offered for sale." Colby also recalled that during this time he was handling for Donovan's law firm the case of an "exile Rumanian financier," which meshes with a July 8, 1948, FBI report that a "suspected Rumanian spy" had hired a Donovan associate and agreed "to pay $15,000 to find out what the FBI had on him."

That allegation set off alarms at the Bureau, and Donovan was watched more closely than ever. Colby later claimed that the Rumanian's case concerned only "an intense dispute with another exile Rumanian financier" over "access to some timberland." He did recall, though, that the opposing counsel in the Rumanian case was Frank Wisner, three floors above in 2 Wall Street, who had also been with OSS.

That Wisner worked in the same building must have been conducive to whatever Donovan was doing by way of contract intelligence, for Wisner soon became the U.S. government's official point man for covert actions in Europe. A pudgy man from Mississippi, third in his class at University of Virginia Law School, Wisner had quit CIG in disgust over its lack of resources, but by spring 1948 he was back in government again, working for George Kennan at State, and sitting on the State–Army–Navy–Air Force Coordinating Committee (SANACC), which aimed to counter communist influence in Europe. Kennan and Wisner were now convinced that containment should consist in more than the U.S.'s stating its case; according to SANACC documents, Wisner wanted to assist "native anticommunist elements" in "psychological warfare (black), clandestine warfare, subversion, sabotage, and miscellaneous operations such as assassination, target capture, and rescue of downed airmen." Five million dollars was to be spent on the project, which was code-named "Blood-stone."

But Wisner didn't want to leave a money trail. Because the problem was "essentially one of a political nature," disbursements should be handled "in such a manner as to conceal the fact that their source is the U.S. Government." There was a need, as Wisner put it, for some "private American organization" to "dovetail with this plan generally." The Dono-van-Stephenson enterprise afforded such commercial cover, and another Donovan operation, a private committee established to assist Russians who had escaped across the Iron Curtain, offered the chance to recruit a "Legion of Liberation."

Donovan was not a very "deniable" asset, however, especially vis-à-vis the FBI, and the situation became somewhat more complicated after fall 1948, when Bloodstone was incorporated into CIA as the Office of Policy Coordination. It was still headed by Wisner, who was still, apparently, linked to Donovan's private network. Indeed, FBI files describe a March 1949 "controversy between Admiral Hillenkoetter, Director of CIA, and Frank Wisner . . . over the possibility of Wisner's outfit transmitting infor-mation to General 'Wild Bill' Donovan."

Whatever the exact nature of Wisner's ongoing relationship with Dono-van, OPC was soon hiring its personnel almost exclusively from Donovan's reservoir of OSS veterans. Wisner recruited paratroopers like Colby, who knew how to fight behind the lines; intellectuals like Tom Braden and Cord Meyer, who could penetrate international labor and student organi-zations; and eccentrics such as E. Howard Hunt, who thought up things like an animated version of Orwell's *Animal Farm* for distribution in the Third World. This OSS-driven expansionism completed the creation of CIA, defined its buccaneering extralegal ethos, and caused what one FBI agent termed "ten million headaches for old J. Edgar."

Frank Wisner became the new Donald Downes. Not only did he have an OSS background, a weight problem, and family wealth, he outdid Downes in missionary idealism, zeal for action at the expense of security, and the habit of domestic trespassing. Wisner's people might be out in Cincinnati, perhaps recruiting refugees to parachute into the Carpathian mountains, or printing up black propaganda about the Czech wheat crop, when some ordinary citizen would take notice and contact the Bureau about the doings of "suspicious foreigners." DeLoach had to sit down with some of those characters, including Wisner himself, and try to explain: "Guys, you can't *do* that. Your operation just won't work, it's gonna *blow*. People suspect you. They know damn well you're not Defense. You aren't properly backstopped."

In one case, CIA got in some trouble for poaching on Hoover's turf by monitoring Nazi rocket scientists resettled into American life under a program known as Project Paperclip. When two Paperclip scientists were being followed around by a suspicious character at Ohio State University in the mid-1950s, one of the scientists called the FBI and said, "It must be the Russians." On looking into it, DeLoach discovered that the scientists were being followed by CIA.

Of themselves such flaps did not amount to much, but their frequency—and the overall principle of trespass—caused the Bureau to take Wisner's transgressions quite seriously. Hoover would "just go into orbit" because Wisner's "gang of weirdos" was operating in the U.S., remembered one FBI agent familiar with the period. "They ran all around the country, and didn't coordinate with anybody. Freelancers all over the place! They drove us nuts. You talk about Hoover's feelings toward CIA, the mistakes that OPC made in the early years were definitely a source of tension. Hoover didn't understand what in the hell they were trying to do."

What Wisner's agents were trying to do was roll back communism in Europe, and Wisner himself was not particularly concerned with the legality or morality of what it would take to accomplish that, let alone whether he was violating jurisdictional guidelines. Nevertheless, to set some ground rules for OPC's domestic presence, Lawrence Houston prepared an FBI-CIA delimitation statement, carving out the separate jurisdictions of each. "The Office of Policy Coordination recognizes the primary responsibility of the FBI in the field of United States domestic security," the September 1948 document announced, "and the FBI acknowledges that it is essential for the Office of Policy Coordination to have direct dealings with [foreign] individuals and groups." But such declarations of good intent did little to smooth disputes as OPC expanded into places like Mexico.

BOTH AGENCIES HAD interests in Mexico City, because the Soviet Embassy there was considered a major base for intelligence operations in the United States. David Phillips, who served in Mexico City, would characterize it as "a hugger-mugger metropolis of cloak-and-dagger operations." Those operations could range from the conventional surveillances and dead-drops to the CIA practice of disrupting communist rallies with devastatingly pungent stink bombs. It was the perfect environment for an imaginative, colorful character like OPC's E. Howard Hunt, a wiry, mustachioed man who moonlighted as an author of paperback mysteries.

Briefed by Wisner before leaving Washington, Hunt had been warned that Hoover maintained "a large and active station" at the Mexico City embassy, and that the FBI was likely to be unhelpfully "jealous of its prerogatives in Mexico." The situation was worsened by the fact that CIA's station chief in Mexico was a former FBI agent who was "thoroughly disliked" by the embassy's legal attaché. Arriving in Mexico City in late summer 1950, a tropical straw hat snapped low over his eyes, Hunt found relations with the local FBI office cold indeed. But he did not give up on the possibility of effective liaison, and the G-men warmed when they realized that Hunt shared their enthusiasm for hunting and fishing. That goodwill was cemented when Hunt used CIA money to finance an FBI-dominated duck-hunting club only forty-five minutes from the embassy. Still, when an FBI agent asked him one day if he knew the whereabouts of the former Spanish Republican guerrilla general known as "El Campesino," Hunt denied knowledge of his whereabouts, though El Campesino was actually concealed in a Cuernavaca safe house, where he was telling his life story to a CIA biographer. The Bureau, too, had a habit of keeping CIA ignorant of matters that were judged "too important" to share, such as the hunt for atom spies in Mexico.

Julius and Ethel Rosenberg's recently uncovered atom-spy ring had been much in the news when, early on the morning of August 17, 1950, the U.S. ambassador to Mexico summoned Hunt to a meeting at the embassy. Waiting for him there were the ambassador, CIA's station chief, and the resident FBI legal attaché. Angrily the ambassador denounced the FBI chief in Mexico for having effected the arrest and expulsion of one of the Rosenbergs' accomplices. Morton Sobell, a fugitive from the FBI, had been hiding in Mexico, and the Soviets had provided him with contact instructions. At a certain date and time, Sobell was to have appeared by a statue of Christopher Columbus near the U.S. Embassy, where he would be approached by a man carrying a folded newspaper under his arm. Prearranged code words were to have been exchanged in conversation, after which Sobell would have been smuggled out of Mexico on a Soviet "fishing trawler." Through informants, however, the FBI's legal attaché had located him in a seedy motel just outside the city. With the cooperation of Mexican police, Sobell had been arrested—kidnapped, really—and put in a car driven by FBI agents. Driving in relays, they reached the border in just under twenty-four hours and delivered Sobell to their colleagues on the American side. Had there been a road accident, the ambassador kept repeating, the whole episode would have become public knowledge and soured U.S.-Mexican relations. Besides which, as Hunt pointed out, "Sobell, while in Mexico, should have been a CIA responsibility and not a Bureau target." That the Bureau hadn't even told CIA Sobell was a suspect suggested that liaison in treason cases was shaky at best.

In fact, the situation was even worse than Hunt knew, for the FBI was holding back on more than the atom spies. It was also hiding information which might have helped CIA unmask a Soviet mole named Kim Philby.

HUNT DID NOT KNOW IT, but Sobell and the Rosenbergs had come to the FBI's attention through deciphered Soviet World War II cable traffic, known by the cryptonym "Venona." OSS had managed to obtain fragmentary pages of Soviet codes from Finnish intelligence in 1944, and these had been passed to cipher experts at the Army Security Agency (ASA) at Fort Meade, Maryland. There, by a complex, laborious process, the codes were applied to Soviet cables intercepted by the British, and messages were slowly deciphered which held clues to the identities of spies. Those leads—or "serials," as they were known in the trade—were passed to the FBI, where they were overseen by Harvey's erstwhile assistant Lamphere. "Venona was more important to us than anyone has ever publicly let on," one of Lamphere's colleagues would recall. "It gave us a window on Soviet subversion everywhere, especially in Latin America. It was hard-core stuff."

But while Lamphere was chasing down those leads, he kept CIA, and his former boss Harvey, ignorant. "When I started on what has been called Venona, we were the only agency getting the material," Lamphere later said. "Frank Rowlett, who headed the intelligence division at ASA, had personally briefed me on the importance of keeping it Top Secret between the two agencies, and I tried to emphasize this all the way to the top of the FBI. CIA knew nothing of the code break."

By spring 1949, Lamphere had concluded that a Soviet agent identified in the Venona traffic as "Homer" must be someone who had served in the British Embassy in Washington. Investigation concentrated on sweepers, cleaners, and bottlewashers, Latvian grandmothers and the like, but nothing much came of it. Still, it was possible that the British Embassy remained insecure. The Homer serial was certainly information "essential to the national security," which the Bureau therefore should have shared with CIA.

But it did not. "The Homer investigation was strictly an MI5-FBI matter," Lamphere admitted. "CIA did not figure in it." CIA's director never made "written request" for the information—how could he, when he did not know it existed?—so Hoover was technically in compliance with the law. Perhaps he did not trust the security of CIA any more than OSS. He did, however, choose to keep the British informed of their search for Homer by entrusting leads to MI6's Washington representative.

This man was a charmer—an aristocrat in unpressed clothes who drank a lot, a good talker even though he stuttered—but there was more to the Bureau's coziness than Kim Philby's charisma, or the fact that he was odds-on favorite to become the next director of British intelligence. The Bureau also wanted him on their side in the struggle against Central Intelligence. "In the years just after the war, the Director became more concerned with the challenge to the FBI from the just-forming CIA, and stopped looking askance at the British," Lamphere later said. "It personally did not take me long after I arrived in 1947 to know that [FBI Assistant Director] Mickey Ladd was playing off British intelligence against CIA, and that we should place more reliance on the Brits than in asking CIA for assistance in the foreign counterintelligence field."

Philby, meanwhile, was playing a game of his own. He had been fully briefed on the FBI-CIA feud before leaving London, and his official mission was to bring MI6 gently into closer cooperation with CIA without offending Hoover. "CIA and SIS had agreed to close collaboration over a wide range of issues which inevitably meant more day-to-day contact than SIS would have with the FBI," Philby later wrote. "Nothing about this change of policy could be acknowledged," however, because "the FBI, taking its cue from the prima donna Hoover, was childishly sensitive on the subject of CIA. . . . My assignment was therefore to tighten links with CIA and loosen those with the FBI without the FBI noticing. It did not take much reflection to convince me that such a task was impossible and absurd. The only sensible course was to get on with CIA on subjects of common interest and take on the chin the unavoidable resentment of Hoover's men . . . and be ready to apologize for the bricks which my position would force me to drop from time to time."

Philby did not at all mind pulling MI6 closer to the Agency. As a member of Britain's "ruling class," he felt more at home with CIA's bluebloods than with the more proletarian FBI. It made sense, then, that the one CIA officer Philby could not abide was former G-man William Harvey. "The first time he dined in my house," Philby recalled, Harvey "fell asleep over the coffee and sat snoring gently until midnight when his wife took him away, saying: 'Come now, Daddy, it's time you were in bed.' " But Philby had to liaise with Harvey on counterintelligence matters, and could not afford to snub him, so Harvey and his wife were among the guests invited to a party Philby gave for his FBI and CIA colleagues on January 19, 1951, at his big house on Wisconsin Avenue.

"Generally, at the party, the FBI and CIA groups tended not to mingle, and chatted apart from each other," recalled Lamphere, who attended. "During cocktails I listened to a discussion among several of the CIA people which concerned intelligence priorities—blue-sky stuff. I found it too far out for me, not oriented enough toward reality. I was more comfortable speaking with Bill Harvey." They were joined by Libby Harvey, who'd already had a lot to drink and did not feel comfortable around the other CIA wives. Somehow she became Lamphere's dinner partner, and he spent most of the meal attempting to quiet her. She hated Mrs. Philby's cold roast beef, and loudly said, "Isn't this God-awful" about every detail of the food and service. The end of dinner came none too quickly for Lamphere, who left the party as soon as he could politely manage.

But Bill and Libby stayed, and were on hand when Philby's permanent houseguest, Guy Burgess, arrived on the scene. He was a second secretary at the British Embassy in Washington, a fairly obvious homosexual, and a bad drunk. "He would have been all right if only the Harvey woman had left him alone, but she'd heard that Guy was a brilliant quick sketch artist and she kept pestering him to draw her," Philby would later say. "Finally Guy said, 'Oh, all right then.' He got his pad and dashed something off. He'd done this terrible caricature of her"—other witnesses described it as pornographic—"and when she saw it she was deeply hurt. I rang Bill the next day and took him to lunch and apologized on Burgess's behalf. Bill said, 'Forget it,' but clearly he didn't."

The Burgess incident raised in Harvey's mind the question of why Philby would be associated with such a reprehensible character, and this question assumed importance after May 25, 1951, when Burgess disappeared with another Foreign Office man, Donald Maclean, who had served in the British Embassy in Washington during the war. Maclean was suspected by the British of being a Soviet spy, and it was assumed that Burgess and Maclean had gone to Moscow. The clinching piece of evidence implicating Maclean was that he traveled twice a week to New York to meet his Soviet controller, which matched Homer's movements as established through the Venona decrypts.

The Bureau still did not tell CIA about its search for Homer, or about suspicions that Homer was Maclean. But after CIA forwarded Hoover a "written request" for information on Maclean and Burgess, the FBI provided background material on the two missing men. One source said that shortly before leaving America, Burgess had repeatedly complained that he wanted to get away from the "very muddled" Western world, and had expressed a love of life in the Middle East, especially the Moslem countries, "where he said men were dominant and women are in the background." According to another Bureau source, Maclean's foreign-service career had been skidding since a drunken rage in May 1950, when he broke into the apartment of an American girl in Cairo, emptied drawers, upset furniture, threw dishes in the bathtub, and beat up the girl. The episode had been suppressed by the U.S. Embassy at British request, but Americans in Cairo talked openly about Maclean as "one of a ring of 12 people who were regarded as homosexuals and possibly dope addicts," who were "devoted to each other" and "dressed up in women's clothes." The Bureau's Security Division even pondered the possibility that Burgess and Maclean had gone to Buenos Aires disguised as women to contact their Soviet handlers.

But there remained the question of why the two men had fled just at this juncture. Was it merely coincidence that they had disappeared as Maclean was coming under suspicion of being Homer? Or had he been tipped by yet another Soviet mole in Washington or London?

The Bureau seemed to buy Philby's thesis that Maclean must have detected MI5 surveillance in London, that Burgess had been Maclean's cutout with Soviet intelligence, and the Soviets decided to withdraw both men because the Western net was closing. "I must admit that I initially doubted that Philby was an active Soviet spy," Lamphere would later say. "I reasoned that a real Soviet agent would have worked harder at establishing closer relations with me and with the other key people; I understood that Philby had concentrated on the CIA, which was certainly a KGB target, but why hadn't he taken the opportunity to penetrate the FBI as well? Since Philby hadn't spent much time on us, I temporarily concluded that he must not have been an active spy." Not until much later did Lamphere realize that Philby had "no need" to rely on him for FBI counterintelligence data, because, in their attempt to play the British against CIA, Ladd and Boyd were routinely *giving* it to Philby. "We were working closely with the British because we trusted their abilities more than we did those of the fledgling CIA, but in the process, many things about our current cases came into Philby's hands, and presumably were passed by him to the KGB."

Harvey was not so willing to believe Philby's story, however. If feelings usually got in the way of cold reasoning, sometimes they leavened it, and his personal dislike for Philby meant that Harvey was prepared to think the worst. Even before the defections of Burgess and Maclean, he had been quietly digging into Philby's background, and had found a number of damning circumstances. Philby had covered the Spanish Civil War for the London *Times*, which fit the allegation of a prewar Soviet defector, Walter Krivitsky, that the Soviets had recruited a British journalist in Spain. He had once been married to a Communist Party activist in Vienna. He had been in Istanbul in 1946 when the Soviets somehow found out that one of their officers, Konstantin Volkov, was about to defect to the British, and prevented him from doing so. Over the past few years in Washington, he had been cut in on any number of CIA operations in Eastern Europe which inexplicably went bad. After Burgess and Maclean bolted, Harvey came to believe that Philby had tipped them off. The pieces of the puzzle all fit. By June 12, Harvey had formally accused Philby of being a Soviet agent.

Throughout 1951, the Bureau pressed its own worldwide investigation into Philby's career. Hoover complained to Hillenkoetter that Harvey's scenario rested on "considerable data not previously known to us," and disseminated to CIA such tidbits as the fact that Philby was "fairly far to the left" in 1934, when he lived in Vienna. But Harvey had beat the Bureau to it. They were going over old ground, and coming up with the same answer. By summer 1951, Lamphere was discussing Philby in lectures to FBI field agents as "a major spy."

The occasion of Philby's flushing-out would have been a good time to consider the damage done by interagency animosity, both in securing Philby access to America's secrets, and in blinding the intelligence community for so long to the guilt of Philby and Maclean. Would the FBI have been less eager to please Philby by sharing secrets if it had not been trying to play him against CIA? More to the point, would the British traitors have been uncovered earlier if CIA had been in on the Venona work? Lamphere recalled that certain Agency officers "never forgave me totally because we had not furnished information on Maclean, and the code break, until after the disappearance of Maclean and Burgess in 1951."

For all its attempts to blame the Philby affair on the FBI, however, CIA, too, had been badly burned. Philby had dealt directly with Wisner and Hillenkoetter, and had known about many of OPC's projects for Eastern Europe. The hard lesson for both CIA and FBI was that their own secrets could be lost through liaison, even if they themselves weren't penetrated.

At least, no one *thought* U.S. intelligence was penetrated by the Soviets. Not yet. But in Philby's wake, the FBI's institutional mind began to magnify certain doubts about the loyalty of CIA personnel, and a big witch-hunt was about to begin.

CHAPTER SIX

A POISONED CHALICE

IAN FLEMING KNEW from his attempts to mediate the Hoover-Donovan feud that Central Intelligence could not survive, let alone earn the respect of the British services, unless it was headed by someone willing to step hard on the FBI director's toes. Those toes were "covered with corns," as Bond's boss warned him in *Live and Let Die*, but in October 1950 CIA finally got a director who did not care. He was the incarnation of everything Fleming and the British loved about America. New World culture might be corrupt—in Fleming's words, "bad but plentiful food, shiny toys such as the automobile and the television, and the 'quick buck' "—and its style might be dreadful—"chilly white nylon shirts with white points to the collars, garishly patterned foulard ties, overcoats with over-buttressed shoulders"—but James Bond envied the American spirit. In Americans there still lived the rugged energy and individualist drive which had characterized England's Victorian age. "We don't show any teeth any more— just gums," a disillusioned old boy would tell Bond, but American intelligence had men who could still bite. CIA now had the man whom Churchill himself had nicknamed "Bulldog," and it was due to this man, more than any other, that the British were eventually forced to acknowledge the superiority of America's Central Intelligence, and J. Edgar Hoover its permanence.

Yet his tenure would also climax in what Agency and Bureau men would later call one of the "lowest" times in the history of interagency relations, for Hoover came down hard on suspected communists in the Agency, and investigated one outgoing CIA director as a possible Soviet spy.

WALTER BEDELL SMITH, FBI files noted, was "a man of great personal force." As CIA analyst Ray Cline recalled, "It was often said he was the most even-tempered man in the world—he was always angry." That irascibility had made the career military officer a valuable chief of staff for Eisenhower, in whose service Smith had gained an ulcerous stomach and more decorations than he could wear. He had never gone to college but had an encyclopedic mind, and his conversation was interlaced with lengthy verbatim quotations from military authorities. He was antisocial and yet could be, as an associate put it, "one of the most loyal friends you could have; if you were his man, he would really back you." Unbending when he believed himself right, which was all the time, he was frank to the point of indiscretion, and had a proclivity for popping off. The only other bad thing you might say about Smith was that he drove himself too hard and always seemed to be tired. Said one of his colleagues, interviewed by the FBI during a background check: "If Smith is not the ablest, he is one of the three ablest men in my generation anywhere in the world." Kim Philby, who worried after the defection of Maclean that Smith might suspect him of treason, put it somewhat differently: "He had a cold, fishy eye and a precision-tool brain. . . . Smith, I had an uneasy feeling, would be apt to think that two and two made four rather than five."

In 1946, Truman had tried to project a tough military image in foreign affairs by appointing Smith U.S. ambassador to the Soviet Union. That was truly style over substance, for America's military was shrinking by a million men a month, and her policy in Eastern Europe was no tougher than appeasement could ever be, but Smith did what was later regarded as a good job under strained circumstances. He had, for instance, personally undertaken the impossible task of negotiating with Stalin over the Soviets' Berlin blockade. By March 1949, Truman had wanted a softer image to complement the tougher actions of his covert containment policy, and Smith came home to be commanding general of the First Army at Governor's Island, New York, while his name began surfacing in press discussions about replacement of the indecisive Hillenkoetter.

On August 18, 1950, after Smith's appointment was announced, the FBI's New York SAC, Edward Scheidt, went to see Smith in his office at Governors' Island. The DCI-designate was "extremely cordial and friendly in his manner," and "spoke in terms of the highest praise of the Director and the FBI," Scheidt recorded. Smith said he knew he faced a difficult task at CIA, since it was easy for outsiders to criticize the secret work of an intelligence agency even when it had been well done. He was aware that CIA had many bureaucratic rivals, and ended the interview by telling the FBI man, "I'm afraid I'm accepting a poisoned chalice."

But at least Smith acknowledged the difficulty of the situation, and would meet his problems square-on. Consulting Houston, Lyman Kirkpatrick, Dulles, and others, he decided to concentrate immediately on three areas: the Agency's poor analytical capacity, which had failed to foresee the Korean War; its personnel, who were undisciplined and not always competent; and its relations with the FBI, which were extremely strained. Historians of CIA would credit Smith with "saving the Agency" by taking quick action in response to all three problems: setting up a new research-and-analysis division under Yale Professor Sherman Kent; starting a career-officer training program under Colonel Matthew Baird; and dealing firmly but fairly with the director of the FBI.

When Smith arrived in Washington in early October, he moved with characteristic directness to arrange an introductory luncheon with Hoover in which interagency problems could be discussed. He found, however, that, despite Hoover's offer "to call on me at any time we of the FBI may be of service," extended in a letter of congratulation on Smith's appointment as DCI, the director was not available to see him. When passed the message that Smith would "await your pleasure regarding the available date, time and any other arrangements at your convenience," Hoover only scrawled: "I am leaving the city at noon tomorrow & my return is indefinite." For the moment, Smith would have to content himself with meeting DeLoach.

They saw each other on October 9, in Hillenkoetter's office at CIA, where the outgoing DCI was boxing up his personal property. After going through the formalities—"General Smith advised of his admiration for the Director and the FBI several times during the conversation" and "indicated his desire to carry on the same close personal liaison relationship with the Bureau as his predecessor, Admiral Hillenkoetter, had enjoyed"—Smith followed DeLoach into the hall outside Hillenkoetter's office and apologized, in a hushed tone, for the poor state of liaison during his predecessor's tenure. Smith had heard from high officials in Washington that "various units of CIA" had attempted to "usurp the FBI's jurisdiction from time to time" under Hillenkoetter, but he wished Mr. Hoover to know he would not tolerate such actions. He hoped Hoover would accept his invitation to discuss these matters during a confidential luncheon hour whenever it might be convenient. DeLoach said he would relay the CIA director's thoughts to Mr. Hoover, and did so when he got back to his office at the Bureau.

"General Smith is quite brusque in personality," DeLoach reported, "[but] he seems to be anxious to start off on the right foot at CIA. He has undoubtedly been briefed thoroughly by Admiral Hillenkoetter regarding the numerous occasions in which CIA has 'blundered' to the embarrassment of the U.S. Government and other intelligence agencies. He, of course, fully realizes that one of CIA's principal claims to existence will be through the medium of cooperating with the FBI and receiving domestic intelligence material upon which CIA can base work of their own. General Smith, therefore, desires to set the initial stage in exhibiting cooperation. . . . The Liaison Section will be guided by your wishes in accepting General Smith's invitation."

Hoover did soon agree to a luncheon date with Smith, although exactly how it came about remains a matter of some dispute. William Sullivan would recall seeing a letter from Smith to Hoover during the first days of Smith's tenure, which said, in effect, "Whether you, Mr. Hoover, like me or not has nothing to do with the cooperation between two government agencies and it is mandatory for you to give the CIA full cooperation within your limits. If it is not done, if you want to fight this, I'll fight you all over Washington." Sullivan alleged that "Hoover put his tail between his legs and backed off at that time, even requesting our CIA liaison man to set up a luncheon with him and Smith." DeLoach, however, would maintain that the lunch was scheduled only after he went to CIA to complain about intimidation of FBI legal attachés in foreign embassies. "Several former FBI agents, then serving with CIA, attempted to close down FBI operations as well as to wrest the title of 'Legal Attaché' from the FBI," DeLoach said. "It was necessary for me to call upon Gen. Smith at Mr. Hoover's instructions and indicate that if such tactics persisted, the FBI would withdraw its personnel from all foreign offices, leaving the CIA to furnish the intelligence that was needed at the time." As DeLoach told it, "Smith became very angry because the lowly FBI was telling him to go fuck himself. He was so mad that when he tried to lift his coffee cup it was shaking so badly that he put it down. He said, 'I've got a mind to throw you out of my office.' I said, 'General, neither you nor any man in your agency is man enough to throw me out.' Twenty minutes after I got back to the Bureau a handwritten message arrived from Smith inviting Hoover to lunch. Hoover told me to accept."

That Sullivan and DeLoach should recall the mere setting up of a luncheon to be a matter of such melodrama is indicative of just how bad relations seemed. But the FBI and CIA directors did meet for lunch at twelve-thirty on October 17.

"What seems to be the problem between the two organizations?" Smith asked as soon as they had sat down. "Why can't we get along?"

The director of the FBI was equally direct. "One of the problems is the former FBI men working for CIA, who are continually proselytizing FBI men to join them, and criticizing the FBI, and in particular Bill Harvey."

After the luncheon, Smith ordered his executive assistant, Lyman Kirkpatrick, to talk to the ex-FBI men in the Agency. "The law was laid down in unmistakable terms," Kirkpatrick later wrote. "There would be no attempt to recruit from the FBI. There would be no criticism of the FBI. Any problems were to be forwarded to the assistant director for solution. Any deviation from the instructions was to be the grounds for instant dismissal." Harvey, especially, was ordered not to do anything that might unduly upset Hoover.

Yet despite the luncheon pledge "to establish a system for the quick solution of mutual problems," contacts remained spotty and tense. The FBI director apparently felt that CIA harbored its share of "pink pansies," and it was probably in that context that Hoover told Smith, at their luncheon, that he would have DeLoach furnish a digested summary of a new book by Indiana zoology professor Alfred S. Kinsey, *Sexual Behavior in the Human Male*. (DeLoach brought it over the following day.) But in February 1951, when Smith asked for Hoover's help in vetting employees, he was turned down because the FBI was "pretty busy." He also became frustrated with Hoover's inaccessibility. Smith always declined to speak to anyone else when Hoover was unavailable, according to FBI files, and simply "hung up." A Bureau memo tersely stated in July 1951 that "Files reflect limited contacts with General Smith."

Smith meanwhile enjoyed little success in trying to win from Hoover a seat on the Interdepartmental Intelligence Committee (IIC), the board of the "Big Three" (ONI, G-2, FBI) which Hoover had chaired since the days of the "twilight zone" problem. The IIC still met on matters of domestic and hemispheric security, but it refused to "perform estimates," i.e., to analyze intelligence. Smith wanted to change that by obtaining an IIC seat for CIA. When these requests were rebuffed, the task of persuading Hoover was assigned to Allen Dulles, deputy director of plans. Smith laid down the line that Dulles should take: The matter was too important for those involved to quibble about the media of exchange or details of protocol. CIA was willing to give to the FBI whatever information it obtained overseas, but it would make no special collection effort for the FBI unless it got something in return. Dulles accomplished nothing, however, and in November Smith took up the task himself, at another luncheon with Hoover. The FBI director was genial, but adamantly refused the Agency a permanent IIC seat. The best Smith could get out of him was a pledge that CIA would be specially invited to attend the IIC whenever, in Hoover's judgment, Smith's people had a legitimate interest in the subject under discussion. A Top Secret CIA history noted ruefully, "In this case, [Smith's] usually irresistible force came up against an immovable object."

SMITH'S FAILURE TO WIN a seat on the IIC made it all too clear that FBI-CIA relations were in need of a serious overhaul, and by late 1951 there was agitation at both agencies for the removal of liaison officer DeLoach. "As time went on and as Hoover, Tolson and Ladd came to realize CIA was there to stay, things improved, but as long as DeLoach was CIA liaison there was constant friction," Lamphere recalled. "He reflected the Director's negative attitude toward the CIA by working to exacerbate the problems between the two agencies, rather than to tamp them down."

FBI Security Division man William Sullivan backed Lamphere's assessment. "I heard about him from some former FBI agents who were working at CIA. The word around was that DeLoach was consciously driving a wedge between the two agencies. DeLoach played on the FBI Director's jealousy by hinting to Hoover that the CIA was planning to extend its field of operations to the United States. To Hoover, that was like waving a red flag in front of a bull, and he was furious when he heard it. My CIA contacts saw through DeLoach's game and came to me in alarm to discuss the ever-widening gap between the two agencies. They asked if I could do anything to remove DeLoach from his liaison job, but I didn't have the authority."

It seems likely that the DeLoach problem was raised at the second Smith-Hoover luncheon, in November 1951, from which DeLoach was conspicuously absent, and at which Smith set out the "personalities problem." DeLoach was gone within a month, but in earning the ire of CIA he had not, it seems, provoked any disapproval from his own director; he was promoted to the FBI's Inspection Staff. Reflecting on his tenure afterward, DeLoach denied that he had consciously tried to undermine the Agency, but admitted that his attitude toward it had been shaped by Hoover's own, and by the overall delicacy and novelty of the situation. CIA liaison was a tricky job—"at times similar to walking a tightrope, attempting to maintain good relations between the two agencies while adequately representing the FBI. Special Agents who later handled the liaison assignment worked under vastly different conditions inasmuch as CIA had become a reality."

"I'M SORT OF A LIAISON between the Central Intelligence Agency and our friends at the FBI," Felix Leiter told James Bond in *Live and Let Die*. They were drinking martinis in Bond's room at the St. Regis Hotel. Bond had come to New York to help shut down an international bullion-smuggling ring, but first Leiter had to brief him on the jurisdictional subtleties.

"It's the FBI's case," Leiter said, "at least the American end of it is— but as you know there are some big overseas angles which are CIA's territory, so we're running it jointly." Leiter's job, as Bond understood it, was to "marry up the two halves" of the operation.

The liaison officer seemed to know and enjoy his business, and he caused Bond to reflect that Americans could be good people. Leiter's movements and speech were slow, but his eyes were sharp and his words were always well chosen. He had a uniquely intimidating charm, the kind that would make anyone think twice about crossing him. He was a tall man with flappy ears, huge rough hands, and a deep, rumbling belly laugh that made people want to be his friend. Yet Bond had the feeling that there was plenty of speed and strength in him, and that he would be a tough and cruel fighter, whether in a dark alley or in the mazes of bureaucratic Washington.

As it happened, this was an uncannily apt description of the man who became FBI-CIA liaison officer in March 1952, the very month Fleming created Bond.

• • •

SAM PAPICH, THE SON of a Montana copper miner, had played football at Northwestern University. At 190 pounds he had been the lightest tackle in the Big Ten, but was scrappy and strong enough to lead a lot of plays— getting a full running start, targeting a defensive back, and just *cracking* up through him as the wingback motored past and fifty-five thousand people roared. After graduating with an engineering degree in 1936, Papich worked at a Chicago insurance firm during the day, went to law school nights, and on weekends was a tackle for the Chicago Gunners, a pro team financed by a lumber company. During his second pro season he messed up his knees and was finished with the football. He had meanwhile met some FBI agents through his insurance work, however, and soon his G-friends were recommending him to the FBI. It sounded like the kind of work he could do, and the agents he knew seemed truly worthy of their status as veritable American Knights. He joined in March 1941, and was quickly assigned to SIS.

Working under Bud Foxworth in New York, one of Papich's early assignments was to follow Dusko Popov around the city, checking and double-checking on him, and helping unload the butterfly trays when Popov returned from Brazil. Papich himself was then posted undercover to Latin America, where he became known as an especially adept agent-handler. After the German surrender, he returned briefly to the States to marry, then was made legal attaché in Rio de Janeiro. It was a nice place to start a marriage, but by 1947 CIA was taking over the FBI's Latin American operations, and Sam and his young bride were feeling a little homesick. After turning down an offer from CIA, Papich made his way back to Washington, sat down with J. Edgar, asked specifically for San Francisco, and was sent to work there against the Mafia. After five years, he was recalled to Washington for headquarters assignment. He didn't want to go; he didn't like headquarters, though he was told he was going to be doing bank-robbery cases. But when he got there, they wanted him to be the new CIA liaison.

Papich didn't particularly want the position. In the three months since DeLoach had moved on, another liaison officer, Charles Bates, had already tried the job, found it too frustrating, and requested reassignment. Given Hoover's open dislike of CIA, the liaison post was bound to be one of the Bureau's real "battle stations." Still, Papich rather liked the idea of a challenge, an impossible mission, and he liked spy work. He was also willing to help out Hoover, a man for whom he had little personal affection but immense professional respect. Hoover needed someone to "buffer" him from daily headaches with the Agency, and his deputies had recommended that he appoint someone with good CI experience. The director would even throw in a nice raise and promotion. So Papich took the job.

He began by reading the FBI's liaison files, which covered disputes concerning CIA's creation, and subsequent misunderstandings about jurisdictions. "Reading those files gave me a picture of two warring agencies," Papich remembered. "It *was* that bad." He felt that some of the FBI's animus against CIA was justified, especially on the matter of OSS-CIA security problems, but thought much of the rest was misgiven. The FBI hadn't grasped the whole intelligence picture, the scene. It hadn't seen the importance of working with CIA on Venona, of sharing certain serials, of matching up the foreign with the domestic. Hoover had been biased against Harvey, and some agents had likewise confused the personal with the professional. The Bureau should have let certain things slide with Wisner's OPC; there was no reason to ring J. Edgar's bells every time Ukrainian nationalists met in the recreation center of some Eastern Orthodox church. Papich would have to undo much damage done.

But as he got out there and tried to undo it, Papich began to understand the difficulties that had confronted DeLoach. On one of his very first visits to CIA, he was offended by an officer who failed to show him common courtesy and respect, and they nearly came to blows. Soon afterward, Papich was in Bedell Smith's office, and there was a disagreement, and Smith said to him, "You go back down to Ninth Street and tell J. Edgar to stick it up his ass!" Papich wasn't about to tell Hoover any such thing, but he scribbled in his notebook, as if taking down the CIA director's exact words, until Smith suddenly sucked in his cheeks and said, "Let's calm down." They put the work aside for a few minutes, and Smith took him into his side office, a little snack room, to have a cup of coffee, and the dispute began to clear.

The Smith episode taught Papich a valuable lesson: when CIA and FBI met outside the context of headquarters work, it was possible to relate as decent human beings getting on with the secret war against the Soviets. Thereafter, when he could, he met socially with Wisner, or Harvey, or whoever it was, playing tennis or going to football games. Such contacts had produced only limited benefits under DeLoach, but by summer 1952 it was clear that Sam Papich was helping to smooth relations.

"Most people at CIA liked Sam very much," Lawrence Houston said. "Difference in background was not a problem with Sam—I didn't even know what Sam's background was—but he was able to talk to anyone on a nice, easy basis. Sometimes we'd just sit around and talk. I liked him. He led a rough life, but he had the confidence of both sides, which was remarkable, in that job. He was one of the major influences keeping relations as good as they were."

FBI agents agreed that there was a kind of sea-change under Papich. "Things improved when Sam took over liaison," Lamphere would say. "My view, shared I think by Sam, was that we should think first on what was good for the United States and that problems between the two agencies, which were inevitable, should be worked out without having them grow like a cancer. In many instances I thought the FBI was being unreasonable in making big problems out of fairly small ones."

Perhaps the main reason relations began to improve was that Papich had the "mind-set" of a foreign-intelligence officer, having been one himself. He was by nature "action-oriented," and empathized with those at CIA, such as Wisner, whose domestic adventurism raised Hoover's hackles. Wisner made mistakes, and caused problems, but Papich always had more respect for the guy who was gung-ho than the one writing memoranda and coming up with do's and don't's, but mostly don't's. Moreover, Papich understood the code of extralegal virtue that undergirded CIA's entire operational existence. He knew there wasn't a day when some foreign-intelligence officer, somewhere in the world, wasn't violating the laws of some country, simply by being there. He also knew that, whatever foreign-domestic distinction might be mandated by the National Security Act, CIA had to operate in the United States. And on a more personal level, having lived undercover three years in Latin America, separated from a fiancée and family who knew nothing of his real activities, he sympathized with CIA officers who had to live two lives, undercover with the State Department in Greece or France, lying to their children, enduring marital breakups from the strains of a secret foreign life.

Of course, no matter how well Papich might have understood the clandestine mentality, he could not prevent it from clashing with Hoover's own. Several imbroglios were caused when CIA's Domestic Operations Division tried to recruit foreign officials in the U.S. without cutting Hoover in. CIA's constant requests for bugs or taps or "bag jobs" (burglaries) on foreign targets in the U.S. were another "red flag" before Hoover's eyes. Wisner would press Papich: "Why the hell can't you fellas give us coverage on this case?" And Papich would have to say, "That's illegal." Not that the FBI didn't "put out" for CIA under certain protections, such as an understanding with the Justice Department or the White House, but, overall, CIA's extralegal activities in the United States caused problems for an agency that was supposed to enforce laws, not be a party to their breach. Though it was not yet clear to Papich in 1952, a whole chain of such disputes would mar liaison over the next two decades.

Still, it was inevitable that the Bureau should move closer to CIA under Papich—especially in Philby's wake. After Philby was kicked out of the country by Bedell Smith in late 1951, just as DeLoach was kicked upstairs,

FBI reliance on the British decreased markedly. If Hoover wanted any help at all in the foreign-intelligence sphere, he simply had to rely more on CIA.

But Papich soon learned that this reliance would be tempered by the very factor that forged it. For if Philby's treason had the effect of pulling FBI closer to CIA, it also served to feed a general climate of suspicion, in which the Bureau would probe Central Intelligence for Soviet moles.

IAN FLEMING HAD URGED William Donovan back in July 1941 to "Make an example of someone at an early date for indiscretion, and continue to act ruthlessly where lack of security is concerned," and much of CIA's trouble during the McCarthyist period might have been avoided if Donovan had followed Fleming's advice. Although William Quinn had thought the problem solved by Hoover's vettings of the Bentley suspects in late 1945, it seemed probable that others, uncaught, had burrowed into the Agency. As CIA counterintelligence specialist James Angleton later acknowledged, there was "a very grave problem of the security standards of the Agency coming from World War Two . . . [when] OSS had many people who were loyal to General Donovan, but also had loyalties to the opposition." Papich recalled that "CIA's Office of Security ran a long campaign to ferret out those who potentially might be problems. I guess you could call it an ongoing housecleaning."

Much of the suspicion came from Venona. The decrypted Soviet cables suggested that there had been at least fourteen Soviet penetrations in or close to OSS—meaning that Bentley had identified perhaps only half of the agents—and it did not take a professor of logic to grasp the implications for an agency dominated, at its highest levels, by OSS veterans. When Donovan was pushing the idea of a strong centralized intelligence organization in October 1946, Hoover's deputy Michael Ladd objected that such an entity would inevitably be a platform for leftist "coloration and biases," given "the number of the type of people Donovan proposes to employ, especially 'foreign-born experts.' " Hoover agreed heartily, scrawling flatly on one memo: "OSS was a breeding ground for Commies." Lamphere, Papich, and others who often secretly sided with CIA against Hoover did not think their director was wrong on this point. "The FBI knew that a number of OSS men ended up in CIA, and we knew of a number of instances where OSS had Communists in their ranks knowingly," Lamphere recalled. "This tainted our view of CIA in the early days."

Great attention was paid to persons considered security risks on the basis of sexual preference. This was not motivated by homophobia per se, but by a fear that the Soviets could play on homosexuals' own fears of stigmatization by threatening to "out" them if they did not cooperate. For instance, the prominent journalist Joseph Alsop had reportedly gone to both FBI and CIA and said that the KGB threatened to expose his homosexuality unless he did their bidding. The "homo factor" thus became important in FBI investigation of prospective CIA employees, including Donald Downes. The ubiquitous COI-OSS operative, a burr in the FBI's side in Washington, Mexico City, and Morocco, was denied the necessary security clearance when some OSS colleagues conceded that he was probably "a pervert."

The homo factor hit closer to CIA's operational heart in 1950, when it forced Frank Wisner's best deputy, Carmel Offie, out into the cold. Offie was a popular "walker" in Washington society; no Georgetown dinner party was really complete without him. His many contacts on the Continent proved invaluable to Wisner in developing an underground railway for the quiet movement of anticommunist exiles to and from Eastern Europe, but his private proclivities came to the attention of the FBI when he was arrested for soliciting a male prostitute in Lafayette Park, just across Pennsylvania Avenue from the White House. By February 1950, the Bureau was surveilling him. A number of "unknown subjects" were spotted leaving and entering his home, and one of them carried a mysterious envelope which appeared to contain "three cylindrical objects about the size of Ediphone records." When its file on "Carmel Offie, a well-known homosexual," was forwarded to CIA, the Bureau was certain that Offie was not only a security risk but a Soviet agent. It is not clear on what grounds the Bureau so concluded, but after reading the FBI material, William Harvey, then still running Staff C, agreed that Offie was quite probably a Soviet mole.

Still, the Agency did not fire Offie. Wisner defended his man against Harvey and the FBI, and Hoover grew impatient. When CIA Security Director Sheffield Edwards, caught in the middle, failed to arrange some kind of compromise, the case against Offie was leaked to Senator Joseph McCarthy, probably by someone at the FBI. Wisner had no choice but to sack his man, but the Bureau did not find the Agency helpful when it tried to get the government to prosecute Offie. The director of CIA had a statutory right to protect "sources and methods," including the identities of current and former personnel which might be exposed at an Offie trial, and CIA's refusal to cooperate meant that Offie could not be tried. "The usual 'brush off' all around," a disgusted Hoover complained to one underling.

The FBI next fixed on OPC's John Paton Davies. A former assistant to Bedell Smith in Moscow, Davies had worked with Wisner on Bloodstone and had proposed a project code-named Tawney Pippet, which was to finance covertly a procommunist think-tank in the U.S., in order to control it and gain intelligence—much as Lenin's secret police had once created the Trust, or Britain's XX Committee had created the Tricycle ring. But one OPC agent, alarmed at the prospect of funding America's enemies, passed word of the project to Hoover. The FBI dug into Davies' past, and learned that he had once recommended that the U.S. back communist rebels in China. The Bureau also believed that Davies had recommended that CIA employ certain communists, then lied to Senate investigators about it. Davies was fired.

But each FBI victory, rather than sating suspicions, only fueled demands for another sacrifice. In a way, the Agency brought this on itself, or its director did. When called to testify before HUAC, General Smith told the truth; in so doing, he crippled his own career, and endangered the very existence of CIA.

"I believe there are Communists in my own organization," he testified on October 13, 1952. "I believe that they are so adroit that they have infiltrated practically every security organization of Government." General Smith so assumed, he said, because CIA had discovered "one or two" communist penetrations, and he believed that in the future they would discover more. CIA was doing its best to screen out security risks, Smith said, but the security of government employees was mainly the business of the FBI. "I have . . . no internal security responsibility in the United States, and am prohibited by law from exercising any of these functions," Smith reminded the committee, adding: "I should say the FBI is almost entirely penetration proof. They employ only Americans and they operate only in the United States."

Smith's remarks were noted by the FBI, and despite the DCI's apparently flattering reference to the security of the Bureau's personnel, Papich's supervisor in the liaison section, V. P. Keay, concluded Smith "was not at all impressive as a witness," having shown "ignorance of important subjects," a "lack of clear thought," and "a general ineptness in handling questions." Public reaction to the CIA director's words proved the Bureau correct on at least the last point. Rather than earning the country's trust, Smith's candor caused a groundswell of grass-roots agitation against the "commie-dominated" CIA. As a chastened Smith told Papich, "That's what happens when you talk too much." The CIA director realized only too late that press reaction to his testimony was "natural" in the political climate of a presidential-election season—his old boss, Eisenhower, was running against Adlai Stevenson—and he knew that he had placed himself in a "jam." If Eisenhower had not cooperated by ordering "no use" of

Smith's testimony in Republican speeches, CIA undoubtedly would have been subjected to even more embarrassing press coverage.

His previous relationship with Ike had seemed to assure that he could stay in the job if he wanted it after Eisenhower's November triumph, but Papich could read the signs, even if Smith could not. Eisenhower and his former chief of staff did not have the relationship they once had, and there was no way the incoming president was going to keep a DCI who had undercut his own Agency by "popping off" about communist infiltration. By Christmas 1952, FBI memos recorded "rumors that General Smith might be leaving CIA," and on January 12 Eisenhower told Smith that he wanted to "make a change." Smith would become undersecretary of state for administration, and Allen Dulles would be the next Director of Central Intelligence.

General Smith closed up his desk on January 23, but before leaving his office he telephoned Hoover. For the first time in a long while, the director of the FBI was available to take his call. The outgoing DCI duly expressed appreciation for the "courtesies and cooperation" which had been extended to him during his days at CIA. Hoover noted in a memo that Smith was "most verbose in his praise" for the "fine work" Sam Papich had done as liaison. The outgoing DCI expressed a desire for continued contacts when he assumed his new duties, which would include the weeding out of security risks at State, and he hoped Hoover would come over for lunch once he was settled in. The FBI director said he would be glad to, but he never did.

ALLEN WELSH DULLES was essentially the same man he had been when Donald Downes met him just after Pearl Harbor, in the New York office of Donovan's COI. The milk-white mustache was a little fuller, perhaps, and the dome of his forehead higher and more wrinkled with the worries of the past decade, during which he had become a seasoned veteran of secret intelligence. In World War II, Dulles had been Donovan's star operative in Europe, operating mostly out of Switzerland, and after a stint at the prestigious New York law firm of Sullivan and Cromwell, he had been made CIA's deputy director for plans (DDP) in 1950. Soon he had been moved up to the number-two slot, deputy director of central intelligence (DDCI), and in that capacity had overseen daily operations. For all his familiarity with the intimate workings of the institution, Dulles was not an ideal administrator, and was in fact something of a bumbler. One intelligence officer who worked with him noted that Dulles "had a habit of talking around a problem, not coming to grips with it. Sometimes, he seemed to be ruminating aloud—and pretty diffusedly at that." But the same officer found Dulles to be "good, comfortable, predictable, pipe-sucking, whiskey-sipping company." In this sense, Dulles was much like Donovan: professionally bold, but personally mild. He was popular with his men in a way that no one since Donovan had managed to be, and was much admired and respected by Sam Papich, too. "Allen Dulles was a great man," Papich would say. "A real gentleman, regardless of what you read and what you hear. In many ways he was a *gentle* man. But action-oriented, and very dedicated to CIA."

Hoover did not share the feelings of his liaison officer, at least not at first. The distrust went back to Dulles' 1949 report to the National Security Council, in which a larger domestic role had been urged for CIA. Later it was also said that Hoover had suspected Dulles of "secret communist leanings." For the first few years of Dulles' tenure, he and J. Edgar "didn't have much of a personal relationship," as Papich put it, but Dulles himself attributed that less to personal chemistry than to the dynamics of bureaucracy. In any case, Hoover's hostility persisted throughout the 1950s, and agents in the FBI's Security Division would recall several symptomatic episodes. In 1954, according to William Sullivan, Hoover decided to share the Bureau's Venona material with the director of the Royal Canadian Mounted Police after withholding it for a decade. "When he asks why we kept it from them for ten years," Sullivan asked Hoover, "what will I tell him?" "Blame it on the CIA," Hoover reportedly instructed. Sullivan understood that he cooperated with CIA at his own peril, and when he worked with Richard Helms and others at the Agency, he had to do it "behind Hoover's back." On one occasion, when Hoover cut back funds needed to pay an agent on what Sullivan considered a vital national-security case, Helms supplied $9,000 from CIA so that the FBI could obtain the information.

Hoover's resentment of CIA was so fierce that it could even be used as a lever to advance one's Bureau career. By mid-1953 Robert Lamphere was due for a raise, but a recent letter of censure for a minor infraction of Hoover's code would have precluded that. Lamphere went to Assistant Director Allan H. Belmont and threatened to "pull a Harvey": He was going to work for the Agency if he didn't get his raise. Over the next few weeks, Lamphere got not one raise but three. "I was very lucky to get what I wanted after spouting off," Lamphere remembered, "but I knew better than to ever try that ploy again."

So much for irritants on the Bureau's side. As far as the CIA was concerned, the situation was not helped by the fact that, during Dulles' first days as director, his agency came under sustained attack by Senator

Joseph McCarthy, who fired away with material fed to him, it seems, by the FBI.

FIRST THERE WAS THE CASE of CIA officer Cord Meyer, Jr. He came from an old family, and had a distinguished Marine career in World War II. A Japanese hand grenade had blown out one of his eyes, and since then he had worn a glass one. After gaining some recognition as a literary talent when the *Atlantic* published "Waves of Darkness," a short story about his wartime experience, Meyer became active during the late 1940s in the World Federalist movement, a leftist group which proposed putting all mankind under one government. The FBI had looked into the World Federalists, and had apparently given Meyer's name to McCarthy, who in turn pressed the Bureau to investigate him further. By September 1951, Meyer was working for Frank Wisner and Tom Braden in CIA; some said he had "run" there for the "protection" of Dulles, who knew Meyer's father. But the Bureau was not put off Meyer's track by his alleged special relation to the DCI, any more than by the fact that he had spearheaded the expulsion of communists from the Federalists. On August 31, 1953, Meyer was in his office discussing with a branch chief certain lines of action they planned to follow in Europe when the phone rang and he was requested to go see Richard Helms, then second-in-command of the Agency's clandestine operations under Wisner. Helms seemed uncomfortable as Meyer sat down opposite his desk.

"I've got a rough one," Helms said, offering him a cigarette. "They've apparently found something in your past that looks serious." The allegations in an FBI report on him were so serious, in fact, that he would have to resign immediately, without pay. The "information" included FBI allegations that someone who met Meyer in 1948 "concluded, on the basis of that contact, that you must be in the Communist Party," as well as reports that Meyer associated with persons such as journalist Theodore White and poet Richard Wilbur, who were "associated with Communist front organizations." Additionally, Meyer's wife, Mary Pinchot, had "registered as a member of the American Labor Party of New York in 1944, at which time it was reportedly under extreme left-wing or Communist domination."

As he read the allegations, Meyer's first reaction was incredulity, followed by relief and then by indignation. No old friend turned out to have been a Soviet agent, which was one of the fears he had conjured up while waiting to see the charges. But he was warned that the situation was grave, and that his reply to the charges should be "extremely complete and detailed." For the next few weeks, Meyer worked diligently on his response. He happened to know many communists, because he moved in intellectual circles and had been in with the World Federalists; he had worked to weaken communism in that organization and was now trying to do the same in the international labor movement. He listed dozens of people who could swear to his ultimate loyalty, handed his rebuttal to Houston, and waited. Finally, on Thanksgiving Day, Meyer received a call from Director Dulles; he was acquitted.

Meyer never did discover who at the FBI had been out to get him, or why. In later years, he worked closely with FBI officials on a number of occasions and came to respect and like most of them. They never raised with him the subject of his suspension, and he never asked them about it. But ultimately, he and other CIA officers thought Hoover's Bureau was to blame for the McCarthyist disaster. It went back to their wartime incompetence in counterespionage. For all Hoover's early anticommunism, the FBI had been remarkably uninterested in pursuing Chambers' and Krivitsky's early tips about a huge Soviet ring in government. Even when Elizabeth Bentley and William Harvey confirmed the truth of Chambers' warnings, the FBI should have moved more aggressively. If proper pre-emptive action had been taken then, McCarthy would have been denied the ammunition that he used so effectively in charging that communist infiltration had been condoned, and communist agents befriended, by traitors at the highest levels of American life. As it was, McCarthy was able to make a big show of attacking men with impeccable credentials and character references from the Eastern liberal establishment, men like Offie, Davies—and Meyer. If the nation's best sons were to be suspected of treason, Meyer reflected, "where did suspicion end?"

Not with Meyer. Others at CIA were closely watched; Robert Amory, deputy director for intelligence from 1953 to 1961, later said he saw evidence that the Bureau tapped his office phone. No one, not even such an archetype of American capitalism as Nelson Rockefeller, was above doubt. At the beginning of the Eisenhower administration, Bedell Smith had opposed Rockefeller's appointment as special assistant to the president for Cold War operations because Rockefeller was, Smith said, "a communist."

Allen Dulles, who was then taking over as CIA director, considered it unthinkable that Rockefeller was a traitor, and told the president that he had learned of other stupid statements by Smith, such as "World War III is to start tomorrow." The Rockefeller episode soon evaporated, and was remembered as just one more mark against the irascible general, but two months later there was cause for even more serious concern about his character. It was suspected that Smith himself, while serving as CIA director, might have been a Soviet spy.

PERHAPS FITTINGLY, such an outrageously sensational allegation first found its way into the FBI's Smith file in a January 1951 crank letter postmarked Palm City, California. According to the anonymous informant, "The Communist Party used the Main Event at the Ocean Park Calif Wrestling Arena to send a message over television to Party members (The match between Lord Byron & Count on Friday Jan. 12, 1951)—I do not know the signs & signals but I understand the fake right arm injury meant some trouble for the right arm of Communism in other words DOPE. The Count went to the rope for relief more in this match than ever before signifying something. Another tip. The U.S. Attorney General Office used a news broadcast over a San Diego Calif radio station tonight to warn & give legal assistance to some Communists who might be in hot water. Walter B. Smith of Central Intelligence Agency, Washington, D.C. will stand investigation for communistic activities."

Exactly two years later, on the day after Eisenhower's decision to send the general packing, the State Department asked the FBI to see whether Smith might be a security risk. On the surface, this was a routine request. In the wake of McCarthy's charges, the Senate had resolved that State should not appoint any personnel without full FBI background checks. But Smith's case was complicated by his connections to John Paton Davies. The idea took hold that Davies must have had powerful sponsors who advanced his career, and those who supported Davies against his FBI accusers soon became suspect, too. When Davies came under scrutiny in 1952, Smith got "seriously involved in the case" and was "bedeviled" by it, according to a Top Secret CIA account, after telling investigators that Davies was "a very loyal and very capable officer of sound judgement." It was only days after his final refusal to condemn Davies, in January 1953, that Smith's own career came under review. An "Urgent" FBI teletype went out from headquarters to various field offices, ordering a "thorough investigation as to character, loyalty, reputation, associates and qualifications of Smith. Account for his entire adult life." Findings were to be reported surreptitiously to the director through one of his assistants.

At first pass, the suspicions against Smith seemed absurd, as they would against anyone who could list "Dwight D. Eisenhower" as a reference on a personnel security questionnaire. One of Smith's former bosses in government believed that "the general had occupied such high positions, always cleared for secret matters, that inquiries into his loyalty were useless," and even telephoned the FBI to complain about its "foolish" attempts to pacify Senator McCarthy. The FBI noted that Smith's book *My Three Years in Moscow* had been "critical of Russia and the spread of communism," and that the general was given to saying, "The Communists embrace you only to destroy you."

And yet ... through the dark prism of suspicion, certain facts about Smith were not flattering. One of his favorite devices, when being questioned too closely by congressmen, was to divert attention from the subject by saying, "Now, as I recall, Marshal Stalin once told me ..." That always made a big impression; there were not many men in Washington who could recall what Stalin, the archenemy, had once told them. But how close had Smith been to Stalin, exactly? Although Smith claimed in his HUAC testimony to have "realized fully" the "conspirational designs" of Russia "around 1943," he elsewhere admitted that in the days immediately following the Nazi surrender he went through a period of thinking that "the leopard might have changed its spots," and that there might be "a way of working out a modus vivendi with the Communist countries." He had thought backing communist coalition governments in China and Italy "a wise thing to do," in the belief that "our communists are different." He had attended a January 1946 Red Army Day Dinner at New York City's Waldorf Astoria hotel, sponsored by the National Council of Soviet-American Friendship. He had said, "The Soviet Union is setting a higher cultural standing within its borders. At least according to my taste, the Soviet ballet, the puppet theaters, and things of that sort are based on a higher cultural level than that in this country." At the Waldorf dinner, he had shared the dais with persons the FBI considered "leading Soviet sympathizers," such as Max Yergan, "Communist leader of the National Negro Congress," and Lillian Hellman, the "pro-Soviet playwright." Also present were Edmund J. Barach, a close friend of Julius Rosenberg and Philip Jaffe; the FBI was sure that Jaffe, Barach, and Rosenberg were Soviet spies. Indeed, FBI investigators believed they had uncovered a pattern of contacts between Smith and suspected Soviet agents. He had met with Barach on at least one other occasion, at the Soviet consulate in New York City, and the general's name had come up in the FBI's investigation of China expert Owen Lattimore, a close friend of Davies. . . .

Bureau files do not show whether investigators ever assembled anything more than such a McCarthyist mélange of associational guilt. The special inquiry appeared to have concluded on May 6, 1953, when Hoover sent a summary of its results to the White House. Forty years later, that summary would be among 197 pages from Smith's FBI file withheld from the public on national-security grounds. The State Department would similarly refuse to release any documents stating the FBI's conclusions. A later FBI memo to the Army stated flatly that "This investigation [reported to the White House on May 6] developed no derogatory information concerning Walter Bedell Smith." But on May 21 the case was apparently open again, and serious enough to be expanded internationally. Hoover's legats interviewed Smith associates in Moscow, Karachi, Berlin, Cairo, Tokyo, and Rome.

What was going on? Although the first investigation may have been mustered merely to preclude McCarthyist attacks, or as some private vendetta by Foster Dulles against Smith, Bureau files show no apparent rationale for the second investigation, and no indication of its results. One possibility is that State Department security chief R. W. McCleod, a former FBI man, was put onto Smith by the Venona intercepts, which were still being worked by McCleod's old colleagues at the Bureau. For instance, Venona held a suggestive reference to one "Agent 19," who had provided Stalin with high-level details of Top Secret British-U.S. agreements in 1945 and 1946. Smith would have had access to those details while managing Eisenhower's paper flow, and then as ambassador to Moscow. Averell Harriman, who preceded Smith as ambassador, would have had the same access, and he, too, would later be investigated as a possible Soviet mole. Yet Lamphere, who was trying to track down Agent 19 for the FBI at the time, later insisted that he knew "nothing" of any suspicions against Smith.

In June 1953, despite Hoover's orders that the inquiry be handled "surreptitiously," news of it somehow reached Smith himself, who reacted to it by denigrating the FBI. The only man the FBI interviewed, Smith said in a banquet speech, was one who didn't get along with him, but who couldn't think of anything bad to say. When Smith's remarks reached Hoover, Papich went to Smith's office at State to complain about such incorrect and "derogatory" statements. Smith insisted that his intention was only to tell a funny story at a banquet. Reading his liaison man's account of the conversation, Hoover sniffed: "He has a most peculiar sense of humor. At least it isn't appreciated by me."

Nor did Hoover look kindly on allegations by Smith that the Bureau harbored homosexuals. During a discussion one Saturday morning with an FBI informant in August 1953, Smith noted that, though Senator McCarthy had found CIA "a juicy target," the FBI was "not so lily white." Some time ago, Smith said, when the Bureau was giving its people polygraph tests, it was discovered that one sixteen-year veteran was a lifelong homosexual, and "old J. Edgar almost dropped dead when he heard about it." Papich again went to see Smith, telling him that Hoover wondered who he was talking about and what the facts were. Smith denied ever saying any such thing, but the FBI did not believe him, and the whole business boiled up into a dramatic confrontation between Smith and Papich in the general's office on August 13.

After "considerable prodding" at the Agency, Papich had learned that "CIA had possession of information which should have been given to the Bureau long ago, but apparently CIA felt that the information should not have been disseminated to the Bureau." There *had* been a homosexual in the FBI. He had been identified not by Bureau polygraphers, but by CIA, when he applied for Agency employment. The Agency had denied his application but had never informed the Bureau about this man, who was still working at FBI headquarters. Papich explained that apparently the case was "pinned down," but damage had already been done to the Bureau through malicious rumors circulating in Washington.

Smith asked Papich why he was calling all this to his attention. Papich took a deep breath. He had respect and admiration for everything that Smith had done for the country, but felt that he was obliged to be blunt. He had been following the matter very closely, and, as far as he was concerned, Smith had undoubtedly originated the rumor.

The general turned purple. "I don't know why I deal with you!" he screamed. Then he paused for several seconds, and calmly added, "Sam, I do not know. It is possible that I did start the rumor. This is very possible." Smith claimed that he hadn't known of the case during his tenure as DCI, and that, if Allen Dulles had failed to disseminate the information, it was only because "Dulles has a great fear of Mr. Hoover." So, too, did the general. The interview ended with a palliative Smith telling Papich, "I do not want to fight the FBI Director."

"Well handled by Papich," Hoover wrote on an FBI summary of the episode. "Smith is a 'stinker' & not a little one either."

The general resigned from government service in August 1954, one of 273 persons to leave the State Department after being investigated by the FBI. Officially, he retired for "health reasons," but suspicions lingered that Smith was a communist agent. In 1956 his pattern of contact with suspected Soviet spies was discovered to include onetime close associate Edward Ellis Smith, CIA's first man in Moscow, who confessed to having been compromised by the KGB during Bedell Smith's tenure as ambassador. A later KGB defector alleged that the Soviets had compromised and recruited as an agent a U.S. ambassador to the Soviet Union, though the defector did not know whether it was Smith, or his predecessor Averell Harriman, or someone else. But in Smith's home, after his death in 1961, scores of still-classified government documents were found, including directives on dozens of military campaigns—most of them stamped Secret, Top Secret, or Eyes Only. And an official CIA account of Smith's tenure, partially declassified in 1992, would contain a suggestive deletion. Immediately after discussion of John Davies' suspected disloyalty and Smith's entrance into the State Department—the very juncture at which Smith came under FBI investigation, and where one would expect some treatment of the suspicions against him—there would be only the words: "thirty six–page chapter deleted."

AT SEVENTY YEARS OLD, Bill Donovan knew that he was going to die, but he was not simply going to fade away. He had hoped desperately for seven years to be named CIA director when the Republicans reclaimed the White House, and was crushed when Dulles, some twenty years his junior, received the post. Putting his field-energetic but disorganized former protégé in charge of Central Intelligence was akin to "making a marvelous telegraph operator the head of Western Union," Donovan believed, but there was nothing he could do. Privately, he blamed the FBI director for his failure to become DCI, and OSS veterans later claimed that Hoover had been "leaking some very damaging personal information about Donovan to President Eisenhower . . . when Donovan was under serious consideration for appointment as the Director of the CIA." The genesis of the rumor appears to have been a deeply resented dig by the Bureau into the question of Donovan's loyalty.

Tracking his movements upon direct orders from Hoover—"We must certainly follow and keep alert to his manipulations, as they bode no good for FBI"—informants continued to locate Donovan around the blurry margins of clandestine service. In February 1950, a U.S. Naval Intelligence source reported that Donovan had gone secretly to China with General Claire Chennault, ostensibly to take possession of some airplanes whose ownership was in dispute, but actually "for espionage purposes and to establish air bases for bombing Russia in event of a war with that country." In September 1951, Donovan was said to be "in Italy on an undercover assignment checking on the murder of Captain Holohan," an OSS commando killed in the mountains of Italy in 1945 while carrying $100,000 in covert funds, which was never found. When Donovan returned from a foreign journey in May 1951 with one of his arms in a sling, the Bureau noted rumors that Wild Bill was "wounded in a fight between intelligence agents in Arabia."

Other reports indicated that Donovan was still in close touch with CIA. A special CIA liaison officer was appointed to maintain contact with him; FBI records imply that this was Security Director Edwards. In September 1950, as Bedell Smith was settling in as DCI, Smith and Dulles had called on Donovan in New York to discuss matters, and on the 21st of the month Donovan sent Smith the first of many letters transmitting old OSS documents, giving advice on organization, and recommending former OSS personnel. That Donovan was sending Smith OSS records and intelligence from other sources did not prevent the two men from being "rather patronizing in their attitudes toward one another," as Lawrence Houston later said, and CIA soon had its fill of Donovan. In November, when DeLoach advised Edwards of a report that Donovan had hired former OSS-CIA security man James Bielaski to investigate Elizabeth Bentley, Edwards was all in favor of reining Donovan in. He told DeLoach that he received approximately six letters each week from Donovan, advising him how to run CIA. Edwards said he was tired of such "trivial tripe" and that he was going to tell Donovan that he should keep his hands off governmental affairs. Hoover noted in blue ink, "I thought Edwards would get fed up with Gen. D."

Yet as late as August 1952, after Papich had replaced DeLoach, the Bureau's Liaison Section was still receiving allegations from an ONI source—soon confirmed by the Agency itself—that "Donovan was employed in some capacity by CIA." The source claimed to know of "150 pounds of confidential CIA material [designated] for transmittal to General William Donovan at his law address in New York City." The material, a secret study of Chinese terrain, had been sent to Donovan by "a CIA operator in Tokyo"—probably Thomas Bland, who had been with OSS in Berne. "ONI has been endeavoring for quite some time to determine whether or not Donovan is an employee of CIA," Hoover was told. The ONI sources had "contacted CIA, told them of the material and asked if Donovan was a CIA employee. The individual at CIA . . . did advise that Donovan was 'a part-time consultant.' "

Whatever Donovan was doing for CIA, he could not have been content with such a sideline role. In March 1953, after he was named a consultant to the Mutual Security Agency (MSA), which distributed foreign aid, the Bureau heard that "Donovan wanted to set up an intelligence office in connection with his work for Mutual Security." When MSA belatedly asked the Bureau for a routine check of its files "for any subversive derogatory data" on Donovan, an FBI agent warned MSA "of Donovan's attempts to subvert the Bureau in the domestic intelligence field," and stressed that "it would be better procedure to check *before* such appointments are made or announced." MSA claimed that Donovan was being used only intermittently, but Hoover remained concerned, jotting on one memo: "All Donovan needs in anything is an entering wedge."

An apparent solution to the "Donovan problem" appeared in June 1953, when Eisenhower decided to make him ambassador to Thailand.

But like Smith and all other State nominees, Donovan had to undergo a full FBI field investigation. A special inquiry into the former OSS Director began with "Urgent" cables to FBI field offices on June 15, and Donovan's well-known indifference toward communists in OSS soon led the Bureau down long, dark avenues of suspicion. Informants described Donovan as "soft and mushy" and a "bubblehead" because he never "got tough" with communists. It was also noted that Donovan had formed a committee asking President Eisenhower to oust Senator McCarthy, and that his law firm not only harbored communist sympathizers, but defended suspected Soviet spies. "There is considerable information regarding [Donovan's] 'soft policy' toward pro-Communists," the inquiry supervisor informed Assistant Director Ladd on July 17, and "running out and documenting this information" was going to cause a "delay in completing this case."

What disturbed FBI investigators most about Donovan was not that he had allowed communists to work for OSS, and thereby risked compromise of U.S. secrets to the Soviets. The real problem was rather that Donovan willfully impeded investigation of suspected spies, and thereby prevented full inquiry into secrets lost. Even before Pearl Harbor, as early as November 1941, a memo warned Hoover: "The Donovan office has ordered all existing lists (those prior to November 1st) of its employees destroyed so that newspapers could not learn how many Communists and phonies had been on their pay roll prior to this date." In September 1942, Donovan advised the Bureau he would "take no action" in the matter of a communist employee, Donald Niven Wheeler. In 1943, OSS received information that Assistant Treasury Secretary Harry Dexter White was a Soviet agent, but Donovan protected White, the FBI believed, "because he was one of the main contacts in the Treasury Department for unvouchered funds used by OSS in their operations." In early 1945, according to Bentley, Donovan had called OSS officer Maurice Halperin and told him that he knew he was a Soviet agent, yet had withheld that information from the FBI, and in 1947 he had offered Halperin free legal counsel. And in 1948, Donovan had launched a concerted offensive against Elizabeth Bentley, the prized FBI source who named so many OSS officers as Soviet agents, by hiring James Bielaski to investigate her and "break down her testimony." Donovan claimed he was only standing by men he believed in. But to FBI investigators conducting the special inquiry in June and July 1953, he certainly seemed to have taken things a bit too far.

What did it all mean? Donovan himself had written, in the context of criticizing the FBI's loyalty work, that "intelligence . . . must take several cases and by the use of the technique of analysis and synthesis, evaluate the material and seek a pattern." In Donovan's own loyalty case, the pattern was damning indeed. The entire grain of his career had gone against everything the FBI tried to do on the matter of domestic subversion. Was Donovan merely trying to spite his old enemy, Hoover? Was he first duped by communists, then embarrassed into covering up his blunders? Could he be viewed as a (perhaps unwitting) agent of communist influence, in the sense that the cumulative effect of his actions, over twenty years, had helped the Soviet cause? Might he not even be a Soviet spy?

Army counterintelligence investigators, trying to run down wartime security leaks, had pondered this last possibility in 1952, and had asked the FBI if it possessed any evidence that Donovan might have been a "subversive." The FBI had replied negatively then, but by July 15, 1953, when the results of its special Donovan inquiry were sent to the Secretary of State Dulles, the Bureau could not be so sure. Donovan's long tolerance of communism was noted prominently in the case summary, and though there was no clear evidence of disloyalty, Hoover personally stressed to Dulles that this was "not to be construed as a clearance."

Dulles and Eisenhower sent Donovan to Bangkok anyway, probably grateful to have him out of Washington. In his one year as ambassador, Donovan helped turn Thailand into the anticommunist bulwark of Southeast Asia, but the Bureau continued to marshal suspicions against him. On April 16, 1954, an informant told the FBI that a Mrs. Hugo Steiner, a native of Germany, was shipping large quantities of microfilm to Wild Bill in Thailand, and might be sending "classified information" she obtained from Donovan to "unfriendly nations." Questioned by the FBI, Steiner claimed she was employed by Donovan to research "sabotage during the American Revolution." Twelve days after this report reached Hoover, the FBI began a "correlation search" into Donovan, and over the next year and a half compiled a massive seven-hundred-page catalogue of his alleged sins, much of which would remain classified, nearly forty years later, on national-security grounds. Donovan's people later claimed that during this period microphones were discovered in his New York law office, and that they had been planted by the FBI. The Bureau's suspicions may even have rubbed off on the Agency: according to former OSS officer Richard Dunlop, Donovan found himself being followed, in Thailand, "by what he at first took to be Soviet agents. Then . . . he learned that the agents were from the CIA. Allen Dulles apparently did not trust his old mentor."

On returning from Thailand for health reasons in August 1954, Donovan again took up the practice of law, and lost more than one case from lack of preparation. He was slipping, but he still dreamed that he might replace Dulles. He spent the rest of the 1950s waiting for the calls that never came, exiled by presidential ingratitude, insensibly sinking into the languid indifference of private life. Former OSS men remarked sadly that "once he had direct access to the president; now his audience might be a Junior Chamber of Commerce or a Women's Club luncheon."

It was perhaps an easy excuse to credit the old soldier's decline to his archenemy Hoover, but the belief died hard among his admirers. There was a lingering suspicion that Hoover had collected "dirt" on Donovan and used it to keep him from becoming DCI. Old Donovan hands like Helms would allege that Hoover played "a very skillful game" with knowledge of the sexual habits of prominent people. Houston would hint darkly that "The last thing Wild Bill would have done was collect information about people and use it against them—which Hoover did *all* the time." If that kind of talk was an underground river in Washington during the FBI director's lifetime, and a standard anti-Hoover allegation after his death, embittered OSS veterans were its fountainhead.

Down to the end of the century, FBI and CIA men would each tilt at the honor of the other's legendary founder, and the personal and interagency rivalries informed a smarmy politics of reputation. Hoover was said to have spread the rumor that Donovan had contracted syphilis in orgies with prostitutes, while Donovan's men may have been the genesis of a Mafia–homosexual blackmail thesis advanced after Hoover's death. OSS veterans said that Hoover lived "queerly," and decades later ex-CIA men like Richard Helms would insist that the FBI Director had refused, first to acknowledge, and then to vigorously prosecute, the Mafia. By some poorly sourced accounts, Donovan ordered a secret probe of Hoover's relationship with Clyde Tolson; journalist Anthony Summers has even speculated that this Donovan investigation yielded a "sex photograph" which later fell into the hands of underworld figure Meyer Lansky, perhaps via OSS officers who served in Italy. Summers suggests "that Edgar had tried and failed to find smear material on General Donovan, that Donovan in turn found smear material on him and that the material found its way to a top mobster, to be used against Edgar for the rest of his life." There is no proof of such a scenario, however; nor does it explain why such material was never used for its alleged purpose: to keep Hoover from hurting Donovan's career.

Whatever effect Hoover's machinations did have on the decline of Donovan's professional fortunes became irrelevant after February 1957, however, when Wild Bill suffered a stroke. He lived out most of the next two years in his apartment overlooking the East River, seldom leaving his bed. Loyal to the last, OSS colleagues like Houston came to visit when they could. Propped up with pillows, Donovan stared out a window toward the east, and told his nurse he saw Russian tanks rolling across Queensboro Bridge to take Manhattan. On February 8, 1959, at age seventy-six, he died.

Hoover sent Mrs. Donovan a note of condolence, but Top Secret memoranda cynically recorded FBI worries that CIA might soon attempt a refurbishment of Donovan's reputation. "There is a good possibility that an autobiography of Donovan will be published in the not too distant future," Hoover's number-three man, Assistant Director Al Belmont, was cautioned on the day after Donovan's death. "Because of his colorful career, it can be anticipated a movie will follow the book. CIA undoubtedly will take every opportunity to make certain that the movie places CIA in a favorable light."

Neither the autobiography nor the movie ever came into being, but in his waning months there had occurred an event by which Donovan would always be remembered, and which no Hooverian hostility could ever taint. After his first stroke, in 1957, CIA had decided to award its architect and spiritual father the National Security Medal, the highest award the Agency could offer, and just about the only one left for a man who was one of the most decorated soldiers in American military history. Having recently seen Donovan and knowing his health was fading, Houston went to Dulles and suggested "that we get this medal to the old boy while he's still going." Dulles said, "You take one of the Air Force planes and go up now." Houston did; he pinned the medal on Donovan's pajama top, then asked his old boss about a portrait CIA planned to have done. Donovan was making fairly good sense at that time, and they talked about which artist might do it. Houston returned to Washington, and the portrait was started from photographs. Then, in spring 1958, Donovan had a second stroke, and was badly off, so CIA had him flown down to Walter Reed Army Hospital in Washington, where the intensive care was the best in the world. Houston and Colby and others would go out and see him; on some days he was pretty good, and on others he would just babble at the ceiling. But finally they got his portrait done, and hung it on the ground floor of the Administration Building, where Donovan had started up his central-intelligence dream with COI almost eighteen years before; now it was headquarters of CIA. Houston checked with Donovan's nurse to find what appeared to be a good day, went out, and picked him up. As they drove toward CIA, the old man's mind was really wandering, and he was very nervous that maybe children would get in front of the car. But they pulled up to CIA headquarters and Houston said, "Come on in, General. I've got something to show you." They led him in, and showed him the portrait—a pretty good likeness of Wild Bill. He looked at it, and he *straightened up.*

Full attention! He stood there, and said, "Great! Great!" And with that he stomped out, sort of parade-stepped to the car. They drove off, and Donovan took a piece of paper and a pencil out of his pocket, and he started writing: "Memorandum to the President." Then his hand just trailed down the paper; he was gone.

CHAPTER SEVEN

THE GRAY GHOST

IAN FLEMING'S FAVORITE NOVELIST, John Buchan, created in *The Thirty-nine Steps* a character for whom one whole chapter was named: "The Dry-Fly Fisherman." Richard Hannay, the hero of Buchan's stories, met him at a waterfall. The fisherman nodded to Hannay, leaned his delicate ten-foot split-cane rod against a nearby bridge, and stared at the surface of the waters. His kind blue eyes seemed to go very deep. He had a square, cleft jaw and a broad, lined brow; Hannay had never seen a shrewder face. But his hair was prematurely gray and thin about the temples, and there were lines of overwork below the eyes; his big frame seemed built for a much heavier man, his shoulders were stooped, and his skin was drained of color, like that of someone who got too little fresh air. He made a few cryptic remarks, then invited Hannay into his adjacent country home; they drank good champagne, dined, and smoked. Hannay's host swung his long legs over the side of a chair and identified himself as Sir Walter Bullivant, the country's counterintelligence chief. He would become Hannay's mentor and boss, and the prototype for master spy-catchers in fiction and in fact.

If Fleming himself never really made a Bullivant type the focus of his fictions—"the white-collar boys" could "catch spies," while Agent 007 would attack SMERSH, "the threat that made them spy"—that was one reason the Bond books would be dismissed by Dulles and others as "unrealistic." Dulles did not think that professional intelligence officers, as a rule, went on "perilous or glamorous missions" or became involved with "luscious dames." He would, however, say: "A useful analogy is to the art of angling. The fisherman's preparation for the catch, his consideration of the weather, the light, the currents, the depth of the water, the right bait or fly to use, the time of day to fish, the spot he chooses and the patience he shows are all a part of the art and essential to success. In fact, I have found that good fishermen tend to make good intelligence officers."

So it was with the man whom Dulles thought CIA's best intelligence officer of all, a dry-fly fisherman who much resembled Buchan's Bullivant. For the twenty years following December 20, 1954, he would be the FBI's main point of liaison. His separate peace with Papich would help break a network of Soviet agents in New York, lead the two agencies into a joint project to open the mail of U.S. citizens, and limit fallout when the FBI's prize spy prisoner was swapped for a CIA pilot downed in Russia. Yet he would also bring to the Agency a way of thinking that crystallized FBI-CIA differences, and which would ultimately rip relations apart.

BY SUMMER 1954, a whole slew of traumas and setbacks had demonstrated the need for a revamped national counterintelligence effort. The Bentley, Hiss, Fuchs, and Rosenberg cases had destroyed the country's early naïveté. The Burgess-Maclean affair alerted the intelligence establishment that its secrets could go, even if its own operations weren't penetrated. The McCarthyist period brought home the need to prevent such morale-sapping episodes by prophylactic measures. That need was felt particularly acutely by Houston, Edwards, and others concerned with personnel security at CIA, who had tangled with the FBI over Offie and Meyer and various loyalty cases, and who didn't feel the Agency was getting proper investigative help from the Bureau. It was not so much a lack of help, as the wrong kind. CIA was all for getting tips from Hoover, but wanted to handle its own security problems internally, without the Bureau or HUAC or anyone else sneezing into the soup.

A start at reform had been made in June, when Dulles and Hoover worked out, via Houston and Attorney General William P. Rogers, a procedure for FBI investigation of "irregularities" involving CIA employees. Misconduct of any kind was to be the province of CIA's Office of Security, which had to jump into a situation immediately—not only to preserve CIA's public reputation, but to protect secrets which might be compromised by the curiosity of the FBI. Every so often, some CIA officer would fall afoul of the administrative charter, or, on rare occasions, flee an automobile accident, or leave a satchel full of classified documents in a taxicab, and Papich would turn the case over to Sheffield Edwards. One CIA officer had to resign after the FBI discovered that his house was stacked to the ceiling with secret government papers; he wasn't passing them out to the enemy, just building up a library for himself, for writing books, and apparently it helped him, because he later became a top expert in foreign policy. The Bureau could have recommended that the man be prosecuted for unlawful possession of government documents, but CIA's policy was to handle and resolve everything internally, fearing that secrets would be lost through the "discovery" process in a trial, and the FBI went along.

But DCI Dulles knew that counterintelligence involved more than just letting the Agency take care of its own; it mattered what kind of care was taken. There was a demonstrable need to be more cautious, more concerned with the principles of compartmentation and "need to know." If Dulles' people were going to succeed, the security of sources, operations, and personnel was *everything*. That was the lesson taught by Wisner's OPC, at least in the view of William Harvey's counterintelligence people. If Cord Meyer was trying to suborn the editor of a newspaper, or Wisner to work with a guerrilla leader in the mountains, it was crucial to know whether one's agent might be an informant for the security service. But OPC wanted only action. As one of Harvey's colleagues was admonished, "Goddamn it, we don't want counterintelligence, we want *guerrillas!*" Because of progress in radio detection, and because the adversary controlled Trust-style opposition groups, the task of infiltrating commandos was more difficult than it had been even ten years earlier—yet there didn't seem to be any shift in tactics from world war to Cold War. Wisner's men were still fighting the Nazis, still dropping people behind the lines, and it took the spectacular failures of OPC's covert actions, in Poland, Albania, and the Ukraine, to teach the wisdom of Harvey's more cautious approach.

Additional pressures came from outside the Agency. The White House was getting mail urging that Hoover be made director of CIA, or that the Agency be folded into the FBI; J. Edgar would kick out the commies as he had chased down Dillinger, and only then would the nation's secrets be safe. One concerned citizen complained that CIA had been puffed into existence by Donovan's press campaign, and that Hoover's more efficient SIS had been taken over by the Agency because Hoover refused to publicize the FBI's successes; "the public and even Congress never even heard of [SIS], nor did it get any publicity, nor did J. Edgar Hoover or the men in charge get pictures in the paper entitled 'Superspy.' " Eisenhower responded to the pressure as any politician would, by appointing a committee to look into it. The inquiry was headed by Lieutenant General James Doolittle, and the sixty-nine-page Doolittle Report, presented to Eisenhower in September 1954, proposed some radical reforms.

Most signally, the report urged CIA to assume the country's leading counterintelligence role. The National Security Council had given the job of collating counterintelligence to CIA in December 1947, but there was a consensus, Harvey's Staff C notwithstanding, that countering enemy intelligence was the FBI's job. That would have to change. The United States needed to abandon the law-enforcement route for a "more ruthless" approach, the Doolittle Report stressed, and that new ruthlessness must be applied to "intensification of CIA's counterintelligence efforts to prevent or detect and eliminate penetrations." The situation required a new strategy, a new concept for American life, one which would spill across normally restricted areas, legal channels, and departmental lines.

It also required a new chief of counterintelligence, for in mid-1953 Harvey had been made Chief of Base in Berlin. The outgoing Bedell Smith had told Papich early that year that Harvey was probably going to be posted abroad. "As you know," Hoover was reminded in a summary of that conversation, "[Harvey] has been the center of many controversies." But there was more to the decision than a desire to keep Harvey out of Hoover's way. Harvey himself had wanted to leave Staff C, because he hoped to rise in the Agency and, compared with other disciplines, counterintelligence was considered career-ending. Harvey didn't have much of a chance to manage people, the way he would if he were running agents in even the smallest foreign station, and thus wasn't as easily marked for promotion; already, while he was stalled in Staff C, two less knowledgeable men with overseas experience had overtaken him. He added an extra martini at lunch, and when the chiefship of Berlin Base came free, he asked for the job and got it. Divided into Russian, British, French, and American zones, isolated in the heartland of communist Germany, Berlin was the hotbed of the Cold War. It was, too, a welcome reprieve from the hassles and obstructionism of the FBI. It would be almost nine years before Harvey worked again in Washington, though, as he would find, that was not long enough to outrun Hoover's memory.

SAM PAPICH MET CIA's new counterintelligence chief in a large corner office of L Building, where a row of windows looked out on the Lincoln Memorial—or would have, if Venetian blinds had not been shut against the light. Six secretaries in the anteroom testified to the new appointee's power, as did the long row of black safes in his inner sanctum, and the piles of documents. Red priority stickers were everywhere in the mass of papers, like poppies pushing through a field of snow. In all other respects, the office was undistinctive, typical CIA; there wasn't much on the walls. But in a high leather-backed chair behind the desk was as singular a man as Papich had ever seen.

His black hair was slicked back from a pale forehead, a bony blade of nose, sunken cheeks, and elegantly pointed chin—a chiseled, cadaverous face that had been proposed, only half facetiously, as a logo for CIA. His deep-set eyes were emphasized by arched brows, framed by horn-rimmed bifocals, and lit with a kind of controlled fire. He was thirty-seven years old, and well over six feet tall, but his gaunt frame was stooped and slightly twisted, making him seem, as one colleague said, half his height and twice his age. Clasped to his shirt pocket was a plastic picture-ID, required wearing for anyone inside headquarters, and around its edges were twenty-four boxes filled with red letters, signifying the security clearances that gave him access to more restricted areas, and more secrets, than any man except the Agency's director.

James Jesus Angleton was one of only a handful of people—Harvey was another—who would ever become truly legendary within the faceless bureaucracy of knowledge that was CIA. A chain-smoking poetry enthusiast, ace fly-fisherman, and grower of rare orchids, Angleton had been recruited into OSS after graduating from Yale. He had served under Norman Pearson in X-2 and had been particularly adept at burning and turning Nazi stay-behinds in Italy. After the war, he had been put in charge of a so-called Special Desk to handle such tasks as liaison with the Israelis and the British. That latter experience had stamped him with a general suspiciousness, for he had lunched regularly with Kim Philby and detected nothing until it was too late. Some of his Special Desk duties had also caused Angleton to clash with DeLoach the few times they met, so Papich was not entirely surprised that when he first encountered Angleton, in that corner office of L Building, they got into "a real fight."

After preliminary greetings, the new counterintelligence chief lit a cigarette, leaned across his desk, and, in his gravelly burr, brought up a case that had allegedly been mishandled by the Bureau. It had been damaging to CIA, and Angleton made a big deal about it—maybe with good reason, but Papich disagreed with him. It got to a bitter stage; they were shouting insults. Finally, Papich just walked out. Maybe Angleton was testing him, to make clear that he was going to dominate liaison. Well, thought Papich, he's not going to.

They saw each other again the next day, and managed to act cordially. Before too long, small talk brought out that they were from neighboring big-sky states, and they both liked fly-fishing. They went off one weekend to do a little angling for brown trout in the freestone streams of West Virginia, and after that they were friends. Papich was impressed by the fact that Angleton would never just cast a fly; he would always spend a half-hour or so just stalking along the riverbank, examining the insect life, and then craft lures to imitate the species along that particular stretch of shore—brown ants, inchworms, soldier beetles, whatever he saw. Angleton had mastered the esoteric lore and literature of the discipline, which dated back to fifteenth-century Scotland; he could loop his line through the air and splash it onto the waters *just so*, in imitation of a hatching fly, and his vest and hat were decorated with traditional fly designs, in all their exotic colors and types and names: Flamingo Zonker, Yellow Goofus Bug, Egg-Sucking Leach. Angleton knew them all, but his standby was the Gray Ghost, a classic American freestone-river design— ocher floss-silk body ribbed with flat silver tinsel, black silk nose, white buck tail, and gray cock hackles sweeping sleekly back, like wings. Given Angleton's own spookish demeanor and suspicious outlook, "Gray Ghost" became one of his nicknames, and colleagues thought it the one that fit him best.

The fishing trips sealed what would become a close working relationship, and Papich became a serious student of Angleton's counterintelligence philosophy. To Angleton, catching spies was much like landing trout. It was all about patience, research, deception. Yet CI was not merely a body of knowledge; it was also a way of seeing things. It meant transcending the details of a case, putting tactical problems in a strategic perspective, gaining a larger view. Angleton felt that too much of the country's conception of CI, as promoted by detective entertainments and the FBI's own actions, was "spy versus spy." That was like fighting soldier-to-soldier using bayonets, as opposed to understanding *why* the soldiers were being put face to face. That was counterespionage, not counterintelligence. What CI really required, most of all, was a good dollop of focused historical research—not the random digestion of massive mounds of fact, but purposeful, teleological analysis, looking for patterns over a long period of time. His work against the Nazis had taught him that patient accumulation of fact allowed one to decipher the enemy's thinking, and thus anticipate his moves. If one could not read the enemy's files, one could at least read his mind.

Trying to read the Soviet mind on CIA-FBI relations, Angleton considered it logical that the KGB would try to split America's CI community along its pre-existent fault line. "When the enemy is united, divide him"— so the ancient Chinese strategist Sun Tzu had counseled in *The Art of War*—a work which, through the Mongol-Tartars, had greatly influenced Russian strategy, and which, in English translation, Angleton had read more than once. "Drive a wedge. . . . Separate the enemy's allies from him. Make them mutually suspicious so that they drift apart. Then you can plot against them." The West itself was trying to split Rumania and Hungary from Moscow, and to play Soviet military intelligence (the GRU) against the KGB. Just so, Angleton reasoned, the Soviets wanted to sow schisms between the Americans and the British, and between CIA and FBI. "That was part and parcel of Jim's basic philosophy—he didn't want that to happen," Papich would later say. "It was one of the worst things that could happen, because once you destroy a relationship between services, you've destroyed the effectiveness of *both* services."

Though the CI chief was not yet sure exactly how the Soviets would make interagency trouble, he guessed they would try to capitalize on a "dissociation of sensibility." (The phrase came from a famous essay by Angleton's favorite poet, T. S. Eliot, who used it to describe thematic dualisms in literature; Angleton used it to describe the tension between Hoover's law-enforcement mentality and CIA's double-agent approach.) Angleton also supposed the KGB would try to slip between jurisdictional cracks. Just as a fly-fisherman, spotting a brown trout nibbling near the surface of the shallows, would cast from beyond its field of vision, so would the Soviets profit from interagency blind spots. If such schemes were not thwarted by close liaison, American CI would be essentially at war with itself, and the game could be lost. "Counter-intelligence," Angleton liked to say, "is only as good as relations between the CIA and FBI."

AN EARLY TEST of the new cooperation came when Papich tried to broker a joint FBI-CIA operation to kidnap a Soviet spy in the Middle East. Elizabeth Bentley had told Harvey back in 1946 that her controller, an American known to her only as "Jack," had been operating a big net of agents; by 1953, FBI counterintelligence man Robert Lamphere was sure that "Jack" was an American man named Joseph Katz. Subpoenaed by HUAC, Katz had fled to Israel, where, being of the Jewish faith, he was automatically eligible for citizenship. The U.S. did not have an extradition treaty with Israel, but Angleton's close ties to Israeli intelligence offered certain possibilities. Lamphere had met Angleton back when he was running Special Desk, and though they had little direct contact, Lamphere had always got excellent results whenever he asked, via liaison, for Angleton to do something overseas. Now the three formulated a joint FBI-CIA operation to return Katz to the United States. The key to the operation would be luring Katz onto a U.S.-registered boat, outside Israel's territorial waters, where Lamphere could make a legal arrest. It was going to be risky, but Lamphere outlined the plan in a memo to Hoover, who gave preliminary approval. "He didn't like the idea of the joint CIA-FBI operation," Lamphere said, "but had been made to understand that the FBI did not have the resources or contacts in Israel to pull off this one, whereas the CIA did."

Papich and Lamphere got all their shots, and were ready to fly to Israel, when Hoover took a last-hour look at the whole operation and scotched it. The FBI director told them that he'd talked to a deputy attorney general, and had got the distinct impression that Angleton had informed

Justice of the plan. Feeling that this was supposed to be an FBI expedition, and that CIA had overstepped its jurisdiction by going to Justice, Hoover called the whole thing off. Angleton insisted that he'd never had any such conversation with Justice, and Lamphere told Hoover that Justice probably knew about it because he, Lamphere, had cut them a copy of the planning memo, but there was no moving the director.

Of course, the team was extremely disappointed. "I was chagrined on two counts," Lamphere remembered. "One, both Sam Papich and I had wanted this joint operation to improve relations between the FBI and the CIA—and the result had been just the opposite, a further rupture between the agencies. Two, I was disappointed that my one best hope to reopen the Bentley case and prosecute some of the key figures was now gone." Lamphere was so disgusted with Hoover's bull-headedness that he soon resigned from the Bureau.

Angleton also was peeved. He went to Papich and said, "Why the hell did the boss turn this one down?" Papich thought the director was probably concerned that another agency—and another foreign service, the Mossad—had too much operational control. He recounted how some botched operations with local police in the hunt for Dillinger had taught Hoover to participate in joint projects only if he could control the show. That didn't wash too well with Angleton. It sickened him that, despite the best-laid plans of FBI and CIA men, Soviet spies like Katz still could count on the "dissociation" of American counterintelligence.

RUNNING OPERATIONS SILENTLY, without Hoover's direct knowledge, produced much better results. In one case, Angleton got the Bureau access to a New York mob lawyer. The man was a rascal, but there was no counting the cases the FBI prosecuted on the basis of his cooperation, all involving corruption within unions and city government—and all for *free*, just given over by Angleton. Papich also worked with CIA people on projects spearheaded by Angleton in the cryptographic field, while the Agency, for its part, serviced countless FBI requests for coverage of American communist leaders traveling abroad. Since the great majority of Soviet and Eastern-bloc operations against the U.S. were originated overseas, CIA was naturally able to supply more leads for the FBI than conversely, but the Agency got its share of dividends. Angleton would ask the Bureau to undertake "black bag" jobs against certain domestic targets, and the Bureau would sometimes do so.

But good relations at the working level were always constrained by tensions at the top. Angleton's own relations with Hoover were cordial the few times they met, but looking back a quarter-century later, the CI chief would realize that during all those years, from the 1950s through the mid-1970s, "there weren't more than three or four meetings" between Hoover and the directors of CIA, except where they bumped into one another at a national-security conference. There was no question in Angleton's mind but that this adversely affected CI. On the other hand, Angleton had to admit that Hoover had some good reasons to be wary of CIA. In October 1955, for instance, Papich carried over a letter from Hoover suggesting that Donald Maclean might have compromised CIA employees. Maclean had been "a frequent visitor" at CIA, according to a Bureau source, and was alleged to have "dated two of your stenographers." An FBI search of logs kept by the door guards at CIA's "O" Building, in front of the Lincoln Pool, showed that Maclean often entered that particular building after hours. While there was no firm proof that he had dated any CIA women, such episodes did not increase Hoover's trust of CIA.

Hoover's sometimes petty power plays were none too helpful, either. FBI man William Sullivan later alleged that the FBI planted stories critical of the CIA, and it appears that, in September 1955, the FBI director went public with the accusations against Philby in a way that embarrassed the Agency. Columnist Walter Winchell, a Hoover friend, reported on his popular Sunday-night radio show that Burgess and Maclean had escaped to Moscow after being tipped off by "another top British intelligence agent" who had been in Washington; Winchell said that "the FBI refused to give this man any information for over three years," which was false, but that "other American intelligence departments opened up their very secret files for him," which of course was true. Hoover also tried to sour the opinion of Joseph Kennedy about CIA in February 1956, when the Boston power-broker was named a member of the president's Board of Consultants on Foreign Intelligence Activities. "I discussed with Mr. Kennedy generally some of the weaknesses which we have observed in the operations of CIA," Hoover told his top deputies after a private meeting in his headquarters office, "particularly as to the organizational-set-up and the compartmentation that exists within that agency." Nor would Hoover keep out of the Washington paper-mill Attorney General Rogers' July 28, 1958, statement that "he [Rogers] just wished the FBI was doing the intelligence work abroad instead of CIA."

WITH THAT KIND OF SENTIMENT radiating down, it was unsurprising that the two agencies were unable to agree in some important areas, including the storage and retrieval of secrets. The issue arose because Angleton, shortly after becoming Chief/CI, started computerizing documents on the huge vacuum-tube punch-card monsters then being made by IBM. With IBM's help, he developed an innovative computerized microfilm file-index known as Walnut; the project began with Abwehr documents captured in World War II and spread from there. In 1955, Angleton persuaded Dulles to create a U.S. Intelligence Board Committee on Documentation (CODIB) to promote community-wide computerization, but the FBI was not interested in applying computers to its name-trace or identification work. "We've got three warehouses, full of papers, and files, and thousands of people, who can run around and work the files," Hoover's CODIB man insisted. Nor did CODIB ever achieve interagency standards to ease the exchange of data; CIA and FBI couldn't even agree on the order of "header" items in a biographic record. "Do you want last name first, then first name and middle initial, followed by date of birth, followed by place of birth?" That question was debated for eight years, and it was not surprising to those within bureaucratic Washington, let alone familiar with FBI-CIA difficulties, that during the entire existence of CODIB, from 1955 to 1963, so simple a problem was never resolved.

While CODIB stalled over minutiae, a deeper problem for centralized analysis stemmed from the FBI's antianalytical bias. Rocca built an extensive research section, but the FBI's, headed by Bill Sullivan, was comparatively small, and was directed mostly at the CPUSA, not the KGB. That always rankled Papich. "If, over a period of five years, X number of Soviets had visited New Mexico near Los Alamos, and had been seen driving around—well, who were they, what were their backgrounds? Could the Bureau draw any conclusion as to what the target was? What the hell did it all mean? We'd zero in on an individual, primarily to develop evidence for prosecution, but we did very little big-picture thinking. That all goes back to our law-enforcement nature."

But if the Bureau was little interested in CIA's historical research, Angleton's CI shop, for its part, benefited greatly from FBI tips on the way the Soviets worked. For the first two years of Angleton's tenure, the Bureau couldn't tell CIA much it didn't know already, but that began to change in 1957, when the Yale choir made its maiden trip to Moscow, and the Soviets began opening up, a little bit, to the world. After that, CIA had a lot to learn from the Bureau's debriefings of returning American tourists. The real epiphany was to come that same year, when Angleton's cooperation gave the Bureau its biggest break so far in the secret war against Soviet spies. Even so, it was a cooperation that would have to be hidden from Hoover—and the FBI would repay it by risking the safety of CIA's only mole in Moscow.

• • •

ON MAY 4, 1957, a rumpled, mustachioed, dark-haired man entered the U.S. Embassy in Paris with liquor on his breath. Through a thick Finnish accent, Reino Hayhannen told the State Department's duty officer that he had important national security information to share with the United States. The duty officer turned him over to the FBI's resident legal attaché, who considered him "a weirdo," took him outside and put him into a taxicab with instructions on how to get to the CIA's offices, telling him, "It's clearly a case for the CIA." But as soon as one of CIA's officers heard Hayhannen's story, he got on the phone to the legal attaché and insisted: "This guy doesn't belong to us, he belongs to the FBI." The walk-in was passed back and forth two or three times until finally someone in the CIA offices listened to him.

Hayhannen claimed to belong to a network of spies in the New York City area, and identified himself as a Soviet "illegal." In CI jargon, an illegal was any foreign-intelligence officer dispatched to the United States under a false identity, in violation of immigration law. Although technically no spy openly declared his profession and all spying was against the law, most intelligence personnel were "legal" in the sense that they were affiliated with their home nation's embassy and performed some nominal diplomatic functions to justify their presence in-country. Illegals, by contrast, might enter the U.S. under totally fictitious identities, often taken from tombstones. They would never make open contact with their sponsors' embassy, and could live relatively undetected, especially in a polyglot place like New York. Once past the customs barriers of his unwitting hosts, the saying went, a Soviet illegal disappeared like a diamond into an inkwell. It was assumed that illegals aimed to get employment that would permit easy access to scientific and technical information, and that they hoped to penetrate the intelligence community and perhaps even enter political life. Beyond that little was known, because the FBI had never caught a Soviet illegal, or had the chance to debrief one.

"I'm on my way into East Germany, for a meeting with my controllers," he told the CIA officer at Paris Station, "and I don't want to go. I want to cooperate with the United States government." Hayhannen's bizarre behavior soon instilled doubts about whether that might be such a good idea, however. "I live in Peekskill, New York," he said, "and to prove I'm in Peekskill, I'm going to send a message to my wife." Picking up his left hand, he began to beat out a message in Morse code on his chest. Christ, thought the CIA officer, this man is insane. But then Hayhannen showed an American passport obtained by using a false birth certificate, and started reeling off information—about his training, meetings he'd had in Vienna, identities of KGB officers, secret caches of funds. He even promised to lead the FBI to his Soviet controller, a mysterious Brooklyn resident known to him only as "Mark."

This information was immediately cabled Blue-Bottle (highest security) from Paris Station to CIA headquarters in Washington. In essence the station chief said to Frank Wisner, who by then was deputy director for plans: We can't hold him, we can't detain him. We don't want to get involved with the French. We want an immediate reply.

Wisner deferred to Angleton, who consulted Papich, who assessed the situation in Angleton's basement at three in the morning. Papich thought he could get the cooperation of General Joseph Swing, head of the Immigration Service, to put Hayhannen in quarantine. If it was determined Hayhannen was a phony, they could always deport him. Certainly Hayhannen was an unstable character, and Hoover wasn't about to bring him to the United States on his own, but a lot of Bureau cases could develop if they played it right. There was nothing really in it for CIA, except the risk of bringing in a "crazy" or a false defector, but finally Angleton just said, "Let's get the character over here, and see what happens."

Hayhannen was put on a plane from Paris. His CIA bodyguards almost ended up shooting him during the night flight across the Atlantic, because he was drunk and irrational and tried to kick some windows out of the plane. In fact, he was bombed most of the time, and it did not take long to grasp that he was an alcoholic. Once in America, he put down about a fifth of vodka every day, until the Bureau got him into quarantine. They then debriefed him about his boyhood in Finland and Leningrad, how he joined Soviet intelligence to "get ahead," his extensive training before coming to the U.S. in October 1952, and his work for the Soviets since then, mostly servicing dead-drops of other agents. His house in Peekskill was found to contain a codebook and secret writing materials. There was no question about it, the man was a Soviet spy.

But Hoover read the writeups and said, "This guy's an alcoholic—let's drop him."

At that point, Angleton moved in. CIA took formal custody of Hayhannen, put him in one of its own safehouses in Manhattan, a better layout in a more secure location, and kept him available for debriefing by the lead FBI agent on the case, Larry McWilliams.

"Mac," as everyone called him, was stout, sharp-eyed, and streetwise, his nasal Queens dialect rich in profanity and in words like "discomboober-ated" or "psychophants," which he made up as he went along. For all his tough exterior, Mac was a thoughtful man, educated at the University of Idaho, and he was fascinated by CI; he wasn't out talking to some tenth-grade hood, but was dealing with abstractions. He couldn't ask, How am I going to handle a Soviet? without wondering, Now, what's this organization behind him? How do they plan? Those were the questions that made McWilliams lay up nights, thinking. He kept a pad and pencil next to the bed, in case he had an idea about a case. And since May 12, when he had drawn the straw to go get Hayhannen at Idlewild Airport, he had been doing a lot of scribbling. He sensed they were on to something really big, and eventually Hoover did, too. After seeing the "take" from Hayhannen's weeks of interrogation in the CIA safehouse, the FBI director happily reclaimed the case as it turned into a hunt for Hayhannen's American controller, the mysterious Mark.

As a "cutout" between Mark and the presumably large ring of agents he controlled, Hayhannen's basic task had been to pick up and deliver packages containing money or microfilm. One drop was the Symphony Theater, a movie house at Broadway and 95th Street, on the right side of the balcony, second row from the rear. Mark liked this location, Hayhannen told McWilliams, because two people meeting there could leave by different exits. Another spot was in Riverside Park at 96th Street, where a hole in the railroad fence could hide magnetic containers. Hayhannen had seldom seen Mark himself, but Mark had once taken him to an art studio he kept in Brooklyn. The Finn couldn't remember where it was, exactly, but he was able to give basic directions and a good description.

After a frantic few days, Mac's crew was sure that Mark's place could only be in the Ovington Building, on Fulton Street in Brooklyn Heights, which rented out studios to writers and artists. It was determined that Mark had occupied number 505, directly under the author Norman Mailer. FBI agents were dispersed at sentinel points all around the Ovington—on benches in a park across from the building entrances, in an adjacent post office, and some just walking around like locals. A command post was set up on the roof and upper floors of the highest building in the neighborhood, the Hotel Touraine, two blocks down Fulton, where agents watched through binoculars. The watch went on for weeks, without result, until, at 10:45 p.m. on May 23, someone returned to Studio 505.

He was middle-aged, bald, with glasses and a fringe of gray hair. He diddled around, then put on a dark straw summer hat with a bright-white band, and came out the front entrance with a coat over his arm. A pack of surveillance pursued him to the subway stop at Borough Hall. Special agent Joseph C. MacDonald followed him into an elevator down to the tracks, and into a subway car. Both men got off at the City Hall station, in Manhattan. MacDonald tailed the man in the straw hat to 28th Street and Fifth Avenue, where he vanished.

But the watch was kept at the Brooklyn studio, where, three weeks later, on June 13, the man again appeared. Again he was tracked into Manhattan, and this time a number of agents were already waiting around 28th and Fifth; they saw him enter the Hotel Latham. A check at the front desk revealed that he was registered as Martin Collins.

Though McWilliams was convinced that the man was an illegal, the Bureau still had no admissible evidence that he was an espionage agent. But if they held off from arresting him, there was the chance he might slip away. Mac consulted Papich, who got Immigration to approve the man's arrest on suspicion of being in the country illegally. At seven o'clock on the morning of June 21, the occupant of Room 839 at the Hotel Latham heard a knock on the door and someone saying, "FBI."

He opened the door a crack. The G-men pushed it open and entered as a naked, groggy man stood there, blinking. They let him put in his false teeth and pull on yesterday's clothes, and then he was handcuffed. They tried to ask him questions, but he would not talk. He gave his name as "Rudolf Ivanovich Abel," but would say no more.

Mac's boys searched the room, but didn't find much except, in the wastepaper basket, a piece of two-by-four. Just a block of wood. No one could figure out what it was, but it had to have some significance; you didn't just find pieces of two-by-four in Manhattan hotels. Finally, one of the agents got disgusted and threw it against the wall. It split open. Inside was a cavity containing microfilm.

Developed at the FBI's laboratory, the film was found to contain a brief message in code. The message itself was not particularly illuminating, because it referred to purported spies only by first names, but this and other clues among Abel's effects—cipher books, locations of dead drops—corroborated the essence of Hayhannen's story. Rudolf Abel, the FBI was sure, was an illegal who handled not just Hayhannen, but a whole ring of Soviet spies. Of course, there was still much they didn't know about all the agents Abel had handled, especially since Abel himself refused to talk. Aside from Hayhannen, all McWilliams knew was that Abel had a lot of contact with certain Upper West Siders named Silverman, Levine, Dinnerstein, Schwartz, Fink, Feifer, Ginzburg, etc., who all seemed to be of the same background and outlook: young, well-educated, Jewish, ambitious participants in the intellectual life around Columbia University, politically involved, signers of petitions to ban the bomb, active in the Democratic Party. Later, the Bureau was able to identify a couple who were Soviet agents, Helen and Peter Kroger, whose drops Abel had serviced. But for the moment, Hayhannen's word and the evidence in Abel's apartment were enough to have Abel indicted for conspiring to betray secrets on "the disposition of this country's armed forces and its atomic energy program." After a trial that received considerable publicity, at which Hayhannen was the chief witness against him, Abel was convicted on all counts. He was sentenced to life imprisonment, and passed time in an Atlanta jail by doing calculus problems on the walls. Hayhannen was returned to his home in Peekskill, where, after a few years of freedom, he drank himself to death.

McWilliams and the FBI came out of it somewhat better. Mac got to meet Hoover, and was marked as someone who might rise. As a result of national headlines about FBI capture of the "Top Red Spy in America," more people started to hear about the Bureau's work in counterintelligence, and young G-men started to gravitate toward it. And the new body of knowledge about Soviet illegal networks became the basis of a two-week FBI counterespionage course at Quantico. The course was nothing like what Papich and McWilliams and others in the FBI's "CI Club" believed it should be, but it was a start, and there was no question but that the Abel case had enlarged their knowledge of what was going on. "The Abel case was the watershed for all of us," McWilliams said, "because up until then, I don't think anybody, including CIA, really knew the deep, penetrating M.O. of the Soviet intelligence. We started to wake up and find out what the hell was really going on. And when that thing broke, my God, we were inundated with interest from the Canadians, the Australians, the French—everybody wanted to know what we knew. There was just a convulsion of activity."

Papich always credited Angleton. "The Rudolf Abel case was a great example of cooperation," Papich said. "And it was one of Jim's great accomplishments. If not for him, the whole thing would have gone down the drain. It was his influence that led to the decision to bring Hayhannen from France to the U.S.A. If Angleton hadn't taken that position—well, I think maybe Hayhannen might have defected to the French. I don't know what he would have done. He was a nut! Maybe nobody would have accepted him."

But even if born of teamwork, the Abel-Hayhannen case would also lead to infighting. Having learned from Hayhannen that when illegal agents wished to meet their principals they wrote to a particular address in the Soviet Union, the Bureau's CI men reasoned that if they could intercept communications directed to that particular address, they might net a good number of spies. In January 1958, Hoover therefore gave permission "to institute confidential inquiries with appropriate Post Office officials to determine the feasibility of covering outgoing correspondence from the U.S. to the U.S.S.R., looking toward picking up a communication dispatched to the aforementioned address." But when the FBI's New York SAC inquired about the possibility, Chief Postal Inspector David Stephens told him he could not authorize Post Office cooperation because "something had happened in Washington on a similar matter." Hoover was on the verge of discovering that CIA was already opening mail in New York, but had been hiding that fact from the FBI.

LIKE WIRETAPPING and surreptitious entry, mail-opening had been practiced by Allied intelligence during World War II, and like those activities it was carried over into the Cold War. The operation had been run jointly by Harvey's Staff C (under the cryptonym "HT/LINGUAL") and Edwards' Office of Security until it was officially transferred to Angleton's reorganized CI Staff for "rations and quarters" in 1955. Angleton thought HT/LINGUAL "probably the most important overview that counterintelligence had." Precisely because the enemy regarded America's mails as inviolate, mail coverage was likely to provide clues to the identities of Soviet agents.

Angleton understood that the mail-opening operation was illegal, and that if it were ever exposed, "serious public reaction in the United States would probably occur." The Fourth Amendment to the Constitution stated pretty clearly that "The right of the people to be secure in their persons, houses, and papers and effects against unreasonable searches and seizures shall not be violated, and no warrant shall issue, but upon probable cause, supported by oath or affirmation, and particularly describing the place to be searched and the persons or things to be seized." But Angleton could rationalize mail-opening on several counts. The Fourth Amendment applied only to *unreasonable* searches and seizures, which left it open as to whether reading suspected Soviet spies' mail to Moscow was reasonable. Since 1947, every president and every attorney general had agreed that warrantless wiretaps could sometimes be reasonable, and if there was an exception to the Fourth Amendment for trespass via electronic surveillance, it did not take much imagination to extend that to trespass via surreptitious entry, or mail-opening. Every law had its exceptions; the laws of God and man clearly said it was wrong to kill or steal, and those laws did not say "except in the time of war," but everyone knew that a wartime exception was read into them. Angleton believed that any restrictions on government mail-opening must similarly have read into them an exception that would allow CIA to cover mail in time of secret war. Abraham Lincoln had authorized the Pinkerton Detective Service to open mail to catch Confederate spies; why could the country not do the same to identify Nazi or communist agents? As no less a founding father than Thomas Jefferson had once observed: "A strict observance of the written law is doubtless one of the highest duties of a good citizen, but it is not the highest. The laws of necessity, of self-preservation, are of higher obligation. To lose our country by a scrupulous adherence to the written law, would be to lose law itself, with life, liberty, and property, and all those who are enjoying them with us; thus sacrificing the end to the means."

Besides, it was not as if CIA were going into every person's mailbox. The program was carefully controlled, the targeting highly selective, the watch-listing terms tighter than those Attorney General Tom Clark had used when getting authorization for telephone taps from President Truman. The entire intent and motivation of the program involved the question of foreign entanglements, counterintelligence objects. A real effort was made to avoid harming the innocent, and there was a consensus among those who knew of the operation that nobody except Soviet spies was disadvantaged by having the CIA read his mail.

Of course, nobody ever *knew* his mail was being opened, either, because it was carefully done by trained personnel of the Technical Services Division within CIA. The envelopes were collected within a restricted secure area of Federal Building No. 111 (Jamaica Airmail Facility), adjoining Idlewild Airport, and couriered to CIA's New York City office. Each evening, a six-man team of CIA technicians, fluent in Russian and proficient in holographs and flaps, would photograph envelope exteriors with a Diebold camera, and select some for opening. Perhaps two-thirds were chosen at random; the others were culled from a "watch list" which included, at various times, people like Linus Pauling, Bella Abzug, Senator Hubert Humphrey, John Steinbeck, Edward Albee, Thomas Merton, Jay Rockefeller, Martin Luther King, and Richard Nixon. The method of opening which had been taught to the CIA officers during their one-week Technical Services Division "flaps-and-seals" course was to hold the envelope over a steaming teakettle to soften the sealant, then slip a narrow stick under the flap. When you got good at it, it could be done in as little as five seconds. After the letters were photographed, they were replaced in the envelopes, were resealed and returned to the mails the following morning. CIA's inspector general, Lyman Kirkpatrick, came by to see the new operation after it was set up and wrote approvingly: "This is a highly efficient way to get the job done and the investigators enjoy the work and appreciate the opportunity to earn overtime pay."

It was understood by all at the Agency who knew about the program, however, that J. Edgar Hoover would be somewhat less happy about its existence. In early 1952, when the operation began, there had been some bad blood between Hoover and the chief of the Postal Inspection Service; also, CIA and FBI had been barely talking to each other. The habit of secrecy persisted even as relations improved under Papich, partly because any "confession" would have to account for why the Agency had failed to consult the Bureau in the first place. Angleton well knew that, in addition to foreign intelligence, the program would produce "information affecting Internal Security," and when he proposed to Dulles that his new CI Staff disseminate HT/LINGUAL information "to other Agency components," security chief Sheffield Edwards had therefore added by hand on Angleton's proposal: "and to the FBI." But Edwards' writing it did not make it so. Angleton later explained that he held back because no matter how well he got on personally with Papich, "relations with the FBI were pretty spotty."

In January 1958, Postal Inspector Stephens informed Angleton that the Bureau desired to begin its own mail coverage in New York. Angleton consulted Dulles, and they agreed that there was no choice but to disclose the program to Hoover before the FBI uncovered it anyway. On January 21, Angleton met with Sam Papich "on a personal basis"—late that night, among the orchids in his greenhouse, after they had been doing some drinking—and told him that CIA was opening mail. The project was one of the largest and most sensitive of all CIA covert operations, Angleton said, and its sole purpose was a *foreign* one—to identify persons behind the Iron Curtain who had family relations in the U.S. That was hardly the only objective of HT/LINGUAL, however, and when Hoover heard about it, he made it clear he considered the project a serious violation of turf. Papich anticipated, as he later said, that "all hell was going to break loose."

But Hoover's blood went from boiling to merely simmering when Papich convinced him, via assistant director Al Belmont, that CIA had some jurisdictional right to conduct mail coverage—and that the situation was actually a potential windfall for the FBI. Instead of having to start its own coverage from scratch, it could enjoy the benefits of CIA's operation, without any of the expenses or responsibilities. "The question immediately arises as to whether CIA in effecting this coverage in New York has invaded our jurisdiction," Belmont wrote Hoover. "In this regard, it is believed that they have a legitimate right in the objectives for which the coverage was set up, namely, the development of contacts and sources of information behind the Iron Curtain. . . . At the same time, there is an internal security objective here in which, because of our responsibilities, we have a definite interest, namely, the identification of illegal agents who may be in the United States. While recognizing this interest, it is not believed that the Bureau should assume this coverage because of the inherent dangers in the sensitive nature of it, its complexity, size, and expense. It is believed that we can capitalize on this coverage by pointing out to CIA our internal security objectives and holding them responsible to share their coverage with us."

Hoover marked the memo: "O.K." Two days later, on January 24,

Papich was sent to CIA headquarters to "point out" Hoover's position to Angleton, Edwards, and John Maury, head of the Agency's Soviet Russia Division.

Without mentioning Angleton's "personal" admission to him, Papich announced that he had reason to believe CIA was opening mail in New York. CIA's representatives acknowledged it, gave Papich a briefing, and offered to "handle leads" for the Bureau. The FBI would be the only other agency to receive raw copies of the material. In return, the FBI must restrict HT/LINGUAL materials to special-agent supervisors, who regularly handled sensitive information. FBI field offices would receive the product only after it had been sanitized. Films must never be placed in case files, though files could contain coded cross-references to allow retrieval.

Hoover agreed to CIA's terms, and the FBI was made part of the operation, which became known in the Bureau as Hunter Project. As the joint enterprise became part of Papich's liaison routine, he would pick up a batch of Hunter reports at the Agency each week and take them to a special desk in the Soviet Section at the FBI's Domestic Intelligence Division. Over the following fifteen years, Papich would personally carry in his briefcase over fifty-seven thousand Hunter reports from CIA to FBI headquarters. An internal Agency study would eventually acknowledge that since the Bureau received more disseminations than any single branch of the Agency, "the FBI is receiving the major benefit from this project." The Hunter reports included such items as indications that someone might be serving as a Soviet courier, news about Russian social and art clubs in the U.S., and contacts between American citizens and Soviet agents. The Bureau found CIA's Hunter reports helpful in evaluating what they already had on some suspects, and closed a few cases as a result of that supportive information.

Still, the project did not provide leads resulting in identification of a single illegal agent. FBI counterintelligence specialist William Branigan thought most of the material received, maybe as much as 95 percent of it, was just "junk." Certainly it was far inferior to the take from the Bureau's own mail-opening program, which they continued to hide from CIA even after the Agency had "come clean" about its own.

The FBI had begun to open the mail of suspected Nazi spies during summer 1940, when six of Foxworth's special agents, in Bermuda, were taught to do it by the British. Hoover stopped the practice at war's end, but reapproved coverage in the Washington, D.C., area in September 1951. As in the Agency's operation, the FBI's opened mail between Moscow and the U.S.. But unlike CIA's, the Bureau's program had been formally approved by the attorney general (Smith and Dulles, wanting to preserve deniability for the Executive Branch, relied on "implicit consent"). And whereas the Agency's "shotgun" approach aimed to get general intelligence on the USSR, the Bureau's operation was targeted specifically against long-term Soviet illegals. CIA's program provided a lot of positive intelligence about wheat crops in Siberia, but the FBI's located three illegals in New York and Washington; identified U.S.-trained scientists of Chinese descent who returned to China, which yielded vital positive intelligence about weapons research abroad; saved the government tens of millions of dollars by catching a Defense intelligence employee who was offering to sell weapons systems to the Soviets; and discovered that suspected Soviet spy Joseph Katz was living in Haifa, Israel (whence 1955's abortive Angleton-Papich-Lamphere mission had hoped to extract him). The FBI's method was also quicker than the Agency's. CIA's Technical Services Division had tried to develop an "oven" to mass-moisten a hundred letters at once, but it never worked right, and the kettle-and-stick technique remained the state of the Agency's art. The FBI's machine, however, took one or two seconds for a single letter, compared with five to fifteen for CIA's. The Bureau's technological knowledge would certainly have improved the efficiency of the national CI effort if shared with the Agency, but the FBI did not disclose the existence of its mail coverage to Angleton or anyone else at CIA.

Why not?

"It is perhaps difficult to answer," FBI CI man Don Moore would later say. "Perhaps I could liken it to a defector in place in the KGB. You don't want to tell anybody his name, the location, the title, or anything like that. Not that you don't trust them completely, but the fact is that anytime one additional person becomes aware of it, there is a potential for the information to go further." Moore's colleague Branigan did not believe that the Bureau had any obligation to inform CIA, since mail coverage was "strictly a domestic situation involving a person in the United States, solely within the jurisdiction of the FBI."

An argument could be made, of course, that, just as CIA infringed on the FBI's turf by opening Americans' mail in New York, the FBI's "take" had positive foreign-intelligence value, and therefore should have been shared with the Agency. McWilliams and others in the FBI's New York Field Office thought so, and in 1960 recommended informing CIA. Hoover demurred, even when it was pointed out to him that if the Agency knew about the FBI coverage, it could provide a list of known Soviet mail-drops in Europe.

Papich, meanwhile, had been intermittently lobbying Hoover for permission to disclose the FBI's program to CIA as a basic reciprocation of courtesies after Angleton's 1958 mail-opening "confession." Hoover refused, reminding him that the Agency had disclosed its operation only after it had been exposed by other means. All the more reason for the Bureau to come clean now, Papich said: if the Agency found out about the FBI's program on its own, the Bureau would lose the moral high ground when it came to criticizing CIA for not sharing information. After three years of stalling, Hoover finally saw that side of it, and in January 1961 Papich told Angleton about the Bureau's mail-opening operation. He apologized for holding back, and requested the exchange of lists on known and suspected mail-drops, both domestic and abroad.

Angleton yelled at him for a few minutes, but agreed to the exchange of lists. CIA supplied McWilliams' shop in New York with a list of sixteen drops and "accommodation addresses" in Western Europe, and Angleton also offered the FBI use of an Agency laboratory in Manhattan to screen intercepted letters for secret writings such as microdots. The Bureau had its own screening capacity, however—set up twenty years earlier to process the microdots provided by Dusko Popov—and they never did use the CIA's shop, because the boss didn't let them. When informed in a memo that CIA had built a dot-lab in the Bureau's yard, Hoover wrote in anger: "Another inroad!"

FOR ALL THE FUSS over mail-opening, it was another time-honored espionage practice—penetration—that tipped the Agency to two new Soviet illegals in New York, who had probably been sent to replace Abel or Hayhannen. Perhaps fittingly, given its corrosive interagency implications, the case began with Hoover's bête noire, William King Harvey, in Berlin.

October 1957 found Harvey riding high. After taking over Berlin Base four years earlier, he had conceived and carried out an epic-scale penetration into the Soviet sector: a six-hundred-yard-long tunnel under the East-West border, which allowed CIA to tap cables carrying Soviet telephone traffic. Harvey also digested the "take" from informants run by expert agent-handlers like George Kisevalter, and got prize "product" from Kisevalter's best agent: Pyotr Popov, a lieutenant colonel in Soviet Military Intelligence (GRU).

Popov had contacted CIA officers in Vienna in November 1952, represented himself as a patriotic Russian disillusioned with communist tyranny, and offered to work as an agent-in-place. Since then, he had provided CIA with the innermost secrets of the Soviet military. "This one man's reporting," said CIA Soviet Division officer Harry Rositzke, "saved the Pentagon at least a half-billion dollars in its research and development program." After summer 1957, when Popov was assigned to East Berlin, he also provided identities and travel plans of illegals transiting that city.

The very first agent Popov was assigned to handle, Margarita Tairova, was headed for New York City.

The Tairova tip was one of Popov's many coups for CIA, but when told of it by Kisevalter, Harvey said: "Oh shit, oh damn!" CIA would have to inform the FBI, who would pursue the case with the law-enforcement approach Harvey had found so frustrating in his own years there. If the FBI surveilled Tairova and she detected it, Moscow might deduce that her mission had been blown, and begin monitoring those very few persons—Popov among them—who knew her travel plans. Harvey and Kisevalter worked all night on a cable to Soviet Russia Division chief Jack Maury, trying to convey the situation's delicacy and danger.

When Maury read the cable, he saw the problem. He urged Dulles that the Bureau be kept out of the case. Dulles sympathized, but decided that the FBI had to be informed. The matter was turned over to Angleton, who immediately got Papich involved and stressed the sensitivity of the situation.

Nevertheless, from the moment she stepped off the plane on November 27, Tairova was followed by a dozen FBI agents. She made contact with a man, soon determined to be her husband, Walter, and moved in with him on Manhattan's Upper West Side. The FBI kept watch from an abandoned apartment across the street, where Mac's agents suspended their sandwiches from the ceiling to keep the roaches away. Then, on March 12, 1958, the couple simply disappeared. Popov later reported that Margarita had resurfaced in Moscow, complaining that the FBI had surveilled her from day one. The KGB was trying to determine how her travel plans could have leaked. Popov had been grilled about the matter, and though he believed he had deflected any suspicion, Kisevalter and Harvey weren't so sure. They offered their mole the chance to defect; Popov refused. He was arrested less than a year later, and the Soviets eventually announced his execution as a CIA spy.

There was no proving, of course, that the FBI's handling of the Tairovas' tip had put the KGB on to Popov. They might have caught on to him, for instance, by tailing Kisevalter or other CIA men who met with him in Europe. Harvey and others at the Agency, however, were prone to blame the Bureau. Even FBI CI men like James Nolan privately thought the loss was "partly Hoover's fault."

But CIA's counterintelligence chief did not react by complaining about Hoover. Angleton was considering the possibility, he told Papich, that Tairova might have been strictly a "throwaway" lead, planted on Popov to see if it would be leaked to the West. If so, Popov had been suspected *before* he was assigned to work with illegals in Berlin, and well before the

FBI was ever cut into the case. That would mean that Popov was probably compromised by a Soviet mole in CIA. In this sense, the most profound legacy of the Popov disaster was that CIA could not know for sure whether its agent had been blown by FBI incompetence, or by Soviet penetration. Only one thing was certain: as long as there was the mere possibility of Soviet moles, Angleton would have to do his damnedest to root them out.

ONE OF ANGLETON'S early leads to the possible identity of a KGB mole had been a report from Popov himself, before he was executed, suggesting a leak in CIA's Top Secret U-2 spyplane program. In April 1958, Popov had reported hearing a drunken colonel boast that the KGB had many technical details on a new high-altitude spycraft America was routing over the Soviet Union. Details of this revolutionary plane had been tightly held within the U.S. government; the leak could only have come from somewhere within the project itself. Soviet knowledge of these flights raised a number of troubling issues for Dulles, such as whether Soviet anti-aircraft operators, knowing the altitudes at which these planes flew, might be able to program their guided missiles accordingly and shoot one down.

The answer to that came on May 1, 1960. The U-2 was over Sverdlovsk, its pilot later said, when there was an explosion and an orange flash. The aircraft went out of control. The pilot threw open the cockpit and parachuted to earth. Within hours, the Soviets announced the downing of a CIA plane and the capture of its pilot, Francis Gary Powers. An Eisenhower-Khrushchev summit was ruined. The U.S., exposed as a violator of international law, lost prestige.

The FBI closely monitored public opinion toward CIA's role in the affair. The New York *Mirror* ventured that "if the FBI instead of CIA had been conducting the operation . . . no such error would have resulted." The agent who clipped the piece recommended against sending the newspaper any letter of appreciation, which "might tend to lend approval to his comparison of the FBI with CIA," but was overruled by former liaison officer DeLoach. Any critic of the Agency, it seemed, was by extension the Bureau's friend.

But for all their appreciation of a good anti-CIA angle to a major news story, Hoover and others at the FBI wondered whether the affair could be written off as merely Agency incompetence. There might have been leaks in the operation. The radio for coded transmissions had broken down at the U-2 control base at Adana, Turkey, so a CIA officer had decided to violate procedure and relay permission for Powers' flight on an insecure circuit that could have been monitored by the Soviets. CIA investigators interrogated Turkish janitors who might have been paid by the Soviets to sabotage the spycraft, and U.S. military counterintelligence officers at Peshawar, Pakistan, where Powers had taken off, believed they had foiled a tampering attempt, by persons unknown, against the U-2 on the eve of its departure. Perhaps there had been another sabotage plot that had not been detected. By midsummer 1960, the Bureau was even considering a theory then circulating in British anticommunist circles—that the U-2 had been hijacked by the Soviets according to a carefully orchestrated plan similar to that in Ian Fleming's novel *Thunderball*, in which a NATO jet was hijacked by a special unit of Bond's nemesis, SPECTRE.

Quoting "a report sent from behind the Iron Curtain by the Russian underground movement," an FBI source in Britain alleged that "For five years there has existed, with its headquarters in the Soviet Union, a special intelligence group with agents scattered throughout the world. Its task is to steal new types of aircraft and other material secrets from the West. The group, known by the code-name "Molnia"—lightning—is under the command of a Colonel Jurii Petrovitch Smolnikov. And it is claimed in leading Communist Party circles that Molnia was not only responsible for capturing the American plane, but since it was formed in 1955 has successfully stolen from under the noses of Western Counter-Intelligence 27 other aircraft; the last one being British. This British plane landed at Pribaltica with one or two members of its crew still in a drugged state." According to the British source, Powers' U-2 was captured by Molnia "so that Khrushchev could deliberately wreck the Paris Summit Conference and use the spotlight of world publicity to blame President Eisenhower for the failure."

Fantastic as it was, the Molnia theory at least offered one way to resolve a running dispute about the U-2's altitude when struck. Khrushchev claimed it had been at sixty-eight thousand feet, but U.S. intelligence officials did not believe Soviet anti-aircraft rockets could operate effectively at that altitude. Either the plane had "flamed out" at sixty-eight thousand feet, and was not struck by rockets until it was somewhere between twenty and forty thousand, or it had been forced down by other means. That the U-2 had lost altitude and been forced down from a height of only thirty thousand feet, as "high Washington sources" reportedly believed, and as NATO radar allegedly confirmed, could be explained by the fact that agents of Molnia had allegedly drugged Powers prior to takeoff, with a "slow-acting dope to take effect over the heart of Russia."

Of course, it was possible that Powers had not been drugged at all, but had simply landed the plane in the Soviet Union and defected to the Soviets. Perhaps he had been a Soviet agent for some time. CIA officials were struck by the fact that, strangely enough, Powers' plane was not "pretty well destroyed," as the Soviets claimed, but had "apparently leveled off and made something of a soft landing." Other "evidence" was circumstantial at best: Powers had failed to use the ejector seat, which would have automatically destroyed the top-secret plane; he was reportedly being treated well in Moscow, with books to read and a small yard in which he could exercise and take sunbaths; he was given a tour of the city and described it as "beautiful"; Khrushchev would not dare to put Powers on trial if he were not sure that Powers would admit every charge laid against him. This line of reasoning gained some currency as various anticommunist sophists of the John Birch variety began giving lectures at rotary clubs in American middletowns, stating, according to FBI documents, "that Powers was not shot down by the USSR, and indicated he defected and is presently living in Russia and receiving pay from Russia." In the atmosphere of mounting hysteria, Attorney General Rogers came under considerable public pressure to "turn the FBI loose," as one concerned citizen recommended, to see if "the Central Intelligence Agency was, or is, infiltrated by Soviet agents."

Hoover personally was disturbed by the"most peculiar" circumstances of Powers' ejection. Powers confirmed the Soviet account of the incident when pleading guilty to charges of espionage in a KGB court on July 7, but Hoover was intrigued by the skeptical analysis of Sir Philip Livingstone, a former director general of RAF medical air services. "It is utterly impossible for a pilot to bail out [at 68,000 feet] without using ejection equipment," Livingstone said. "He would be destroyed instantly by the slipstream and air pressure. Should he survive this, he could not last more than 45 seconds without the oxygen equipment attached to the ejection seat, and the 50-below cold would make life impossible."

Hoover noted also that "Oliver Powers, father of the U-2 pilot, was quoted as stating that his son's plane had not been shot down by the Soviets. The father allegedly obtained this information when he visited his son in Moscow." The Soviets had quickly publicized a statement, attributed to Powers, denying that he had ever told his father any such thing, but that only made the situation seem more suspicious. It came to Hoover's attention that Powers' home state was Georgia, and HUAC investigators had previously alleged "that there was a Soviet agent in Georgia named Powers." CIA's top management suggested to Agency General Counsel Lawrence Houston that Powers had deliberately flown his plane into Soviet hands and defected. Dulles himself told Eisenhower, according to information in Powers' FBI file, "that he would not be surprised if Powers personally implicated the President himself and then announced dramatically that he has decided to remain in Russia and work for peace."

By October .1960, there were so many unanswered questions about Powers' loyalty that Hoover authorized a complete investigation into the CIA pilot—his parents, his political views, his financial status (any substantial deposits recently?)—to determine whether he had been known to have communist sympathies or was actually an agent of the Soviets. Papich began furnishing leads to CIA on October 10, and the investigation continued through at least June 1961, when the Agency was sharing with the Bureau its pilot's medical records. It is unclear when the Bureau reached its conclusion about Powers' loyalty, or what that conclusion was. Years later, when the Bureau's file on Powers was finally declassified, the FBI's verdict remained blacked out, as the Bureau explained, "per CIA request." Sam Papich and others familiar with the details of the FBI's Powers investigation declined to discuss it.

A few facts gleaned from unredacted passages in the FBI documents, however, suggest that Bureau suspicions about CIA's pilot were never quite dissipated. On February 10, 1962, it was decided to move Powers' FBI file from headquarters to the Bureau's Special Mail Room, 1315 Identification Building, where only files of the most extreme sensitivity were stored. And the Bureau prepared for the contingency that Powers might be infiltrated back into the United States as an illegal agent, perhaps after being brainwashed or undergoing plastic surgery. A notice was posted in the FBI's Identification Division to be alert "in the event any fingerprints in the future are received in Ident identical with" those of Powers, or any of six other U.S. airmen missing since July 1, 1960, in the vicinity of the Barents Sea. "This action is believed desirable," a Bureau memo urged, "in view of the possibility that the Russians may try to use any of these men for their own purposes in the United States under different names."

Despite the general suspicions against Powers, Papich was advised by CIA in January 1961 that secret negotiations were under way to swap him for Rudolf Abel, who was serving out his life sentence in a Georgia prison. Within the week, Hoover wrote Attorney General Rogers to express his opposition to CIA's proposed spy-trade. "It would appear that [Abel's] past experiences make him of particular value to Soviet operations directed against this country," Hoover noted. It was hoped that Abel might eventually break down in captivity and tell the Bureau much more than they already knew about KGB illegal networks, but that obviously would not happen if he were returned to the USSR. Moreover, Powers' loyalty to the United States was not certain. "It would be catastrophic," Hoover warned, "if the United States arranged for Powers' release and he then refused to come home." On another memo Hoover scrawled: "They may get their 'fingers burned' " by giving up Abel and getting "nothing in return. . . . If they are determined to play with fire & make 'deals' with such ratters [as Powers] they will pay the price."

The Attorney General sided with CIA, however, and Powers and Abel were exchanged on February 10, 1962, on the Glienecker Bridge connecting East and West Berlin. Powers was trundled off to a CIA safehouse in Oxford, Maryland, where for eight days he was interrogated by one of Angleton's men. The FBI was cut in on some of the take beginning February 16. Thirty years later, that information remained classified by the Bureau "per CIA request," and CIA transcripts of the debriefings would remain Top Secret as well. Lawrence Houston eventually disclosed that in the course of their debriefing of Powers, "we were getting slightly different stories." Powers later compared CIA's questioning to that which he received while imprisoned by the Soviets.

The affair ended as it had begun, with negative press about the Agency; all of it went into Hoover's files. The public got a peek into the life of a CIA family when Barbara Powers was hospitalized for a drug overdose in April 1962, two months after her husband's return, and they were divorced soon after, when he ran off with a CIA psychiatrist. Powers' ex-wife then began to write a memoir, which the FBI noted would "be giving the inside story on CIA and the Agency's personnel," with emphasis on "sex and drinking." In June of that year, the Agency was taken to task for incompetence by two journalists, David Wise and Thomas Ross, in their best-selling book *The U-2 Affair*; CIA officials assured the Bureau "that approximately 75% of the book is pure fiction," that the authors had "collected some factual data and then filled in the gaps with fabricated material," but newspaper reviews of the book became part of Powers' FBI file.

Hoover might have found some consolation in the mudbath Central Intelligence was still taking over the U-2 incident, but he remained sore to the end about Abel, the spy who got away. When columnist Rowland Evans reported that the directors of CIA and FBI "were unanimous in recommending the exchange," Hoover practically engraved in the article's margin with his pen: "I never did any such thing!"

The mystery of Powers' downing never was cleared up. Senator Barry Goldwater believed there was much more to the story than CIA ever publicly admitted. Attorney General Robert Kennedy thought Powers should be tried for treason. Selmer Nilsen, a Norwegian fisherman and convicted spy who covered the U-2 airbase at Bodde, Sweden for Soviet intelligence, alleged in 1975 that the U-2 had been downed by a bomb planted in its tail by a Soviet agent before its takeoff from Peshawar. Nilsen had been told about the bomb, he said, by a KGB officer in Moscow, at a May 1960 party to celebrate the downing of the U-2. When asked about Nilsen's allegations, Powers, then working as a traffic reporter for KNBC-TV news in Los Angeles, insisted that the U-2 planes were inspected so closely before takeoff that "it would have to be an inside job."

In 1981, one of the CIA officers who had worked on security for the U-2 program, Edwin Wilson, was arrested by the FBI for collaborating with Libyan, East German, and Soviet intelligence. Wilson could have been the source of the U-2 leak that Popov brought to CIA's attention in April 1958, and might also have contributed to Powers' downing. In the late 1950s, while posted at the U-2 base in Adana, Wilson had watched over some of Powers' flights, and had even kept tabs on Powers himself. Wilson had been transferred back to the U.S. more than a year before Powers was shot down, but he might have given the Soviets enough general data for them to attempt sabotage. He might also have given the KGB a psychological profile of Powers, to be used in an attempted recruitment. But no firm evidence of either scenario has ever emerged.

Powers died in August 1977, when his Bell Jet Ranger helicopter crashed just outside Van Nuys Airport. Apparently he had run out of fuel. Conspiracy theorists thought that explanation suspicious, since Powers' fuel gauge had supposedly been repaired the night before, and since CIA was known to maintain a presence at Van Nuys Airport, where certain joint research projects with Lockheed Aircraft were carried out. Agency spokesmen dismissed newspaper speculation that Powers had been killed by CIA, perhaps in retaliation for some unknown transgression, as "absurd."

But CIA had long since lost the moral high ground on such matters, and the benefit of any doubt. By then it was known publicly that CIA did kill people, or had sometimes tried to. Indeed, even as Powers was swapped for Abel in 1962, William Harvey was hard at work on one such plot. These schemes would be the source of much displeasure to J. Edgar Hoover, and the cause of much interest to President John F. Kennedy. After Kennedy was killed, these plots would also become a matter of dark fascination for President Lyndon Johnson, and for some of Harvey's agents, who saw a sinister connection between CIA's assassination plans and the actions of yet another man who might have given U-2 secrets to the Soviets. This individual, whom Powers himself later blamed for his capture, was a discharged Marine radar operator who had worked at CIA's U-2 base in Atsugi, Japan, and who had defected to the Soviet Union six months before Powers was downed. His name was Lee Harvey Oswald.

CHAPTER EIGHT

LICENSED TO KILL

CAMELOT GLISTENED and glittered and gleamed in all its splendor in late April 1962, when President and Mrs. John Fitzgerald Kennedy held a reception for forty-nine Nobel laureates in the East Room of the White House. In a sea-foam-green evening gown by Oleg Cassini, the first lady greeted guests including Berkeley chemist Linus Pauling, who had spent the day picketing her husband's decision to allow nuclear testing on Christmas Island. "I think this is the most extraordinary collection of talent, of human knowledge, that has ever been gathered together at the White House," JFK said in his dinner toast, "with the possible exception of when Thomas Jefferson dined alone." After a reading from Sinclair Lewis' *Main Street,* deriding the cultural sophistication of the average American, there was jazz dancing to a Marine combo. Soviet Ambassador Anatoliy Dobrynin whisked his wife through a fox trot, insisting the step was "typical Russian." Years later, when it became known that CIA was involved in assassination plots during his administration, glorious classy evenings such as this led JFK's advisers to believe it "totally out of character" for Kennedy to be privy to such dirty, deadly matters. Yet even while he presided at the "Easter egghead hunt," as it was jokingly known, his brother Bobby was at CIA Station JM/WAVE in Miami, assuring America's James Bond of White House support for the killing of a foreign head of state.

For the Kennedys, ethics was aesthetics, and aesthetics was athletics. The fighting-Irish spirit of their touch-football games was well adapted to an organization created by an Irish football hero, Wild Bill Donovan. CIA men quickly learned that they could get approval for covert projects by lacing memoranda with language like, "If we do this, we might uncork the touchdown play." The new enthusiasm for secret, even illegal work was present even in Postmaster General James Day, who okayed CIA mail-opening as long there were no "reverberations." And it was certainly present in JFK's approach to the problem of Fidel Castro.

The idea of covertly unseating Castro was first suggested to Kennedy by Ian Fleming at a Georgetown dinner party on Sunday, March 13, 1960. When asked what Bond might do if assigned to get rid of Castro, Fleming told JFK there were three things that really mattered to the Cubans: money, religion, and sex. Therefore, CIA should scatter counterfeit Cuban money over Havana, with leaflets saying it came compliments of the U.S.A.; next, the Agency should conjure up some religious image in the sky, which would imply that God was against communism; finally, CIA should cause Fidel Castro to lose his facial hair, for without macho bearded Cubans there could be no revolution.

By 1962, all three of Fleming's anti-Castro schemes were attempted or at least seriously being considered by the Kennedy government, but the reliance on Fleming's ideas went beyond his dinner-party palaver. During JFK's first four days in power, CIA's Richard Bissell was urged twice by "the White House," as he later said, to develop an "Executive Action Capability" to "eliminate the effectiveness" of troublesome foreign leaders. CIA, in other words, was to have assets like Fleming's "oo" agents, who were licensed to kill. And when Kennedy asked in November 1961 to meet "America's James Bond," he was introduced to William Harvey. The meeting lasted only a few moments; no official record was kept of it. The next day, Harvey was officially tasked with eliminating Castro.

Harvey had already been working on assassination matters for more than a year. After the White House asked Bissell to create an Executive Action Capability, Harvey had been charged with the effort, known as ZR/RIFLE, but in doing so he only formalized a campaign that had been under way during the final summer of the Eisenhower administration. Spearheading the effort had been Vice-President Richard Nixon, who believed, as he recorded in a 1959 memo, that Castro was "either incredibly naive about communism or under communist discipline." Nixon's executive assistant for national-security affairs, General Robert E. Cushman, had pressured CIA on the "elimination of Fidel Castro," as Agency documents described it, as part of a planned invasion of Cuba. While the Agency's Western Hemisphere Division conceived a military landing at Bay of Pigs, Harvey worked with CIA security chief Sheffield Edwards to neutralize the Cuban leader.

Harvey may have given some consideration to Fleming's dinner-party ideas, which were taken to Dulles by CIA officer John Bross, who had also been at Kennedy's table. But it was a Fleming conception not mentioned at that staid gathering—an idea put forth in the novel Fleming had just finished—which, coincidentally or not, became the linchpin of Harvey's plots. Just as James Bond, in *On Her Majesty's Secret Service*, worked with the Mafia to terminate an enemy regarded as far more sinister, so CIA would now team with U.S. mobsters to kill Castro.

Robert Maheu, a former FBI agent who sometimes performed freelance "operational support" for CIA, was tapped to recruit suave Los

Angeles wiseguy Johnny Rosselli. Maheu flew west and met Rosselli at Hollywood's Brown Derby restaurant in August 1960. The mobster carried himself like a movie star; he wore Ray-Ban Wayfarer sunglasses indoors, and moved with cool ease in a double-breasted linen suit; he was tanned, and his clay-brown face contrasted suavely with his gray-white slicked-back hair. He was known in the underworld as the Silver Fox. When Maheu proposed a "cutout" operation, which would give the Agency total deniability, Rosselli's first response was to laugh in his face.

"The Feds are tracking me everywhere I go!" he said. He couldn't even visit his tailor without being followed by FBI agents.

But as Maheu pressed him, Rosselli saw a chance perhaps to immunize himself from future FBI persecution by cooperating with CIA. In October, he put Maheu in touch with Chicago Mafia chieftain Sam "Momo" Giancana and with Santos Trafficante, kingpin of Florida's "Gold Coast Syndicate." Trafficante often traveled to Havana, ostensibly to determine whether Mafia-owned casinos were going to be nationalized; he purportedly knew a disaffected Cuban official who could get close to the dictator. Since Castro frequently drank tea, coffee, or bouillon, a liquid poison would be particularly well suited for the job. Maheu said he would talk to the operation's sponsors and see what he could do.

But the Mafiosi were apparently doing some talking of their own, to people who had nothing to do with the operation. On October 18, 1960, Hoover wrote Dulles to report that, according to "a source whose reliability has not been tested," Sam Giancana had stated during a recent conversation with friends "that Fidel Castro was to be done away with very shortly." Giancana claimed that "he had already met with the assassin-to-be on three occasions," that "everything has been perfected for the killing of Castro," and that the assassin had arranged with a woman, not further described, "to drop a pill in some food or drink of Castro's."

Giancana had not talked about CIA in connection with the anti-Castro attempt, but the FBI soon found out about his links to the Agency through what one of Edwards' men called "a Keystone Cops episode" in Las Vegas. Maheu had arranged for a wiretap on the phone in comedian Dan Rowan's Las Vegas hotel room, to see if Giancana's moll, Phyllis McGuire, was having an affair with Rowan. As a favor to Maheu, CIA agreed to pay up to $1,000 for the tapping device. On the afternoon of Halloween 1960, one of Maheu's employees, Ed DuBois, broke into Rowan's suite to install a bug, but took a break in the middle of the job, leaving his equipment unattended. A maid discovered it and called the local sheriff. Maheu's wire-man was arrested. His bail was paid by Rosselli, attracting the attention of the FBI. Interrogated by the Bureau, DuBois admitted that he had been hired by Maheu. Two FBI agents called on Maheu and read him a formal statement of his legal rights. According to previous arrangement with CIA, Maheu told the FBI only that the tap had been part of an operation he was running "on behalf of the CIA relative to anti-Castro activities," and suggested the Bureau contact Sheff Edwards at the Agency.

At that point, the matter became Sam Papich's problem. Edwards approached him on May 3, 1961, and said, "Sam, we got problems." He told Papich that CIA was using Maheu because of his contacts with Giancana, who might be useful "in connection with CIA's clandestine efforts against the Castro government." None of Giancana's efforts had yet materialized, Edwards said, but "several of the plans still are working and may eventually pay off." Edwards himself claimed to be deliberately ignorant of the details of such a "dirty business." He did know the overall objective, he said, but could not reveal it to Papich or anyone else at the FBI. Edwards also told Papich that CIA would fight the FBI if it tried to prosecute Maheu, because any public legal action might disclose sensitive information about CIA's failed invasion of Cuba at the Bay of Pigs, which had gone down only two weeks before.

"Of course, all hell broke loose in the FBI," Papich said. "There was a definite increase in tensions. Here was CIA, coddling characters the Bureau was supposed to be investigating. That irritated the hell out of Hoover—and when J. Edgar got mad, boy, he got mad!" Of course, a lot of it fell on Papich. "Why are they dealing with these types?" Hoover roared at him. "Did they think it would be okay with us? What the hell kind of understanding have you given them?" Papich just stood there and took it. Everyone at the Bureau felt it was the stupidest thing CIA had ever tried. You couldn't make a deal with those crooks without their owning you after that. Once they were in bed with you, they *had* you.

Angry as Hoover was, however, the Maheu-Giancana affair at least gave him the means of killing two birds with one bolt. Robert Kennedy's conscription of FBI agents into Justice Department task forces for anti-Mafia work, and Hoover's determined resistance to this policy, had become a cause of much friction between the FBI director and the Kennedys. The attorney general believed Hoover to be an obstacle to prosecutions, and had even told reporters that Hoover believed the Mafia did not exist. The Las Vegas incident thus offered Hoover the chance not only to embarrass CIA, but to show Kennedy he was serious about the Mafia. He tattled to RFK in a memo that CIA had been using Maheu and other "hoodlum elements" in unspecified "anti-Castro activities." The Bureau was "conducting a full investigation," and "the field has been instructed to press investigation vigorously."

Indeed, as Maheu later related, FBI agents were "beginning to tail us

. . . very interested in our every move." G-men began spending a lot of time in the restaurant of Miami Beach's Fontainebleau hotel, unofficial headquarters of the anti-Castro plots, while Maheu fretted that all the "heat" would cool the mobsters' ardor for assassination. If the CIA plots didn't offer security from FBI harassment, why bother? "It was just further proof of what you always hear: one branch of the government doesn't know what the other is doing," Maheu reflected. "I knew my phone was tapped, too, so I tried to make things easy on the government. I'd purposely call the CIA from my hotel room rather than from a pay phone. That way the FBI could listen in, and save both agencies some extra work."

In May 1961, with the FBI on to its assets, and with its Cuban networks in shambles after the bungled beach landings, CIA suspended its anti-Castro plots—but not its plottings. Most U.S. "wet work" had been subcontracted to the British in World War II, and Harvey wondered whether it could be so again. In October, he consulted British MI5 emissary Peter Wright, who had come to Washington for a conference on technical surveillance. As Wright later told it, they were drinking whiskey in a Virginia hunting lodge owned by CIA when Harvey's voice dropped to a low monotone. Could Her Majesty's Secret Service be of assistance in "hitting" Castro? "We'd certainly have that capability," Wright told him, "but I doubt we would use it nowadays. We're not in it anymore, Bill. We got out a couple years ago, after Suez. We're the junior partner in the alliance, remember? It's your responsibility now."

"Well," Harvey said, "we're developing a new capability in the company to handle these kinds of problems, and we're in the market for the requisite expertise." He spoke of the need for a deniable "delivery mechanism."

"The French!" Wright said brightly. "Have you tried them? It's more their type of thing."

Out of the question. De Gaulle didn't trust Americans.

"Have you thought of approaching William Stephenson? A lot of the old-timers say he ran this kind of thing in New York during the war. Used some Italian, apparently, when there was no other way of sorting a German shipping spy. Probably the Mafia, for all I know."

So Harvey was back where he began, with the mob. In November 1961, after JFK had said to him, "So you're our James Bond," Harvey had pondered the file on Johnny Rosselli, stamped "INACTIVE CONTACT." He hesitated to get involved with a such a Bureau-tainted asset. But by the first week of April 1962, he knew his own job would be in jeopardy if he didn't do something; nor was it in his nature to do nothing. He met the Mafioso in a cocktail lounge at Miami Airport.

The two men could not have been more incongruous. Rosselli was tanned and coiffed, sporting alligator shoes and a $2,000 watch, while Harvey was fat and fashionless, in his usual brown suit. But Harvey immediately liked Rosselli and instinctively trusted him. He saw a man much like himself, a dedicated anticommunist whose motive in wanting to kill Castro was nothing more complicated than patriotism, a man who had never requested a cent for his services, not even expenses—although Harvey must have realized that the gangster had maneuvered himself into an excellent position from which to stave off prosecution by the Justice Department. Rosselli, for his part, looked at Harvey and saw a hard-drinking man with a revolver-bulge in his jacket, and thought, "This guy's one of us." Over the coming months, as Harvey and Rosselli sat up nights drinking and talking around motel pools, scheming to undo Castro, they became good friends.

But the FBI crowded in again. In February 1962, Papich spoke to Edwards about possible prosecutions in the Las Vegas wiretap case. Edwards protested that "any prosecution in the matter would endanger sensitive sources and methods . . . and would not be in the national interest." Harvey was kept apprised of those FBI pressures, which eventually made Edwards so nervous that he told CIA counsel Lawrence Houston about the project. Houston was given the misleading idea that the operation had been ended, as was Attorney General Robert Kennedy, whom Houston briefed about it on May 7. Lest the lie be found out, Edwards even falsified a memo for CIA files, stating that Harvey had terminated the project.

That same false impression was given the FBI through Sam Papich, whom a frustrated Harvey approached in pursuit of a separate peace. As he conferred with Harvey after hours, it dawned on Papich, though he was never told in so many words, that the Agency had been plotting with the Mafia to kill Fidel Castro. Papich argued about it with him—"You're not going to win on this one, you can't deal with these characters"—but Harvey insisted that he had to continue an "open relationship" with Rosselli. "Even though Harvey claimed that CIA had canceled, annulled the whole operation on Cuba, they still had their goddamn problem," Papich recalled. "They couldn't tell those Mafia types to go to hell. They were in bed with 'em." As Harvey himself would later say, one by-product of CIA's assassination schemes was "a very pregnant possibility . . . of this government being blackmailed either by Cubans for political purposes or by figures in organized crime for their own self-protection or aggrandizement." Hoping therefore to keep Rosselli well disposed toward CIA, and to anticipate any upcoming troubles—and also because he just plain liked him—Harvey kept in touch with the gangster. He promised Papich that any contacts with Rosselli would of course be reported to the Bureau, and that any intelligence on their domestic criminal activities would be forwarded to Hoover.

Harvey then blithely returned to plotting the very violence he assured Papich had been foresworn. A new set of poison pills was provided to one of Trafficante's exile teams. But any discovery of his Rosselli-Trafficante schemes was now likely to land him in deep trouble, because he had no official Agency sanction; he would be proceeding on his own. That much became clear during the Cuban Missile Crisis, when the Bureau informed CIA that the attorney general did not want any "crackpot" individuals or organizations going to Cuba "at this particularly sensitive time"—especially not any "who might make assassination attempts." Harvey disregarded the order and dispatched a special commando team to Cuba. The FBI's Miami office had been surveilling Harvey's Cuban exiles in Miami, and reported the team's departure to Hoover, who told RFK. The attorney general took a great deal of exception to Harvey's recklessness at a time when the world seemed to be at the lip of thermonuclear extinction. He went to CIA's leadership and told them their man was "out of control." Harvey's immediate boss, Richard Helms, felt he had taken to "drinking a bit too much" and become "somewhat too flamboyant," and he knew that he did not help relations with Hoover. The Rosselli connection was to be shut down, and Harvey was to be transferred—demoted, really—to chief of station in Rome.

On June 20, 1963, Harvey met Rosselli in Washington for a goodbye bash before flying off to his new assignment in "the old country," as Rosselli called it. Since it was going to be his last meeting with the mobster for a while, Harvey figured he didn't have to tell Agency people about the contact, and certainly not Papich or anyone at the FBI, even though he had promised them he would.

Again the Bureau found him out. Papich had assured Hoover at the beginning of 1963 that Harvey and CIA were no longer seeking Castro's assassination, and in Hoover's mind that freed up the Bureau to move against Rosselli and his friends. When Harvey drove out to National Airport to meet Rosselli, he was spotted by FBI agents who had been surveilling the mobster. The pair were trailed to Tino's Continental Restaurant in Georgetown. Not recognizing Harvey but sensing that he was something more than an underworld crony, the G-men contacted Papich, reportedly reaching him at James Angleton's dinner table. Angleton and Papich immediately identified Harvey from the physical description given by the agents. The next day, Papich told Harvey that his unauthorized contact with Rosselli would have to be brought to Hoover's attention. A sullen, hungover Harvey requested only that Papich give him a warning call if it seemed likely that Hoover was going to make a big stink. Harvey thought it wise to describe the incident to his immediate superior, Deputy Director for Plans Richard Helms, who agreed that there was no need to brief the DCI unless a call from Hoover was expected.

Blessedly, Hoover left him alone. Occupying his full allotment of two airline seats, America's James Bond lifted away from Washington in early July 1963, grateful that the final stroke by his old nemesis had been an act of mercy.

DESPITE AGENCY ASSURANCES to Hoover, CIA kept trying to kill Castro after Harvey departed the scene. In midsummer 1963, the Cuban account was turned over to Desmond FitzGerald, formerly chief of the Agency's Far East Division, who asked his staff to determine whether a tropical seashell could be fitted with explosives and placed in an area where Castro liked to scuba-dive. The idea was discarded by Helms, who thought it "cockeyed," but FitzGerald came up with other imaginative schemes. One was to have the leader of a U.S. delegation to Cuba present Castro with a poisoned wetsuit as a "gift of friendship." Technical Services actually obtained a top-quality wetsuit, coated its inside with a fungus that would cause a chronic skin disease called "Madura foot," and dusted the oxygen hose with a tubercule bacillus, but the plot was ruined when the U.S. delegation coincidentally presented Castro with another, uncontaminated suit on its own initiative.

More serious was a series of events relating to Rolando Cubela, a Cuban who was CIA's only "mole" within Castro's inner circle. During Castro's revolution, Cubela had belonged to a communist-guerrilla cell at the University of Havana, and had led a daring raid on the Presidential Palace in 1957, which made him a national hero and turned the momentum of the conflict in favor of the rebels. After Castro's triumph in January 1959, Cubela was named to the number-two position in the new Interior Ministry, in charge of state security. He also served as president of the FEU, Castro's revolutionary national student organization, a position which frequently required him to travel abroad. On one such trip to Brazil, in early 1961, Cubela contacted CIA officers, said he was disillusioned with the increasingly communist drift of Castro's regime, and volunteered to work for CIA.

Cubela struck his American contacts as somewhat mercurial, even irrational, but there was no refusing someone who could help plot a coup against Castro. He was brought into CIA's files under the cryptonym "AM/LASH." For almost a year and a half, CIA lost contact with their new agent; when he suddenly turned up again, in a safehouse in São Paulo, Brazil, on September 7, 1963, he volunteered to arrange Fidel's "execution." The offer was relayed to FitzGerald, at CIA headquarters, who authorized CIA officials in Brazil to tell Cubela that his proposal was under consideration at "the highest levels" of the U.S. government. On returning to Havana, AM/LASH made increasing contact with CIA's operatives in the city, and kept pressing for U.S. government help in arranging Castro's death. When he went abroad again on October 29, FitzGerald met with him to discuss the idea. To assure Cubela that the American government took him seriously, FitzGerald described himself as a "personal representative of Robert F. Kennedy." Cubela repeatedly asked for an assassination device, especially a "high-powered rifle with telescopic sights that could be used to kill Castro from a distance." FitzGerald said he would do what he could, and scheduled their next meeting for November 22, 1963.

All along, FitzGerald and others at CIA had assumed that Cubela was a bona-fide agent, and that the AM/LASH operation was secure. If he and it were not, the consequences could be catastrophic. As Harvey had put down in his ZR/RIFLE notes almost three years earlier, there was always the chance that CIA assassination plots, if discovered by intended victims or their allies, might spur "retaliation," or even pre-emptive retribution. President Kennedy himself had realized back in November 1961 that, if U.S. officials were identified with assassination attempts on foreign leaders such as Castro, "we would all be targets." Yet here was a U.S. official, FitzGerald, meeting with AM/LASH as the "personal representative" of the president's brother, planning the assassination of the most important communist leader outside of Moscow or Peking. When Fitz-Gerald's anti-Castro task force met on September 12, five days after Cubela's offer to kill Castro, it was agreed that "there was a strong likelihood that Castro would retaliate in some way" if it were discovered that CIA was plotting with Cubela to kill him. They went ahead, however, on the assumption that Castro would not find out.

In light of later events, it would be important to determine, as the title of one CIA memo asked, "What Could Castro Have Known?" There could be little question but that the Cuban dictator was at least aware of CIA assistance to guerrilla groups generally. It was common knowledge in Miami's Cuban exile community that Castro routinely sent false defectors to infiltrate and keep him informed of any plots, and Castro later boasted, "We knew more about what they did than they did themselves." Even before the bungled Bay of Pigs invasion, operational security was so poor that Agency activities in Miami frequently came to the attention of the FBI. During summer 1960, for instance, a German-born CIA officer, who used the alias Frank Bender, met a Cuban exile leader in a Miami motel room with too-thin walls. The occupant of the adjoining room was a stenographer whose brother worked for the FBI. She was bothered by the acrid smoke from Bender's cheap cigar, which drifted under the door between the two rooms. Suspicious of Bender's German accent, she listened and took shorthand notes, which she then turned over to her brother. The FBI recognized the nature of the conversation, and Papich passed the notes to the CIA, whose officers were deeply embarrassed.

The circle of anti-Castro plotters hired by Edwards and run by Harvey was similarly porous. There had been loose talk by Sam Giancana about a "girl" who was supposed to put "pills" in Castro's coffee, and those rumors, too, had been reported by Papich to a shamed Edwards at CIA. Harvey himself worried that Castro might know about the attempts. "Given the capabilities of Castro's security apparata, and the general sieve-like character of the Cuban community in exile and the number of people who knew at least something of the operation," Harvey later said, "I think and thought at the time that it was quite conceivable that it had been penetrated."

But where the Harvey-era plots had been dogged by generalized suspicion, the FBI had more definite evidence that CIA's post-Harvey plots were in danger of compromise. On October 10, 1963, the Bureau was told by an informant in Miami that CIA had been meeting with "a Cuban official" identified as Rolando Cubela. According to a memo that same day from the FBI's Miami Field Office to headquarters, the Miami informant knew the date and location of one of Cubela's meetings with CIA. Since Castro's agents had thoroughly penetrated the same Miami Cuban community in which the Bureau informant gossiped and lived, there was a serious danger that CIA's meetings with Cubela might be known to Castro.

The Bureau could not have failed to know that such information would have been desired or valued by CIA. There had been a routine pattern of cooperation on matters pertaining to the Cuban-exile community in Miami since March 1962, when the two agencies began conducting joint debriefings to exploit what a CIA memo called the "intelligence potential of Cuban 'colonies'" in Miami and New Orleans. The Agency had regularly forwarded to Hoover, via Papich, updated lists of anti-Castro organizations, and the Bureau had kept CIA current about the doings of such Castro fronts as the Fair Play for Cuba Committee. That the Bureau had learned that the Agency was meeting with Cubela should certainly have prompted CIA to scrutinize the security of the Cubela operation.

But the October 1963 report was not passed to CIA.

Nor did the Bureau tell the Agency about allegations that Santos Trafficante, the key figure in CIA's pre-Cubela assassination attempts, was also really working for Castro—and that the president's life might be in danger. This information came to the FBI from Jose Aleman, an anti-Castro exile in Miami. Aleman had been a co-conspirator with Cubela during the revolution, but afterward became disillusioned with Castro's overt Marxism and emigrated to the U.S. By September 1962, one of Aleman's distant cousins, who had allegedly helped spring Trafficante from a Cuban jail, had introduced Aleman to the mobster at a Miami Beach hotel. Disturbed by what had transpired at that meeting, Aleman immediately began informing on Trafficante to George Davis and Paul Scranton of the FBI's Miami Field Office. Trafficante had offered to get him a loan from Jimmy Hoffa's International Brotherhood of Teamsters, and while they were on that subject, Trafficante had mentioned, in passing, that because of the Kennedy administration's harassment of certain individuals, JFK was finished. According to Aleman, Trafficante had said simply, "He is going to be hit."

Such words would seem ominous enough in hindsight, but at the time Trafficante's hints were apparently judged mere gangland braggadocio. Aleman got little reaction from the FBI when, starting in late 1962 and continuing through the summer of 1963, three Cubans he had known in Havana appeared in Miami and then left for Texas. Aleman suspected them of being Cuban agents and, he later said, told this to the Bureau. "I advised the FBI in long conversations that I thought something was going to happen," Aleman said. "I was telling them to be careful." Thirty years later, with Bureau records of his debriefings remaining classified, Aleman's accusations would resist positive confirmation. But FBI agent Davis, when advised of Aleman's allegations, would affirm: "He's a reliable individual."

A possible threat to the president's life was only part of Aleman's dark message. He was also convinced that Trafficante was tied in to Cubela, and that both Trafficante and Cubela were agents of Fidel Castro. He did not then know that Trafficante was the point man for CIA's attempts on Castro's life, or that Cubela was CIA's "mole" in Castro's junta. He only knew that Cubela and Trafficante were "linked" and that, as he said, "something was wrong in some way." Cubela was a closet communist, and the whole Trafficante story was suspicious. Both before and after the revolution, Trafficante had run a corrupt *bolita* (numbers racket) that was used to pay off Castro's secret agents. (Aleman did not know it, but such suspicions were paralleled in a Federal Bureau of Narcotics memo dated July 21, 1961, reporting rumors that Castro had kept Trafficante confined after the revolution merely "to make it appear that he had a personal dislike for Castro, when in fact Trafficante is an agent of Castro," his "outlet for illegal contraband in the country." The Narcotics Bureau memo also confirmed Aleman on the *bolita* scheme, stating outright, "Fidel

Castro has operatives in Miami making heavy bets with Santos Trafficante Jr.'s organization.")

But the FBI made no attempts to verify Aleman's ramblings about Cubela's and Trafficante's loyalties. The agents were interested primarily in the Mafioso's business dealings, because he was on RFK's "ten most wanted" list and the Bureau was under intense pressure from the White House to develop evidence for prosecution. Besides, there was no "law" against being in bed with Castro.

Of course, it would have behooved the Bureau to refer Aleman to CIA, or at least to have referred his allegations there through Papich, if the potential importance of Aleman's allegations to the Agency had been understood. But the Agency had never told the Bureau that they were using Trafficante to plot Castro's death; even with Papich, Harvey had refused to name anyone beyond Rosselli. Nor had CIA ever told the Bureau it was using Cubela. The FBI therefore had no way of knowing that Cubela or Trafficante would be of special interest to the Agency. They might have passed on Aleman's information under the aegis of routine cooperation on Cuban matters in the U.S., but even after Cubela's Agency connections became known to the Bureau in October 1963, they did not. If they had, CIA might have investigated the matter and concluded that Cubela and Trafficante were agents of Castro, as Aleman alleged, and that both had kept Castro abreast of CIA attempts to kill him. As it happened, the Agency did not reach these conclusions until after President Kennedy was dead, when a re-examination of the Cubela case turned up two disturbing coincidences.

The first was the timing of CIA's meeting with Cubela in Paris, at which the Cuban was promised that the Agency would provide him with everything he needed to kill Castro—according to CIA records, "telescopic scope, silencer, all the money he wanted." In the meantime, Cubela was given a ballpoint pen rigged with a hypodermic needle so fine that a victim would not perceive its insertion. It was suggested to Cubela that he use the deadly but commercially available poison Blackleaf-40. The Cuban did not think much of the device, and asked CIA to "come up with something more sophisticated." This meeting occurred on November 22, and it was interrupted by the news from Dallas. As a CIA report stonily stated: "At the very moment President Kennedy was shot, a CIA officer was meeting with a Cuban agent in Paris and giving him an assassination device for use against Castro."

The second coincidence also suggested a link between CIA's Cubela plots and danger to President Kennedy. Incredibly, on Saturday, September 7, 1963—the very day that Cubela, in Brazil, was meeting with U.S. intelligence officers and offering to kill Castro—the Cuban dictator just happened to go to the Brazilian Embassy in Havana. Finding a U.S. reporter, Daniel Harker, Castro approached him, and said: "United States leaders should think that if they are aiding terrorist plans to eliminate Cuban leaders, they themselves will not be safe. Let Kennedy and his brother Robert take care of themselves since they, too, can be the cause of an attempt which will cause their death."

CERTAINLY THE FBI had little reason to suspect in November 1963 that CIA assets, originally recruited to kill Castro, might have really been "turned around" by Castro to go after President Kennedy. That was the theory of President Lyndon Johnson, after he read a 1967 CIA study on the Cubela-Trafficante plots, but in fall 1963 that belief would have presupposed the bringing together of facts which CIA and FBI knew separately, but which were not integrated in any single counterintelligence brain. Even so, the events of November 22 might have been prevented if CIA had told the Bureau everything it knew about contacts between the KGB and Lee Harvey Oswald.

The two agencies had been exchanging data on Oswald at irregular intervals since November 2, 1957, when a CIA memo recorded that "Mr. Papich would like to know what we know about this ex-Marine who recently defected in the USSR." Two days later, Papich was advised that CIA "had no info on subject." After Oswald's return to the United States in June 1962, the FBI kept a loose watch on his activities—he had come back with a Russian wife, which was suspicious in its own right—and right up through November 1963, FBI reports on Oswald's pro-Castro pamphleteering were finding their way into Oswald's file at CIA. The Agency could do no more than receive these reports and file them, because Oswald was a U.S. citizen in the United States, and clearly an FBI charge.

But the jurisdiction blurred when Oswald traveled to Mexico in late September 1963. A CIA station officer in Mexico later affirmed that Oswald "became a person of great interest to us" as a result of that visit. "We thought at first that Oswald might be a dangerous potential defector from the USA to the Soviet Union . . . so we kept a special watch on him and his activities." Yet even if he was in a foreign country, Oswald was still an American citizen, and CIA was not supposed to investigate Americans without a special request from the FBI. No such request had been received in the Oswald case; his presence in Mexico was detected by accident. As the Agency informed the Bureau on October 10, 1963:

1. On 1 October 1963 a reliable source reported that an American male, who identified himself as Lee OSWALD, contacted the Soviet Embassy in

Mexico City inquiring whether the Embassy had received any news concerning a telegram which had been sent to Washington. The American was described as approximately 35 years old, with an athletic build, about six feet tall, with a receding hairline.

2. It is believed that OSWALD may be identical to Lee Henry [*sic*] OSWALD, born on 8 October 1939 in New Orleans, Louisiana, a former U.S. Marine who defected to the Soviet Union in October 1959 and later made arrangement through the United States Embassy in Moscow to return to the United States with his Russian-born wife . . . and their child.

3. The information in paragraph one is being disseminated to your representatives in Mexico City. Any further information received on this subject will be furnished you.

It wasn't. On October 9, the day before FBI was informed of Oswald's visit, the CIA station in Mexico City had cabled headquarters with additional data, suggesting that Oswald might be even more "dangerous" than first feared. According to the cable, an American male speaking broken Russian, who "said his name was Lee Oswald," visited the Soviet Embassy on September 28 and spoke with Consul Valeriy V. Kostikov. The Agency had obtained that information by tapping the embassy's phones in Mexico City, and also had some highly placed informants within the embassy, who confirmed the Oswald-Kostikov meeting. According to a later CIA memo, it was suspected that Kostikov, while "functioning overtly as a consul," was also "a staff officer of the KGB . . . connected with the Thirteenth, or 'liquid affairs' department, whose responsibilities include assassination." Although it is unclear when CIA's suspicions about Kostikov first arose, a declassified CIA document shows that they existed by at least November 23, 1963, when one of Angleton's staffers shared the Agency's fears with Papich. Two officials who later saw secret files on the case, however, insist that CIA's worries about Kostikov and Department 13 went back even earlier. According to Clarence Kelley, one of Hoover's successors as FBI director, and James Johnston, a counsel to the Senate Intelligence Committee, CIA suspected that Kostikov was an assassinations specialist in October 1963. If Kelley and Johnston are correct, any report to the FBI of Oswald's meeting with Kostikov should have given the Bureau clear grounds for reopening its security case on Oswald, and for watching him quite closely on November 22.

But things did not happen that way. On October 18, CIA did advise the FBI that Oswald had met with Kostikov—but failed to mention their belief that Kostikov was an assassinations specialist for the KGB. Kelley, who in 1975 reviewed the problem of CIA-FBI cooperation on the Oswald case, saw the Kostikov blunder as typical of "the reluctance-to-share attitude prevalent throughout all government agencies at the time. Not only did the CIA withhold the true identity of Kostikov, but they also made it clear that the information they were willing to mete out was 'of the highest confidentiality,' and should go no further. . . . Thus, the one FBI agent responsible for maintaining surveillance on Oswald was kept in the dark."

That "one agent" was James Hosty of the Dallas Field Office, who had held the "Oswald ticket" in Texas for almost a year and a half. Hosty thought Oswald strange, but had no reason, at the time, to believe he was dangerous. "There's no question but that I *should* have known about Kostikov, who he was, and the threat he represented," an embittered Hosty later said. "I first heard of the Oswald meeting with Kostikov a full month before the assassination—but somebody forgot to let Dallas know exactly how dangerous Kostikov was."

Presumably CIA had its own reasons for not telling the FBI who Kostikov was. Perhaps it wanted to protect the security of its technical and human sources within the Soviet Embassy. Perhaps it was feared that Hoover would do something heavy-handed, as he had been doing since the days of Dusko Popov in 1941, and as he had done in the case of another Popov, Pyotr, in 1958. If the Bureau suddenly saw Oswald as a subversive meeting with a KGB assassinations specialist, instead of a crank meeting a friendly consular official, and interrogated Oswald or sent legal attachés sniffing around Mexico City, instead of letting CIA handle that end of it—the KGB would surely suspect a leak in its operations, and the Agency could lose its most important sources in Mexico. Perhaps, too, CIA simply assumed that the FBI already knew who Kostikov was. A weak set of excuses, to be sure, but no better ones may be mustered to explain why CIA failed to tell the FBI that Kostikov was a suspected member of KGB's Department 13.

"That omission," Kelley later said, "cost JFK his life. Had Jim Hosty and the Dallas office known the nature of the Russian with whom Oswald had met at the Soviet Embassy in Mexico City, the FBI in Dallas would have (after learning that the President was coming to Dallas) undoubtedly taken all necessary steps to neutralize Oswald—perhaps by interviewing him on November 22. And history would have taken a different turn. . . . Had our intelligence communities pooled their information on Oswald, had the Oswald–Kostikov–Mexico City information been distributed to the New Orleans and Dallas field offices in time for them to act then, without a doubt, JFK would not have died in Dallas on November 22, 1963."

TO ALLEGE THAT CIA-FBI fumbling contributed to President Kennedy's death was not necessarily to say that Kostikov, or the KGB, ordered

Kennedy killed. Soviet intelligence officers, like those of any nation, routinely carried out consular work unrelated to their clandestine functions, in order to preserve diplomatic "cover"; perhaps Kostikov had simply been helping Oswald with his visa request. Nor did the FBI, believing CIA's anti-Castro plots to have been terminated with Harvey's transfer, have any reason to suspect that Kennedy had been killed to avenge attempts on Castro's life. But whereas the FBI refused to believe that Oswald had acted as part of any communist conspiracy, CIA, in coming years, would not be so eager to dismiss the possibility. If liaison problems contributed to the Dallas tragedy, they would even more thoroughly impede its investigation, and devolve into a projected fight that precluded the truth from being inarguably known. The fight would be bound up with the search for Soviet moles, sparked by a 1961 defector, and would ultimately lead to a formal break in relations between FBI and CIA.

BOOK THREE

THE POETRY OF DECEPTION

CHAPTER NINE

A MIND OF WINTER

THE DEFECTION OF A KGB major on December 15, 1961, was one of the few encouraging auguries on an otherwise unsettling Friday for the U.S. government. President Kennedy had boarded Air Force One for a weekend visit to Venezuela, pleased that a contract had been awarded Lockheed for a rocket to the moon, but disturbed by developments in Europe. Six months after Khrushchev had built a wall between East and West Berlin, the U.S. was still trying to resolve the crisis diplomatically, but French President Charles de Gaulle was dividing NATO by objecting to America's hardline position, and on this very day France had closed her skies to UN aircraft. Washington was trying, similarly, to split the Soviet bloc by selling thirty thousand tons of edible oils to Yugoslavia. It was a frustrating maze, this game of foreign relations in the Cold War, but the ultimate price of failure was implicit in the Pentagon's terse announcement this day that it would stockpile crushed-bulgur survival wafers in atomic-fallout shelters. It probably would have comforted Kennedy little to hear that such biscuits might never be necessary, according to the new KGB defector, because the Soviets had hatched a plan for defeating the West without waging war.

The KGB man had come over just after noon Washington time, or 6:00 p.m. in Helsinki. In a blinding snowstorm, he had approached the Haapatie Street doorstep of CIA's station chief, Frank Friberg. Within hours, Friberg was on a U.S. Air Force jet with the stocky, sharp-eyed KGB major, who gave his name as Anatoliy Golitsyn. Neither Friberg nor anyone else at CIA had any inkling, at the time, that Golitsyn would become perhaps the most controversial and divisive defector of the Cold

War, a catalyst and symbol of the deep and philosophical forces that were already spinning FBI and CIA into collision.

For the moment, Golitsyn's defection sent a much-needed frisson of excitement through CIA's new headquarters at Langley, Virginia. A half-hour drive from downtown Washington, D.C., cloaked by several thousand acres of Virginia forest and ringed by a huge parking lot, the main building was a seven-story modernistic monster; some thought it looked like a giant milk crate. The Agency had moved in only the month before, and one could still smell the paint in the corridors, but already there was nostalgia for the ratty old tempo buildings, and the type of man that had worked in them. In the golden days of OSS, and on through the fifties, clandestine operations had been managed mostly by men whose families had helped create the American institutions it was CIA's duty to defend. But by the early 1960s, after Bedell Smith and Allen Dulles had improved foreign intelligence to something between a science and an art, its practice was at once degraded from a noble calling into a teachable trade. Bill Donovan's bold Easterners were being replaced by prudent professionals, and what had been a private club was becoming a public-service bureaucracy. Nothing betokened this change more than the huge Langley parking lot, with its special sections reserved for area divisions, directorates, and watch staffs. That was too orderly, too much like a corporation. Veteran CIA officers quipped that, should an Agency officer be captured by hostile forces, he was authorized to answer only three questions: name, grade, and parking-space number.

Dulles' departure also symbolized the change. Earlier in the year, a CIA-backed army of anti-Castro exiles had bungled badly in the attempt to invade Cuba at the Bay of Pigs. It was a gung-ho operation in the classic Donovan style, even to the point of poor security, and Castro's militia had been waiting on the beaches when CIA's commandos landed. The operation had embarrassed President Kennedy, and Dulles had hung on just long enough to dedicate the new headquarters that November.

His successor, millionaire Republican shipbuilder John McCone, had no experience in spying. Ordinarily, the Agency's deputy director for plans (DDP) would have been overseeing things until McCone settled in, but Richard Bissell, too, was on the ropes. He'd been in on the Bay of Pigs planning, and there was pressure for him to go; he was spending the holidays trying to decide. So it was by default, more than design, that one of Bissell's senior officers in the Department of Plans, forty-eight-year-old OSS veteran Richard Helms, had come to be running the secret operations of CIA.

Helms' background was tradecraft, contacting and running agents, and through much of the 1950s he'd been chief of a division responsible for secret operations in Central and Eastern Europe. Helms was the ultimate professional; depending on circumstance, he could be friendly as a grand-father, or cold as a witch. He gave back-slapping pep talks to new chiefs of station—"Ring the gong for us out there in Malaya, Dave!"—but was rumored to have fired an Agency tennis partner who tried to presume on their friendship for personal advancement. Tall, with thinning black hair, he was a man without any other memorable qualities except supreme emotional control and a ruthless dedication to his work.

Helms sensed immediately the importance of Anatoliy Golitsyn, who by Christmas was being debriefed at Ashford Farm, a scenic CIA property near the Choptank River in Maryland. KGB defectors were rare enough, but Golitsyn was a major, and few higher-ranking KGB men had ever defected. He had served in Moscow Center, processing the "take" from spies in NATO, and when CIA officers tested him with a batch of NATO documents in which both fake and real papers had been mixed, he quickly identified the real ones. But Golitsyn was less an "operations" officer than a scholar and historian; he had spent years studying at KGB think tanks, including the KGB Higher Institute, where he earned the equivalent of a Ph.D. in spying. As a theoretician, Golitsyn could tell CIA not only *what* the KGB was doing, but *how* and *why*.

One document Golitsyn provided was particularly suggestive. Among the package of papers he turned over to CIA debriefers the week before Christmas was one describing a new KGB "disinformation directorate," Department D, which Golitsyn said was to implement the Soviets' grand strategy for winning without fighting. According to a CIA Soviet Division officer who saw the document, "It described the need for disinformation in KGB intelligence work. It stated that just catching American spies isn't enough, because the enemy can always start again with new ones. Therefore, said this KGB document, disinformation operations are essential. And among the purposes of such operations, as I recall the words of the document, the first one mentioned is 'to negate and discredit authentic information the enemy has obtained.' The last of the four or five purposes the secret KGB document listed was 'to penetrate deeper into the enemy service.' "

Golitsyn intimated that Soviet disinformation operations were designed to support a new "long-range plan," by which "the world balance of power" was to be "shifted inconspicuously in communist favor," but declined to elaborate with anyone except President Kennedy. Helms refused to allow that—it was unwise to let defectors become too convinced of their own importance—so a fuller exposition of the KGB's master strategy would have to wait. But by early January 1962, Golitsyn had tantalized his han-dlers with at least three leads about the KGB's practical activities. First, he said, the KGB had penetrated every intelligence service in NATO, including CIA. Second, the KGB would send false defectors after Golitsyn, to deflect from his leads. Finally, KGB Department 13, which handled assassinations and sabotage, was plotting to kill a Western political figure.

Helms did not attach too much urgency to this last warning. Golitsyn could not specify the target of the plot—his best guess was perhaps an opposition figure in Northern Europe—and CIA could not just approach the thousand or so European persons who fit that description, and say, "Be careful."

Nor could much be done with Golitsyn's warning about false defectors who would allegedly follow him . . . except, perhaps, to wait alertly.

But Golitsyn's leads about Soviet moles were quite "live." Generally, he said, a "cancer" of penetrations had been growing in CIA since it was OSS; specifically, the Agency harbored a Soviet spy of Slavic background, whose name began with "K" and ended in "sky." This agent was known within the KGB as "Sasha," and had spent time in Germany. Golitsyn believed that Sasha might have been activated by the KGB in 1957, when V. M. Kovshuk, head of the American Department in the KGB's First Chief Directorate, had visited Washington. The defector also suspected that this spy might have been in a position to tell the KGB about an American-British electronic-surveillance project, code-named "Easy Chair." Those clues added impetus to the investigation of a CIA employee who was already under suspicion when Golitsyn arrived.

His name was Peter Karlow. He had been born Klibansky, the last name of his Russian émigré father; he had served for six years in Germany, where he ran a CIA laboratory near Frankfurt; he had been stationed in the United States in 1957, when Kovshuk visited; as an officer in CIA's Technical Services Division, he had been CIA chairman of the Easy Chair project. It was in that capacity that he had come under suspicion of compromising information before Golitsyn came over; apparently a high number of science-and-technology projects had been compromised. Karlow had also served in OSS, losing a leg in the Mediterreanean theater. Perhaps he had even been one of the original "Venona 14," the moles mentioned in Soviet cable traffic as having served in OSS.

Still, Helms knew there wasn't much that the Office of Security could actually do about the suspicions of Karlow. CIA could not tap his phone, break into his house, or even follow him around. Those were domestic operations, the province of J. Edgar Hoover. The only thing for it was to turn the Karlow serial over to the FBI.

Helms was apprehensive about that. From personal involvement in the Cord Meyer case ten years before, he realized how easily FBI loyalty investigations could cause interagency friction. And as one of the few

CIA-headquarters officers who had known about Pyotr Popov, CIA's mole in Moscow, Helms knew the potential danger posed by ten-ton FBI surveillances. If Karlow really was guilty, it would be crucial that he not detect the suspicions against him. Otherwise he might cease behavior, such as contact with Soviet cutouts, that could establish his guilt. If, on the other hand, he was innocent—as Helms truly hoped—it would be equally vital that a complete, secure, foolproof inquiry be conducted, without nagging questions about whether FBI indiscretion had prejudiced the outcome. Only then could Karlow's reputation be fully restored.

But Helms, ever the professional, suppressed his doubts and followed standard operating procedure. On January 9, 1962, the Peter Karlow serial was officially passed to J. Edgar Hoover and the FBI.

SIX DAYS AFTER getting the tip from CIA, the Bureau began what Hoover termed "a discreet investigation" by openly knocking on the door of Karlow's home. There was a suspicious German couple down the street who might be spies for a hostile country, the G-men said. Could the Bureau use Karlow's garage to set up listening equipment? Karlow consented; the next morning, his own phone sounded tapped. As a Technical man himself, Karlow knew the signs. He also thought it was odd that the gas company insisted on cleaning his fireplace—for free. Obviously, he was under some kind of suspicion.

As Papich informed Sheffield Edwards in early February, the FBI coverage established, among other things, that "certain meetings . . . had been held in the recreation room in the basement of the home of the Subject," at which had been present some former and present CIA Technical people from Karlow's days in Germany. Papich also reminded the Agency security director, as Edwards recorded, that "the general aim of the FBI was, of course, prosecution if a criminal case can be established." Edwards said CIA had an "open view" on that, though "the primary interest of this Agency, of course," was simply to find out if Karlow was a KGB agent, "and if so what Agency information has been compromised by Subject." As long as the Bureau did not interfere with those objectives, CIA "desired that the FBI conduct a full covert investigation."

The Bureau complied, maintaining its surveillance of Karlow throughout 1962. On one occasion, agents followed Karlow to Philadelphia, where he entered a storefront carrying a box, then emerged three hours later without it. According to the Bureau surveillance report, "Nothing can be observed within the business establishment inasmuch as Venetian blinds extend across the entire window in front of the store and are kept tightly closed." But by February of the following year there was still no firm evidence against Karlow, and Hoover, tired of playing out the case, wanted results. Karlow was summoned to the FBI's Washington Field Office, where he was told by special agents Maurice Taylor and Peter Brent: "You have the right to remain silent." After a week of hostile grilling, in which he consistently denied being a Soviet agent, Karlow composed a letter to Helms. "I wish to help the FBI in any way I can, both to resolve the case and to clear my name. I have nothing to confess and nothing to conceal. I realize that, through an incredible error . . . I have come so deeply under suspicion of treason that my career in CIA is ended." But, Karlow insisted, "I intend to fight any suspicions or allegations of disloyalty or indiscretion in any way that I can, inside and outside CIA and government, until any personal implication or blemish on my record is removed."

He never had a chance. The next day, Helms coolly informed him that the matter was out of CIA's hands; it was entirely within the FBI's jurisdiction. Karlow went home on administrative leave. Meanwhile, according to CIA counsel Lawrence Houston, "Allegations were coming in from the Bureau about Karlow's relationship with a Russian who turned out to be a defector. It led to an employee hearing board, which determined that probably he should no longer be on the staff." On July 5, Karlow limped through the Agency parking lot on his wooden leg and drove away from Langley for the last time.

But Houston, among others, didn't think his old OSS colleague would ever have worked for the communists, and was always bothered by the case. "I was sure there was something wrong about this," Houston recalled. "And a year or two, a couple of years, later, I went back and asked our people down in Security, and they checked with the Bureau. The Bureau said, 'Oh, we had the wrong guy.' " Two FBI agents who reviewed the case, Courtland Jones and Alexander Neale, confirmed that the FBI ultimately found Karlow innocent.

"I thought that was absolutely inexcusable," Houston said. "But there had already been so much damage done to Peter's reputation, and so much of our business depends on trust, and he had already moved on with his life, and was pretty bitter toward CIA. So he wasn't put back on the rolls. Only years later, when the truth finally came out, was he given a rather nice decoration for his long and valuable service, and a good financial settlement for the damage to his career."

INTERAGENCY RECRIMINATION over the Karlow and other molehunt cases was still some years away in the early 1960s, but dispute over one source of the Karlow serial—CIA's new KGB defector—was quick in coming. It is unclear exactly when and how the FBI first learned of

Anatoliy Golitsyn, but by June 1962 the Bureau knew all about him. Hoover had one of his infamous eruptions, insisting that McCone explain why he hadn't been immediately informed.

The FBI director had some basis for complaint. Although it was "accepted procedure" for defectors to be "handled by CIA through the interrogation and resettling periods," it was also standard practice to convene an interagency defector committee once the man was safely west. That way, each agency could decide for itself whether the individual was of any interest, and, if so, how urgent and immediate that agency's need to debrief him was. Typically, the FBI claimed a priority need to interrogate any KGB defector about any Soviet operations within the United States. Things were working more smoothly in this regard than in 1949, when the two sides had scuffled over Ansimov in a Washington restaurant, but a year before Golitsyn there had been a big flap over the Bureau's lack of access to a former colonel in Polish intelligence, Michael Goleniewski, who had made his initial contact with the U.S. through a letter addressed to Hoover personally. The Agency had obtained this letter in Switzerland and had run Goleniewski as an agent in place, then smuggled him west and debriefed him, all without letting the FBI know what was going on. After that episode, Dulles had promised to make it "standard procedure" to let the Bureau know, in a timely manner, about any intelligence defectors. If standard procedure had been followed, then, the Peter Karlow serial would have come to the Bureau in January and would have been a Bureau case from the outset.

But real life wasn't always so simple. Defectors were complicated human beings under extreme emotional duress, and the relation between any defector or agent and his handler, or principal, was intrinsically fragile. To introduce any new outside elements while trying to build bonds of trust was dangerous. As Angleton later put it: "Now, assuming an agent of ours comes to the United States, we are presented with a problem, therefore, of: Is he to be transferred to the jurisdiction of the FBI? The moment the answer is yes, we are subjecting that individual to risk." Angleton recognized that "in order not to jeopardize the domestic activities of the Bureau, and at the same time to give them the full benefits of the individual," there had to be "a coordinating process with them," but defector-handling was necessarily "a gray area." That was so, Angleton would say, "not because of jealousies or internecine fighting"—although there was certainly enough of that to go around—but "by virtue of the actuality of a principal-agent relationship."

That was especially true in regard to Golitsyn, who was as difficult an agent as his principals had ever handled. He had been testy with Friberg and various CIA personnel on the way from Helsinki, fearing that inadequate precautions had been taken for his safety, and his mood had not improved at CIA's Ashford Farm. There, under Victorian eaves shagged with ice, his own mind had gone cold. His information, he kept insisting, was so important that he must deal directly with the president of the United States. This access was denied him, and he was sulking. All CIA needed to alienate Golitsyn further was to bring in a bunch of flatfooted cops from the FBI. So the Agency had tried to hide Golitsyn from Hoover, at least until the defector warmed to his hosts. And even after the FBI had learned about Golitsyn, McCone refused to make him available.

The ensuing bureaucratic battle was exacerbated by personal hostility between Hoover and McCone. For all the problems Dulles had caused, Hoover much preferred the bumbling, genial ways of a Donovan man to McCone's all-business administrative approach, which was in fact much akin to Hoover's own. "By the early sixties, Mr. Hoover had developed a respect for Dulles," Papich recalled. "They didn't like each other necessarily, but each knew what to expect." McCone not only ruined that familiarity, but never even tried to make friends with the legendary Hoover. The new DCI was as frosty as his hair was white, his spirit unleavened even by the instinct for camaraderie that was well developed even in the irascible Bedell Smith. "No question, McCone was *tough*," Papich allowed. "He probably would have liked to toss Hoover into the Potomac."

Relations between FBI and CIA became increasingly strained over the question of Bureau access to Golitsyn. President Kennedy had to be brought into the dispute, which was embarrassing to both agencies, as well as highly annoying to the president. McCone reluctantly acceded, and shortly after the Rudolf Abel–Francis Gary Powers exchange of February 10, 1962, Papich and Don Moore, the FBI's Soviet counterintelligence chief, met Golitsyn at the Mayflower Hotel in downtown Washington, just four blocks from the White House.

"That Mayflower meeting covered a lot of ground," Papich recalled. The FBI debriefers started about nine o'clock in the morning, stopped for a sandwich, went on, stopped for another sandwich about six, then continued until ten o'clock that night. They questioned Golitsyn about his KGB training, and about Soviet personnel at consulates, embassies, the United Nations. Moore displayed surveillance photos of Soviet diplomats, saying each time, 'Do you know this man?' "

Golitsyn was gruff. "No," he mostly said, but there were several he recognized.

"What do you know about him?" the agents would ask.

He never knew very much. Or, if he did, he would say, "Yeah, I know him, but I'm not going to tell you any more now." And so, despite the wide range of topics covered, the meeting was not very productive for the

FBI. "We were disappointed with Golitsyn, because most of the hot stuff he gave related to agents overseas," Papich said. "And it was clear that Golitsyn knew a lot more than he was telling. He was a cagey character. He was worried that we would just wring him out for what he knew, and then he wouldn't have any bargaining power anymore. So he was going to give out his information to us in pieces. He was a bright, arrogant bastard; he even tried asking *us* questions, to improve his own base of knowledge. Well, we weren't going to give him any information, and that didn't make him happy. I don't think he saw us as people who could do him good, anyway, unless he could have access to the boss. He would have loved to have sat down with J. Edgar; he was that type. But Hoover—no way was he going to meet with any Soviet defector."

Moore was even less charmed than Papich, and later claimed to have been put off by Golitsyn's analysis of the recent Abel-Powers exchange, which was much in the news. Though Papich could not recall Golitsyn's speaking of the Abel case, Moore remembered Golitsyn theorizing that, just as the KGB would have tried to turn Powers into a double agent before returning him, so the FBI would have tried to double Abel before sending him back to Moscow. At any rate, the KGB would certainly have expected the FBI to do that, Golitsyn warned, and if the FBI had in fact doubled Abel, the KGB would certainly try to turn him back against the Bureau in a deception game.

"You give me Abel's secret messages," Golitsyn allegedly pleaded. "You need me to analyze them. You give me reports, I give you facts."

Moore, who had an intimate familiarity with the Abel case, knew that the Soviet illegal had not been doubled by the FBI. The reasoning struck him as convoluted, speculative, overly conspiratorial. Besides which, Golitsyn was too haughty, too sure of himself. Moore decided that he simply didn't like the man. "Frankly," he would say, "that Golitsyn was a pain in the ass from the word go."

But KGB officers don't come along very often, so Moore didn't pass up the chance to meet the defector again, a few weeks later, at a yellow-brick CIA technical-research facility on 23rd Street in Northwest Washington, adjacent to the old OSS buildings. This time, Moore brought along his deputy, William Branigan, as well as Intelligence Division chief William Sullivan and Russian-speaking special agent Alekso Poptanich. Angleton headed a six-man Agency contingent, whom Moore knew as a man who wouldn't even take off his jacket when Papich arranged an interagency poker game. Golitsyn stood and addressed the group, which sat around a massive mahogany table. Beware of false defectors who will come after me, he said. And beware the Soviet long-range plan. He displayed a chart which he had sketched on a sheet of canary paper. In the middle was the

KGB, with arms stretching everywhere like an octopus to other states in the Soviet bloc, even to Albania and Yugoslavia, which supposedly were outside Moscow's sphere of influence. Golitsyn spoke of "phony splits" and "false liberalization" in the communist world, and secret channels of coordination. He was short on detail, but kept using the word "disinformation."

The G-men were unimpressed. There was some coughing and shifting of elbows. A silence when Golitsyn waited for questions. A longer one when he said he could be more specific about the Soviet strategy only with Hoover or his boss, Attorney General Robert Kennedy.

Poptanich, who sat beside the defector, asked in Russian about Soviet spies in the United States. Golitsyn looked at him and said nothing.

Angleton, who kept his head down, was scribbling in indigo ink on a notepad, drawing a flock of waterfowl on a pond. He said, in his gravelly voice, that he thought Golitsyn should see "Bobby."

The KGB man was led from the room while the point was argued. FBI men were against letting Golitsyn see their superiors, because they feared losing control of him. CIA officers thought Golitsyn's message was potentially so important that he should be allowed higher access; only then would he open up. The debate ended in impasse.

When Golitsyn was ushered back in, he was questioned closely by Poptanich and Branigan, each of whom had years of field experience in counterespionage. They got some ancillary explanation of KGB organization and pecking orders, but little else. "He couldn't tell us with any accuracy what the Soviet situation was in Washington, for instance," Branigan griped. "He just didn't know."

Papich, who arranged the meeting but did not attend, thought that at least part of the problem was the FBI's inability to understand the Soviet mind-set. "We didn't have a single agent that ever worked, or lived, or was assigned in the Soviet Union. We had several fellows, like Poptanich, who could handle the language, but they didn't have that foreign experience. We didn't think like them. And what we, in the FBI, meant by counterintelligence was not what a KGB man like Golitsyn had in mind. So naturally, Poptanich was disgusted because he got nowhere trying to talk to Golitsyn."

Despite his patent failure to win the defector's trust, however, an Annual Report of Performance Rating noted that Poptanich had recently "participated in the interrogation of a Soviet defector and his knowledge of the Russian language and mores of the Russian people proved most helpful relative thereto." His supervisor, Branigan, lauded Poptanich's refusal to be intimidated by Golitsyn or by CIA pressure. Poptanich had indeed hewn to what was becoming an FBI party platform on the Soviet defector; as Branigan put it: "The FBI was not happy with Golitsyn and did not respect him."

GOLITSYN'S REPUTATION WAS meanwhile rising swiftly at CIA, especially since one of his dark predictions seemed to be coming true. On June 5, 1962, Yuri Nosenko, a KGB security officer with the Soviet Disarmament Commission, approached an American diplomat at U.S.-Soviet disarmament talks in Geneva, Switzerland, and whispered that he wished to talk privately with U.S. intelligence. He was met in a safehouse by young CIA officer Tennent H. "Pete" Bagley. After offering Nosenko some liquor and peanuts, Bagley said he would appreciate the Soviet's speaking clearly and slowly, and in English wherever possible. Nosenko then delivered a great number of sentences, fast, in Russian, while swigging whiskey and munching nuts. Because of the language problem, Bagley had to puzzle out much of what Nosenko said from a tape of the conversation, which had been made automatically by a recorder in the wall, but even then there were gaps. In the early 1960s, portable tape recorders were not the refined machines they later became, and there was much ambient noise. The machine would pick up the crumpling of paper, the scraping of a match, the drone of a distant airplane, yet fail to record key words or phrases. The essence of Nosenko's message, however, was clear: he was in financial trouble, and would work for CIA as an agent-in-place. To prove his sincerity, he would tell what he knew about KGB penetration of CIA. After hearing him out, Bagley cabled headquarters that Nosenko had "conclusively proven his bona fides."

But when Bagley flew home that weekend to make a full report, Angleton was skeptical. All of Nosenko's information was of the "throwaway" variety, the CI chief said. Nosenko spoke of Department D, but only after Golitsyn had already disclosed it. Nosenko gave specific locations of microphones at the U.S. Embassy in Moscow, but Golitsyn had provided approximate locations of some of the microphones six months earlier. Nosenko also said that Pytor Popov had been detected in 1959 by a special KGB "spy dust" sprayed on the shoes of his Western contacts, not blown by a mole in CIA, and that "Sasha" was a low-ranking Army officer, not a high-ranking Agency man. Might not Nosenko be a false defector, intended to throw CIA off the trail of its mole(s)?

Bagley eventually bought that logic. He wondered what disinformation Nosenko would try to feed CIA when he next made contact, as he promised to do whenever he was outside the Soviet bloc. Thanks to Golitsyn, CIA was "keyed in" to an apparent KGB deception game right from the start.

Golitsyn himself was becoming increasingly impatient with his hosts, however, and with the lack of access they afforded him to higher-ups. He wondered if the British might be more appreciative, especially because he had information which had already allowed them to confront Kim Philby and force a confession. Golitsyn therefore flew to Britain to help MI5 hunt for moles, arriving on January 24—the very day that Kim Philby, after confessing, eluded Western surveillance and hopped onto a Soviet freighter in Beirut. CIA agents converged on Philby's apartment and confiscated a typewriter ribbon; they turned it over to the FBI, who found no leads. Philby soon afterward surfaced in the Soviet Union.

Golitsyn returned to the U.S. in June 1963, after his identity was partially leaked to the British press, and was taken under wing by Angleton, who believed that, with the proper approach, he could be immensely valuable. Though the defector still did not see President Kennedy, Angleton did get him an appointment with RFK. Golitsyn held back from the attorney general what he knew about long-range Soviet strategy, but during fall 1963 he began to open up to Angleton, whom he befriended and considered an intellectual equal. In late-night drinking sessions, Angleton elicited from Golitsyn the logic of KGB penetration, and details of the Soviet strategy for winning without fighting.

Angleton then tried to get Golitsyn to share his big secrets directly with Papich, perhaps hoping that the liaison officer could in turn arrange a meeting between the KGB defector and Hoover. The chance came one Saturday afternoon, when both Papich and Golitsyn happened to be over at Angleton's North Arlington home.

"I'm going to be gone for a while," Angleton said.

He stepped out, leaving Golitsyn and Papich sitting in armchairs in the living room. Papich made his pitch.

"We're both of Slav background," he began. He related how his family had immigrated from Yugoslavia, what the country meant to him. Even if it was just an extemporaneous spiel, Papich meant every word of it. Golitsyn was listening intently. "You're just like my father, in many respects," Papich went on. "You've come here and you've got freedom that you never had before. Your children are going to have freedom they never had before. You've got a future here that you never would have had." And so on, until finally there was a silence.

"Are you finished?" Golitsyn asked.

"Yes."

"Thank you," the defector said, and then went quiet. He had no questions, no observations; he wasn't going to share details of the Soviet Union's master plan with any FBI man except Hoover, no matter how favorably recommended by Angleton.

But Angleton himself was willing to share the defector's theories with Papich in long talks after work at their homes. They lived only a few blocks apart, in North Arlington, and Papich would find himself at two or three o'clock in the morning in the backyard greenhouse where Angleton grew orchids. The hobby had become a full-blown obsession for Angleton, who frequently traveled as an orchid salesman for cover on sensitive missions abroad. When he took his custom hybrids to flower shows, he showed them with the professionals, and sometimes won prizes. It was always warm in the orchid house, and Angleton would be diddling around with his plants while they talked, but it got them away from the families, and there were a couple of old wood benches where Papich could sit down. So it was among the leafy shadows and eternal summer of the greenhouse that Papich learned the details of what Golitsyn called the Soviets' "long-range plan."

Greatly simplified, this plan called for massive political warfare, buttressed by secret intelligence deceptions. At the Twentieth Communist World Congress, in 1959, the U.S.A. had been designated the Main Enemy, but at the same time it had been decided to try a new approach. There was to be a thaw in relations, and a return to Leninist deceptions like the Trust and the New Economic Program (NEP), which had once convinced the U.S. that the Soviets were reforming. The KGB was to be reorganized to project an image of disunity and weakness in the communist world. By playing up false splits between communist nations, the Soviets would hope to divide and confuse the West, ultimately weakening it. Over the short term, the objective was economic aid to the communist world; over the long term, the goal was to end the Cold War, which would cause the U.S. to disarm.

Papich was skeptical. Even if the KGB had been divided, as Golitsyn said, into an elite "inner" core which knew about such things as secret bloc coordination, and a much larger "outer" KGB, which did not, hundreds if not thousands of people would eventually have to know. How could such a big secret be totally kept from the West?

The answer, Angleton said, was contained in the question. Human nature being what it was, such a secret surely couldn't be kept forever; therefore, the Soviets must exploit human nature to keep the West from believing the secret, once it was out. That would not be too difficult, for the Western mind naturally wanted to believe in Soviet weakness and evolution, and probably would, if that false message came from a plurality of Soviet sources—especially when those sources provided other information that was checkably true. Where the NEP had used Western contacts with the Trust to inject its reformist message into British intelligence, Golitsyn said, the KGB would now create a new "Trust" of anticommunists—defectors and "walk-ins" from Soviet intelligence. False information would even be planted on genuine defectors and unimportant agents in the KGB, on the assumption that these would be cultivated by the West—a process Golitsyn compared to the deliberate misbriefing of "doomed pilots" in World War II. Disinformants would confirm the reality of bogus schisms within the communist world, perpetuate a false picture of communist designs, and deflect from true information provided by defectors such as Golitsyn. Nosenko could be part of that strategy, Angleton reasoned, even if his information overlapped with Golitsyn's on many counts; eventually, once his credibility was established, he would take CIA for a ride. Disinformation messages would be shifted over time, to accord with Western preconceptions, and the net effect would be to keep the West from taking seriously the idea of any secret Soviet plot.

Papich was still not convinced. How would the Soviets know whether and when certain information was believed by CIA, and when and how to shift their messages accordingly?

Angleton smiled. Here at last, he said, was the "final cause" of Soviet penetration, its ultimate logic, the key to KGB strategy. Although the most obvious purpose of any Soviet mole was simply to relay secrets to Moscow Center, the most valuable type of secret was knowledge of how KGB disinformation was being interpreted, so that it could be tailored to Western perspectives. The penetration and disinformation agents were to work in tandem: the "outside" men supplying the disinformation, and the "inside" reporting what was thought of it. If operating successfully, that "feedback loop" would leave Western intelligence agencies, and their sponsor governments, completely at the mercy of the KGB—unable to distinguish falsehood from fact.

And Golitsyn believed, as did Angleton, that the Soviets had indeed penetrated Western intelligence to the point where such a feedback loop could successfully operate. The defector employed a medical analogy to describe the severity of the problem: "When the patient refuses to recognize it exists, it grows and spreads, with bad cells infecting good cells." Western intelligence was "sick" from the cancer of penetration at various levels. The French and British and other services were already dead; CIA had been penetrated broadly at a fairly low level, and was gravely ill; the FBI, because of at least three penetrations in its New York and Washington field offices, was "dying."

"I listened with great interest to what Jim was getting from Golitsyn," Papich later said. "To a certain extent, Jim sold me a message on that; some people might say I was Jim's man at the FBI. I was very much concerned about all of our vulnerabilities, because our inclination at the FBI was sometimes to accept things at face value, to be impressed only when a defector gave us *cases*. Well, the whole idea of disinformation agents made me realize that we had to look at all our cases goddamned carefully."

But Papich immediately understood that the new Angleton-Golitsyn line was bound to be "controversial" and "irritating," especially to FBI officers who had already soured on Golitsyn. When Papich relayed the essence of Golitsyn's thesis to others at the FBI, it was rejected out of hand. Privately, G-men like Don Moore and William Branigan would make fun of what they called Golitsyn's "Monster Plot," while simply telling Papich and Angleton that the idea was "too speculative." Strictly speaking, that was true; though CIA had established Golitsyn's bona fides, his account of the new long-range strategy had not yet been independently confirmed. The Agency could document a secret KGB meeting in May 1959 and some subsequent reorganization, and could glean a return to Leninism from open party sources, and even Nosenko had confirmed the existence of Department D. But otherwise everything rested ultimately on Golitsyn's word. "We need confirmation; we need more detail," the FBI counterespionage experts told Papich.

The liaison officer sensed that there were other reasons why his colleagues didn't want to believe Golitsyn. Hoover had always said, "An attack on any employee of the FBI will be considered an attack on me personally," and in alleging that three employees in Hoover's two most important field offices were Soviet agents, Golitsyn caused a closing of ranks against the very possibility. Whereas the Bureau was only too eager to chase down alleged Soviet moles in CIA, it stubbornly refused to investigate Golitsyn's allegations about communist spies in the FBI, saying that the defector's leads were not specific enough. Angleton countered by suggesting, through Papich, that Golitsyn's memory might be jogged, or his deductions sharpened, if he were allowed to view certain FBI personnel and operational files in sanitized form, with sensitive methods and sources concealed. But the Bureau flatly refused all CIA requests to examine its files. "We never gave Golitsyn any of our material, despite Jim's many requests that we do so," FBI counterintelligence man James Nolan recalled.

Yet Papich knew that FBI resentment of CIA's star defector ran even deeper than unwillingness to believe the KGB had penetrated the Bureau. There was also a will to believe that the Bureau had successfully penetrated the KGB. Indeed, the FBI had just recently made its first-ever recruitments within Soviet intelligence, and though Golitsyn would cast them as probable disinformation agents, the Bureau wanted to believe they were bona fide.

The first of the FBI's two new sources was forty-year-old Aleksei Isidorovich Kulak, nicknamed "Fatso" by his Bureau handlers and officially code-named "Fedora." He served as a consultant to the United Nations Scientific Committee on the Effects of Atomic Radiation, but his real task was to collect scientific and technological secrets from KGB spies in the U.S. One afternoon in March 1962, he simply walked into the FBI's New York Field Office, on Manhattan's Upper East Side, and claimed to be disenchanted by lack of advancement within the KGB's First Chief Directorate. For cash, he would provide the FBI with the identities of other KGB officers, furnish Soviet military-technological "wish lists," and report on Red Army missile capacity and nuclear-development plans.

The second new FBI source was Dmitri Fedorovich Polyakov, code-named "Top Hat." An officer in the GRU and a junior military attaché at the UN, he approached an FBI agent in New York in early 1962. Claiming to be disillusioned because he had to remit 90 percent of his salary to Moscow, he agreed to further meetings in a room at the Cameron Hotel, on West 86th Street. Soon he was serving up the identities of GRU cipher clerks, gossiping about political developments in Moscow, and bad-mouthing guidance systems on Soviet missiles (so inaccurate, he said, that they could not hit Miami from Cuba).

Fedora and Top Hat were so prized and so jealously protected by the Bureau that for much of 1962 their existence was hidden from CIA. Theoretically, enough contextual information about both men should have been turned over to CIA for Angleton to assess their bona fides, even if their true identities were obscured. But Hoover bypassed Angleton and sent reports based on Fedora's and Top Hat's information straight to President Kennedy. When one report described Fedora as "a source of unknown reliability," the FBI director took up his infamous blue-inked fountain pen and slashed out the "un."

By 1963, CIA had to be informed of both sources, however, because both were begging the FBI to supply "feed material," doctored or low-grade intelligence, to keep their KGB superiors happy. That was a complicated process which required careful coordination. Military secrets had to be cleared by Military Intelligence, naval secrets by Naval Intelligence, etc. The game would be lost, moreover, if doctored intelligence passed by the FBI did not cohere with what the Soviets might be getting from doubles run separately by CIA. Indeed, the necessity of coordination in such double-agent schemes had been one of the great CI lessons taught by the Dusko Popov and Kopff-Baarn cases of World War II. So by 1963, CIA had been brought into the feeding of Fedora and Top Hat.

"They checked with us, and there was a mechanism for clearance of feed material for the two UN diplomats," Angleton's deputy Scotty Miler confirmed. "They didn't tell us all the details of how they were met and how they were handled, but that wasn't really important. We knew enough, not only from Golitsyn, but from other sources, that we weren't too sure the agents were kosher. And it was our business to tell the FBI why we didn't think Fedora and Top Hat were for real: because they weren't giving the proper poop, because they were asking for things that fit in with what we thought the Soviets could check on, and because of what they told us about Soviet objectives, some of which was counter to Golitsyn."

There were other caution flags. It seemed odd to Papich, as to Angleton, that, after almost a half-century without a Soviet walk-in, the FBI should suddenly get two of them. Their reporting ranged across compartments, which was odd in the notoriously compartmented KGB. And much of what they provided was dated. "They gave us cases," Papich said, "but most of them we knew already."

Those few cases the Bureau hadn't known about seemed of dubious value, at least to Papich and Angleton. In 1963, for instance, Fedora said that the Soviets had a spy in a British nuclear-research facility. Suspicion soon hovered over Giuseppe Martelli, a physicist at Culham Laboratory. Investigation revealed rendezvous information locked in a drawer in his desk, and partially used coding pads for secret communications. But, according to MI5's Peter Wright, "no evidence had been found that Martelli had access to secrets or was passing them to a foreign power." To Angleton and Papich, as to Wright, the Martelli case seemed clearly of the "throwaway variety," as if designed to build up the credibility of the source at little real cost to Soviet operations.

The very nature of Fedora's approach to the FBI caused suspicion. "I got turned off on Fedora right from the beginning," Papich said. "If you're doing something, and you've been trained in such-and-such a way, overall, you're going to try to adhere to orthodox principles. In football, for instance, you're going to punt on fourth down, for the most part. And in espionage, you're not just going to stroll into the enemy camp in broad daylight and volunteer. But what the hell did Fedora do? He walked into our goddamn office in New York! Right on 72nd Street, not too far away from the Soviet consulate. And you don't do that if you're going to defect, knowing that it's surveilled by your own people. If you do it that way, and you're a bona-fide agent, you're going to get your head chopped off."

But when Papich made that case to Don Moore, the Bureau's Soviet CI chief, he got nowhere. "Sam, maybe just walking in one day was the best way of doing it, because it's what the Soviets would least expect," Papich would recall Moore as saying. "He knew just where to go, which floor. He had confidence he wasn't going to get burned, he had confidence he wasn't being tailed by his own people—all that traffic and whatnot in New York, who the hell was going to see him going into the field office? That's not the way we would do it, but he did it that way, and people don't always adhere to orthodox principles. Sometimes you're not going to punt on fourth down. Sonny Jurgensen sometimes didn't; sometimes he'd throw a pass. Well, the same thing can happen in counterintelligence."

THOUGH GOLITSYN WAS beginning to widen their long-standing philosophical split, FBI and CIA did manage to team up at the field level in a number of cases during the early 1960s. Good cooperation did exist alongside strong disagreement. In some areas, Papich effected liaison so smoothly that the net effect was a sort of "golden days" during the Kennedy period, which obscured the deeper conflicts already being formed over molehunts, deception theory, and even assassination.

In general, liaison was most effective when practical or case-oriented, at least from the FBI's point of view. In 1961, for instance, before CIA's new Moscow Station Chief Paul Garbler was dispatched to the USSR, Angleton reportedly gave him a number of cases developed with Papich. "I've been working with the FBI," Angleton told Garbler at a goodbye party at William Harvey's house. "We've got a couple of cases where the source has returned to the Soviet Union and we want to maintain contact. I'll let you know the details tomorrow and you tell me if you can handle it." At some point, the Bureau had even been cut in on Colonel Oleg Penkovskiy, the GRU colonel who had been working for CIA for two years. In spring 1962, when it was believed that Penkovskiy might visit Washington, a complicated FBI-CIA watch was kept on all planes arriving from Europe. The agencies' instructions to Penkovskiy read, in part: "Go to the Washington monument approaching it on foot from Constitution Avenue and Fifteenth Street. Walk around the monument. You will see one of your friends. If he is holding a newspaper do not contact him. If he is not holding a newspaper follow him to a waiting car." But Penkovskiy was executed before he ever made it to the United States.

When clear security interests seemed at stake, Hoover did not mind acquiescing in certain of CIA's extralegal adventures. From February 21 to March 19, 1963, FBI-CIA cooperation in the Hunter mail-opening project was expanded to include correspondence with Latin America; the FBI provided CIA about 180 names for watch-listing. During this period, the two agencies also collaborated on a "black-bag job"—a burglary—of the French Embassy in Washington, D.C. This operation had the cooperation of Philippe de Vosjoli, the French Western Hemisphere intelligence chief, who remained inside the embassy after midnight and let the team in. The objective was apparently to see what material French intelligence agents in the U.S. might be passing to their superiors in Paris, some of whom Golitsyn and Vosjoli suspected were working for Moscow.

Cooperation likewise bloomed in Mexico City, where CIA's Station Chief David Atlee Phillips worked well with Clark Anderson, the FBI legal attaché, on the case of an American military traitor. A mole in the Cuban Embassy had given CIA a letter offering to reveal American military secrets. The letter provided a room and telephone number at a local hotel and asked for a private meeting. "Before assuming responsibility for the case [Anderson] wanted to be sure the man was an American," Phillips related. "He asked if I had an agent who could contact him under the guise of a Cuban intelligence officer responding to the message and find out more about the stranger's proposal. I had just such an agent, 'Enrique,' who spoke fluent English." The two agencies arranged for Enrique to meet the letter-writer in a Mexico City restaurant, with Phillips seated at the next table, not four feet away, listening. As Phillips reported the next day to Anderson, it turned out the novice spy was a middle-grade United States military officer who needed enough money to allow him to flee a hen-pecking wife. "I don't know how the case turned out," Phillips said, "but it must have been a surprise and a shock to the disloyal military man when, eventually, there was a knock on his door from the FBI."

Despite such teamwork, however, the Bureau still faced digs about being a bunch of flatfeet. "In the world of intelligence, FBI agents—that is, career FBI men who have been through the FBI Academy, as distinct from sub-agents who only work outside the Bureau—stand out just about like pink carnations in a vase of red roses," wrote former OPC officer James McCargar in a 1963 book published under the pseudonym Christopher Felix. "Perhaps the widespread comments on their heavy preference for gabardine have now led the Bureau's agents to change into less uniform garb. But experience tells me no one has been able to do anything about their expressionless faces and their transparent reticence. They are of a mold—not unlike the comic strips' Dick Tracy, who any fan knows only laughs once a year and can keep his counsel for as long as five years at a time, no matter how baffled his Chief becomes."

Such jibes were good-natured enough, returned in kind by Papich and others at the Bureau, and seen as part of the good macho shit-giving tradition that boys learn on playgrounds. Disputes about defectors remained theoretical and far from explosive, and there was some afterglow from the mutual respect Dulles had managed to establish with Hoover. In his own book, published the same year as McCargar's, the retired DCI saw interagency relations as a virtual continuum of rainbows, broken only by the blackness of misinformation.

"There are [certain] kinds of myths ... of the spiteful or backbiting sort, that one sometimes hears in more restricted and 'knowing' circles," Dulles wrote. "Since the FBI and the CIA work very closely in the field of counterintelligence, it was to be expected that rumors would come to life in some quarters that they were working against each other, or in competition, and that relations between them are not good. The facts of the matter are that relations between them are on a wholly satisfactory basis. Each agency passes to the other all information that belongs to its special province. There is no failure of coordination."

Dulles should have known better, even if he was merely engaging in PR. Liaison was generally good during 1963, but there had been plenty of bungles even during the latter years of Dulles' own tenure, and there were bigger problems looming. Even as Dulles wrote, a failure of coordination on the Cubela-Trafficante plots, and poor FBI-CIA coverage of Oswald in Mexico, had perhaps been factoring into the imminent death of President Kennedy. Soon, too, interagency infighting would preclude the truth about that tragic event from being fully known. Only then, as CIA and FBI struggled to reconcile conflicting views on the assassination, would the full importance of the defectors controversy, and the molehunt, begin to emerge.

CHAPTER TEN

SINISTER IMPLICATIONS

A CHILL MIST CAME off Lake Geneva on the evening of January 23, 1964, nine weeks after the assassination of President Kennedy. A CIA officer hung back in the shadows across from Cinéma ABC at 42 Rue Rhône, watching people buy tickets in the strong pool of light under the marquee for *Dr. Strangelove*. An electrified trolley rattled past, blocking his view for a moment, but then he saw his man. Casually and at the same moment, they walked toward each other. Amidst the jostle of entering and exiting patrons, a matchbook changed hands invisibly.

The KGB man was a full block away before he opened it and read the ballpoint: "20 Chemin François Lemann." After an hour of taxis and buses for countersurveillance, he met the CIA man at the safehouse.

They drank. The KGB officer got drunk. He offered "to come over."

An escape was plotted. On February 4, the KGB agent failed to turn up for lunch with the rest of the Soviet delegation in the dining room of the Palais des Nations. Most of the Soviets were flying that night to Moscow, so no one had noticed when he removed his things from the hotel on Avenue Wendt. By noon he was in the back seat of a sedan with tinted glass and diplomatic plates, disguised as a U.S. Army officer, smoking American cigarettes, wending through the Alps toward Germany.

The KGB defector's debriefing would soon assume an awesome significance, for he was America's only source of information on Lee Harvey Oswald's "lost years" in the USSR. Both FBI and CIA agreed that this man could answer the riddle of a possible Soviet role in President Kennedy's death. The fight would come over whether he spoke the truth.

FROM ITS INCEPTION, the official U.S. government investigation into JFK's death put politics, or policy, at a premium to fact. Obvious delinquencies and cover-ups would later lead conspiracy theorists to suspect government complicity in the assassination. In fact, what was covered up was indications of a communist role. On November 23, Helms' assistant, Thomas Karamessines, was put in a state of near-panic upon hearing that Mexican authorities were about to arrest and interrogate Silvia Duran, a Cuban consular official who had met with Oswald and, it later developed, had sex with him several times during his visit. As Karamessines later said, "CIA feared that the Cubans were responsible for the assassination, and that Duran might reveal this during an interrogation." That, in turn, might lead to an international crisis that could literally mean the end of the world. Faced with the absolute ultimate in "situation ethics," Karamessines sent a flash cable to Mexico Station: "Arrest of Silvia Duran is extremely serious matter. . . . Request you insure that her arrest is kept absolutely secret, that no information from her is published or leaked, that all such info is cabled to us." When U.S. Ambassador to Mexico Thomas Mann questioned Duran's insistence that her only contact with Oswald had been to process his visa request, Helms cabled Mexico Station chief David Atlee Phillips, warning that the ambassador must not go public with his fears. "There is distinct feeling here," Helms wrote, "that Ambassador is pushing this case too hard . . . and that we could well create flap with Cubans which could have serious repercussions."

The FBI, too, acted to obscure any possible communist connection. Within hours of the president's death, two key Kostikov-related documents—the October 18 cable from CIA, stating that Kostikov had met with Oswald, and a Hunter (mail-opening) report, indicating that Oswald had mentioned Kostikov in a November 9 note to the Soviet Embassy—

were removed from the Dallas office by order of Assistant Director William C. Sullivan. When special agent James Hosty was called to testify before the Warren Commission in 1964, he found that FBI files which he had intended to cite about the Kostikov connection were missing. Without those documents, he could not testify about their contents. When he returned from the hearings, the Kostikov documents had mysteriously appeared back in his file with a note attached: "Removed from Hosty's in-box on November 22." The withholding of that Kostikov information from the public had been ordered, Clarence Kelley later concluded after viewing the FBI assassination files, "because the White House seemingly considered the risk of a confrontation with the Soviet Union over the Kennedy assassination was too great."

It was just such a desire to avoid world war, in fact, that led to creation of the Warren Commission. After John McCone briefed Robert Kennedy and new president Lyndon Johnson about CIA's anti-Castro plots on November 24, both RFK and Johnson were haunted by suspicions that the president had been killed in retaliation for attempts on Castro's life. The next day, worried that evidence of Soviet-Cuban complicity "could lead us into a war that could cost forty million lives," Johnson directed that "speculation about Oswald's motivation should be cut off, and we should have some basis for rebutting the thought that this was a Communist conspiracy." Thus arose, on November 29, an official commission of inquiry under Chief Justice Earl Warren. "The President told me how serious the situation was," Warren recalled. "He said there had been wild rumors, and that there was the international situation to think of. . . . If the public became aroused against Castro and Khrushchev there might be war." Commission members were soon confronted by the same conspiracy conundrum: "If we find out it was the Russians," one commission lawyer wondered aloud during a staff meeting, "will it mean World War III?"

Even if Warren's commission had wanted to find a communist role, however, staff lawyers quickly realized that the FBI, which would end up doing most of the legwork, was unlikely to provide them with evidence that would lead down that avenue. The Bureau had already come under fire for failing to protect JFK. If it were to be shown that Hoover had failed to detect and thwart a foreign conspiracy, the FBI director might well lose his job. Commission members knew that Hoover would do whatever it took to shield the FBI from criticism; early on, the staff learned that the FBI had hidden the fact that agent James Hosty's name was in Oswald's address book (Marina had written it there after Hosty visited her house, a few weeks before the assassination, to ask about Oswald).

Hoover's duplicity on that matter, and more sociological factors, soon led to a subtle bias at the commission toward the Agency and against the

Bureau. Commission lawyers admired their sophisticated CIA contacts, many from the same Ivy League schools they had attended. FBI men, by contrast, seemed plodding. CIA analysts did not dissuade commission members of that opinion. They, too, felt that the FBI had been derelict in its handling of Oswald

The Bureau, for its part, was not entirely happy with the cooperation it was getting from CIA. After November 23, when the Agency told the FBI that Kostikov was "an identified KGB officer" associated with the group "responsible for sabotage and assassination," the Agency was under great pressure to explain why it hadn't earlier warned the FBI that Oswald might be dangerous. "We do not participate in the actual work of protecting the president or planning his trips within the U.S.A.," one CIA report stated weakly, by way of rationalization.

FBI investigators could also have stood to know about the Castro schemes, and CIA officers fretted that the Bureau might make a connection between the Mafia plots and Kennedy's death. Sheffield Edwards met Johnny Rosselli after the Kennedy assassination, perhaps to discuss Rosselli's belief that Castro had "doubled" Trafficante's hit squad and turned it back against the president—but Edwards worried that the FBI was tailing them and spying on the meetings. Perhaps it was just such FBI surveillance that led Papich to query CIA in January 1964 whether they were plotting to kill the Cuban leader. The official answer, as Papich recorded in a memo, was that "The Agency currently is not involved in any activity which includes plans to assassinate Castro." That information was passed to the two FBI section chiefs working the JFK assassination, and to the Bureau supervisors responsible for anti-Castro activities, who got the misleading impression that CIA had never conspired to kill Castro. Papich, being a good soldier, revealed nothing of his knowledge of the earlier CIA plots, which he (and those few others at the FBI who knew about them) believed had only reached the "discussion stage." The Bureau's expert on Cuban matters was never informed of the CIA-Mafia schemes, or of Castro's September 7 retaliation threat—which seemed to the FBI expert, when he learned of it years later, "a pointed signal."

The Bureau's bitterness only deepened, moreover, as it shared postassassination leads with CIA, but felt it got little in return. For instance, on November 23, according to Bureau documents, the FBI briefed a "Mr. George Bush of the Central Intelligence Agency" on matters relating to the assassination. Although he denied it, there would later be speculation that "George Bush" was the future president, who was at the time managing a Texas-based offshore-oil firm. That position might have put him in contact with George DeMohrenschildt, a Texas-based petroleum engineer who specialized in scouting offshore sites. DeMohrenschildt, a Russian émigré investigated by the FBI for alleged communist affiliations, had been Oswald's closest Dallas contact before the assassination.

But even as the FBI shared its information with CIA's George Bush, whoever he was, yet another Agency failure to warn the FBI of imminent danger was about to obstruct permanently any probe into a possible conspiracy. Within twenty-four hours of the president's death, CIA analysts prepared a memorandum covering the facts they knew at the time. As James Johnston, staff lawyer for a later congressional reinvestigation of the Dallas tragedy, described the memo's contents: "They [CIA] knew that Oswald had once defected to the Soviet Union. They knew that he made a trip to Mexico City two months before the assassination and talked to Soviet Vice Consul Kostikov about a visa. And they believed that Kostikov was a KGB assassination and sabotage expert. From this, their memorandum argued, there was reason enough to believe that Oswald was part of a foreign plot. If this were true, CIA analysts predicted, then Oswald himself might be killed before he could talk."

The gist of the memorandum, according to Johnston, was to be passed through CIA liaison to the FBI—with the warning that Oswald could be in danger. "Unfortunately, relations between the two agencies were strained, and liaison was awkward," Johnston later lamented. Oswald, while in police custody, was killed by Dallas nightclub owner Jack Ruby on November 24, before the FBI received the message.

ON NOVEMBER 26, 1963, perhaps out of anger over CIA's failure to warn the FBI about Oswald's safety, President Johnson gave the FBI the lead responsibility for investigating JFK's death. By some accounts, the Agency initially welcomed playing second fiddle, because it wanted its own efforts to be as independent as possible. But within a day of Johnson's decision, the FBI's expanded duties seemed to be having just the reverse effect. CIA's Mexico City station refused to cooperate with a Bureau team that tried to wrest away its list of informants, and on November 27 FBI legat Clark Anderson cabled headquarters to complain that, according to the CIA people in Mexico City, only the Agency had "jurisdiction in getting investigative results abroad." An FBI supervisor was sent down from Washington to try to clear up the dispute. CIA Station Chief David Phillips reluctantly agreed to let the Bureau run the show. But it was not long before a special Warren Commission delegation had to travel to Mexico to handle problems of coordination, especially in the area of possible Cuban involvement.

One difficulty was that the FBI, being a domestic law-enforcement agency, did not have enough foreign contacts to conduct a meaningful investigation. For instance, after a Mexican woman and her daughter claimed to have seen Oswald with two other gringos at a party at the Cuban Embassy, the FBI interviewed her twice but, having no way to confirm or deny the story, simply left it alone. Nor did the Bureau conduct any follow-up investigation to determine the identity of a "mystery passenger" who had reportedly departed Mexico City for Havana aboard a Cubana Airlines jet on November 22. The FBI similarly failed to follow up on information received by CIA headquarters from its Mexico Station on December 3, 1963, about the suspicious activities of Gilberto Lopez, a Cuban-American who left the U.S. for Cuba the day after the assassination. Lopez's itinerary was confirmed by several sources, including one who reported hearing, according to a March 20, 1964, memo to the director of CIA from Mexico Station, "that Gilberto Lopez, U.S. citizen, was involved in President Kennedy's assassination." The Lopez case was passed to the FBI, but, as a later CIA memo tersely recorded, "FBI furnished no further info on subject." Grilled years later by a Senate committee, the FBI agents handling the Oswald investigation could not account for their failure to pursue the Lopez lead.

Liaison did improve after Angleton's CI Staff took over CIA's assassination probe in early 1964. The move was ordered by Helms, he later said, because the CI Staff "had through the years the responsibility for carrying on liaison with the FBI, [and] was in a better position and used to dealing with the Bureau." That was only the official reason for the shift, however. Unofficially, Helms wanted to remove the Agency's Soviet Division, which Angleton believed was penetrated by the KGB, from any direct role in investigating possible KGB complicity in the president's death.

In most areas, Angleton had little difficulty coordinating with the Bureau. Shortly after assuming control of CIA's inquiry, for example, he contacted FBI Assistant Director Sullivan and said, "It would be well for both McCone and Hoover to be aware that the Commission might ask the same questions wondering whether they would get different replies from the heads of the two agencies." The CI chief therefore suggested that the heads of the two organizations rehearse their answers so as not to tell conflicting stories. Examples of possible questions and how they should be answered: "(1) Q. Was Oswald ever an agent of the CIA? A. No. (2) Q. Does the CIA have any credible evidence showing that a conspiracy existed to assassinate President Kennedy? A. No."

Despite Angleton's good relations with Sullivan and Papich, however, there was an inability to reconcile the larger, institutional difference in mind-sets. Told by Angleton staffer Birch O'Neal on November 27 that Kostikov's KGB role was known "on the basis of an analysis," Papich pressed: "Do you have anything more specific which would pinpoint him as being a member of that department?" O'Neal admitted the case was wholly deductive, but agreed to prepare a statement for Hoover, laying out the case. "Keep it right down, very brief and very simple," Papich reminded him. O'Neal conferred with a CIA colleague, probably someone in Raymond Rocca's CI-research section, who indicated his "firm belief" that Kostikov was a KGB assassinations specialist and agreed to outline CIA analysis of the point. But it was to be four years before the FBI finally accepted, on the basis of other, nonanalytical CIA reporting, that Kostikov was a KGB assassinations man. That suspension of belief allowed the Bureau considerably more freedom to assure a suspicious public that Oswald had been a lone loony.

That conclusion, reached officially by the FBI on December 9, 1963, had in fact colored the Bureau's investigation from the start. As Mexico City legat Anderson later said, he proceeded at all times under the "impression," conveyed to him by Bureau headquarters, that Oswald was the sole assassin and not part of any conspiracy. He therefore "tried to stress," to the skeptical ambassador and to his CIA contacts, "that every bit of information that we had developed in Washington, at Dallas, and elsewhere, indicated that this was a lone job." That conclusion was bolstered around the turn of the year, when the Bureau sent Jack and Morris Childs, two FBI moles working in the American Communist Party as part of an operation code-named Solo, to visit the Cuban Embassy. The Childses reported that Oswald had indeed discussed assassination with the Cubans, but that the offer had been turned down.

This report matched most FBI agents' intuitions. Neither the KGB nor its Cuban offshoot, the highly professional DGI, would have hired an unstable loser like Oswald, the Bureau's reasoning ran. Nor would Castro or Khrushchev have risked U.S. discovery and retaliation—such as an invasion of Cuba, or even world war—merely to replace a liberal like Kennedy with the more conservative Lyndon Johnson. Nor would speculation about a communist role serve either the country or the Bureau well. Therefore William Sullivan leaked, on what he later said were Hoover's orders, the news that "An exhaustive FBI report now nearly ready for the White House will indicate that Lee Harvey Oswald was the lone and unaided assassin of President Kennedy."

That story, which ran nationally on December 13, caused a direct clash between Hoover and McCone. After the Bureau's ability to conduct an "exhaustive" inquiry in three weeks was questioned by columnist Drew Pearson, Hoover suspected that McCone was leaking anti-Bureau information. According to a heavily redacted December 1963 FBI memo, "Relations with the CIA," which later turned up in the FBI's file on Pearson, Hoover was upset because "Information developed by Mr. DeLoach has indicated that John McCone, Director, CIA, has attacked the Bureau in a vicious and underhanded manner characterized with sheer dishonesty." There should be a "firm and forthright confrontation" with the CIA director, the FBI memo urged, to discourage any such future "attack against the Bureau." Hoover jotted "OK."

Papich went to McCone and told him, diplomatically but directly, of the FBI director's concerns. On December 16, McCone telephoned Hoover to appease him.

"I know the importance the President places on this investigation you are making," McCone said. "He asked me personally whether CIA was giving you full support. I said we were, but I just wanted to be sure that you felt so."

Hoover was soothed when McCone agreed the main responsibility for the investigation fell on the Bureau. If the Bureau said there was no foreign plot, CIA would play along—especially since that was the answer the White House wanted publicized.

While the public record was being censored, however, Angleton was considering more carefully, and secretly, the specter of a possible KGB plot. After an all-nighter at FBI headquarters, Papich had driven to Langley and was in Angleton's office by 10:30 a.m. on the day after the assassination, where the CI chief apprised him of certain "sinister implications." Angleton was bothered by Golitsyn's ominous 1961 warning about the KGB's plotting to kill a "Western political leader," by the mystery of Oswald's travels in the USSR, and by other unresolved questions. CIA had heard, for instance, that Kostikov had planned in advance to leave Mexico on November 22, and that a Cubana Airlines flight to Havana was delayed for six hours on the tarmac in Mexico City on the night of the assassination, awaiting an unidentified passenger. The man had finally arrived at the airport in a twin-engine aircraft, then failed to go through Customs, where he would have needed to identify himself by displaying a passport. The Cubana plane took off and the mysterious passenger rode in the cockpit to Havana, precluding any identification by the passengers. Mexican surveillance soon established that Kostikov had remained in Mexico City, but Angleton still wondered who the passenger had been, why he flew to Cuba on the day the president died, and why he had taken such pains to conceal his identity.

Similar questions swirled around Gilberto Lopez, the Cuban-American who, by some reports to CIA, had been involved in Kennedy's death, and whose actions the FBI inexplicably failed to probe. Lopez had lived in Tampa, which was Santos Trafficante's base of operations, and he had visited Cuba for several weeks during May 1962, precisely when Trafficante had claimed to be sending his agents into Cuba to poison Castro.

Lopez was active in the Fair Play for Cuba Committee, whose leaflets Oswald had distributed, and his wife and others characterized Lopez as pro-Castro. It was also known that Lopez had a brother in the Cuban military who was studying in the Soviet Union. On November 17, 1963, the day President Kennedy's Dallas limousine route was announced, Lopez was at a get-together of the Tampa Chapter of the Fair Play for Cuba Committee, where color slides of Cuba were shown. CIA knew from several informants that Lopez had been at the residence for some time waiting for an important telephone call—the "go ahead order" for him to leave the United States. Lopez obtained a Mexican tourist card at the Honorary Consulate of Mexico in Tampa on November 20. Then he had departed for Texas. What he did there was not known. At twelve noon on the day after the assassination, according to a CIA source, "Lopez entered Mexico on foot from Laredo, Texas . . . and proceeded by bus to Mexico [City,] where he entered Cuban Embassy. On 27 Nov he left Embassy for Cuba on Cubana flight 465 and was the only passenger allowed on the plane." Thereafter, Lopez was reportedly not working in Cuba but spent most of his time playing dominoes—strange and luxurious treatment, indeed, for a purported dissident who had once defected to Cuba's main enemy.

Also pointing to a possible Cuban role were CIA phone taps on November 26. On that morning, Cuban figurehead President Osvaldo Dorticos, in Havana, telephoned his ambassador in Mexico City, Joaquín Hernández Armas, to inquire whether Silvia Duran, the Cuban Embassy employee who had spent time with Oswald during his visit, had been asked anything about "money" by the Mexican authorities. Armas said she had not been, but in closing the phone call, the CIA report said, "Dorticos again asked if Duran had been questioned about 'money.' Hernandez said no." Nonetheless, Mann, the U.S. ambassador, told Washington he believed "that Dorticos' preoccupation with the money angle of interrogation of Silvia Duran" corroborated "the strong possibility that a down payment was made to Oswald in the Cuban Embassy here, presumably with promise of a subsequent payment after assassination," and that the purpose of Oswald's journey to Mexico had been to receive that payment and to "set up get away route." Although CIA intercepted another phone call between Dorticos and Hernández Armas the following day, in which the Cuban president said his question about money referred to another matter, Angleton wondered whether the Cubans hadn't perhaps discovered—from a penetration of CIA?—that the previous day's conversation was tapped, and had staged a corrective or clarifying call especially for CIA's hearing.

In any case, Angleton believed that Oswald's trip to Mexico City would certainly have been orthodox behavior if he were affiliated with some foreign intelligence service, such as the Soviet KGB or Cuban DGI. Agents periodically left their home countries to meet their handlers in safehouses, and Oswald's six days in Mexico City got him out of the FBI's reach. Other mysterious aspects of Oswald's odd character, which the FBI and the Warren Commission casually dismissed, seemed perfectly explicable to Angleton as espionage "tradecraft." Oswald used aliases and post-office boxes, and lived apart from his family. His possessions had been found to include a book which had certain letters cut out, giving the impression that this might have formed the base or key for a cipher system. It was also noted that letters from Oswald to his mother regarding his desire to return to the United States seemed dictated, since they contained none of his usual grammatical errors, and used legal language with which he could not have been familiar. He was in communication with foreign-linked organizations such as the Fair Play for Cuba Committee, which agents often used to relay innocent-sounding messages. After the assassination, he fled to a movie theater, prompting KGB defector Pyotr Deriabin to observe in a memo to CIA: "Certainly, we know the KGB's penchant for using theaters for meeting places." The Russian émigré DeMohrenschildt had found him a job briefly in 1962 at Jaggars-Stonewall, a Dallas photographics firm which prepared U.S. intelligence maps based on U-2 photographs; co-workers said he had indicated a detailed knowledge of microdots. Also suspicious was Oswald's counterfeiting of identity documents. The counterfeits were inferior by CIA standards, but how and why had Oswald learned to make them?

One possibility, taken seriously by Angleton and many others at CIA, was that Oswald had learned his tradecraft in Russia. A CIA report of the period asserted flatly that both Oswald and his Soviet-born wife, Marina, had been recruited by the KGB, and noted that Oswald, while living in the Soviet Union, had obtained a hunting license but never went hunting. "This would have been a good method for the KGB to meet and train him," the report said. CIA analysts speculated that the Soviets were running a terrorist training camp in Minsk, where Oswald had lived, and considered whether he might not have been "programmed" or brainwashed by Soviet mind-control specialists using LSD. Other questions hung unanswered: Why had Oswald maintained contact with the Soviet Embassy in Washington? What was the purpose of his contacts with Kostikov? Had he made other contacts with Kostikov, which CIA didn't know about? Oswald had refused a lie-detector examination on those matters. That he was murdered before he could be interrogated in detail, as CIA analysts had warned, only fueled suspicion.

But what would the Soviets possibly gain from Kennedy's death that would be worth the risk of U.S. retaliation? From a pragmatic Western perspective, there seemed little profit indeed, but Angleton thought about the problem with more subtlety. First of all, the nuclear age precluded any massive U.S. retaliation—as Johnson's craven cover-ups of all possible communist connections were already demonstrating. Second, if the Soviets had truly penetrated the Soviet Division at CIA, as Angleton believed, the KGB might even have hoped to steer U.S. investigation of the crime. As for the Soviet motive: Out was Kennedy, a charismatic leader who could "sell" a socially conscious anticommunism in the Third World and even to Western liberals. In was Johnson, who would only "heighten the contradictions" between East and West and therefore hasten (by Leninist dialectical reasoning) the ultimate collapse of late capitalism.

Angleton also took seriously the observations marshaled in a November 27 memo by defector Deriabin, who cited the Kennedy administration's opposition to long-term credits to the Soviets, which he said were vital to survival of the USSR. Johnson, by contrast, came from an agricultural state and had always supported grain sales to Russia. Moreover, Western pressure on the USSR "would automatically ease up" if the KGB murdered the president. As evidence, Deriabin noted a "conciliatory telegram" by a frightened and disoriented Lyndon Johnson to Khrushchev. A more amenable America would "strengthen Khrushchev's hand" at a time when the Soviet leader was under intensifying internal pressures because of mismanagement of the 1963 harvest and disputes with China. Kennedy's death, as Deriabin put it, thus "effectively diverts the Soviets' attention from their internal problems. It directly affects Khrushchev's longevity." Finally, Deriabin ventured that "the death of President Kennedy, whether a planned operation or not, will serve the most obvious purpose of providing proof of the power and omniscience of the KGB." Much later, Angleton would obliquely compare the Soviets' probable motivation to a famous scene in Mario Puzo's novel *The Godfather*, in which a Mafia chieftain puts a horse's head into the bed of a stubborn film producer, in order to demonstrate "pure power."

Although Angleton's critics would later excoriate him for entertaining what seemed paranoid theories, it was his job as CI chief to consider every possibility. "In my conversations with Jim, he never excluded that maybe we were missing something on Soviet involvement," Papich recalled. "He and I had a lot of discussions on that. As far as we knew, Oswald acted alone. But Jim felt that we couldn't be *sure* until we had the full story on Oswald's possible links to the KGB. That meant getting the full story on his stay in Russia."

It also meant a fight with the FBI over whether that story could be believed, once it was obtained from a new Soviet defector—a man who said he could resolve, fully and finally, all questions about whether Oswald had been acting as a KGB agent when he killed President Kennedy.

ON FEBRUARY 4, 1964, Yuri Nosenko was met at Geneva's ABC Cinéma by Pete Bagley, the CIA officer who had debriefed him two years earlier. Bagley still believed that Nosenko was a provocateur, sent in part to discredit Golitsyn. But, with Angleton's blessing, Bagley was to continue playing along, to see what the Soviets' game might be. Trouble began, though, as they sat down in the safehouse.

"I'm not going home," Nosenko said.

Bagley was stunned. In 1962, Nosenko had made a big point of saying he would never defect, because he loved his family and country too much.

"Why do you want to defect?" Bagley asked. "Didn't you tell us you never would?"

The Soviet could offer only a vague answer. "Well, I think the KGB may suspect me. I have decided to make a new life."

"How about your family?"

Nosenko changed the subject to Lee Harvey Oswald. He could speak definitively about his government's relations with the alleged assassin, Nosenko said, because he had personally overseen Oswald's KGB file. Nosenko insisted, according to a Top Secret CIA summary, that "the KGB was frightened of Oswald" and would "absolutely not" have attempted to recruit him. "The thrust of [Nosenko's] account was that neither Oswald nor his wife had at any time been of any interest whatsoever to Soviet authorities, that there had not ever been thought given to recruiting either of them as agents and that, in fact, the Soviets were glad to get rid of them both."

Bagley helped Nosenko escape from Geneva, and rode with him through Switzerland to Germany. But the defector had not gone beyond a U.S. Army base in Frankfurt before Bagley's boss, Soviet Division chief David Murphy, expressed renewed certainty that Nosenko was "a plant." Bagley agreed, and together they told Angleton their doubts about Nosenko's Oswald story. Although they could not irrefutably disprove it, because it did not contradict any data in CIA files, Nosenko's mere ability to tell the tale rested on a tripod of incredibles. Of the thousands of KGB officers throughout the world, CIA had secret relations with only one, after Golitsyn, yet he just happened to have participated directly in the Oswald case—not only once, but on three separate occasions: (1) when Oswald came to Russia in 1959; (2) when Oswald applied for a visa to return to Russia in 1963; and (3) when the Kremlin leadership caused a definitive review of the whole KGB file on Oswald after the assassination. That Nosenko was thus in a perfect position to testify to KGB innocence in JFK's death seemed to Bagley a result of such neatly aligned coincidence that one had to suspect deliberate planning.

Nor did Bagley or Murphy believe Nosenko's claim that the KGB would not have at least talked to Oswald. The KGB, as a matter of procedure, didn't ignore foreigners, period, and certainly not a U.S. Marine like Oswald, who had worked at an operational base for CIA's U-2 spyplanes in Atsugi, Japan. Deriabin told Murphy that the KGB "would be like a pool of piranhas [on such] an American swimming into their sea."

But why would Nosenko, or the KGB, lie about Oswald's Soviet links? Was it because they had conspired to kill the president? If so, and if the KGB had indeed dispatched Nosenko to cover up the plot, how could they have tailored his Oswald story so neatly as to contradict nothing in CIA files? Was it because they had a secret helper inside CIA?

To Bagley, the implications were ugly. There were going to be doors he didn't want to open, corridors he wouldn't want to look down. But the case was there; it would not go away. The burden had fallen on him, and he would do his duty.

"DO WE KNOW ANYTHING about this?" Hoover scribbled on a news clipping which intimated that a new KGB defector, Yuri Nosenko, might have information about Oswald. It was February 11, 1964, and that very day Nosenko had arrived in the U.S. by Air Force jet and been spirited to a CIA safehouse in Virginia. Reading in a news clipping that "The defection to the United States of Yuri Nossenko [sic], Soviet secret police officer, is definitely a victory for our Central Intelligence Agency.... It's good to see the CIA win one," Hoover underlined "CIA," almost as if to complain: It should have been the FBI. "We are closely following CIA in its efforts to resolve the bona fides of subject's defection," a deputy assured Hoover, but CIA wasn't giving over much. Hoover scrawled boldly at the bottom of one memo: *Keep after it.*"

On February 13, the Agency provided a brief update on Nosenko's background and KGB career, but by month's end the Bureau had received nothing on what Nosenko might know about the president's apparent assassin. The FBI director therefore ordered his underlings: "We must press CIA to make Nosenko completely available to us."

CIA acceded. A team of FBI debriefers went to see Nosenko at a CIA safehouse on February 26 and again on March 3 and 4. Alekso Poptanich, Maurice Taylor, and Donald E. Walter, all of the Washington Field Office, questioned Nosenko for about two hours, mostly in English, employing

Russian only when Nosenko became confused. "Source was at ease and very cooperative during this session," the FBI director was informed in a Top Secret airtel. The FBI men liked Nosenko and instinctively trusted him. Whereas the earlier KGB defector Golitsyn had been a "son of a bitch" to the FBI, Nosenko was warm and friendly. Although they had denied Golitsyn access to any files, the FBI now shared Warren Commission documents with Nosenko. And although the Bureau had been offered custody of the defector, according to Bagley, "for as long as they wanted," the interrogators decided after only six hours with him that they had got the whole story on Oswald. "I accepted it at face value," Poptanich later said of Nosenko's information. "We had no reason not to believe [Nosenko]. You have to start with the basic premise that you accept the information, and then you go out and verify it or disprove it, and that is what we did with almost all the information we got from Nosenko." Since none of it could be disproved, Poptanich reasoned, it all must be true.

The FBI's final determination on that matter, however, would rest with headquarters, where the "Nosenko ticket" was held by Larry McWilliams. Mac didn't really have a problem with Nosenko's statement that the KGB was essentially uninterested in an American defector who, as it turned out, could have given them information pertaining to his work as a U-2 radar operator. The way he saw it, the Soviets had a good intelligence network, and all Oswald's information was dated, useless except for propaganda purposes. If Oswald was unstable and they couldn't control him, it made sense that they probably would never touch him. What was more, Mac learned that Fedora, the Bureau's KGB mole in New York, had confirmed Nosenko's rank and importance within the KGB, and had said that his defection caused a major crisis in Soviet intelligence. Fedora even confirmed Nosenko's allegation that he had received a telegram recalling him to the USSR on February 4, which had caused CIA to accept his defection without further delay. Nosenko's authenticity was seemingly confirmed, too, when he provided information about a Soviet scheme to filch secret documents from the U.S. Armed Forces Courier Center at Orly Airport, Paris. FBI suspicion focused on Robert Lee Johnson, an Army sergeant at Orly, who confessed to doing just what Nosenko said he had done. Johnson was convicted of espionage and sentenced to twenty-five years. Mac thought it inconceivable that the Soviets would sacrifice such a valuable agent just to establish Nosenko's bona fides.

But the basic reason for judging Nosenko to be truthful about Oswald was that his story accorded with what the Bureau already believed about the assassination. "The FBI does not perceive any significant evidence of foreign involvement in the assassination of President Kennedy," a Bureau memo concluded, based on Mac's analysis, "nor does the FBI perceive any credible evidence that Nosenko's defection was a Soviet ploy to mask Soviet governmental involvement in the assassination. *Therefore*, the FBI is satisfied that Nosenko reported the facts about Oswald as he knew them [emphasis added]."

When informed of this assessment, CIA officers felt that the Bureau's line of logic was exactly backward. Only if it was first determined that Nosenko reported facts as he knew them could the U.S. be sure that there was no "significant evidence of foreign involvement in the assassination of President Kennedy," and that Nosenko's defection was not "a Soviet ploy."

The ensuing interagency dispute over Nosenko's bona fides crystallized twenty years of difference over CIA philosophy. Angleton's pattern-recognition method, which found in the study of poetry a relevance to the detecting of strategic deceptions, was set squarely against Hoover's criminal-evidenciary approach. "It wasn't just tension," McWilliams later said. "It was a *raging dispute*. Some of the conferences that we had—I mean, they were damn near knock-down drag-out. We—Don Moore, Bill Branigan, and I—we would sit down around a table with people from the Agency and disagree like hell."

The CIA contingent consisted of Angleton and some people from his shop, along with the two top men in the Soviet Division, Bagley and Murphy, who took the lead in arguing against Nosenko. Murphy's involvement did not help CIA's case, for he was not especially beloved by the Bureau. "I don't know if I ever trusted Murphy," McWilliams said. "I just had a feeling."

Murphy began his assault on the FBI's position by noting that most of Nosenko's information was "cold." The Orly courier-vault operation, for instance, had been shut down by the Soviets a year before Nosenko's tip, because Sergeant Johnson had lost his access to the vault and was being publicly exposed by a neurotic wife.

The G-men countered with a roster of American citizens identified by Nosenko as subjects of KGB interest, and a number of Soviet diplomats named by him as KGB officers. Under no circumstances, the FBI agents argued, would the Soviets "blow" such sensitive information merely to establish a disinformation agent's bona fides.

Bagley responded by alleging that Nosenko had lied to the FBI. As proof he cited Nosenko's claim that, after judging Oswald to be "abnormal," he (Nosenko) had instructed a fellow KGB man in the Tourist Department, one "Krupnov," to advise Oswald to leave the USSR at the expiration of his visa. CIA already knew, from information provided by Golitsyn, that Krupnov was not in the KGB's Tourist Department at this time. Nosenko himself had admitted this to CIA, but could not account for the error. He had also conceded, in the time since he had talked to the FBI, that he had lied about receiving a telegram recalling him to Moscow on February 4. He said he made up the story so that CIA would take him. He even admitted lying about his rank. He was not Lieutenant Colonel Nosenko, merely a captain.

The FBI men were unmoved by those revelations. Mac later opined: "Bagley was a bright guy who thought wrong. They didn't have enough common sense over there at CIA, they didn't understand enough about the evaluation of a human being, like we had gathered through years of working with criminals. Any first-year FBI man finds out, when he cops a guy and he's trying to build himself up, he's going to lie like hell, with a lot of truth. And it's an FBI agent's responsibility to gradually find out the truth from the lie. CIA didn't understand that."

When McWilliams expressed himself to that effect, in much politer terms, Angleton stared him down from across the table. Maybe lying was natural, the CI chief said, but there was something decidedly artificial about the way a certain FBI source—the great Fedora—had confirmed Nosenko's false rank, his bogus recall telegram, even his incorrect story about Krupnov. "There was a concern that Fedora corroborated information from Nosenko that later proved to be false, and that this might somehow taint the value of Fedora, too," Angleton's deputy Scott Miler recalled. "That was our position. The FBI disagreed. They said, 'No,' except for Papich and a few people, like Sullivan, who agreed that it was goddamned suspicious. They never really addressed the issue of the telegram that Fedora had reported on. They just kind of walked away from that."

Instead, the Bureau tried to knock out the prop on which CIA's suspicions of Nosenko and Fedora ultimately rested—viz., Anatoliy Golitsyn. True, FBI agents argued, Nosenko had provided much information that overlapped Golitsyn's. But maybe this just meant that they had access to the same information in Moscow.

"The KGB is more compartmented than that," Murphy argued.

"How do we know that?" Mac asked.

"Golitsyn told us," Murphy said.

They were back again to the source of the problem. "CIA never seemed to comprehend that Golitsyn wasn't a walking genius," Mac recalled. "This overall buying of Golitsyn perverted their entire thinking, and did cause trouble on whether we should accept or reject Nosenko."

The conferences resolved nothing. But CIA didn't give up.

"All this stuff would come over on Nosenko, 'proving' he was a fake— at that time, we wouldn't even reply to it," Mac said. "None of that god-damned stuff that they sent over convinced us that he wasn't real. The

FBI never bought Nosenko being a plant, never bought it from the word go. We just didn't accept it."

The crisis deepened as Bagley pressured the Bureau to reinterview Nosenko about Oswald. He griped to Papich that the two FBI reports he had read left "many important questions unanswered," and inspired "no confidence in the FBI's ability to cover the Soviet phase." He asked his Soviet Russia staff to prepare forty-four additional questions for the G-men to put to the defector. How had the KGB evaluated Oswald's "operational potential"? Was his hotel room bugged? If so, was it a routine bug, or was it installed especially for Oswald? What "take" was there, if any? Was Oswald physically surveilled? His mail monitored? Precisely when and by whom was it decided that the KGB had no interest in the former spyplane-radar operator? Who, exactly, found Oswald bleeding in his hotel room after his apparent suicide attempt? To what hospital was Oswald taken? Why was the U.S. Embassy not informed?

Bagley also desired to know more about Marina Oswald. How did Lee Harvey meet his wife? What were the KGB sources on her? How was it that she was "stupid and not educated" and at the same time a graduate pharmacist? How could Nosenko explain the fact that Marina claimed not to know who her father was and bore her mother's surname, thus indicating that she was born out of wedlock, yet also had the patronymic "Nikolayevna" ("Nikolai's daughter"), indicating that her father was known? On what grounds did the KGB consider Marina "anti-Soviet" at the time she wished to leave the USSR with Oswald—and why did these factors not prevent her from being promoted in her job after her marriage? How did it happen that there were so few difficulties in the way of Marina's marriage to a foreigner and departure from the country with him, when similar situations in the past usually resulted in prolonged and often unsuccessful negotiations with the Soviet government?

"We passed [those questions] to the CI Staff, which was our channel and liaison to the Bureau," Bagley related. "The questions were hand carried over to the FBI for the approval Hoover required. There was a big back and forth about whether they would or wouldn't service these questions in their dealings with Nosenko." On March 6, Angleton told Bagley that his questions "would not be asked."

Bagley was furious. He called up Papich and complained that it would not be possible to complete his job in the Oswald case if he could not get the pertinent information.

Papich calmly replied that in Director Hoover's view, assessing Oswald's stay in Russia was not CIA's "job" to complete, but the FBI's.

Bagley tried a different tack. If Hoover would not allow the FBI to reinterrogate Nosenko on Oswald, could CIA at least provide some questions for the Bureau to put to Marina? CIA had no access to the woman, and had never interrogated her about her husband and compared it with what Nosenko was giving them. Papich agreed to review CIA questions for Marina, but reminded Bagley not to include any hint that FBI would report back to the Agency. So Bagley passed along questions for Marina, as suggestions, hoping that the FBI might relay the answers back to CIA.

The answers never came. Years later, Bagley was still bitter, because "none of our questions were, I gather, ever serviced by the Bureau." Of course, CIA could have put its Oswald questions to Nosenko directly; he was, after all, in CIA custody. But custody did not amount to jurisdiction. CIA technically could not bring Nosenko's Oswald information to bear on the assassination inquiry. That was the FBI's turf, and what CIA wanted more than anything was for the G-men to develop their own reasons for doubting the defector. "I think we were constrained, that the Bureau felt very strongly it was their responsibility," Bagley explained. "Believe me, we were extremely conscious of this, and if my memory is right, I believe we were enjoined at the time not to question him."

Some CIA officers began to wonder whether there might be more to Hoover's territorialism than the usual jurisdictional jealousy. Perhaps the FBI had been biased on the Nosenko question by Hoover's need to protect the Bureau from censure for failing to prevent a possible foreign plot. "Any bureaucracy has vested interests, and acceptance of Nosenko's information tended to excuse the FBI for its failure to have Oswald under surveillance," Angleton's man Miler believed. "It was in the best interests of the FBI to accept Nosenko's story."

When Angleton himself candidly conveyed such doubts to Papich, during late-night sessions in the greenhouse, the FBI man begged to differ. If Hoover had in any way felt that the Soviets or Cubans were involved, he wasn't going to leave himself vulnerable by not pursuing those angles. Besides, the boss wasn't out in the field chasing down those leads himself, but merely reading what was coming to him from the fellows in the field and at the desks. They did present to him that there was no evidence of foreign involvement, and he bought that view. Nor was he familiar enough with the Nosenko case to have forced through his own views on it. He had followed it in the beginning, but recently he had inked documents with comments like, "How long have we had the Nosenko case? Memo should indicate just who Nosenko is."

On March 6, however, Hoover was familiar enough with Nosenko's information to unilaterally pass it to the Warren Commission. "In the event you desire to have Nosenko appear," he coaxed, "it is suggested that you try to make arrangements with the Central Intelligence Agency, which Agency has custody of Nosenko." This unsolicited offer caused considerable excitement at the commission. That same day, Warren staffer Lee J. Rankin wrote Helms to say that, because of "a report from the Federal Bureau of Investigation . . . it appears to us that Nosenko's defection, whether or not it is authentic, is of very great interest." Commission staffers wanted to discuss the matter with Helms as soon as possible.

Helms came to see them in Rankin's office at Justice on March 12. He brought along Angleton's research chief, Ray Rocca, as well as Dave Murphy, whose Soviet Bloc Division had formal charge of Nosenko. Helms tried to explain that, though the FBI might be in a position to report Nosenko's information to the commission, only CIA was in a position to judge whether Nosenko, and his information, were bona fide. At the moment, CIA had serious reservations about his authenticity, but Helms recommended that the commission "await further developments."

The commission did not want to wait. They were quite worried, in fact, that the President's assassin might have had intelligence connections, and began to complain about "the inability of any of the governmental agencies to fill in the very large gaps still existing in Lee Harvey Oswald's visit to Mexico." Rocca's explanation for the Agency's performance was that CIA's contribution was limited to "the FBI's investigation on this point." For the same reason, CIA was "limited in its possibility of assisting" any assessment of "information from an unspecified source that [Jack] Ruby was in Havana in 1963 under a Czech passport."

Rankin frowned. Did that mean that the FBI and CIA were failing to cooperate?

Helms replied that there were always "understandable human problems in conducting any liaison on any subject," but that "by and large the procedures for dealing with other agencies" were "effective."

On that, the meeting ended, but by June 24, commission members were pressing McCone for a "final answer" on whether Nosenko's Oswald story should be believed. This request tripped wires at Langley.

"Director McCone asked me to go down and see Chief Justice Warren and explain that CIA and FBI disagreed about Nosenko," Helms recalled. "We met privately in a room in Commission Headquarters and I gave the reasons why we couldn't establish Nosenko's bona fides." Helms, duly respectful in the presence of the chief justice, spoke softly but to the point. Some of Nosenko's information, he said, contradicted what CIA had from other sources. Nosenko alleged, for instance, that there were no Soviet regulations which would have prevented Oswald from traveling from Minsk to Moscow without first obtaining permission to do so. But both CIA and the State Department knew that such regulations existed. CIA was not even able to satisfy itself that Nosenko had ever supervised Oswald's file, and there were many inconsistencies in his story, which, even if it had been consistent, would have made no sense to CIA. Helms was sorry, but "whatever the FBI" had told the Warren Commission about Nosenko's Oswald information, Justice Warren should consider the fact that CIA could not vouch for Nosenko's claim that Oswald had "no KGB contacts." Therefore, such information should not become part of the Warren Commission record.

The chief justice nodded in seeming assent, but his commission could not decide whether to side with CIA or FBI until July 24, when a full complement of its members, including former DCI Dulles, heard a CIA delegation frame the problem in truly chilling terms. "Nosenko is a KGB plant," Bagley pronounced, while Helms and Murphy looked on, "and may be publicly exposed as such some time after the appearance of the Commission's report. Once Nosenko is exposed as a KGB plant, there will arise the danger that his information will be mirror-read by the press and public, leading to conclusions that the USSR did direct the assassination."

That was enough to settle the question. The commission had been founded for no other reason than to avert rumors which might cost "forty million lives," and later that afternoon decided it would be "undesirable to include any Nosenko information" in its report. The defector's FBI debriefings would remain classified in commission files.

Hoover was not happy about that. "When the Warren people sided with us, it cut across Mr. Hoover's assertion that the Russians had had nothing to do with the assassination," Helms said. "So there was some irritation in the Bureau about it."

THOUGH CIA HAD "WON," for the moment, on Nosenko, there remained the problem of what to do with him. While Nosenko was on a vacation in Hawaii with CIA officers, Helms pondered the options. If the Soviet Division was indeed penetrated by the KGB, it would be important to isolate Nosenko physically from that division, to keep the Soviets from getting feedback on his interrogation, as well as to keep him from updating his story (as, Angleton later related, he already seemed to have some means of doing). It would also be necessary to keep Nosenko away from alcohol, since he had a habit of getting in bar fights, and from reporters, who were pressing for details about the defector who had only weeks earlier been in the headlines. Too, the agents of KGB Department 13 might try to kill Nosenko, even if he was a plant, since that might serve to establish his authenticity in CIA's minds. Some form of incarceration was therefore going to be required, at least for a time.

Helms consulted the Soviet Division and the CI Staff about what form the incarceration should take. Bagley and Murphy argued that conditions should be "Spartan" and should coincide with "hostile interrogation." Nosenko was bogus, but they needed to confront him, and "break" him on collateral information. Angleton objected, however. He wanted to "play" Nosenko like a prize trout, and thought that the key to elicitation was to keep the subject feeling secure. Helms opted for the Soviet Division's hostile approach, since it promised a quicker answer to what could be an embarrassing problem for the Agency. The Justice Department approved Nosenko's being jailed on CIA property, and Nosenko returned from Hawaiian fun and sun to be "fluttered" by a CIA polygrapher. Questions were yelled at him, and he failed the exam. He was installed in a small cell, where two debriefers played bad-cop, worse-cop. They caught him in a flat lie when he denied knowledge of an operation involving an American, of which CIA had a record—and which Nosenko had claimed to know about in a 1962 interview taped by Bagley.

"The transcript must be wrong," Nosenko said.

His questioners brought in a tape recorder.

"You don't remember this operation? Here is your voice."

Nosenko heard himself giving details of the operation.

"I was drunk," Nosenko said. But this failed to explain how he could have spoken correctly about an operation while drunk yet known nothing about it while sober.

Nosenko was next shown a travel warrant he had given Bagley in Geneva, back in 1962, as proof of his KGB identity. It was made out to "Lieutenant Colonel" Yuri Nosenko. But Nosenko had already admitted to lying about his rank; he was merely a captain. Why, then, had the KGB made out a travel warrant with this false information?

Nosenko admitted that he "looked bad," even to himself, but as spring warmed to summer, Nosenko stuck to his story, contributing nothing new except to complain about the heat in the attic. A blower was installed to keep the air moving, and as it became evident that the defector was not going to crack anytime soon, CIA would have to find more suitable quarters for a longer-term incarceration. It was therefore decided to intern Nosenko in a small cell at CIA's training facility at Camp Peary, Virginia, in the same malarial lowland between the James and York rivers where America's first English settlers had failed to survive in 1607. Nosenko's new home was twelve by twelve feet, windowless, with one naked sixty-watt bulb above a narrow steel bed. The walls, floor, and ceiling were formed of steel-reinforced concrete, to prevent tunneling. The toilet flushed, but it was right there in the open. There was an adjoining interrogation room, and out back an exercise yard, surrounded by a chain-link fence topped with barbed wire. Helms came out to see the place, which he judged to be satisfactory.

Nosenko was put in. He was under twenty-four-hour visual surveillance through the door. His diet was kept bland, and he could not brush his teeth. He was allowed no reading material, and his guards were provided with earphones so that he could not overhear their TV. To pass the time, Nosenko tried to make a tiny chess set from blanket threads, but each time it was noticed and taken away. He began talking to himself, and sometimes, lying on his bed at night, he would toss aside his blankets and shout about things flickering against the ceiling. At other times, he would just sit along the bed's edge, clasping the yellow soles of his feet in the palms of his hands, screaming: "Let me talk to the FBI!"

CHAPTER ELEVEN

MOLEHUNT

IN SEPTEMBER 1964, the Warren Commission formally found that Oswald was the lone assassin of President Kennedy, but Angleton's secret probe continued throughout the decade. "The Warren Commission report should have left a wider window for [the] contingency . . . that there was Soviet and/or Cuban (KGB and/or DGI) connection with Oswald," a Top Secret CIA review later related. "That, indeed, was the opinion at the working level, particularly in the counterintelligence component in the CIA." Like the idea that Nosenko was bogus, such suspicions were inseparable from Golitsyn's allegations about moles, for, if Department 13 had in fact conspired to kill the president, they would have surely wanted to control the investigation afterward. As it happened, routine procedure dictated that CIA's Soviet Division be responsible for determining whether there was any KGB connection—but this was the very division which Angleton suspected was infiltrated by the KGB. And if the Soviets had indeed penetrated the Soviet Division and received feedback from it, that would, in turn, explain how it could have tailored for Nosenko a perfectly uncheckable "legend" for Oswald's Soviet years. Thus, part of the reason Angleton's CI shop had taken over the Kennedy probe in December 1963 was a fear of manipulation by Soviet moles.

But then Nosenko had arrived, only one month later, which put the Soviet Division right back in the middle of things. Had the KGB determined to send him only after their moles' access to the assassination probe was cut off, and the KGB's ability to manipulate it ended? Nosenko's timely arrival with a manipulative message was one more whorl that fit the general pattern, and one more reason for Angleton to pursue Golitsyn's penetration leads with renewed vigor. As coming years were to show, however, the hunt for moles could only succeed if FBI and CIA played on the same team to find them.

To DIRECT THE SEARCH for penetrations, Angleton had created a Special Investigations Group (SIG) eventually headed by Newton Scott Miler. A husky man with the unflappable face of a big-league baseball umpire, Miler had been chief of station in Ethiopia before joining Angleton's CI Staff. Managing the molehunt on a daily basis was a thankless job, likely to take years and yet never be resolved unless a confession was gained. All the while, Miler would be doing business on a daily basis with some of the people he was investigating, yet he had to deal with them as if nothing were wrong. "The whole idea was to avoid speculation or rumors to avoid creating a general climate of suspicion," Miler would say. "All we had was an allegation. That didn't make the guy guilty. It didn't make him innocent. But there had to be an investigation. And at some point, procedure usually required that this be done in conjunction with the FBI."

Alas, sharing a case with the Bureau could sometimes work against CIA's desire to keep things hushed. From the Agency's standpoint, the best way to neutralize a spy was to ask for his cooperation, play him, use him as penetration or as a deception channel. But Miler knew that the Bureau's way of neutralizing a suspect was often to confront him, arrest him, "and really destroy him, in the sense that he was no longer useful."

So it had been in the case of Peter Karlow. One year of obvious surveillance, capped by a "hell week" of interrogation, was not CIA's way of doing things. Angletonian CI would have preferred to see Karlow transferred to an out-of-the-way station where CIA could quietly wait for him to make contact with the Soviets. Perhaps, after a time, CIA would obtain data exonerating him; or, if damning evidence was obtained, Karlow might be asked to become a double agent. But because the FBI had made Karlow aware of the suspicions against him and forced him out, none of that was possible. Notwithstanding the Bureau's later admission of error, CIA could probably never know for sure whether Karlow was a Soviet spy.

"The idea that the FBI wasn't doing its job, and wasn't capable of doing its job, was an attitude that permeated a lot of our search for penetrations, and caused some conflict between the FBI and the CIA," Miler later lamented.

It wasn't just that Hoover himself didn't understand counterintelligence, as even his own men acknowledged. It was the way his organization was made to reflect that ignorance. Because of the Bureau's lack of interest in historical research, Miler found it "awfully difficult, in what has become known as the 'molehunt,' to follow up anything that wasn't totally specific. We couldn't just go to the FBI and say, 'It has to do with this area, this kind of information, and in 1953 our suspect was here, in 1954 he was there. Go after it.' The FBI wasn't equipped to do that; they didn't have the base of knowledge to investigate penetrations. On a number of occasions, Bill Sullivan, without really explaining the whole situation to Hoover, tried to set up a research section, under Larry McWilliams, to study counterintelligence cases, and McWilliams would come over and meet with us. But when it came down to the nitty-gritty, and they needed somebody to be legal attaché, suddenly McWilliams was sent off to Copenhagen, and there's no research section anymore. When Sullivan tried to say, 'Look, boss, I need this research,' Hoover would just say, 'Nuh-uh, you don't. It's not part of your job, boy.' "

Because it lacked a sufficient system to search for patterns in the past, the Bureau's assistance was limited to legwork, to black-bag jobs or surveillance, in the present. But Hoover was even less enthusiastic about helping CIA with physical or technical surveillance than he was about building a CI database. Following a suspect twenty-four hours daily was labor-intensive, and FBI manpower was extremely limited. To service a CIA request, agents would have to be taken off a criminal case. Hoover had done that for more than a year with Peter Karlow, with no prosecution or profit of any kind to show for it. With termination of coverage on Karlow in April 1963, Helms and Angleton asked Papich for "across-the-board" telephone taps on other suspected Soviet spies, but Hoover had refused to comply, because CIA did not have enough evidence for a warrant.

By November 1964, as Nosenko was being transferred to Camp Peary, and as new leads were being developed from Golitsyn's tips, Miler and Angleton thus felt a vital need for closer FBI cooperation in the search for moles. Helms took the matter to McCone, who agreed to raise the subject with Hoover. That was the kind of high-level support the molehunt project needed, and the result was a joint operation to investigate suspected Soviet spies in CIA.

The targets, as Papich recalled, "were selected as a result of information or analysis from Golitsyn." The defector was insisting that the breadth and depth of CIA secrets he'd seen in Moscow could not have come from any one man, and suggested that the Agency try to find the original "tumor" from which the "cancer" of penetration had spread. Golitsyn believed that the problem had begun with OSS recruitment of former Nazi intelligence assets during the waning days of World War II, and suspicion soon focused on an ex-Nazi spy who had gone into OSS, Igor Orlov.

On Soviet orders, Orlov had parachuted into Prussia in 1944, to penetrate Russian-émigré groups behind the advancing Red Army lines, only to be shredded by Nazi anti-aircraft fire as he floated down. Captured, and recovered from his wounds, Orlov went to work for the Nazis until war's end; he then became active in a Ukrainian exile group before becoming a contract agent-handler at CIA's Berlin Base from 1949 to 1956. Orlov neatly matched the "Sasha" profile provided by Golitsyn: a name beginning with "K" and ending in "sky" (Orlov had formerly been known as Alexander Koptatzky); his diminutive name was "Sasha"; he had worked in Germany; and an unusually high percentage of his operations had gone bad.

By the time he became a suspect in the joint FBI-CIA molehunt, Orlov had emigrated to the U.S. with his wife, Eleanor, and opened a picture-frame shop in Alexandria, Virginia. He was there one afternoon in early March 1965 when six men appeared in hats and dark suits, looking quite serious. Sasha wondered if they were Mormons. One of them rang the bell. "FBI," he said. "We'd like to search the building. Espionage."

Each morning for the next six weeks, Sasha reported to a nearby FBI office for interrogation. The framing gallery was staked out, with two G-men sitting inside at all times, never taking off their hats, staring down every customer who might be one of Sasha's Soviet contacts. The Bureau even sent over one of its best double agents, welding engineer John Huminik, to see if he could spot any of the Soviet spies he had met, but Huminik never saw anyone he recognized.

At some point during his ordeal, Sasha managed to evade FBI surveillance and visited the Soviet Embassy. Perhaps, as he told his wife, he was simply tired of being persecuted in his adoptive country; perhaps, as Angleton later ventured, he was a scared spy running for cover. In any case, the Soviets promised Sasha asylum, and, with KGB assistance, an escape plan was hatched. But on the day he and his family were to have redefected, Orlov suddenly came home, smiling.

"Guess what?" he said to his wife. "The FBI let me go. They apologized and said I can go on with my life. Tomorrow we are free."

The Orlovs thought that meant the government had decided Sasha was innocent. In fact, the FBI had called off its participation in the CIA molehunt because of deepening disagreements over defectors, and because John Edgar Hoover was seventy years old.

• • •

AFTER JANUARY 1, 1965, the FBI director was subject to a government law requiring retirement, and it was illegal for him to head the country's leading law-enforcement agency unless he was annually reappointed by the president. Hoover acutely sensed that any embarrassment to the Bureau could reflect unfavorably on his leadership, providing an excuse not to renew him. Surveillance suddenly became a potential cause of embarrassment, because the new attorney general, Nicholas Katzenbach, and his deputy, Ramsey Clark, were refusing to authorize warrantless surveillance of suspected spies. Hoover had been routinely conducting such coverage for over a quarter-century, operating basically out of a 1939 directive by President Roosevelt which enabled the FBI to cope with problems "clearly and directly" related to foreign interests. But even if tacitly sanctioned by presidents and attorneys general, warrantless coverage could be regarded as illegal from a certain constitutional point of view. The FBI had never been caught, but the consequences of exposure had increased as Hoover's grip on power loosened, and as he failed to find the political backing that had been there before. "Hoover wasn't going to do a surveillance on anybody unless he got that goddamn thing supported by the attorney general, by the president, or both," Papich recalled. "That's how he survived as long as he did. And when he didn't get that support, this was a time when a lot of troubles developed. We were getting requests from CIA for coverage that we had provided before, but now we were turning them down."

A more moderate adjustment in surveillance policy might have been urged on Hoover by Al Belmont, regarded as the FBI Counterintelligence Section's best friend at the top. But when Belmont retired in spring 1965, the way was clear to a termination of molehunt surveillances. "When Al Belmont left—nobody writes about this, but, boy—Hoover lost his helmsman," Papich would later reflect. "Al was great at communicating between J. Edgar and the field. The Bureau was never the same after that. That was the era when you really had your problems."

Belmont was replaced by Deke DeLoach, who, it will be remembered, had served as FBI liaison to CIA during the darkest years of interagency relations, from 1948 to 1952. His view of CIA had been shaped by unpleasant experiences with William Harvey and Frank Wisner and their "shakedown cruises" on FBI turf. Now, as the new number-three man, DeLoach was charged with making the Bureau run smoothly and keeping it out of political trouble.

If he needed any excuse to recommend against continued cooperation in CIA's molehunt, DeLoach got it from congressional hearings led by Louisiana Senator Russell Long. In late 1964 and into spring 1965, Long began looking into allegations that Government agencies illegally spied on Americans. These inquiries caused CIA to temporarily suspend its mail-opening program, by February 27, 1965, the FBI director was urging his men, too, to play it safe. "I would have no hesitance in discontinuing all techniques—technical coverage, microphones, trash covers, mail covers, etc.," Hoover wrote on a memo reporting the Long Subcommittee's proceedings. "While it might handicap us, I doubt they are as valuable as some believe." By late April, Hoover's "no hesitance in discontinuing" warrantless coverage had caused the coverage to be discontinued. At the same time, ostensibly because the joint FBI-CIA molehunt had failed to gain evidence which might support warrant-backed, legal surveillance, he ordered his men to withdraw from the project.

But Angleton apparently believed that Hoover's legalism was a mere pretext for ending the hunt. The deeper reason, it was feared, was that Hoover had come to suspect that the main source of the mole allegations, Anatoliy Golitsyn, might himself be a disinformant under KGB control. It is unclear when Hoover's suspicion first emerged, but it was well known to Angleton by 1967, when he reprimanded Soviet Division officer Bagley, who was writing a report on the Nosenko matter, for questioning Golitsyn's veracity. According to Bagley's memo of one of their arguments, "Chief CI [Angleton] said he did not see how CIA could submit a final report to the Bureau if it contained suggestions that Golitsyn had lied to us about certain aspects of Nosenko's past. He recalled that the Director of the FBI had stated that in his opinion Golitsyn himself was a provocateur and a penetration agent."

There seem to have been two pillars to Hoover's position. First was the fact that Golitsyn kept asking to see FBI files. If Golitsyn redefected, or was in contact with Soviet agents, or even if he was genuine but was kidnapped by the Russians, FBI secrets could be lost; therefore, the intensity of his interest in Bureau files evoked great distrust. Second, Golitsyn's disinformation thesis had led to a situation where, as Miler put it, "You had a bunch of CIA guys throwing darts at the FBI's sources." These sources included a GRU officer, known to the FBI as "Nick Nack," who had briefly been posted in New York; Nosenko, of course; Fedora and Top Hat, the two KGB officers under UN cover; and a third KGB recruitment inside the United Nations, code-named AE/SHAMROCK, whose true identity has never been revealed.

This "third man"—a KGB officer under diplomatic cover, run jointly by FBI and CIA—had first contacted the Bureau in New York in 1965 and provided leads to espionage cases in France and Britain. His information overlapped with much of what the U.S. already knew about these cases from Fedora and Nick Nack, and Angleton judged him to be bogus. When "Shamrock" appeared, even Bill Sullivan began to doubt the FBI's good fortune in getting so many sources at the UN.

Desperate to know what was going on, Sullivan finally broke down and let Golitsyn see some science-and-technology aspects of the Fedora and Top Hat cases. Hoover, and Sullivan's own deputies, were kept ignorant of this. With Golitsyn's help, Sullivan re-examined some of the take on Soviet missile-guidance systems, and found that "the lines of disinformation didn't cross." At least some of the sources had to be lying, or perhaps deliberately misbriefed. Perhaps they all were.

Although Hoover did not know that Sullivan had shared FBI data with Golitsyn, he did know that the defector's theories had caused CIA to doubt the Bureau's recruitments. Now those doubts seemed to be infecting even the FBI. Hoover wondered: might not Golitsyn have been dispatched by the KGB to destroy the FBI's intelligence gathering efforts? The possibility had at least to be considered. That all of the FBI's prized sources had been developed *after* Golitsyn's defection—how could he have been sent to discredit sources which did not yet exist?—did not necessarily exclude a KGB deception plan. Perhaps Golitsyn had been planted simply to discredit *all future* KGB sources, no matter who they were.

In any case, with Golitsyn implicitly discrediting much of what the FBI was doing in counterintelligence, Hoover was hardly disposed to cooperate in CIA enterprises such as molehunts, which, if successful, might buttress the very arguments that were undercutting Hoover's treasured informants. Angleton, at any rate, seems to have reasoned that it was such thoughts that had led the Bureau to decline many of CIA's domestic-coverage requests.

Thus, after being held open for three consecutive ninety-day periods, the coverage of Sasha Orlov had not been renewed. The FBI's official rationale for shutting down the case was that they were unable to establish that he was a Soviet spy. There was a significant amount of high-grade circumstantial evidence, but nothing more. A lie-detector test had suggested deception, but that was not the same as legal proof. What could the Bureau do? "We haven't proved anything," Hoover finally said. "Close it."

American counterintelligence entered a frustrating phase. Larry McWilliams recalled one occasion when Angleton's shop sent over a request for the FBI to cover five people that they suspected of being Soviet moles. "It's a waste of time," DeLoach said. "Suppose anything goes wrong, and we're caught in this thing. Who's got the bag on it?" A memo went up to Hoover, and he concurred.

"Coverage at that time—if you were going to have to cover something that was really worthwhile, it was terrible," Papich remembered. "Hell, there were Soviet agents in the area, in the country, that we couldn't cover electronically. We just generally cut down our input on identifying spies, and even the old Venona work was stopped. Jim Angleton believed that, whether it was for prosecution or not, these people should be identified; they might still be around. But J. Edgar didn't want to be told what targets he should cover, particularly if there was no demonstrable evidence that it was going to benefit the FBI. He's sticking his neck out, but it's for another agency—he's not going to go along with that, especially when Congress was becoming curious, and there were new political considerations."

Angleton understood Hoover's need for political support, but he did not enjoy the consequences of the cutback. "Thousands of man-hours would have been saved if the Bureau had been willing to place taps on [suspected traitors'] telephones," he later said. He could only shake his head at the "clumsy bureaucratic actions." Consensus in the CI Staff was that the Orlov serial, and the joint molehunt generally, were issues important enough to take to a higher level, to Helms and thence to McCone, with the argument that national security transcended the priorities of a rival service. McCone would not have been afraid to "go to the mat" with Hoover, but by April 28 he was gone, and the man who took his place was not inclined to fight anyone over anything.

WESTERN HEMISPHERE OFFICER David Atlee Phillips had been busy in his division's operations room at Langley on April 29, monitoring a civil war in the Dominican Republic, leaning over a teletype, when someone touched him on the shoulder. It was Dick Helms. Like many others in the Department of Plans, Phillips had been hoping that Helms would become DCI after a Washington-wearied McCone announced plans to retire to California. But now Helms said, "Dave, meet our new Director—Admiral William Raborn."

Helms moved aside to present a short, stocky, sixtyish man, his white-skinned face veined with red lines, his eyes crow's-footed from years of squinting across seas. Raborn grunted, then stalked about the hectic room, fascinated by the clattering machines. He had been on the job about fourteen hours. Formerly in charge of the Navy's Polaris-missile development program, he had brought it in two years early and under budget, and that achievement had prompted President Johnson to appoint him DCI. He was a diehard, sentimental patriot, and the day before, when Johnson had introduced him to the CIA leadership, tears had coursed down Raborn's crimson cheeks and formed tiny drops on the point of his chin. He knew little about the intelligence business and apparently nothing about foreign affairs, and he was soon frustrating Helms, the Agency's new DDCI, and Helms' successor as DDP, Desmond FitzGerald, with silly questions. Hearing that CIA's likely choice in the Dominican Republic was between dictatorship and oligarchy, Raborn asked, "Who is this fellow Oligarchy, anyway?"

Although uniformly disliked at CIA, Raborn was quite popular at the FBI. Indeed, Hoover got on extremely well with him, just as he had with the first woebegone admiral who held the post, Sidney Souers, back in 1946. "Hoover and the Admiral held many common views and were in frequent contact," Phillips recalled. Presumably that was because Raborn, like Souers, was an ineffectual leader who posed no threat to Hoover's domain, and who happily allowed Hoover to expand into CIA's yard. Indeed, FBI encroachment into CIA jurisdiction during the Caribbean crisis was to show how fully Hoover was capable of dominating a lesser leader.

Raborn had been CIA director for less than a week when President Johnson elected to dispatch twenty-five thousand Marines to the Dominican Republic to avert a communist takeover, and not long afterward Johnson followed up by sending in the FBI. Phillips, who was to become CIA's new station chief in Santo Domingo, presumed that the president "wanted to be able to explain to Congress and the American public, in the event of fiasco, that it had occurred despite the fact that he had committed his 'first team'—not only the CIA . . . but the then highly respected FBI as well." William Sullivan also believed that sending G-men to Santo Domingo was essentially a public-relations ploy. DeLoach was becoming one of LBJ's best friends, and apparently he had convinced the president that bad press about the invasion could be negated by ordering a legion of American Knights to join the fight against the Red Menace.

"It made a great story," Sullivan recalled. "Hoover, with his dream of a worldwide intelligence network, jumped through the usual hoops to carry out Johnson's scheme. The whole phony set-up made me angry, especially as I was put in charge of the operation, and I dragged my heels before assigning any agents to go down there, putting off the inevitable. In May of 1965 when I finally wrote the memo requesting permission to send the men down, Hoover wrote 'It's about time' on the bottom. Naturally, the CIA was horrified to find the FBI operating in the Dominican Republic, as horrified as the FBI would have been had Johnson ordered the CIA to investigate a case in New York City. Richard Helms, deputy director of the CIA, found out about it in the newspapers, so I called him to arrange a meeting. He offered to come over to see me, but I knew that thirty seconds after Helms entered the building Hoover would have been told, so I went over his way. We sat down and looked at each other, almost numb with disbelief. We agreed to work together and to try to keep our agents out of each other's operations. . . . Of course, this arrangement had to be kept from Hoover or I would have been fired."

After meeting with Sullivan, Helms called in Phillips for the traditional send-off chat he gave all outgoing station chiefs. Phillips, who was all packed and ready to leave, wondered what Helms' inevitable one-liner would be this time. Ring the gong for us in Santo Domingo? Show them how to run an intelligence service down there?

Helms said, "Get along with the FBI."

He seemed relieved when Phillips told him he had been working in Mexico City for the past four years with Clark Anderson, "a personal friend and a fine guy" who was now heading the FBI unit on the island. Phillips and Anderson had managed to contain the substantial interagency tensions in Mexico during the JFK-Oswald investigation, or lack thereof; if they could not keep things on track in the Dominican Republic, no one could.

But Phillips was not prepared for what he encountered when he arrived in Santo Domingo. CIA's station was staffed by fewer than a dozen people, including secretaries, but the FBI had flown in twice as many agents to make recruitments and file basic reports. Though most of them did speak Spanish, they seemed to have little savvy for foreign-intelligence work. Instead of blending into the environment like CIA case officers, who wore traditional collarless *guayabarra* shirts and tropical straw hats, Hoover's heroes advertised their presence in gray summerweight suits and snap-brim fedoras. "They didn't even have 3 × 5 cards, a basic tool of an intelligence organization, or a more than cursory knowledge of the local situation," Phillips later smirked. "Only CIA was able to provide intelligence from the rebel zone."

Phillips immediately went to see Anderson, who was operating out of the U.S. Embassy, to discuss how they could work together. The FBI man was frank. "Here I am with twenty-four men. My instructions are to gather intelligence. None of us knows anything of the local political and military situation and our experience is in criminal, not political investigation. J. Edgar has told us to start churning out reports. What do we do?"

Phillips and Anderson contrived a program for cooperation. "The important element," Phillips recollected, "was that we would keep from trying to recruit and handle the same agents by a frank review of our candidates. We met every morning. Clark would identify potential sources. I would tell him whether we had already recruited the agent, or if we had tried with dubious results. One does not often identify agents to another government agency, but in Santo Domingo Clark and I violated the rules. If one of his officers recruited a source, he would advise me."

Though coordination became trickier as CIA's presence grew to half a hundred men over the coming year, the rival agencies did manage, by all accounts, to "get along" in the Dominican Republic. Sullivan approvingly noted that CIA and FBI had worked in Santo Domingo "like hand in glove." It was in Washington, as usual, that problems emerged.

After order was finally restored to the island under CIA-backed Héctor García-Godoy, who appointed a number of "left-of-center" types to form a coalition, Phillips was suddenly recalled to Washington for an audience with Admiral Raborn. Hoover had complained to him that some of Godoy's new men in the Dominican government were secret communists. Phillips assured the admiral that this was not accurate, but Raborn seemed more inclined to believe the insinuations of the FBI director than the perceptions of his own men on the scene. Phillips felt frustrated and undercut, but when he ran into Helms in the locker room of the Langley gym, he was again enjoined to get along with the FBI. So he returned to Santo Domingo, met with the new president, and raised, as tactfully as he could, J. Edgar Hoover's concern that García-Godoy was placing "secret communists" in his government.

"Mr. Phillips," Godoy replied acidly, "this is *my* country. I am the President. I will not do it. To me you are nothing but a foreign spy." The CIA station chief hastily backpedaled and apologized, and said no more of the FBI's concerns.

When Phillips' tour on the island was finished, in August 1967, he was summoned to the White House. President Johnson offered him a Dr. Pepper and said: "I want to thank you for getting along with the FBI." But the president was apparently telling Phillips only part of the story. If happy that the two agencies had managed to work together, Johnson was apparently somewhat more impressed with the Bureau's reporting on the crisis than the Agency's. Probably that was because the domestic-based FBI, by operating overseas, had been able to fuse both domestic and foreign data on the conflict. Dominican exiles were plotting strategy in San Juan, Puerto Rico, and by covering that angle, the FBI could predict events with some degree of certainty. Consequently, LBJ had ordered Hoover to establish a permanent office in Santo Domingo—a move not resisted by Admiral Raborn, but resented by DDCI Helms. "At the time I was not aware of the severity of the strain on relations between J. Edgar Hoover and Helms," Phillips recalled. "But the schism with Hoover was sharp, with overtones that affected Agency relations for years."

WEDGE

. . .

NOTWITHSTANDING THE FRICTION which came out of the Dominican affair, some attempt was made during Raborn's tenure to regularize coordination on cases which crossed jurisdictions. The need for a new mechanism was shown not only in the Caribbean crisis but in the December 1965 transfer to Burma of Top Hat (Polyakov), who had been one of the FBI's top sources in New York. Policy was that Polyakov had to be turned over to a CIA officer overseas, disrupting the tenuous relation between agent and handling officer. CIA officers did sit down with Polyakov's FBI handler, and got some guidance on how the GRU man acted, and reacted, but the Agency picked up the contact in Burma—not the FBI. That not only put the agent in a psychologically uncomfortable position, but made his former handling officer reliant on someone else's contact reports, which might not be totally accurate. Even if a meeting were recorded and transcribed, the new handler would miss facial expressions and body language which could be easily picked up by his old contact, and the new case officer might be snowed where the old might have said: He's not really telling the truth on this one, and I'll go after him on it. "I think everyone realized we needed a little more flexibility, not draw the line that it had to be the CIA or FBI, exclusively," Scotty Miler recalled. "To me, to Jim, and to Sam, it always just made sense that you would coordinate this."

On February 7, 1966, a formal agreement was finally negotiated to cover the "overlap" problem. The "heart" of the understanding, according to Papich, was that CIA would "seek concurrence and coordination of the FBI" before engaging in clandestine activity in the United States, and that the Bureau would "concur and coordinate if the proposed action does not conflict with any operation, current or planned, including active investigation." When an agent recruited by CIA abroad arrived in the United States, the FBI would be advised and the two agencies would confer. The Agency could continue its handling for "foreign intelligence purposes" as long as it briefed the Bureau, and the FBI would become involved where there were "internal security factors." When Bureau sources went abroad, however, CIA's superior foreign tradecraft dictated that it take control. The Agency did offer to institute foreign-intelligence-training courses, including report-writing and analysis, for FBI personnel. But Hoover turned the offer down.

FOUR MONTHS AFTER the arrangement was formalized, almost as if to test it, a new KGB man dropped into the laps of both agencies, promising to solve both the problem of Nosenko's legitimacy and the molehunt. He arrived, and the case began, just as J. Edgar's honeymoon with the ineffectual Raborn ended.

Faced with a near-mutiny among CIA staffers, President Johnson fired Admiral Raborn and on June 30, 1966, replaced him with Richard Helms. The move was greeted enthusiastically at CIA—here at last was a clandestine-service officer who had risen from the ranks to run the place—but Helms quickly showed that he could be professional to the point of inflicting pain. A big status symbol for senior officers since moving to Langley in 1961 had been a key to the DCI's elevator, but when Helms decided there were just "too damn many" people riding up with him, he took some of the keys away, and that was a real blow for those who lost the perk. Reaction at the FBI, too, was mixed; Sam Papich saw "eye to eye" with Helms on most things, and found it "easy to communicate with him," but Hoover reacted somewhat differently.

Within a few days of being appointed DCI, Helms thought it would be polite to call on the FBI director. Hoover received him, which was a good start, since it was not at all a given that he would. Helms put aside his feelings about the Dominican intrusion and politely, quietly said that he had just "come to visit," to seek any thoughts Hoover might have about the CIA directorship, or on the relationship between their agencies. Hoover started to talk, and a half hour later he was still talking. As soon as he reasonably could, Helms excused himself, thanked Hoover, and went back to Langley. On the way out, he thought, If that's the way business with Mr. Hoover is going to go, there's no sense in my visiting him. And Helms never did again.

So began what a later in-house CIA historian would term "a very long span of time during which the Director of the Central Intelligence Agency and Mr. Hoover were barely on speaking terms," when "it was very difficult for the two Agencies to get along." Helms did see Hoover sometimes at embassy receptions given by the Royal Canadian Mounted Police when their director came to Washington, and Helms made an effort to chat with the FBI director on those few occasions, because most of the other people at the reception either were afraid to talk to Hoover or didn't want to talk to him. But for the most part Helms was as close to Hoover as the telephone and not any closer. They always referred to each other as "Mr. Helms" and "Mr. Hoover," and never got beyond the "Mr." in all the time they worked together. Helms sensed acutely that Hoover still regarded CIA "essentially as a rival."

Through Papich, Helms pressed Hoover to increase telephone taps, and to resume the joint FBI-CIA molehunt and its attendant surveillances, but Hoover refused. Some of the Bureau's own people, especially Sullivan and his deputy, Charles Brennan, confided to their Agency contacts that they felt the FBI was shirking its duties—but who was going to confront the old man?

Helms, for one, had more pressing matters on his mind during that summer of 1966—most particularly, a case that began on Saturday, June 18, with the ringing of a telephone at his Georgetown home. The call was from KGB officer Igor Kochnov, offering to work as an agent-in-place.

Under the new jurisdictional agreement, Kochnov would be run jointly, and both CIA and FBI officers reportedly showed up to debrief him at a Virginia coffee shop. Kochnov alleged that Yuri Nosenko was a genuine defector, that Igor Orlov was indeed the Soviet agent known as "Sasha," and that Orlov had contacted the Soviet Embassy in Washington in 1965. The FBI checked its surveillance records of the Soviet Embassy and discovered that this was true, though they had somehow overlooked it. But because much of his information was "dated" and seemed to support Nosenko, Angleton and Miler suspected that Kochnov was a provocateur. When Kochnov asked for information about Nosenko, ostensibly to help himself climb the ladder in Moscow, CIA suspected that Kochnov had been sent to give the Soviets feedback on Nosenko, whose incarceration would have sealed off the defector from any KGB moles in CIA's Soviet Division.

But Angleton did want to play the Kochnov case out, to see what would happen. The two agencies therefore coordinated to recruit a previous defector, Soviet Naval officer Nicholas Shadrin, into a double-agent game, ostensibly to further Kochnov's KGB career. The operation, code-named "Kittyhawk," was run jointly by Bruce Solie, in CIA's Office of Security, and Elbert Turner of the FBI's Washington Field Office. Kochnov was allowed to contact Shadrin and ask him about the whereabouts of Golitsyn and Nosenko, and Shadrin was permitted to tell the truth, which was that he had no idea. Shadrin also began to pass doctored naval secrets to the Soviets.

Paradoxically, while Angleton thought that the Kittyhawk game offered a good way of getting FBI and CIA to work together, he decided that this teamwork was only possible if he himself held back. Specifically—and Helms agreed to this—it was decided not to let the FBI know that CIA doubted Kochnov's bona fides. Hoover's patience with such pronouncements had clearly been evaporating since Angleton had impugned the credibility of the Bureau's "third man" at the UN, but balming J. Edgar was only a secondary cause for the concealment. The primary one was to avoid giving Kochnov himself any hint of the suspicions against him. Angleton did not regard Turner as an especially adept or experienced case officer, and he knew that Russians, who lived in a society where they could not always speak freely, were adept at reading posture, facial expressions, the flicking of eyes. Americans tended to be open people, inept at reading other people's body language, let alone hiding their own. CIA officers were trained to override some of this cultural conditioning, but FBI agents, who thrived on public trust, cultivated openness as a virtue. Though Solie was experienced enough to hide his thoughts, Turner might inadvertently tip Kochnov to what was up. It would be better for all concerned if the FBI were kept in the dark.

Better, that is, for everyone but Shadrin. But the demonstration of that tragic truth was still nine years away.

In the meantime, Kittyhawk's implication of Orlov did promise to reconcile the agencies in that part of the molehunt. Angleton, it seemed, had been right about Sasha, and the Bureau had been wrong to shut down their surveillance. After being told that Sasha had visited the Soviet Embassy the previous year, the FBI asked him to explain himself. He said that he had gone there simply to ask for "my mother's address." But where Angleton thought this an obvious lie, Turner and other FBI agents said they believed Orlov. If he really were a spy, they reasoned, he wouldn't have gone to the embassy, which was watched by the FBI; he would have some more secure means of staying in touch. Angleton never let the case go, and would frequently put FBI man James Nolan on the defensive by asking, "Have you cracked the case? What's new on Orlov?" To see whether the Orlovs' shop was a front, while at the same time sending a false message that Sasha was not under suspicion, Nolan sent a stream of FBI agents into the gallery on their "free time" with unframed portraits of Director Hoover, but no physical or electronic coverage was imposed.

Angleton fared even less well when he tried to get the FBI to surveil some of Orlov's former handlers at CIA. Beginning in late summer 1966, leads were passed to Papich, who sent them to his bosses—who passed them back again. "It's a bunch of nonsense," Papich was told. "Where's their evidence?" The Bureau wasn't interested in a case unless it promised to lead to prosecution. Miler understood that Hoover was only obeying the law, but he was frustrated when FBI asked him not to give them any more cases until he had something a little more solid.

"There was a CIA request for shotgun surveillance of Orlov's handlers, which we failed to go by," Larry McWilliams recalled. "As marvelous as it is to be an agency where you can say, 'Let's do this!,' it's certainly a different thing if you have to stay within the rules of law. Besides, we didn't buy Golitsyn's reasoning in the first place. So, where CIA would call it lack of cooperation, we called it lack of common sense."

Among the suspected moles the Bureau declined to surveil was Paul Garbler, who had been Sasha Orlov's handler at Berlin Base from 1952 to 1955. Garbler had also been CIA station chief in Moscow from November 1961 through February 1964, which theoretically put him in a position to help craft Nosenko's uncheckable Oswald legend, as well as to betray a CIA-MI6 mole in the GRU, Oleg Penkovskiy, who was executed in 1963. After February 1964, Garbler had been chief of operations for the Soviet Division at headquarters, which placed him in the perfect spot to provide the KGB with feedback about Nosenko. Garbler's father, it was discovered, had emigrated from Russia, and Angleton's staff also learned that, while posted in Korea from 1950 to 1952, Garbler had been a tennis partner to British MI6 officer George Blake, who confessed in 1961 to being a Soviet spy. Garbler's case was referred to the Bureau, who reportedly investigated his sex life, bank accounts, and parents, but never called him in for an interview, and never instituted electronic or physical coverage. Unable either to formally charge or to clear him, Helms quietly arranged Garbler's transfer to a less sensitive post.

The Bureau also turned down a request to investigate Richard Kovich, another "Sasha" suspect in CIA's Soviet Division. Kovich had served in Berlin and handled Orlov, his name began with "K," he spoke Russian and had a Slavic background—all of which meant he matched Golitsyn's mock-up. He had also supported George Kisevalter in the running of Colonel Pyotr Popov, CIA's first mole in the GRU, in 1953, and again from 1955 to 1958—which meant that he could have conceivably burned Popov, who was executed in 1959. From August to October 1964, Kovich had assisted the FBI in running their KGB source at the UN, Fedora, alias Aleksei Kulak, which meant that he might have given the KGB feedback on Fedora's alleged disinformation. Since then Kovich had been a "headhunter" for the Soviet Division, ready to make a recruitment pitch to a Soviet intelligence officer whenever and wherever division chief Dave Murphy desired. On December 2, 1965, Helms wrote Hoover to request physical surveillance of Kovich during what was regarded as a "particularly critical period of time" of CIA's investigation. Concerned about "evidence that he will contact a Soviet installation in this country," Helms urged: "If this should occur this agency desires to know whether your Bureau would take the necessary steps to prevent Kovich from entering any Soviet installation." But the FBI declined Helms' request.

Nor was Hoover enthusiastic about investigating CIA's Soviet Division chief. David Murphy had worked closely with Sasha Orlov while chief of CIA's Munich operations base from 1949 to 1953, and while he was deputy chief of CIA's Berlin Base from 1953 to 1959, Murphy's backyard had actually adjoined Sasha's. Murphy's first wife had been a White Russian from China who emigrated to San Francisco, and Miler knew from his own Far East experiences that there were a lot of communist-controlled émigrés coming out of that part of the world. Murphy had recommended that CIA hire a man named Andy Yankovsky, who built a network of agents in North Korea, almost all of whom were caught. The Soviet Division chief also had a habit of getting into well-publicized tussles with KGB agents in places like Tokyo and Vienna; the persistence of the pattern suggested that such episodes might have been "staged" by the KGB handlers as an excuse for contact, or to establish his anti-Soviet bona fides (as if to say: they would never get into fistfights with their own man). Finally, as chief of the Soviet Division from 1963 on, Murphy would naturally have been the ideal KGB source of feedback on Nosenko and other suspected disinformation efforts. Although CIA's top management had been loath to sic the FBI on Murphy without damning evidence, in late 1966, one of Murphy's underlings, Peter Kapusta, called Papich at 2:00 a.m. and accused his boss of being a Soviet spy. But the FBI viewed the Murphy matter strictly as an internal CIA problem, and even though Kapusta's allegation was complemented by circumstantial material from Angleton, the Bureau did not investigate.

Hoover's refusal to help CIA root out security problems continued for years, and dismayed FBI Intelligence Division chief William Sullivan. In early 1971, Sullivan later said, Angleton turned to the Bureau for a domestic investigation because he "believed four or five guys were agents, including two guys still in the agency and three or four who had been high-level. They were suspected of having dealings with foreign intelligence agents." Sullivan consulted Hoover, who "refused on the grounds that it was the responsibility of the CIA. However, in this case he realized that he might be put in a compromising position by suggesting that the CIA conduct domestic investigations, so reluctantly he told me to go ahead, but he instructed me to conduct just the semblance of an investigation." In other words, "It was a brush-off. CIA was never satisfied with the FBI, and I can't blame them. We did hit or miss jobs. We were constantly cutting the throats of CIA."

Papich, who had to carry the bad news to Angleton on the FBI's numerous refusals and sham inquiries, was circumspect about what happened. "I think where Jim Angleton may have made mistakes is in—and, then, maybe not, maybe history'll prove that he was right, as he was right about looking at Soviet deception—but I say he may have selected the wrong targets within the Agency. And he may not have, I don't know."

In the end, that very uncertainty would be the most tragic legacy of FBI-CIA disagreement in the molehunt. Without full, "clean," timely investigations by the FBI, the suspects' careers and reputations could never be totally restored. In effect, they were blacklisted. Garbler was transferred from headquarters to CIA's tiny station in Trinidad; Kovich was demoted to a lower-security assignment at Camp Peary; Murphy landed as station chief in Paris. All eventually retired in frustration.

"These individuals were under scrutiny," Helms recalled, "and they were put in jobs that were not particularly sensitive, so that if they were indeed a Russian agent, or a Polish agent, or a penetration of some kind, they could not continue to send valuable information to the home office. None of these people were ever taken off the payroll, because I had a policy that nobody was going to be forced to leave the Agency until a clear case was made that there was a reason for this. Suspicion was not enough. So none of these people were fired, and none of them were at least directly penalized financially. And if some people were hurt in the process, *I'm sorry!*" There was a rare edge of emotion in his voice when he spoke of the matter, even thirty years later. "But this is not a game for the soft-hearted."

Alas, Helms' defensiveness would reveal yet another legacy of the unsuccessful search for penetrations, and it was a dangerous one. Because no legal evidence was ever developed against high-level moles in CIA, and because Karlow, Kovich, and Garbler were later officially cleared by the Agency and given generous financial settlements, it became fashionable to believe that CIA had never been penetrated at all. Eventually Golitsyn's allegations would be dismissed as paranoia, Angleton would be denounced by colleagues and historians as a merciless inquisitor, and CIA, as an institution, would overcorrect by taking an approach to counterintelligence that could best be summed up by the phrase: "Relax, we have nothing to worry about." That transformation would not be formally effected until the 1970s, and its impact not fully felt until a decade after that, but it was rooted in the failure to find moles by the end of 1966.

CHAPTER TWELVE
_____

WEDGE

RICHARD HELMS HAD a predicament. By October 1966, it was clear that Yuri Nosenko could not remain incarcerated indefinitely. CIA's Office of Security, which had built Nosenko's jail and was keeping him in it, had begun to grumble. Security man Solie had been impressed by Kochnov's claim that Nosenko was bona fide, and began protesting to Security Director Howard Osborn about "the illegality of the Agency's position in handling a defector under these conditions for such a long period of time." Congressmen and journalists were getting curious; as early as January 1965, Angleton had been bothered by a query from Senator Everett Dirksen, based on a letter from a constituent, concerning the "whereabouts" of Nosenko. The CI chief told Papich that, though Dirksen's correspondent was probably just a "curious individual who followed the publicity previously given to Nosenko," CIA nevertheless did "not wish to discount the possibility that there may be more to this inquiry"—the black hand of the KGB, perhaps?—and so requested "an appropriate check" by the FBI's Soviet Section to "determine the purpose" of Dirksen's query. Nothing sinister was found behind Dirksen's request, but journalist David Wise in 1966 discovered a reference to Nosenko in a listing of still-classified Warren Commission documents. CIA feared that Wise's article would "immediately result in newspaper inquiries as to the whereabouts of . . . Nosenko," and Helms was forced to violate the usual code of "plausible deniability" by briefing President Johnson on the Nosenko situation. "Through the years, we have been working with the FBI in an effort to establish whether he is a KGB agent on assignment or a bona fide defector," Helms wrote the president, adding that public access to Nosenko was "not feasible" because "This question is still not resolved."

The thing to do was resolve it. On August 23, 1966, Helms set a limit of sixty days for Bagley, who still oversaw the Nosenko case, to "wind it up." That resulted in a period of frenetic activity, because Bagley felt that it was impossible to prove Nosenko's guilt and couldn't conceive of any way of getting at the truth unless some additional measures were taken. More polygraph tests were administered; their results were interpreted as indicating deception, but no firm proof was gained. Bagley proposed that Nosenko be interrogated under the influence of sodium amytal, believed to lower a subject's defenses, but Helms refused to permit any interrogations using drugs. Finally, the sixty days ran out, and Bagley was asked how CIA could "clean up traces of a situation in which CIA could be accused of illegally holding Nosenko." Of seven options put down by Bagley, the last three were chilling: "5. Liquidate the man. 6. Render him incapable of giving coherent story (special dose of drug, etc.). Possible aim, commitment to looney bin. 7. Commitment to looney bin without making him nuts." Helms decided that the case simply could not go on in such a fashion, so he took it to his new DDCI, Admiral Rufus Taylor, and said, "It's all yours."

Taylor quickly moved not only to head off a possible scandal over conditions of Nosenko's incarceration, but to contain the "enormous damage" which the dispute had already done to relations between CIA and

FBI. He took a two-pronged approach. Bagley was to begin work on a massive report detailing the history of the case and setting down all the evidence. At the same time, the defector would be turned over to Bruce Solie at CIA's Office of Security, who could work with the FBI in the attempt to square Nosenko's information with Golitsyn's. That latter task was easier ordered than performed, however, and it was also to be seen how Bagley's and Solie's projects would be rectified if they happened to come to different results. It would be almost two years before such matters brought FBI-CIA relations to their most desperate and dangerous phase—catalyzing disagreement over Golitsyn's thesis, exacerbating irritation over suspected CIA support for Israeli nuclear espionage, and eventually climaxing in a major crisis over the otherwise minor case of a man who disappeared in Denver. In the meantime, new questions about the assassination, raised both publicly and in secret, would make the problem of Nosenko's bona fides and message ever more pressing.

THE NEW THINKING was spurred by FBI reports about the insecurity of CIA's fall-1963 plottings with Rolando Cubela, alias AM/LASH, to assassinate Fidel Castro. As early as October 1963, it will be recalled, the Bureau had possessed indications that CIA's Cubela contacts might have been known to Castro, but these indications had not been shared with CIA. Consequently, Cubela continued to receive caches of weapons, silencers, pistols, and explosives from CIA until June 1965, when the Bureau finally did relay data that caused the Agency to reassess security. Eladio del Valle, a Cuban exile who was an old friend of both Cubela and Trafficante, tipped the Bureau that the mobster was secretly in league with Cubela and had discussed with him the Castro plots before November 22, 1963. That report caused Joseph Langosch, a CIA officer who had helped Fitzgerald run Cubela, to conclude that the Cubela plot to kill Castro "had been an insecure operation prior to the assassination [of Kennedy]." Not long afterward, del Valle's head was split open by an ax; the murder was never solved. All contact with Cubela was terminated by a cable to Miami and European stations on June 23, 1965, which cited "Convincing proof that entire AM/LASH group insecure and that further contact with key members of group constitutes a menace to CIA operations." That menacing group was eventually taken to include Santos Trafficante, who had been suspected by FBI informant José Aleman of being a Cuban agent. "Fidel reportedly knew that this group was plotting against him and once enlisted its support," Langosch noted. "Hence, we cannot rule out the possibility of provocation." The question "What Could Castro Have Known?" could only be answered: He could have known everything, right from the start. The question then became: What, If Anything, Had Castro Done About It?

Johnny Rosselli, Trafficante's co-conspirator in CIA's 1962 anti-Castro plots, soon came forward to say that Castro, once he learned about the plots against his life, had gone after Kennedy. In early fall 1966, Rosselli confided to his attorney, Robert Morgan, that the three-man CIA assassination team of "Trafficante mob" recruits dispatched to Cuba to kill Castro in September 1962 had come under Cuban influence or control and returned to the United States to kill President Kennedy. Rosselli's attorney called the office of columnist Drew Pearson, who was known to be tight with Chief Justice Warren, and Pearson dispatched his assistant, Jack Anderson, to extract details from Rosselli. Though it took Anderson several months to get the story—Rosselli feared that other mobsters would kill him for "talking"—by late January 1967 he had given it over. Pearson met with Warren and relayed the allegation; Warren informed President Johnson, who promptly ordered a full accounting. Scott Breckinridge, of CIA's Office of the Inspector General, was instructed to summarize the history of CIA's attempts to kill Castro, to assess how widely these schemes were known outside the Agency, and consider whether these plots might have been "turned around" to cause Kennedy's death.

In the course of his inquiry, Breckinridge somberly surmised that CIA's plots were probably known not only to Castro but also to the FBI. "As far as we know, the FBI has not been told the sensitive operational details," Breckinridge noted, "but it would be naive to assume that they have not by now put two and two together and come out with the right answer. They know of CIA's involvement with Rosselli and Giancana as a result of the Las Vegas wiretapping incident. From the Chicago newspaper stories of August 1963, and from Giancana's own statement, it appears that they know this related to Cuba. When Rosselli's story reached them . . . all of the pieces should have fallen into place. They should by now have concluded that CIA plotted the assassination of Castro and used U.S. gangster elements in the operation." Breckinridge felt his hunch confirmed in a May 3 conversation with Sam Papich, who commented that Rosselli had the FBI "over a barrel" because of "that operation." Papich said he doubted that the FBI would be able to do anything about mobsters such as Rosselli or Trafficante because of "their previous activities with your people."

The liaison officer's insight, if pushed to its logical end, contained an implication that was chilling indeed. If Trafficante and his assassins were immunized from prosecution because of participation in CIA's anti-Castro plots, could they not have had a "free shot" against President Kennedy? And could not communist intelligence, by using anti-Castro assets tainted by "CIA fingerprints," force the U.S. government to cover up any and all evidence of a communist role—as, indeed, the government had done? Couldn't the conspirators have reasoned that the U.S. government would never go after the assassins, or declare war on their suspected foreign sponsors, over evidence which, viewed from the public's perspective, might also implicate CIA? If Trafficante and/or Cubela were secretly working with Castro—as Aleman had originally alleged, and as Breckinridge himself reportedly believed—there was the troubling possibility that any mischief they made in Castro's behalf could not only be undertaken under immunity from prosecution but, as Angleton later hinted, "ghost[ed] ... to the doorstep of CIA." Because the U.S. government would be forced to obscure its own seeming links to the plot, any official investigation would be a de facto cover-up which, when exposed as such, would undermine the country's confidence in its most basic institutions. Finally, as KGB defector Pyotr Deriabin had hinted four days after the killing, the U.S. intelligence community would be demoralized by such a demonstration of "pure power" by its enemies, who would have effectively said: We can reach out and do this, and you can't do a thing to punish us.

The poetry of that possible deception struck Lyndon Johnson with all the force of legal proof. Before reading Breckinridge's May 1967 study on the Cubela-Trafficante plots, the president thought the notion of a Castro plot no more credible than the idea that the first lady was "taking dope." But after reading the Breckinridge Report, Johnson was persuaded, as he later told columnist Marianne Means, that his predecessor was liquidated "either under the influence or the orders of Castro." Johnson also confided to his close adviser Joseph Califano: "I will tell you something that will rock you. Kennedy was trying to get Castro, but Castro got him first."

Yet CIA believed, from Golitsyn and other defectors, that Castro's intelligence service, as that of any Soviet-bloc country, would not have undertaken such a sensitive operation without KGB knowledge and guidance—and so the Nosenko problem gained urgency. As one CIA memo noted, "the belief that there was Soviet and/or Cuban (KGB and/or DGI) connection with Oswald" would "persist and grow" until there was "a full disclosure" of "all elements of Oswald's handling and stay in the Soviet Union and his contacts in Mexico City"—or until Nosenko was broken. By summer 1967, as Helms later admitted, the Agency's investigation of Nosenko "reflected the concern or working hypothesis among many officers working on these matters that the Soviets might have been involved in this [i.e., the Kennedy assassination] in some fashion and that Cubans might have been involved. . . . That was obviously a matter of prime concern, and since Nosenko was in the Agency's hands this became one of the most difficult issues to face that the Agency had ever faced."

It was especially difficult because, by February 1967, New Orleans District Attorney Jim Garrison was forcing CIA's hand by publicly alleging that the Agency had killed Kennedy. Garrison had ties to Trafficante's close friend, reputed New Orleans underboss Carlos Marcello, and Garrison's self-styled "investigation," initiated just after Rosselli began to "sing," seemed to confirm precisely what the "turnaround" thesis postulated: when any hint of Cuban or Soviet involvement in JFK's death threatened to surface publicly, it would be matched by allegations implicating the Agency. Public opinion was meanwhile increasingly restive, after several best-selling attacks on the Warren Report, and Helms worried that CIA incarceration of Nosenko, a KGB defector who alleged CIA innocence, might even be mirror-read by the public as evidence of Agency guilt. That was just one more reason the Nosenko situation had become volatile, and Helms moved to defuse it before it could explode.

IN NOVEMBER 1967, Nosenko was blindfolded, handcuffed, and driven from his cell at Camp Peary to a luxurious townhouse near Washington. After being held prisoner for 1,277 days, he was now given considerable freedom of independent movement, was allowed to brush his teeth, and lived perhaps as well as anyone in Washington. In his plush new pad, Nosenko was questioned daily by Bruce Solie and other sympathetic Security people. They went through his career, and all KGB cases and personnel known to him. To Solie, it was "immediately apparent" that Nosenko was bona fide.

In January 1968, however, Pete Bagley completed a nine-hundred-page report which reached exactly the opposite conclusion, as did a study conducted independently by Scotty Miler. Though perhaps only codifying what had been believed since summer 1962, two of the most powerful "black" pieces on the U.S. intelligence chessboard, CIA's Soviet Russia Division and CI Staff, had now officially allied themselves firmly against Nosenko. But the white queen had yet to be heard from.

When Hoover was advised of Bagley's evaluation, he sensed that it could have grave consequences for his beloved Bureau. So Angleton, at least, seems to have later psychologized: if Nosenko was now found to be phony, this not only undermined the authority of Fedora, Hoover's KGB source at the UN, who had backed up Nosenko's story, but might force a new inquiry into Oswald's foreign connections, and expose all the FBI mistakes which had caused Hoover to concede: "There is no question in my mind but that we failed in carrying through some of the most salient aspects of the Oswald investigation." The director therefore abandoned his historical resistance to joint FBI-CIA operations by assigning Bert Turner, and several other FBI agents who accepted Nosenko's authenticity, to work with Solie toward the defector's total rehabilitation.

Solie and the Bureau were an easy "fit." He had worked closely with the FBI on many cases, including the ongoing Shadrin-Kochnov double-agent game, and, because his job was to see CI as simple security, he shared the G-men's open disdain for convoluted, theoretical constructs of the Angleton-Golitsyn school. "Solie was a security type, not an analyst, so we felt comfortable with him," FBI Soviet-CI man Bill Branigan said. "He was a rock."

The main emphasis in the Solie-FBI debriefings was in obtaining new counterespionage leads, and those "serials" were then taken as proof of Nosenko's bona fides. "An analysis of this case clearly indicates that Mr. Nosenko has been an extremely valuable source, one who has identified many hundreds of Soviet Intelligence Officers," Solie wrote in a rebuttal to Bagley's nine-hundred-page indictment. It was noted that "a considerable quantity of useful information on the organization of the KGB, its operational doctrine, and methods," including the identities of "nearly 2200" Soviet intelligence officers or recruitment targets, had been "forwarded to the Federal Bureau of Investigation based on data from Mr. Nosenko." The report went on to list some of those leads, including a loyalty investigation of ABC correspondent Sam Jaffe, and "remarks in regard to personalities in the pocket book entitled, *Svetlana, the Incredible Story of Stalin's Daughter.*"

When Scotty Miler read Solie's report, he pronounced it "a whitewash." The whole project, he believed, was based on a false premise—namely, that the Soviets would never have "thrown away" so much information to establish a disinformant's bona fides. What difference did it make, really, if Nosenko named twenty-two hundred KGB officers in 1963? It was nice to have in the files, but what good did it do, particularly if twenty-one hundred of those guys were going to be in Moscow the rest of their lives? As for the "spies" Nosenko burned, none of them was actually in a position to provide secrets to the Soviets—not Sergeant Johnson, not Jaffe, not any of them. Miler concluded: "To give him merit badges on any of that stuff is bullshit."

Perhaps most puzzling of all, Solie had devoted almost no effort to getting Nosenko's Oswald story straight. On January 3, 1968, Solie had asked Nosenko to write out an account of everything he did in the Oswald investigation. After reading this version, Solie concluded that there was "no conflict" between Nosenko's new Oswald story and the one given

Bagley in 1964. But it would have been difficult for Solie to have found any conflict between the two stories, because, by his own admission, he never compared them. Although he conceded that Nosenko's Oswald information was "an important part to be considered" in establishing Nosenko's authenticity, Solie never questioned Nosenko about what he wrote, or about Oswald generally, because he "never had any reason" to doubt Nosenko's story in the first place. Years later, during the reinvestigation of President Kennedy's death by the House Select Committee on Assassinations, Solie was asked in a sworn deposition whether he thought it possible that Nosenko could be lying about Oswald and still be bona fide. "I do not consider that he was lying about Oswald," Solie said. His questioners were taken aback by this dogmatic attitude, and asked him to clarify it. But Solie simply repeated: "I do not consider it." The questioners tried a different tack: if it were proved that Nosenko was lying about Oswald, would that change Solie's opinion about Nosenko? "It sure would." So why hadn't he asked Nosenko about Oswald? The CIA man passed that buck to the FBI. "As far as our office was concerned, the Oswald matter was an FBI matter," he said. "They would be in a much better position for that judgement than I would be."

Miler was frustrated, but with both the CI Staff and SR Division against Nosenko, and only Security for him, Nosenko's attackers seemed in a good position to outflank his defenders during CIA's final disposition of the case. Before that could happen, however, the FBI officially got into the Nosenko sweepstakes with a report of its own. In a Top Secret working paper disseminated to CIA on October 1, 1968, Bert Turner cited "significant confirmatory information" obtained during the Bureau's 1967–68 interrogations, and found "no substantial basis to conclude that Nosenko was not a bona fide defector."

Deputy DCI Rufus Taylor, who was managing the the case for Helms, now had four reports to consider: Bagley's and Miler's, indicting Nosenko, partly on Golitsynist grounds, and Solie's and Turner's, which supported Nosenko largely because of his utility to the FBI. Bureaucratically speaking, the score was tied, and Taylor would have the swing vote. Three days after receiving the FBI's report, he had made up his mind.

"The FBI summary notes that a minimum of 9 new cases have been developed as a result of this re-examination and that new information of considerable importance on old cases not previously available resulted from this effort. Thus, I conclude that Nosenko should be accepted as a bona fide defector. In addition, I recommend that we now proceed with the resettlement and rehabilitation of Nosenko with sufficient dispatch to permit his full freedom by 1 January 1969."

To discuss just how Nosenko should be freed, Taylor suggested that

Helms convene "the relevant personalities" at a final meeting in mid-October. Present at the big table in the DCI's seventh-floor Conference Room were Helms, Taylor, Inspector General Gordon Stewart, Solie and others from Security, the new SR chief, and a CI contingent headed by Rocca; Angleton was in the hospital with a minor illness. Everyone agreed that Nosenko should be quietly released, but Miler and the CI faction insisted that all past and future data obtained from Nosenko be tagged: "From a defector whose bona fides have not been established." That angered Nosenko's many defenders, especially Taylor.

All eyes were on Helms. He was preoccupied with getting Nosenko resettled, but he had never resolved the case in his own mind, and he hesitated to sign off on any document or make any final decision about Nosenko's bona fides. He therefore determined to cut the pie in half. The CI caveat about Nosenko's bona fides would stand; in that sense, the Angletonian skeptics had won. But as Taylor recommended, CIA's prisoner would be relocated, employed as a consultant to the Agency, compensated for the time of his incarceration, and made freely available to the FBI for the development of leads. The Agency would also take the official position that Nosenko had been "truthful and honest" in his Solie-FBI debriefings. In that sense the skeptics had lost, Solie and the FBI had won, and a de-facto acceptance of Nosenko had been achieved.

Even so, CIA officials worried whether tensions with the FBI had been fully resolved. Taylor warned Helms that, despite acceptance of the Solie report, "the FBI just might level official criticism at this Agency for its previous handling of this case." Because Solie had conducted Nosenko's re-examination with "finesse and candor," Taylor was "inclined to doubt that the FBI [would] wish to make an issue of our previous actions," but there was no telling what Hoover might do. The Bureau's Washington Field Office interviewed Nosenko regularly after December 8, 1968, but CIA and FBI were unable to agree on the "proper characterization to be used in reporting information from the subject"—i.e., on whether Nosenko was telling the truth. No more than a tacit approval of Nosenko's future information could be given without the consent of Angleton's shop. The FBI was free to interview Nosenko, but his information couldn't be disseminated to the Justice Department, or to the White House, as "solid" or "reliable" intelligence.

That epistemological roadblock greatly annoyed Hoover, and the seventy-three-year-old director was becoming increasingly testy over constant clashes with CIA. Even if the Nosenko dispute did not provoke him to punitive actions, any number of other episodes might. Indeed, even as Solie and Taylor had been smoothing out FBI resentment over Nosenko, Hoover was riled by an Angletonian scheme that harked back to the days of Wisner's OPC mischief, and canceled out whatever goodwill Taylor and Solie had won.

SINCE THE EARLY 1950S, Angleton had been in charge of KK/MOUNTAIN, CIA's "Israeli account," and the forging of a special relationship with Israel's Mossad was to be one of his great legacies. The Mossad would become by consensus the most efficient spy service in the world, and it could be said that this had something to with Angleton's role as mentor to its various chiefs. Millions of U.S. dollars also must have helped, in exchange for which the Mossad agreed to act as U.S. intermediaries or surrogates in certain situations throughout the world. But the intimacy of U.S.-Israeli intelligence relations was not unproblematic from the law-enforcement perspective, especially when it was suspected that Israeli agents might be spying on their patrons.

In September 1968, Angleton arranged for Israeli intelligence officer Rafi Eitan to visit the United States. Eitan was a seasoned Mossad officer known as "Rafi the Smelly," because he had had to wade through sewage on a 1947 sabotage mission; he had scored his greatest coup in organizing the commando team that kidnapped Adolf Eichmann in 1960. Eitan had been recently put in charge of Lakam, the Mossad's Science Liaison Bureau, which aimed to keep Israel's defenses technologically superior to those of any likely aggressor. During his 1968 trip, Eitan and three other Israelis visited a Nuclear Materials and Equipment Corporation (NUMEC) uranium-processing plant in Apollo, Pennsylvania, which enriched uranium for Westinghouse, the U.S. Navy, and other contractees. After Eitan's visit, an audit by the Atomic Energy Commission (AEC) determined that two hundred pounds of enriched uranium, enough to make six atomic bombs, could not be accounted for.

The AEC suspected that NUMEC's founder and president, Zalman Shapiro, might have helped Eitan smuggle the uranium to Israel, and since the case seemed to have both foreign and domestic angles, both the FBI and CIA were informed. Neither agency could agree, however, on whose problem Israeli espionage really was. Perhaps because spying by a U.S. ally was such a sensitive issue, no one wanted official responsibility for the problem. A former congressional investigator who reviewed the Senate and House intelligence committees' files on Shapiro later told journalist Seymour Hersh about a yearlong war of memoranda: "The CIA was saying to Hoover, 'You're responsible for counterintelligence in America. Investigate Shapiro, and if he's a spy, catch him.' Hoover's answer was, "Go to Israel and get inside Dimona [the Israeli nuclear program], and if you find it [evidence of the Shapiro uranium], let us know.'

It was kind of a game. The memos were hysterical—they went back and forth."

But Hoover, at least, was playing a double game. Though he refused, on the one hand, CIA's formal requests to investigate Shapiro, the FBI was already investigating Shapiro under a massive counterintelligence program whose existence was hidden from the Agency. After Israel's Six-Day War against the Arab nations in 1967, which impressed upon Tel Aviv the importance of technological advantage, the FBI had noted that an increasing number of Israeli experts and business executives were visiting the United States. Reports started filtering back from U.S. executives who had been approached by Lakam agents. In 1968, under a super-secret project code-named "Scope," the FBI began tracking Israeli scientific delegations in the U.S., as well as the movements of Israeli Embassy personnel. Knowing that Angleton's CI shop was eager to maintain cooperation with Israeli intelligence and would likely not have thought too highly of the program, the FBI did not disclose it to CIA.

Shapiro was put under active FBI surveillance, and it was determined that he was under Mossad influence, though there was no firm evidence that he had smuggled the uranium. A Scope assessment of Eitan's visit did conclude that it was part of a Lakam effort to divert uranium from the NUMEC plant to Israel, but no formal charges were ever brought against Shapiro or Eitan. Nevertheless, the Bureau was concerned enough about Eitan's mischief to expand Scope in 1968–69 to include wiretapping and bugging of the Israeli Embassy in Washington. Consequently, some Israelis were asked to leave the country.

The Agency's resistance to those expulsions caused Hoover to suspect that Helms, too, might be playing a double game, and that CIA might be a partner in the very espionage it had asked the Bureau to investigate. Among the targets tracked by Scope in 1969 was Israeli professor Yuval Ne'eman, a former colonel in Israeli Military Intelligence, who made frequent and lengthy stays in the United States. The FBI watched him as he visited Lawrence Livermore Laboratory near the University of California at Berkeley, and Caltech's Jet Propulsion Laboratory in La Cañada, near Pasadena. As a result of that surveillance, FBI officials believed they had conclusive evidence that Ne'eman was working for Lakam, and finally they confronted him. Ne'eman was ordered to register formally as a foreign agent of the Israeli government or risk deportation. Knowing that registering as an agent would automatically deny him access to most research facilities, Ne'eman stubbornly pretended innocence. The G-men then revealed all they had learned about his activities in-country. Horrified, Ne'eman contacted Mossad's station chief in Washington, D.C., and asked for help. The station chief decided to circumvent the FBI by appealing to CIA.

A few days later, Angleton suggested to William Sullivan that it would be in the U.S. national interest if the Bureau left Ne'eman alone. Angleton was negotiating an expanded U.S.-Israeli intelligence-cooperation deal, he said, and he didn't want the Bureau's hounding of Ne'eman to put that arrangement at risk. Papich relayed the message and the FBI backed off, but Hoover was furious. Not since the days of Wisner's OPC, when foreign nationals had been running wild all over the country, had the Agency asked the Bureau to countenance such mischief. At the very least, the Agency's foreign liaison interests were in direct conflict with the FBI's domestic imperatives. "As was typical," recalled an FBI deputy director, "intelligence cooperation superseded effective counterintelligence here to protect our secrets. The Israelis knew that was our tendency, and they took advantage of it."

Also typical was that the whole matter of U.S.-Israeli technological cooperation, like so much conflict between CIA and FBI in the late 1960s, may have been ultimately rooted in Angleton's reliance on Anatoliy Golitsyn. If Angleton was, in fact, helping Rafi Eitan build Israel's atomic capabilities, he was almost certainly doing so in the attempt to maintain a pro-Western nuclear counterweight to the Ba'ath socialist government of Iraq, whose role as a Soviet client was a subject of much Golitsynist suspicion. The defector believed that the Soviets would cultivate Third World client states as part of the KGB's long-range plan, and when Saddam Hussein's own writings proclaimed that the Soviet-Iraqi alliance was based on a unity of long-term "strategic interests," Golitsyn began to see Saddam as a key rook or knight in the Soviet endgame. Chilling, then, was Leonid Brezhnev's 1968 gift to Saddam of a nuclear "research reactor," at Tuwaitha, on the east bank of the Tigris River. It was only a week after this that Angleton arranged for Eitan to visit the NUMEC in Pennsylvania, and only a few months later asked for Ne'eman to be allowed continued access to rocket-propulsion secrets; the sequence of events may not have been coincidental. It may well have been Golitsyn's concerns that caused CIA to condone one of the great ironies of the Cold War: the smuggling of technology gleaned from ex-Nazi rocket scientists, at the Jet Propulsion Laboratory and elsewhere, for the delivery of nuclear devices in defense of a Jewish state.

THAT EVEN THE MOST otiose of FBI-CIA conflicts in the late 1960s could be traced back to Anatoliy Golitsyn was testimony to just how divisive the defector's message was proving to be. As the decade neared a close, the long-standing war over which axis would guide U.S. counterintelligence, CIA-Golitsyn or FBI-Nosenko, reached a point of crisis. Papich would maintain that Hoover's own opinion on Golitsyn was not unilaterally formed—that the boss "pretty much relied on the analysis and the viewpoints of his men, no question about it"—but Hoover clearly had a close acquaintance with the impact of the Golitsyn thesis on FBI reporting from Soviet sources, and in one case it deeply embarrassed him.

In 1970, British intelligence had "turned" Oleg Lyalin, a KGB man under diplomatic cover in London. They sent over intelligence digests containing his material to the FBI for circulation through to the CIA, and on up to the president. Hoover was so proud of the fact that Lyalin's information had been obtained from the British by his agency that during a vacation in Florida, when he called on President Nixon at his holiday home on Key Biscayne, the FBI director went out of his way to ask, "How do you like the British reports from their source Lyalin, Mr. President?"

"What reports?" replied Nixon. He had never received them.

Hoover turned red with rage. Calls to CIA determined that all intelligence from Lyalin had been dead-ended in Angleton's safe. The CI chief suspected that Lyalin was yet another disinformation agent, as predicted by Golitsyn, and had refused to circulate the documents to Nixon.

If Lyalin had been the first such source to be knocked down by Golitsyn, Hoover might have been able to tolerate Angleton's skepticism. But, coming at the end of a decade which had seen CIA disparage a whole series of FBI sources, the Lyalin affair turned Hoover irrevocably against Angleton and Golitsyn—and against Sam Papich, who was still trying to merge the incommensurate mind-sets.

"There's no question about it, I did present the views of Jim Angleton and his people on defectors," Papich reflected. "And I mean I made it clear that they should be considered. I needled the hell out of Hoover and a lot of people. I definitely knew there were people in the Bureau that completely disagreed with me. You can run into FBI agents and they'll tell you, 'Sam's a great friend of mine, but, boy, did he get sucked in by CIA.' But I honestly felt Jim's criticism could help correct us where we were weak, on disinformation. So I questioned the Bureau's position on Nosenko and Fedora. I gave my reasons for it. And I presented CIA's views. Of course, at CIA I presented the FBI's position. To me, it wasn't a matter of rooting for one or the other team, depending on your loyalties. Goddamn it, it was just a matter of analyzing what you had there."

That attitude was killing his FBI career. "Sam routinely took on Hoover," Larry McWilliams would say, still in awe more than twenty years later. "When Hoover demanded that certain things be written up in certain ways for his own purposes, Sam refused him. He said, 'There's two sides to this argument—ours, and CIA's.' Well, that was his end."

In 1969, Papich started getting the message that he wasn't "fitting into the picture." There were little hints—not being invited to "closed meetings," and getting little blue ink digs on interoffice memoranda: *Does this fellow Papich have all his marbles today?* Papich had been around long enough to know Hoover's tactics, and by early 1970 had come to the conclusion "that I was no longer useful as a liaison man."

He probably could have hung on at some post out in the field, but Papich was fifty-seven years old, and he felt physically and mentally beaten. There was no sense staying with an organization that did not really want him anymore, and at such a cost to his family life. He was lucky to have a wife who was considerate about the long days and lost weekends, but it wasn't doing her any good, and it was getting to him, too. He hoped to spend more time with his son, Bill, who was coming home disillusioned from an army tour in Vietnam, cursing Nixon and all the policymakers for fighting a political war, not going in to win, and Sam didn't argue with him. He'd seen in Washington the way decisions were based on all manner of considerations but merit, and it sickened him, too. He didn't like Washington, never did want to work at headquarters, and, looking back, he thought it amazing that he had lasted almost twenty years in that atmosphere—getting into disagreements with Dulles, with Bedell Smith, John McCone, Dick Helms, "bouncing among all those wheels in both agencies like a goddamned tennis ball."

But he had a lot of good friends at both agencies, and no misgivings. Relations between the two outfits had developed and grown. In the beginning, back in 1952, it was just Papich and CIA, but gradually he had got people to see each other, and now, despite all the differences over defectors, which would with luck clear up, G-men and spooks were working together on cases in New York and Washington and all over the country, whether Hoover wanted them to or not. That wasn't all the liaison man's doing, but he had incited it and inspired it to some extent. At the very least, he had left the secret world a better place for his having been there, which was something few men could safely say. He would do it all again, if he could relive the past. But he had no future in the FBI.

On February 15, 1970, Papich submitted a letter to Hoover, giving five weeks' notice of retirement. This letter was an unusual document. Interlarded among traditional kudos to the legendary director were a number of polite but implicitly critical pleas for the FBI to move more aggressively, and work more closely with CIA, against foreign spies. The United States had "never faced the kind of sophisticated and dangerous Soviet-bloc espionage" that it did now, and the Bureau needed to make some changes if it were to meet the new level of threat. The FBI had no real CI training program, and "nothing in the way of computerized counterintelligence," and, given the Soviets' excellent capability of monitoring telephonic communications from Lourdes, Cuba, steps needed to be taken to secure the lines of FBI communication between Washington and New York. The Bureau should also try to see CIA's side on certain issues, like requests for technical coverage, and Papich later admitted "taking off on the whole subject of defector bona fides." Urging a reconciliation between warring CI philosophies, Papich ended by expressing the hope that Hoover would appoint a new liaison officer who "might more easily smooth over the difficulties between the two agencies."

But this criticism boomeranged, reinforcing Hoover's desire to continue in his old ways. Papich later acknowledged that his letter "really shook up J. Edgar," as he had hoped it would, but he hadn't anticipated Hoover's furious accusation that the letter had been "drafted by the CIA." Nor had he any idea that his criticism would boil up all the resentment which had been building in Hoover's soul—stirred by the penetration and defection controversies of the 1960s, but really brewing ever since Donovan's men had started invading his turf back in the summer of 1941.

"I want to abolish the Liaison Section," Hoover barked at one of his deputies, Mark Felt, after reading Papich's letter. "It's costing us a quarter of a million dollars a year, and other agencies obviously benefit from it more than we do. Let the supervisors handle their own contacts with other agencies." Felt said he would look into it—"I think we can work out something which will be effective"—but privately he was horrified. "Papich had an extremely effective working relationship with the CIA," Felt later wrote, "from the lowest supervisor to Richard Helms." His reputation, even among those who thought him too Angletonian for a G-man, was that of "an honest and sincere man with high professional competence and an insatiable appetite for work. More importantly, in an area potentially fraught with jealousy, intrigue and deceit, he had the trust of the CIA and the respect of the FBI, if not its Director." But it was Hoover who counted, not his men, and clearly he had made up his mind.

Of course, a pretext was needed for such a drastic move as the breaking off of liaison with CIA. Hoover and Felt found it in a bizarre case twenty-five hundred miles to the west, which had begun the spring before.

JUST AFTER MIDNIGHT on Sunday, March 9, 1969, at a ranch-style home on a snowy hill in Boulder, Colorado, a pretty young woman had locked herself in her first-floor bedroom, opened the window, and screamed for help. When a neighbor ran over and helped her to the ground, he noticed about her a strong odor of what smelled like chloroform. Boulder police, summoned to the scene of this domestic disturbance, were met at the door by another woman, later described by officers as "the fullback type." She had graying hair, a ruddy complexion, and horn-rimmed glasses; she gave her name as Galya Storm Tannenbaum. She said she was "doing a little work for Immigration now and then," and had been attempting to have the screaming woman, Mrs. Thomas Riha, sign some type of immigration papers which had to do with "divorce proceedings."

Lurking submissively behind the imposing Tannenbaum was a man who looked like Gary Cooper. This was University of Colorado history professor Thomas Riha, a thirty-nine-year-old Czech émigré, and the screaming woman's husband. Police sensed immediately that he and Tannenbaum were lovers, a classic case of "opposites attract."

But why had Riha's wife been screaming?

When interviewed at the neighbor's house where she had taken refuge, Mrs. Riha said she had been in bed when she heard whispered voices in the study and awoke to sense a strange odor. Feeling dizzy, she opened her window and called for assistance. Under her bedcovers, police found a small bottle containing what was subsequently determined to be ether.

Nevertheless, police concluded that "no foul play" was involved. They were not particularly concerned that, when asked for proof of her employment with Immigration, Tannenbaum stated it was in her car, but failed to produce it. It would be some months before police learned that the name of Julia Galya Storm Tannenbaum had appeared in the wills of two persons whose deaths had been described by authorities as suicidal and accidental, respectively.

That pattern would loom in significance after March 16, when Professor Riha failed to show up for a faculty meeting. Colleagues came by his house, looked through the kitchen window, and saw a table set for a breakfast never eaten. They never saw their friend again. Police soon discovered that Riha had recently transferred the title to his car, house, and furniture to Tannenbaum. In January 1970, she was arrested for forging the will of another Colorado man, who had recently died with cyanide in his blood. The local police chief told Scott Werner, the special agent in charge of the FBI's Denver Field Office, that Riha had probably been murdered by Tannenbaum. But before any direct evidence could be developed, a District Court declared her legally insane, and she was carted off to a Boulder mental hospital. There she became known to fellow inmates as "a kind of witch of the ward," and it was not long before she was found dead by cyanide poisoning, with a suicide note in the pocket of her dress.

Newspapers were meanwhile speculating that Riha was a victim of international intrigue—"either kidnapped by the Russians, or picked up by the CIA or the FBI." His colleagues told reporters of generalized suspicions that Riha had intelligence links, but could produce no proof. In fact, Riha had been of some interest to both CIA and FBI since emigrating from Czechoslovakia in 1947. Fluent in five foreign languages, he had taken a leave of absence from doctoral work in the Harvard history department to study at Moscow University, from June 1958 to September 1959, leaving Russia just as Lee Harvey Oswald arrived. The Bureau debriefed him on his return, and cross-referenced its Riha file: "Soviet Intelligence Services—Recruitment of Students." The FBI report noted, "It is not believed at this time that Riha possesses any double agent potential," but a later Bureau document disclosed "that at one time subject was of some interest to CIA."

After Riha's disappearance, Angleton and his staffers were left to wonder, as Miler would put it, "whether there was an STB [Czech intelligence] or KGB connection." Angleton naturally tried to connect the Riha affair with the larger events of the day: Was it significant that Riha, a Czech, disappeared just after the Prague Spring? Was it possible that Riha was a deep-cover, long-term illegal after the manner of Rudolf Abel? If so, had he bolted after being tipped by an "emergency contact" that he might be exposed by one of several recent Czech defectors? "We never could find out," Miler later said. "There was information that he was in Czechoslovakia, but we never got anything more; we never could confirm it." Indeed, Papich advised his superiors in April 1969 of CIA's belief that the Czechoslovakia story was "without foundation," although the University of Colorado had been publicizing that angle to quiet rumors. The Agency had also stipulated that, despite its previous interest in Riha, it was "not utilizing subject in any capacity," and did not know where he had gone.

CIA repeated that disclaimer publicly, but by late 1969 it had failed to neutralize speculation about an Agency role in Riha's decampment. As a result, CIA's man in Boulder, a nonoperational "domestic contact," worried that the Agency might be "kicked off campus." He therefore told University President Joseph Smiley, who was very concerned about Riha, that the professor's absence was "merely a marital matter" and that Riha was all right. The CIA officer attributed that information to an FBI agent, and pledged Smiley to secrecy.

But Smiley fumbled the ball. By January 1970, he had inadvertently told reporters that government officials had assured him that Riha was safe, and Denver SAC Werner suspected that CIA might have leaked this information. Werner's inquiries produced "some equivocation" from CIA officials, and by January 28 he was lamenting "unfavorable relations" with

CIA in Denver. Finally, just as the sun sank behind the Rockies on February 10, CIA's domestic-contact agent in Denver, Mike Todorovich, called Werner and came clean. He admitted that a "CIA representative in Boulder" had told Smiley that Riha was all right. Todorovich alleged that both he and the Boulder officer had "got this information from an FBI agent in Boulder."

Werner demanded to know the name of the FBI agent. Todorovich demurred. Werner began shouting. Until he had the name, he would assume CIA was lying.

Four days later, FBI headquarters was told that Smiley was trying to float a retraction. His information about Riha was based on someone else's "honest mistake." Smiley thought this "cleared the air." But Hoover wrote: "I don't. I still want name of our agent which [CIA representative] gave to Dr. Smiley."

Sam Papich was still on duty for a few weeks, closing out his files and cleaning out his office, and his main project before retiring was now to get the name of the offending agent from CIA. On February 17, according to FBI records, "Liaison Agent Papich vigorously protested . . . to CIA, charging the Agency with impeding our inquiry." Papich pointed out that CIA's "stubborn refusal to divulge the identity of the Bureau agent involved was unacceptable because we had no information to support the information attributed to our agent." As a result of Papich's protest, a CIA official telephoned the Agency's Boulder officer and insisted that he divulge the identity of the G-man. The officer refused as "a matter of personal honor," and offered to resign before squealing.

Papich went higher. On February 20, he visited Helms in his seventh-floor office at Langley, went through the background of the case, and asked Helms to help him. The DCI maintained that he did not have the identity of the FBI agent, but said that CIA's Boulder officer had been recalled to HQ and would be "interviewed in detail" by Helms personally. In the meantime, Helms was requesting his subordinates to prepare a report covering all CIA knew on the matter. Helms advised that he considered this "a most serious development" and fully recognized "the gravity of the situation," since it had a "bearing on relations between the two agencies and the highly important work of both organizations."

The CIA officer arrived in Washington on February 24, and Helms heard him out. Two days later, Papich carried a Personal and Confidential letter from Helms to Hoover.

The FBI director read it at his desk, with blue pen poised.

"Dear Mr. Hoover," Helms began. "Mr. Papich has informed me that you wish to have the identity of the FBI agent who was the source of certain information communicated to an employee of this Agency. I have reviewed this complicated case and have requested [my employee] to reveal the identity of his source.

"As a point of honor and personal integrity," Helms wrote, his man "was adamant that he could not disclose the identity of his source, and had maintained this position under further pressure from me stating that in defense of it he was prepared to submit his resignation immediately." The officer had given out his Riha story merely to counter media speculation that U.S. intelligence had killed or kidnapped the professor. He had tried to coordinate this white-propaganda process with SAC Werner, but the FBI man had instead "engaged in an oral exchange during which he remarked that our representative in Boulder was 'lying.' "

Hoover scribbled, "Werner acted properly."

Helms went on: "I feel that poor judgement was employed in passing the information in question. This should only have been done with specific FBI approval." At the same time, Helms had "no reason to doubt" that his man had "acted honestly" and "reported to me in good faith," being "sincerely interested in preserving a sound working relationship between the CIA and the FBI."

Hoover wrote: "I do not agree."

"I hope sincerely," Helms continued, "that this recent incident will not impair our mutual efforts in making certain that we have not overlooked factors possibly having a significant bearing on U.S. intelligence and internal security interests. I shall pursue this matter through our respective liaison offices.

"In closing, Mr. Hoover, I wish to state that this Agency can only fully perform its duties in the furtherance of the national security when it has the closest coordination and teamwork with the Federal Bureau of Investigation. Furthermore, it is necessary that we continue to conduct our business in an atmosphere of mutual respect. I trust that we can coordinate closely any future developments or actions in these cases, in order to prevent the airing in public of conflicts or differences between the two agencies."

Hoover's comment: "Helms forgets that it is a two way street."

"I strongly feel that there are representatives of the news media who are eager to exploit alleged differences on a national scale. Disturbing as this experience has been, I wish to thank you in the interests of our common cause for having communicated with me in such a forthright and candid manner. Sincerely, Richard Helms."

Underneath the DCI's signature, Hoover wrote: "This is not satisfactory. I want our Denver office to have absolutely no contacts with CIA. I want direct liaison here with CIA to be terminated & any contact with CIA in the future to be by letter only. H."

When Sam Papich read those words, his blood ran cold. He rushed into Hoover's office and beseeched him in the strongest terms to reconsider, pleading that a close relationship between the two agencies was vital to an effective national counterintelligence effort. The intricacy of CI cases, combined with the speed of travel and communication, required direct personal contact between the FBI agents and more than a dozen CIA officers daily. Communicating by mail would be an unworkable situation, Papich warned. By cutting off liaison, Hoover would only "drive a wedge" between FBI and CIA, accomplishing in one capricious instant what the KGB had been patiently trying to do for years. This wedge would create a dangerous gap, which communist intelligence would naturally exploit.

"I was very strongly denouncing the cutoff of liaison," Papich allowed. "You know, I'd been working my butt off for years to build bridges, and the boss severs relations with the Agency, just kind of overnight—yeah, I blew my stack."

Hoover listened quietly. Then he said, "My decision stands," and went back to work on the pile of papers before him.

That afternoon, Papich informed Helms that no "new Papich" would be coming around after his retirement, because Hoover had "terminated" the liaison-officer position. Papich was despondent, and Helms was grim.

The outgoing liaison agent tried one last time to reason with Hoover, in a memo on March 2. "I hope that you will share my alarm," Papich wrote, being "absolutely convinced that the intelligence services of Great Britain, France, West Germany and others," including the FBI and CIA, were "well penetrated by the Soviets." It was important for the agencies to work together in rooting out these penetrations; the KGB must not profit from interagency differences. "The break in relations between the FBI and CIA will provide a basis for promoting further rifts," he warned Hoover. "I appeal to you to leave the door open."

Hoover did not respond to Papich's letter. Instead, that same day he sent a Secret Coded Urgent teletype to all FBI field offices in cities where CIA also had a presence. "IMMEDIATELY DISCONTINUE ALL CONTACT WITH THE LOCAL CIA OFFICE," the message read.

No one pretended that Hoover had decided to break liaison simply in a "fit of pique" over the unsolved disappearance of a Czech professor. After all, he had endured far worse transgressions by men like Bill Donovan, Donald Downes, William Harvey, and Frank Wisner, but had never cut off relations because of them. And if it was often true, as CIA's Lyman Kirkpatrick observed, that "superficial and insignificant mistakes resulted in greater adverse reaction than the important ones," it was no less true that the impact of seemingly trivial errors could be magnified, so to speak, at the end of a bad day, when one was looking for an excuse to blow up.

For Hoover it had been a bad *decade*, coming after two others which, from the perspective of interagency relations, were less than wholly good. Scotty Miler and others at CIA later told Senate investigators that the deeper causes of the liaison rupture included the Bureau's lack of CI savvy and research resources, differences of opinion on possible moles, and, most especially, disputes over the bona fides of Nosenko and Golitsyn. The Riha episode, as Angleton later said, was simply "the straw that broke the camel's back."

"I LEFT UNDER A CLOUD," Sam Papich recalled. "It was standard for any retiree to get a letter from J. Edgar, and a picture taken with him. But I got nothing. Quite honestly, I'm not bitter about it, but that's the way it was."

Papich insisted that his retirement ceremony be kept "quite brief," but it went on for a couple of hours, because so many people wanted to talk to him. He was loaded down with gifts of one kind or another, mostly fishing equipment, and he had to get help carrying it all out to his car. It was almost like what Hoover himself would get from his men for Christmas, and what he had once got from the public, back during the Dillinger days. The comparison was not lost on G-men like McWilliams. "To me, and to everyone else I knew, Sam was a jewel. What happened to him, with Hoover, was a travesty. Sam should have been running the goddamned place, after Hoover." CIA officers like Raymond Rocca would revere Papich as a martyr to the true CI cause—"an outstanding person, who really understood, and because of that, suffered much."

The Papich legend only grew when, in coming years, he stood virtually alone among disillusioned ex-FBI men in refraining from blasting Hoover, supporting him even in private conversation with his closest friends. How, people asked him, can you look at Hoover with any sympathy or support or kindness, after what he did? Papich would just say, "Well, I disagreed with the man, but on the other hand I had some great assignments under him." And then he would change the subject.

BOOK FOUR

CHAOS

CHAPTER THIRTEEN
THE HYDRA
PROJECT

WHEN J. EDGAR HOOVER broke liaison with CIA on February 26, 1970, America was quite a different country than it had been when Sam Papich joined the secret world some thirty years before. As Papich drove home to North Arlington that night, after the worst day of his life, the news on the radio did nothing to cheer him. In Saigon, the U.S. Marine Corps command announced that five American soldiers had been charged with murdering eleven South Vietnamese women and five children while on patrol south of Danang. At the University of California in Santa Barbara, hundreds of peace demonstrators smashed store windows, burned a Bank of America, and hurled firebombs at police, who dropped tear-gas grenades from helicopters and begged Governor Ronald Reagan to declare a state of emergency. In San Francisco, a District Court judge heard a civil suit by David Hilliard, a leader of the Black Panther Party, challenging the constitutionality of the law banning threats against the president's life. When, in coming days, Papich tried to escape this troubled world by going to see a movie with his wife, now that he had time, he discovered just how far the changes had reached. There were ads for X-rated films in the movie pages of the *Post*, unthinkable only a few years earlier, and—as if to symptomize the malaise of confusion that had struck the secret world, as well as society—Alfred Hitchcock had made his first boring thriller, *Topaz*, from the Leon Uris novel about an irascible Soviet defector modeled on Anatoliy Golitsyn. Uris' story ended happily, with the defector's daughter giving a piano recital of an original composition called *The American Dream*, whereas Golitsyn's daughter, a talented artist, had fallen in with a bad crowd, and died of a drug overdose.

The cultural revolution had made itself felt even among Golitsyn's keepers at CIA. The first sign had been beards. It was nothing new for CIA officers to come home full-whiskered from postings in Asia and Africa—the kind of places where one thought: Well, if I'm ever going to grow a beard, this is the place to grow one—but by the late 1960s a lot of people were not shaving them, and Agency headquarters had begun filling with sideburns and goatees and muttonchops, which lent something of the atmosphere of a steamboat pilots' convention. The next transformation was women wearing slacks, which traumatized the old guard, particularly West Pointers and other military types. Then came the addition of young computer programmers and systems analysts, at a time when, nationwide, there weren't really very many, so CIA was competing against RCA and IBM, and therefore not only had to pay considerable salaries to these new people but had to take them in sandals, with hair down to their shoulders, and all that sort of thing. Director Helms would deflect complaints by saying, "You know, we just don't need to have the same kind of mold applied to all our personnel, we need to have some young people who are part of that culture." On the other hand, when he first saw an employee in the Executive Dining Room wearing a high black turtleneck shirt, no coat or tie, and a medallion around his neck, his eyebrows did go up.

But there was one institution where the traditional American way of life seemed purely preserved, her old customs and mores protected intact. J. Edgar Hoover's FBI remained in a cultural time warp. One could walk down its spit-polished corridors, past crew-cut crusaders in suits and hats, and get the impression that it was 1959. The only hints of change were at Hoover's 30th Street hermitage, where his living room displayed a large stereo, the kind that flashed colored lights as different notes were hit. The director's beloved backyard grass had also been torn up for easy-care AstroTurf after James E. Crawford, his chauffeur and gardener, had been disabled by a brain tumor; Hoover never wanted anyone around the house he didn't know, a prudent prejudice for someone who'd received over a thousand threatening letters from left-wing revolutionaries in 1969. FBI sedans were parked under the elms at either end of his street, agents sitting there all night or whenever he was home, and motorcading with him in the mornings. "It was great," one of Hoover's neighbors would remember. "You could cancel your insurance when they were out there."

In fracturing daily interface with the Agency, however, Hoover had crippled the Bureau's efforts to cover and comprehend the same domestic disturbances which now endangered his life. Of course, though Papich no longer came over each day, that didn't stop communication by courier pouch, and superficially the rupture might have seemed a mere inconvenience, surmounted by telephone calls over newly installed secure lines, and through meetings on the sly. Helms, for one, refused to appear disturbed by the development, precisely because he knew that Hoover expected some kind of reaction. General consensus, though, was that the country was in trouble. Scotty Miler believed that Hoover's move had injured U.S. counterintelligence, and FBI CI man Charles Brennan "very definitely" believed, as he later said, "that this adversely affected the operations of the FBI." Many G-men, such as William Sullivan, saw the breach as a principal impediment to FBI's domestic collection efforts, especially regarding the possibility of foreign sponsorship to terrorism and dissent.

The disruption of FBI efforts was particularly troubling to Sullivan and others because, coincidentally enough, on the very afternoon Hoover terminated direct contacts with CIA, the U.S. Army announced it would no longer monitor antiwar dissent. The FBI had now to carry sole responsibility for investigating political disorder and violence. That was an impossible duty, and the Bureau's inability to perform it would drive two U.S. presidents to desperate measures in the attempt to conjoin the rival halves of U.S. counterintelligence.

THE BUREAU HAD BEEN monitoring ideological "subversives" since FDR's antifascist edict in 1936, and on up through the McCarthyist period, but 1960 marked a new era of drastic social change, posing new problems which should have brought about better-defined legislation. Failing that, the Bureau fell back on guidance from presidents. In the early 1960s, the FBI had begun unlawfully burglarizing Ku Klux Klan headquarters in Louisiana, obtaining its membership list and financial records, then subjecting suspected troublemakers to surveillance, and sometimes arresting them before murders were committed. The tail-side of that coin was investigation of civil-rights leader Martin Luther King, Jr., whose most trusted adviser, Stanley Levison, was believed by the Bureau to be a key financial backer and organizer for the American Communist Party. The Justice Department also sanctioned COINTELPRO ("counterintelligence program") operations against the communists and other radical groups. If, for instance, Professor Jones was a member of the Socialist Workers Party and was running for the school board, a friendly neighborhood FBI agent might send a letter to the local newspaper saying, "You may not know it, but this bird is a Marxist fanatic."

Although Papich and some others at the Bureau had been quiet critics of COINTELPRO projects—not because such operations were judged immoral, but because "we were not trained to do that kind of psychological-warfare work"—there was no going back after the mid-1960s, when political protest turned increasingly violent. The hope of civil-rights progress within a democratic framework imposed by Northern white liberals seemed symbolically to die with Jack Kennedy, and despite Lyndon Johnson's strong support for voting rights and welfare bills, sit-ins soon gave way to riots. Early in 1965, leading New Left theoretician Franz Fanon pronounced that "violence invests character with positive and creative qualities"; the next year H. Rap Brown, who had once directed nonviolent protest as head of the Student National Coordinating Committee (SNCC), declared that "Violence is as American as apple pie." From SNCC was born the Black Panther Party, an urban-guerrilla group that was armed and, by its own declarations, very dangerous.

By spring 1967 the goals, tactics, and rhetoric of the Black Power movement were taken up by the largely white "free-speech," countercultural, and antiwar movements which had been building at college campuses since 1964, and the result was an amorphous phenomenon that came to be called the New Left. This was really a disjointed collection of individuals, ranging from those who simply grew long hair and experimented in the drug scene, to several millions of middle-class students concerned with the Vietnam situation, but including a relatively small core of radical revolutionaries, probably no more than a few thousand, who formed the active membership of groups like Students for a Democratic Society (SDS) and the Youth International Party (Yippies). These groups denounced the old American Communist Party and Soviet Union as moribund and defunct, aligned themselves with Third World revolutionary movements (China, Cuba, the Vietcong), and openly advocated the violent overthrow of America's "bourgeois" constitutional democracy. Until that happened, they hoped that the Constitution would protect their right to organize massive antiestablishment demonstrations such as those during 1967's "Summer of Love," which became the worst period of racial riots and the largest political protests America had ever known.

Pressure on the FBI to stoke up its investigations increased when President Johnson concluded that the protest movement must be the product of a foreign conspiracy. That theory had been presented to him by Republican Senator John Tower of Texas, who had tried to give a conciliatory speech from the steps of Sproul Hall at Berkeley, only to be drowned out by "all the rhetoric of the Communist anti-American propaganda mill." Tower considered himself lucky to get away with his life, and was sure that, however "indigenous" the sentiment, the scale and seeming coordination of radical action must be due to "external influence." That set Johnson to thinking. Was it any accident, he wondered, that a number of Black Panthers had reportedly traveled to Algeria, North Korea, and Cuba, then come back denouncing his Great Society welfare programs as a "capitalist trick"? For that matter, what were Jane Fonda and other dissidents doing in North Vietnam? When polls showed that a majority of the American people still supported military intervention in Southeast Asia, a cause that was "so clearly right for the country," as Johnson muttered to his advisers, how could it be "so widely attacked if there were not some foreign force behind it"?

But the FBI's ability to verify Johnson's hunch, or disprove it as paranoia, was crimped by Hoover's new hesitance to undertake warrantless surveillance. Johnson's push for coverage on subversives had come just four months after Hoover rejected, for the last time, requests for black-bag jobs and other illegal methods, and when the FBI prepared a study for the White House in July 1967, the lack of intelligence resulted in a weak thesis. "Certainly there was evidence of Communist direction," recalled the FBI's Charles Brennan, but that "direction" seemed to be primarily in the form of "ideological guidance." There was "no evidence" that dissidence was being "funded from abroad." As far as the FBI could tell, they were dealing with middle- and upper-income people, whom Brennan considered "credit card revolutionaries."

The president would not be persuaded on that point. The American conservative mind had always regarded left-wing dissidence as something external, an alien import, rather than as, say, a consequence of the political right's own failure to articulate a consistent moral basis for capitalism. Unfathomed was the fact that communist revolutionaries took much of their moral inspiration from ideals like altruism or collectivism, whose roots could be traced to the brother's-keeper ethics of Christianity. Nor were pacifist movements, or their tendency to turn violent, novel phenomena in American history. New England's Transcendentalists had been devoutly antiwar until slavery became an issue, whereupon they purchased rifles and ammunition for the abolitionist guerrilla leader John Brown. Once the Civil War broke out, bloody "peace" riots had nearly cost Abraham Lincoln his re-election. But Lyndon Johnson certainly did not see the problem in that kind of historical or intellectual context, and by August 1967, unhappy with Hoover's "product," he was already turning to Central Intelligence.

PRESIDENTIAL PRESSURE ON antiwar matters created an immediate problem for Richard Helms. Surveillance of domestic dissidence was really the FBI's duty, even if uncovering their suspected foreign links could be a legitimate CIA job. How, then, could Helms comply with LBJ's request without encroaching on J. Edgar's AstroTurf? *Very carefully*, and probably not even then. Setting aside the whole molehunt fiasco, post-McCarthyist cooperation between CIA and FBI on the foreign connections of certain

American citizens had been shaky since February 1963, when McCone formally established a Domestic Operations Division (DOD). The stated purpose of the unit was "to exercise centralized responsibility for the direction, support, and coordination of clandestine operational activities of the Clandestine Services conducted within the United States." Naturally, CIA was careful to stipulate some feared foreign connection to legitimize each domestic operation. The DOD must coordinate action "against foreign targets in response to established operational requirements. . . . Nothing in this instruction shall be construed to vest in DOD responsibility for the conduct of clandestine internal security or counterintelligence operations in the United States." Though distrustful as ever of CIA's designs, Hoover had agreed to compromises and "working arrangements," such as the February 1966 deal which gave CIA some operational leeway.

Yet the Agency's aim seems to have been somewhat imperialistic from the start. According to McCone's 1963 directive, "The essential relationship of DOD to divisions and staffs parallels that of a foreign field station. The future establishment of subordinate bases is envisioned." CIA officer Victor Marchetti would recall that, after creation of the DOD, many clandestine officers under Helms continued "to press for additional operational duties in the United States, claiming that the FBI was not sophisticated enough to cope with the KGB."

Even before Hoover's mid-1960s "conversion" to civil libertarianism, there had been a feeling that the FBI was not providing enough support domestically, let alone the right kind. Since the FBI's statistical reporting procedure measured effectiveness in numbers of prosecutions, Hoover was reluctant to approve certain kinds of investigations, such as the "leaks" of government secrets to the press, which tended to be undertaken less on legal than on political grounds. CIA found that situation unsettling, given its statutory responsibility for protecting intelligence sources and methods, and therefore sometimes put together its own "plumber" units to stop the leaks. In 1959, for instance, a foreign newspaper correspondent and two U.S. writers were the object of CIA telephone taps, which Allen Dulles authorized without consulting the FBI, and two American newspaper reporters were the target of an Agency tap again in 1963. Discovery of such projects inevitably led to FBI criticism of CIA for violating its charter, and to what Marks termed "constant bureaucratic bickering." But Hoover's final January 1967 refusal to do bag jobs only increased pressure on CIA to conduct its leak investigations.

Within a month of that decision, in fact, the Agency had initiated its largest plumbing operation to date, one which would eventually become a "desk" to handle domestic subversive matters for LBJ. When *Ramparts* magazine, a New Left organ, exposed CIA sponsorship of the liberal but anticommunist National Student Association—yet another domestic incursion which Hoover could not have heartily welcomed—the question arose: Who had blabbed? Were there any links between the *Ramparts* crowd and hostile intelligence? CIA's Richard Ober was ordered to find out, and began building computerized files on all individuals and groups, American or otherwise, with *Ramparts* "connections."

Ober was working on that project out of the CI shop, and when Helms' clandestine-operations chief, Tom Karamessines, asked Angleton on August 15 to find someone to run a new Agency unit for Overseas Coverage of Subversive Student and Related Matters, Angleton chose Ober, who had already keyed in information on several hundred Americans for the *Ramparts* database. Much as Angleton had once created a Special Investigations Group (SIG) to hunt for Soviet moles, he now created a Special Operations Group (SOG), to search for communist connections to domestic disorder. The SOG would be under Angleton's CI Staff for rations and quarters, but Ober would run the SOG as Miler ran the SIG—"tightly controlled, and tightly compartmented." Because CIA was now keeping files on the political activities of certain Americans, there was, as in the case of its continuing mail-openings, a special need for discretion. Angleton himself would not have access to many of Ober's documents, not even the carbons, and the new unit quickly became known as "the deep snow section."

No attempt was made to hide Ober's function totally from the FBI; the most that could be done was to mask it. "Because of the pressure placed upon Helms, a new desk has been created at the Agency for the explicit purpose of collecting information coming into the Agency and having any significant bearing on possible racial disturbances in the U.S.," an FBI memo tersely recorded. Technically, coverage of racial disorder was an internal security function, but the president had directly ordered it, and Hoover had to sit still. To reassure the FBI director, Helms had stressed that CIA was only to collect information concerning U.S. racial agitators who might travel abroad, and Karamessines had mandated that Ober feed his findings to "appropriate departments and agencies which have the responsibility domestically," which meant mostly the FBI. Not mentioned was Ober's burgeoning database, or the collection of information on New Left activists—or the fact that, rather than restricting itself to servicing the Bureau's requests for coverage of American dissidents, CIA had launched its own program, which would operate and report to the president independently of the FBI's, and compete with it. As Karamessines confided to Angleton, the SOG had "definite domestic counterintelligence aspects."

Merging Ober's preliminary take with tidbits from the HT/LINGUAL mail-openings, Angleton and Miler thought they discerned some patterns suggesting foreign involvement. Some American leftists went to Cuba as part of the so-called Venceremos Brigade and came back as well-trained guerrillas and saboteurs, presumably after being trained by Soviet-bloc intelligence. Other activists flew from New York to Stockholm to Berlin, then disappeared for three weeks, only to come out in Prague. Mail intercepts showed that certain individuals who traveled to Moscow and North Korea were at least keeping Soviet institutions informed of their plans and actions—nothing illegal in that, but it was suggestive. And how could these students or occupational radicals afford to travel so much? Unlike Brennan and other FBI men, who created the concept of "credit card revolutionaries" to cover that contingency, Miler thought there was more to it than bourgeois parental largesse. After all, the FBI thesis could not cover racial radicals, like Julius Lester or Rap Brown or the Black Panthers, and even for the New Left it was demographically and sociologically suspect. How many parents of that generation approved of their children's activities? How many of them said, "Son, here's $2,000—grow your hair long, visit Hanoi, and blow up the Pentagon"? Some activists were "red-diaper babies," whose parents had gone to New York's City College and organized garment workers and talked social justice at the breakfast table, but being a professional socialist was not like running Standard Oil. People like Abbie Hoffman or Jerry Rubin or Mark Rudd were not preppy WASPs or trust-fund brats, but working-class Jewish kids from places like Queens, New York. Yet, when they went to Prague for two weeks and stopped over in Paris, they weren't doing it on bicycles, and they weren't staying in hostels at $2.00 a night. Whence came the cash?

From Soviet "peace fronts," perhaps? Nothing could be demonstrated, of course, without bag jobs on the U.S. offices of such groups, but Angleton's CI Staff knew from Golitsyn and other defectors that in 1949 the Soviet Politburo had determined to sponsor what it called "the peace movement" in the West, by funding "front" organizations and recruiting agents of influence. Party ideologist Mikhail Suslov had ordered that "Particular attention should be devoted to drawing into the peace movement" both "youth" and "political and public leaders." And after 1963, it seemed, a large number of young and radical political leaders had been associated with the Institute for Policy Studies (IPS), a Washington-based think tank heavily endowed by de-facto Soviet influence agent Samuel Rubin. After emigrating from the USSR in the 1920s, Rubin became a member of the Communist Party of the U.S.A., and despite being a communist, he made a fortune in Faberge, Inc., which he founded in 1936. Rubin sold the lucrative family business in 1963, the same year that IPS was established with his money, and by the mid-1960s the institute had brought together such militants as Stokely Carmichael, Tom Hayden, Jerry Rubin, H. Rap Brown, and many other representatives from SNCC and SDS. When seven black militant groups, including the Panthers, met in December 1966 to form a black-power alliance, they did so at IPS headquarters. Rubin's daughter, Cora Weiss, led Women Strike for Peace, and had mobilized thousands of women from thirty-five states in a march on the Pentagon on February 15, 1967. When American radicals met with foreign counterparts in Bratislava, Czechoslovakia, in September 1967, to coordinate a massive international "day of action" on October 1, IPS fellow Christopher Jencks was there to meet with North Vietnamese and Vietcong representatives. There was no evidence that IPS was serving as a "paymaster" for the Panthers or Yippies, and there would have been nothing illegal about it if it had been. But given the Rubin connection, the pattern of IPS involvement in radical action did seem significant from the CI perspective.

From other viewpoints at CIA, however, it seemed Ober and Angleton had come up with only patterns of suspicion, not conclusive facts. There were no photographs of KGB or Czech intelligence officers handing SDS leaders suitcases of cash, no taped conversations showing radicals to be acting on orders of a foreign power, no "hard evidence" that IPS people who went to Cuba had done anything but cut sugarcane. "Within the Agency itself, there were those who took a very staunch stand that there was no foreign involvement," Angleton recalled. "And these were fairly senior individuals, mainly on the overt side of the business. This attitude was very definitely that there was nothing to it; namely, foreign contact."

As he had a habit of doing, Helms carefully split the difference. There was no conclusive proof of foreign sponsorship, direction, or control, he reported to President Johnson on November 15, but demonstrations had been "coordinated" by meetings in communist Prague. There might be more to the situation than met the eye, but CIA simply had not been able to cover important angles. In particular, the Agency lacked data on "finances, foreign embassy contacts in the U.S., and campus radicals"—which, as Helms reminded the president, "could only be met by levying requirements on the FBI."

Johnson probably did not grasp exactly what Helms was asking. The FBI, which had always had the leading role in monitoring domestic dissent, was used to "levying requirements" on CIA for coverage of radicals—not the other way around. In 1960, Papich had made it standard operating procedure to inform CIA about the overseas travel of American "subversives," as a Bureau manual explained, "to place stops [requests for coverage] with appropriate security services abroad to be advised of the activities of these subjects." Although CIA provided the same kind of information to the FBI for domestic "stops" on suspected foreign agents, such as communist diplomats, there was no precedent for CIA's asking Hoover: Give us all your files on American student radicals, bug the Black Panthers for us, and, while you're at it, burglarize IPS.

But the White House wanted results, not a lesson in bureaucratic delicacies. Badgered by Johnson to work "with" CIA, Hoover finally consented, in July 1968, to service Agency "requirements" in a field which had for thirty-two years been the monopoly of the FBI. Henceforth the Agency was to get all FBI reports on dissidents and their known contacts, and Ober would cross-index them in a special CIA computer system, Hydra. To safeguard the ultra-sensitive fact that CIA was keeping files on the activities of American political activists, Karamessines limited headquarters distribution of such intelligence by creating a special reporting cryptonym, MH/CHAOS.

It is unclear whether and to what extent the FBI knew about CIA's work under Chaos, which on a few occasions shaded into outright domestic spying. Tom Charles Huston, who kept an eye on domestic intelligence for the White House, later mused that "Hoover would have had an absolute stroke if he had known that CIA had an Operation Chaos going on." FBI agent Jay Aldhizer, who worked Black Power cases, later complained: "I never knew that the Agency was involved in domestic programs. Stokely Carmichael—the Bureau was always trying to get information on him, and since he lived in Africa, we expected CIA to give us all kinds of good scoop. But it was probably one of the lowest priorities CIA had, you know? Maybe people above me, at higher levels, knew, and the Agency would keep them posted, but I've always held that against the Agency. I always felt like they had a lot of information that they probably never disseminated to the Bureau, that could have helped us with what we were trying to do."

Miler and others would insist however, that Ober's work was known to the Bureau, at least in a general way, and that the problems came not so much over turf as over "how information was handled" at the working levels. "It was like in the Tairova case—that *kind* of thing," Miler said. "Could we rely on X field office? Did they have the manpower to follow up our leads, or would they use too much, and blow the source? So we were careful about what we passed them, and I'm not sure they knew how much data we were collecting."

Though the full scope and nature of Chaos was apparently kept hidden from the Bureau, consensus at the Agency was that Ober's work was a proper counterintelligence function. If there was any "gray area" or unavoidable overlap with FBI work, it was only because one had to consider both the foreign and domestic sides. Miler felt that the problem "pretty fairly graphically illustrated the impossibility of this demarcation between the domestic and the foreign responsibilities. Where do you divide the line? Unless there is real centralization, and very good coordination, between the Bureau and the CIA, you aren't going to get the kinds of leads and basic information that permit you to follow up. We were supposed to know what Eldridge Cleaver was doing in Algeria. In a logical sense, it seems easy, but it's complicated, also, by the fact that, in order to go that way, you have to know what's going on here. How did a Black Panther leader know that he would get sanctuary in Algiers if he fled there, unless he had somebody telling him that here? How did he make those connections, and who was involved? Those ordinarily might have been questions for the FBI. But the idea was that the FBI didn't know enough." After all, their work stopped at the border. As Ober put it: "Obviously, if you're talking about links between the foreign individuals or groups of people in the United States, to understand any link you need some information on either end."

Operation Chaos thus led to some unlikely interagency teamings in places like Mexico City, where old CIA hands like Joseph Burkholder Smith were serving out their final days. When Smith arrived in 1969, he found that Chaos work with the Bureau was the first and most frustrating priority of Sam Archer, Mexico Station's resident CI officer. Precisely because Archer's information had been collected "jointly with the FBI," Smith noted, "more station space was taken up by files than by people. . . . J. Edgar Hoover insisted that all FBI memoranda be written on especially heavy bond paper, thicker than the paper used by any other agency of the U.S. government. Any file containing FBI memos quickly became fuller than any file which didn't." And much of what was in the FBI memos, according to Smith, was merely the product of poorly targeted paranoia. The first thing Smith learned was that the initials "ACGM" stood for "American Communist Group in Mexico"; the one thing that seemed to make the ACGM a "group" in the FBI's view was that all had fled the United States during the McCarthy era. The file of every person identified as ACGM was filled with telephone-tap transcripts, surveillance reports, and informant accounts—but no firm evidence of contacts with communist intelligence.

Ober believed that better results might be obtained by opening the mail of dissidents in the U.S., rather than tapping the phones of those abroad, and had suggested as much to Papich on January 16, 1969. The Bureau should not overlook Hunter Project, the FBI-CIA mail-opening venture, for "development of leads in the New Left and Black Nationalist fields," and the Bureau might wish to consider "placing stops on certain key personalities." But when Papich dutifully reported Ober's idea to Hoover, it was killed by cold blue ink: "stops on black extremists not warranted at this time."

HOOVER'S HESITANCE TO HELP CIA increase dissident coverage coincided with Richard Nixon's arrival in the White House, and marked a gambit by the FBI director, not only to reclaim his lost role as leading political policeman, but to usurp CIA's authority abroad by playing the "Nixon card." Hoover and the president went back a long way, had seen each other socially at least a hundred times—"Shit, Hoover was my crony," White House tapes caught Nixon saying—and they still considered themselves old friends, partly because both had been active against suspected communists in the McCarthyist era. Nixon had no such ties with Helms, who was asked to stay on as DCI, but who quickly found himself reporting to the president through National Security Adviser Henry Kissinger or Attorney General John Mitchell. Hoover, however, retained his personal access to Nixon, and used it to convince him that an expansion of FBI jurisdiction was the best way to uncover foreign sponsorship of domestic unrest.

Like LBJ before him, Nixon suspected that leftist troublemakers "were being aided and abetted, if not actually inspired, by Communist countries," as his chief of staff, H. R. Haldeman, recalled. After only a few days in office, he called in both Helms and Hoover—separately, of course—to push for better coverage. Each blamed his problems largely on the other agency, but Hoover's case was apparently enhanced because Nixon liked him, and owed him a favor: according to William Sullivan, Nixon had asked Hoover not to investigate Mitchell before his confirmation hearings, as was done with all other attorneys general.

"By merely making the request of Hoover," Sullivan recalled, "Nixon put himself right in the director's pocket. Never a man to let any advantage go to waste, Hoover used his leverage with Nixon when the president called him over to the White House . . . to complain about the quality of domestic intelligence being supplied by the FBI. Hoover smoothly changed the subject from domestic to foreign intelligence and sold Nixon on the idea that he should be permitted to expand our international intelligence network. Hoover proposed that Nixon allow the FBI to reopen the overseas offices that had, with some exceptions, been closed or only minimally functional for so many years." Hoover reportedly told Nixon: "When these offices are fully operational, Mr. President, I will give you better information than the CIA." Nixon gave the go-ahead, prompting an outburst from presidential counsel John Ehrlichman, who had hoped the president would hire a new FBI director. "That goddamned Hoover! He swung Nixon around!"

Sullivan likewise thought Hoover had "sold Nixon a bill of goods," but Papich and others supported putting G-men in more embassies—with the understanding that there would be coordination with CIA. He and Angleton agreed that there were a lot of things on certain operations overseas that the FBI could do with locals that were just not right for CIA to be doing. For example, FBI, being law enforcement, could deal with its overseas counterparts, such as Scotland Yard, in getting certain information, or instituting a certain type of an operation, though still coordinating with CI. They could conduct interviews—as FBI agents. As Papich contended, "There was a very important role for FBI overseas."

Richard Helms was not so sure. The president assured him that Hoover's legats would stick strictly to the investigation of crimes, but Helms was not going to abet any further overseas encroachment—even if his own men requested it. When William Colby asked to borrow some G-men for Operation Phoenix, a counterinsurgency program aimed at neutralizing double agents in rural South Vietnam, he was turned down.

For the better part of a year, the Bureau's overseas expansion went smoothly, especially in Northern Europe, where experienced CI men like Larry McWilliams were sent to help effect it. As assistant legal attaché in London during the mid-1960s, on leave from the Nosenko furor, McWilliams had worked well with Scotland Yard, and, despite differences of philosophy, had managed to get along well with CIA since his 1950s adventures in Pigeon's Paradise. In 1970, as Mac moved the FBI into Norway, Sweden, Denmark, and Finland, his first step was always to drop in on the local CIA station to broker a "special arrangement." If he wanted to meet the security chief in Finland, he couldn't just go up there "cold," but would use CIA to set things up. That was the Papich-Angleton conception of how things should work, and it was shared by Mac and most everyone else but Hoover. "I don't think the boss ever knew the system was operating like that," McWilliams said. "In fact, I'm positive he never knew, because before I even got over there, I was told, by some higher-ups, 'If you're working closely with the Agency, make sure that CIA never sends a communication back with a copy for the Bureau. We're supposed to be striking out on our own.' So I know that Hoover didn't know about that dependence on CIA, because he probably would have canceled it."

But when obeyed by less imaginative agents in places like the Middle East, Hoover's demand for FBI "independence" soon caused trouble. "We were making a lot of people angry," Sullivan later wrote. "Our men overseas were under instructions from Hoover to send everything straight to him, without clearing it first with the ambassador, the CIA, or the State Department. Two of our men in Israel sent in some incorrect information, and when Hoover unwittingly sent it on to Kissinger and Nixon, the people at the State Department hit the ceiling. A real flap developed, and Nixon finally had to tell Hoover—it couldn't have been easy—that our agents had to clear their reports through the ambassador and the CIA before sending them on to the United States. That really cramped Hoover's style. He liked to go around ambassadors, the CIA, military intelligence, and everyone else who stood between the director and the president."

By fall 1969, in fact, President Nixon, like Johnson before him, was already beginning to "go around" Hoover to CIA. This time it happened through the graces of Attorney General Mitchell, who was "keeping an eye on intelligence matters and on covert action matters," as Helms perceived. Mitchell felt that Hoover was "too timid" about using wiretaps and other "black" techniques against American radicals, and admired Helms' more aggressive approach. Helms ended up consulting with Mitchell, as the DCI later conceded, "on a variety of problems affecting CIA that an Attorney General would not normally have been privy to." Mitchell was intensely interested in CIA's mail-openings, and also liked the work CIA's Office of Security had been doing in Operation Merrimac, a sister project to Ober's initial *Ramparts* inquiry, which used construction workers to gather intelligence on IPS-linked groups who might potentially attack CIA installations. Impressed by Helms' fighting spirit, Mitchell urged him to expand CIA's domestic coverage.

What Mitchell was asking, *as asked,* was very likely against the law, and Helms told him so. Merrimac could be justified by a need to protect "sources and methods," and Chaos by "foreign collection," but outright domestic coverage would violate CIA's charter. Still, the matter kept coming up in the context of feelers—as Helms recounted, "How can we do a better job, isn't there somebody else that can take on some of these things if the FBI isn't doing them as well as they should?" Despite Helms' hinting that flat-out CIA monitoring of U.S. dissent was illegal, and despite the continuing failure of Chaos and Merrimac to prove anything, the White House did not stop pressing.

Helms was also getting pressure from the working level, as Ober and the CI Staff felt increasingly that they needed more room to work in Hoover's yard. So by September 1969, Helms approved the development of "new sources" to feed Hydra and Chaos. One was MK/SOURDOUGH, a project to cover mail coming into the San Francisco Bay area from communist China and Vietnam. Technical Services experts flew out from Langley for three-week shifts, and, according to blind notes assembled by one participant in early 1970, the setup yielded "leads for domestic operations (Asian operations) and the FBI." Sourdough was soon augmented by a dramatic expansion of Chaos collection; the net was cast so wide that virtually all opponents of U.S. policy could be monitored. In October 1969, Ober for the first time "fully tasked" CIA's Domestic Contact Service (DCS, successor to DOD) to collect intelligence on "black militants; radical youth groups; radical underground press; antiwar groups; and deserter/draft resister movements." This new thrust produced such silliness as a CIA memo to the FBI listing all contributors to *The New York Review of Books*, and such seriousness as the burrowing of CIA moles into radical groups *inside* the United States.

Where possible, those penetrations were to be attempted with the assistance of the FBI, and one of Sam Papich's last meaningful actions as liaison officer was to accomplish that smoothly. Of forty potential recruits evaluated by Ober at CIA, roughly half were current or former FBI informants, lured by the romance of a foreign-intelligence assignment or in some cases already planning to travel overseas. Eighteen of those FBI referrals were hired, and then, to avoid being "caught out" as secret squares, underwent a "reddening" process. They held "rap" sessions to hone their facility in leftist theory and jargon. Arrangements were made for novice narcotics users to experiment sufficiently with marijuana and LSD. The agents were ordered not to shampoo, shave, or shower for a full week before their infiltration attempts. The Bureau provided questions for the agents' debriefings, and one of the CIA handlers consistently amazed the Bureau with the amount of data he could pull from the recruits; he was "like a vacuum cleaner." G-men who liaised with CIA on the project were so impressed that they soon levied requests for the agents to cover domestic targets when they returned from overseas missions.

Some of CIA's assets, however, refused to work with the Bureau. Principal among them was one who was described in a CIA memo as having "particularly good entree into the highest levels of the domestic radical community," and who thus reported some "extremely personal data." In the fall of 1969, it was determined that this prize source could not be sent overseas for many months and, in the meantime, would be debriefed for purely domestic information about his associates, "in part because he did not wish to deal with the FBI." There is some evidence to suggest that this Chaos agent might have been LSD guru Timothy Leary, who was "liberated" in September 1970 from a minimum-security prison in Lompoc, California, by members of the Weather Underground, a new and extremely militant group, and had then found his way to the Algerian headquarters of Black Panther leader Eldridge Cleaver. Later Leary turned state's evidence against the Weathermen who rescued him, giving a complete account of the escape and naming the "commandos" who took part. In 1966, Leary had had a "bad trip" at the hands of the FBI when then special agent G. Gordon Liddy led a raid on Leary's "acid estate" in Millbrook, New York, an event which could explain Leary's reluctance, if he was working with CIA, to cooperate also with the Bureau.

If Leary was indeed a Chaos agent, his infiltration-by-staged-rescue into the Weather Underground would certainly have made sense, for the Weathermen had become a top-priority counterintelligence target. After October 1968, when IPS wired bail to Weathermen arrested for overturning cars and smashing windows, Angleton staffers saw the group as yet another tentacle of the Samuel Rubin octopus. The September 1969 return of the group's "queen bee," Bernadine Dohrn, from her summer in Cuba had marked the beginning of a violent new phase of protest, which the Weathermen christened "Days of Rage." In October, they instigated a mêlée in Chicago; they raked police headquarters in Cambridge, Massachusetts, with sniper fire on November 8; they bombed Chicago police cars three weeks before Christmas. At December's end, a three-day "Wargasm Conference" of four hundred Weathermen was convened in Flint, Michigan, to plan their transformation into a PLO-style terrorist group, complete with guerrilla cells, safehouses, weapons caches, and bomb factories. Dohrn took the stage in a Flint ballroom in brown hot-pants, admonishing her "honky" colleagues to emulate the actions of Charles Manson's followers, arrested the month before for brutally murdering pregnant actress Sharon Tate and six other purported symbols of establishment life. Dohrn held up three fingers in a Manson "fork salute," mimicking the ivory-handled carving fork which had been found by police protruding from the stomach of one Manson victim; this replaced the two-fingered "peace sign" as the revolutionary greeting favored by the group. After three evenings of drug-fueled orgies in the nave of a Flint Catholic church, a select cadre of the most trusted Weathermen set up their first underground action cell—"The Fork"—in a townhouse on 11th Street in New York's Greenwich Village. But on March 6, 1970, one stoned Weatherman accidentally crossed wires while constructing a bomb he planned to detonate at Fort Dix, New Jersey, during an Army dance. The townhouse was totally destroyed, and three Weathermen were killed, but two others, Kathy Boudin and Cathy Wilkerson, escaped.

The townhouse explosion not only dramatized the full menace of the Weather Underground's intentions, but also demonstrated the inability of the nation's estranged CI agencies to anticipate the new level of threat, or to track the living suspects. The Bureau had not had any Weathermen under surveillance, and had no penetrations in the group. CIA's own Chaos agents were still in training at the time, so all that could be done was to hope for a break from FBI. But Bureau clumsiness soon negated an instance of bald luck that could have made the case. When the entire top leadership of the Weathermen, including Dohrn, went to see a movie at a theater just around the corner from the FBI's New York Field Office, they were spotted by a special agent, who waited till the lights dimmed, then approached one of them and said, "Excuse me, would you please step out into the lobby?" The fugitives, though high on LSD, scattered simultaneously toward different exits, and they all escaped.

Most galling of all, though, was the Secret Urgent teletype that had gone out from FBI Headquarters just four days before the 11th Street blast, breaking Bureau contacts with domestic CIA offices. That did not make it very easy for G-men who "held the tickets" on Boudin, Wilkerson, and other fugitives to swap leads with their opposite numbers at the Agency, who might supply the "Moscow connections" and other foreign-based clues. It was in that desperate, frustrating, violent atmosphere that one of Hoover's closest deputies now betrayed him, hatching a secret plan to restore FBI-CIA liaison.

CHAPTER FOURTEEN

THE SULLIVAN PLOT

HOOVER'S JUDAS WAS William C. Sullivan, the FBI's assistant director for domestic intelligence. A short man approaching sixty, Sullivan was regarded in the Bureau as something of a character, much as William Harvey once had been. He was one of the Bureau's few liberal Democrats, and an intellectual in the "nutty professor mode." His home and office were stacked with books, and Bureau efficiency reports consistently noted that "This agent does not always present a neat appearance." But his eccentricities were tolerated by Hoover because of his thirst for eighteen-hour days, his gift for brilliant, logical conversation, and his unquestionable loyalty. Hoover called him "the son I never had" until 1971, when Sullivan stood accused of being "more on the side of CIA . . . than the FBI."

Sullivan's good relations with CIA dated to 1961, when he began representing the FBI on the United States Intelligence Board (USIB), chaired by CIA's director. Sullivan was impressed by the exchange of ideas, especially compared to what he felt was groupthink in FBI meetings. "Everyone was uninhibited; every man spoke his mind. There was very little back-scratching going on; these were able, intelligent men who had done their homework." After 1966, Sullivan was much taken with Helms, who had "a great knowledge of intelligence operations but [who] in running the board ... always avoided any parochial approach." By decade's end Sullivan was smitten also with Angleton, and became CIA's main point of contact with the Bureau when Papich retired. "After I left, I understand that Sullivan saw Jim a lot more," Papich said. "These contacts were not known to Hoover. I don't know how solidly Bill bought into all of Jim's doubts, but he saw our vulnerabilities to penetration."

Indeed, Sullivan became convinced that the Soviets had placed several moles in the FBI's New York Field Office. But he had reached that conclusion "more from being persuaded by Angleton than from the FBI," according to McWilliams, and Hoover had consequently been of little help in finding the alleged FBI moles. When Sullivan had recommended gradually transferring people out of the espionage section in New York and replacing them with all new men—a shotgun approach that had been used by Helms and Angleton on the supposedly porous CIA Soviet Division—Hoover declined. "Some smart newspaperman is bound to find out that we are transferring people out of the New York Office," he told Sullivan. That was an eerily intuitive prediction, for reporters would eventually find out about CIA's mole transfers, and the Agency's reputation would be hurt by cries of "Witch-hunt!" Hoover spared the FBI that public relations trauma, but in Sullivan's view he also ensured that the Bureau would remain insecure.

Even before the liaison break, Sullivan had outlined the "Hoover problem" in a secret letter to Helms, but Helms felt that there was nothing either of them could do about it as long as Hoover was in control. "Bill, I'm with you, you know that," Sullivan would recall Helms as saying. "But as long as Hoover remains in the bureau there's not a damn thing that I can do, and I don't think anyone else will back you, either."

"Well, I'll try to do something on my own," Sullivan said.

"You haven't a chance," Helms warned. "But if there's anything I can do to help without coming out into the open as an opponent to Hoover, I'll back you."

Sullivan had lain low for a while after that, but the explosion of the Weather Underground's townhouse, just after the liaison break, gave him a pretext for proposing reform. Within hours of the news from New York, he composed a memo to Hoover.

Noting "CIA criticism which could generate from Agency belief that the Bureau has failed to cooperate and offer necessary assistance in collection of positive intelligence in the United States," Sullivan undertook to "briefly comment on policy of cooperation we have adopted with CIA." Careful not to let his own sympathies show, he cited "CIA belief that more aggressive action should have been taken in field of collecting positive intelligence in the United States," which "would mean increased technical surveillance, coverage, development of informants." Sullivan noted especially a refusal of CIA technical-coverage requests in October 1969; perhaps those requests had concerned the Weathermen, who had been achieving real notoriety then, in the Days of Rage, and who were the prime subject of CI concern on March 6, when Sullivan wrote. Noting that "our policy of cooperation with CIA . . . calls for guarding our jurisdiction but shows our willingness to cooperate with CIA," Sullivan concluded by recommending "that we . . . forthrightly ask CIA if it is satisfied with the status quo, and if not what do they have to suggest as changes."

In essence, Sullivan was trying to broker an interagency meeting of the minds, but by cloaking his proposal as a pre-emptive brief against "CIA criticism," he obtained Hoover's backing. On March 11, Hoover wrote Helms and asked for his views on FBI-CIA relations.

Helms' reply was crafty. "Dear Mr. Hoover," he wrote, "We endorse *your proposal* for a reexamination and bespeak *your desires* as to how this might be conducted [emphasis added]." Helms was smart enough to give credit where it wasn't due. Since Hoover had asked, however, Helms would raise a few subjects "deserving of your personal consideration," such as the question of bugs on domestic targets.

"For several years your Bureau has been receptive to requirements and leads which resulted in valuable coverage," Helms diplomatically lied, softening Hoover for what came next: "On 2 October 1969, two related requests for audio coverage were submitted by this Agency pertaining to positive intelligence targets. . . . Your Bureau replied that henceforth the Agency should refer all such cases directly to the Attorney General for approval. It is suggested that the question of audio coverage be repeated between representatives of your Bureau and this Agency." The DCI then extended the olive branch of technical assistance ("our most sophisticated equipment . . . offered you at cost or gratis") before gingerly raising the subject of the FBI's ability to collect information on such domestic threats as the Weathermen.

"I realize that your personnel are now somewhat at a disadvantage in carrying out the evaluating and reporting procedures necessary for the conduct of positive intelligence," Helms wrote. In the past, CIA had offered to institute positive-intelligence-training courses, including report writing and analysis, for FBI personnel, and Helms wished "to reiterate our willingness to provide such instruction." In the same mode, Helms suggested that FBI agents attend CIA seminars on "opposition Services" such as the KGB, "in order to keep abreast of new developments." The DCI ended by tendering the understatement that "there may be room for improving the quality of liaison."

Hoover's reply fell considerably short of what CIA or Sullivan wanted. The Bureau was eager to continue receiving "certain technical equipment developed by the Agency," but "inclusion of positive intelligence courses in our training curricula" would not be "feasible." As for "New Left and racial extremist matters," there was "already a considerable exchange of information between our agencies," and the only problem with it, according to Hoover, was that "we are definitely in need of additional information from your Agency as to the foreign aspects of the extremist movement in the United States, including foreign funding in support of local extremist organizations." Nor was Hoover about to go back to his old ways when it came to "black" techniques, let alone approve any restoration of formal liaison.

The only concession to Helms—or to Sullivan—was Hoover's approval of "seminars between specialists of our two agencies in selective areas of interest when justified by specific circumstances." That was only a tossed bone, but Sullivan retrieved it, and dropped it directly into the lap of a secret ally in the White House.

SULLIVAN'S COVERT PARTNER IN his plot against Hoover was a slight young man, just twenty-nine, with two-inch sideburns and a penchant for quoting the Federalist Papers. Tom Charles Huston had been a leader of the conservative Young Americans for Freedom, a U.S. Army captain assigned to the Defense Intelligence Agency, then a part-time volunteer for Nixon's 1968 campaign before joining the president's speechwriting-and-research staff under Pat Buchanan. On June 5, 1969, presidential counsel John Ehrlichman had asked Huston to report on foreign financing of revolutionary protest activity, choosing him for essentially the same reason that one might choose a black to examine racial problems. Huston was interested in the subject and, being under thirty and slightly "hip," presumably knew more about "the radical scene" than anyone else in the administration.

It was in that context that Huston had first come into contact with Sullivan, on June 19, in the Executive Office Building. "President Nixon has designated me to look into the entire intelligence operation in this country, to see whether we can improve it," Huston said. As Sullivan later told it, Huston ran down a list of student riots that had "caught the FBI completely by surprise," and chastised the Bureau for "lack of cooperation with other intelligence agencies, which was jeopardizing national security." Since Sullivan was as dissatisfied with Hoover's performance as Huston was, he assured the younger man that he would have his cooperation in pressuring Hoover to improve.

Sullivan assumed the role of mentor in what followed. One day after meeting Sullivan, Huston sent all U.S. intelligence agencies a memo on White House letterhead which clearly echoed the "Sullivan line," asking what gaps might exist "because of either inadequate resources or a low priority of attention." Sullivan later said that "Hoover hit the roof" when he read Huston's memo, and this set back the Sullivan-Huston initiative by about a year, but the two men kept in contact by phone, and often lunched together. Huston came increasingly under Sullivan's spell—"I do not think there was anyone in the government who I respected more than Mr. Sullivan"—and the young White House intellectual soon developed a theory on domestic dissent that reflected Sullivan's interest in the history of communism. Sullivan pointed out that Russia's revolt against the czars had really begun with a general university strike in 1899, which was soon co-opted by radicals. Student bodies and faculties became politicized, and Bolsheviks shrewdly incited acts which would bring repression, knowing that this, in turn would radicalize moderate dissidents. After two hundred demonstrators were killed in the "Bloody Sunday" of January 1905, Russian campuses were closed, and the country turned forever against its established form of rule. Sullivan thought communist dialecticians and campus radicals were now similarly hoping for "a [U.S.] police state that could be brought on by law-and-order overcorrection," which would turn the American public against its leaders.

Such a complex and subtle scenario could only be "preemptively resisted," Sullivan led Huston to believe, if the White House were to put liberal intelligence professionals, as opposed to conservative law-enforcement types, in charge of a secret counteroffensive. CIA should assume the leading role; the FBI "had neither the manpower nor the minds to do it." At the very least, failing such radical surgery, "the quality of data on domestic radicals could be vastly improved by increased FBI-CIA cooperation." The younger man listened ruefully as Sullivan recounted how, on "hundreds of occasions," Hoover arbitrarily denied CIA coverage requests in such language as "Screw the CIA—let them do their own work!" It was with Huston's backing, then, that Sullivan wrote Hoover about FBI-CIA relations on March 6, 1970, and then intrigued to parlay the FBI director's single concession—approval of "meetings between CIA and Bureau representatives"—into a restoration of liaison.

Sullivan began by lining up support for his plan at CIA, asking Angleton for what amounted to a shopping list of items for Huston to take to the president. Not wanting to diffuse presidential attention, Angleton cited only two areas for improvement. The first was electronic surveillance, which CIA needed for coverage on subversives and suspected moles. The second was a resumption of regular personal liaison, even if only in the form of "periodic seminars to coordinate our information." Those were just the issues that Huston hand-carried to Nixon on April 22, in what was to be Huston's only meeting alone with the president. After White House photographers lurched in for the obligatory handshake-shot, Huston had exactly ten minutes to make his pitch. The only way to restore CIA-FBI liaison and to get Hoover to resume warrantless coverages, Huston said, was for the president himself to give a "hot foot" to the FBI director. That could by done by forcing a series of sit-downs between CIA and FBI officials, such as Hoover himself had reluctantly authorized in his letter to Helms—with the difference that the president himself would chair the first meeting, and a White House representative would oversee subsequent sessions, until agreement was reached.

Nixon's chief of staff, H. R. Haldeman, would recall that "this recommendation fell on predictably fertile soil when it reached the President," for "Huston was saying exactly what Nixon was thinking." It was agreed that Nixon should meet as soon as possible with intelligence-community leaders regarding "gaps" in coverage, and that Huston himself would convene regular interagency meetings for "liaison with FBI and CIA on domestic violence, if they wouldn't liaison with each other." For symbolism, other agencies would be brought into the process, and Nixon would name Hoover "chairman" of the overall effort. For substance, William Sullivan would be in charge of any working-level groups, and would supply a two-page "talking paper" for the president to use in briefing the IC chiefs.

The plan was to have been put into effect in May, but Nixon's invasion of Cambodia on April 29 disrupted the entire White House schedule, delaying the Huston-Sullivan initiative another month. In the meantime, four student protesters were shot to death at Kent State, echoing Russia's Bloody Sunday, and the shutdown of campuses that spring also followed the Russian pattern. A series of meetings to coordinate and revivify domestic intelligence therefore "became even more important," as Huston later said. Haldeman reflected that "Kent State . . . marked a turning point for Nixon," a junction on the way toward Watergate, and the president's meeting with his intelligence chiefs on June 5 was among the earliest in a series of interlinked episodes—almost all of them involving FBI-CIA relations—which would eventually drive Nixon from office.

"THE PRESIDENT CHEWED OUR BUTTS," one participant remembered. The June 5 session lasted less than an hour, but Nixon presented a stern, angry front to Hoover, Helms, and Directors Noel Gayler and Donald Bennett of the National Security Agency and Defense Intelligence Agency. Huston was seated near the president, while Haldeman and Ehrlichman lurked on the sidelines. Nixon announced that he was forming a "special committee to study intelligence gaps, how to close them, and to enhance interagency coordination." He paused and looked deliberately at Hoover, then at Helms.

"Are you people getting along, working well together?"

Hoover frowned. "Well yes, we're doing very well."

Helms, caught off balance, was unprepared to challenge or contradict. He murmured his agreement.

Huston felt a sinking in his chest. Looking back years later, he saw such deception and bureaucratic timidity as emblematic of the difficulties he faced. For the moment, though, he took solace in the president's flat declaration that Hoover would chair a new Interagency Committee on Intelligence (ICI), and tried not to blush as the president announced to the much older men around the table that "this very capable young man," Tom Charles Huston, would monitor all meetings, to ensure "the scope of the review which I have in mind."

But Huston was merely a screen for his mentor, and the ICI would fold or flourish as Sullivan's show. The assistant FBI director was put in charge of the ICI staff, and his first move was to schedule a "planning session" in Hoover's office the following Monday. Hoover went through the motions of compliance, convening his fellow intelligence directors at the Bureau to plan the writing of a special report to the President, which Nixon wanted on his desk by June 25. The FBI director stressed that the president was unhappy with intelligence on domestic dissent, and admitted that he, Hoover, was himself worried about possible dissident links to Cuba, China, and Iron Curtain countries. No wonder the president wanted "a historical study made of intelligence operations in the United States and the present security problems of the country." Hoover hoped that the ICI would be able to satisfy the White House in this, and he asked the other directors if they had anything to add.

None did. Huston, seated on Hoover's left, cleared his throat.

"I didn't hear the president say that we should prepare a historical document," Huston said. "I understood President Nixon to say that he was dissatisfied with present-day operations and what the president really wants to know is what the present-day problems are in the security and intelligence fields. Further, the president wants to know to what extent they are being solved and *what we can do* to elevate the quality of our intelligence operations."

There was a long, long stretch of quiet. Then Gayler said, "Yes, Mr. Hoover, that was also my understanding." Bennett and Helms backed Huston as well.

Hoover "became crimson," according to Sullivan, to whom the director now turned. "Well, you're the one in charge of the working committee. Go ahead—do a study and prepare a report." He then asked the other directors to assign staffers to the project, and abruptly adjourned the meeting. As the intelligence chiefs filed out, Hoover muttered that Huston was a "hippie intellectual." Sullivan recalled that "From that moment on, Hoover hated Huston. He never called him by his right name, and in our conversations he never referred to him by any other name except that 'hippie.' "

For the moment it did not matter what Hoover thought of Huston, because Sullivan would be running the meetings from now on. The very next day, he chaired the first of four ICI "drafting discussions" at Langley. Huston carpooled out there with the FBI contingent—Sullivan, Don Moore, and William Cregar, who had been Sam Papich's assistant during the final days of liaison, and who was favored to succeed Papich if the position were ever restored. Sullivan understood the importance of a continuing White House imprimatur, so he let his mouthpiece, Huston, lead the discussion. With Sullivan's nodded approval, Huston tasked the FBI to prepare a report on the possible "domestic" improvements, CIA on the "foreign."

Angleton, wreathed as usual in a blue haze of cigarette smoke, monitored the proceedings with considerable interest. For someone so inexperienced, Huston was extremely aware of the gaps in CI coverage. Angleton realized that Sullivan and Huston had become close over the past year, and he knew what Sullivan's concerns were in terms of gaps. Huston certainly reflected those concerns. Angleton also knew that Sullivan didn't usually waste his time, and wouldn't be putting them through all this unless there was an excellent chance something could come of it. The key was the White House role. Huston's letter from the president seemed a clear-cut edict, declaring him the ultimate authority for domestic security in the Executive Branch. But could this young man ride herd over Hoover?

Angleton was at least prepared to let him try. The CI chief had "enormous respect" for Hoover, as he later said, and "understood the problems he had in sustaining the reputation of the FBI," but recentralizing the CI community must take precedence over parochial concerns. Angleton was ready to "practically drop everything" he was doing, as he later said, to resolve "conflicts [that] had grown specifically between the CIA and the FBI."

Helms, however, was wary of the unlit way before them. "I thought, since the president was so forcefully behind it, since he called the meeting to start it off, the improvements would probably come into being. But I didn't want to mix in domestic politics or law enforcement; that was somebody else's job." Helms made only a brief appearance as "host" for the first planning meeting, since it was being held in his headquarters, and then, as Angleton noted, "took off." He would not attend any more working meetings, but Angleton would keep him current as the ICI prepared its report to the president.

A preliminary report, authored by Sullivan on June 17, proposed a Permanent Interagency Committee to force FBI and CIA to work together. Huston thought that was "the most important recommendation" that could be made to the White House, but the draft also recommended the development of more "campus sources" (not specifying whether by FBI or CIA), and the resumption of warrantless surveillance. For tactical purposes, Sullivan would first submit the draft to Gayler, Bennett, and Helms, and only then to Hoover, saying, "This report has already been approved by the other three Directors." Consensus was that Sullivan had a good strategy, and the other agencies would play along. No one suspected that, the very next day, Sullivan would betray them all, disavowing his own report and realigning with Hoover.

ON THE EVENING OF JUNE 18, Sullivan learned that he would be promoted to number-three man at the Bureau, to replace the retiring Deke DeLoach. That put Sullivan in "pole position" for the directorship after Hoover—and offered an alternate route for realization of the Sullivan-Huston plan. Sullivan apparently calculated that he had more to gain by advancing his career, at the temporary expense of his plan, than by advancing the plan at possible long-term expense to his career. He had been playing a double game with Hoover, but now he tripled back.

"It is clear that there could be problems involved for the Bureau," Sullivan wrote Hoover the next day, passing along a copy of the "Huston" plan he had previously promised to hide from his boss. Hoover's new number-three opposed "the relaxation of investigative restraints which affect the Bureau," and even attacked the existence of the ICI and its mandate to improve coordination: "I do not agree with the scope of this proposed committee nor do I feel an effort should be made at this time to engage in any combined preparations of intelligence estimates." Within hours, Hoover called in Sullivan, thanked him for the heads-up, and scowled: "That hippie is behind this. Well, they're not going to put the responsibility for these programs on me." The FBI director was not merely opposed to a resumption of "black" coverage. According to Sullivan, "The provisions for better interagency coordination were anathema to him; he believed that he and the FBI operated best independently and unilaterally." As Hoover put it, "We've got enough damned coordination in government now, too much in fact!"

This sudden opposition to the ICI's work, even if secretly engineered by Sullivan, did pose something of a problem for him. His working subcommittee was supposed to produce a "final report" for signing just five days hence, and if one was not ready by then, Sullivan would have to take the blame. So he asked Hoover: why not just add footnotes to the ICI report, stating the Bureau's objections? Such a policy was allowed by the USIB, on which Sullivan sat. Hoover consented, and Sullivan had a secretary completely redo the draft before the fourth and final working meeting at Langley.

When the "final draft" of the report was distributed at the ICI's meeting, the other intelligence directors got all stirred up. If Hoover could add footnotes, why couldn't they? Huston pleaded that with only one day left before the official signing of the report, there was no time for additional changes. Helms acquiesced, knowing that there was no fighting both Hoover and the White House deadline, but Gayler and Bennett remained "mad as the dickens." Huston asked them to "live with" the situation until he could cover their concerns in a memo to the president.

Admiral Gayler expressed his contempt by arriving five minutes late for the three o'clock signing ceremony on June 25. The other directors and their aides were already seated at the long rectangular conference table in the FBI director's ceremonial outer office. Hoover greeted him by saying, "We hope this is not characteristic of the Navy." Gayler merely glowered at him.

After praising the participants for their "cooperative spirit," Hoover began reading page one of the report aloud.

"We couldn't believe what we were hearing," remembered Sullivan, who had promised everyone that the meeting would take only ten to fifteen minutes: these were busy men with full schedules, and how long could it take to sign a piece of paper? But, whether from senility or spite, Hoover was reading the entire report, all forty-three pages of it, as if it were a speech. At the end of every page, he would look up and query each of his chiefs, ostensibly giving them a chance to add any footnotes they wished. "Mr. Helms, do you have anything to add on page one?" he'd ask, and when Helms did not, he went on to Admiral Gayler, General Bennett, the others, and finally to "Mr. Hutchinson," or one of the half-dozen other names he used for Huston. Helms, sitting to Hoover's right, casually leaned back in his chair and winked behind the director's back at Huston, who was praying they'd get through the whole thing without anyone speaking out about Hoover's footnotes. But Admiral Gayler was practically biting through his lip, and he looked as if he was about to snap. Finally, he did. So did General Bennett. Hoover's dissenting footnotes, they protested, had essentially torpedoed the whole ICI process, which was supposed to bring *agreement* on various points of contention.

Hoover appeared to have trouble swallowing. He was obviously stunned that these men had dared raise critical objections during what was supposed to be a pro-forma reading. Huston looked toward Helms, who tried to smooth the waters by referring to the "special burdens of the FBI." Hoover remained visibly upset, however, and quickly skimmed through the rest of the pages. Despite objections to the FBI footnotes, everyone signed the report, and Nixon's deadline was met. Hoover reminded the rival chiefs to have all working papers destroyed, and ended the meeting. In all, it had taken an hour and a half.

Huston put the signed copy of the report into his briefcase, carried it back up Pennsylvania Avenue to the White House, and prepared a covering memo for Haldeman, who managed the presidential paper-flow. Trying to capture "the real result and attitude of the committee," Huston characterized Helms as "most cooperative and helpful," Hoover as a "stumbling block." Should the president adopt the ICI's recommendations, Huston recommended a face-to-face "stroking session" with Hoover, in which Nixon would explain that he was "counting on Edgar's cooperation." That was the only way of winning cooperation from a man who was "getting old and worried about his legend," and who was, quite simply, "bullheaded as hell."

Three weeks later, on July 14, Haldeman told Huston the president had "approved" all the recommendations, including an Intelligence Evaluation Committee to recoordinate foreign and domestic intelligence, and the lifting of FBI coverage restrictions which had been impeding molehunt and antiwar projects. Huston got nothing in writing, however. Ascribing that lack to a need to preserve presidential "deniability" concerning such matters as warrantless coverage, he prepared his own memo, noting Nixon's approval, and sent it to the intelligence chiefs. But the bureaucratically seasoned chiefs equated Nixon's failure to offer written authorization as a lack of support, and joked about Huston's signature on the plan. "They passed that one down about as low as it could go," remarked Bennett's assistant, James Stilwell. Nixon and Haldeman "didn't have the guts" to sign it themselves, and the use of Huston as a possible scapegoat indicated "what a hot potato it was." Indeed, even without Nixon's signature, presidential approval of certain terms in Sullivan's attempted CIA-FBI truce would later constitute article II of the House Judiciary Committee's 1974 Articles of Impeachment.

But if Nixon erred by orally approving the Sullivan Plan, he compounded his mistake by not agreeing to Huston's proposed "stroking session" with Hoover. According to Sullivan, Hoover "had yet another eruption" after reading Huston's approval memo; no hippie intellectual was going to order him around in the name of the president. He stormed straight into the office of Attorney General Mitchell, restating his objections to both warrantless coverage and permanent interagency coordination. At first Mitchell didn't know what Hoover was talking about, because, on Sullivan's urging, Huston had left him out of the ICI process. After Hoover filled him in, he was angry about being bypassed. Two days later, Mitchell met with Nixon and suggested that the ICI recommendations, "in toto," were not the kind of thing the president should put his name to—especially when the FBI director was so staunchly against it. If the White House tried to "buck Edgar," the FBI could always have the Huston recommendations leaked, which at the least would bring the enterprise to a sudden halt, and at most could land the White House in serious legal trouble.

Nixon agreed. That afternoon, Huston got a call from Haldeman, saying that the president had decided to "revoke" the approval memo and "reconsider" its recommendations. "In terms of lack of any coordination among the intelligence agencies," a dejected Huston told Sullivan, they were "back to ground zero." Within a few weeks, Huston was officially demoted to a "floater" position. He kept in contact with Sullivan and other CI friends via a special scrambler phone concealed in his office safe, and tried to remain their White House advocate on issues of "interagency" concern; on September 10, he wrote Haldeman on the need for "improved intelligence community coordination" against air hijacking—referring to Hoover, predictably enough, as "the chief obstacle." But Huston was disenchanted with his own diminished role at the White House, and with Sullivan's continuing inability to fix FBI-CIA liaison; he soon quit government for a private law practice. Like so many idealistic young intellectuals who had come to Washington, Huston had found that there was nothing so powerless as an idea whose time the bureaucrats would not let come.

. . .

THE FAILURE OF Sullivan's plot caused a groundswell of sentiment, even within the FBI itself, for Hoover's removal. His own men increasingly complained to one another, after hours, that Hoover was simply too old and out of touch. "The boss was just surrounded with a number of syco-phants, and a lot of them were as old as he was," McWilliams remembered. "His secretary, Helen Gandy, must have been about seventy-four; Tolson, well into his seventies, was three-quarters dead. We were run by a geriatric society. Hoover was a damned recluse, the average guy never really saw him, and for all we knew the man was taking a nap in the afternoon."

Hoover's old friend President Nixon was losing patience. Helms heard that Nixon "really wanted to get rid of Mr. Hoover, and was wondering how to get rid of him." White House sources confidentially told Helms that Nixon "did not feel that Mr. Hoover was doing a very good job of getting a hold on dissent in the country—principally, dissent on the Vietnamese War, and how much of it was foreign-inspired." Haldeman later corroborated the rumors that reached Helms. "As far as [President Nixon] was concerned, the FBI was a failure; it hadn't found Communist backing for the antiwar organizations which he was sure was there. And Hoover had cut off FBI liaison with the CIA. . . . The jealousies among various intelligence agencies were working at a white-hot pitch." An exas-perated Nixon complained to his chief of staff: "Those guys spend all their time fighting each other."

Shortly after the collapse of the Sullivan Plan, Mitchell had approached Deke DeLoach, then working for PepsiCo, to see "what would be the best way to get rid of Mr. Hoover." DeLoach was astonished that such an act would even be contemplated, but thought to himself: If they're going to do it anyhow, let's try to work something out so the boss can leave in grace. He suggested that Nixon make Hoover director emeritus, let him keep a small office and his secretary, because he didn't know how to order grocer-ies or handle correspondence, and also his bulletproof Cadillac and driver, because the boss didn't know how to drive. "Let the President do it, not you," DeLoach recommended, "and call upon him for consultation every once in a while on matters of espionage or organized crime." Mitchell said, "Good idea, I'll do it."

Two weeks later, DeLoach heard that Nixon had invited the director for breakfast and told him exactly what DeLoach suggested, but that Hoover "kept right on talking," as if he hadn't heard what the president said. Mitchell confided that Nixon didn't have "guts enough" to tell Hoo-ver he wanted a new director. The story went around that Nixon had said,

"I wanted to see you to discuss with you the issue of retirement," prompting a shocked Hoover to reply, "Why, that's ridiculous. You're still a young man."

CLEARLY THERE WAS NO getting rid of Hoover, but the White House was still determined to find a path around him. Huston himself had hinted as much when the Sullivan Plan was withdrawn. "He seemed to exude the attitude, 'What the White House wanted, the White House would get,'" a Navy observer at the Huston proceedings recalled. "If Hoover didn't want to play, it would be played some other way."

Reanimating the Sullivan Plan became a running project among the president's men, and the onus fell on presidential counsel John Dean. A sharp young California lawyer who had worked under Mitchell at Justice, Dean had the political savvy Huston lacked. He did not possess the counterintelligence knowledge Huston had garnered through tutorials with Sullivan, but in late August 1970 CIA gave him a security clearance so he could see a copy of the Sullivan proposal. Two Office of Security men made him promise to keep the document locked in a combination safe, to move it only in the company of a CIA guard, and to avoid talking into lamps, flowerpots, or paintings in any foreign hotel. Dean agreed, and was handed a sheaf of papers labeled "Top Secret/Handle Via COMINT Channels Only."

"You've got to be kidding," Dean laughed to Haldeman after he read the plan. "This sounds like something the people on 'Mission Impossible' would dream up." When Haldeman solemnly asked Dean to see what he could do to implement the plan, Dean suddenly realized that "These were the hottest papers I had ever touched." They called for removal of legal restraints on wiretaps, mail intercepts, and burglaries, as well as a legally dubious expansion of CIA coverage. Dean hesitated to mix in such matters, so he stalled for a few weeks until Mitchell assured him that "the President loves all this stuff." The hint was obvious: Dean had to take some action on the plan. But what could anyone do, Dean asked, if Hoover was so set against it?

Mitchell had an idea, though probably it was not his own. He had just lunched that day with Helms at Langley, to discuss the "possibility of improved interagency coordination." If an Intelligence Evaluation Committee (IEC) could be brought into being, as the Sullivan Plan proposed, it might become a forum for the continued pursuit of other objectives. Mitchell therefore approved putting the IEC under the Justice Department, so the Bureau could be forced to join. Similarly, to gain Hoover's confidence, the IEC would operate "within the FBI," being staffed by G-men and chaired by the Bureau's director, though he could easily be outvoted.

Hoover could smell a setup. He declined to chair the group, and did his best, or his worst, to delay the IEC's debut until December 3, 1970. Under the direction of Assistant Attorney General Robert Mardian, the IEC would aim, as Mardian later stated, "to increase formal liaison among the intelligence agencies, since Hoover had broken it off the previous summer." Most of the participants were old "Huston Plan" hands. As experienced CI men, they were soon disillusioned with the new group. Neither its creator, Dean, nor its leader, Mardian, had the foggiest conception of counterintelligence, and the IEC itself had no operational powers or resources, no leverage to implement the additional Huston recommendations, and therefore could put no "bite" into the eighty-five staff reports and "intelligence calendars" it sent to Dean at the White House.

Dean's failure to improve interagency cooperation, or to loosen legal restraints, caused counterintelligence professionals to cast about for alternative solutions, including the possibility that Sam Papich might once again work his magic. After "doing nothing" for a few months, Papich had become a consultant to the Joint Chiefs of Staff, helping assemble a "bible" on strategic deception, and then moved to the consulting staff of the President's Foreign Intelligence Advisory Board (PFIAB), a part-time civilian body intended as an independent White House watchdog. "That was great, because I had access to everything the board was getting from all the agencies," Papich said. "So I had some role in continuing developments in the whole area of counterintelligence, both FBI and CIA." Speaking with the authority of a two-decade liaison officer, Papich effectively represented the Agency's need for closer cooperation with the Bureau, especially in the area of electronic coverage. The board was persuaded to the point where it met with Mitchell and challenged him to do what other attorneys general had done—namely, authorize warrantless work. Mitchell promised to prepare a memo authorizing a return to previous policies, but eventually just sent the board a sheet of paper indicating, as Papich recalled, "that in no way did he agree to do anything that involved sticking his neck out. So the problem was still there."

BY SUMMER 1971, impatient for better coverage on antiwar matters, the White House was quietly encouraging CIA and FBI to encroach on each other's turf. Helms complied by continuing with Chaos, which was still kept hidden from Hoover. Hoover complied by resuming his overseas expansion, which was to be concealed from Helms. When asked by Secretary of State William P. Rogers if Helms knew about the planned expansion, Hoover told him, according to his own memo of the conversation, "that he did not, and I did not believe the President was desirous for him to know. . . . I assume he [the president] did not notify the CIA and certainly we have not."

But William Sullivan knew about the FBI's proposed enlargement, and he took up CIA's role in objecting to it. On June 8, Sullivan commented on a Bureau planning memo that "more is not better" when it came to FBI overseas work, although, "by juggling statistics, you can prove almost anything." A Hoover loyalist duly reported to the FBI director, "Mr. Sullivan apparently does not realize that this is being considered at the specific request of the White House. . . . Accordingly, I recommend that Sullivan's observations be disregarded at this time." Sullivan's remarks were indeed ignored, but his insubordination was not, and the matter came to confrontation in fall 1971, when news of the expansion somehow reached columnists Rowland Evans and Robert Novak, who attacked Hoover for trespassing into CIA's domain. "The arguments advanced and the language used were exactly the same as Sullivan had used within the Bureau," FBI Assistant Director Felt recalled, and Sullivan later admitted leaking the story. Some at the Bureau speculated that Sullivan was opposing Hoover perhaps because he knew that his friends in CIA, who resented what they considered FBI incursions into their jurisdiction, would be pleased by his position. In a "Strictly Confidential Memo for the Director's Personal Files," Hoover assistant R. R. Beaver warned: "It appears more definite to me that he [Sullivan] is more on the side of CIA . . . than the FBI."

Some thought that Sullivan's stand on the overseas expansion merely served as a pretext for Hoover to attack his deputy for other supposed transgressions, especially his involvement in the Huston process. James Nolan believed Hoover might have recognized the Huston Plan "as a Bill Sullivan thing," and Felt, too, thought it "more than possible that Hoover, because of the intrigue of the efforts on imposing the Huston Plan, had been informed by Tolson of what Sullivan was up to—and he may have decided to use this [overseas-expansion] incident to clamp down hard on a rampaging subordinate." Then again, maybe it was sin enough simply to be identified as "more on the side of CIA"; according to Sullivan, Hoover had "falsely accused me of writing the two fine letters which Sam J. Papich . . . had written trying to prevent [Hoover] from further damaging the Bureau." Perhaps, too, Hoover had heard rumors, as had Felt, that Sullivan "would be the new Director within a few months, placed on the throne by friends in the White House." In any case, Sullivan arrived at his office on the morning of October 1 to find that he had been locked out.

Sullivan's parting shot, as Sam Papich's had been, was an appeal for closer work with CIA. "I never wrote [Papich's protest] letters but I would have been proud to have done so," Sullivan told Hoover in his official letter of resignation, dated October 6. "Had you listened to Mr. Papich, one of the finest and most able men this Bureau ever had, we would not be in the horrible condition we are in today and there would have been no need of my writing this letter to you. Like myself, Mr. Papich was most fond of the Bureau but he saw it was deteriorating and tried to prevent it. After the reception his two fine letters received he knew the cause was hopeless and retired. Perhaps I should have done the same thing at the time but I still clung to the hope that changes could be brought about orderly and quietly. . . ." Now, however, Sullivan saw things as they really were: "You want the FBI to have as little to do jointly as possible with other members of the community. It is suggested that this be changed. We should pool our assets in behalf of national security. You have always been hostile toward CIA despite the usual polite exchange of letters. We should work very closely together in every respect, pool assets, work cases jointly where facts warrant, etc. Breaking liaison with CIA was not rational."

But Hoover was unaffected by such arguments, and was unruffled when they were echoed four days later by reporter Robert M. Smith, in a lead story on the front page of *The New York Times.*:

FBI IS SAID TO HAVE CUT DIRECT LIAISON WITH CIA
Hoover Move in Quarrel 1½ Years Ago Causes Concern Among
Intelligence Officials About Coping With Spies

The information was attributed to "authoritative sources," but Sullivan's hand was transparent to those who had worked with him. "To offset some of the danger" posed by the breakdown of liaison, Smith wrote, "officials of the FBI and CIA have held private meetings, unknown to Mr. Hoover, at which they exchanged information. . . . The suspension of direct contact is one of the factors prompting leading members of the intelligence community to feel that Mr. Hoover must be deposed as Director of the FBI. . . . They fear the 76-year-old Director will do nothing to repair the breakdown in liaison between the two agencies and will try to remain as long as he can at the post he has held for 46 years."

Asked if it was true that the Bureau had broken direct liaison with CIA, an FBI spokesman told Smith, "It is not true." He added, "The FBI has always maintained liaison with CIA, and it is very close and effective liaison."

When asked the same question, CIA had no comment.

THREE MONTHS BEFORE Sullivan's final dramatic exit, his "failure to bring Hoover into line" had already, as Sullivan later realized, "forced the White House to forget about the FBI and look elsewhere for men to do the kind of investigative work Nixon, Mitchell, Haldeman, Ehrlichman, Dean, and the others felt was necessary." As the Sullivan plot was catalyzed by the Weatherman townhouse explosion, so the new approach was triggered by an event with which the CI community seemed unequipped to deal—viz., the June 1971 report from Hoover's pet KGB source at the United Nations, Aleksei Isidorovich Kulak (Fedora), that a sheaf of Defense Department documents had been delivered to the Soviet Embassy in Washington. The White House had not been too concerned when those same "Pentagon Papers," which chronicled America's Vietnam buildup, had been leaked to *The New York Times* on June 13 by former Rand Corporation analyst Daniel Ellsberg. But the notion that a "complete set" had been passed to the KGB rattled Nixon and Henry Kissinger. Though CIA officers such as Angleton, accepting the Golitsyn thesis, believed that Fedora was a disinformant, Hoover had passed his tip to the White House as intelligence "from a source who has proved reliable in the past." That caused Kissinger to wonder whether Ellsberg, who had lectured at Kissinger's Defense Policy Seminars at Harvard in the mid-1960s, might be a Soviet agent. "Henry had a problem because Ellsberg had been one of his 'boys,' " Haldeman recalled. "Ellsberg, according to Henry, had weird sexual habits, used drugs, and enjoyed helicopter flights in which he would take potshots at the Vietnamese below." Ellsberg had also undergone a mysterious transformation from hawk to dove and, by leaking the Pentagon Papers to the press, and possibly by carrying them to the Soviets, had undermined Kissinger's secret efforts to negotiate an end to the Vietnam War on terms favorable to the U.S.—or so Kissinger told the USIB.

Sullivan, who was then still three months from his final confrontation with Hoover, would recall that "the USIB unanimously requested the FBI to investigate the case." Unanimously, that is, except for the FBI. Sullivan realized sadly "that not one among this prestigious board comprised of brilliant men, including Helms, could take a stand against Hoover and say, 'Look here, you're responsible for intelligence investigations within the United States. You *are* responsible. Now get off your ass and do it.' " Helms had tried to get Hoover "off his ass" by personally meeting with him in spring 1971, and Dean had attempted to do it through the IEC, as had Sullivan himself, but all had been beaten. Even the White House had backed off him, after the Huston process. Indeed, it was the "failure to implement the Huston Plan," as Haldeman recalled, that "set the stage for the drama surrounding the release of the Pentagon Papers. By this time, Nixon had given up on the FBI and CIA for any real help. . . . But he was still determined something had to be done."

What the White House did was to set up under Ehrlichman a "Special Investigations Unit," which came to be known as the Plumbers, because its first assignment was to fix the Pentagon Papers leak. Appropriately enough, for a unit which was to investigate the *foreign* connections of *domestic* dissidents, such as Ellsberg, its key operatives were former CIA and FBI men. George Gordon Liddy had been named for Lord Byron, and had a relationship to reality that was grimly adventurous; he would hold his hand over an open flame to intimidate colleagues, and in the FBI had sometimes acted erratically, deflating the car tires of citizens who did not cooperate in Bureau probes. Edward Howard Hunt was regarded as "a bit of a romantic" by Helms, who had allowed him to write an "American James Bond" series, but Hunt had been case officer to many Miami Cubans during the Bay of Pigs period, and his ongoing contacts with the Cubans would be vital to the Plumbers' work. James McCord, an electronic-surveillance specialist, had incurred Hoover's wrath by leaving the FBI for CIA's Office of Security in 1951; he had been assigned to protect Yuri Nosenko before retiring from CIA in August 1970, just after the collapse of the Huston-Sullivan Plan. By the time McCord joined Hunt and Liddy, the Plumbers were doing some of the black-bag operations that Hoover had refused to do, while relying on CIA for certain kinds of "assistance." In July 1971, Liddy received from CIA a 9mm parabellum pistol and false documentation; Hunt obtained from the Agency a miniature camera and tape recorder, which could be concealed in his tobacco pouch, as well as a red wig and a speech-altering device. On August 26, Hunt delivered some film to Langley, where it was developed; one picture showed Liddy standing in front of the decimated files of Ellsberg's psychiatrist.

The next day, a shocked Helms ordered CIA to cut all contacts with Hunt, who seemed to be crossing over a line. Although Ehrlichman promised to restrain him, Helms staunchly refused to provide any further "rations and quarters" for the freelance White House spies, and a few months later, after failing to prove that Ellsberg was a Soviet agent, the Special Investigations Unit was officially "disbanded." Yet both Liddy and Hunt remained as White House "security consultants" and continued to receive CIA help into early 1972, when they added McCord to their group. Liddy and McCord went on the payroll of the Committee to Re-elect the

President (CREEP), while Hunt worked across the street, at a private security firm. That reorganization was simply a shell game; the Plumbers continued as a White House "operational arm."

But if the original mandate of the Plumbers had been to do what CIA and FBI between them could not do—find foreign links to domestic dissidence—the Plumbers' operations now began to focus on the upcoming presidential election. Under exotic code names such as "Crystal," "Quartz," and "Odessa," the Plumbers would at various times perform such pranks as "inviting" all Washington's black diplomats to a Democratic Party function, even hiring limousines to drop them off there, only to have the blacks discover they hadn't really been invited. Other plans called for such domestic-espionage operations as "photographing key documents" and sexually compromising Democrats. Many of the operations were openly proposed to Mitchell, who now headed CREEP, and to Dean, who was still trying to be the Kissinger of domestic security. "The most incredible thing I have ever laid my eyes on," Dean later said of the Liddy proposals. "All in codes, and involving black bag operations, kidnapping, providing prostitutes, uh, to weaken the opposition, bugging, uh, mugging teams. It was just an incredible thing. Mitchell virtually sat there puffing and laughing."

Yet by spring 1972, the Plumbers themselves were quite serious about one climactic political-warfare assignment, one which would both fulfill the spirit of the Huston-Sullivan Plan and show what an evil precedent that plan had set. At the time, Huston hadn't thought anyone in the ICI process was motivated by a desire to protect the president politically, to secure his re-election, to embarrass the Democrats, or to engage in any partisan purpose. But the danger, as Huston discovered only too late, was that some people would be motivated by political rather than national-security considerations, or perhaps conflate the two rationales. The danger was that they would move from the kid with a bomb to the kid with a picket sign, and from the kid with a picket sign to the kid with the bumper sticker of the opposing candidate, and just keep going down the line. The danger was that if the national-security rationale could be used by sincere, honest, responsible people, it could also be used by duplicitous, dishonest, irresponsible men. The danger, as Huston, Sullivan, and all the world were about to learn, was that laws would be broken not by people like Dick Helms and Jim Angleton, who were targeting Weatherman terrorists or suspected Soviet moles, but by people like G. Gordon Liddy and E. Howard Hunt, who were targeting the headquarters of the Democratic National Committee at Watergate.

CHAPTER FIFTEEN

SMOKING GUN

A WET HAZE OBSCURED the Goddess of Freedom atop the United States Capitol on May 3, 1972. At the base of the building a black automobile braked gently to a stop; it was a hearse. Eight Marine pallbearers started slowly up the thirty-five steps, bearing the flag-draped coffin past a column of honor guards. A drizzle thickened to rain, and the Marines almost lost their footing; two suffered ruptures as they struggled up. But they reached the bronze doors of the Rotunda, and then were under the awesome dome. There, upon the catafalque once built for Abraham Lincoln, they placed the body of John Edgar Hoover, dead from heart failure the day before.

A few hours later, as Hoover lay in state, an antiwar demonstration began on the steps outside—and then a demonstration against the demonstration. As actress Jane Fonda took the megaphone, there moved also along the margins of the crowd nine Miami Cubans, hired by the Plumbers to be ready to repulse a rush for Hoover's casket. But the only trouble occurred when the Cubans, who could not contain themselves, got into scuffles while shouting "Traitors! Castro-lovers! Communists!"

The Cubans' leader, Eugenio "Macho" Martinez, recounted those details proudly to his controllers, G. Gordon Liddy and E. Howard Hunt, who drove over afterward and picked him up. It was getting dark as they headed down Virginia Avenue and Liddy pointed to the complex of structures called Watergate.

"That's our next job, Macho," Liddy said.

"What is it?"

"Democratic National Headquarters—and after McGovern's nominated, it'll be his headquarters, too."

"There's a report," Hunt broke in, "that Castro's been getting money to the Democrats. The idea is to photograph the list of contributors the Democrats are required to keep. Once we have those lists, we can have them checked to determine whether the contributors are bona fide or merely fronts for Castro or Hanoi money."

They drove on into the night, plotting how to tie domestic antiwar personalities to foreign communists—precisely what the feuding FBI and CIA had largely failed to do since 1967. That failure had caused creation of the Plumbers, as has been seen, but the FBI-CIA wedge was to figure even more fundamentally in White House attempts to cover up the Plumbers' crimes, causing the worst political scandal in American history.

AMERICA'S DOWNHILL SLIDE to Watergate had really begun shortly after Nixon assumed office, when he ordered White House counsel John Ehrlichman to get all the "facts and documents" about CIA's plots to remove Castro. As vice-president, Nixon had played a catalyzing role in the Bay of Pigs plan, of which the Maheu-Giancana plot had been one aspect. Though assassination had not been formally "authorized" by the White House before Kennedy came along, the push to get rid of Castro had really begun in April 1959, when Nixon's executive assistant for national-security affairs, General Robert E. Cushman, began pressuring CIA for "action" on the Castro problem. The result had been the Bay of Pigs, secret deals with the Mafia, and, eventually, the 1967 report by CIA's Scott Breckenridge, which had caused LBJ to believe that President Kennedy was killed by Castro in a "turnaround plot." But by summer 1969, six months after Ehrlichman had asked CIA for all it had on the Castro operations, the Agency had still not handed over the Breckenridge Report. Ehrlichman had complained to Haldeman, "Those bastards in Langley are holding back something. They just dig in their heels and say the President can't have it. Period. Imagine that! The Commander-in-Chief wants to see a document, and the spooks say he can't have it. From the way they're protecting it, it must be pure dynamite."

In an attempt to pry the secrets loose, Nixon named Cushman, the very former staffer who had been his liaison with CIA on anti-Castro matters, to be the Agency's deputy director. This produced a Helms visit to the White House, during which Ehrlichman hoped that Nixon would give a direct order "to turn that document [i.e., the inspector general's anti-Castro report] over to me." After Helms' long secret conversation with Nixon, however, Ehrlichman had appeared in Haldeman's office, dropped into a chair, and just stared furiously, speechless. When asked what happened, Ehrlichman had finally said, "I am now to *forget* all about that CIA document. In fact, I am to cease and desist from trying to obtain it."

But by 1972, the matter had come up again. Robert Maheu, who had been CIA's go-between for Rosselli and Trafficante, was a close friend of Democratic National Committee chairman Lawrence O'Brien. The Cuban security service must have good evidence of attempts against their leader's life, and Castro himself would probably do all he could to help the progressive McGovern, including pass evidence of anti-Castro plots undertaken on Nixon's watch. The Democratic Party also encompassed Johnson staffers who must have known of the Breckenridge Report, and who knew that LBJ thought it implicated a vengeful Castro in JFK's death. If the anti-Castro plots could have caused Kennedy's assassination, and if Nixon had in part caused the anti-Castro plots, Nixon might then be blamed by the Democrats for causing the Dallas tragedy.

To ensure that Nixon would not be hit with any such "surprise" allegations, two countermeasures were adopted. First, as a moral equalizer and counterblackmail device, Hunt tried to prove that JFK had ordered the 1963 assassination of South Vietnamese President Diem. Examining Saigon-Washington cable traffic, Hunt noticed that, "the closer one approached the assassination period, the more frequently were cables missing." So Hunt decided to "improve" the existing cables with a razor blade and a Xerox machine, until he came up with something more "incriminating."

Second, it was decided to burglarize the Democratic National Headquarters at the Watergate Apartments complex, to see how much the opposition really knew about the anti-Castro plots. As burglar Frank Sturgis later explained: "One of the things we were looking for in the Democratic National Committee's files, and in some other Washington file cabinets, too, was a thick secret memorandum from the Castro government addressed confidentially to the Democrats' platform committee. The Cubans were providing an itemized list of all the [CIA] abuses. The complaints were especially bitter about various attempts to assassinate the Castro brothers."

From the start, there had been one great obstacle to such a precipitous act as breaking into Democratic headquarters: the fear that Hoover's FBI would not look the other way if the Plumbers were caught. But Hunt and his henchmen could assume a new boldness in May 1972, when Hoover was finally gone.

SECRETARIES AND ADMINISTRATIVE assistants at FBI headquarters had begun to cry at the announcement of the director's death, while numbed G-men tried to comfort them. Looking back, most FBI men would find it difficult to assess their exact feelings. Few felt any sense of personal loss; Clyde Tolson had been Hoover's only real friend. Nor had the director been an easy man to work for; he was tough and irascible and would not accept even 98-percent perfection. He was, however, respected and admired as few men ever would be. He had been a fierce fighter for justice, and for the old America that seemed in danger of passing with him. For all his flaws, he had made the FBI into the finest law-enforcement agency in the world. It just did not seem possible that such a man could leave the scene so suddenly.

This was the uncertain atmosphere into which ex–submarine commander L. Patrick Gray, the new FBI chief, was now thrust. A hardworking, methodical Connecticut lawyer, Gray had been a Nixon organizer in 1960 and a sort of man Friday to the 1968 transition team, working all day at stand-up desks until he was made an assistant to the attorney general. On the morning after Hoover's death, when people were sitting around the office of Acting Attorney General Richard Kleindienst, considering who should be named FBI director, someone suggested, Why not Pat Gray? After Nixon's difficulties with the independent, unyielding, world-famous Hoover, the president must have liked the idea of a loyal, team-playing unknown. At two-fifteen on the afternoon of May 3, Gray was called into the Oval Office, shook the president's hand, and heard him say, "I am going to name you Acting Director of the Federal Bureau of Investigation."

Gray was honored but deeply surprised, since his relationship with the president had been marginal and impersonal. In retrospect, Gray thought that he should have called to mind the old adage about things that seem too good to be true. . . . But at the time, he looked upon his new job as a return to the service of his country, analogous to that which he had rendered in the Navy. And, like a good ship's captain, he moved immediately to avoid a mutiny among his men.

"Frankly, most of us were hoping that the President would select an insider," Mark Felt told the new director. That was true enough, though actually Felt had been hoping that *he* would be the new director, as had a clutch of other top Hoover deputies. None of them would be of much help to Gray as he tried to learn how things worked, and no one told him anything unless he asked; no one bothered to inform him that the two little red buckets under his desk were burn baskets, or that his office included a shredding machine. Gray fought back by winning the allegiance of special agents in the Bureau's field offices.

"He was a dynamic guy and went around making speeches," recalled special agent Jay Aldhizer. "He said, 'We are going to make some changes, you don't have to wear white shirts anymore. You can drink coffee at the desk.' There was a very definite relaxation, immediately. Gray wanted to create something new, and get us looking toward the future, and for a little while there was a real sense of renewal."

There was also an instant opening up to CIA. With Hoover gone, the way was clear for an official restoration of liaison, both at headquarters and in the field. Indeed, with Hoover dead, and total interface permitted, the need for a liaison officer was no longer so clear-cut; instead of going through a single middleman, such as Papich, personnel dealt with their opposite numbers at the other agency. Hence, despite the dire significance once attached to Hoover's scrapping of the liaison-officer position, it would be some months before Gray appointed a new liaison man.

But new tensions with CIA were not so long in coming. Gray was on a morale-boosting mission to the FBI's Los Angeles Field Office on Saturday, June 17, when he got a call from Felt, who had replaced Tolson as the Bureau's number-two man. "At approximately 2:30 this morning," Felt recalled telling Gray, "a security guard at the Watergate complex noticed a partially open basement stairwell door which had tapes placed across the spring bolt to prevent it from locking. He removed the tape but when he saw the same door taped again about forty minutes later, he telephoned the police at once and they were on the scene within minutes. The police surprised and arrested five individuals at Democratic headquarters and they were identified as James Walter McCord, Jr., Bernard L. Barker, Frank Anthony Fiorini, Virginio R. Gonzales, and Eugenio Martinez. They had in their possession burglary tools and photographic equipment. Several ceiling panels had been removed, as well as an air vent cover. They had been taking apart the telephone equipment. All of them were wearing surgical-type plastic gloves. It looks like they were getting ready to install more eavesdropping equipment or to repair or put new batteries in equipment already there."

"Have they said what they were doing?" Gray asked.

"They haven't said one word. Trying to get information from these people is like trying to interview the Black Panther Party. They didn't even call an attorney but one showed up anyway. It's very mysterious." Felt added that the arrested men had been carrying $2,400 cash, including three new hundred-dollar bills, and that a search of their rooms at the Watergate had turned up thirty-five crisp new hundreds of the same series. Also found was an envelope containing a personal check made out by E. Howard Hunt. The FBI knew Hunt had been a CIA employee, and had worked on "highly sensitive matters" for the White House, but was now officially with Mullen Company, a private security firm.

None of it made any sense to Gray. Obviously the police had broken up some kind of political-espionage business, but he wondered, for no reason he could name, whether there wasn't more to the affair. He was haunted by the thought that somehow the Watergate burglary was connected to CIA.

. . .

THE CENTRAL INTELLIGENCE AGENCY first heard about the Watergate break-in, according to its own records, at 5 p.m. that Saturday afternoon, when an inquiry about the arrested men was received from reporter Bob Woodward at the Washington *Post*. That call was soon followed by one from the FBI, advising that McCord and Hunt had been identified as former officers of CIA. By 8:45 p.m., the case had been taken to Director of Security Howard Osborn. It was one of Osborn's routine duties to inform Helms of any trouble in the extended Agency family, and that included events like suicides, break-ins, rapes, and other bad things that happened in a big city like Washington. But when Osborn called Helms at 10 p.m. that evening, the DCI knew that this episode was different; he sensed, he later said, that the Watergate affair would be "big news from the moment it happened." Not only were Hunt and McCord former CIA officers, but all of the Miami Cubans had worked for the Agency during the Bay of Pigs episode, and one of them was still a contract agent on the payroll.

Ideally, Helms would have liked to settle the matter quietly, without publicity, according to the 1955 agreement between CIA and Justice, which called for the Agency to investigate its own. But that agreement applied only to current Agency employees, and in any case the incident was already public knowledge. All Helms could do, for the moment, was to call Gray, disavow any knowledge of what the Agency's ex-employees were up to, and warn: "These fellows may have some connection with Ehrlichman. You'd better watch out."

Monday morning, at his regular 9 a.m. staff meeting, Helms went around the table on the break-in. Cord Meyer, sitting in for DDP Karamessines, remembered "a unanimous expression of total ignorance and surprise," but also "general concern that the public and press would suspect some Agency involvement because of Hunt's and McCord's past connection to the Agency." To prevent that from happening, Helms set out a fundamental strategy. "Stay cool, stay clean, keep away from this," Helms said. "Volunteer nothing, because it will only be used to involve us." William Colby, Helms announced, would deal with outside parties seeking cooperation from CIA. According to Colby's own account, Helms asked him to "coordinate the Agency's efforts" in deflecting public suspicions of a CIA role in the affair.

Just such a deflection of suspicion away from CIA was accomplished by Deep Throat, a source who began feeding leads to *Post* reporter Woodward, by the reporter's own account, on June 19—only hours after Helms launched CIA's damage-control plan. Woodward's later description of Deep Throat as having "an aggregate of information flowing in and out of many stations" would seem a pointed signal to someone in Langley. Woodward also said that Deep Throat had an "extremely sensitive" position in the Executive Branch, which would perfectly fit someone at CIA, who (according to Woodward) did not like getting calls at the office. The use of an underground parking garage for clandestine meetings would seem to evidence a certain skill at "tradecraft." Furthermore, with the exception of Helms and his DDCI, CIA officers were not political appointees, and therefore their careers, unlike those of Dean and most other possible Throats, would not have automatically fallen with Nixon's own. Woodward himself would later all but confirm that Deep Throat was a spook. "As you know, I'm not going to discuss the identity of Deep Throat or any other of my confidential sources who are still alive. But let me just say that [the] suggestion that we were being used by the intelligence community was of concern to us at the time and afterward."

Could Deep Throat have perhaps been Colby? Much of the information Colby provided to the FBI in the days after the burglary was immediately leaked to the press, as Colby later admitted, though he blamed those leaks on the Bureau. Colby was a political liberal, and no great fan of the Nixon White House; as Helms' damage-control officer on Watergate, he would be perfectly positioned to leak; he was later rumored to use underground parking structures for secret meetings of a personal nature. Moreover, the final pages of Colby's 1978 book, *Honorable Men*, would contain a suggestive reference to Throat. Discussing how "the public must be informed of what intelligence is doing in its name," Colby cites "unofficial leaks" as one means of so informing the citizenry; sometimes material is made available to the media though "its source in the intelligence community is obscured from the people who use it." Colby then immediately raises the subject of Deep Throat, and although one might expect him to resent the role of Throat as a competitor in controlling public perceptions of Watergate, he actually characterizes Throat as a force for national good: "Deep Throat remains a secret," Colby says, "but the public has benefitted from his information."

Woodward's clues suggest, however, that Throat was more likely another CIA officer present at the June 19 damage-control meeting. This was Cord Meyer. Woodward describes Throat as a chain-smoker and heavy drinker, which Meyer was and Colby was not. Throat was an intellectual who "knew too much literature too well," and Meyer was an award-winning literary talent. Throat's appearance bespoke "too many battles," and Meyer had a glass eye from the Battle of Iwo Jima. Meyer also reportedly bore a special grudge against Nixon because of his complicity in the McCarthyist drama which had once almost cost Meyer his CIA job; he was even said to have made digs at CIA secretaries who wore Nixon campaign buttons on their blouses. Meyer was practically a charter member of the Old Boys Network of Yale graduates who had gone on to work in intelligence, and Woodward, too, was a member of this club. In fact,

Meyer may well have become acquainted with Woodward during the latter's 1969–70 tenure as a Washington briefer in naval intelligence: as part of his daily rounds, Woodward sometimes addressed top people in CIA's Department of Plans, where Meyer was then the number-two man. Moreover, Throat knew all about Hunt's activities—his first tips and most of his early leads concerned Hunt—and Meyer was one of the few at CIA who knew, even before the Watergate burglary, that Hunt was working for the White House. On March 27, 1972, for instance, when CIA's domestic contact office in Miami queried Langley about Hunt's frequent contacts with Cuban exiles, Meyer cabled back that Hunt was in Miami on White House work and that Miami Station should "cool it," i.e., not concern itself with Hunt. Meyer, it should also be noted, possessed great family wealth— his father controlled a lot of real estate in Manhattan—which would explain why Throat could afford not to come forward for big bucks (the advance for his book even now, two decades later, would be colossal). But perhaps most important, Meyer had extremely intimate connections with Ben Bradlee, Woodward's boss at the *Post*. Indeed, they were in-laws, having both married sisters from the socially prominent Pinchot family. Meyer's interface with Bradlee could have had a close professional aspect as well, since Meyer's main duty at CIA was to penetrate and influence leftist but anticommunist organs of opinion. Among other things, Meyer's close relationship to the editor of the *Post* might have accounted for the special access that allowed Throat to get to Woodward's morning copy of the *Post* and scribble on it times for secret meetings.

In any case, while Deep Throat, whoever he was, deflected press attention from CIA, Colby deflected requests from the FBI's Alexandria office for information on the burglars. "The immediate problem," Colby recalled, "was how we could give the FBI facts about the activities of former CIA personnel without revealing the operational jobs they had done in the past and the people with whom they dealt. We had to be concerned with the protection of legitimate operational secrets and with ensuring that the Agency was not dragged into something it had nothing to do with while responding to quite appropriate FBI inquiries." As he was "pondering this problem," Colby was informed that Howard Hunt had received a red wig and miniature camera from CIA during summer 1971; Colby and Helms then determined to conceal this information from the Bureau. "Neither Helms nor I saw any need to volunteer this information to the FBI," Colby conceded, "since it did not have anything to do with the Watergate break-in a year later. Our strategy, Helms stressed, was to respond to legitimate requests by the investigators for information on the individuals involved in Watergate or any other directly related questions. But we had no obligation to rush forward with peripheral information not significant to the investigation at hand and likely to create misunderstandings and public excitement about a possible—and nonexistent—CIA role in the activity under investigation."

At month's end, Helms affirmed that his strategy required not being overly helpful to the Bureau. Leaving aside the White House's concerns, Helms did have some real worry about FBI inquiries into Hunt, who, if not acting on CIA's behalf when working for the Plumbers, nevertheless had many Agency friends and connections. These were not the things the White House wanted covered up, but Helms did not want them volunteered. "In short," Helms directed, "it is up to the FBI to lay some cards on the table. Otherwise, we are unable to be of help. In addition, we still adhere to the request that they confine themselves to the personalities already arrested or directly under suspicion and that they desist from expanding this investigation into other areas which may well, eventually, run afoul of our operations."

Unsurprisingly, that policy caused the Bureau to believe that CIA was being "less than cooperative," as Felt recalled, "with inquiries from the FBI running into a stone wall or, worse still, encountering outright deception." When CIA got a tip on June 19 that burglar Eugenio Martinez's car had been left at Miami Airport, it waited two days before informing the FBI, probably so as to "sanitize" the car of any "compromising" data about Martinez's relations with the Agency. When the FBI asked to interview Martinez's CIA case officer, Robert Ritchie, they were told, first, that he had gone on an "African safari," then that he had been reassigned to Indochina and would not be available for questioning. And when the Bureau asked about a "Mr. Pennington," who had reportedly once been James McCord's supervisor, CIA furnished a summary on Cecil H. Pennington, a former employee who had no connection with McCord. The lead turned into a dead end for the FBI, just as CIA had hoped; it was more than a year before the Bureau learned that the man they wanted was Lee R. Pennington, a contract agent for CIA's Security Research Staff, who on June 21 or 22, according to the later sworn testimony of an Agency security officer, had "entered Mr. McCord's office at home, destroying any indication of connections between the Agency and Mr. McCord." When confronted on such matters by Mark Felt, Colby airily brushed aside the FBI man's complaints by saying that "we were trying to keep publicity away from CIA."

DESPITE CIA'S PATENT LACK of cooperation, a detailed investigative report on the Watergate incident was waiting on Pat Gray's desk at 7:45 a.m. on June 20, when he returned to headquarters from California. The

Bureau now knew that the burglars' cash came from the Mexican bank account of one Kenneth Dahlberg; it was also known that Eugenio Martinez was on a "retainer of $100 per month" from CIA "to report on the Cuban exile community." Thus, the "money chain" seemed to involve, at its near end, a current CIA contract agent and several ex–CIA officers, while leading overseas, into CIA's jurisdiction.

Gray telephoned Helms: could he confirm or deny that CIA was involved?

Helms could deny. He said that he knew nothing about Dahlberg or the Mexican bank, and that Martinez, though under contract to CIA, had not been acting on Agency orders during the burglary. Just as the FBI couldn't control all its stool pigeons in the underworld, or be held accountable if an FBI informant "whacked" a rival casino owner, so a CIA contract informant like Martinez could get into all kinds of trouble on his own— could beat up his girlfriend, steal a car, or burglarize a building—but that didn't mean he was doing it at Agency behest. Similarly, Hunt's and McCord's former work for CIA did not mean that Helms had any way of "keeping a string" on them. When they walked out the door, "they turned in their badge"; the notion that one never really "retired" from CIA was a false if widely held myth.

Gray murmured that he understood, but Helms sensed his message wasn't getting across very well. In Gray's mind, as in that of the public, distinctions between current and former, or between contract and full-time, employees didn't really make any difference. Helms knew that, and yet he was surprised that the issue kept coming up. He couldn't understand why Gray kept thinking that CIA was somehow involved. It seemed strange.

THE PRESIDENT OF the United States had been sitting in his boxer shorts, sipping coffee in the kitchen of his vacation home in Key Biscayne on Sunday morning, June 18, when he saw a small article about the Watergate burglary on page 30 of *The New York Times*. Two decades of investigation would uncover no evidence that Nixon or any of his advisers knew about the burglary in advance, but if Hunt and Liddy were perhaps schooled enough in notions of deniability and compartmentation to keep their bosses "clean," by the evening of June 20, their first night back in Washington from Key Biscayne, the Plumbers' bosses were dirtying themselves, conspiring to cover up White House links to the crime by playing CIA against the FBI. As a lever, to force CIA into cooperation, the White House would use its knowledge of an operation which had gone wrong, perhaps tragically so, because of lack of coordination between the rival agencies.

It began with cryptic hints from Nixon. Haldeman was at home unpacking, he later said, when he got a call from the president. They talked about Watergate. The president said: "Tell Ehrlichman this whole group of Cubans is tied to the Bay of Pigs."

"The Bay of Pigs?"

"Ehrlichman will know what I mean."

As he drifted to sleep that night, a puzzled Haldeman considered the president's suggestion. He recalled Ehrlichman's failed attempts to get the Breckenridge Report from CIA, and wondered, as had Ehrlichman, what could be "pure dynamite" about the Agency's attempts to unseat Castro.

The next morning, after the regular White House staff meeting, Haldeman followed Ehrlichman to his office and gave him the president's message. Ehrlichman's eyebrows arched, and he smiled. "Our brothers at Langley? He's suggesting I twist or break a few arms?" Ehrlichman leaned back in his chair, tapping a pencil on the edge of his desk. He paused for a long beat, then said. "All right. Message accepted."

Haldeman heard nothing more on the matter until the morning of June 23, when he met Nixon in the Oval Office, alone. Their talk was secretly recorded by a White House taping system, recently installed to help detect leaks; by keeping a verifiable log of who had heard what from the horse's mouth, Nixon hoped to be able to confront leakers with irrefutable proof. "Now on the investigation, you know, the Democratic break-in thing," Nixon said, "the FBI is not under control, because Gray doesn't know exactly how to control them, and they have—their investigation is now leading into some productive areas, because they've been able to trace the money." Specifically, the FBI had implicated campaign contributor Kenneth Dahlberg. But Gray's apparent belief that Dahlberg was connected with CIA suggested to Nixon a way out. "The only way to solve this, and we're set up beautifully to do it, is for us to have [Deputy Director of Central Intelligence Vernon] Walters call Pat Gray and say, 'Stay the hell out of this. This is, ah, business here that we don't want you to go any further on.' That's not an unusual development. 'We've got a signal from across the river to, to put the hold on this.' And that will fit rather well because the FBI agents who are working this case, at this point, feel that's what it is. This is CIA."

But was it CIA? Haldeman wanted to know. Nixon was "not sure" whether Watergate was, in fact, a "CIA thing," but he thought it was a good plan—and CIA would roll over when told. "We protected Helms from a hell of a lot of things," the president said. "Hunt—that will uncover a lot of things. You open that scab there's a hell of a lot of things and that we just feel it would be very detrimental to have this thing go any further. This involves these Cubans, Hunt, and a lot of hanky-panky that we have nothing to do with ourselves." Haldeman didn't know what hanky-panky he was talking about, but Nixon wasn't finished. He gazed out the window, then turned to Haldeman. "Play it tough. That's the way they play it and that's the way we're going to play it. . . . They should call the FBI in and say that 'We wish for the good of the country don't go any further into this case.' Period."

As Haldeman left the Oval Office, the doors opened and a motion-picture camera crew entered. They were making a film for screening at the Republican Convention, and they wanted to get some footage of Nixon functioning at his finest as president, on a typical glorious day, discussing great problems of state. No one would know that they were seeing the man one minute after he began the massive cover-up that would cause his downfall and disgrace.

"Guess what," Haldeman said to Ehrlichman, meeting up with him in the hall outside. "It's Bay of Pigs time again. The man will never quit." He explained that they were to meet Walters and Helms as soon as they could, and play the Cuban card, to force Walters into calling off the FBI.

"Well, the President has a point. It will put pressure on Helms. But this time you're going to push the red button, not me. I've had it on that route."

The red button? Haldeman still had no idea what all this meant. He figured that Helms would know, but wondered if Walters, who was new to CIA, would also understand.

THREE-STAR GENERAL Vernon Walters was the Orson Welles of American intelligence—a portly, cultured epicure who could hold forth fluently in any one of eight languages while consuming impressive amounts of food and wine. As a defense attaché and official government interpreter, Walters had been with then Vice-President Nixon in Caracas when a crowd stopped their car and started breaking the windows, and had been struck by the courage and calmness Nixon showed while they waited for Venezuelan guardsmen to clear the riot. As he entered the White House on June 23, with Richard Helms, Walters sensed that he was going to be asked again to serve Nixon, but he also sensed a certain tension among the President's men. There was the usual shaking of hands as they entered, but no small talk.

Haldeman started right in by saying that Watergate was "creating a lot of noise," causing problems that "the opposition" was "attempting to maximize." The FBI investigation might lead to "some important people . . . in Mexico."

After a pause, Haldeman asked Helms what the "Agency connection" was in Watergate.

"We're *not* connected," Helms instantly said. His tone was of injured innocence. "No sir, no way." Indeed, Helms had twice told Director Gray by phone that there was no CIA involvement. Nor did Helms think CIA operations would be jeopardized by the FBI's inquiries.

"Nevertheless," Haldeman said, turning to Walters, "it is the President's wish that you, General Walters, go to see Director Gray, and tell him that the further pursuit of this investigation will uncover some activity or assets of the CIA in Mexico. Tell him that if he pursues the Mexican part of the financing of this business it will uncover CIA assets or schemes for moving money."

Helms began to protest, but Haldeman cut him off.

"The President asked me to tell you this entire affair may be connected to the Bay of Pigs, and if it opens up, the Bay of Pigs may be blown, and the FBI may uncover some things that—"

Total chaos in the room. Helms clutched the arms of his chair, jutted forward, and screamed: "Don't throw that dead cat at us! Bay of Pigs has nothing to do with this! That was years ago! I have no concern about the Bay of Pigs!"

Dead silence. Jesus Christ, Haldeman wondered, *What was such dynamite* in the Agency's attempts to get rid of Castro?

"I'm just following my instructions, Dick. This is what the President told me to relay to you."

Helms was settling back, trying to calm himself. "All right," he said at last. The whole atmosphere had changed; Nixon had sure been right about the Agency's attempts to remove the Cuban leader.

"What is the purpose of this?" Helms cautiously asked.

Ehrlichman, who previously had only nodded or smiled in agreement with Haldeman, said simply: "General Walters should get down to see Gray just as fast as he can."

Walters said nothing. Helms rose. The meeting was over.

Haldeman went back to see the president and informed him that his strategy had worked. Nixon smiled grimly. He did not tell Haldeman why mere allusion to the Agency's anti-Castro operations could be used, in essence, to blackmail CIA, but three years later, when CIA's Cubela-Trafficante assassination plots were investigated and publicized by the U.S. Senate, Haldeman finally thought he knew. These operations contained in them the Agency's "High Holy," its darkest, most damaging secret. As Haldeman surmised:

It seems that in all of those Nixon references to the Bay of Pigs, he was actually referring to the Kennedy assassination. As an outgrowth of the Bay of Pigs, CIA made several attempts on Fidel Castro's life. The Deputy Director of Plans at CIA at the time was a man named Richard Helms. Unfortunately, Castro knew of the assassination attempts all the time. . . . After Kennedy was killed, CIA launched a fantastic cover-up. Many of the facts about Oswald unavoidably pointed to a Cuban connection. . . . CIA literally erased any connection between Kennedy's assassination and CIA.

Haldeman figured that Nixon must have learned about this High Holy during his long secret conversation with Helms in summer 1969, after Ehrlichman pressed to see that CIA "mystery document," the Inspector General's Report. So when Haldeman, at Nixon's behest, had told Helms, "It's likely to blow the whole Bay of Pigs," he had really been—he came to believe—"reminding Helms, not so gently, of the cover-up of CIA assassination attempts on the hero of the Bay of Pigs, Fidel Castro—a CIA operation that may have triggered the Kennedy tragedy and which Helms desperately wanted to hide."

RICHARD HELMS MADE no mention of the Kennedy assassination as he stood talking with his deputy downstairs, on June 23, by their car on West Executive Avenue. Instead, he shared with Walters his puzzlement about the White House's concerns. The references to Mexico were quite unclear to him, but he had been dealing with the White House for a long time, and sometimes a president, or a Haldeman, somebody in high authority, had information Helms did not. It would have been presumptuous to press any harder as to how they had come up with this strategy, or who was behind it. After all, here were Haldeman and Ehrlichman, the two most senior officials in the White House next to the president himself, and Helms had to assume they had the proper authority. That had to be the working assumption of anyone competing for the president's personal attention, really needing and rarely getting it.

But why, Helms wondered aloud, had Walters been chosen to go see Gray? Perhaps, Walters suggested, Haldeman thought that he was a good bet because he was military; a lot of people had the mistaken belief that military types obeyed blindly, because they were used to taking orders. Or maybe Haldeman had heard reports of past friction between the FBI and the CIA, between Hoover and Helms, and wanted a fresh relationship to grow between Walters and the new FBI director.

Helms frowned, but the notion of Gray's newness to the job did suggest to him a way of framing Walters' request: as a perfectly legitimate CIA reminder to a rookie bureaucrat. "I think you should put this to Acting Director Gray, since he is a new Acting Director of the FBI, within these legitimate limits: That there is a longstanding delimitation agreement that if the FBI runs into CIA operations, or CIA runs into FBI operations, one side notifies the other."

Walters nodded. Helms, still frowning, got into the car and drove back to Langley.

PROMPTLY AT TWO-THIRTY that afternoon, Walters called on Gray and saw him alone. It was the first time any CIA official had been inside the FBI director's office since Helms had visited Hoover in June 1966. They expressed pleasure at meeting one another; Walters had intended to call on Gray, and so forth. After a few minutes of such pleasantries, Walters casually said that he had just talked to some senior staff member at the White House. He mentioned no names, and Gray asked for none. Those unnamed White House persons wanted Gray to be told that the FBI investigation into the Mexican money chain might uncover covert CIA assets or sources. Though the investigation had not touched any current Agency projects, its continuation "south of the border" could "trespass upon some of our covert projects and, in view of the fact that the five men involved were under arrest, it would be best to taper off the matter there."

Gray understood that statement to mean that CIA had an interest in Kenneth Dahlberg, who had bankrolled the burglers. But that clearly contradicted what Helms had twice told him—that there was no CIA involvement. The contradiction was a little strange, but not necessarily sinister. There was so much compartmentation in the Agency, Gray figured, that the left hand didn't always know what the right was doing.

Walters next relayed what Helms had said about the FBI-CIA agreement not to expose each other's sources, and added, incorrectly, that the Bureau had always "scrupulously" respected it. Gray had not read that agreement, and had not even heard of it, but it seemed logical. He didn't yet know exactly how the FBI would proceed, but understood what Walters was trying to say. His problem was how to "low key" the investigation now that it was launched. A large sum of money had been floating around; there was the matter of a check on a Mexican bank for $89,000, and some $81,000 that had been sent to Mexico, for purposes unknown.

"A most awkward matter to come up during an election year," Gray said ominously as they wound up the session.

Walters returned to his office at CIA and made a report of the meeting to Helms, then talked to the Western Hemisphere desk. Nobody felt that the ongoing FBI investigation could jeopardize any Agency activities.

Walters wondered why the White House wanted him to lie.

HOOVER'S CRITICS COULD SAY what they wanted—and they dared to say a lot more about him once he was dead—but no one ever doubted that he would have refused to let CIA, or the White House, tell the Bureau how to conduct a criminal investigation. The Watergate cover-up, even his most severe detractors would admit, could not have happened on Hoover's watch.

But L. Patrick Gray was no J. Edgar Hoover. After meeting Walters on June 23, Gray telephoned Dean, assuring him that the FBI would hold up its interviews temporarily and "work around this problem." Dean seemed satisfied. Gray then informed Assistant Director Charles Bates that the FBI might have uncovered "a CIA money chain," but must abide by the CIA-FBI agreement relating to exposure of Agency operations. Bates, who had been liaison to CIA for three months between Papich and De-Loach, believed that Gray was being perhaps a bit too willing to call off the dogs; he urged: "Under no circumstances should the FBI back off an investigation at the request of CIA without forcing them to reveal completely their interest in the matter." But Gray ordered that the Bureau refrain from interviewing Dahlberg, as well as Manuel Ogarrio, a Mexico City lawyer whose checks, like Kenneth Dahlberg's, had found their way into the CREEP account accessed by Barker. Bates' anger only built as, at Helms' request, Gray also directed that the FBI not interview CIA men Karl Wagner and John Caswell, whose names had been found in a little telephone-address notebook belonging to Hunt. By the first week of July, Bates and other FBI agents were on the verge of rebellion, especially over their inability to follow the Mexican money trail by interrogating Ogarrio and Dahlberg. On July 5, Gray finally called up Walters and put the heat on.

"We have done everything we can do to trace the money except interview those two men," Gray complained. "Either you have got an interest in Ogarrio and Dahlberg or you haven't, and if you have I need it in writing or I am going to go ahead and interview those people."

The next morning, Walters delivered a document indicating that CIA had no interest in either man, no matter what the White House said. Walters didn't care if he had to resign; he would not write any letter saying that the FBI's investigation was endangering CIA operations in Mexico. He did not see why he or Gray should jeopardize the integrity of their agencies to protect some White House figures who had acted imprudently. General Walters then told Gray he had to be quite frank with him, and described the White House meeting in which Haldeman had ordered him to warn Gray off. Leaning back in the red overstuffed leather chair in which he was sitting and putting his hands behind his head, he said that he had come into an inheritance, was not concerned about his pension, and wasn't going to let "these kids" kick him around anymore. Someone should tell the president that certain White House aides were encouraging CIA to deceive the FBI—a course of action which, if made public, could be "electorally mortal."

Gray said firmly, "You should call the president, you know him better than I."

Walters said, "No, I think you should, because these are persons that FBI wishes to interview."

They did not settle on who, if anyone, would make such a call, but, after Walters departed, Gray ordered the immediate interviews of Ogarrio and Dahlberg. Then he sat at his desk quietly and pondered Walters' revelations. He was unsettled enough to believe that Nixon should know what was going on, but it was a pretty awesome thing to call the president of the United States. He decided to relay the message through one of the president's advisers, Clark MacGregor, who was close to Nixon and had his confidence.

About a half-hour later, at 11:28 a.m., the president telephoned Gray, who was somewhat surprised that his call was returned so quickly. Nixon congratulated him for the FBI's successful termination of a hijacking the previous day in San Francisco. Gray thanked him, then said awkwardly: "Mr. President, there is something that I want to speak to you about. Walters and I feel that people on your staff are trying to mortally wound you by confusing the question of CIA interest in, or not in, people the FBI wishes to interview."

He expected Nixon to ask which staff members were meant, but he did not. There was a slight pause. The president said, "Pat, you just continue to conduct your thorough and aggressive investigation."

Gray warned that the case could not be covered up. He and General Walters felt that Nixon should "get rid of the people" who were trying to do so.

Nixon asked, "No matter how high?"

Yes, Gray replied, that was his recommendation.

FOR THE MOMENT, President Nixon decided not to get rid of himself, or Haldeman, or Ehrlichman, or Dean. Instead, he responded to Gray's advice by axing the chief obstacle to the cover-up—Richard Helms—whose refusal to let CIA take the hit for Watergate was opening the way for an FBI investigation that would lead into the Oval Office. By summer's end, the Bureau successfully followed the Ogarrio-Dahlberg money trail away from CIA to CREEP, while a similar deflection of suspicions from the Agency, toward the president's men, was accomplished by Deep Throat's continued reporting to Woodward. Nothing was uncovered to keep Nixon from defeating George McGovern, but the die had been cast, for Helms as for Nixon. "By refusing to participate in the Watergate cover-up," Cord Meyer ventured, "Helms preserved the institutional integrity of the CIA, but he also ensured the end of his career as director."

Nixon decided to replace Helms with James Schlesinger, a relatively unknown forty-eight-year-old economist in the Bureau of the Budget. A politicized intellectual with white hair and the habit of taking off his eyeglasses and chewing absently on one endpiece, Schlesinger had recently made what old-school CIA analysts like Ray Cline regarded as "a very sensible study of Central Intelligence." Informed of the president's decision even before Helms, Schlesinger suggested that Helms' sixtieth birthday, the following spring, would be a more appropriate time to make the switch, since Helms' own policy required automatic retirement at that age. But on November 20, Nixon called Helms in and asked him to become ambassador to Iran, effective the following February. Not feeling quite ready to quit government, but more than happy to escape Washington, Helms accepted the post.

Before leaving, Helms briefed Schlesinger on operational matters, and liaison relationships, especially with the FBI. The Bureau was getting set to send over a regular liaison officer again, to supplant ad-hoc contacts that had been occurring surreptitiously in Hoover's last two years, and openly and with great frequency in the months since his death. After they had successfully resisted the White House cover-up scheme, a sense of secret alliance and shared integrity bound CIA officers like Helms, Walters, and Colby to FBI men like Gray and Bates. Nor was the Bureau objecting anymore to the DCI's wearing of his second hat, as leader of the intelligence community as a whole, and there was now a golden opportunity for the new director to expand into that role by a more activist chairing of interagency boards, and the assumption of more control over the preparation of national estimates. By the end of his tenure Helms regarded the traditional FBI-CIA problem as "absolutely no problem at all." That was surely an overstatement, but it was emblematic of the new feeling that Helms was given a farewell lunch by the acting director of the FBI, which was, Helms thought, "simply new in history." He only hoped his old

Agency itself would withstand the storm of controversy he sensed was about to break.

THE FIRST CRACKS of thunder came three weeks after Helms flew to Iran, during Gray's long-postponed confirmation hearings. The Senate Judiciary Committee had previously been busy with antitrust hearings against ITT, Gray had been out for most of November, convalescing from abdominal surgery, and Nixon had wanted to evaluate Gray's performance. But in late February 1973, Nixon finally had sent Gray's name to Capitol Hill. That was a strange decision indeed, inasmuch as Gray was certain to be grilled about the FBI's Watergate work. Ehrlichman and others had therefore strongly opposed Gray's nomination, but Nixon had gone ahead—perhaps because Gray had been a Nixon loyalist since 1960, and had only been trying to look out for the president by ratting on Dean and Ehrlichman in July; perhaps because Nixon feared Gray might expose the Watergate cover-up if unceremoniously dismissed for his loyal service. In any case, the hearings were a total disaster.

They began on February 28, with Gray insisting that the FBI had conducted "a full-court press" on Watergate. He then volunteered, without being asked, that he had routinely furnished Watergate investigation summaries to the White House. That unleashed angry badgering from senators such as Robert C. Byrd of West Virginia, who believed that Gray had been, wittingly or not, abetting a White House cover-up. To appease them, Gray said they could review all the FBI Watergate files they wished, but in that he was promptly overruled by the White House. By early April, senators had so many questions about how Gray had conducted himself as acting director, and whether his Watergate investigation had been independent of the White House, that his prospects seemed weak. Gray himself was meanwhile beginning to have some questions about the president he had been trying to serve, and he withdrew his name from nomination. "In the service of my country, I withstood hours and hours of depth charging, shelling, bombing," Gray later reflected, "but I never expected to run into a Watergate in the service of the President of the United States, and I ran into a buzzsaw, obviously."

Gray was succeeded by William Ruckelshaus, former head of the Environmental Protection Agency. On his desk when he arrived was a telegram protesting his appointment, bearing the names of all Bureau SACs. No one could figure out why he was made director, and neither could he.

"When Gray got in trouble, and Ruckelshaus came in—I think that was probably the worst time in the Bureau," special agent Jay Aldhizer recalled. "You had a director who was compromised by White House aides." With the selection of Ruckelshaus, who didn't really know what to do, the debacle was complete; all the old pride was almost gone.

Morale was plunging at CIA, too. Schlesinger had "arrived at Langley running," as William Colby would later say, "his shirt-tails flying, determined, with that bulldog, abrasive temperament of his, to set off a wave of change." By late 1973, he had fired over 7 percent of the Agency's officers, mostly from the clandestine side. There was a general sense that Schlesinger was "Nixon's revenge" against the Agency for not cooperating in the cover-up of Watergate.

But already the Watergate scandal had passed the point where the FBI or CIA could do anything to contain it, even if Schlesinger and Ruckelshaus, each selected at least partially for anticipated political subservience, had been willing to comply. Nixon's attempt to play CIA against FBI, described in August 1973 by Gray, and also alleged by Dean, initially lacked any firm public proof. But such proof existed in the secret White House taping system, which Watergate prosecutors had learned about from former staffers scrambling for leniency. When the president refused to release any of the tapes, his public-approval rating sank like an anvil, 37 points in the seven months ending August 14, according to one Gallup poll; his 31-percent rating was the lowest of any president in twenty years. At Disney World, on November 17, he insisted, "I am not a crook," but he was not believed. Even so, Nixon might have run out his term had not the Supreme Court ruled, on May 31, 1974, that he had to turn over his White House recordings to a Watergate special prosecutor. Among the sixty-four tapes ordered released was one revealing that on June 23, 1972, Nixon had ordered Haldeman to use CIA to obstruct FBI inquiries. When finally released, on August 5, 1974, that tape provided irrefutable proof that Nixon had conspired in a cover-up, and thus immediately became known as the "smoking gun."

It "mortally wounded" the president, just as Walters had predicted. Nixon's attempt to exploit the wedge between foreign and domestic counterintelligence became article I of the Articles of Impeachment drawn up against him. His earlier attempt to close that same FBI-CIA wedge, by relaxing legal restraints on CI coverage under the Huston-Sullivan Plan, constituted article II. The looming certainty of a Senate vote on these two articles led directly to President Nixon's pre-emptive resignation on August 9, 1974.

It is one of the neglected significances of history that both articles of impeachment were rooted in the secret war between CIA and FBI. Nixon's personality may have driven the events that culminated in Watergate, but their form was dictated by the uniquely bicameral context of counterintelligence. If there had been no break in liaison, no disputes on domestic CI coverage, no need for the Huston Plan, no cause for creation of the Plumbers, no forty-year feud to inspire a cover-up scheme, and no separate left hand of American CI to restrain the right, Watergate probably would never have happened at all.

Nor, for that matter, would there have ensued the post-Watergate chain of cause and effect—leadership changes, and investigations into CIA and FBI work—which would radically alter the nature of recently restored liaison, create new twilight-zone problems, and ultimately lead—as Cord Meyer put it, "like a string of exploding Chinese firecrackers"—to the devastation of American counterintelligence.

CHAPTER SIXTEEN

BLOWBACK

TRASH SWIRLED THROUGH the great Langley parking lot on May 11, 1973, as William Egan Colby locked up his car and began the long walk toward CIA headquarters. Unremarkable-looking, of average height, middle-aged, with mild eyes blinking behind glasses, he looked like any suburban commuter anywhere in the world. He had almost nothing in common with James Bond; therefore, Colby was exactly what the Agency wanted its officers to look like in real life. Though he had been made director of CIA only the day before, he had deliberately parked up against the fence on the far side of West Parking, instead of in the director's garage, and now he was striding the equivalent distance of the enormous Pentagon parking lot. He was doing this to make a point: among other changes, CIA had to become "more democratic."

Colby was an ACLU member and a onetime union-organizer who had joined CIA as the best route for a noncommunist liberal to do good. After serving as CIA's Far East Division chief from 1962 to 1967, and then as the architect of Operation Phoenix, a rural "pacification" program in Vietnam, he had returned to Washington in 1970 and absorbed certain themes floated by the campus movement of the sixties: self-determination by the young, equal opportunity, ethnic diversity. He instituted parking spaces for the handicapped and a program of minority hiring, and would go down to the regular employee dining room for lunch and invite junior officers to eat with him. That impressed most young people, who came to regard Colby as the epitome of egalitarianism, but it depressed senior officers, who eventually came to regard Colby as CIA's answer to California's perk-abhorring governor, Jerry "Moonbeam" Brown. To veteran clandestine operators, who already feared Colby as Schlesinger's hatchet man, the symbolic rejection of senior-officer privileges was but one more drag on morale. "It all changed under Colby," one CIA official recalled. "There was graffiti on the walls in the bathrooms, a different outlook toward pride in the organization, and a general decline of discipline."

But Colby was going to remake CIA whether it made him popular or not. During the two years of down-time between the Watergate burglars' arrest and Nixon's resignation, he changed the face of CIA counterintelligence, and with it the nature of CIA-FBI liaison. After Nixon's departure, by going public with Chaos and other CIA "Family Jewels," Colby would spur what was later viewed as an overcorrective "regulation" of intelligence. Yet official inquiry into the Colby-era revelations would also offer a forum for examination of interagency disputes, and several government bodies would recommend remedies for FBI-CIA conflict. James Angleton, and others who felt themselves victimized by the Colby changes, could only hope that such scrutiny would resolve some old turf problems. Then again, perhaps that was asking too much.

IN HIS DETERMINATION to transform the Agency, Colby shared a sense of mission with the FBI's new director, who arrived shortly after Colby took over at Langley. Clarence Kelley had become acting FBI director on July 7, 1973, when the hapless Ruckelshaus' unpopularity forced Nixon to appoint someone who would be respected. Kansas City Police Chief Kelley, a special agent himself for over twenty years, was a husky, blunt-featured man—Babe Ruth with bifocals, some said. He had once been an FBI firearms instructor, and was generally considered "a man's kind of guy, as opposed to the shoe clerks who ran the Bureau." Yet his simple, police-chief exterior hid a sharpness of insight, and a tendency to think long-term. He was willing to try new, decidedly anti-Hooverian techniques to improve the Bureau's performance, and to patch up relations with CIA.

Shortly after Kelley took over, Colby dialed him up with a formal offer of peace. "Look, I don't care what hell the past was all about," Colby said. "Let's communicate. Why don't you bring all your senior officers out to the Agency, and we'll give you lunch." Kelley came over with his top deputies, and there was what Colby considered "a good, long session. I put the word out, you know—'We *will* cooperate.' It was something I felt needed to be done."

The next few months saw a flurry of pro-forma concessions by each side. On August 29, Colby essentially ceded primacy to the FBI in covering Americans abroad, and restricted Operation Chaos to a passive collection of information upon FBI request. In November, Kelley killed the FBI's Scope campaign, which had been targeting Israeli scientists in the U.S. since 1968, much to the Agency's displeasure. At the same time, Kelley reinstated the formal position of liaison officer with CIA.

Although interagency meetings had been held openly, and much more frequently, after Hoover's death, liaison during the early Watergate era had been conducted mostly at the top levels, on an ad hoc basis, by Walters, Angleton, and Colby. Gray had been warned, by anti-CIA deputies such as Felt, against appointing "another Papich," who would only come under CIA domination and perhaps steer the FBI away from real Agency involvement in Watergate. Helms, meanwhile, had not wanted any FBI people roaming the halls at Langley, where they might pick up loose hypotheses about Hunt or McCord, until it was clear that the Bureau was not going to unfairly pin Watergate on the Agency. Hence, despite the dire significance once attached to Hoover's scrapping of the liaison-officer position, no new Papich had materialized during the Pat Gray period.

But by November 1972, Papich's onetime assistant William Cregar had not only taken the lead in managing the daily mail flow to CIA, but was coordinating Soviet CI with Angleton's shop. During the Ruckelshaus-Schlesinger interlude, Cregar had become the FBI's de-facto liaison officer, and when Kelley came in, Cregar was officially given the job. Like Papich, Cregar had been a college- and pro-football star—first as an All-American guard at Holy Cross, and then for the Pittsburgh Steelers—before joining the FBI in the early 1950s. His athletic career and big-jock approach to life were often remarked on, not only by spooks at the Agency, but even by his colleagues at the FBI. "Bill really was the football-player archetype," one of his colleagues would later say. "I mean, imagine John Madden running around after Soviet spies instead of coaching the Oakland Raiders—that was Bill Cregar. He was just that way—absolutely outrageous to interact with. He was built like a bull—and would act like a bull, at times. Always a very up-front man. He never was subtle, or too introspective." Recalled Jay Aldhizer, who worked under him: "Cregar had a high profile in the intelligence community. Definitely a flamboyant personality, with a desk-pounding, get-what-I-want type of relationship with CIA."

Cregar might easily have been shunned by the Agency as just another gun-toting Bureau bigfoot, if not for one salient fact: he knew CI. In the late 1960s, he had started coming to interagency meetings more or less as Papich's deputy and detail man; he had kept minutes for the working meetings at Langley during summer 1970, when Sullivan was pushing the

"Huston Plan," and had been a strong backer of that project. "Hoover put us out of business in 1966 and 1967 when he placed sharp restrictions on intelligence collection," Cregar would later say. "I was a Soviet specialist and I wanted better coverage of the Soviets. I felt that we needed technical coverage on every Soviet in the country. I didn't give a damn about the Black Panthers myself, but I did about the Russians. I saw these meetings as a perfect opportunity to get back the methods we needed." His pro-Agency stance at the Huston-Sullivan meetings had endeared Cregar to Angleton and others at CIA, and he met secretly with CI officers many times after the Huston-Sullivan Plan collapsed. "Cregar liked CIA, and they liked him; they trusted Cregar, and he trusted them," Aldhizer would say, expressing the general view. "If a matter of CIA interest ever worked its way up to him, the Agency got a good hearing. So he had developed a lot of his own contacts, and could pick up the phone, call somebody at the Agency if he had a problem, and they'd get right to it. He was in daily communication with them—and I think, operationally, he got very involved."

So involved, apparently, that the whole nature of the liaison position had to be changed. There was so much business with CIA—in new areas like terrorism and drug smuggling, as well as in more traditional spheres like security checks, the travel of diplomats, and the search for penetrations—that one man could no longer manage it all. Papich couldn't, by the end of his tenure, which was why he had brought in Cregar, but the problem had moved even beyond that level, and Cregar had to split up the duties among various people at the FBI. Junior agents like Fred J. Cassidy handled routine correspondence and liaison, and sat in on meetings with specific divisions at CIA, freeing up Cregar, who still oversaw the whole, to work important joint operations. The result was a degree of cooperation that not even Papich, hampered by the jealousies of Hoover, had been able to attain. "Under Bill Cregar, we had a number of cases we ran together, or shared information on—black areas I still can't talk about—where I didn't see any essential distinction between the two outfits," James Nolan attested. "We were working as one team."

Cregar also achieved the long-sought Papich goal of agent exchange, or at least what amounted to a "student-exchange" program. Beginning in late 1972, seven CIA officers began participating in Bureau training programs at Quantico, Virginia, and a few G-men enrolled in ultra-secret sessions at Langley. Among the latter was Larry McWilliams, who was among the first select group to attend a two-week mid-level CIA course. "CIA officers in that class were just fascinated by us, like we'd just stepped off a flying saucer," Mac remembered. Sometimes when a question was asked, a CIA officer would sort of turn around in his seat and jokingly say, "Maybe one of these cops can answer it," and after the laughter died, an FBI man usually would. FBI agents likewise warmed to guest lecturers from the Agency. An old hand from Angleton's shop might be in from 3:00 to 6:00 p.m., though only halfway through his lecture by 6:00, and the FBI students would say, "Hey, can we sit around? You want to go to dinner, have a beer?" FBI overseers were initially hesitant about such unchaperoned contacts, but soon relaxed their vigilance. As Mac put it, "We knew, if we couldn't trust these students by now, and if we couldn't trust CIA not to screw us, we were failures."

As a result of such cross-pollination, young FBI agents became well versed in Angletonian counterintelligence, and disinformation became an established topic in the Bureau's basic CI course. Mac and others still disagreed with Angleton over the bona fides of Nosenko, Fedora, and Top Hat, and there was still no embrace of the difficult Golitsyn, but deception theories were at least "in play." FBI counterspy work was generally deprovincialized, as G-men working Czech or other "Satellite" accounts would be given the opportunity to handle Soviet cases, to see the bigger picture. There was an improved compartmentation of secrets, and a tightening of access to classified documents within the Bureau. The net effect was that FBI counterintelligence became more like CIA, as McWilliams had hoped would happen: "This big difference in philosophy was what we were trying, through these schools, to break down."

To break down that philosophical barrier was also the goal of William Colby, who was meanwhile remaking CIA counterintelligence along the lines of the FBI. The irony of that parallel push for change was a dramatic "switch" of great historical importance: while the FBI adopted much of CIA's Anglo-Angletonian contextualism, CIA counterintelligence adopted the FBI's old anti-intellectual approach. Perhaps they passed in the night, but never were the twain to meet.

HOOVER HAD SEEMED "a gruff old man" when Colby was invited to the FBI in early 1973 for a ritual handshake, but Colby harbored, as he later said, "the highest respect for the first-class, professional, outfit Hoover had built," and especially admired the "discipline and professionalism" of FBI personnel. CIA needed a little more of that, Colby thought. Most of all, the Agency needed to stick to practical reality, something the FBI had never had a problem doing. Colby felt that CIA counterintelligence had become altogether too dependent on the theses of Anatoliy Golitsyn, and that an inordinate fear of disinformation agents and moles had paralyzed CIA's collection efforts, especially in the communist world. He grasped also that Angleton's belief in a long-range Soviet plan complicated full

Agency support for the policy of détente, which, as Henry Kissinger would say, began by rejecting the notion that Soviet strategy necessarily followed a long-range plan. At a time when Nixon and Kissinger had been opening up to China, Angleton had even arranged a meeting—derisively dubbed the "Flat Earth Conference" by some attendees—at which Golitsyn argued that the Sino-Soviet split was a disinformation stunt. Colby didn't want to fire Angleton, preferring to ease him out, but he was going to remake CI operations on the FBI model, whether Angleton remained as CI chief or no.

"I just thought CI should be an inherent part of the intelligence process," Colby later explained. "Do your counterintelligence as an aspect of your positive intelligence. Make it part of a case officer's professional background." In practice, that would mean that every case officer would have the task of establishing the bona fides of his own recruitments. Angleton's CI Staff would no longer have an automatic role in agent assessment, and would be largely cut out of the process. No one doubted that this would cause agent-handlers to take their sources' information at face value, and to downplay the possibility of provocation—just as the FBI, until recently, had always tended to do. The rationale was evident in a cable that went out, under Colby's direction, to CIA chiefs of station throughout the world, setting out a new policy in the handling of "walk-ins," as unsolicited agents were known. "Analysis of REDTOP [communist] walk-ins in recent years clearly indicates that REDTOP services have *not* been using sophisticated and serious walk-ins as a provocation technique. However, fear of provocation has been more responsible for bad handling of walk-ins than any other cause. We have concluded that we do ourselves a real disservice if we shy away from promising cases because of fear of provocation. We are willing to run any apparently useful case for a reasonable period and can do so in such a way that little or no harm will be done if the case should turn out to be controlled."

Miler was incredulous. "To me, Colby's idea that every case officer could be his own CI officer was a bunch of crap. How could one man possibly know enough about foreign intelligence services to do a good job? If an agent came to you with the blueprints for, say, an Iraqi supergun, how were you going to know enough even to ask an intelligent question?" The notion of a multidextrous CI-FI officer seemed akin to the ideal socialist man in Marx and Engels' utopia, who would get up each morning and plow his field, and in the afternoon he'd write a symphony—no division of labor at all, everybody would know everything. Angleton and Miler felt Colby's approach to CI was no more feasible than setting up the communists' impossible dream.

Even some of Angleton's critics within the Agency wondered whether a field agent could really have enough background knowledge to make such assessments, but Colby had an answer to that objection. To ensure that each case officer would know all he needed to know in assessing a recruitment, Colby decided that CIA's files, like the FBI's, should be decompartmentalized; Angleton would no longer control who got to see CI aspects of a case. Effective July 1, 1973, the CI Staff was "decentralized," and would serve only in an auxiliary or advisory capacity. Even most FBI liaison was stripped from Angleton and given to the DDP and Office of Security.

As Colby would later allow, "Taking away FBI liaison was designed to lead [Angleton] to read the handwriting on the wall." But the move had other effects, which Colby could not have foreseen. Under Colby's decompartmentalization, liaison with the FBI in security cases could mean exposing Agency secrets to unnecessary risk. If the two agencies had wreaked much havoc on national security by not telling each other things, there had always been a healthy, positive aspect to that, a legitimate concern that the other organization might not be as secure, or might treat carelessly secrets that were not its own. By 1975, Colby would prove that it was possible to bungle not only by holding back, but by telling too much.

THE CASE IN QUESTION had begun back in February 1968, when a Soviet Golf-class submarine was cruising 750 miles northwest of Hawaii, armed with nuclear-tipped SSN-5 missiles. A malfunction trapped hydrogen in the vent system, and a spark caused the flammable gas to explode. The ship's hull plates were torn open, tons of water poured in, and she sank. By May, the Soviets had given up hope of ever finding her. But the computerized U.S. Sea Spider tracking system knew exactly where she lay, like a lost treasure ship, with a wealth of intelligence about Soviet military capabilities. So, by June 1968, CIA's deputy director for science and technology, Carl Duckett, had proposed a mission to the bottom of the sea.

"You must be crazy!" Helms had said. But Duckett convinced Helms that the mission could be accomplished if CIA tapped the technical genius of one of its longtime contractees, Howard Hughes. Under the code name "Jennifer," CIA and Hughes began building a mother-ship that would be longer than two football fields and as tall as a twenty-three-story building. The showpiece of the ship would be a "pipe string," lengths of thirty-foot pipe joinable into segments, which would descend three miles underwater to the wreck. Attached at the end of the pipe string would be a great mechanical claw. Since there was no way to hide construction of such a leviathan vessel, a cover story had to be conceived. CIA settled on an expedition to mine for minerals, ostensibly by a company called Glomar

Research. The ship took five years to build, and Hughes himself died in the interim. But his successors delivered the *Hughes Glomar Explorer* on time and under budget ($70 million). On June 20, 1974, it left Long Beach Harbor on its secret mission.

A few days later, as the *Explorer* was almost at the sub site, CIA's Office of Security came to Colby with troubling news. On June 5, Hughes' offices in Los Angeles had been burglarized. A memo describing the sub-recovery operation could not be found. The true nature of the expedition might be known to the Soviets, who might lodge a UN protest or board the ship in international waters. Colby decided to proceed until the full extent of Soviet knowledge was established; in the meantime, every effort would be made to recover the stolen paper. Since CIA had no authority to conduct domestic operations, Colby contacted Kelley and explained the dire implications. Kelley promised that the Bureau would conduct a "full-court press."

On July 5, when the *Explorer* reached the recovery area, Soviet "fishing trawlers" also showed up at the scene. They made no attempts to board, however, and Hughes had specially designed the ship to reveal little to ignorant observers. Secret underwater gates slid back, the pipe string descended, the claw grappled the submarine. But in securing the hull, the giant steel fingers were bent, and the sub came loose; half was broken off during raising. Because of seasonal swells, further attempts would have to wait until the next "weather window," in July 1975. Even as the *Explorer* headed home, planning for this second operation, to be known as Project Matador, was under way at Langley. All the hardware existed, and next time they'd get it all—if only security could be maintained a little longer.

The Bureau kept after the Hughes memo. By Christmas 1974, the search had turned up nothing. An elaborate scheme was concocted to trap the burglars, and $1 million in secret federal contingency funds was authorized to finance the plan. But some at CIA worried that the size and openness of the FBI's "full-court press" might blow the Jennifer secret in the act of trying to protect it. In fact, that was what happened.

Though the FBI had generally increased its compartmentation of classified data, it had not devised a way to keep its director from being careless with CIA secrets. In an attempt to gain local cooperation in the memo search, Kelley had confidentially advised Los Angeles Police Chief Ed Davis of the Jennifer Project. Someone from Davis' office then leaked to the Los Angeles *Times*, which ran the story on February 7, 1975, with a front-page banner headline: "U.S. REPORTED AFTER SOVIET SUB."

So ended the treasure hunt. Because FBI indiscretion had exposed the first operation, another CIA trip to the sub site would be detected before the ship left its moorings, and Colby was not about to risk an international flap at the height of détente. The ship was sold to Lockheed. The Hughes burglary was never solved, the missing memo never found. Some of the blame was the LAPD's, of course, but that compromise could not have occurred if Colby himself hadn't told the FBI more than they needed to know. It was one more operation that had gone bad at the seam between law enforcement and intelligence—costing, in this case, $70 million, five years' labor, and a trove of secrets.

COLBY HAD APPEARED to colleagues to be in a state of increasing agitation during 1974, and not because of the sub-recovery project alone. The same pro-détente viewpoint which made him fear Soviet protest over the *Explorer* mission also imposed upon him a mounting desire to be rid of James Angleton. Despite being stripped of many powers, Angleton still used his position as CI chief as a sort of bully pulpit to inveigh against U.S.-Soviet rapprochement. Since decentralization had not caused Angleton to take the hint, Colby called him into his office on December 17 and suggested that he retire. Angleton refused. Colby now sought a pretext for forcing his outright removal, and found it in the jurisdictional twilight zone where Angleton had cooperated most closely with the FBI.

The next day, Colby spoke by telephone with journalist Seymour Hersh and invited him to a meeting in his office at Langley. When they met, on December 20, Colby told Hersh about CIA's Chaos and mail-opening operations, placing the blame for them on the CI Staff. In fact, Angleton had neither created nor overseen either program directly. He had, however, lobbied to continue both projects when Colby wanted to kill them, arguing that the FBI depended greatly on such "product" (even if, in the case of Chaos, the FBI had no "need to know" how CIA obtained the information). In any case, there could be no question that Angleton had done things of dubious legality, and Hersh was given proof of that. After briefing Hersh, Colby summoned Angleton and informed him that *The New York Times* would be exposing the operations, and linking them to Angleton, who now had no choice but to resign. His top deputies, Miler and Rocca, would also have to go.

His old FBI friend Donald Moore was in the corridor as the CI chief shuffled out of Colby's office. Angleton's posture was more bent than ever, his face dark and defeated. Behind his horn-rimmed glasses, the usually sharp eyes were blurred with pain.

Moore took him by the arm. "Jesus, Jim, it can't be that bad," Moore said. "What's the matter?"

"It's horrible," Angleton rasped. "It's awful. You'll soon read all about it."

WEDGE

• • •

"OH, MY GOD! Oh, my God! They're not supposed to have any counter-intelligence in this country! We had an agreement with them that they weren't to do anything unless they checked with us," Hersh quoted a former senior FBI official, probably William Sullivan, as saying. "They double-crossed me all along." Toward the end of the article, which *The New York Times* ran on its front page December 22, Hersh briefly considered the proposition advanced by some Angleton defenders—viz., "that the laws were fuzzy in connection with the so-called 'gray' area of CIA-FBI operations"—but Colby was given the last word: "I really see less of a gray area in that regard. I believe that there is really no authority . . . that can be used for [domestic operations]."

The American public was as shocked as Hersh's "senior FBI" official professed to be, and as unforgiving as Colby. Hersh's article was followed by revelations of other CIA "Family Jewels," such as mind-control experiments and the Castro-assassination plots, prompting Senator Frank Church to characterize that Agency as "a rogue elephant rampaging out of control." Novelists like Robert Ludlum soon depicted the U.S. government as hatching conspiracies far more diabolical than any Angleton had ever attributed to the Soviets—a development not appreciated by Ludlum's college roommate, who had become one of Colby's top troubleshooters, and who "got tired of getting up in the morning to face the same old accusations about 'dirty work,' even from my wife and children."

Morale at CIA sank to an all-time low, and stayed there for five years. It wasn't that officials weren't prepared for "blowback," the trade term for negative publicity or unintended repercussions from an operation. It was the scale and tone of the reaction, and their own government's role in it, that came as a shock. As various governmental inquiries assumed the aura of inquisition, CIA's legal counsel reminded all employees of their rights under the Miranda decision. Officers like Dave Phillips considered that "a pretty meager reward for twenty-five of the best years I could muster working for my country," and it stung all the more because it came just when so much CIA had fought for seemed in vain. The domino theory of communist expansionism in the Third World, so long ridiculed as right-wing paranoia, seemed actually to have come to pass; Angola, South Yemen, South Vietnam, Laos, Cambodia, all went communist in the space of a few months. America herself seemed lost, and preoccupied with themes of decline. Inflation had made it a lean Christmas for many families, and the sense of foreboding was tapped into by disaster movies like *The Towering Inferno, Airport 1975*, and *Earthquake*, all of which were playing as the Hersh story broke.

Debate about authority and blame for Chaos continued in the papers over the Christmas holidays, as it would in various public forums for the next five years. A *Times* editorial took the Hersh line that Chaos flowed from the "unchecked independent initiative" of Angleton's CI Staff, but noted "the decision in 1970 of J. Edgar Hoover, late director of the Federal Bureau of Investigation, to cut off working relations with the CIA. Since the agency could no longer rely on the FBI, the body legally charged with internal security, it was pushed into its own domestic surveillance. . . . Professional rivalries are endemic among secret services, but this particular feud, stretching back to the predecessor organization of CIA, has had deplorable implications for national security."

Early in the new year, a presidentially appointed Commission on CIA Activities Within the United States, headed by Vice-President Nelson Rockefeller, devoted a fair portion of its labors to the Agency-Bureau feud. Clarence Kelley assured the commission that there was no longer any problem, but Helms, called to testify, thought things could be improved, for starters, if the Bureau were given the "source-protection" duties which had been "an albatross" to directors of central intelligence since 1947. The commission did not list Helms' suggestion among its recommendations to President Gerald Ford in June 1975, but did urge an improvement in FBI counterintelligence, which would, it was hoped, remove Langley's need to meddle in gray areas. The Bureau should develop an analytical capability, and, to help that happen, CIA officers should continue lecturing at Quantico, despite the worry of William Colby that this might be illegal. "There is no impropriety in the CIA's furnishing information concerning [counterintelligence] techniques and developments to the FBI," the commission found. "The statutory prohibition on internal security functions . . . was intended to promote coordination, not compartmentation of intelligence between governmental departments."

Of course, there were limits to what the Agency could do domestically. It could not tap phones, infiltrate dissident groups, "or otherwise engage in activities that would require a warrant if conducted by a law enforcement agency." The only exception would be when there was "a clear danger to Agency installations, operations or personnel" and Bureau coverage was "inadequate." That left open the question of who would decide whether FBI coverage was "adequate," and by what criteria. The commission did not think that this would be problematic, "provided that proper coordination with the FBI is accomplished." To that end, Colby and Clarence Kelley should submit to the National Security Council "a detailed agreement setting forth the jurisdiction of each agency and providing for effective liaison with respect to all matters of mutual concern." But the Rockefeller Commission's words carried no legal force; they were only recommendations. Colby and Kelley insisted that the problems of the past would not recur in the future, and no new jurisdictional-liaison agreement materialized.

More severe were the 1976 conclusions of a Senate Select Committee chaired by Frank Church. Senator Church was particularly galled that the agencies had withheld their deepest secrets not only from Congress, but from each other. "These agencies are fiefdoms!" he pronounced in disgust. "CIA does not want the FBI to know what particular things it may be up to and vice versa." The committee proposed reconciliation of mindsets, clarification of jurisdictions, and establishment of an NSC-level mechanism to resolve defector and molehunt disputes, but in some areas could not see how to eliminate the twilight zone. Which agency, for instance, should be allowed to infiltrate a domestic radical group whose members traveled overseas? Since the committee felt that "CIA should not infiltrate groups within the United States for any purpose," this left only the FBI. But the FBI would lose its jurisdiction as soon as the infiltrating agent left the country. The most the committee could suggest was "setting restraints on the investigation of Americans by the FBI, and applying those restraints to the surveillance of Americans overseas, by any arm of the government." Since CIA was not allowed to collect any information about Americans in the United States, this truly put overseas coverage of Americans in a no-man's-land. But it was the best the senators could do.

President Ford did issue an executive order in February 1976, attempting to lay down some fresh chalk lines on the turf. The order declared that CIA "shall not engage in . . . physical surveillance against a United States person outside the United States," unless that person "is reasonably believed to be acting on behalf of a foreign power or engaging in . . . activities threatening the national security." Otherwise, however, the sole measure taken to smooth liaison was creation of yet another panel of talking heads, in the long and luckless tradition that had begun with Franklin Roosevelt's Interdepartmental Intelligence Committee in 1939. The new National Foreign Intelligence Board was to effect "coordination of national intelligence products" and the "maintenance of effective interface" between intelligence agencies. It was to be chaired by CIA's director; two other CIA men would sit on it, and one each from the other agencies, including a representative of the FBI director. Its first task was to resolve acrimony over the joint Kittyhawk operation, which had just gone tragically bad.

REACTIVATING IGOR KOCHNOV, a purported mole in the KGB, had been one of the first moves by Angleton's successors in CIA counterintelligence. The new CI chief was nominally George Kalaris, an old Southeast Asia hand and friend of Colby's who did not pretend to know CI, and was happy to let his assistant, Leonard McCoy, have the run of Angleton's shop. McCoy did not have any real CI experience, either, but he had a great interest in Kochnov, alias Kittyhawk, who in 1966 had offered to serve as a U.S. mole in Soviet intelligence. A condition of that offer had been that the U.S. help him "recruit" Russian naval defector Nicholas Shadrin into "working" for the KGB. Kochnov had returned to Moscow after Shadrin began feeding doctored naval secrets to the Soviets, but, almost nine years later, he had not been heard from. In keeping with the main theme of Colby's CIA—recruitment of agents—McCoy now determined to get in touch with Kochov. Although Angleton had concluded that the Soviet was a provocateur, McCoy had no such doubts. Hoping to lure him to a secret meeting, a CIA Soviet Division officer made a "brush" contact with Kochnov in the Moscow subways. A Shadrin-Kochnov meeting was arranged, in Vienna, as an excuse for the Soviet to leave the USSR.

Kittyhawk was supposed to be a joint enterprise, and its reactivation had apparently been arranged with the FBI's consent, or at least with its blessing, but there were strains between the Bureau's CI Club and the new CI Staff. After Colby decentralized CIA counterintelligence and stripped it of liaison, Cregar, who had a good rapport with Angleton, had largely ignored the change. In 1974, after Cregar was promoted to assistant director for foreign counterintelligence, liaison officer Frank Schwartz had also continued to see Angleton, and the CI Chief's sudden firing had caused genuine alarm at the Bureau. It wasn't that FBI men made Angleton out as any kind of saint. There was general sentiment that, much like Hoover, he had stayed in the same position too long. There was also some resentment against Angleton for hiding Chaos, and a lingering sense that he had been wrong about the bona fides of Nosenko and the value of Golitsyn. But men like McWilliams and Cregar would have much preferred Angleton to Leonard McCoy, who now adopted all the positions which the post-Hoover FBI had rejected: double-agent games were worthless, compartmentation was not so important, and disinformation agents did not exist. That ran directly counter to what the FBI's James Nolan now argued, in a paper alleging that both Fedora and Top Hat were bogus. The great counterintelligence flip-flop was thus complete As far as the Agency's new CI Staff was concerned, the FBI was paranoid. To the Bureau's CI Club, it seemed CIA did not really have any counterintelligence anymore—especially since Angleton's successors had actually *burned* 99 percent of his CI files. The disagreements became so bitter that Cregar had cut off almost all contact between the two units, and so personal that McWilliams would say, even years later, "McCoy is a horse's ass, and I hope that's going on the record."

Those were the two sides that were supposed to share the Kittyhawk game in November 1975, when McCoy arranged an FBI-CIA meeting on the case. If FBI agents needed any further reason to disapprove of McCoy, they were now stunned to learn that their good buddy Bruce Solie, of CIA's Office of Security, had been cut out of the operation. Solie had always been Kittyhawk's CIA handler, but now McCoy wanted to send a Soviet Division officer who had met Kittyhawk in the early 1960s in Karachi, Pakistan. Sending that officer was risky, because if the KGB identified him entering Vienna, looked up his postings, and found that he had been assigned to Karachi at the same time as Kochnov, who was now also coming to town, they might wonder whether the CIA man had come to Vienna to meet the Soviet. When FBI agent William Branigan objected along those lines, McCoy proposed, as a compromise, that Shadrin be handled by McCoy's assistant, Cynthia Hausmann. The FBI was not told that Hausmann had been publicly identified as a CIA officer by rogue former agent Philip Agee.

The FBI was also not told about Angleton's longstanding doubts on Kittyhawk. Because he suspected Kochnov of being a provocateur, Angleton always held that Shadrin should not be allowed to meet him in "unfriendly" foreign environments like Vienna, where the KGB had built a substantial apparat. Although the CI Chief had not believed that the FBI had a clear "need to know" of his suspicions, the interagency planning meeting on Shadrin's trip to Vienna would have been a good occasion for Angleton's successors to cut the Bureau in. Barring any warning from McCoy, however, Shadrin's FBI handlers continued to believe that the whole Kittyhawk operation was secure. With Shadrin in no apparent danger from the Soviets, the Bureau decided that it could afford not to surveil Shadrin's contacts with the KGB in Vienna.

Shadrin and his wife, Ewa, arrived in Vienna on December 18, 1975, ostensibly on their way to skiing in the Alps. Shadrin went to a meeting with two KGB officers, returned, and was debriefed by Hausmann in the bathroom of his suite at the Hotel Bristol. His wife had thought he seemed edgy before he went to a second meeting with the KGB, from which he failed to return. Ewa contacted Hausmann, who was not at an emergency number when Ewa first called it, and who seemed unconcerned until the next morning—by which time the local CIA station was in a panic. Not only had Shadrin apparently been kidnapped by the Soviets, but a KGB-backed terrorist known as Carlos the Jackal had taken an entire meeting of OPEC ministers hostage in downtown Vienna, and Richard Welch, CIA station chief in Athens, had been gunned down by terrorists. The three moves came within a few hours of each other, and shared some common elements. Welch's identity, like Hausmann's, had been compromised by Agee. Carlos' KGB case officer, Colonel Viktor Simenov, was also Agee's handler. If not a wilderness of mirrors, this was at least a tangled spider-web, and Angleton would probably have seen the synchronicity of Welch's death, Shadrin's vanishing, and Carlos' OPEC takeover as evidence of a coordinated effort. But Angleton was not chief of counterintelligence anymore.

Ewa Shadrin returned to the United States without Nick, who was never seen again. A later Soviet defector said he had died from too much chloroform in a KGB sedan. Igor Kochnov was never heard from. Eventually both CIA and FBI judged him to have been a provocateur, as Angleton had contended.

Blame for the Shadrin bungle was debated to no result by the new National Foreign Intelligence Board. The FBI made much of the fact that Hausmann had not been at the emergency number; that kind of disciplinary lapse would have never happened in the house that Hoover built. CIA blamed the Bureau for calling off surveillance on Shadrin. The Bureau countered that they would have surveilled him if they had known about Angleton's doubts on Kochnov. CIA should have also explained that the Votivkirche, where Shadrin had agreed to meet the KGB, was a perfect spot for safe, fixed-point surveillance, because it was overlooked by the U.S. consulate. The Bureau was relying on CIA's judgment; Vienna was not exactly FBI turf. "What the hell," Branigan's colleague Eugene Peterson recalled, "Vienna is a place on the Danube, and the guy wrote waltzes there. That's about all we know about Vienna." Branigan would later be incredulous that CIA had not explained the situation more fully. "All we ever knew was that we didn't want anybody out there pussyfooting around," he said. "You had to be stupid not to look out that window. . . . Anybody knows that."

Outside the FBI, however, the consensus was that Shadrin's disappearance had been the fault of neither side, and both—a classic case of an operation's falling into interagency cracks. "It was a case being run on sort of the boundary line between the FBI and the CIA, and it just didn't get the attention it deserved," Shadrin's friend General Sam Wilson, of Defense Intelligence, later said. Colby, though maintaining that the FBI's guilt ran as deep as CIA's, would also see a "system failure" of sorts. "Clearly it did fall into that chasm between us. By not raising the subject, that he shouldn't go to this meeting without some kind of countersurveillance—that was our mistake. But the FBI were handling him, so it was sort of their operation, and I don't think they told the station very much about it, enough to realize what might happen. The station knew they were going to make the meeting, but there was a drop of the ball there. In other words, if it could have been a CIA case, and the CIA station would have been in charge of it, they probably would have arranged a countersurveillance. But since it was an FBI case—you know, there's a reluctance—probably the Bureau didn't want to be bossed around too much, and our people didn't want to try to focus on what was really FBI business."

THE SHADRIN DISASTER did little to shore up Colby's career as DCI. Many within his own agency thought he was too forthcoming with Congress and the media, which in 1975 had teased out other CIA "Family Jewels." President Ford sensed that if the publicly vilified CIA "was to have the substance as well as the image of a significant change, we had to appoint a new man to preside over it." Colby was fired and replaced in January 1976 by George Bush, a Republican Party loyalist, who restored morale by freezing the Schlesinger-Colby firings of clandestine operatives.

With Ford's electoral defeat, Bush was succeeded in January 1977 by Admiral Stansfield Turner. The Agency found him a rough man to work for, and he would become probably the least popular DCI since William Raborn. Turner came in, as Pete Bagley observed, "very much from outside, " but, unlike Bush, he was never welcomed into the club. The admiral always referred to his ward as "the CIA," instead of simply "CIA," as other directors had learned to do; it was a minor point that symbolized a major estrangement. If he had entered the service of his country a generation earlier, he might have contributed much to the establishment of the U.S. intelligence community, for he had a sharp mind and the willingness to entertain bold ideas. But CIA did not want those qualities from its director in the late 1970s.

Turner did not help matters by his approach to the job. On the surface, his cerebral self-confidence could often be mistaken for pomposity. He had a deep conviction that his own ideas were right; deputies seldom felt they could influence his judgment. But most troubling was Turner's decision to lay off eight hundred of the Agency's most experienced foreign-intelligence officers. "When I came into the Agency, they had all these old fuds sitting up there, who were good guys, in their day," Turner recalled, "but a fifty-nine-year-old spy is passé. You need maybe one or two to run the place, but you don't need them sitting around. Cord Meyer, one of the great old hands of human intelligence, was a special assistant to my deputy when I got there. There was just *nothing for him to do.* They gave him a make-work job, because he didn't want to retire. But spies have to retire a lot earlier than most people, because it's a young person's game. You don't go running around the back alleys of Bucharest at sixty-five."

The old hands, however, were not usually replaced by young ones. For the most part, they were replaced by machines. Turner had decided to shift CIA's operational emphasis from human to "technical" collection—from case officers and spies to listening devices and satellites. That had its logic, especially since covert action had become such an embarrassment and a liability to CIA during the Church period. But it was understandably unpopular with the collectors and analysts of human intelligence, who had traditionally been the spine of the Agency.

Sometimes Turner felt more welcomed by the FBI than by his own people. He himself professed great respect for the Bureau—"I never looked down my nose at any of the FBI people I dealt with; they were just as suave, just as smooth, just as educated as anyone; I had known a couple of FBI men personally, before I got into CIA. I was hardly installed as DCI when Clarence Kelley invited me and my wife to have dinner in the FBI building one evening with him and all of his top people and their wives. I think he made one or two other overtures, including having me come to lunch with him in the White House mess."

Operational interface was eroding, however, because of a recent change in liaison. Although impressed by Vernon Wannamer, who replaced Frank Schwartz as liaison officer, Turner seldom saw him. In 1975, partly to protest the McCoy regime at CIA, Cregar had bucked down the liaison position from "supergrade" in the civil-service pay scale. Thereafter, few men stayed in position long enough to get the trust of both sides. Liaison officers lost their operational roles and became largely errand boys and social secretaries, setting up meetings and carrying mail. Wannamer and his successor, James Whalen, could do little to prevent disputes over such matters as the intractable "Chaos problem"—the surveillance of American citizens—which became a recurring irritant on Turner's watch.

"I would get frustrated because CIA would be listening to a telephone tap in Bolivia or Panama, and all of sudden a Latino with an American accent would get on the line, and by CIA's own rules we had to drop that tap," Turner recalled. "These were CIA-imposed rules, they weren't the law, but in the inquisitorial atmosphere of the Church-Committee era, we didn't want to take any chances. Looking back, we probably should have had some kind of arrangement to turn that material over to the FBI, so that they could have maintained the tap." At the time, however, this idea had been rejected. By dragging the principals into court, the FBI might jeopardize the lives of agents CIA had placed inside narcotics rings (their cohorts were likely to be suspicious when they got off). "There was a case in Colombia in which that was something of a problem between us and the FBI. We said, 'Sure, we helped you get this information, and track these people down, but we just can't go to court with this.' "

In other cases, CIA failed to track Americans overseas at all. In January 1977, two young Californians, Christopher Boyce and Daulton Lee, were arrested by Mexican police for selling the KGB code material from Project Pyramider, a communications system for U.S. Rhyolite surveillance satellites. (The case later became the basis for a book and movie, *The Falcon and the Snowman*.) Boyce, a clerk for the TRW Corporation in Redondo Beach, was caught when his courier, Lee, was spotted by Mexican police loitering around the Soviet Embassy in Mexico City. It developed that Lee had gone to the embassy previously, before any secrets were passed, but CIA had not picked that up. Cregar and others at the Bureau were aghast. Had the Agency become so timid, in the wake of recriminations over Chaos, that it didn't cover American citizens at the Soviet Embassy in Mexico, as had been routine in Lee Harvey Oswald's time? Ex-CIA men grumbled, "In the old days, we would have had coverage." To Turner, though, matters were not so simple. If Lee's role in passing CIA secrets was not yet known, did the 1976 executive order allow routine surveillance of Lee outside the Soviet Embassy? If CIA did cover Lee, could it relay this knowledge to the FBI? Or did it have to "sit" on the information, as it did when an American voice came on the line with Colombian drug dealers?

When the case was discussed at a conference of current and former CI specialists, minutes of the meeting recorded that "A number of former senior intelligence officers [said] that the lead agency [CIA] should have coordinated its efforts with the FBI." Others believed the episode represented an FBI failure to recognize that new weapons systems would logically be major Soviet intelligence targets; this guidance should have been provided the Bureau by CIA. A member of the House Intelligence Oversight Committee worried that the Boyce-Lee case showed "that no one is responsible, no one is really in charge and that this, in turn, does argue in favor of some new coordinating mechanism."

The need for a new mechanism was also shown by the unraveling of a case code-named "Magic Dragon." In May 1977 a U.S. naval officer's Vietnamese wife, Dung Krall, known by the cryptonym "Keyseat," was approached by Vietnamese intelligence and asked to serve as a courier. After reporting this overture to the FBI and CIA, Krall pretended to accept the Vietnamese offer, and began receiving batches of State Department documents from a man she identified as Vietnamese antiwar crusader David Truong, who was receiving them from a State Department employee, Ronald Humphrey. Truong and Humphrey were arrested by the FBI in January 1978, but the prosecutions would rest entirely on the willingness of Dung Krall to testify. That was where Magic Dragon fell apart. Kelley told Attorney General Griffin Bell that Mrs. Krall would be happy to appear in court, but an angry Turner insisted that Krall would not be available, since she still wanted to work for CIA overseas. Bell then dispatched his deputy, John Martin, to interview Krall, who was in London, in front of both CIA and FBI officials, to see if the contradiction could be resolved. Krall told the delegation she needed time to think about it, but afterward a CIA officer sneaked back into Krall's apartment and persuaded her not to cooperate with the FBI. When the Bureau learned of that double-cross, it protested to Bell, who personally drove over to Langley, walked into Turner's seventh-floor office, announced that the woman would testify, and ordered CIA to have "no more contact with Krall." Turner acceded, but was bitter about Kelley's apparent lack of concern for the safety of CIA sources.

HUMPHREY AND TRUONG were convicted and sentenced to fifteen years each for espionage, but interagency disagreements in the Truong case had attracted President Jimmy Carter's attention, and gave him the idea of replacing Republican-appointed Kelley with someone more likely to play on Turner's team. In February 1978, Carter personally interviewed all the candidates, and the one he chose was William Hedgecock Webster. Webster was a Missourian, as was Kelley, but he came from cosmopolitan St. Louis, whereas Kelley was from more rustic Kansas City, and that symbolized the difference between the men. Both were lawyers, but Kelley had become an FBI agent and police chief, whereas Webster had been a District Court and federal appellate judge for five years before making Carter's shortlist. Ultimately, Webster was chosen over other qualified men because he was a good friend of Turner, and thus offered the prospect of a détente between CIA and FBI.

The future directors had met in 1941 at Amherst College, where Turner had gone before Annapolis, and where Webster belonged to an adjoining fraternity house. Both were Christian Scientists, and they had maintained contact over the years, while Webster was in law practice and Turner was coming up through the Navy. When Webster went to a bar-association meeting in Honolulu, Turner arranged for him to see captured Japanese footage of Pearl Harbor, and Webster got to ride on the admiral's barge. Sometimes they still played early-morning tennis at Washington's Naval Observatory—a fact which, for symbolism's sake, they went out of their way to advertise after Webster became FBI director. Additionally, as Turner would recount, "About once every eight weeks we had lunch with a small number of people from both staffs to demonstrate our personal commitment to harmonious relations." Webster felt that was the kind of signal needed, because "deep down in the system, most people wanted it to work." FBI agent Jay Aldhizer would affirm that the Turner-Webster effect "filtered down, and it was hard for an assistant director or anyone else under Webster to not get along with the Agency."

But the two friends did have their share of shouting matches, though never in front of subordinates. In one instance, Turner recollected, "I signed something that made the FBI think we were trying to take over their duties for counterintelligence in this country. That was not what I intended the order to mean, but it was not good, on my part. Bill called me up and said, 'I'm mad as hell at you!' It was a good thing we were buddies, because in earlier times things would have begun to get out of control."

The Turner-Webster friendship was increasingly tested as the FBI director urged Attorney General Bell to prosecute more spies. "It wasn't a simple thing," Webster recalled. "Whether the government actually went ahead and prosecuted a spy was not actually the FBI's province, though we could decide whether or not to refer cases for prosecution. But I actively supported Griffin Bell, and urged him to go forward against spies who did not enjoy diplomatic immunity." The main rationale for that push was public awareness. Webster's theory was, "You try people in the courtroom, and that's how you convince the public that hostile intelligence is recruiting defense employees, breaking into briefcases, and so on." Webster also wanted to send a stark message to the KGB at a time when the sheer numbers of Soviet and bloc personnel in the United States, a legacy of détente, were simply overwhelming the Bureau. The FBI figured that a minimum of eight hundred Soviet-bloc intelligence officers were working permanently in-country, but Webster had fewer than two hundred agents to track them. He needed all the help he could get, and that meant not only prosecutions, but hair-trigger deportations and especially the denial of visas. It also meant overcoming his old friend's objections.

"It was the War of the Granting of Visas," Webster said. "Often the denial of visas would coincide with some effort by CIA to do something, where they feared retaliation. The Agency didn't necessarily want hostile intelligence here any more than we did, but they wanted to be sure none of this endangered their ability to put people in place elsewhere. And it was true that, the more actively aggressive and public FBI activities were, in prosecution or expulsion, the more likely the Soviets would be to retaliate against CIA, particularly in the Soviet Union. So our interests appeared to be competing. In most cases, CIA wanted to learn, like they were looking at ants under glass. My job was to wreck the whole ant farm, at least all the tunnels in this country. Sometimes I acceded to CIA; in others I went ahead despite Stan's objections. It was a question of *balance*."

If so, it was a balance that tipped dramatically in favor of the Bureau, through a series of battles in spring and summer 1978. The trouble began in May, at a shopping center in Woodbridge, New Jersey. In a double-agent operation code-named "Lemonade," the FBI had dangled a Navy man to a Soviet spy ring operating out of a yacht in the Caribbean. Two Soviet UN staffers had consequently come to Woodbridge to retrieve microfilm of doctored antisubmarine secrets, which the Navy man had left in an orange-juice carton. Arrested in the act were Rudolf P. Cherneyev and Vladik A. Enger. When Webster referred their case to Justice for prosecution, Turner protested that this would "start a spy war." The matter was taken to President Carter, who sided with Justice and the FBI. "I was mad," Turner recounted. "It was nowhere near a resignation issue; it wasn't going to wreck CIA, so I went along. But of course, the spy war did develop." Indeed, the KGB seized two Americans, practically as hostages: F. Jay Crawford, Moscow service manager for International Harvester, and Martha Petersen, an employee of the U.S. Embassy in Moscow. After Cherneyev and Enger were convicted, which let the FBI make its point to the public, a trade was finally effected, which took pressure off CIA. So ended the "spy war" of spring and summer 1978, but a new skirmish soon erupted.

In March of that year, former CIA watch officer William Kampiles had flown to Athens and given the Soviets a System Technical Manual for the U.S. KH-11 surveillance satellite. Its loss destroyed U.S. ability to verify Soviet compliance with the Strategic Arms Limitation Treaty (SALT); Kampiles had sold this information for $3,000. When CIA photointerpreters noticed that the Soviets were evading the KH-11, the FBI was asked to investigate a possible leak, and Kampiles was arrested in August. Again Webster had a chance to raise public consciousness at a trial; again Turner protested. CIA did not want to produce as evidence a copy of the KH-11 manual, but Bureau officials were not particularly sympathetic. "The case was embarrassing to CIA to begin with," James Nolan said. "Here was some little flunky, who had not only gotten access to an extremely sensitive document, but the Agency didn't know it was gone. The whole thing was a case that I think they would have liked to see go quietly into the woodwork somewhere"—especially since the Agency discovered that an additional fourteen copies of the manual could not be found.

The dispute over prosecution was settled when President Carter sided with Webster. That was Turner's second defeat in two months, and it marked a major turning point in U.S. policy toward spies. But there was another aspect of the case with important CI implications. Several months before his arrest, Kampiles had offered to become a double agent for CIA, and had written the Agency a memo admitting contact with the KGB in Athens. Yet CIA had refused to talk to him, and had not even opened his letter until the Soviets began hiding their missiles. When asked at Kampiles' trial why CIA had not looked into the Kampiles case sooner, Soviet Division officers said they worried it might be improper for CIA to be investigating "a U.S. person." Such activity had been forbidden by Executive Order 12036, issued by President Carter in January 1978. CIA was allowed to conduct "counterintelligence" activities outside the United States, and to coordinate CI domestically, but Carter had redefined CI so that Kampiles was merely a "personnel, documents, or communications security" probe, which could not be undertaken against a United States citizen, or anyone in the U.S., without a judicial warrant. Since there was no firm evidence, in April 1978, that Kampiles had yet violated any criminal statutes, CIA could hardly request the FBI to conduct a criminal investigation.

"Only when there are suspicions that a law has been broken can the FBI conduct surveillance," Turner later said. "That may not come until many secrets have been lost. We pay a price for respecting the rights of our citizens, and therefore must accept that our counterintelligence efforts will never be as effective as the KGB's."

AMONG THE OTHER PRICES paid for respecting the rights of American citizens was a virtual ban on FBI or CIA coverage of Americans abroad, at places like Jonestown, Guyana. In the age of Operation Chaos, the FBI and CIA would have been all over a communist revolutionary like the Reverend Jim Jones, who claimed to be "the dual reincarnation of Christ and Marx," and whose People's Temple offered daily training in guerrilla warfare. That much the U.S. government knew from Jones' chief radio operator, Mike Carter, who had defected from the cult in 1977, after serving as a courier between Jones and the Soviet Embassy in Guyana. But neither CIA nor FBI would investigate Jones overseas. Restrictions on the coverage of Americans had caused CIA to believe that Jonestown was the province of the FBI, and the Bureau to believe it was Agency turf.

Although Carter's executive order would have allowed CIA to cover Americans abroad if "the person being surveilled is reasonably believed to be acting on behalf of a foreign power," that loophole was closed on October 25, 1978, when Congress, in an attempt to prevent any future Operation Chaos or mail-opening projects, passed the Foreign Intelligence Surveillance Act (FISA). Under FISA, warrants were required for all surveillance, even when a suspected foreign agent was being monitored. Requests for warrants had to be submitted to a special FISA court, whose judges were sworn to secrecy. Both Turner and Webster welcomed the procedure, if somewhat warily, because it at least promised to keep Congress off their backs, while giving FBI and CIA coverage legal footing. But CI officers at the working levels of both agencies were less enthusiastic about the new regulations, especially since they seemed to impose an impossible paradox. The meeting minutes of a 1979 interagency CI colloquium recorded a general complaint that, "In order to convince a judge to issue a warrant, it was necessary to show that sufficient evidence existed, 'probable cause,' yet the collection of that evidence could only be done through surveillance of some sort. A Catch-22 situation!"

Because there were stiff penalties for violating FISA, each agency began to look to the other in the coverage of Americans, whereas previously each would simply have invaded the other's turf. Both agencies thus refused to accept information volunteered by a private American ham-radio operator, who monitored shortwave-radio conversations between People's Temple members in Jonestown and San Francisco, and who kept a detailed two-hundred-page memo log which referred to planned acts of "self-defense." The FBI did look into an allegation that Jones was holding Americans in Jonestown, but no evidence of forced confinement had been developed, and the probe was terminated because no violation of the federal kidnapping statute had occurred. A congressional postmortem on Jonestown observed that "No conclusive evidence is available to indicate that the CIA was acquiring information on Mr. Jones. . . . In this same connection it should be noted that under [laws] which prohibit intelligence gathering on U.S. citizens, the CIA was legally proscribed from engaging in any activities vis-à-vis People's Temple."

It was therefore left for U.S. Congressman Leo Ryan, an NBC camera crew, and American journalists to go in. This direct, open, hostile intelligence-gathering method was the devil's trigger, destabilizing Jones' already irrational mind. On November 18, 1978, Ryan was shot and killed, and Jones' armed lieutenants prepared two fifty-gallon drums of Kool-Aid punch containing cyanide. Anyone who refused to drink would be injected with the solution. A tape recording made by Jones preserved his final act of dialectical heroism. His last words were, "We didn't commit suicide, we committed an act of revolution!" Over the next few days, nearly a thousand corpses, still clad in bell-bottoms and tube tops, were flown home to the U.S. on military transport, in steel "tempo" coffins not used since the Vietnam War. Jones' will, drafted by Lee Harvey Oswald's lawyer, Mark Lane, bequeathed most of the People's Temple estate—$7 million—to the Communist Party of the U.S.A. and to the Soviet Union.

Stansfield Turner would later let on that an overcautious, tiptoeing approach had kept CIA's man in Guyana, twenty-year veteran Richard Dwyer, from getting too involved. "I do remember getting into the Jim Jones case," Turner said, "and all I can say is that the CIA did not handle that well. I recall something about us not getting to the airfield on time. We had indications that something could go wrong, I will say that, but not the kind that would hold up in court. It was the decision of our person there. It wasn't something where I administered punishment, but he wasn't the kind of person I'd promote next week, if you know what I mean. Whatever we did down there, we didn't do it with the kind of smoothness we should have. I don't know that it would have stopped the suicides, but it was an issue. It was a case involving Americans, and that was FBI, so we stayed around the edges."

Webster later explained that the FBI had taken just the opposite position. "The Bureau did a lot of investigation of the Jones organization, on the West Coast, church groups and what they were doing there," Webster said. "But what was the jurisdiction overseas? It's pretty hard to find."

Several months after Jonestown, current and former CI officials from both agencies held a round-table discussion on how to close coverage gaps. It was noted in a record of the session: "In the case of the People's Temple, which concerned the activities of a group of American citizens abroad, neither agency felt they could intervene. The CIA did not act because American citizens were involved, while the FBI had declined to enter the case because it was primarily a religious matter beyond U.S. borders."

That was Monday-morning quarterbacking, of course, but no other kind was possible in the case, for U.S. intelligence had played the Jonestown game with no quarterback at all. Both agencies did become actively involved after the mass deaths, when FISA permitted; until then, nothing meaningful was done. Nor could it have been, legally. Only Congressman Ryan and NBC News had the authority to gather information on Jones. The post-Watergate regulation of American intelligence had thus achieved an irony that was at once tragic and absurd. Congress and the media could collect intelligence on Americans, but America's intelligence agencies could not.

JIM WHALEN, FBI liaison officer to CIA, quit just after Jonestown, saying that a year of the job was about all he could take. As with the other liaison officers who followed Cregar, people had just seemed to bypass him, and he felt he just hadn't been able to make any impact on the situation. But the new liaison man was determined to be different.

A slim, soft-spoken Virginian, John T. "Jay" Aldhizer was not physically prepossessing. Compared with Papich, DeLoach, and Cregar, who had all been college or pro football players, he seemed about as intimidating as a high-school math teacher. But he had a way of putting people at ease, which was a good quality for a liaison officer, and he was also willing to stay in the job for a while, to work at it, to establish some of the continuity that the position had lacked since Cregar.

That commitment was crucial, for it would take at least two years for Aldhizer just to get to know all the relevant personalities at CIA, and to learn the organizational ropes, and often he would only be cut in when something was already a problem. "That was a big drawback," he recalled. "As long as things were going smoothly, and Joe Blow in the Agency knew who to deal with in the Bureau, and vice versa, everything went along okay. But it *broke down.*"

An early test for Aldhizer came during the Iranian hostage crisis. The seizure of the U.S. Embassy in Teheran on November 4, 1979, created a unique turf problem. The Bureau had jurisdiction in the recovery of American hostages under some U.S. kidnapping laws, but the Agency had a clear interest because many of the hostages were being held in CIA offices at the embassy. Turner was considering a number of paramilitary rescue operations, in coordination with the Joint Chiefs of Staff, while Webster was facing a difficult hostage-negotiation dilemma. Both tracks were constrained by President Carter's indecision, but Aldhizer meanwhile had to make sure that negotiations with the kidnappers didn't interfere with what CIA was trying to do, and vice versa. He also had to put a lot of people from the FBI's criminal division in touch with Farsi translators, and fast. Where else to get them but Langley? The dimensions of the crisis somehow made bureaucratic infighting seem out of place, and Aldhizer would remember the teamwork during the hostage crisis as one of the "high points" of his liaison work.

But the Iranian situation spilled over into other spheres, causing unexpected conflicts. Because the Iranians' declared reason for seizing the embassy had been to protest a U.S. decision to repatriate the Shah, it was important that safe-havens be kept open for him in other countries. One of the countries that was considering inviting the Shah was the Bahamas, where both CIA and FBI were trying to capture the world's most wanted man, fugitive financier Robert Vesco. Accused of defrauding investors of $220 million and making an illegal campaign contribution of $200,000 to Richard Nixon's re-election campaign, Vesco had fled the country in 1972. After he had been on the run seven years, CIA learned that he was hiding on Cistern Cay, where he paid government officials for protection, and rented a palatial house on a high sea-bluff. The FBI moved in on Vesco in late 1979 under Operation Kingfish, which used a fifty-five-foot pleasure yacht and a crew of scuba-diving G-men dressed up as Arabs. They anchored a mile or so from Vesco's house, and set up a concealed camera with a huge telescopic lens. The idea was to catch Bahamian officials taking bribes, and then use that knowledge as a lever to gain cooperation in a plan to abduct Vesco, jab him with a drugged needle, and transport him to a U.S. submarine-testing base in the Bahamas, where he could be legally arrested and flown back to the mainland.

Operation Kingfish was delayed, however, when CIA's station chief in Nassau invoked certain policy considerations. It was important not to offend or embarrass certain Bahamian officials. At issue was potential sanctuary not only for the Shah of Iran, but for another recently deposed U.S.-backed potentate, former Nicaraguan president Anastasio Somoza. The Agency also feared that any heavy-handed seizure of Vesco could upset negotiations with the Bahamians over continued U.S. rights to the submarine-testing base. While the final move in Kingfish was being debated in Washington, Vesco was tipped to the FBI's decidedly unclandestine presence nearby, and slipped out one night by boat. Between them, FBI and CIA had blown America's best chance at nabbing the notorious financier, who soon took refuge in Sandinista-ruled Nicaragua, and then in Castro's Cuba.

The FBI blamed CIA for the costly hiatus, but the Agency was irate that FBI flatfeet had spooked Vesco, especially since CIA was running its own (warrant-backed) coverage of Vesco in the Bahamas and felt it had a "handle" on him there. A CIA memo of Vesco's Cistern Cay period noted "spectral analysis" of the fugitive's radio broadcasts, as well as coverage of his mail and telephone, and even referred to the accuracy of "NOAA [satellite] material." The Agency had Vesco like Webster's proverbial ant under glass, and the FBI had disturbed the environment.

One of the factors in CIA's resistance to Kingfish—viz., Agency support and concern for the Shah of Iran—was to foil yet another FBI investigation, only three months later, which aimed at the extradition of Panamanian Military Intelligence chief Manuel Noriega. In January 1980, FBI agents in Miami began investigating Noriega's involvement in illegal arms trafficking from the U.S. to the Castro-backed Sandinista guerrillas who had recently overthrown Somoza. As it happened, however, the Shah was wintering in Panama City until accommodations in the Bahamas could be arranged, and Noriega was personally charged with his security after the Ayatollah Khomeini publicly announced that Carlos the Jackal had been hired to assassinate the Shah. Thus was Frank Gibbons, the FBI's legal attaché in Panama, warned in late January by CIA's Panama station chief, Joe Kisyonaga, that the Panamanian government would be embarrassed if the one man most directly concerned with the Shah's safety were to be indicted. CIA's concern about Noriega certainly ran deeper than it let on to the Bureau, however, since Noriega, despite known contacts with Cuban intelligence, had been put on CIA's payroll during William Colby's tenure as DCI, and was given control of an Agency slush fund for the recruitment and payment of agents in Panama. Hauling Noriega into court threatened not only the Shah but could expose CIA's long-standing relationship with Noriega. The upshot was that the Bureau was called off CIA's man in Panama. "Unfortunately," the investigating agents' supervisor recorded in a memo, "those of us in law enforcement in Miami find ourselves frequently attempting to enforce the laws of the United States, but simultaneously being caught between foreign policy considerations over which we have no control (and often no knowledge)."

BY SUMMER 1980, the need for improved FBI-CIA liaison was a recurring theme in overhaul proposals, especially in books and lectures by retired CIA officers. Former Soviet Division officer Harry Rositzke urged a truly binding coordinating authority "to assure that no Soviet agent profits from American rivalry." William Colby urged "an act of Congress defining the roles and rules for American intelligence," in which the division between CIA's foreign intelligence mission and the FBI's internal-security activities . . . should be plainly stated." And at a colloquium of current and former CI officials, former CIA molehunter Miler urged that CI be put "on a functional not a geographic basis." When there were problems, the NSC must "harmonize relationships" by "establishing authoritative coordination."

Miler's audience was generally receptive, but there was considerable hand-wringing about just how to "harmonize relationships" without sacrificing flexibility. "The problem was also raised of how to close gaps in coverage when some activities were under the jurisdiction of the FBI and some under that of the CIA," noted a summary of the discussion. "Former professionals believed that reorganization and the passage of new legislation [to improve FBI-CIA coordination] was not the answer [since] coordination between the agencies could not be legislated." But many participants felt that such bold plans must be tried if the U.S. was to replace what the minutes-keeper referred to as "a rotting root system."

Sensitive to such complaints, Turner and Webster in 1980 attempted to force the two agencies together operationally in at least one important area: the recruitment of Soviet intelligence personnel in Washington. Code-named "Courtship," the project was to capitalize on contacts established by Aldhizer, Nolan, and Cregar with CIA's Soviet Division. Whenever a Soviet visitor entered the U.S., an FBI counterintelligence squad would be assigned to determine whether he was KGB. Courtship was then to have first pick among intelligence officers considered prime targets for recruitment or compromise, and FBI agents assessed the targets with assistance from CIA psychologists. KGB officers were tailed by FBI operatives who favored Impala sedans and made a habit of staring into the Soviets' eyes in supermarkets and shopping malls; the idea was to compose a psychological portrait. Once a target was chosen, the FBI-CIA squad would work exclusively on him until they succeeded or failed, and then move on to the next one.

It was to be several years before Courtship recruited its first target, however, and creation of the new unit could not stem a general feeling that there was need for a more fundamental rejuvenation. Turner believed CIA needed more help from the FBI or must again enter the domestic field; he also sensed that he himself had gone too far in trying to keep CIA operating legally. He tried to give his officers more leeway, but it was too late; already he symbolized the timidity which seemed to have caused a string of American losses in the Third World, most recently in Nicaragua and Iran. By November 1980, Turner's deputies were on the verge of mutiny. One of Turner's senior executives, who later became president of the Association of Foreign Intelligence Officers, recalled: "Ever since the Donovan days, it was a tradition that you stood up when the Director came into the room. That was a very clear indication of how you felt about him. But I remember once when Turner walked in. Nobody stood."

Ronald Reagan and the Republicans made an issue of the "debilitated" CIA and its director in the 1980 presidential-election campaign. Turner hoped that he might be kept on even if Carter lost, but it was hard for him to remain optimistic. On election eve, when he half jokingly asked for a secret straw vote of his top fifteen deputies, the result was: Carter, 2; Reagan, 13. That stinging rebuke, delivered by some of the most politically liberal individuals in government, would just about reflect the proportion of Reagan's electoral-college victory. The morning after the election, there was manifest elation in the corridors at Langley; CIA officers weren't quite jumping up and down, but there were a lot of smiles, and people were walking more briskly. No one thought the Agency's problems would be over, but there was hope that they could be confronted forthrightly, with a renewed sense of mission. For most of the next eight years, that would be true. Thus were old turf problems to assume new forms, shaped largely by aggressive post-Carter attempts at the "rollback" of Soviet interests around the world.

BOOK FIVE

TWILIGHT FOR CHAMELEONS

CHAPTER SEVENTEEN

THE LAST
BUCCANEERS

IN MANY WAYS, William Casey was the second coming of Wild Bill Donovan. The parallels were striking; it was almost as if the old OSS director had been cloned. Both were blue-eyed, white-haired, husky-framed, sloppily dressed, Irish Catholic lawyers from the state of New York; both were disorganized, Republican, workaholic millionaires and anti-bureaucratic idea men; and both disliked J. Edgar Hoover and distrusted his FBI. Casey had served in OSS, then gone on to work alongside William Colby at Donovan's New York law firm; he did not return to intelligence until decades later, but Wild Bill had been one of the great influences in his life. The moral tenor of Casey's command at CIA, and the cause of much consequent conflict with the Bureau, was perhaps best expressed by Clair George, who for three years ran Casey's clandestine operations. "William Casey," George would say, "was the last great buccaneer from OSS."

Like his operational philosophy, the new director's antipathy to the FBI went all the way back to World War II. As chief of OSS Special Branch in the European Theater of Operations, Casey had seen firsthand how Hoover tried "to walk off with a slice of [Donovan's] franchise," and felt that his mentor had spent "an inordinate amount of time fighting a legal and bureaucratic war for survival." Casey also believed that Hoover's withholding of the Dusko Popov questionnaire from Donovan had caused the disaster at Pearl Harbor. Casey had, moreover, been a friend of André Dewavrin, whose 1945 nomination for the U.S. Distinguished Service Cross had been staunchly fought by Hoover. And while spending several weeks on a 1946 committee advising Truman about peacetime intelligence, Casey had been depressed by Hoover's attempts to stunt CIA at birth. Even twenty-five years later, when Casey was named to head the Securities and Exchange Commission, Hoover was making life difficult for him—unearthing a plagiarism suit over a tax-code manual Casey had prepared, which almost kept him from assuming the SEC post.

That Hoover was no longer around did not keep the Bureau from causing problems for the new director. He had not been at Langley long before Webster launched a criminal investigation into Casey himself, in the so-called Debategate scandal. White House Chief of Staff James Baker alleged that Casey had provided him, before a campaign debate, with Carter's briefing papers. Casey denied this. The FBI questioned Casey on three occasions, rifled Republican files, and turned up a memo suggesting a Reagan mole inside Carter's camp. Although no "smoking gun" was found to implicate Casey, the episode could not have warmed him toward the FBI.

But if Casey would always see law enforcement as a threat to his secret projects, he still had to get along with Webster. The hard-driving Irishman and the more genteel Webster were not a natural match, but they were not going to go through any Mongoose and Cobra routines, either. They did some things together. Casey took Webster on a trip to New Zealand, probably for a meeting of the CAZAB, a semiannual conference of Western CI executives begun by James Angleton in 1967. The Bureau's CI Club felt that Casey was more sensitive to its counterespionage needs than Turner had been. It seemed that relations might not necessarily worsen with Turner's departure, as Aldhizer initially fretted. It would be several years before the Bureau learned that Casey was hiding things from them, even breaking the law behind their backs.

For the moment, there was a drawing-together. The Bureau's CI Club took solace in the retirements of George Kalaris and especially the anti-Angletonian Leonard McCoy. New CIA counterintelligence chief David Blee was not overtly hostile to traditional CI, and that helped close the "mind-set" gap. On the Agency side, there was some brief concern when FBI Assistant Director Cregar retired in 1981; the new Intelligence Division chief, Ed O'Malley, had few previous contacts with the Agency, and was by nature so reserved that Agency people complained to Aldhizer, "Ed won't talk to me." But the new relationships were helped along when Aldhizer scheduled a few interagency softball games, pitting the Bureau's Intelligence Division against CIA's Counterintelligence Staff. CIA won the first contest, the FBI took the second, then swept an abbreviated double-header—which Aldhizer would good-naturedly cite as evidence that "there were better athletes in the Bureau than in CIA." There were also some interagency poker games, and O'Malley was seen as "one of us" by CIA's Office of Security after he cleaned their clocks.

Above all, however, O'Malley came to be admired at Langley for pulling good pranks. After Casey's first DDO, Max Hugel, resigned for alleged securities violations in summer 1981, O'Malley asked the Bureau's crime lab to white him out of a group photo taken at an interagency luncheon. That especially tickled CIA officers, because Hugel, a Casey business partner who had no intelligence experience, was widely resented as a bad choice for the job. Agency techs were in turn inspired to airbrush the head of Casey's number-two man, Admiral Bobby Ray Inman, onto a *Playgirl* magazine centerfold. The finished product became an instant classic at the Bureau, where Inman, because of his resistance to loosening FBI domestic-collection rules, was not especially liked.

But the Bureau did not take kindly, either, to the relaxing of restraints on CIA's domestic work. On one occasion, Casey gathered various agencies over at Langley to talk about CI, in the imperious tone of: *This is what we're going to do.* "That was not the way to go about it with guys like Jim Nolan," Aldhizer recalled. "It was a definite move by the Agency to get involved in FBI turf. And man, there was some fur flying."

In fact, Casey wanted to remove all the post-Angleton restraints on CIA. He got Attorney General Ed Meese to back him. When Meese made the case at a White House intelligence round-table on January 26, 1981, the first Monday of the new administration, Webster immediately spoke up to disagree. Perhaps the Turner-Carter school had put too great a premium on civil liberties, but there were good reasons to be cautious about what CIA could do within the country. Webster's own Bureau, which had sole jurisdiction in such matters, did not feel especially hindered by legal restrictions. He could use more resources, and he would not mind having a formal charter to spell out what the FBI could do, in positive terms, rather than simply saying what it could not. Otherwise, however, he was in favor of preserving the status quo.

Casey did not argue the point, but CIA's legal staff soon redrafted Carter's executive order on intelligence in a way that would let the Agency run operations and conduct electronic surveillance within the U.S. Casey initialed his approval. The draft order was then promptly leaked to the press—perhaps by the FBI, or perhaps by Inman. "Intelligence Groups Seek Power to Gain Data on U.S. Citizens," warned *The New York Times'* front-page headline on March 10, 1981. The American Civil Liberties Union was prepared for a full counteroffensive, and the draft order was quickly watered down.

Still, Reagan's Executive Order 12333, issued on December 4, 1981, did give the Agency greater domestic powers. Carter had only allowed CIA a "coordinating" role domestically, but Reagan now permitted the Agency to "conduct counterintelligence activities within the United States, in coordination with the Bureau, as required by procedures agreed upon by the Director of Central Intelligence and the Attorney General." On that foundation Casey created a Senior Interagency Group–Intelligence (SIG–I), chaired by himself, to "resolve interagency differences concerning the implementation of counterintelligence policy." The SIG began hashing out arrangements, some of them designed to blur traditional foreign-domestic distinctions. Casey was allowed to request the FBI to collect foreign intelligence. Agency personnel, upon approval of the Agency's Foreign Resources Division Chief, were permitted "to use [U.S.] athletic, entertainment, or cultural facilities that are open to members of the general public . . . for the purpose of maintaining cover or to develop sources." That meant Nolan's agent-handlers could meet their moles in Bangkok or Beirut, and CIA officers could hit on diplomats at the Kennedy Center, or debrief tourists returning from Nicaragua. This went well beyond the arrangement Papich had brokered in 1966, which had let CIA work at home but had not allowed the FBI to follow cases abroad.

But if the SIG could help keep fieldwork on track, it could not resolve differences of philosophy. When Casey wanted to expand the use of random polygraphs on persons in national-security work, Webster expressed uneasiness over the reliability and intrusiveness of that technique. When the FBI pushed to reduce the number of Soviet diplomats in the U.S., Casey could not help thinking of Hoover's opposition to Donovan's proposed OSS-NKVD exchange, and warned the president that the Soviets would retaliate by cutting the number of U.S. intelligence agents allowed under diplomatic cover in Moscow. (Indeed, when acting Soviet military attaché Yevgeniy Barmyantsev was expelled after receiving bogus "classified documents" from an FBI double agent in 1982, the Soviets kicked out of Moscow Richard W. Osborne, a first secretary at the U.S. Embassy, and Lewis C. Thomas, an attaché and electronics expert.) And when a longtime CIA asset, Nassar Haro, was named chief of the Mexico City police elite DFS intelligence division in 1982, the FBI created an embarrassing problem for Casey by refusing to halt their investigation of Haro's connections to a California car-theft ring. Casey had to lobby Justice directly to scuttle the case, arguing—over cables of protest from the Bureau's legal attaché—that Haro was an "essential contact" who helped track suspected terrorists, as well as communist agents and diplomats.

To some within the administration, such episodes proved that the new executive order had done enough to break down bureaucratic barriers between FBI and CIA. There were even rumblings for creating a new counterintelligence superagency, which would combine foreign and domestic CI. The movement was launched by a conservative "firespitter" on the Reagan transition team, Senate aide Angelo Codevilla, who had attended colloquia at which Miler and others lamented the intractability of FBI-CIA bungles. Within the new administration the superagency idea was taken up by Kenneth DeGraffenreid, a forty-one-year-old ex–Navy flier who had worked briefly at the Defense Intelligence Agency before being named senior director of intelligence programs at the National Security Council. DeGraffenreid protested eloquently at NSC meetings that Reagan's draft order on intelligence did not offer any meaningful mechanism to harmonize interagency relations, but only such toothless prescriptions as: "all agencies and departments should seek to ensure full and free exchange of information." DeGraffenreid urged abandonment of the arbitrary foreign-domestic split, which was not a distinction observed by the Soviets or, for that matter, any other country in the world. Counterintelligence, he argued, should be handled by an agency like Britain's MI5, which could follow its cases both at home and abroad, and be headed by a "czar" who would have all the country's CI tools at his fingertips.

Although the czar idea was soon squelched because of Orwellian fears for Americans' rights, DeGraffenreid did not give up, and in January 1982 the president ordered a wide counterintelligence study into his ideas. DeGraffenreid was not happy with the forum, however, which was an interagency "task force" headed by Webster. The group was to examine the quality of CIA and FBI counterintelligence—spy-catching, double agents, and deception operations—but the examination was to be done by parties with vested interests, who could hardly be expected to offer up their empires to radical reform. The task force did set up an interagency group in 1983 in the attempt to forge a unified policy on background investigations and security clearances, but even that body failed to produce consensus, as events were soon to prove.

STILL, ONE OF THE STANDARD OBJECTIONS to DeGraffenreid's ideas was that, in joint operations like Courtship, the two agencies were already working as a single unit. Indeed, Reagan had not been in power long before Courtship made its first two recruitments in the KGB's Washington residency. The first to be landed was Valery Martynov, an officer of the "Line X" or scientific-espionage section, who had seemed to CIA's psychologists to be a good target because he was enamored of Western life and eager to please Americans. That assessment proved correct, and, beginning in fall 1982, Martynov met at least once weekly with CIA and FBI men to trade secrets for cash. He provided KGB "shopping lists," detailing the technological secrets Moscow most desperately wanted to steal, and explained some of the Soviets' own espionage gadgetry. He said, for instance, that the KGB supplied its agents with communications devices that propelled themselves underwater for several miles before surfacing to send coded bursts to Soviet satellites, thus concealing the agent's location from any Western interceptors.

Only a few months after recruiting Martynov, Courtship struck success again, with Sergei Motorin, a political-intelligence officer who was "persuaded" to help the West after the FBI photographed him trading a case of Russian vodka for a Japanese stereo system. The take from Motorin included insight into Soviet disinformation techniques, and echoed some of what Golitsyn had given over twenty years before. Motorin related how Moscow Center periodically tasked each KGB officer to mention the same bit of information to every American he met; the data might relate to Soviet missile strength, Kremlin power struggles, or Yuri Andropov's image as a jazz-loving "reformer" who had given up hope for communist world-conquest. "So you had a hundred guys saying the same sentence." Motorin told his stunned handlers. "Everyone agrees it must be true. In fact, it's a lie."

To make sure the agents themselves were telling the truth, the FBI shared their take with the counterintelligence officer in CIA's Soviet Europe Division, Aldrich Hazen Ames. Better known to his colleagues as Rick, Ames was a "legacy": his father, a career CIA officer, had been an analyst on Angleton's staff. Except for his mustache, Rick Ames actually looked a bit like the legendary CI chief—thin, graying, nondescript, unassuming, withdrawn. But even if he was not very gregarious, FBI agents found him "a nice guy," and considered him an expert on Soviet intelligence. He vetted Martynov's and Motorin's information against what CIA already knew, and pronounced both agents to be bona fide sources.

The FBI retained the lead role in running Martynov and Motorin, but O'Malley did not object to parallel attempts at penetration by CIA. Courtship, he thought, could be a good umbrella for both agencies' work. Beginning in March 1984, he even approved Ames' visiting Soviet diplomatic sites in Washington, to size up and "pitch" potential recruits. All O'Malley asked was that Ames keep the Bureau posted on his contacts. Ames gave his word.

WHILE FBI AND CIA teamed to penetrate the Soviet Embassy in Washington, considerably less cooperation was marshaled against Soviet attempts to penetrate the U.S. Embassy in Moscow. When French intelligence warned in late 1983 that a Soviet bug had been found in a coding machine at the French Embassy, the State Department asked a team of FBI security experts to determine whether the Soviets might also have bugged communications at the U.S. Embassy. The Bureau had some predication in the probe because the embassy was technically "U.S. soil." After sweeping the outpost—including the top three floors, which were occupied by CIA—the FBI agents returned with a devastating critique of security weaknesses. Their findings were presented to the president and his advisers in a slide show by the FBI's David Major. Whereas the Soviet Embassy in Washington perched atop Mount Alto, the District's second-highest location and an ideal site for intercepting government communications, the U.S. Embassy in Moscow had been built on low, swampy ground by the Mosvka River, which made it an ideal target for Soviet interception efforts. That inequality, a product of political considerations during the William Colby years, had been compounded by the decision to allow a Soviet émigré to serve as design engineer for the U.S. embassy. The building had been honeycombed by bugs in its walls and chimneys. The émigré eventually returned to the Soviet Union and was promoted by the KGB. Finally, Major reported, an FBI team, in a test, had been able to infiltrate communications rooms on CIA's three "secure" floors, without being detected by guards or alarm systems. Conceivably, then, the KGB could do the same.

After Major's startling allegations, CIA was put in charge of a committee to examine the problems, and concluded that some of them did not exist. For instance, the Agency questioned whether it was really possible to break into the communications room, as Major said the FBI team had proved. To impugn the Bureau's methodology, CIA pointed to Operation Gunman, an FBI-NSA follow-up investigation which discovered Soviet bugs in seventeen embassy typewriters in spring 1984. Since some of the typewriter bugs were battery-powered, the Bureau concluded that the KGB must have had a way of getting into secure areas of the embassy to replace those batteries. It was suggested that chimney flues had been enlarged so that trained midgets or children could climb up into the CIA station, or that a Soviet spider-man was scaling the embassy wall at night, squeezing through a tiny window and making his way to the code room. But a CIA–State Department study pronounced that the flues had not been enlarged, and also claimed that the "spider-man" window was nailed shut, with years of Russian bird droppings on the seal. The FBI maintained that such findings did not invalidate its earlier conclusions, and called for a congressionally approved study of the situation that would involve all intelligence agencies. But CIA vetoed that idea, arguing that Casey alone had the right, by law, to protect intelligence sources and methods. Such matters were debated for three years without agreement. Frustrated White House officials like DeGraffenreid worried that the embassy was a disaster waiting to happen.

OTHER SECURITY PROBLEMS were meanwhile emerging from the case of a suspected mole in CIA. In 1973, after defecting from Czechoslovakia, Karl Koecher had obtained work in AE/SCREEN, a sensitive translation unit in CIA's Soviet Russia Division. Koecher's Czech-born wife, Hana, served as a courier, using her work as a diamond grader as an excuse to travel to the jewelry centers of Europe, hiding CIA documents in cigarette packs and trading them to Czech agents for cash. Karl Koecher also met handlers in the U.S., and it was probably through routine surveillance on suspected Czech agents that the FBI began developing its case against Koecher in late 1982. O'Malley immediately warned Casey, who curbed Koecher's access to secrets. The Bureau then let the case run for more than two years, hoping that Koecher might lead them to other spies, as well as offer proof of his treason that would hold up in court. But by November 1984, the Bureau had met neither objective, and Koecher seemed to sense he was under suspicion. He scheduled a trip to Vienna, which would be an easy platform for redefection to Czechoslovakia. Kenneth M. Geide, the FBI agent in charge of the Koecher case, and Jerry G. Brown, chief of CIA's security-analysis group, therefore decided to stake the case on a massive bluff.

On November 15, FBI agents approached Karl Koecher in New York City and asked him to sit down for "a talk." A few minutes later, Koecher was in a two-bedroom suite on the 26th floor of the Barbizon Plaza Hotel, overlooking Central Park. "We know who you are and what you are and what you've done since you arrived in this country," Geide said. He proposed using Koecher in a double-agent game which would allow him and Hana to move to Austria—and escape prosecution—as long as he would help fill in some "blanks." Koecher launched into an admission of his spying activities. He was then released, presumably after being given a CIA mission to perform in Austria. The FBI even offered to take the Koechers to the airport for their scheduled flight to Vienna, on November 26. But when the Koechers showed up at the Barbizon Plaza with their suitcases, they were put in handcuffs.

When the case was forwarded the next day to Justice Department internal security chief John L. Martin, he was shocked by what appeared to be a confusion in CIA-FBI treatment of Koecher. Apparently the Agency had actually wanted to turn him into a double agent, while the

Bureau had wanted to prosecute him all along. At the last moment, the Bureau had convinced CIA that Koecher should not be allowed to visit Vienna. Geide and Brown had offered him immunity from prosecution, and made other false promises, which they had no power to confer, and which the FBI had no intention of fulfilling. In short, Martin believed that the confession had been obtained improperly, and wondered if it would hold up in court. It eventually did, but largely because Koecher muffed his own defense, insulting his lawyer's taste in clothes and making careless admissions while in jail.

The Bureau and the Agency even disagreed in their damage assessments of the case. CIA believed that Koecher had been an important spy, an impression the Soviets seemed to confirm by agreeing to exchange dissident Anatoliy Shcharansky for the Koechers in Berlin. But O'Malley and others at the FBI were not so sure that Koecher was all CIA made him out to be. He was only a translator, after all, not a case officer or an agent-handler or an analyst. He did not work in Langley, but in one of the outbuildings in Arlington, Virginia. He claimed to have "burned" a Soviet mole in Moscow, Alexander Ogorodnikov, who was arrested by the KGB in 1977 and reportedly died in custody. But an FBI polygraph test showed that Koecher was being deceptive about what information he had given communist intelligence. Koecher himself later told journalist Ronald Kessler that he made up some of his admissions. The question had to be entertained: Was Koecher merely taking the fall for a much-higher-level penetration of CIA? Had he been briefed by his communist handlers on what to "confess to," to protect another agent—on promise of an eventual spy trade, and a hero's life in Prague? Those were black thoughts, but other startling discoveries in the case—including the participation of some CIA employees in sexual orgies arranged by the Koechers—indicated potentially cancerous security problems at the Agency. Especially scandalized was Philip A. Parker, who in March 1983 replaced the retiring Nolan as O'Malley's deputy. "As far as we in the FBI were concerned," Parker would say, "there was no real counterintelligence function in the Agency's CI Staff."

THE ACCURACY OF Parker's assessment was borne out on a hot, muggy morning in July 1985, on a rain-slicked road outside Moscow. A five-car convoy closed on a yellow sedan, which pulled over to the gravel median. Its driver got out. As uniformed officers approached him, he reached into his vest pocket—presumably to show identification, but perhaps to draw a gun. There was a struggle, shouting, then chloroform. The suspect was hustled into a white van. The cars caravaned back toward Dzerzhinsky Square, blue lights flashing. The KGB had arrested Adolf G. Tolkachev, a missile-avionics expert, for passing information to CIA.

The "burn" did not stop there. By year's end, the Soviets had rolled up virtually all Western sources in Moscow. At least twelve Soviet citizens were caught spying for Langley, and at least six were reportedly put to death. Casey's spies were shut down in other parts of the world, too. Panicked moles, sensing they were under suspicion, defected in Athens and London. Both Courtship recruitments, Martynov and Motorin, were recalled to Moscow and later reported shot. Just as Mikhail Gorbachev was coming to power, just as the Agency had its greatest need to know what was going on, all the Agency's eyes had been poked out at once. As one of Casey's confidants would later write, "It was like the beginning of a spy novel, but no one knew what to do."

How had the Soviets pinpointed so many spies? By persistent tailing of their American handlers? Through bugs at the U.S. Embassy? Or by tips from a highly placed mole?

In early August 1985, counterintelligence professionals received an easy answer to this riddle. Too easy, perhaps. But before it could be cross-checked and tested and probed, the answer, or twin halves of it, would slip between the right and left hands of American CI. Thereafter, it would have to be taken on faith.

ON THURSDAY, August 1, 1985, KGB officer Vitaliy Yurchenko defected to CIA at the United States Embassy in Rome. He was a thickset man with a shaggy mustache and facial warts. The tips were missing from the middle and ring fingers on his right hand, caught in a winch when he had worked as a submarine repairman in the Soviet Navy. From the Navy he had transferred to the KGB, rising swiftly. Just a few months earlier, Yurchenko told his CIA handlers, he had been made deputy chief of the KGB's First Department. That made him responsible for all KGB operations in North America.

Cabled to Langley, that latter biographical tidbit caused considerable excitement among Casey and his deputies, who were trying to puzzle out how their networks were being blown. If Yurchenko was all he claimed to be, and if there was a mole in the Agency, Yurchenko would almost certainly know who it was.

The next day, Yurchenko landed at Andrews Air Force Base aboard a C-5A transport jet, and was driven in an FBI motorcade to a luxury condominium five miles from Langley. Waiting there were debriefers from both the Bureau and the Agency. Representing CIA were Rick

Ames, the Soviet division's CI chief, and Colin Thompson, an agent-handler. The FBI team was headed by Mike Rochford.

"Do you know of any penetrations in CIA?" they asked Yurchenko.

Only a former Agency trainee, the Soviet said. He did not know the man's real name, just his cryptonym: "Robert." This spy had been groomed and briefed for assignment to Moscow Station, but was fired because he was considered a drug addict or an alcoholic. He had visited the Soviet Embassy in Washington in 1983, then traveled to St. Anton, Austria, for a meeting with the Soviets. According to Yurchenko, it was on the basis of Robert's information—and by the use of an invisible "spy dust" on Western diplomats who posted letters to secret agents—that the KGB had rolled up CIA's Moscow network.

Yurchenko's tip created an immediate crisis for Gus Hathaway, a lanky, gray-templed clandestine services veteran who had recently become chief of CIA counterintelligence. From Yurchenko's description, Hathaway knew that Robert could only be the thirty-four-year-old former trainee Edward Lee Howard. An Army brat and altar boy before serving with the Peace Corps in rural Colombia, Howard had applied to CIA in part because of a Walter Mitty complex. "As a kid I used to see James Bond movies," he later said. "The guy steals; he gets away with things, like any of us would like to do." In 1981, Howard was accepted into training at Camp Peary, and by spring of 1983 was slated to be posted to Moscow, his first overseas assignment. He was given a battery of polygraph exams, as are all CIA officers before leaving on extended foreign missions. He admitted to stealing from a woman's purse during an airplane flight, and to using cocaine while on CIA's payroll, but apparently was holding back even more. After the results were analyzed, Howard's supervisor, USSR desk chief Thomas Mills, told him that the tests indicated deception, and said, "We'd like you to resign."

Standard procedure would have been to alert the FBI right then, in 1984, that Howard was a potential traitor, a man who might bear watching. But CIA had decided not to share the case. Why the Bureau should not be told about Howard would later become a matter of much speculation. The generally accepted view was that the Agency was simply embarrassed, and wanted to keep its own failures in-house. Nor was there, as yet, any evidence that Howard had broken the law.

But the Howard case, and CIA's withholding of it, had not ended there. A few days after being cut loose, Howard called a secret number at Moscow Station and left a message for the station chief, apparently as some sort of joke. The Agency was troubled by this bizarre behavior, but again it was decided not to brief the FBI. Instead, CIA sent Howard to a psychiatrist, to whom he confessed that he had contemplated selling details of CIA operational methods in Moscow. Howard said he had even loitered outside the Soviet Embassy in Washington, but had not gone in. For a third time, CIA officials wondered whether to inform the FBI of Howard, and for a third time decided not to.

But now that Yurchenko had tipped the joint FBI-CIA debriefing team about "Robert," the Howard matter was coming to a head. CIA could not stall forever; at some stage the Bureau must be informed. This would not be pleasant. To admit to the FBI that Robert's identity was already known to CIA would mean admitting to a pattern of deceit and incompetence lasting more than two years.

In the old days, CIA officials could have rationalized that it was difficult to discern when a mere "security breach" became a more serious counter-espionage case worth bringing to the Bureau. But Reagan's executive order precluded that kind of waffling. "In any case involving serious or continuing breeches of security," Reagan had spelled out, CI must "recommend to the Attorney General that the case be referred to the FBI for further investigation." CIA's deception of the FBI in the Howard case was not only monumentally stupid; it was also illegal.

Yet if the Agency had held out for two years, it could do so for a few days more. Thus, when Parker entered the office of O'Malley's successor, James Geer, on Monday, August 5, 1985, and announced, "CIA has a problem," the FBI still did not know any more than what Yurchenko had said. Parker told Geer that two special agents from the Washington Field Office were already out at Langley, trying to help the Agency figure out who Robert might be. Until the Agency told the FBI who he was, there was nothing anyone could do.

Monday passed. Tuesday. No word from Langley. They were checking their files, Aldhizer reported. As soon as they knew anything, the Bureau would hear. It did not occur to Parker that CIA might be up to something. He felt he had always played it straight with the Agency, and assumed they would always play it pretty straight with him. When CIA finally told him, on Wednesday, August 7, that Robert was unquestionably one Edward Lee Howard, Parker had no reason to suspect that the five-day lag was due to anything other than CIA's painstaking analysis of its files.

But by late August, the truth began filtering back to Parker from the Washington Field Office. He realized that "from the moment the news came in [from Yurchenko] they knew exactly who it was." His best guess as to why CIA had held off those extra five days: "Maybe it took that long to figure out how the hell they were going to tell us."

The concealment was costly. On August 6, as the Bureau patiently awaited word about Robert's identity, Howard had taken a plane to Vienna, where he had almost certainly met his Soviet controllers. If the

Agency had let on right away that Robert was Howard, and if he had been under surveillance during the meeting in Vienna, the FBI could have had enough evidence to make an arrest. As it was, he had returned to the U.S. before the Bureau even knew he was gone. CIA's dishonesty had probably caused them their best chance to nail a spy.

"That was the low point of my work as a liaison officer," Jay Aldhizer admitted. "We were playing softball with these guys who were supposed to tell us."

The Agency's duplicity continued even after the Bureau was told about Howard. As the FBI began surveilling him and placed a tap on his phone, CIA failed to disclose that another of its former officers, William Bosch, had been Howard's best friend at Langley, and that the two still saw each other frequently. Bosch was potentially a source for some very good leads, but the Bureau found him only by rooting through Howard's long-distance phone calls one at a time and cross-checking each number against a computer base of names.

CIA had a reason for holding back about Bosch: it was feared that he might tip Howard to the Bureau's inquiries. In fact, Howard did learn that the FBI was on to him, although it is unclear whether he was originally warned by Bosch, or by someone else—a mole in CIA?—earlier on. Certainly, the timing of Howard's August visit to Vienna, just days after Yurchenko came over but before the FBI knew about him, suggested a leak in Langley. In any case, if Howard had not hatched an escape plan with his Soviet handlers on August 6, in Vienna, he did so in September, after a phone call from Bosch.

The success of Howard's scheme would hinge on the quality of the countersurveillance training he had received from FBI agents guest-lecturing at CIA. As part of the cross-pollination arranged by Aldhizer, Howard and many other Agency trainees had absorbed all the Bureau could teach about eluding watchers and pursuers. Now Howard would use that knowledge, which came of interagency cooperation, to pull off an action that would drive the agencies further apart.

At four-thirty on the afternoon of September 21, Howard and his wife, Mary, left their home in Santa Fe, New Mexico, and drove to a restaurant nestled between art galleries. At about seven o'clock, they paid the check and his wife took the wheel. She turned through a number of residential side streets. On one of them, as they turned a sharp corner at fifteen miles per hour, Howard opened his door and rolled out onto a well-tended lawn. He landed hard on one arm and almost broke it, but scrambled into bushes by a high fence. In the car, a Styrofoam dummy popped up in his place, complete with wig and clothes. It was still daylight as his wife pulled into their garage at home with the fake Howard beside her on the front seat. A Bureau surveillance team duly noted that the pair had returned from their date. Howard's disappearance was not detected until late the following evening; by then he was already on his way to Moscow. Instead of a life in jail, and a confession which would help CIA assess the damage he had done, he would have a long, thorough debriefing by the KGB, and occasional dinners with Kim Philby.

THE AGENCY WAS ALMOST hysterically upset with the Bureau for blowing the Howard stakeout. Not since Hoover's ham-handed surveillance of the Tairovas, twenty-eight years before, had the FBI performed so poorly on an important target. Casey wanted to know how Howard had managed to drive off in broad daylight. Webster lamely explained that the lookout man was a rookie agent who had been watching a video monitor. There were problems with reflection and glare, because the sun was strong in the desert. CIA officials acidly suggested that the Bureau might want to use some of its counterintelligence budget to invest in sunglasses. The rookie FBI agent was disciplined and soon resigned.

CIA's outrage was somewhat hypocritical, however. The Bureau's botched surveillance was an end-play only made possible by the Agency's own withholding in the case. It had been Langley's five-day delay, after all, that caused the FBI to miss evidence which would have allowed an immediate arrest.

While the two agencies pointed fingers over Howard's loss, tensions surged over the handling of the source who had sparked the suspicions against Howard in the first place. After their initial joint debriefing of Vitaliy Yurchenko, the two agencies had alternated days, and the defector soon spent much of his time with his Bureau interrogator, Mike Rochford, complaining about alleged maltreatment by CIA. His Agency handler, Colin Thompson, was taciturn and, according to Yurchenko, generally not nice. The Agency sent guards to sleep in Yurchenko's room, and would not allow him to visit Russian-language bookstores. The Bureau, by contrast, had bought him golf clubs and seemed to show some genuine concern for his well-being. The net result was a good-cop/bad-cop effect, but Rochford and other FBI agents didn't see the need for such a Manichean approach. After all, the man had risked his life to help the West. He should be treated not as a prisoner but as a hero.

CIA officers, however, thought it wrong to believe that a more "popular" handler was necessarily a better one. It was a cardinal mistake to let defectors obtain an exaggerated sense of their own worth. Remembering names and dates and other details from years past was grueling, exasperating work, and defectors, like other sources, should be made to understand that their treatment would be pegged to performance. CIA, moreover, had the difficult job of establishing a defector's bona fides, of analyzing his information against everything else that was known, whereas the FBI had the easier and more fun job of pumping him for information and running down leads. Finally, as the saying went, kids were always great when they were someone else's. Since CIA had formal responsibility for defector resettlement, the Bureau didn't have to deal with the frustrations that came from having to care for and feed these exiles for the rest of their lives, didn't have to deal with their infantile behavior and adult needs, didn't have to find them jobs and sex and happiness.

In an attempt to revive Yurchenko's apparently sputtering spirits, the two agencies did agree that Thompson and Rochford could take him on a two-week tour of the American Southwest. But because of interagency differences, the trip was a disaster. After several days of scenic driving through dramatic gorges of rust-colored prehistoric rock, they arrived in Las Vegas. When Yurchenko expressed a strong desire for female companionship, Thompson, the CIA man, suggested that Yurchenko be allowed to hire a prostitute. But Rochford, the FBI man, refused. The Bureau was a publicly respected law-enforcement agency, and would not get involved with things like that. To Thompson, that typified the cop mentality that had for so long prejudiced CIA officers against the Bureau. Here was a man who had come thousands of miles, betrayed his own country to help the United States—and Uncle Sam couldn't even get him laid?

But even if FBI puritanism contributed to Yurchenko's apparent unhappiness, it was CIA that would receive most of the blame for the unprecedented scenario that then began to unfold. Back in Washington, on November 2, Yurchenko was allowed to go to dinner at a Georgetown bistro, accompanied by only one Agency security guard. The Russian calmly ordered bisque, lobster, and a carafe of white wine, then suddenly dashed out of the restaurant and disappeared among the dark streets. A fifty-man search team of FBI and CIA officials descended on the neighborhood, keeping in touch by walkie-talkies and car radios. By 5 a.m., when they regrouped at the Bureau's Washington Field Office, it was clear that Yurchenko had slipped the net.

Not until two days later did the agencies learn where he had gone. A press conference was called at the Soviet Embassy complex at Mount Alto, in Northwest Washington. "I was forcibly abducted [by CIA] in Rome," Yurchenko announced. He claimed not to have betrayed any real secrets, but to have instead used the debriefing sessions to learn about U.S. defector-interrogation methods. Then he boarded an Aeroflot plane at Dulles Airport, gave a thumbs-up to news cameramen, and was gone.

What had happened? Was Yurchenko a bona-fide defector who had simply got homesick and cut a deal with his former employers? Had the KGB offered him leniency in exchange for assistance in embarrassing the United States? Or was Yurchenko's original "defection" to CIA some elaborate ruse? Had he been dispatched to sacrifice the used-up Howard and protect a higher-level mole? If so, why would the KGB have put the game at risk by having him re-defect?

Officially and publicly, both CIA and FBI claimed Yurchenko had been bona fide, but each blamed the other for causing his redefection. FBI agents told journalists that Yurchenko had gone back because the Agency was mean to him. The Agency countered that it had offered Yurchenko $1 million for his information and then taken him on a two-week vacation, which was hardly treating him as a prisoner. Yurchenko had more likely been upset because he had requested that his defection not be publicized, yet FBI agents repeatedly showed him news clips about it. "That is when he began thinking maybe he'd made a big mistake," one anonymous CIA official told *The New York Times*.

Privately, an even more serious dispute was raging. In a virtual replay of the Nosenko case, the two agencies disagreed as to whether Yurchenko had been a bona-fide defector. Though the Bureau had absorbed some of Angleton's skepticism after Hoover's death, it was now nudging back toward the old face-value approach. The shift had begun with the retirement of Cregar, gained momentum with the 1983 departure of Nolan, and was sealed by the retirement of O'Malley, on the very day Yurchenko arrived. O'Malley's successor as FBI intelligence chief, James Geer, was a dedicated golfer who had previously run the Bureau's forensic crime lab. His sardonic attitude toward CI was evident in a plaque on his office wall, engraved with a passage from Eric Ambler's spy thriller *Light of Day*: "I think if I were asked to single out one specific group of men, one category as being the most suspicious, unbelieving, unreasonable, petty, inhuman, sadistic, double-crossing set of bastards in any language, I would say without hesitation the people who run counterespionage departments." Geer preferred simple, obvious explanations to unprovable and complex ones, arrests over double-agent games, action over theory. Whereas Nolan had declared the FBI's old KGB informant Fedora bogus, Geer's team reversed the Bureau to its original position—an assessment seemingly confirmed by Yurchenko's claim that there had "never been anything but genuine defectors." To Geer, as to Yurchenko's FBI handler, Rochford, there was no question that Yurchenko was legitimate. It was unthinkable that the KGB would have given over good live leads like Pelton and Howard for any reason, and least of all to establish the bona fides of an agent who would later redefect.

"Bullshit!" the FBI men soon heard their Agency counterparts saying. Ames stood by Yurchenko, but most of his colleagues thought Yurchenko had been a false defector. This determination was reached despite Angleton's legacy, rather than because of it. Hathaway thought that Angleton's obsession with moles and false defectors paralyzed the Agency; Thompson had served briefly on Angleton's CI Staff and was bored. But neither could believe in Yurchenko. The man himself now said he had been a loyal KGB man all along. Why not believe him? Both of the agents he had exposed, Howard and Pelton, had lost access to U.S. secrets, and therefore would have been perfect "chicken feed." They were live cases from the FBI's prosecutorial point of view, but dead to the KGB—just as Nosenko's leads had been.

There were other parallels with Nosenko. Both defectors claimed that priceless CIA assets in Moscow had been compromised by spy dust, not by Soviet moles. Both made claims about KGB recruitments of U.S. journalists in Moscow which were admitted by the FBI to be without substance (Nosenko had implicated ABC's Sam Jaffe, Yurchenko the Washington *Post*'s Dusko Doder). Both claimed not to know things they should know, if they really were who they said they were. (Yurchenko, though supposedly running all KGB agents in North America, knew of no illegals, and could report on no approaches made to the Soviets by "dangled" U.S. agents.) Indeed, Yurchenko seemed to follow the Nosenko script so closely that CI staffers had found themselves referring to records on that earlier case for clues as to what the Soviets might be up to with Yurchenko. Particularly suggestive was a February 1964 memo by then Soviet Division chief David Murphy, suggesting that Nosenko's defection was part of "a massive propaganda assault on CIA in which Subject, *most probably as a 're-defected CIA agent,'* will play a major but not necessarily the sole role." [Emphasis added.] But whereas Murphy had once argued for Nosenko's incarceration, in part to prevent that prediction from being fulfilled, CIA had decided on the opposite approach, perhaps to see whether Yurchenko would follow the script that Murphy had outlined.

Thus had they sent Yurchenko to a restaurant a few blocks from the Soviet Embassy on November 2, with a single unarmed guard, and waited to see what he would do. Yurchenko had then done what Murphy predicted in 1964, right down to the "propaganda assault." If it was difficult for the FBI to comprehend why the Soviets would deliberately impugn Yurchenko's bona fides by engineering his return to the USSR, it was equally difficult for CIA to fathom why, if Yurchenko was a truly disloyal KGB officer, he had not been executed or imprisoned, but was attending parties and had reportedly been promoted. One possibility was that the KGB had not originally *planned* to reel in Yurchenko, but had done so after learning, perhaps from a CIA mole, that Yurchenko was under suspicion of being bogus. That way, the KGB would at least keep him from cracking under CIA interrogation, and could confuse and demoralize American intelligence in the bargain. In any case, with so many questions about Yurchenko, CIA certainly questioned his basic "message," which seemed to be: No false defectors, no moles—relax, there's nothing to worry about.

That the United States nevertheless had much to worry about became clear in the weeks after Yurchenko's redefection. At least four more CIA agents were burned, and a third FBI source in the Washington embassy was hustled back to Moscow and executed. These sources had all been recruited after Howard left CIA, and Hathaway began to doubt whether Howard had been in a position to blow any of the cases that had been going bad. But if Howard hadn't burned those operations, how had they been compromised? Was there another traitor still roaming the halls at Langley? The possibility that Howard and Yurchenko had been tipped to the suspicions against them certainly suggested as much.

On the hunch that Yurchenko had been sent to deflect suspicion from a still-active mole in CIA, Hathaway found himself doing just what Angleton had done in 1967. He recommended to Clair George, Casey's chief of operations, that a number of officers in the Soviet Europe Division be quietly transferred to less sensitive posts. That not only cut off their access to some of CIA's most precious secrets, but also gave CIA's Office of Security a convenient excuse for "routinely" polygraphing them on their way to foreign assignments. All the SE officers passed their polygraphs, but Thomas Mills and Colin Thompson took the hint and retired. Ames stayed with the Agency, in Rome.

WHILE AMERICAN secret agents were being caught overseas, a number of foreign spies were also being uncovered in the U.S. Twenty-six American citizens were arrested for espionage by the end of 1985, the so-called "Year of the Spy." In some of these cases, FBI and CIA worked together well. For example, when a polygraph test showed signs of deception, Sharon Scranage, a CIA operations-support assistant in Ghana, confessed to turning over classified information to her Ghanaian lover. Scranage's treason had already led to the arrest of eight CIA agents in Ghana, and some of her information was also apparently passed by Ghanaian intelligence to the KGB. Scranage cooperated in a joint operation by the FBI and CIA's Office of Security to trap her lover, who was arrested in Virginia. He was then exchanged for CIA's imprisoned sources and their families, who settled in the U.S. Scranage was sentenced to two years in jail.

Too often, however, the agencies muffed. In one case, after a mole in Chinese intelligence tipped the Agency that a spy in CIA had traveled to China for a banquet, FBI agents pored over airline-passenger lists and came across a customs declaration signed by a retired CIA analyst, Larry Wu-Tai Chin. Chin confessed to being a Chinese-communist mole for more than thirty years. He had retired from CIA in 1981, and was under investigation by the FBI after February 1983, but in 1984 CIA had asked him to come back to work full-time as a consultant. Reportedly this was because they were oblivious to the Bureau's suspicions, although it seems possible that CIA had been told about Chin and was using him for deception or bait.

In another well-publicized episode, Berkeley graduate student Clifford Stoll tried to warn U.S. intelligence that someone was trying to "hack into" sensitive databanks at Lawrence Livermore Laboratory, but CIA and FBI each disclaimed responsibility in electronic espionage. East German agents continued downloading data for months until Stoll, frustrated by the bureaucratic run-around, baited a trap for the hackers and cracked the case himself.

Reviewing the litany of CI failures in September 1986, a Senate Intelligence Committee report isolated one overarching problem: "constant risk of fragmentation and conflict among organizations with different methods and priorities." In an apparent allusion to the Yurchenko affair, the Committee noted that "Disputes over the bona fides of defectors have plagued the U.S. intelligence community. . . . Such differences are unavoidable, but they should not disrupt interagency cooperation." Above all, there was a "need for earlier involvement of the FBI . . . in cases of suspected espionage." In a pointed reference to the Howard case, the Committee recommended that "The decision as to whether the circumstances justify investigation in varying degrees should be made by the FBI, in light of its counterintelligence experience, not by the employing agency. . . . When offices or agencies have held back from bringing in the FBI, events have often gotten out of control."

With such high-level attention to the unique problems of American CI, it seemed for a time that increased awareness might translate into actual reform. The Agency and the Bureau signed a "memorandum of understanding," intended to bolster cooperation on CIA espionage cases within the United States, and there was wide support for creation of a central CI "brain center." James Angleton had been building such a capacity for twenty years, with as much FBI input as Papich could arrange, until Bill Colby's people torched 95 percent of the product. But in 1987, at a CI colloquium, Leonard McCoy and George Kalaris declared themselves in favor of recentralization. "The department and geographic CI boundaries that the United States has established are not honored by the primary opposition services, which use them to defeat us," the retired officers observed. "Opposition services recruit in one area and run the case in another. Further, they move agents and operations officers about the map at will. This engenders among U.S. counterintelligence agencies a cumbersome, lumbering process that seldom catches up with opposition actions. . . . The United States must eliminate the opposition's advantage in this area by bringing its . . . primary CI bodies together at the sources of [American] vulnerability." Naturally, there was debate about whether CIA or FBI should have the main CI coordinating job. A former White House official added that it mattered less who was in charge than that someone be in charge.

A single boss seemed especially needed in the ongoing hunt for a Soviet mole in CIA. Counterintelligence officials on both sides had suspected treason since Yurchenko's redefection, but separate CIA and FBI probes were languishing, riven by competition and bickering. Despite suspicions on Hathaway's CI staff, Casey's top managers played down the possibility of a mole, and blocked independent FBI scrutiny of CIA's failed operations. When the Bureau raised objections, Casey's executives argued that they could take care of their own security problems, thank you.

In the end, little was done to end the infighting. There was no true recentralization of CI, no radical reorientation. When Reagan tried to get a handle on KGB espionage by ordering eighty Soviet officials to leave the country, as Webster recommended, CIA officials blamed "counterintelligence drum beaters" at the FBI for jeopardizing U.S. diplomatic slots in Moscow. When the Senior Interagency Group willfully disregarded most of the Senate's ninety-five recommendations for fixing CI, a distracted Reagan did nothing. Ken DeGraffenreid, still observing from the National Security Council, lamented "the bureaucratics involved, the turf considerations [that] simply prevented the movement to action," while "interest and attention . . . flagged in some quarters of the Executive branch."

Unsolved, meanwhile, were the "mole mysteries" that had seemed to swirl around the Howard and Yurchenko affairs, fueling FBI distrust of CIA. If Geer, Parker, and others at the Bureau did not believe that Yurchenko had been sent to deflect fears of Soviet penetration of the Agency, they nevertheless did not have difficulty believing that CIA might be riddled with moles. In the wake of the Howard and Yurchenko episodes, there was what Parker called "a healthy paranoia about CIA personnel security—a natural concern, especially where sensitive information and sources had to be shared."

What Parker and DeGraffenreid had learned was that Casey was not really a CI man. Despite Republican rhetoric about the Carter-Turner CIA being soft on Soviet spies, Casey himself wasn't much tougher. Here again, Casey had been influenced, and probably blinkered, by the OSS-Donovan legacy. Wild Bill had always thought the best defense was a good offense; the way to do counterintelligence was to get out there and hit the enemy. So did his protégé, who chose to emphasize positive collection and covert action. When ex-DCI William Colby, another OSS veteran, had personally counseled the incoming Casey to aggressively develop human penetrations in Moscow—even if it meant getting burned by bogus agents—Casey had bought the logic. Casey himself, it was said, tried to set the example by personally bugging the office of a friendly foreign-intelligence chief during an official visit. The new DCI had issued a call for heroes, and the operational mode of CIA was to be one of bold risk-taking, not orchid-growing patience and caution.

A MORE MEANINGFUL REFORM was effected by Casey in the sphere of counterterrorism (CT), an area Aldhizer considered "ripe for Agency-Bureau problems." In part, the increased threat of terrorism was a necessary risk of renewed commitment overseas. Reagan had promised not to let "a single inch of earth" go communist on his watch, and in March 1981 Casey wrote a fateful memo outlining a covert plan, later known as the Reagan Doctrine, to "roll back" communism by aiding "resistance" forces around the world. Yet the implementation of that vision would require being in places like Lebanon, El Salvador, and Grenada, and retaliating against Soviet proxies like Libya. If terrorism had been a problem for Carter, who was disengaging from overseas commitments, what would it mean for Reagan, who now went where Carter had feared to tread?

The answer came on April 18, 1983, when an explosion shook all of West Beirut, spewing glass and metal, melting traffic lights, and turning the U.S. Embassy to smoking ruins. Sixty-seven people were left dead, including a half-dozen CIA officers. At the moment of the explosion, Casey's Middle East expert, Robert C. Ames, had been chairing a first-floor conference on terrorism. There was suspicion that news of Ames' visit had leaked, and that the attack had been timed to kill him.

Casey wanted to draw on the Bureau's forensic expertise, and had immediately requested that special agents get involved. Aldhizer arranged that. But after only a few days, the FBI team came back in a state of extreme agitation, claiming that a team of CIA officers, who flew from Langley to Beirut to pursue their own bombing inquiries, had not fully cooperated. Just as the Agency wanted to investigate its own men when they got into security trouble, so it now wanted to bury its heroes and find their killers. That brief was given the CIA crew by the new Beirut station chief. William Buckley was usually a quiet, reserved person, passionate only about collecting toy soldiers, but he was distraught over the loss of his colleagues, and took it out on the meddling G-men—or so they had been made to feel. Apparently there had been some yelling and even some shoving in the hotel rooms that had to serve as embassy offices. "Man alive, it was a *bad scene*," Aldhizer recalled. He tried to explain to the FBI agents: "If you turn that thing around, and a bomb went off in the New York Field Office and killed a bunch of your friends, and you were working your tails off to find out who did it, and all of a sudden CIA butts into the investigation—how would you feel?"

But the Bureau's Criminal Division still bore a grudge about its treatment overseas, and fallout from the Beirut episode contaminated the routine exchange of information in other fields. In one case, an Agency source provided a tip, relayed to the Bureau, that caused Webster to send agents from several field divisions out into the Florida Everglades at night, but all for nothing; the lead was false. Bureau tempers were already short, because of the Beirut snub, and a letter came down from Floyd Clark, assistant director of the Bureau's Criminal Division, which Aldhizer was ordered to carry to Langley. It contained language like, "You had our agents out in the middle of the night, chopping through swamps, all because you didn't handle this source correctly." Clair George, Casey's chief of operations, replied with what bureaucrats called "a screamer." Its essence was, Don't you tell us about your guys' having to work overnight in the swamps when we just had *x* number of guys killed in a bombing in Beirut. Don't tell me about sacrifice! Aldhizer was concerned by the Clark-George exchange, because a lot of people underneath saw it, and ill will radiated down. He tried to arrange a meeting between George and Clark, two guys that needed to get along, but never was able to pull it off.

Aldhizer was able to convene a conference at Langley on the Beirut-embassy situation, however. The session devolved into a shouting, name-calling match between Buckley and several representatives of the Bureau's Criminal Division. But the exchange was apparently cathartic. After presenting Buckley with an FBI-logo cap as a peace gift, the Bureau team went back to Beirut and did what Buckley considered a "bang-up" investigation, tracing a piece of axle from the truck used in the bombing to a factory in Iran, and eventually pinning the act on the Popular Front for the Liberation of Palestine, an Iranian-backed group.

But by the time the FBI reached that conclusion, Buckley himself had been kidnapped by Iranian-sponsored terrorists, in April 1984. An FBI team specializing in kidnapping cases was brought in to help hunt for him. Things went more smoothly this time, but "that kind of teamwork aspect was extremely sensitive," as Aldhizer would say. "It all boils down, a lot of times, to nothing more than *turf*."

To pool U.S. efforts in such cases, Reagan approved creation of a Restricted Interagency Group for Terrorism (RIG-T). The DCI held the chair, but the working group was run by one representative each from CIA, FBI, and the NSC. Casey selected all three reps for their gung-ho, risk-taking styles. Duane C. "Dewey" Clarridge, from CIA, was one of Casey's favorite "shooters," a suave hawk who had until recently been running Casey's contra war in Nicaragua. Oliver "Buck" Revell, the FBI's assistant director for criminal investigations, was dissatisfied with the Bureau's tendency to conduct CT "on a case-by-case basis rather than correlating the information to have a more thorough knowledge of the overall threat," and welcomed a more activist CIA counterterrorism. But above all Casey was impressed by the NSC's man on the RIG, an imaginative, gutsy Marine lieutenant-colonel, Oliver North. Casey hoped that "Ollie," as he affectionately termed him, just might be able to pool FBI and CIA resources to get Buckley back.

North's first plan was to ransom Buckley before he could be tortured into revealing CIA secrets. He made contact with some DEA informants, heroin traffickers in the Middle East, who claimed to be in touch with Buckley's captors. But the Agency would not put up any money unless it got proof that North's sources were telling the truth. The Bureau meanwhile worried that use of its funds to pay drug dealers might violate U.S. law. North therefore went around both agencies, appealing to Texas superpatriot and billionaire gadfly Ross Perot, who in 1980 had financed a successful private rescue attempt of U.S. citizens from Iran. With $100,000 down and the promise of $2 million to follow, North proposed to bankroll a joint CIA-FBI operation, which would ideally culminate on a yacht off Cyprus, where Buckley would be swapped for cash. Clarridge was in favor of using the Perot money, but Revell initially expressed his disapproval; the plan seemed like a violation of American policy, which was not to deal with hostage takers. Revell discussed the idea with Webster, who similarly disliked it. Because the operation was going to take place outside the U.S, and under the auspices of a private donor, the FBI, after expressing disapproval, did not try to stop it. But before the project could get under way, good coordination between CIA and FBI proved that North was being snookered. After North's informant visited Beirut and returned with a newspaper on which Buckley's initials were allegedly scrawled, CIA submitted the handwriting to FBI lab for analysis. Their conclusion: the handwriting was not the station chief's.

North's next plan was to kidnap Imad Mugniyeh, a Lebanese Shiite cleric who headed the Islamic Jihad, the organization that was holding

Buckley, then trade hostage for hostage. Mugniyeh was to visit France in the fall of 1985, and though the French weren't likely to cooperate in such a controversial operation, North wanted to strike without French consent. Clarridge took the idea to Casey, who liked it. But the idea was fiercely resisted by Webster, who believed the risk of exposure was too great. He also predicted that, if the United States undertook the kidnapping, the French would never again cooperate with the United States on other fronts. Reluctantly Casey agreed, and North shelved the idea.

Discord similarly plagued CT policy during a rash of hijackings in late 1985. On one occasion, FBI experts at Quantico wanted to come up with a capability for putting special silencers on pistols. The problem they presented was: How can we shoot a hijacker on one end of a plane, without letting a hijacker on the other end know that we've done his buddy in? Could the Bureau's liaison officer find out if the Agency had such silencers, and if they'd let the Bureau have some? Aldhizer put Quantico in touch with some of his Agency contacts, and an arrangement was made to fly the silencers in from somewhere in the United States. But it turned out that CIA had "coordinated" with the wrong set of people; the silencers belonged to someone else in the Agency. "You can't have them," Aldhizer was told. He went back to Quantico with the bad news.

OUT OF SUCH FRUSTRATIONS was born a new strategy. On January 16, 1986, Reagan authorized Casey to create a new interagency Counterterrorism Center (CTC). Headed by Dewey Clarridge, with a support staff of two hundred CIA officers and ten people on loan from other agencies, the Center was soon a mechanism for unprecedented cross-pollination. CIA even assisted the Bureau in a study to collect and analyze "positive" domestic intelligence, in counterterrorism and other fields. There was some concern about this in the Agency's National Collection Division, which performed that same function by debriefing U.S. citizens. At best, the Bureau would be a competitor, and at worst, it could take NCD's job away. But Aldhizer regarded the move as a real liaison breakthrough.

Operational liaison was a more delicate matter, though, for it raised legal issues that Webster found troubling. Casey had consulted him before creating CTC, and Webster had appreciated that, but he worried that CTC's "pro-active" stance might involve the U.S. in assassinating terrorists, which was banned by executive order. And CTC had not been in existence for more than a month when Webster opposed a CIA plan that would have had the FBI help abduct the suspected hijackers of TWA Flight 847 and fly them to trial in America. Webster had reservations not only because of the possibility of failure and embarrassment, but because such operations could violate international and even U.S. law.

On the latter point, Webster was probably right. Reagan's January finding allowed CIA to seize terrorists overseas, but the FBI lacked jurisdiction until April, when Congress authorized the Bureau to arrest suspects overseas. Even so, Webster had to submit to a lecture from Representative Don Edwards (D-California), himself a former G-man, about the dangers of jurisdiction expansionism—proving how right Webster's initial instincts had been. "That is something that we are not very enthusiastic about in this country, to have the FBI operating overseas and the CIA operating within the confines of the United States," Edwards said. "It is a slippery slope that one must watch very carefully."

But letting CIA and FBI cross geographical lines did allow otherwise impossible working partnerships. One was a scheme to nail Mohammed Hussein Rashid, a genius bomb-maker who beat airport X-ray machines by wiring explosives into Sony Walkmen. Since 1982, the Agency had been monitoring Rashid's actions through a penetration agent code-named "MJ/HOLIDAY," a Palestinian businessman who served as one of Rashid's bomb couriers in Europe. Still, there was dissension when CTC decided to try to kidnap Rashid and bring him to America for trial. Initially CIA had opposed the operation, because Rashid was sponsored by Iraq, and Casey was trying to woo Saddam Hussein away from the Soviet camp. Baghdad was therefore off-limits to CTC. "We were told in no uncertain terms," said a senior FBI official, "that the indictments were not to interfere with our larger policy toward Iraq." When CIA finally did consent to move against Rashid, it wanted to gather intelligence in a way that would not jeopardize its sources. "The FBI wasn't used to investigating abroad, and the CIA didn't want to share any secrets, particularly with lawyers," a Justice Department official recalled.

Webster later acknowledged a problem in "the interface between law enforcement needs and intelligence responsibilities," but he also knew it had to be overcome. "There is never an excuse to say: Well, we're in the intelligence business, and you're in the law enforcement business. Because when dealing with intelligence with terrorism, both sides of the equation are very, very important. . . . So, they [CIA] have to look for switching mechanisms where they can get information to the law enforcement community."

Webster hoped CTC would be such a "switching mechanism," but it had been intended for operational, not prosecutorial coordination. Frustrated FBI officials soon took their complaints to the press. Officials from other agencies had been stymied in trying to get information from CTC and, in some cases, had been "unable to get the CIA to accept their intelligence." A task force headed by Vice-President Bush proposed complementing CTC with an "intelligence-fusion center," to collect, analyze, and distribute intelligence data throughout the government, but no such center emerged.

Nor did CTC seem to be enjoying the operational success Casey had hoped for. FBI and CIA thought they had cornered Rashid in the Sudan, but he escaped through some kind of bungle that no one at either agency will talk about. When terrorists bombed a TWA jet, and then a Berlin discotheque, killing U.S. servicemen; CTC was of little use. A special CTC team was created to recover Buckley, but failed. It later developed that he had died after fourteen months in captivity, apparently having been tortured into revealing all he knew about CIA operations in the Middle East.

ALTHOUGH CTC WAS SLOW to prove its worth, the granting of FBI counterterrorist jurisdiction overseas was a landmark shift, with *operational* consequences that soon were felt. In 1986, the FBI expended approximately eighteen street-agent work-years in cases involving "extraterritorial jurisdiction," creating considerable problems for Jay Aldhizer. "The thing that would go off-track more than anything else," he said, "was operating in the other guy's yard, which had to be coordinated on both sides. The Bureau's attitude toward CIA was, 'We just want to make sure that you know that we're not going to impact on anything you do.' But sometimes we did impact on what they did."

Indeed, the FBI's foreign work could even derail what Casey was doing behind the Bureau's back, in places like Nicaragua. As Webster later realized, the North-Clarridge-Casey nexus produced "circumstances [that] helped create the Iran-contra affair." It started, Webster would recall, "when people at the White House became impatient with the efforts of the intelligence services and others to locate the hostages, and then began to try to form sort of think-tank groups to see if they could come up with new and more imaginative ways of dealing with it. And as they started to do this, these think tanks became operational, and North was an operative person on it." But also born of White House impatience was the FBI's foreign-CT role, which would put the Bureau on to CIA's illegal partnership with North. That partnership was a pure expression of Casey's freebooting, OSS style, and FBI exposure of the project's assets was the final confirmation of an old OSS prejudice—that the interests of law enforcement posed a direct threat to the extralegal imperatives of covert action. Casey lived to see his anti-FBI fears confirmed, but died before it became clear that Hoover's revenge on the ghost of Donovan would cause the worst political scandal since Watergate.

To most CIA officers, Oliver North seemed a reckless, irresponsible, incorrigibly romantic man. Hearing, for instance, that Cubans were deathly afraid of snakes, North proposed strafing Havana with planeloads of vipers. But to Casey, whose idol Donovan had once considered dropping bats over Tokyo, North was an ideal choice for carrying on the contra war. A decorated Vietnam veteran, North wanted to redress perceptions that America was an unreliable ally. For those who had been gullible enough to take America at its word, there had been only disaster, whether at the Bay of Pigs, in Vietnam, or, most recently, in Central America. At a news conference on July 25, 1979, six days after the Sandinistas triumphed, Carter had said, "I do not attribute at all the change in Nicaragua to Cuba," but the first contingent of Cuban "advisers" had been arriving in Managua that very day. Carter was quick to realize his error, and in 1980 authorized Stansfield Turner to funnel $1 million to anti-Sandinista politicians in Nicaragua. Two years later, Casey had turned Carter's contras into a paramilitary force, modeled after OSS-backed anti-Nazi partisans whose work, according to Casey, pointed up "the potential for dissident action against the control centers and lines of communication of a totalitarian power."

But the contras only seemed to drive the Sandinistas further left, much as CIA's abortive invasion of Cuba had caused Castro to ask for direct Soviet assistance. On April 18, 1983, the day that the U.S. Embassy was bombed in Beirut, Sandinista Defense Minister Humberto Ortega even raised the specter of a "Nicaraguan Missile Crisis," saying that his country would consider stationing Soviet nuclear weapons. Top Secret CIA memoranda warned: "The Soviets and Cubans are turning Nicaragua into an armed camp, with military forces far beyond its defensive needs and in a position to intimidate and coerce its neighbors."

By late 1983, the Agency's secret warriors had begun to harass the perimeter of this "armed camp" with daring OSS-style raids. Scuba-diving saboteurs in motorized rubber rafts moved in on Nicaragua's oil reserves at the port of Corinto, under cover of night, and blew them up. But Casey had approved this operation without consulting Congress, and his punishment was an April 1984 measure, sponsored by Representative Edward Boland, which would suspend CIA assistance to the contras in

October of that year. In lieu of direct CIA assistance after that date, North was asked to keep his mentor's contras together, as North would say, "body and soul."

The result was a Panama-registered, privatized anticommunist network. In many ways it resembled the Wisner-Donovan apparat that had been born in 1948, when Casey, Hunt, and other ex–OSS officers had set up Operation Bloodstone. Slush funds were disbursed through "shell" corporations such as Udall Research in Panama City, established by retired General Richard Secord, whose "private" planes would make supply drops. A loop of conspirators was formed, with each insulated from the others by a common go-between, former State Department official Robert Owen. A typical Owen mission involved giving to the contras $10,000 in "humanitarian assistance," via former Agency asset John Hull, a rugged, rich old rancher whose border properties were a contra sanctuary. Owen also met with CIA Costa Rican Station Chief Fernandez to discuss the logistics of aerial resupply. The Creoles and the Miskito Indians along the Caribbean were rising up against the Sandinistas; they could be reached by filling fifty-five-gallon drums with weapons, sealing them watertight, then affixing Chemlites—plastic tubes containing chemicals that, when crushed, interacted to create glowing cylinders. After these drums were kicked out of a plane and hit water, they would glow iridescent green as they floated along the coast, and the waiting Indians would row out in canoes and retrieve them.

Reaching the landlocked contras deeper inside Nicaragua would be somewhat more challenging, but it could be done. Fernandez helped Owen scout for an emergency airstrip in friendly territory, in case mechanical problems or anti-aircraft fire forced down a plane. They decided on a remote site in northwestern Costa Rica. Owen and the CIA man helicoptered up there in August 1985, and Owen returned to Washington with photos and maps.

But Owen home also carried a warning. John Hull and other Enterprise assets were in serious danger of being exposed by Sandinista agents, including some moles who had worked within the contra movement. The "cancer" seemed to have begun with Eden Pastora, a former Sandinista guerrilla hero who had earned the nom-de-guerre "Commander Zero" during a raid on Nicaragua's National Palace. Pastora had served as the Sandinistas' number-two man for internal security, just as Rolando Cubela had for Castro; like his Cuban counterpart, he soon established contact with CIA and claimed disillusionment. Pastora was every bit as mercurial and unpredictable as Cubela had been, but Casey thought he could give the counterrevolution a romantic and democratic face. By 1982, Commander Zero was operating a small contra force out of Costa Rica, along

Nicaragua's southern border. Doubts persisted, however, about his ultimate loyalties. He and his intelligence chief, Julio Bigote, had spent a "lost" year in Cuba before working for CIA. His ranks were "rife with double agents," as one of his colleagues later said. His camp mistress, Marieles Serrano, redefected to Managua in late April 1984 and admitted to being a Sandinista spy. His closest adviser, Carlos Coronel, was judged by CIA to be a Sandinista agent. Pastora himself was believed conceivably disloyal. In spring 1985, a CIA counterintelligence task force descended on the contras' southern front with polygraphs, purging all who failed, such as Arturo Cruz, Jr., and all who refused them, including Pastora.

But this created a "disposal problem." Pastora and his former lieutenants were perfectly positioned to blow details of North's network in Costa Rica. They knew all about Owen and Hull. They knew some of the network's Miami-Cuban mercenaries, and had been privy to the secret logistics of the CIA weapons pipelines. They were in touch with two left-wing expatriate journalists, Martha Honey and her husband, Tony Avirgan—a couple of "commie disinformation experts," Owen warned North, who were "after me and you." These journalists were the kind of people, Owen believed, who might even be getting some of their leads from the Soviet listening post at Lourdes, Cuba, which monitored U.S. telephone traffic. Even if some of their allegations were ludicrous, such as a contra-backed plot against the U.S. ambassador to Costa Rica, they were nevertheless likely to attract the attention of the FBI. "The biggest concern," Owen therefore told North, "is how long the operation will remain covert."

Deniability was a problem at Langley, too. Although nominally run by North at the NSC, contra resupply remained as much a CIA initiative as the "privatized" Mafia plots to kill Castro had been, if not more so. Not only Casey and Fernandez, but CIA officers Clair George, Allen Fiers, Duane Clarridge, and Jay Gruner would all help North's network in various ways. Langley provided flight vectors to Fernandez, who relayed them to Secord's pilots. Clarridge gave North information on arms dealers, and Fiers handed him maps and other intelligence on the Sandinista positions. But since CIA assistance to North's network was palpably illegal, Casey needed to hide it not only from the Sandinistas and the media, but from Congress, the FBI, and even from most officers at Langley. Fiers, chief of the Agency's Central American Task Force, was thus directed by Casey to serve as a "buffer" within the Agency, to keep his colleagues "on the other side of the line." That was similar to what William Harvey and Richard Helms had done in CIA's attempts to kill Castro. But just like Harvey and Helms, Casey failed to consider that no buffer in the world could keep the Federal Bureau of Investigation on the other side of the line.

WEDGE

. . .

THE BUREAU BEGAN investigating the contras and their U.S. backers in earnest on July 22, 1985, when Kevin Currier, in the FBI's antiterrorist unit in Miami, noticed a front-page article in the Miami *Herald*. In what seemed a major scoop, free-lance journalist Martha Honey described a pipeline of contra arms shipments from Florida to Nicaraguan rebels based in Costa Rica. According to Honey, arms were being flown into the jungled Costa Rican border with Nicaragua, where most of the land was controlled by a "wealthy American rancher." This rancher, Honey intimated, had plotted an April 1984 bombing at the jungle camp of independent-minded contra leader Eden Pastora, who was splitting the movement by refusing to align with the other contras. It was unclear from Honey's report whether the operations were carried out with or without U.S. government assistance; either way, they were probably illegal. If there was no government support, the shipments violated the Neutrality Act, which forbade private citizens' participation in foreign conflicts. If there was government support, the shipments violated the Boland Amendment, which banned CIA and other U.S. agencies from giving military aid to the anti-Sandinistas.

Currier opened a Neutrality case and soon teamed with fellow agent George Kiszynski, who specialized in investigating bombings by right-wing Cuban terrorists. Interviews with informants developed no evidence of any bombing plot, but did produce a shortlist of names that kept coming up in connection with contra support: John Hull, Robert Owen, Oliver North.

Alleged CIA links to those men were brought to the Bureau's attention when Jack Terrell, a disillusioned former mercenary, contacted the FBI in early 1986 and fleshed out Honey's allegations. Terrell claimed that despite the Boland Amendment, the Agency was still coordinating the contra war, using North, Owen ("who says he is CIA"), and a "CIA contract man," John Hull. He additionally claimed to have heard of a right-wing plot to kill Lewis Tambs, U.S. ambassador to Costa Rica, and blame it on the Sandinistas. When pressed for proof, however, Terrell admitted that most, and perhaps all, of his information came from Martha Honey.

Terrell's credibility slipped even further when NSA wiretaps on the Nicaraguan Embassy in Washington revealed him to be in regular touch with Sandinista intelligence. His contact was Manuel Martín Cordero-Cuadra, who was posted under diplomatic cover in Washington. In fact, as Terrell later acknowledged, he was working with Cuadra to "attract the attention of Federal law enforcement agencies" to illegal contra resupply.

Terrell was taken under the wing of the Center for Development Policy, an IPS spinoff and Rubin-funded group, where, as Terrell would say, "employees had direct access to Cuban and Nicaraguan officials." Terrell was even "given a list of 40 names and a brief biography of each that told of their role with the Contras," including data on Oliver North, to be "released to the press or anyone else who might have an interest in it."

But even if their motives were open to question, at least some of the information fed to the Bureau by Terrell and Honey checked out, and had to be run down further. Although the alleged plot against the U.S. Ambassador to Costa Rica proved to be nonexistent, reports of gun-running to that country seemed to be grounded in fact. So in March 1986, the agents flew to San José, Costa Rica with Jeffrey Feldman, an assistant U.S. attorney, and met with Ambassador Lewis Tambs at the American Embassy. Feldman took out a diagram showing John Hull's name, and on top of it Robert Owen's, and above that Oliver North's. Feldman hypothesized that North was pumping funds through Owen to Hull, who, in turn, was distributing them to various contra leaders. He believed that these individuals had somehow transported weapons from South Florida to Hull's property near the Nicaraguan border.

The ambassador turned white. The only thing he said was, "Get Fernandez in here." The FBI agents guessed, correctly, that Fernandez was the CIA station chief. Feldman went over the diagram again, saying that he and the FBI agents were looking at "the big picture," meaning not only possible violations of the Neutrality Act, but unauthorized use of Government funds.

The CIA man's reaction, as Feldman recalled, was to "rip the credibility of the various people who were making the allegations." Martha Honey and her husband, Tony Avirgan, were a couple of real left-wingers. Feldman started taking notes: "Honey and Avirgan are Sandinista agents or have ties to Sandinistas." It was alleged that the couple had visited North Vietnam in 1970 and fled the U.S. in 1973, when Avirgan allegedly came under suspicion for some antiwar bombings. After living in several Soviet-bloc countries, the couple had settled in Costa Rica as stringers for international news agencies, specializing in critical coverage of the contra war. They spent Christmases in Nicaragua. By one report, Honey met almost weekly with Valentin P. Chekanov of the Soviet Embassy, whose KGB status was an open secret in San José. During the summer of 1985, Avirgan traveled with unusual frequency to Managua, and he stayed in the Sandinista power center for periods of twelve, six, and four days; he later said he was doing research. His wife, meanwhile, was interviewing former contra commander Eden Pastora and his top people, recently purged by CIA as suspected Sandinista agents. These were the kinds of people who were going after the rancher John Hull, who was not a criminal but a patriotic man.

Feldman asked if Hull worked for CIA.

Fernandez smiled. Hull had helped the Agency coordinate weapons deliveries to the contras prior to the Boland Amendment. Since then, however, he had not been "militarily involved." As a private citizen, Hull had been providing only medical and humanitarian assistance to guerrillas who retreated onto his land. As far as Fernandez knew, the money for that came from Hull's own deep pockets.

"Do you know if John Hull knows Oliver North?" Feldman pressed.

"Certainly," Fernandez said. "I can tell you for a fact that John Hull knows both Rob Owen and Oliver North." But Hull's role was only to coordinate "humanitarian" assistance, Fernandez repeated. Any reports to the contrary were "a hill of beans." Nevertheless, the meeting ended with Fernandez specifically requesting that the Bureau contact him if they planned to "take action against John Hull."

The FBI agents left the meeting feeling that the CIA station chief was bothered by their inquiries. When they saw Fernandez in the embassy after that, he wouldn't even say hello. Feldman decided not to speak in his hotel room, because he felt perhaps that he and the FBI agents were being watched or listened to by CIA. Embassy security officer James Nagel followed the agents wherever they went. After Currier and Kiszysnki interviewed some imprisoned mercenaries, who described weapons flights to Hull's ranch, Nagel warned them: "There are other agencies that have their operational requirements, and you should not interfere with the work of those agencies." The security officer paused, then added in a low voice: "John Hull is a friend of Ronald Reagan, if you know what I mean." The G-men concluded that because CIA was trying to protect Hull, it would not be possible to interview him, and they quit trying.

Returning to Miami on April 4, the FBI delegation tried to sift through what they had learned. "We all thought we were on to something," Currier recalled. Weapons were probably flown to Hull's ranch. Owen had often visited Hull, and also secretly worked for North. North was reportedly close with CIA Director Casey. But no one could figure out what kind of criminal provisions were specified by Boland, or whether the Bureau had developed enough evidence to empanel a grand jury. On such matters they would defer to FBI headquarters.

In Washington, the agent's reports were read with interest by the Bureau's number-three man, Buck Revell. He began to suspect that CIA, through North, might be secretly resupplying the contras. But each time the FBI had a pending Neutrality case, they went to CIA and were told there was "no connection."

JUST AFTER THE FBI AGENTS left their March 31 meeting with the CIA station chief in Costa Rica, Joe Fernandez placed an encrypted call to Oliver North. After hearing about the FBI mission in general terms, North dispatched his courier, Robert Owen, to San José for a full "damage control" assessment. In a memo summarizing his trip, Owen warned that Feldman and the FBI had North's name, and Owen's own, on its conspiracy chart. Given the risk of public exposure, North's network would have to suspend operations. As Owen saw it, suspected hostile agents (Honey, Avirgan, Pastora, Terrell) had caused one arm of the U.S. intelligence community to accuse the other, and had thus neutralized CIA's privatized resupply. Perhaps the pipeline could be opened up again, once things cooled down, but for the moment North and Owen could only devote their energies to denial. "If and when I am contacted by the FBI I will not answer any questions without an attorney present," Owen promised. "Even then, I will not answer any questions. It is the only way I can see to stem the tide."

In a desperate attempt to deflect suspicion from his operatives, North now tried to turn the Bureau against the sources of its leads. Shortly after the FBI agents returned from Costa Rica, North asked the Bureau's Washington Field Office to investigate Terrell, Honey, and Avirgan, to see if they might be involved in a communist "active measures" (political-warfare) campaign against U.S. policy in Central America. In mid-June, North was informed by the Bureau that, although there was evidence of such a campaign, the Bureau was "unable to resolve the identity of the originator of these active measures. Further, [the FBI] has no predication into this investigation."

Within a few weeks, however, the FBI did have grounds to investigate those who threatened North and Casey's work. On July 12, the Bureau received information, from NSA wiretaps on the Nicaraguan Embassy, that Jack Terrell might be contemplating an assassination of President Reagan.

THE FBI DISSEMINATED that news to CIA, and the two agencies began jointly looking into Terrell. The Bureau concluded that he was a "paid agent of Sandinista intelligence," especially after he was observed on July 17 accepting a bag of money from a Nicaraguan diplomat at a Washington

Metro station. A few days later, Terrell traveled to Miami at the same time Reagan did, lending apparent credence to the idea that he might indeed be a Lee Harvey Oswald type. He was closely watched in Miami by special agents Floyd H. Plummer and Gerald D. Perlata, Jr. When Terrell left his room at the Marriott Hotel on July 26 carrying a brown suitcase and small black overnight bag, FBI agents in the lobby advised Plummer by radio that Terrell was checking out and boarding a courtesy bus to the airport. Plummer then entered Terrell's room and searched the trash receptacles. In addition to the various gum wrappers, cigarette butts, and empty cigarette packs, Plummer found a copy of the Miami *Herald*; an article had been torn out, quoting White House statements that North's relationship with the contras did not violate the Boland Amendment. Terrell was then apprehended by the FBI and polygraphed extensively. Although he was eliminated as a threat to the president—Terrell later said he "concocted" the story to "keep [the FBI] interested" in him—the examiner concluded that he was deceptive about his relations with the Nicaraguan government.

But the FBI also concluded that CIA was being deceptive. In the process of investigating Terrell, the FBI began to sense that Duane Clarridge was seeking to protect former CIA employees who had been associated with Terrell in "private" efforts to assist the contras. At the FBI's request, Clarridge gave investigators a heavily deleted file on Terrell's former associates in a group called Civilian Military Assistance, saying that he had provided all available materials. But CIA employees tipped the Justice Department that "another file existed which was the real thing." Armed with the file number, FBI agents returned to Langley and asked to see the material. CIA refused, replying, "We'll see you in court." FBI officials felt Clarridge was withholding the files on Casey's orders.

Still, there was no firm proof of CIA wrongdoing, and a consensus had developed in Washington that FBI agents Currier and Kiszynski were being used by hostile intelligence. The Justice Department ordered that no action to be taken in the case. Throughout the summer of 1986, Leon Kellner, Feldman's boss at Justice, simply refused to reply to the FBI agents' many requests for a grand jury. Currier and Kiszynski felt that something "fishy" was going on, but there was nothing they could do.

BY SEPTEMBER word came down to Costa Rica from Langley that it would be okay to resume supply drops. Apparently it was felt that the Bureau's investigation had been contained by pressure on Justice in Washington. But because the FBI's curiosity had caused a three-month crimp in the pipeline, the Agency had to make up for lost time, and took previously unnecessary risks. Instead of flying at night, along the Pacific Coast, then cutting inland along the Costa Rican border and drifting over Nicaragua, Secord's mercenaries flew in daylight, directly over Nicaragua, with a full payload. They did that six times in a row, always following the same route, right over Sandinista radar and missile batteries. Their defense against state-of-the-art Soviet technology was a "fuzz buster" bought at Radio Shack. On their seventh flight, on October 5, one of Secord's C-123 planes was shot down by a SAM-7 missile. The only survivor, American cargo kicker Eugene Hasenfus, was captured. He said at a press conference that he had been hired by CIA. Documents aboard the plane showed that it was owned by Southern Air Transport, a former CIA "proprietary" or front.

The Hasenfus affair lent sudden credibility to the Bureau's contra case. Hours after the crash, Kellner told Feldman that he felt there was "really something there," and decided to go with it. FBI agents interviewed Southern Air employees, and as the investigation expanded, it threatened to expose the contra venture's covert twin: an initiative to free hostages by selling missile parts to Ayatollah Khomeini's Iran and, as CIA's Allen Fiers would put it, "kicking dollars into the contras' pot."

THREE DAYS AFTER Hasenfus was downed, Oliver North telephoned Buck Revell, warning that a probe of Southern Air Transport might disrupt "Presidentially authorized activity that you are privy to." They were on an open line, so North was talking cryptically, but Revell understood that he meant some kind of Iran initiative.

Revell already knew that North and CIA were up to something in Iran. At a July meeting, North had advised that the president had authorized contact with an Iranian government faction headed by the speaker of the parliament, Hashemi Rafsanjani. Then North had "put in the kicker," as Revell later said. In order to show good faith, the American emissaries had been authorized to arrange the shipment of a small number of anti-tank missiles and other spare parts. In return, the Iranian group had agreed to use their influence in attempting to obtain release of William Buckley and other hostages held by radical Shiites in Lebanon. Clarridge, who also attended the session, seemed unsurprised by the revelation, and Revell thought to himself: Sonofabitch, the Agency already knows. This whole Iran thing is probably Casey's baby. Revell had immediately briefed Webster, who was aghast that CIA—and the White House—would so flagrantly flout America's stated policy of not negotiating with terrorists. There were also rumors, denied by CIA, that the hostage operation was somehow linked to the contras. But because no laws seemed to have been broken, the Bureau had not pushed further into CIA's Iranian enterprise.

North's October 8 call to Revell now changed everything. Revell deduced that if subpoena of Southern Air records could compromise the hostage-negotiation process—if exposure of one operation could reveal the other—the two were probably linked. That meant that the hostage operations, like the Hasenfus flight, might violate the Boland Amendment.

On the chance that a hostage's life might indeed be in danger, the FBI agreed to temporarily suspend its Southern Air investigation, on grounds that it would "most likely trip over legal but very sensitive covert CIA operations not related to Nicaragua." But the Agency lost all credibility after November 21, when Casey testified to Congress that he did not know who arranged the sale of two thousand TOW missiles to Iran. Revell knew from his terrorism work that the Agency had, in fact, been actively involved in that scheme. There was a concern, as Revell warned Webster, about whether CIA was giving Congress "right information." If it deliberately wasn't, it was obstructing justice.

CASEY WAS HOSPITALIZED for a brain tumor in early December, lapsed into semiconsciousness, and died on May 9, 1987, before the Bureau could interrogate him. But by then, Iran-contra revelations had made clear not only to the FBI but to the country at large just how thoroughly the former OSS swashbuckler had considered intelligence work to be above the law. At his funeral, with President Reagan and former President Nixon sitting in a front pew, a Roman Catholic bishop lamented that Casey's anticommunism kept him from understanding "the ethical questions raised" by his church.

The hammer came down hard on Casey's co-conspirators at CIA. After Justice Department investigators uncovered a memo describing diversion of Iranian arms-sales profits to the contras, North was fired, and Attorney General Meese turned the FBI loose. On Casey's advice, North had burned a diary detailing his contacts with CIA; North's secretary, Fawn Hall, had slipped past FBI agents with documents hidden in her undergarments, and shredded so many other memos that the machine jammed; but a team of six FBI agents wearing rubber gloves retrieved other material implicating CIA. A disk found in Hall's office computer held a presidential intelligence "finding" signed by Reagan, retroactively authorizing CIA participation in an earlier Israeli weapons transfer to Iran. Another North memo asked CIA to charge the Iranians an inflated price for a thousand TOW missiles, with the difference being diverted to the contras. A February 1985 document stated flatly, "CIA will provide the advice and information needed by the F.D.N. [a contra group] on the shipping, traffic, and all necessary intelligence on the movement of these aircraft."

Armed with what seemed clear proof of illegal CIA assistance to the contras, FBI agents eventually converged on Langley with search warrants. It was a historically unprecedented moment, with agents opening even the office safe of CIA's deputy director for operations, Clair George. Inside was a document later determined to have prints from both of George's ring fingers, apparently proving that he had misled Congress about CIA support for the contras. George was eventually indicted on ten counts of obstructing congressional and FBI investigations. Station Chief Fernandez was recalled from Costa Rica and placed on administrative leave because the Bureau was closing in. Two other station chiefs were disciplined for helping North. Duane Clarridge, Fiers' predecessor as chief of CIA's Central American Task Force, was indicted on seven counts of perjury and making false statements to FBI agents during the Iran-contra investigation. Even Deputy Director Robert Gates, nominated by Reagan to replace Casey in February 1987, had to withdraw his name because Congress kept grilling him on his knowledge of North's network.

After losing on Gates, and still trying to live down Casey's misdeeds, President Reagan knew that his next nominee must be a man of unquestioned integrity. The list of possible candidates was fairly short, but one of them offered an intriguing prospect. He might be just the man to bring the Agency "under control," and even to end the long-running Bureau-Agency feud. Thus was the Agency's directorship about to pass from Wild Bill Donovan's last buccaneer to one of Hoover's successors at the FBI.

CHAPTER EIGHTEEN

HERE COMES
THE JUDGE

ON TUESDAY MORNING, March 3, 1987, William Webster was working in his corner office at FBI headquarters, high above the traffic of Pennsylvania Avenue, when he received an urgent telephone call from the White House. Ronald Reagan's voice had its usual warmth—the folksy, breathy, slightly scratchy timbre that put one automatically at ease—but today there was a barely detectable trace of weakness. "Bill," the president said after an exchange of pleasantries, "I'd like for you to take over CIA."

The timing of the offer was no accident, Webster knew. In about forty hours, the president was scheduled to deliver his first detailed response to the damaging findings of the Tower Commission, a board he had appointed to investigate the Iran-contra scandal. White House aides had previously hinted that Reagan would announce the new nominee for CIA director before his speech, sending a clear signal that the Agency would be reformed. But the president was having a tough time finding any takers for the post. After Gates' nomination was junked, Republican heavy-weights John Tower, head of the president's Iran-contra board, and James Baker, his chief of staff, had both declined to clean out Casey's stables. As a Washington insider, Webster well knew that he was, at best, the fourth choice for a messy job.

He thanked the president and promised to consider the offer. Leaving the White House on tenterhooks through much of the afternoon, Webster convened his FBI aides, consulted his old friend and former DCI Stan Turner, and talked to his three children. (His wife, Drusilla, had died in 1984.) At sixty-three, he was tiring of the bureaucratic life, and had rather been hoping that he might return to the less demanding, more cerebral work of a federal judge, perhaps even on the Supreme Court. He was also uncertain about just how he would adapt to the culture of secrecy at CIA. "The FBI's one thing," his daughter, Drusilla, told him. "But, Daddy, that other place is scary."

Yet something deep within Webster was stirred by the prospect of running CIA. Part of it was perhaps an Everyman's fascination with for-bidden knowledge, a will to know what no one else knew, a desire to be *inside*. Another part of it was the chance to remake, in his own image, one of the most important institutions in the world. He had done as much in his nine years at the FBI, repolishing its public image and restoring morale after the congressional inquisitions of the 1970s. Surveillance of domestic radicals had been reduced to a level that seemed to satisfy even the American Civil Liberties Union; younger agents had been appointed to key posts; and Webster had kindled loyalty the same way he kept good press: by a painstaking attention to symbolic detail. It was a skill which J. Edgar Hoover had also possessed, and it had been manifest in Webster's first act as FBI director, which was to remove Hoover's bust from his office. Careful image-management had given Webster good relations with Con-gress, and he believed he could count on the House and Senate intelligence subcommittees if he headed CIA. Above all, Webster sincerely wanted to help the president, whom he much admired and liked; he saw CIA reform as part of the larger political picture, an important step in salvaging Republican credibility. After word of his pending nomination leaked out that afternoon—perhaps to force his hand—Webster made up his mind.

It was simply not in him to deliver Ronald Reagan, and by extension the country, a crushing personal blow. Shortly after 6 p.m., he called back the president and accepted the job.

"MAN WHO CLEANED UP FBI WILL TRY FOR ENCORE AT CIA"—or so said newspaper headlines. As Reagan had hoped, Webster's reputation for personal integrity began to restore public confidence in CIA literally overnight. Where Casey's past had included shady stock deals and plagiarism suits settled out of court, colleagues portrayed Webster as "totally honest," "the straightest arrow in Washington," a staid widower with only two vices, tennis and chocolate. As a man who had been studying, upholding, or enforcing the law nearly all his adult life, Judge Webster could be trusted to obey it. Known within the FBI as a strict administrator, as intolerant of mistakes as his religion (Christian Science) and the law he was supposed to uphold, he would surely clamp down on the "cowboys" in CIA's Operations Directorate. "He doesn't cut your head off if you make a mistake," said Jim Adams, who served as Webster's chief deputy at the FBI in 1978, "but if you do anything to weaken the credibility of the institution, he's very tough." Here again, he was more like Hoover than most people realized: that discipline, or the fear of it, translated into respect and enhanced esprit de corps—the "football-coach" or "drill-sergeant" syndrome. Even those who felt his sting benefited from the aura of integrity he had maintained. If his FBI record was not unblemished, his image remained so. On his watch there had been protests over the entrapment of government officials in "Abscam"; lawsuits by disgruntled black and Latino agents who had not advanced; the accidental shooting death of a female agent by her colleagues; the conviction of FBI counterintelligence agent Richard Miller, who swapped secrets for sex with a Soviet mistress; and, not least of all, Howard's escape to Moscow. But as Senate Intelligence Committee Chairman David Boren would say, "No one, not his harshest critics, would question [Webster's] personal integrity or devotion to the rule of law." For Reagan, who after six years was no longer the Teflon president, Webster promised to be at least a Teflon DCI.

He also promised to end the FBI-CIA war, or at least to try. As Webster himself put it, he would be in a "unique position, having occupied director's chairs on both sides, and knowing the arguments on both sides. And there *are* two sides to these arguments." It was only logical, then, that he should judge interagency problems more "objectively" than his predecessors, as one of Webster's aides suggested. *The New York Times* even predicted "a definitive end to a long period of feuding."

Historians of intelligence were circumspect, however. How would Webster, who had been living in the black-and-white world of law enforcement, navigate in a universe that was all shades of gray? "Commanding a corps of clannish, spit-and-polish G-Men is slim preparation for managing the articulate intellectuals, technocrats, and covert operators who make up the CIA," cautioned *Time* magazine. Liaison officer Aldhizer, who heard rumors that Webster might be named, had at first refused to believe them; he was sure "the Agency would never stand for it." Journalist Ronald Kessler compared the move to "choosing the editor of *The New York Times* to head its natural competitor, the *Washington Post*." Historian Thomas Powers ventured that "CIA would rather be run by a Cub Scout den mother than a former head of the FBI."

As Webster's Senate confirmation hearings began that spring, some CIA veterans did feel a certain unease. Intelligence analysts, who wanted to be led by Robert Gates, worried that the FBI director lacked any background in foreign policy or world affairs. Operations officers, who had regarded Casey as a kindred soul, feared that Webster was too cautious, too judicial for a business that demanded risks. Richard Helms, in retirement, came to Webster's defense, pointing out that all DCIs had to be cautious, precisely because of the risks, or else they could end up wrecked on the rocks, like Casey. But to the skeptics, Webster seemed a bureaucrat with a business-school mentality. His longtime friendship with Stan Turner, and his pledge to purge the Agency of anyone remotely connected to Iran-contra, raised the specter of Carter-style cutbacks in covert action. At the very least, his appointment was bound to cause awkward moments, given that thirty-five of his FBI agents were still focusing on CIA's role in contra resupply. Webster tried to soothe Agency fears, during his confirmation hearings, by pledging not to hurry in his housecleaning; by stonewalling Congress on sensitive documents seized by the FBI at Langley; and by backing, in principle, CIA's right to kidnap terrorists overseas. Still, talk in the halls at Langley was that he was Hoover's ultimate reprisal, a final stake-in-the-heart for the old OSS extralegal ethos, driven in by Congress with a mallet called Iran-contra.

Congress believed that Judge Webster was the best man to impose a climate of legality at CIA, and confirmed his nomination. On May 26, leaving his former deputy John Otto temporarily in charge at the FBI, he was sworn in as the fourteenth director of central intelligence. "You are taking over an agency that probably in certain ways wasn't too dissimilar from the FBI at the time you came in," one congressman told Webster. "Lack of mission and purpose, all sorts of activities that shouldn't have gone on—and hopefully you can do the same job at the CIA that you did at the FBI."

That was precisely what some CIA officers worried about—that he would try to turn the place into another FBI. No one doubted that his appointment amounted to an organ transplant or a skin graft; the question was whether the body of the patient, CIA, would accept or reject the alien tissue.

WEBSTER'S FIRST DIFFICULTY was adapting to a new routine. Directing the FBI had been a neatly defined nine-to-five proposition, but CIA was more or less an all-encompassing way of life. At 10 p.m. every evening, an armed Agency courier arrived at Webster's red brick home, on a secluded street off Bradley Boulevard in Bethesda, Maryland, where the widower lived alone with a basset hound. From the courier Webster would receive an early draft of the President's Daily Brief, a top-secret digest of facts and gossip. On a given day it might report on where Soviet leader Mikhail Gorbachev had last been seen, describe movements of other countries' missiles or troops, or psychologically profile foreign dignitaries the president was scheduled to receive. Webster would read it before drifting off to sleep. At 7:15 a.m. the next day, a heavily armored CIA limousine and a "chase car" with security agents would draw up to the curb, to take Webster to the White House. The limousine featured three telephones: one to Langley, one to the president, and one ordinary, outside line, for making personal or social calls. There was little time for the latter, however, as Webster studied new cables that had come in, and updated the President's Brief. At 7:55, he would present the brief at the White House, usually to James Baker, with whom he did not particularly get along. By 8:30, the limousine would sweep Webster through the main guarded entrance gate at Langley, into an underground parking garage. A private elevator took him to his seventh-floor suite. Throughout the day, Webster's CIA guards remained posted just outside the door to his office, in a bulletproof fiberglass cubicle, their faces grayly lit by the monitors they always watched.

Those guards soon became a problem. His daughter's preconceptions about CIA were more on target than Webster expected; there *was* a spook factor. Every few weeks, technicians from CIA's Office of Security swept his home and office for bugs, and checked the special devices that had been installed in his windows to prevent the KGB from listening in by parabolic laser beams. A special detail of personal guards was even assigned to live in the unused parts of the home. When Webster played tennis, the guards insisted on waiting for him courtside, intimidating his opponents. Even in the most genteel of settings, such as cocktail parties, they would hang back along the walls like underworld bouncers, statue-stiff, frowning if anyone asked their names. Webster sometimes wondered whether they were protecting him or watching him. He knew they had their jobs to do, but did grow angry—and threatened to send them to "charm school"—after they were rude to the wife of his new public-affairs officer, William Baker, who had also come over from the Bureau.

In Baker's case, as Webster's, part of the "wooden security guards" problem may have been that he was not exactly "wanted" at CIA. Baker's appointment, announced on Webster's first day of work, had meant retirement for George Lauder, who had served for twenty years in the Operations Directorate and had shared Casey's distrust of the press. Baker promised to be more forthcoming with the outside world. That chilled the blood of veteran clandestine officers, who Baker sensed "were less than enthusiastic about joining forces with an aggressive advocate of public affairs who had just gotten off the boat from the FBI." When he was introduced in the Agency's auditorium, no one clapped. Some in the audience were being investigated by the Bureau for their roles in Iran-contra; others feared for their friends; few supported the idea of a glasnost for secret intelligence. When Baker told the spies that they should now embrace the four "C's" of candor, completeness, consistency, and correctness—all now codified in a new in-house manual on "Briefing Congress"—there was widespread snickering. As one officer later said, "The four C's—God, that was just *so* FBI."

Some officers worried that Langley would be turned into a tour-bus stop, as FBI headquarters had been since the Hoover era, and those fears seemed confirmed by Baker's plans to remake the Agency's family day. It had been the idea of William Colby, back in 1974, to celebrate September 18, the anniversary of CIA's founding, by letting spouses and children come to see where their relatives worked. Webster's PR people now got the idea that the Agency could pass out CIA T-shirts, shorts, and caps to family members. After all, anyone could buy FBI jogging suits and souvenirs at Quantico. But the Office of Security vetoed Baker's plan, fearing that children of covert officers might compromise their parents' identities by wearing the stuff.

Nevertheless, the new regime did manage to make its mark on the 1987 family day. While relatives were visiting Langley, CIA and FBI were executing the final phase of a plan to kidnap a terrorist overseas and bring him to the U.S. for trial. The target was Fawaz Younis, a Lebanese Shiite, who in June 1985 hijacked a Royal Jordanian jet in Beirut, badly pistol-whipped some unarmed government-militia members, then evacuated the plane and blew it up. Planning for Operation Goldenrod, as the hunt for Younis became known, had begun within a few days of Webster's nomination. Although he'd resisted such extractions while FBI director, he now saw the chance to make a symbolic statement—not only as a warning to terrorists, but as reassurance to CIA cowboys who worried that he wouldn't be gung-ho enough. So in spring 1987, the Agency's Counterterrorism Center had dangled an informant into Younis' life, and taped an admission of hijacking. Learning that he needed cash, CTC then lured Younis to a yacht in international waters off Cyprus, ostensibly to meet a narcotics kingpin. To make sure that there would be a "clean" case against him in U.S. courts, Webster let the FBI take the lead when Younis boarded the boat, on September 13. The trap was carefully set to distract his attention: Sunning themselves on deck, as he arrived, were two women in string bikinis, who were actually FBI agents. Younis was caught so completely off guard that, when his feet were kicked out from under him and he was slammed onto the deck, he broke both wrists. He was interrogated for four days on a nearby Navy ammunition ship, then transferred to the U.S. carrier *Saratoga* and flown to the U.S. in a Lockheed S-3 Viking. The plane and its prisoner touched down in Virginia, and the story broke to the press, just as Webster inaugurated anniversary ceremonies at Langley, forty years to the day after CIA was officially founded.

The timing was artful indeed. News stories about the Agency's birthday, instead of just stressing Iran-contra, had an easy "handle" for highlighting the continuing relevance of the post-Casey CIA. The act was symbolic at other levels, too—proving, for instance, that Webster's pledge to improve coordination between CIA and FBI was not just talk. In fact, Goldenrod was apparently the first successful overseas extraction in the long history of FBI-CIA liaison. In 1954, Hoover had nixed a plan to capture suspected Soviet spy Joseph Katz from a yacht off Israel; in 1979, CIA protests had prevented FBI agents disguised as Arab yachtsmen from capturing Robert Vesco in the Bahamas. But now the two agencies had finally pulled one off.

Webster's critics were not satisfied, however. Younis was small fry, not at all one of the world's most wanted terrorists. And by treating the operation as a criminal case, Webster had created certain complications. The courts questioned the legality of Younis' seizure, criticized his extended interrogation in international waters, and threw out some counts because of CTC's rough play. He was eventually convicted of air piracy, but the whole thing would have been much simpler if Webster had just let the Israelis assassinate the man, which was how things had worked in the past. Instead, he had turned it into a media-relations sideshow and courtroom drama, which was essentially taking a J. Edgar Hoover approach.

To his detractors, that seemed to typify what they felt was already a fault in Webster's tenure: an FBI-type emphasis on public image, at the expense of secret substance. In the weeks following Younis' arrest, almost as if to counteract the good publicity from that episode, such sentiments were vented more than once, in the press, by anonymous intelligence officials. The former FBI director, who knew the rules of the PR game, hit back with a blitz of interviews. The theme of this counterattack was that he was learning on the job. He had visited or would soon travel to sixteen countries on a "hello tour"; he was also leaning on Deputy Director Robert Gates, whose specialty was analyzing intelligence. Still, the Washington rumor mill was kept busy with accusations that Webster was a lightweight. He was criticized for enjoying too many perks, for being too detached, for escorting socialites instead of working late. Above all, he was attacked for a failure to adapt to the culture of secrecy. Disgruntled retirees alleged that he had personally blown a sensitive operation in August 1987, when visiting Argentina, by thanking the country's chief of intelligence for cooperating in a case that the Argentines had no need to know about—especially since they were the targets.

Although Webster also stood accused of being a slave to Congress, even his allies there were getting impatient, and they complained openly about one matter in particular, which likewise vexed many at CIA. This was the "aides" problem. Bill Baker was but the most visible member of an "FBI mafia" that had occupied the seventh floor at CIA headquarters. The group included Webster's FBI chief of staff, John Hotis, and a bevy of "special assistants." The assistants all held Ivy League law degrees, but none of them had any background in intelligence. They sealed off the judge like smug law clerks, which was what they were. They always seemed to accompany Webster to Capitol Hill, and intelligence-committee staffers noted the DCI's need to consult them before answering questions. At Langley they became known derisively as the "Munchkins," and one had to go see them if caught violating any of Webster's new edicts, such as the one that forbade smoking in the headquarters building. The consequent edginess of some quite senior CIA officers was not eased when they had to interact with Webster's longtime executive secretary, Peggy Devine. Even at the FBI, her willful protectiveness of Webster's time had earned her the "Dragon Lady" reputation that had once been attached to Hoover's secretary, Helen Gandy. In the bureaucratic context, that was actually something of a compliment; no one doubted the *efficiency* of Devine, or any of the other aides. The problem was not so much who they were as what they wanted to do.

Redrawing the rules for secret operations, for instance. Webster assigned that project to Hotis, who had rewritten FBI guidelines in the Church era, and to Nancy McGregor, a twenty-eight-year-old law clerk. Their restructuring of the Agency's Covert Action Review Group earned the enmity of many old-line intelligence agents, and of conservative policy types in the outside world. Webster himself compared CIA covert activities with the use of undercover agents by the FBI, and new rules reflected the Hooverian "accountability" model that had once driven William Harvey from the Bureau to CIA. In the past, operational review had been a fairly informal process, reflecting the action orientation and administrative looseness that had been a treasured part of the Donovan spirit. Now, as Robert Gates remarked, "they actually sit down and debate the issue. They talk about it; they go through a long checklist." All current covert projects were reviewed, and Webster watched over the proceedings with an osprey's eye. Some operations were tabled or terminated. "The Judge simply asks a lot of difficult questions and requires legal justification for every step taken," one CIA official lamented. "He is not a cowboy."

Webster's long-promised Iran-contra purges brought that point fully home. By the end of 1987, all of Casey's freewheeling favorites were gone. Joseph Fernandez and Allen Fiers were fired; Dewey Clarridge and Clair George took the hint and left. A half-dozen others were reprimanded, their careers effectively killed. George was replaced as head of the Operations Directorate by Richard Stolz, a thirty-one-year Agency veteran with some covert-action experience, who had been a Webster classmate at Amherst. Stolz was not regarded as a bad choice, but there was great resentment about the way some of CIA's best and most dynamic sons had been "hung out to dry" for doing what the White House asked. Some saw a double standard, noting that Webster's 1978 punishments of FBI agents for illegal domestic spying had not been so harshly punitive. He had reasoned then that the G-men acted in good faith, believing their actions authorized by higher-ups; he had not offered CIA officers any such "out."

The purges were followed by a new round of press attacks on Webster, not all of them anonymous. Retired CIA operations man Tom Polgar complained that "the new watchword at the agency seems to be 'Do No Harm'—which is fine for doctors but may not encourage imagination and initiative in secret operations. . . . Initiative is the distinguishing feature of the clandestine operator, but initiative is a tender flower requiring a very special climate. . . . Such conditions can only prevail when it is also well understood that extraordinary demands on the individual and the family will be balanced by extraordinary treatment in an elite."

A part of that extraordinary treatment had always included a certain leeway on matters involving the law, but now the FBI was even sicced on nine CIA Office of Security employees who sold a hundred rare misprinted $1 postage stamps that came across their desks. In the past, such windfalls had been part of the perks, or at most a cause for secret reprimand; after all, if not spotted by the employees, the stamps would have been stuck on letters, with no benefit to anyone. But Webster insisted that the offenders be dragged into court and tried for making a profit off public property. The message could not have been more clear. In big ways and small, CIA's extralegal ethos was under siege. The last buccaneers were being made to walk the plank.

WHILE WEBSTER and his aides were shaking up Langley, they also began a review of relations with the FBI. The lead was taken by Nancy McGregor. A graduate of Barnard College and Harvard Law, McGregor had been one of Webster's administrative assistants at the FBI, and had not been happy about moving to CIA. Arriving at Langley, she found its personnel reticent and not easy to socialize with. She had tried to make an impact by pushing through specific projects; she was instrumental in setting up a day-care center at Langley, although even on such a minor matter the cultures clashed. (After haggling over what seemed excessive security demands, McGregor agreed to segregate the children of parents in CIA "covert" operations from those in "overt" work, and to mark cubbyholes for clothes with first names and numbers only—e.g., "Christopher 3" or "Michelle 7.") McGregor would also change the format for internal Agency reports, which she did not think were written as clearly and logically as the Bureau's. The documents were wordy, circumlocutious, and freighted with jargon and acronyms, which neither she, nor any of the other assistants, nor Webster himself could understand.

That conceptual murkiness became a real problem for McGregor as she waded through Top Secret summaries of cases, such as the Howard-Yurchenko affair, that both CIA and FBI had botched. For elucidation, she talked to some of the personalities involved. She got good cooperation on the FBI side, but at CIA she was hindered by the stubborn unwillingness of senior officials to share information with anyone except the director—and there were even questions about how much they might be holding back from him. CIA's filing system, or systems, also made the job difficult. At the FBI, everything went in one file under an individual's name. But at CIA, there were many different indexes, and it was not easy to know which one to search—or even which ones *existed*. Again, no one came forward to tell her.

As McGregor pieced together the secret histories of cases gone bad, she began to see how each agency rationalized its performance and tried to pin blame on the other. What she didn't see was any easy solution. She figured it would help, however, that a Webster friend had been named to head the FBI.

Aldhizer and some others had been hoping that the White House might effect a "double switch" by giving the Bureau to someone from CIA, such as former Deputy Director John N. McMahon, but Reagan chose instead William Sessions. A tall Texan whose silver hair and outgoing personality made him a natural public emissary, Sessions had been considered a firm but fair-minded federal judge in San Antonio, where he had tried the accused assassins of John Wood, the first federal jurist murdered in the twentieth century. Webster had worked that case hard as FBI director, and the two had been on good terms since then. It wasn't the closeness Webster had with an old college buddy like Stan Turner, but the DCI did hope to achieve a symbiosis at the top, at least for symbolism's sake. The two were photographed together at Washington parties, and Sessions arranged for dedication of a Webster portrait at FBI headquarters. Both men knew that relations between heads of hierarchical agencies could send strong signals. That kind of wisdom had never come easy to hardball corporate lawyers like Donovan or Casey, who came from a world where organizations would sue each other, but it was second nature to veteran federal employees like Sessions and Webster.

But the new dawn was clouded by a change of liaison officers. By the time Iran-contra broke, Jay Aldhizer had had enough. For eight years in the job, longer than anyone except Papich, he had done his best to break down some of the long-standing barriers, or at least to lower them. Though not operationally involved in CI, like Papich and Cregar, he had tried to bring together the personalities. There had been problems, especially in the Howard case, but Aldhizer felt that if the full record of cooperation were ever made public, the mishaps would seem comparatively exceptional and rare. In the last few years alone, the agencies had paired off in thwarting shipments of poison gas to Iraq, monitoring foreign students' access to sensitive materials in U.S. libraries, and pooling technologies in electronic surveillance. Turf-crossings had been managed; the FBI had won acknowledgment of its right to operate overseas, and for five years the Courtship project had been quietly under way. But Aldhizer was nearing fifty, the age when many FBI agents took early retirement and began second careers, with fewer headaches and higher pay. It was time to move on.

Before retiring in January 1987, Aldhizer recommended to Buck Revell that the liaison position be restored to the upper end of the government pay scale, where it had been during Papich and Cregar's day. Although Aldhizer had to interact with secretaries, clerks, and whoever else could help, the majority of the people he dealt with at CIA were supergrades, and though they never made an explicit issue of their superiority in rank, he felt that some of them were pretty well conscious of it. Upgrading the liaison position would also help to keep one person in the job for a while, which Aldhizer thought was especially important with an agency as complex as CIA. It had been two years before he even began to *think* he understood the place, but the natural inclination—and the pattern before he had arrived—was to funnel through as quickly as possible to make supergrade.

Revell promised to consider upgrading the liaison slot, but he never did, and Aldhizer's worries about continuity proved to be well founded. His first successor, Robert Peter, wanted the liaison job badly, but after less than a year he moved on to become deputy legat in Rome. Following Peter, there were a couple of liaison officers, but neither lasted more than a few months.

PETER'S POSTING ABROAD symptomized a growing problem that he himself faced during his brief tenure as liaison officer. As CIA director, Webster continued to encourage FBI overseas expansionism under Sessions, whose agents were pushing for counterspy work abroad. But Chief/CI Hathaway was apprehensive about the competition, and one of his deputies ridiculed the "dial twirlers" that Sessions was sending overseas. "They check to see if safes are locked. . . . But they don't actively look for Americans who have turned coat." Since FBI agents were rarely cleared to see highly classified documents, the naysayers reasoned, they often lacked a "basis to ask informed and penetrating questions." Although FBI counterterrorist agents had received some analytic training under the auspices of the CTC, Bureau CI agents were still thought to be handicapped by "a lack of sophisticated analysis."

As evidence of that shortcoming, CIA skeptics pointed to the FBI's COINTELPRO-style harassment of the Committee in Solidarity with the People of El Salvador (CISPES), a U.S. group that acted as a public-relations arm for Marxist Salvadoran guerrillas. From 1981 to 1985, acting on tips from Frank Varelli, a "defector" from the group, the FBI spent ten work-years monitoring CISPES and 178 affiliated individuals or groups. Special agents purchased "subversive materials" from bookstores, infiltrated CISPES barbecues and bake sales, and discovered that some activists were in contact with former Weather Underground operatives in Dallas. But no charges were ever brought against CISPES members, and after Varelli failed a lie-detector test in 1985, the investigation was shut down. Varelli then joined up with opponents of U.S. Central American policy and, just as Jack Terrell had done to CIA in Iran-contra, exposed FBI operations of questionable legality. Senate investigators concluded that "This was not an investigation to intimidate foes of this administration, as some have alleged," yet chastised the FBI for going off on what amounted to a fruitless commie-hunt without better checking and analysis. Varelli's information, Sessions admitted, "was not adequately verified by the FBI." But why, Senator David Boren pressed Sessions, "were none of Varelli's statements checked out with agencies who were more familiar with Salvadoran affairs, such as the CIA?" Sessions had no answer; he could only say that CIA had not been consulted about Varelli's allegations. Ten man-years of work could have been saved, Sessions conceded, if the Bureau had simply asked for analytical assistance from CIA.

Predictably enough, disclosure of poor liaison in the CISPES affair soon led to renewed rumblings for a superagency or CI "czar." When current and retired intelligence experts called for a top-to-bottom reorganization of CI, at a Washington conference in early 1988, special weight was given to the ideas of those, like former Reagan aides Codevilla and DeGraffenreid, who inveighed against "arbitrary and cumbersome" splits. The main problem, all critics seemed to agree, was that no one person or agency was responsible for countering hostile intelligence. Judge Webster was opposed to radical changes in the CI framework, but he could sense which way the wind was blowing. There was a movement to centralize, and he moved to co-opt it—not only out of bureaucratic savvy, but in a desire to make the system more "cohesive."

In April 1988, at a classified location in Washington, Webster announced the formation of a new interagency Counterintelligence Center at Langley. CIC's boss was the special assistant to the DCI for counterintelligence, Hathaway, who retained his title as Chief/CI. A key goal of the center, Webster explained, was to teach FBI and CIA personnel simply to *recognize* data of value to the other agency, for surely that was a precondition of sharing it. The re-education would be achieved "by putting people in each other's offices." An FBI agent was assigned full-time to the new Center. The Agency also brought into the CI process some research and analytic units; Deputy Director for Intelligence Richard J. Kerr said the Center "was really in the business of trying to do analysis of what was going on, as opposed to looking at individual cases." Centralization of intelligence was put at a premium to investigation, reflecting Webster's heightened interest in looking at the ant farm that hostile intelligence was building, whereas at the FBI his job had been to find the tunnels and fill them.

For all its heralded importance, some of CIC's early missions seemed insignificant, even silly. In May 1988, staffers were quite intent on determining whether the KGB was tapping telephone calls from Nancy Reagan to her astrologer in San Francisco, where the Soviet consulate was known to target microwave-transmitted long-distance traffic. And in 1990, CIC officials traveled to Pensacola, Florida, to question six Army intelligence analysts, all of them with Top Secret security clearances, who had gone AWOL from the 701st Military Intelligence Brigade in Augsburg, West Germany, purportedly to seek and destroy the Antichrist. But those episodes might not have been as trivial as an outsider would initially think. The case of the AWOL analysts did not exactly instill confidence in the nation's personnel security, and their "Antichrist" explanation might have merely been a cover story for other mischief. The first lady, for her part, could have inadvertently given the Soviets a stream of personal and political intelligence simply by saying, over insecure lines: "Ronnie's thinking about changing this policy or that policy. Are the signs right?"

Preoccupied as it was with such matters, CIC was of little help in hashing out agreement on other issues, including a long-sought standardization of Top Secret security clearances. For five years, the Reagan administration had been trying to get the agencies to adopt a single standard, but—as had happened when the Eisenhower administration attempted to force the issue—the agencies were tangled in a fight over who would oversee the new system. "CIA does not want anyone looking over their shoulder," a congressional source told the Washington *Post* in November 1988. A House Intelligence Committee report blamed the failure to implement a common security policy on "turf consciousness."

Yet CIC's first year was not without successes. In June 1988, its analysis caused Canada to oust seventeen alleged KGB officers for spying. And in August, the new unit, working with West German intelligence, broke a major spy network in NATO. The ring had been operating since the early 1970s, perhaps as part of a larger KGB initiative directed by Kim Philby. The key operative was a former U.S. Army sergeant, Clyde Lee Conrad, who until 1985 had guarded a safe that stored documents at a NATO base near Frankfurt. Conrad had reportedly supplied Hungarian Military Intelligence with U.S. Army plans to defend Europe, and the Hungarians had shared the data with Moscow. The case began to unfold as CIA discovered that secrets were being lost but was unable to pinpoint how. CIC took over analysis of the problem, and asked the FBI to tap the calls of a known Hungarian intelligence agent in Washington. That led to surveillance of a Conrad crony who met the Hungarians. The FBI played a key role in supervising the inquiry, and in monitoring the German case for prosecution in the U.S.

Still, there were complaints about cooperation. "There were hints early on that there was a problem," recalled a congressional staffer familiar with the case, "and they [the agencies] didn't coordinate." Because Conrad was no longer actively reporting, CIA suspected that he might be a "throwaway," deliberately burned to protect other Soviet sources in NATO. Geer and the FBI thought this was Angletonian paranoia. They also suspected that CIA's assistance was constrained by a desire to cover up a bizarre and embarrassing irony: Conrad, posing as a Hungarian intelligence agent, was paid $100,000 by CIA for information about an alleged U.S. Army spy ring working for the Hungarians.

After the Conrad flap, Sessions and Webster signed a "Memorandum of Understanding," requiring CIA to brief the Bureau on breaking CI cases "in a timely fashion." But critics contended that something more than the CIC was needed to ensure liaison. In November 1988, a group of current and former experts on spying, the Consortium for the Study of Intelligence, urged creation of a new body to monitor CI. The Consortium's report was prepared by Geer, DeGraffenreid, and DDCI Robert Gates, and endorsed by National Security Adviser Brent Scowcroft, Senate Intelligence chairman Boren, and former President Nixon. Their report said that security failures in the "decade of the spy" had occurred, and were continuing, largely because of inadequate CI coordination. But Judge Webster insisted that everything was fine.

As proof, Webster could soon point to liaison in another case solved by CIC, this one involving an unexpected enemy. American intelligence officials had not been alarmed when François Mitterrand and his socialists came to power in France in 1981, for there was little anti-American or pro-Soviet rhetoric. Unbeknownst to the U.S., however, a special economic spying capacity was created in 1982, when the old French intelligence service, the SDECE, was transformed into the Direction Générale de la Securité Extérieure (DGSE). By January 1987, the new French agency had determined that trade secrets from three U.S. companies could help bolster France's sagging state-run industries: Texas Instruments, Corning Glass, and, most of all, IBM. By the fall of 1987, DGSE had an inside track on Big Blue's strategic business decisions, including bids on contracts for high-tech research. That information helped a French electronics firm, Compagnie des Machines Bull, in some bidding wars. But the DGSE operation began to unravel in February 1989, apparently when a drunken French agent described it in general terms to an American friend. Because the case involved breach of international patent law, Webster arranged for FBI agents to be temporarily attached to the CIA station in Paris. The team achieved a level of cooperation "unprecedented in Agency history," according to one former Agency official, and cracked the case after seven months of patient work. In November 1989, the DGSE moles were found and fired, and French intelligence finally admitted its mischief. To prevent further damage to relations between the two countries, Webster flew over to see the French in January 1990 and "buried the hatchet."

But few counterintelligence cases would have outcomes that were so unambiguous, and CIC was especially stumped by a continuing pattern of losses for U.S. intelligence in Moscow. "Was it communications that were penetrated?" Webster later said, describing the questions being asked by CIA. "Was it human penetration? Was it happening overseas? They were trying to narrow that circle of possibilities." Because Howard couldn't have been responsible for all the rollups, suspicion had fastened again on the Moscow Embassy, especially when two Marine guards, Clayton Lonetree and Arnold Bracy, were arrested for espionage in December 1986. But that happened only after CIA officers interviewed Lonetree for four days without advising him of his rights, letting him have a lawyer, or calling in the FBI. For purposes of prosecution, the interrogations were useless. They proved none too valuable, either, for figuring out why Moscow Station was still burning. Although Bracy initially confessed that he was in love with a Russian woman named Violette, presumably a KGB agent, who had persuaded him to let Soviet agents into the code room, he soon recanted, and all espionage charges against him were eventually dropped. CIA analysts wondered, somewhat convolutedly, whether Bracy might have been put up to his "confession" by the KGB, in order to throw the U.S. off the scent of deeper penetrations. The KGB could have offered Bracy a choice: confess falsely to helping bug the embassy, and then we'll rescue you through a spy swap, so you can live happily ever after with Violette. If you don't, we'll expose your relationship with Violette, declare publicly that you spied for us, and you'll spend the rest of your life in jail. Whatever the reasons for Bracy's confession, CIA in any case determined by 1988 that the embassy's communications had not been compromised at all.

The possibility of human treason therefore assumed a new plausibility, and liaison among the two agencies' molehunters took on a new importance. In acknowledgment of this, Webster and Sessions prepared a "memorandum of understanding," outlining a comprehensive process to ferret out security threats. Its key stipulation was that CIA would keep the FBI promptly informed of security cases, as had clearly not happened with Howard and Bracy. But FBI agents suspected that CIA was still holding back, and sensed a reluctance to probe suspicions fully. One FBI official would remember being told in the late 1980s that "something's funny" in U.S. spy operations, and that several officers on Hathaway's staff had started a probe. But the general consensus at Langley was that CIA had "other things to do."

That lack of institutional support left CIC staffers in a desperate and demoralizing position: seeing Russian sources snuffed out time and again, yet still unable to find the breach in security. Perhaps most disturbing, CIA's operations seemed too carefully "wrapped up and disposed of," always in ways—such as Yurchenko's "spy dust," his tip about Howard, or the Marine guards scandal—that deflected from the idea of a well-placed spy.

Nevertheless, in 1989 CIC found one.

DOWN TO THE END of the Cold War, probably no place in the world was so thick with spies as Vienna. It had been home turf for the KGB since the end of World War II, when the city had been for several years partitioned among the victors, leading to the aura of intrigue dramatized in Graham Greene's thriller *The Third Man*. In the 1950s and '60s, Richard Helms had routinely warned officers bound for Vienna about KGB-sponsored attempts to kidnap or murder CIA assets; in the 1970s, the Soviets had chosen Vienna as the site to abduct and murder Nicholas Shadrin; in the 1980s, the city had been the KGB's favorite place to meet with agents like Ed Howard and Clyde Conrad. But CIA had also built up a considerable apparat in the city. The emphasis was on technical surveillance, especially the tapping of telephones. By 1988, when CIC formed a Security Evaluation Office to boost anti-spy efforts at U.S. embassies, Hathaway had a lot of resources to bring to bear in Vienna, and the Soviets had a lot of fish to get caught in the net.

In early 1989, the CIC tracking program established that a KGB illegal agent, traveling on a Finnish passport as "Reino Gikman," had received a briefcase from the former number-two U.S. diplomat in Vienna, Felix Bloch. An alarmed Hathaway immediately took the case to Webster, explaining that Bloch had access to a broad range of classified secrets, including encoded cable traffic, the identities of CIA officers in the embassy, and even the identities of some Agency sources. Although Bloch was not cleared for some of the most sensitive secrets, he would have known much about the Clayton Lonetree–Moscow embassy case, and could have given the KGB "feedback" on any number of projects. In his capacity as a consular officer, Bloch had also drafted reviews of high-tech exports to the Eastern bloc, consistently urging a soft line on trade restrictions. Bloch's "M.O.," which included sophisticated countersurveillance precautions, suggested that he had been spying for a long time.

On May 14, 1989, Gikman telephoned Bloch at his apartment in Washington, where Bloch was working for the State Department's Canadian-affairs division. CIA was listening on the European end. Gikman, who was in Paris, pretended to be a stamp dealer. Bloch, an avid collector, said he just happened to be flying to Paris that very day. He hoped to see Gikman there the following evening, in the Restaurant Le Meurice. This lead was passed to French intelligence. The two men met as planned.

Bloch placed under the table a black airline-type bag, and the KGB man took it with him when he left. The meeting was monitored by French agents, who learned that Bloch planned to see Gikman again two weeks later, in Brussels.

The Brussels meeting created a predicament for Hathaway. He believed that Belgian intelligence was penetrated by the Soviets, and knew that its director did not have good relations with other Western services. CIA would have to provide its own coverage in Brussels, then. But in doing so, it would be violating a working agreement with the Belgian government. The whole station could be kicked out if the operation blew. Consequently, the Agency's surveillance in Brussels was discreet—perhaps too discreet, for there was confusion about whether Bloch brought a bag to the meeting, and whether he left it with Gikman.

Even so, the Soviets somehow detected the suspicions against Bloch. On June 22, Gikman called Bloch and said, in double-talk, that he wasn't "feeling well." He hoped Bloch didn't "catch the same thing."

Now the Bureau took over the case, but Geer was not at all happy with the way CIA had managed the investigation. As in the Howard episode, the FBI should have been brought in earlier. CIA's surveillance, as usual, had not been conducted with an eye toward prosecution, and now that Bloch seemed to be aware of the suspicions against him, getting such evidence would be almost impossible. Geer wondered, moreover, just how Bloch had found out about the investigation. By September 1989, the FBI was seriously investigating whether leaks about the Bloch investigation might have originated at Langley. *Time* magazine reported that "dozens of FBI agents have been rummaging through CIA.... What the FBI has learned so far is that about 150 officials knew that Bloch was under suspicion. That large number virtually guaranteed early disclosure."

In any case, the KGB's warning to Bloch caused a need for immediate action, before he could flee or destroy evidence. Just hours after his June conversation with Gikman, FBI agents closed in on Bloch and interrogated him for almost three hours, openly accusing him of being a Soviet spy. Sessions later said that confrontation was the "least intrusive mode" of investigation, a view questioned by CIA. Bloch insisted the packages he passed the KGB man contained only stamps. He was not believed, and the Bureau placed him under open twenty-four-hour surveillance. To avoid a reprise of the Howard bungle, the Bureau's coverage verged on overkill. Dozens of FBI agents were on Bloch's tail from the moment he left his house each morning, following him even into public restrooms. In what soon became a media circus, the FBI agents were in turn pursued by a train of reporters. The case dragged on that way until November

1990, when Bloch was finally fired. But he was not arrested or charged, and the much-sought prosecution never materialized.

The Bureau was embarrassed by its inability to nail Bloch, and faulted CIA. Geer felt there should have been better coordination between the FBI and CIA's station in Brussels, working together to develop admissible evidence, and letting the Bureau take the lead as soon as possible. As one CI official told the press, the Bloch case "fell between the cracks."

Again came the calls for a fundamental restructuring, a real centralization of CI. Using unusually harsh language, a Senate Intelligence Committee report found that Webster's CI reforms had "failed" because of "bureaucratic infighting." Senator Boren believed that too many agencies were doing counterintelligence, using different procedures. "That's one of the problems right now," he said. "No one agency in government is really responsible."

Webster had hoped that his new Counterintelligence Center would be responsible. But a 1990 Senate panel, headed by security lawyer Eli Jacobs, found that CIC had failed to overcome fragmentation. "Without some kind of coordinative function," warned one panelist who studied the problem, "people will simply run off, even if they are trying to do right, in all kinds of directions. . . . Correcting this deficiency is the single most important undertaking facing those . . . charged with protecting the nation's secrets." But the panel's ability to correct that deficiency was limited, as Jacobs himself admitted, because "We addressed the counterintelligence problem within the existing organizational framework. We did not examine the need for changes to that framework."

Ken DeGraffenreid did, however. Since November 1989, he had been floating the proposal for a "National Counterintelligence and Security Assessment Center," a toned-down version of the superagency idea. He wanted, in effect, a CI czar to coordinate counterintelligence, much as William Donovan had once been appointed to coordinate foreign collection. Under the CI czar would be some thirty analysts and operators from various national-security agencies. They would identify those secrets most in danger of being stolen; detect and evaluate strategic deception; and collate security measures both at home and abroad. DeGraffenreid realized that his proposal was likely to be fought by both FBI and CIA, but urged the Jacobs panel to consider legislation if the agencies would not go willingly along. "If it takes a hammer," he testified, "maybe it's time for a hammer on these issues."

INSTEAD OF A HAMMER, the Bureau tried a woman's touch. In mid-1989, the position of liaison officer went to FBI agent Barbara Campbell.

This development could be seen as part of a larger trend in Western intelligence—Stella Rimington had already become deputy chief of Britain's FBI equivalent, MI5, and would soon be named its head—but no "affirmative action" had operated in either case. An attractive, married brunette, Campbell came in with a good CI background, having served a half-dozen years in the Soviet Section at headquarters and the Washington Field Office. She was enthusiastic about the liaison job, and impressed Agency officers with her grasp of the issues. A good listener and a quick study, she also had a cool head. Some CIA men had worried, with residual sexism, that she might be too "emotional" in crises, but she always erred on the side of reserve.

Campbell understood that there would always be conflicts, even if the Agency was headed by a former FBI director who was naturally friendly toward his old ward. She knew from experience that CIA would get information and not recognize it as being of value to the Bureau, and that such information wouldn't come over until something substantive happened. At that point, tempers would naturally flare: Why didn't we get this before? How do we know we are getting all the facts now? The problems tended to cluster around CI matters, but were by no means confined to them. Both organizations were so big that there were many things going on between them in computers, medical services, and what Aldhizer had called "offbeat areas." Coordinating the release of documents under the Freedom of Information Act, for instance: because there were no standard government criteria for determining how to sanitize a document, one agency might inadvertently declassify a piece of information that the other had excised. If the requestor had as efficient an operation as intelligence critic Morton Halperin, or as some of the conspiracy theorists, with computer-supported file systems to do the matching, there could be an occasional "Ah! Gotcha! The FBI has released this, and CIA didn't release that—what's the story here?"

Ideally, Campbell would try to keep the parties in contact by arranging for FBI officials to call up their opposite numbers at CIA. In Aldhizer's time, there had been secure green telephones between the organizations, located at various places in the Bureau. By the time Campbell took over, there was a green phone on almost every desk in the Intelligence Division, so that CI agents could dial a five-digit number and talk to their counterparts at Langley. But not all calls to the Agency could be handled by the Intelligence Division, and Bureau people would try to get things done on the regular telephone, "the black line," of which CIA people were deathly afraid. If a CIA employee's name was mentioned on the black line, that might upset the Office of Security, which disciplined personnel whose identities were disclosed. Especially at the lower levels, such episodes could get things tremendously off-track.

At the higher levels, meanwhile, Campbell's task was complicated by a wide purge of CI personnel. At both agencies the moves were seen as reflecting displeasure over continuing CI failures, the Bloch case apparently having been the final straw. Hathaway retired on March 1, 1990, to be replaced by Theodore Price, about whom the Agency was careful to ensure that little was publicly known. By then James Geer, too, had retired, and was replaced by W. Douglas Gow, formerly in charge of the FBI's Washington Field Office. Geer's deputy assistant director, Gary Penrith, was transferred to Newark, and Revell was eventually demoted outright from the FBI's number-three position to chief of the Dallas Field Office. The Bureau's public-affairs office said that Geer had improved cooperation with CIA, but reporters noted that his departure came "at a time of debate between the FBI and CIA over the role of counterintelligence and which agency is best handling the assignment."

The Senate Intelligence Committee was also debating the issue, and sided with the Bureau. In October 1989, after being briefed on the Bloch affair, the Senate introduced a bill compelling CIA to inform the FBI immediately upon learning of any possible espionage by persons subject to U.S. law. "If this provision had been in effect," a Senate Intelligence Committee report said, "initial indications of espionage would have been reported promptly to the FBI, rather than just to . . . agencies without criminal investigative jurisdiction, i.e., CIA." The Committee's leaders, Senators Boren and William Cohen, were so upset with the Agency over its lack of prosecutorial savvy that they even suggested the Bureau should take over the Agency's foreign spy-catching role. "They [the FBI] have the most expertise in the field of counterintelligence," Cohen said.

In the end, Webster was not ceded title to the house that James Angleton had built, but a frustrated Boren warned of future changes. Dividing CI geographically just didn't make sense, he noted, since "obviously the threat [of spying] doesn't stop at the border."

LIKE CASEY, Webster had more success in counterterrorism than in counterintelligence. After its baptism by bombing in Beirut, interagency CT had been aided by Aldhizer's breakthroughs in technical and analytical cooperation, which had laid the framework for the Counter Terrorism Center, and the two sides were used to collaborating by the time Barbara Campbell came along. In March 1989, for instance, the Center brokered a joint FBI-CIA inquiry into the bombing of a van driven by the wife of

Captain Will Rogers III, captain of the U.S. cruiser *Vincennes*, which had mistakenly shot down an Iranian jetliner. CIA analysts convinced FBI forensics experts that the explosive device had used a small fuse of balsa wood, attached to the undercarriage and ignited by engine heat, which would have been destroyed in the blast. And in September 1989, CTC foiled what may have been a plot to assassinate President Bush. After a defector from the Mèdellin cartel told the FBI that drug lords wanted to send hit men to the United States, possibly to kill the president, the CTC tracked four Spanish-speaking suspects to Edmundston, New Brunswick, a small town at the U.S. border. The men were traveling on fake Venezuelan passports, and had loaded three cars with submachine guns and three thousand rounds of ammunition. When arrested, they had been a seven-hour drive from President Bush's summer home in Maine.

But CTC's real test came after December 21, 1988, when Pan Am Flight 103, bound from Frankfurt to the U.S., exploded at thirty thousand feet above Lockerbie, Scotland. Two hundred seventy persons were killed, including, by some accounts, several CIA officers on their way home from a Middle Eastern station for Christmas. The bombing had occurred despite a warning to CIA on December 5, apparently from the Mossad, that a Pan Am flight from Frankfurt to the U.S. would be bombed within two weeks. The tip had not been passed to the FBI for follow-up until after 103 was downed, at which point Sessions declared publicly that "The bureau believes that it was a hoax and not connected to Flight 103." But independent investigations by the House Government Operations Transportation Subcommittee, the Airport Operators Council, and the National Business Travel Association faulted the two agencies for not pooling data before the bombing.

To ensure the sharing of data afterward, CTC was immediately put on the probe. According to one U.S. official, the inquiry nevertheless became a "chaotic mess" of noncooperation. By April 1989, Vincent Cannistraro, one of the Agency's senior officers at CTC, thought Iran had hired a Damascus-based radical Palestinian faction to carry out the operation. So certain was CIA of this that Webster briefed President Bush on the theory. But Neil Gallagher, chief of the FBI's counterterrorism unit, argued that CIA's case was not strong enough to stand up in court. "CIA believe they have a lot, but it's a Styrofoam brick," one FBI agent told the press. The Bureau was meanwhile working on its own thesis, and reportedly kept crucial information from Langley. Those FBI reports that were shared were denigrated by a CIA official under State Department cover as being "like essays from grade school." But Webster recalled the situation differently. "Everybody got into the act quickly in Pan Am 103," he said. "Tremendous cooperation between all of us—CTC made a great contribution to the solution of that case with bits and pieces from FBI forensics, working closely at all levels, and nobody holding anything back."

The big picture, as far as it may be filled in, suggests that cooperation in the 103 case was difficult but good. In early 1990, diligent FBI search at the crash site located a fragment of microchip detonator that had triggered plastic explosives. Campbell turned the chip over to a CIA analyst, who determined that the fragment belonged to a consignment of timers produced by a Swiss firm for the Libyan government. Then came leads from a high-ranking Libyan intelligence officer, Abd Al-Majid Jaaka, who defected to the U.S. in Rome. There were no Hayhannen or Yurchenko problems this time: Jaaka walked into the U.S. Embassy and was interviewed by the FBI's legal attaché, flown to the U.S., placed under CIA care, debriefed by both agencies, and eventually turned back over to the FBI for resettlement under the Federal Witness Protection Program. Jaaka convinced his handlers that two Libyan intelligence officials had prepared the explosives used to blow up the Pan Am jet. The agencies still disagreed about why the bombing happened: the Bureau believed Muammar Qaddafi sought revenge for American air strikes against his country in 1986, whereas CIA felt that Libya was only a proxy for Iranians avenging the *Vincennes*. But by sharing forensic evidence, and jointly debriefing Jaaka, the two agencies had developed a credible case. Campbell had worked hard to broker and maintain that cooperation, and was especially proud when, on the basis of joint FBI-CIA efforts, the United Nations Security Council eventually ordered Libya to surrender for trial the two Libyans accused of preparing the bomb.

When Qaddafi refused, however, Cannistraro and others at CIA, frustrated that the Libyans were "beyond the reach of U.S. law," began to question Webster's legalistic approach to the case. CTC was patiently seeking indictments against the Libyans, which would allow the FBI to arrest them. That might be good public relations, but it would not deter future attacks by state-supported terrorists. To Cannistraro, terrorists themselves were "interchangeable parts," surrogates for state sponsors, and the only way to thwart the surrogates was to "take out" some of the sponsors, perhaps by using the Israelis. In this, Cannistraro was backed by rightwing hawks in Washington, who assailed U.S. CT policy as a "paper tiger with nerf teeth," and by *Newsweek* magazine, which urged that America assassinate terrorist leaders outright. Because Judge Webster would not consider complicity in that kind of business, Cannistraro came to believe that CTC had become too bureaucratic, too much like the FBI, and in September 1990, shortly after Iraq invaded Kuwait, he resigned.

He got out just as CTC, Webster, and FBI-CIA relations generally, were entering their finest hour. As President Bush began sending troops into Saudi Arabia, Iraqi-sponsored terrorist groups declared that they were waiting for a "green light"—possibly the start of war in the Middle East—to attack Western targets. CTC went on full alert. Analysts sifted through thousands of cables, searching for signs of planned attacks and refining profiles of known terrorist cells. CIA had known since at least 1986 that Iraqi embassies in nine European and Asian countries were distributing weapons in diplomatic bags to hit men and terrorists; the goal now became to disrupt the lines of communication between these field assets and their sponsors in Baghdad. By liaising with foreign security services, Webster arranged the arrest or expulsion of Iraqi diplomats, businessmen, and students. He also brokered covert actions of a more sensitive nature. Details of those latter operations remain classified, but Webster's legalism appears to have been somewhat tempered by a wartime expediency. As he himself would say of William Stephenson's adventurism in the U.S. during World War II: "When you're at war, sometimes you need to *reach* to get things done."

Working from Webster's tips, carried to FBI headquaters by Campbell in her briefcase, the Bureau meanwhile monitored thousands of terror suspects in the United States. Special watches were kept on the Trans-Alaska pipeline, on the nation's Strategic Petroleum Reserves in Louisiana and Texas, on landmarks like Grand Central Terminal in New York, and even on Mormon churches—vulnerable because terrorist groups believed they worked closely with CIA. When CIA reported to Campbell that a New Jersey man, Jamal Wariat, had contacted the Iraqis and offered to assassinate President Bush, the FBI dangled an informant posing as an Iraqi intelligence officer, gleaned full details of the plot, then arrested Wariat. Similar teamwork, managed by Campbell, led to the arrest of suspected Palestinian terrorists in New Jersey, and foiled a scheme by Hamid Al-Amri, an intelligence operative assigned to Iraq's United Nations delegation, to kill an Iraqi dissident in California.

By January 16, 1991, as the U.S. began bombing Iraq, both FBI and CIA believed that the terror situation was well under control. On that day, with FBI sharpshooters perched on roofs throughout Capitol Hill, CT experts from both agencies met with congressional leaders and presented evidence of what Senator Boren called "very close coordination between the FBI, in terms of monitoring any threat inside this country, with the intelligence organizations, CIA and other intelligence assets internationally." In counterterrorism, at least for the past few months and for a few weeks more, the wedge no longer was. Campbell hardly slept during the war, but she kept open the information bridges. If there were any interagency gaps in the country's CT defenses, terrorists certainly failed to find them. Attacks against symbols of U.S. influence did occur—a

Woolworth's store in Bonn was firebombed; there were small explosions at U.S. banks in Chile, and sporadic attacks in Lima and Athens—but terrorists scored no major successes. None of those whom Webster considered "the really heavy-hitters," such as the Popular Front or Abu Nidal, got into the act. There were no attacks on U.S. soil. In the murky world of counterterrorism, where success is judged by what does not happen, the scorecard on Desert Storm reflected the worth of the CTC, the continuing education of a former FBI director turned DCI, and the cumulative work of dedicated liaison officers, from Papich to Aldhizer to Campbell, who for decades had been working to make relations as good as they were, when all the chips were down.

CHAPTER NINETEEN

THE FALL OF BABYLON

DESPITE CTC'S UNDENIABLY impressive performance during Desert Storm, Webster himself did not come out of the war quite so well. Although CIA had foiled terrorists, and provided some good tactical data—including precise targeting for bombing runs against Iraqi nuclear installations—General Norman Schwarzkopf had complained about a lack of strategic insight on Iraqi intentions. Even Webster's longtime defender, Senator Boren, griped that "The war might have been avoided if the President had been told six months earlier that this man is thinking of invading his neighbors."

In fact, a CIA analyst had predicted the Kuwait invasion in June, and a warning was conveyed to the White House on August 1, only hours before Saddam attacked. But Webster had not lobbied too hard for that intelligence, perhaps out of fear that this would involve him in policy. Webster often maintained that "It is not our role to shape the policy," and his view on that was so strong that when Bush and his national security advisers started talking about policy matters, Webster insisted on leaving the room. The DCI held that his job was simply to collect and disseminate intelligence—and so, indeed, he had supplied the White House with information about the invasion before it occurred. But because the intelligence had not been prioritized, stressed, or otherwise pushed by Webster, the president's national security advisers had not interpreted it as anything like a warning. This "facts-and-only-the-facts" approach struck some as being pretty close to the old Hoover-style FBI refusal to analyze intelligence or recommend actions, so as to not be blamed for any outcome. The White House was said to want someone with better, or broader, foreign policy knowledge—or, failing that, someone who would go out on analytical limbs.

Some insiders felt that Webster was being made the fall guy for prewar U.S. coddling of Saddam; others saw the quiet hand of former CIA Deputy Director Robert Gates, then serving as assistant to National Security Adviser Brent Scowcroft. Gates had become a welcome member of the Bush-Baker inner circle, and there was a sense that Bush, whose managerial style emphasized personal relationships, would not mind seeing Gates take over CIA.

But perhaps the greatest perceived fault in Webster's tenure was pointed up when the Soviets unexpectedly backed American Gulf policy. Although Moscow maintained more than a thousand military advisers in Iraq, and refused to commit forces for the invasion, the U.S. and the Soviets seemed to be allies for the first time since 1945. In this New World Order, CIA was somewhat "behind events," as Webster conceded. Soviet leader Mikhail Gorbachev had always seemed an inscrutable mystery, and CIA analysts found it impossible to predict what he might do. When he visited the United States in December 1987, an FBI-CIA Courtship task force had gone to elaborate, even absurd lengths to figure him out. He was secretly photographed at cocktail parties by waist cameras disguised as belt buckles, and CIA lip-readers studied hours of FBI films, hoping to decipher any confidential asides to his aides. But no one picked him up saying anything like "I'm going to let Eastern Europe go," and CIA was widely chastised for not seeing what was to come. "For a generation, the Central Intelligence Agency told successive presidents everything they needed to know about the Soviet Union," said Senator Daniel Patrick Moynihan, "except that it was about to fall apart."

Leading Sovietologists both inside and outside CIA seemed baffled indeed by the disarray, for their traditional method of analysis had yielded virtually no clues as to what Gorbachev would do. When the new Soviet leader had assumed power in February 1985 after the death of Konstantin Chernenko, analysts like Roy Medvedev preoccupied themselves with trivial details in the Soviet press, and gained no larger view. "The black mourning frame printed around the second page [where the deceased leader's picture was run] looked rather narrow," Medvedev observed. "It was only half the width of the frame used for Brezhnev and Andropov (3 millimeters rather than 6). It was still, however, a millimeter broader than the frames used for the second-page announcements of the death of senior Politburo members like Marshal Ustinov, who had died a few months previously." There was nothing in the measurement of picture frames to suggest liberalization in the USSR; therefore, no one suggested it.

CIA's top leadership acknowledged that it had fallen short in predicting Gorbachev's reforms, but could provide no real excuse. "Who would have thought that just five years ago we would stand where we are today?" Robert Gates told Congress in late 1991. "Talk about humbling experiences." Gates could have said: Our reporting was poor because our Moscow network was rolled up, coincidentally or not, precisely as Gorbachev was coming into power. Gates did not say this, however. Instead, he suggested that "We're here to help you think through the problem rather than give you some kind of crystal ball prediction." This anti-prediction line was echoed by the Agency's deputy director, Robert Kerr, who told Congress: "Our business is to provide enough understanding of the issue . . . to say here are some possible outcomes. . . . And I think that's the role of intelligence, not to predict outcomes in clear, neat ways. Because that's not doable."

Yet someone *had* predicted glasnost and perestroika, in detail, even before Gorbachev came to power. This person's analysis of events in the communist world had even been provided to the Agency on a regular basis. But the American intelligence community had chosen not to listen— and the roots of that willful deafness could be traced back, ultimately, thirty years, to a series of developments that caused a clash of mind-sets between CIA and FBI.

In 1982, KGB defector Anatoliy Golitsyn had submitted a top-secret manuscript to CIA. In it, he foresaw that leadership of the USSR would by 1986 "or earlier" fall to "a younger man with a more liberal image," who would initiate "changes that would have been beyond the imagination of Marx or the practical reach of Lenin and unthinkable to Stalin." The coming liberalization, Golitsyn said, "would be spectacular and impressive. Formal pronouncements might be made about a reduction in the Communist Party's role; its monopoly would be apparently curtailed. . . . The KGB would be reformed. Dissidents at home would be amnestied; those in exile abroad would be allowed to take up positions in the government. Sakharov might be included in some capacity in the government. . . . Political clubs would be opened to nonmembers of the Communist Party. Leading dissidents might form one or more alternative political parties. Censorship would be relaxed; controversial books, plays, films, and art would be published, performed, and exhibited."

Golitsyn provided an entire chapter of such predictions, containing 194 distinct auguries. Of these, 46 were not falsifiable at the time this book went to press (whether, e.g., Russian "economic ministries" will "be dissolved," it's too early to tell) and another 9 (e.g., Yugoslavia's "prominent role" in East-Bloc liberalization) seemed clearly wrong. Yet of Golitsyn's falsifiable predictions, 139 out of 148 were fulfilled by the end of 1993—an accuracy rate of nearly 94 percent. Among events correctly foreseen: "the return to power of Dubcek and his associates" in Czechoslovakia; the "reemergence of Solidarity" and the formation of a "coalition government" in Poland; a newly "independent" regime in Romania; "economic reforms" in the USSR; and a Soviet repudiation of the Afghanistan invasion. Golitsyn even envisioned that, with the "easing of immigration controls" by East Germany, "pressure could well grow for the solution of the German problem [by] some form of confederation between East and West"—with the result that "demolition of the Berlin Wall might even be contemplated."

Golitsyn received CIA's permission to publish his manuscript in book form, and did so in 1984. But at the time his predictions were made, Sovietologists had little use for Golitsyn or his "new methodology for the study of the communist world." For the man who had once been ridiculed at CIA's infamous "Flat Earth Conference" for claiming that the Sino-Soviet split was false, it must have seemed yet another classic case of "They all laughed at Christopher Columbus." John C. Campbell, reviewing Golitsyn's book in *Foreign Affairs*, politely recommended that it "be taken with several grains of salt," while other critics complained that Golitsyn's analysis "strained credulity" and was "totally inaccurate," or became so exercised as to accuse him of being the "demented" proponent of "cosmic theories." The University of North Carolina's James R. Kuhlman declared that Golitsyn's new methodology would "not withstand rigorous examination"; in the *London Review of Books*, Oxford historian R. W. Johnson dismissed Golitsyn's views as "nonsense." British journalist Tom Mangold even went so far as to say, in 1990—*after* Golitsyn's prescience had become clear—that "As a crystal-ball gazer, Golitsyn has been unimpressive." Mangold reached this conclusion by listing six of Golitsyn's apparently incorrect predictions and ignoring the 139 correct ones.

Golitsyn's analysis was as little appreciated within CIA as it was in the outside world. "Unfortunate is the only term for this book," an Agency reader noted in an official 1985 review. A CIA analyst took Golitsyn to task for making "unsupported allegations without sufficient (or sometimes any) evidence," and for this reason would be "embarrassed to recommend the whole." Golitsyn's case was deductive, based on pattern-recognition and abstract principles; he had no transcript of a secret session in which Gorbachev said he would do all these things. Therefore, his predictions did not need to be taken seriously.

There had been a time, of course, when CIA's conception of "evidence" was considerably less legalistic. This alternate conception, which came out of British literary criticism, had governed OSS/CIA counterintelligence for roughly thirty years, from 1943 to 1973. It had caused considerable conflict between FBI and CIA, in such matters as molehunts and disputes over the bona fides of defectors. Questions about the legitimacy of Yuri Nosenko or the loyalty of Igor Orlov were, to the FBI, only "unsupported allegations without sufficient (or sometimes any) evidence." The FBI's refusal to side with CIA on such questions had limited CI chief James Angleton's ability to prove his suspicions about penetrations, false defectors, and possible KGB complicity in the killing of JFK. The result had been an increase in FBI-CIA tensions, an interagency feud over Golitsyn, a decrease in Angleton's popularity at both agencies, the decentralization of his CI staff, and then his outright dismissal. The clash between Angletonian and Hooverian CI paradigms had then been resolved in a way which remade CIA counterintelligence philosophy according to the simple and direct methodology of the FBI.

If it had been otherwise—if CIA had not lost the war of philosophies to the Bureau; if the FBI had accepted Golitsyn; if Angleton's looser conception of evidence had survived at CIA into the 1980s—the Agency would have perhaps been sensitized to Golitsyn and what he had to say. As it was, however, the defector had been put out to pasture after Angleton left, with a part-time consulting arrangement. He was free to send in "crank memos" and to publish his predictions in a book, but no one at CIA paid him much mind. After all, Golitsyn saw Soviet reforms as part of the Leninist disinformation strategy conceived back in 1959. For the strategy to succeed, the KGB would have to have so deeply deceived and penetrated CIA, with false defectors and moles, that it could effectively control American intelligence. But most at CIA discounted the possibility of false defectors, and there was still no firm proof of any mole. And perhaps most fundamentally, as the philosopher William James once noted, "we tend to disbelieve all facts and theories for which we have no use." Who had any use, in the end, for Golitsyn's belief that the coming glasnost and perestroika would merely constitute the "final phase" of a long-term KGB strategy to "dominate the world"?

One of Golitsyn's predictions, however, could not be ignored, even if one rejected all else he said. This was his observation that "Liberalization in Eastern Europe on the scale suggested could have a social and political impact on the United States itself." Specifically, "anticommunism would be undermined," while Western institutions that owed their existence to the perception of a communist threat, such as NATO and the U.S. intelligence community, "could hardly survive this process." As Gorbachev himself put it in 1987, perestroika was "tantamount to an ideological catastrophe" for the West, because "it frustrat[ed] the chances of using the 'Soviet threat' bugbear, of shadowing the real image of our country with a grotesque and ugly 'enemy image.' " Gorbachev's key adviser Georgi Arbatov was even more explicit about what the Soviets planned. "We are going to do something terrible to you," he told U.S. journalists. "We are going to take away your enemy. The 'image of the enemy' that is being eroded has been absolutely vital for the foreign and military policy of the U.S. and its allies. The destruction of this stereotype is Gorbachev's secret weapon."

As the Soviet Empire fragmented during the late 1980s, U.S. policy professionals began to agree with Arbatov's claim that, in light of developments in the communist world, "America also needs perestroika." Many journalists and politicians now believed that the apparent disappearance of the communist threat made it necessary to reorganize American intelligence. In this new climate, Webster was widely criticized for failing to redefine the Agency's mission.

In April 1991, a year and half after the East Bloc nations (to quote Angleton's favorite poem) "whirled in fractured atoms beyond the circuit of the shuddering Bear," Webster did create a special task force to study what new threats might require CIA attention. But when no new paradigm was found, Senate Intelligence Committee staffers griped that Webster was more interested in his morning tennis matches than in working to refine a "vision." That was probably an unfair rap, since any DCI inevitably looked to the White House for clues to the content of formal change, and Bush himself had long been criticized, even before his election as president, for "the vision thing." The problem ran even deeper than Bush; the plain fact was that U.S. statesmen had been increasingly pragmatic and aphilosophical ever since the Civil War, and America's intelligence community, as its foreign policy, had consequently been passive and reactive until aroused by events. The U.S. had been as unprepared for Saddam's invasion of Kuwait as for the bombing of Pearl Harbor, and as surprised by the enslavement of Eastern Europe as by its liberation. Not until well after each new cataclysm occurred could any coherent new "vision" be produced. When it did not come overnight, the DCI was blamed.

Within CIA ranks, meanwhile, some officers still worried that "Mild Bill" Webster wanted them to uncloak their daggers. Despite his flexibility on legal matters during the Gulf War, some clandestine veterans were bitter about a return to strict clearance procedures. They also complained that Webster didn't do enough to help the disbandment of the Agency's Afghan rebels, and that he was still ignorant, after four years, about key details in the secret world. In some areas that latter charge was plainly false—Webster knew SCUD missiles cold, and could discourse at length about "krytons," used to make triggers for nuclear bombs. In fact, as will be seen, one of the reasons that Webster knew so much about nuclear nonproliferation was that CIA, fearing that legal action might jeopardize sources on Iraq's atomic research, had failed to forward certain data to the FBI. But for the most part Webster did tend toward openness and full liaison, and critics argued that this often conflicted with the DCI's duty to protect secret methods and sources. Sometimes the United States fell down quite hard on that score: in October 1989, two undercover agents, working inside Syria for Jordanian intelligence, were killed by terrorists after their identities were compromised in a diplomatic exchange with Syria. Although in one sense the U.S. was simply conducting good liaison, and may have saved the American ambassador from assassination, the episode also showed that liaison was only as good as the party with whom one liaised—a truth J. Edgar Hoover had applied too often, and Webster perhaps not often enough.

Sensitive to the political weather after thirteen years in Washington, and satisfied but tired from restoring luster to two directorships, Webster resigned in July 1991. McGregor, Hotis, Baker, and his other aides were going or were already gone, but the Webster legacy would survive them. If the "skin graft" had been rejected by the Agency's operational elite, FBI and CIA had nevertheless been joined at the waist, albeit loosely, in the new "fusion center," CIC, and had been linked more tightly in the CTC. But above all, Webster had broken the spell of Casey, who for all his popularity in the DDO had put Langley under the old Chinese curse: "May you live in interesting times." Whenever CIA became too interesting to Congress, or to the public at large, trouble had always followed; but for four years Webster had kept things fairly dull, at least to the outside world. Considering the situation when he arrived, with CIA officers being grilled about Iran-contra on national television, that was probably more than enough, on the ledger sheet, to make up for his failure to invent a new moral compass for American spies.

To define such a vision, however, would be the overriding task of Webster's successor, Robert Gates. Gates would make some good progress in this sphere, assisted by the larger drift of world events. But his efforts would be cut short by a single cancerous lack of liaison, which had occurred on Webster's watch.

IF BILL CASEY HAD BEEN a reincarnation of Donovan, Gates was the second coming of Richard Helms. Although Gates was an analyst from CIA's Directorate of Intelligence, Helms an operative from the clandestine service, both had risen from within to replace less popular outsiders (Raborn, Webster). Like Helms, Gates was well educated but not personally wealthy; the son of a Wichita auto-parts salesman, he took a history major at the College of William and Mary, then drove to Washington in summer 1966 with everything he owned in the back of a Mustang, joining CIA just as Helms became director. Both men were personally cold and professionally driven. Gates had small blue eyes, pale skin, and few interests outside of work; everything about him seemed to symbolize unswerving purpose. A jogger like Helms, he rose before dawn to run on the streets near his home in the Virginia suburbs, and his office was adorned with busts of Churchill and FDR. Neither DCI was bound by ideology; Helms had worked with both Lyndon Johnson and Richard Nixon, and Gates was known as a "chameleon" because of his ability to adapt. During most of the 1980s, he had been one of Casey's favorite right-wing hawks, but before and after that he was a member of the pragmatical "Kissinger Mafia," working closely with Kissinger protégé Brent Scowcroft. Finally, both Helms and Gates would end their public careers in trouble with Congress, trying to counter accusations that CIA had broken the law.

Gates' tenure as DCI even began that way. Originally nominated in 1987, when Casey fell ill, Gates had withdrawn after the confirmation hearings became embroiled in questions about his own actions in Iran-contra. Gates was careful to woo the Senate Intelligence Committee the second time around, but in July 1990 the senators delayed confirmation hearings for two months while again researching the question of whether Gates had any role in the Iran-contra affair. Although testimony in late September suggested that Gates had some early warning about Oliver North's mischief, no damning evidence was found. The Senate approved him by 64 to 31, in a clear victory for President Bush, and on November 12, 1991, Gates was sworn in.

Taking over at Langley, Gates was immediately challenged by accusations that CIA was an "obsolete tool," a Cold War relic whose functions could be better handled by other agencies. Senator Daniel Patrick Moynihan even introduced a bill calling for the Agency to be disbanded. As Gates' spokesmen scrambled to identify new enemies to justify their work, one senior official said CIA was now worried about "green menaces," such as global warming and "hazardous waste disposal." Those claims were justly derided, but other new threats soon convinced most critics that "the world remains a very rough neighborhood," as Gates would say. Most of the newly perceived dangers had domestic and foreign aspects, and countering those threats would thus require close liaison between CIA and FBI.

• • •

THE FIRST NEW THREAT was actually an old one. Russian attorney Dmitri Afanasiev said that "the KGB was abolished after Yeltsin took over," but this was not true. United States newspaper editors believed it was true, for there were headlines like "KGB Network Grinds to Halt," "Gorbachev strips KGB of duties," and, on the front page of *The New York Times Magazine*, "Closing Down the KGB." Even William Sessions believed the hype, and announced plans to shift thirteen hundred agents from counter-KGB work to the Bureau's Criminal Division. In fact, the KGB had not been closed down at all. Its classic espionage functions, and most of its foreign spy staff, had merely been transferred to a new unit, the SVR (Sluzhba Vneshnoi Razvedki, or External Intelligence Service). The chief of the new service, Yevgeny Primakov, claimed that he would not spy against the West, but in 1992 seven Russian intelligence defectors told otherwise. In London, SVR Colonel Viktor Ochenko tipped MI6 to fifty Russian spies. In Paris, Ochenko's leads uncovered Russian penetration of a French nuclear site. In Rome, authorities broke up a ring of twenty-eight SVR agents, the largest Moscow-based network ever revealed in Europe. In Berlin, an employee of the U.S. mission was arrested for helping the Russians target U.S. Air Force personnel. In Brussels, five SVR agents were arrested for compromising a NATO battlefield communications system, as well as secret data on the U.S. space shuttle. And in the United States, a Russian intelligence defector was doling out leads to many hundreds of Americans, possibly more than a thousand, who had been spying for Gorbachev and Yeltsin. Among these spies, American counterintelligence officials came to believe, was a well-placed Soviet agent in Langley.

Clues to his identity came from an unexpected source. After the breaching of the Berlin Wall in November 1989, West German officials captured many secret documents from the East German intelligence service, known as the Stasi. When German security police shared some of the take with the FBI, Bureau intelligence chief Doug Gow was shocked by how effective the Stasi had been. The East Germans had recruited Bonn's top CI officer as a mole; successfully hidden for fifteen years Illich Ramirez Sanchez, the international terrorist known as "Carlos the Jackal"; and even had in their pay a waiter who served President Reagan on a visit to West Berlin. They also seemed to have excellent sources on the internal workings of American intelligence—entirely too excellent, Gow believed.

Although there was no hard evidence of treason, Gow had allowed Campbell to share the files with CIA. After a year, the documents had produced leads on about a dozen American spy suspects, including several within the U.S. government. Gow told reporters in October 1990, "I would think that there are probably a few Americans that are very worried right now."

But for those who did have cause to worry, bureaucracy bought some time. From the very start, CIA and FBI argued over which agency would preside over examination of the Stasi trove. "There was infighting and jockeying," one intelligence official would remember. "It took time to hammer out all the rules. There were personality conflicts." There were also piddling disputes over uniform standards for data retrieval, just as there had been thirty-five years earlier in CODIB, Angleton's attempt to computerize German intelligence files captured from the Nazis. For months, no one could agree on whether the data should be stored on CDs or diskettes. And when agents from the FBI's Washington Field Office tried to run down one live lead, they were stymied by CIA's station chief in Bonn. The station chief, whom his British colleagues dubbed "the poison dwarf," reportedly rebuffed FBI agents' requests for important files and human sources. Robert "Bear" Bryant, the head of the FBI field office, asked his bosses to approve an obstruction-of-justice investigation of the station chief, but his request was turned down.

The bickering was hushed only when German officials came forward with additional information that shamed and shocked everyone. Over the last decade, Bonn said, communist counterspies had identified, exposed, or otherwise compromised every CIA agent in East Germany. More troubling still was that the Stasi had not bothered to shut these sources down, but instead had used them to channel disinformation. Even CIA's less paranoid executives doubted that such massive deception could have been pulled off without an "inside" source who could both pinpoint CIA agents and help steer the Stasi's lying.

CIA finally agreed to join the FBI in a full inquiry. To smooth out the cooperative effort, Gates lunched in November 1991 with Attorney General William P. Barr in the director's dining room at Langley. Through Campbell's mediation a compromise was reached, granting both agencies equal access to the German files, and leading eventually to creation of a joint task force.

The Bureau contingent was headed by Leslie Wiser, a special agent supervisor at the Washington Field Office. The CIA side was overseen by Chief/CI Ted Price, who candidly presented Wiser with evidence of a whole string of CIA losses. Wiser had expected a grim picture, but was shocked to learn just how bad things were. In 1991, the Soviets had caught and killed perhaps the most valuable agent CIA had ever placed in Russian intelligence. The U.S. mole, code-named GT/PROLOGUE, had been head of the American targets section of the KGB's Second Chief Directorate (counterintelligence)—the senior Soviet official in Moscow responsible for catching American spies. Wiser began using CIC computers to comb for patterns. He cross-indexed the names of those CIA officials who had known about the Stasi agents, as well as about GT/PROLOGUE and other cases that had gone bad—Tolkachev, Motorin, Martynov, Gordievsky, Yurchenko, Howard, Bloch. Was there any common denominator?

There was more than one. Roughly two hundred people had not only known the identities of the Stasi agents but had also been privy to one or more earlier failed operations against the Soviet Union. To whittle down the list, investigators queried the defectors who came over in 1992. Unsolved cases from the Stasi files and the defectors began to merge. It became clear that a small group of officers in CIA's Soviet Division and CI Staff had been involved in most or all of the compromised operations. As in 1967 and 1986, all the suspects were quietly transferred. Among them was Rick Ames, the CIA officer who had originally vetted Vitaliy Yurchenko and pronounced him bona fide. Since returning from Rome in 1989, Ames had been made chief of the Soviet Europe Division's Czechoslovak branch. Now he was moved to a less sensitive post, the Black Sea section at CIA's Counter Narcotics Center.

Like the other suspects, Ames was polygraphed. During the first round of questions, his graph showed a jump, suggesting deception, when he was asked if he was withholding any financial information from the government. When the examiners confronted him with that result, he claimed to be distracted by some personal money matters. The explanation was accepted, and the next day Ames was "fluttered" again on the machine. During this second round, Ames did not get the graph totally level, which would have indicated truthfulness, but he did lower it. Like the other suspects, Ames was passed.

Still, CI experts had begun to doubt the reliability of machine-based deception testing. Recently it had been learned that for over twenty years, most U.S spies in Cuba, although they passed polygraphs, had been under Castro's control. German double-agents had also beat the machine. So Wiser and Price could not rule out the possibility that a long-feared mole was among those who had passed the most recent round of lie-detector tests. CIC therefore began dealing "marked cards"—bits of distinctive intelligence—to each of the suspects, to see whether the information made its way to Moscow. If, for instance, only one suspect was given information that a "national" (nonexistent) agent was to meet his handlers at a certain street corner, and the Russians showed up to surveill the meeting, the leak could be traced easily backwards, to the mole.

WHILE THE HUNTERS patiently waited for their prey to spring the trap, Gates was preoccupied for most of 1992 with a dramatic rise in economic spying. Ferreting out French spies in IBM had only been an overture. The intelligence apparat of Matsushita, a Japanese multinational corporation, occupied two floors of a Manhattan skyscraper. Other Japanese firms were bribing executives and recruiting graduate students. New Moscow-based "business ventures," staffed disproportionately with "former" KGB agents, were also targeting technological and economic secrets. The advent of these "friendly spies" only confirmed what Angleton's researcher Raymond Rocca had said years before: that there were "no friendly services . . . only services of friendly foreign powers." Gates believed that nearly twenty governments overall were spying on American business, some by hiring out-of-work spies from Eastern Europe. "We know that foreign intelligence services plant moles in our high-tech companies," he told Congress. "We know that they rifle briefcases of our businessmen who travel in their countries. . . . and I think that the CIA and FBI working together should take a very aggressive program against it."

But working together in economic CI posed special dangers. When the Bureau determined that American companies or businessmen were being spied on overseas, Campbell had to share those data with CIA. The Agency then had to brief U.S. firms and seek their cooperation in tracing leaks or setting traps. Yet some business executives worried that, if they got help in rooting out moles, the Agency would come back later and demand spying or cover arrangements in return. Meanwhile, whenever CIA suspected that an American concern was being targeted in the U.S., it was supposed to take those suspicions to Campbell at the FBI. But the Bureau needed an entirely new and different database to track economic espionage. Until it developed one, cases had to be pursued with ordinary police fieldwork—and without warrantless peeks into the briefcases of foreign executives, whom the FISA classified as "U.S. persons" the instant they stepped onto American soil. When the FBI briefed American firms on operations against them, the information had to be generic enough to protect CIA sources and methods, but specific enough to permit corrective action. Even then, retribution was constrained by foreign policy. Neither CIA nor State—nor, for that matter, American companies—wanted to start a trade war. Given all the interagency angles, congressmen were naturally worried when Gates and Sessions testified on commercial espionage at a congressional hearing in April 1992. "Government agencies are just as persnickety as individuals are," Representative Bill Brooks warned his colleagues. "They're suspicious of each other, just like they are foreign governments."

GATES HAD INITIALLY HOPED that some structural reforms might make cooperation easier. In February 1992, he backed a plan by Senator Boren to "bring about the most sweeping changes in the U.S. intelligence community since the CIA was created in 1947"—and to narrow, in the bargain, the wedge between CIA and FBI. The proposal called for a new National Intelligence Center, a "world-class think-tank," headed by a director of national intelligence, the DNI, to whom CIA's director and the FBI's Intelligence Division would both report.

But if the plan promised to reduce internecine conflict, it also provoked public fears. When leaked to the press, on February 5, 1992, it produced scare headlines of a sort that had not been seen since February 1945, when Donovan's proposed CIA plan was attacked as an "American Gestapo." As previously, it was a politically conservative paper, concerned about "big government," that sounded the alarm. "Senator's Plan Calls for Intelligence 'Czar,'" the Washington *Times* warned in a front-page banner headline. This new czar and his trench-coated Cossacks would have "control over both domestic and foreign counterspying." Even though this would mean that agencies were "compelled to cooperate," various authorities were quoted as saying it was a bad idea. Soviet intelligence defector Stanislav Levchenko urged that domestic and foreign intelligence be kept separate, "to avoid creating anything remotely similar to the KGB."

Senator Boren backpedaled. He said he was not proposing that CIA snoop on Americans, but merely that the new DNI would control the Bureau's counterintelligence budget. Nevertheless, press coverage continued to play up the specter of a national secret police, showing just how sensitive the idea of domestic spying remained in the American mind. Boren's plan died, as did a virtually identical proposal introduced two months later by Gates.

With no fundamental changes in the offing, Gates was still left with the problem of how to close interagency gaps. For instance, when the Bureau tried to block the visa for a Russian UN employee, suspecting he was the new RIS station chief or *rezident*, CIA protested that the Soviets would reciprocally block replacement of America's Moscow station chief, who was nearing completion of his three-year stint. When the FBI complained about loosened travel regulations for Soviet arms-control inspectors in the U.S., CIA countered that parallel privileges for Western arms inspectors in Russia were more than worth the tradeoff. And around the time Webster announced his retirement, Campbell had to calm tempers when Bureau CI agents on surveillance in New York City wound up photographing a CIA officer working the same subject. "It was not what I would call an unusual occurrence," an exasperated FBI official said.

But perhaps the principal spur to Gates was his own admission, during confirmation hearings, that CIA had made mistakes in disseminating information to government agencies about the Bank of Commerce and Credit International (BCCI). Known to regulators as the "Bank of Crooks and Criminals," BCCI fostered a global looting operation that bilked depositors of billions of dollars, but its seizure in August 1991 revealed that the Pakistan-based bank had also run a global intelligence operation, complete with a Mafia-like enforcement squad operating out of Karachi. Called the "black network" by its own members, it offered a self-proclaimed Federal Express service for the delivery of whores, gold, arms, drugs, bribes, extortions, kidnappings, and murders. The network aided Iraqi nuclear smuggling with fake letters of credit and false customs valuations, which constituted one source of CIA interest in BCCI. With the probable complicity of BCCI's president, former Saudi intelligence chief Kamal Adham, the bank briefed CIA on Iraqi transactions, as well as on those of another client, the Abu Nidal terrorist group. And BCCI's Panama City branch had hidden "slush funds" disbursed by CIA to Noriega for various covert projects, such as anti-Sandinista rebels in Nicaragua. In exchange for BCCI's assistance on such matters, CIA had apparently refrained from reporting various BCCI transgressions to financial regulators and law-enforcement agencies. Senate investigators did learn that in 1988 Gates, as deputy director of CIA, had informed U.S. Customs about the bank's role in money laundering. But no memos had been disseminated to the FBI, which had the domestic bank-fraud role, even though CIA knew that BCCI owned First American, a Washington bank. James Nolan believed that "CIA, on BCCI, was hampered by its foreign-targets mind-set. No one thought to say, They've got a branch in downtown Washington, what the hell is that?" Senate investigator Jack Blum was somewhat harsher, alleging that CIA had engineered "an enormous coverup."

After the BCCI imbroglio, Gates announced that an Agency task force had completed a study on coordination with law enforcement. He would not disclose the study's findings, but on April 1, 1992, newspapers reported that CIA was implementing unspecified "procedures" to keep the Bureau informed about possible illegalities, and "to make the scandal-prone agency more accountable, to avoid another Iran-Contra affair." Even as this announcement was made, however, poor FBI-CIA coordination in another bank-fraud investigation was already provoking a new

Iran-contra—type scandal, affecting the course of a presidential election, and jeopardizing one of the most successful covert initiatives of all time.

BEFORE HE WAS FIRED in 1974, James Angleton had joined an initiative with Israeli and British intelligence to prevent Iraq, a Soviet client-state, from building an atomic bomb. Known within the Mossad as Operation Babylon, the project aimed to recruit human sources within Saddam Hussein's nuclear program, and thus to monitor Iraqi progress, so that any punitive actions would proceed from a firm base of knowledge. Where possible, Babylon would even help Iraq buy, smuggle, and assemble the materials for its nuclear program, the better to hurt those efforts later on. To protect sources, a blind eye would be turned toward certain illegalities, if this meant keeping a window on what Saddam was doing. "Jim [Angleton] regarded intelligence as essentially amoral," Angleton's chief of operations, Scotty Miler, would recall. "You can't get in among black hats with a white hat."

Babylon survived Angleton, and by the early 1980s its sources reported that Saddam was getting quite close to actually producing a nuclear device. Aided by CIA satellite intelligence, Israel unleashed a surgical air strike against Iraq's main reactor at Osirak, destroying it on June 7, 1981. Saddam's quest for the bomb had been set back by perhaps a decade, but the Iraqi dictator did not give up his nuclear dreams, and while submerging himself through most of the 1980s in a costly war against Iran, he vowed to conceal and decentralize his new A-bomb projects, so that they could never again be destroyed by a single strike. Huge "industrial" complexes were erected throughout Iraq, many covering thousands of acres. The Agency had plenty of satellite photos of those establishments, but, given strict travel restrictions in Iraq, they had little intelligence about exactly what was going on inside.

To find out, CIA turned to its National Collection Division (NCD), a special component of the Operations Directorate created in 1982 to recruit assets in the international business community. By debriefing those who traveled to or did deals with Iraq, NCD developed extensive files on Saddam's new military projects. Some of the NCD's "non-official cover" operatives, as they were called, operated far from embassies and CIA stations, without diplomatic immunity, and CIA would not acknowledge any links to them. As one senior intelligence officer would put it, "That's about as hairy as it gets." Among the sources accessed were officials at banks used by Iraqi intelligence, including the London branch of BCCI, which was using false customs declarations to assist Iraqi nuclear smuggling.

But the bank that really gave a window on Iraqi procurement was the Atlanta branch of Italy's Banco Lavoro Nazionale (BNL). Since BNL was foreign-owned, the U.S. had legal authority to intercept its communications, and began doing so in 1986. It was learned that many Iraqi entities had almost daily contact with the bank, and that one BNL employee was especially close to Saddam Hussein's son-in-law, Hussein Kamil, who supervised Iraq's nuclear efforts. Kamil was furnishing "shopping lists" to Matrix-Churchill Ltd., a struggling British machine-tools company which Iraq covertly purchased with BNL loans in fall 1987. Matrix officials, in turn, used BNL funds to purchase prefab fiberglass factories, carbide-tipped inserts for machine tools, even a copy of a research thesis by Albert Einstein.

Those transactions were monitored not only by CIA but by MI6, which learned from other sources that Saddam had ordered an all-out push to develop nuclear weapons, to be used on an Iranian city in a "grand-slam" reminiscent of Hiroshima and Nagasaki. Stepping up its antiproliferation efforts with CIA and the Mossad, MI6 recruited three top Matrix executives to be double agents for British intelligence. The major informant was Paul Henderson, who had spied for Western secret services since the 1970s, when he frequently traveled behind the Iron Curtain on business. Upon returning from his various trips to Iraq, Henderson was chauffeured to a London safehouse, where MI6 officers debriefed him about Iraq's nuclear progress.

CIA received "raw" (unanalyzed) reports from Henderson and the other moles, and though for security reasons the U.S. would be kept ignorant of the agents' identities, the Agency was to play the lead role in piecing together and exploiting their "take." In keeping with the Babylon strategy set down by Angleton fifteen years before, CIA decided to play along, to let Saddam get the technology, until such time as another Israeli raid or other punitive actions would be deemed necessary. Shutting down the BNL-Matrix operation would only cause Saddam to set up a new one, which would probably not be known to the West. A crackdown might also endanger the moles within Saddam's network. Such worries were very much on the minds of the moles' controllers, who, according to one British government memo, knew "from secret sources" that Matrix equipment might be used "in uranium enrichment for the development of nuclear weapons," but approved such exports to Iraq "because of the need to protect these sources."

By August 1989, CIA reports revealed a detailed knowledge of Saddam's nuclear efforts. Because the Iraqi effort was so highly centralized in Matrix and BNL, and because CIA and MI6 had penetrated both entities, the Iraqi network was as visible to Western intelligence as the glass-bisected tunnels of Webster's proverbial ant farm. Analysts knew many of the precise locations of the high-tech caves where uranium-enrichment projects were under way, and BNL/Matrix sources tipped CIA whenever equipment was moved. Even better intelligence was promised by the prospect of a Matrix office in Baghdad, which would put CIA and MI6 right in the middle of Saddam's nuclear mischief. The Agency did worry that Saddam's secret networks would become even more complex, making it more difficult to monitor their spread. But as long as BNL funds kept flowing to Saddam, and Matrix-Churchill kept providing the technology, almost nothing could have happened without MI6 and CIA's knowing it.

Except, of course, a raid by the FBI.

THE FBI TEAM that raided BNL's Atlanta branch in August 1989 had been created by the U.S. Justice Department four months earlier, on March 22, in the attempt to pool resources against financial crime. Faced with a wash of failed S&L and bank-fraud cases, Justice had organized FBI agents, federal attorneys, and regulators into local fraud working groups. The Atlanta group had seen no action until a disgruntled BNL employee had tipped the Bureau to "off-the-books" loans. Before alerting its local fraud group, the FBI had put out feelers to the Treasury Department, the local Customs office, the Federal Reserve, and the U.S. attorney in Atlanta—but not to CIA.

Barbara Campbell would wish, in retrospect, that the FBI's Atlanta Field Office had asked her to run a check with the Agency. But she knew it was not feasible for agents working fraud cases, or other criminal matters, to clear every suspected wrongdoer routinely with CIA before making an arrest. The fraud unit would ask her to run a Langley check when agents suspected CIA links, but because the fraud unit was much less attuned to Agency interests than the Intelligence Division, its intuitions about Agency operations were generally poor. There was also a general doubt among criminal agents about whether the Agency would tell the FBI even if it *did* have an interest in a subject of investigation.

So the agents had not checked with CIA before bursting into the twentieth-floor offices of Atlanta's Gas and Light Tower, a few minutes after 5 p.m. on Friday, August 4, 1989. Pushing past stunned secretaries and receptionists at BNL, they went straight for the file cabinets, dumped all the folders onto the floor, and began scooping stray papers into plastic garbage bags. This evidence, and a set of secret gray books, revealed that BNL not only had illegally loaned over $4 billion to Iraq, but was also funding Iraqi nuclear procurement. One of the persons soon wanted for questioning by the FBI was Safia Al-Habobi, Kamil's deputy for nuclear programs.

Because of possible espionage implications, the FBI office in Atlanta kept its Foreign Counterintelligence desk in Washington advised of all developments. It was not long before FBI and Justice investigators began to worry that they might be blowing open some CIA operation. Greatest among the "stumbling blocks" to BNL prosecutions, according to one Justice Department memo, was "what knowledge and role, if any, the Central Intelligence Agency had or played in BNL dealings with foreign governments in general and Iraq more specifically." The U.S. attorney in Atlanta therefore inquired of CIA "Whether the unauthorized BNL-Atlanta funding was orchestrated, approved, or directed by any facet of the U.S. intelligence community prior to August 4, 1989," and whether CIA "had any knowledge of illegal activities at BNL" before the FBI's raid.

A year and a half later, CIA had still not replied. Various excuses were advanced by the Agency for this failure to assist the prosecution, including the idea that it had a faulty filing system. But as Thomas Powers has put it, "Adults need not linger over this explanation." The real reason for nondisclosure was that certain secret CIA reports, if relayed to Campbell or to Main Justice, might be publicly exposed at the trial of BNL's Atlanta branch manager, Christopher Drogoul. Some of these reports had come from sources in British intelligence, and could not be disseminated without violating the "third-agency rule," which stipulated that data passed from one spy service to another could be relayed to a third only with the originating agency's permission.

"CIA was uncomfortable with just what would be discoverable and what wouldn't," recalled one FBI agent who dealt with CIA officers in Rome, where most incidental intelligence on BNL was gathered. The FBI's two top men in Rome at the time were James Frier, the legal attaché, and his deputy, Robert Peter, who in 1987 had briefly succeeded Aldhizer as liaison to CIA. According to Peter and Frier, CIA's Rome station chief asked if he could discuss some of the BNL data he was sending to the U.S. In lunch-table conversations over a few glasses of wine, the FBI men tried to "educate CIA" about the rules of criminal investigation.

"This information is discoverable; this is exculpatory," Frier would remember telling the station chief. "The judge will have to get this."

"Well, it's classified," the station chief said.

"I don't care if it's classified," Frier insisted. "If the judge in Atlanta orders you to bring it in, you're going to have to bring it in. Go back to your own legal people and ask them. Don't count on me."

But the CIA man either did not understand the FBI's advice or did not accept it. He cabled Langley on November 17, 1989, to report that an FBI representative had recommended against submission of the report. Apparently the station chief believed, as did his superiors, that Agency reports would not be subject to discovery in a criminal case unless they had been formally disseminated outside CIA.

If, at this juncture, Agency legal staffers had examined carefully the Classified Information Procedures Act, they would have learned that, FBI counsel notwithstanding, CIA reports were discoverable even if not formally disseminated outside the Agency. They also might have learned from Rome Station that at least one of the reports in question had technically been disseminated outside CIA anyhow, simply by virtue of being shown to the FBI legal attaché. On the other hand, it was undoubtedly more difficult for Justice to "discover" documents which they did not know existed. A CIA desk officer therefore cabled back Rome Station and advised against disseminating secret data to Justice or the FBI. As the officer later said, "it's just as well to have fewer reports that are going to wind up in court."

The prospect of secrets being exposed in court was chilling indeed to CIA officers, as well as their allies in MI6. Not only might documents be submitted as evidence, but double agents like Henderson could be at risk from Iraqi assassins, if Saddam suspected through trial disclosures that they were spies. Technical collection projects—the bugging of BNL's telephone traffic—might also be revealed. The Agency could petition to keep sensitive information out of public purview, but there was no guarantee of success, and the price of failure was too great. As one CIA assessment put it: "The Agency cannot afford to submit so quickly to the preferences of other agencies when its own interests are at risk."

But even as CIA carried out a de-facto coverup in the BNL case, fallout from the precipitous FBI raid was moving matters into a more desperate and dangerous sphere. The BNL bust had dried up Iraq's single largest source of foreign capital. This meant not only that Saddam could no longer fund his nuclear projects, but that he might not be able to meet his foreign-debt payments, since he had been taking out loans to pay off loans. Unless he gained new revenue soon, such as from increased oil sales, the country would soon be bankrupt. So it was that, on August 2, 1990, Saddam sent tanks into oil-rich Kuwait.

Immediately after Iraq's invasion, CIA conducted a special Oval Office briefing on Iraq's nuclear capabilities and reported, based on BNL-Matrix sources, that Saddam was now believed to be only six months to two years from his first bomb. This briefing changed the way President Bush and his advisers viewed the Gulf crisis. It convinced them not only that armed intervention was necessary, but that it must occur before February 1991, when Iraq might conceivably become a nuclear power. CIA also apparently persuaded the administration that Saddam must not suspect BNL, Matrix, and other entities of being operated against him, lest he attempt to move uranium-enrichment equipment from compromised sites. While CIA's National Collection Division debriefed any international businessmen who might know about Saddam's nuclear projects, all had to proceed normally, as if the U.S. knew nothing. Indeed, law-enforcement officials in Atlanta later complained to Congress that Iraqi intelligence agents were permitted to leave the country, and Matrix-Churchill's Cleveland office was permitted to remain open for nearly three months after the invasion. Attorney General Richard L. Thornburgh cautioned congressional investigators that BNL was "a sensitive case with national security concerns," and Sessions, by now partly briefed on Operation Babylon, warned prosecutors that continued prying could cause "serious damage to a very sensitive and important case." The effect of this government pressure, as of CIA's stalling, was to delay indictments in the BNL case—and to safeguard the Agency's knowledge of Saddam's nuclear research.

With the U.S. and Britain thus obstructing justice for purposes of wartime need, Saddam was kept ignorant, and on Sunday, January 16, 1991, U.S. F-117A Stealth bombers swept north from Saudi Arabia, toward the juncture of the Tigris and Euphrates rivers. Precisely because CIA and MI6 assets had helped fund, build, and equip Saddam's nuclear establishment, and thereby penetrated it, allied bombers were able to target and destroy many of Iraq's nuclear facilities during the first forty-eight hours of allied bombing. The scorecard was by no means perfect, and a later congressional inquiry would chastise CIA for underestimating the scope of Saddam's nuclear research. But after the cease-fire, UN inspectors charged with dismantling Iraq's nuclear program were struck by the precision of the intelligence that the U.S. had obtained on Saddam's main atomic facility, Tuwaitha. Although most of the buildings in the complex proper were totally intact, the nuclear-research sectors—the radio-chemistry laboratory, reactor, and isotope separator—were simply *gone*.

Yet such intelligence coups, which the UN inspectors discovered throughout Iraq, came at great political cost. Congressman Henry B. Gonzalez, chairman of the House Banking Committee, had been looking into BNL since before the Gulf War. After asking CIA to release documents in the case, Gonzalez's chief investigator, Dennis Kane, was privately warned against "poking into a vital project—namely, a secret operation to prevent Iraq from getting nuclear bombs." But Kane and Gonzalez thought they smelled an attempt to cover up the Bush administration's prewar decision to "coddle, powder, and diaper Saddam."

Such rhetoric had not made the House Banking Committee popular with Webster, but Gates came in badly needing to prove something to Congress. So he did release to Gonzalez some CIA documents. Among them was a memo suggesting that BNL-Rome knew about Drogoul's illegal loans to Iraq. This memo had been a subject of CIA-FBI confusion in Rome, and it had not been disseminated to FBI headquarters or to Justice, as U.S. prosecutors realized on September 14, 1992. On that date, Gonzalez announced that CIA knew about Italian government complicity in BNL's illegal loans, but allowed Drogoul to stand trial on false charges that he had acted alone.

CIA was forced to concede that it had withheld documents, but claimed it had done so on the advice of the FBI. The Bureau denied this. By October, there had developed a three-way bureaucratic battle royal, with CIA, FBI, and Justice all trading accusations and launching inquiries. Sessions announced the FBI was undertaking its own probe of both CIA and the Justice Department in the case, and assured Senator Boren that this investigation would be "unfettered." But when Sessions had dinner that weekend with a highly placed friend, the friend warned him: word in the intelligence community was that Sessions had become a marked man when he ordered an independent FBI dig into the Italian bank's CIA links. "You'd better protect yourself," the friend said, "or you'll be gone." Three days later, the Justice Department announced that Sessions was being investigated by Justice for alleged ethics violations. In the press, anonymous government officials began attacking his competence to lead. His firing was only a matter of time.

For the moment, however, the main victim was not Sessions but President Bush. Only a year earlier, flush with his victory in the Gulf War, Bush had been riding a colossal 90-percent approval rating, the highest in American history. He had come to seem more vulnerable as the economy soured, but his Gulf victory still could hurt the newly named Democratic ticket, inasmuch as Bill Clinton had once evaded military service, and Al Gore had voted against Desert Storm. Any chance to deflate the Bush administration's victory pride, and take away the moral high ground on Iraq, would therefore serve the Democrats well. Indeed, as Republicans were quick to point out, Gonzalez's main allegations about a BNL "coverup" were made just before the Republican National Convention. Gore began accusing Bush of a "coverup bigger than Watergate," and "Iraq-Gate" attacks became a permanent part of Clinton's basic rally speech in late October, just as Bush was beginning to gain in the polls. In effect, Iraq-Gate allowed Democrats to turn the issue of "character," which Republican strategists had tried to use against Clinton, back against Bush. Even life-long conservatives like William Safire thought Bush was lying to the public over Iraq, and urged fellow Republicans to vote for Clinton.

Then the election was over; Bush had lost, and Iraq-Gate was gone from the headlines, almost as suddenly as it had appeared. The affair had coincided exactly with Clinton's run for the White House; afterward, the Democrats seemed strangely silent on the matter. In August 1993, they quietly disclosed the results of their own investigation, which found that neither Bush nor anyone else in his administration had done anything wrong.

CIA's image had meanwhile been badly battered, especially by the revelation that it had withheld documents. Gates remained strangely unwilling to defend the Agency's actions. The whole Iraq-Gate affair had stricken Langley, like the White House, with a kind of paralysis. Gates might have publicly disclosed that the FBI raid had threatened CIA-MI6 operations against Iraq's bomb, and that CIA had a right to prevent this from happening. He might have said that, just as police allow undercover agents to engage in illicit activities to protect their covers, and offer immunity to collaborators for purposes of rolling up large criminal empires, so, too, intelligence services have the right—indeed, the duty—to protect sources and methods that could save millions of lives from nuclear death, even where this means not providing full support for criminal prosecutions.

But Gates did not say anything of the sort, nor could he have. The very real possibility of Iraqi retaliation against Western agents—including MI6 moles like Paul Henderson—limited CIA's ability to extricate itself from the Iraq-Gate scandal, and prove its continuing relevance after the demise of the USSR, by admitting its penetration of Saddam's nuclear program. Gates also knew that some of Iraq's nuclear-related equipment remained hidden, and calculated that Matrix-BNL intelligence must be guarded jealously for possible use in future U.S. attacks. The wisdom of that policy was proved on January 17, 1993, when U.S. warships in the Persian Gulf launched forty-five Tomahawk missiles at the Zaafraynia nuclear facility, near Baghdad, destroying nuclear lathes that had been made by Matrix-Churchill, paid for by the Atlanta branch of BNL.

THREE DAYS BEFORE the Zaafraynia attack, CIA's inspector general presented Gates with the results of an internal Iraq-Gate inquiry. "The U.S. Intelligence Community and the U.S. Law Enforcement Community have developed in very different ways, under starkly different pressures, to respond to unique missions and objectives," CIA's inspector general wrote. "Some accommodations have been made on each side, yet the two have failed to address adequately the fundamental distinctions in their practices, procedures, and cultures." Given "the increasing intertwining of domestic and international interests," as evident in the BNL affair, CIA had to find "a way to both protect sources and methods and assist criminal prosecutions."

That sounded well and good, but the IG's prescriptions for undoing this Gordian knot, which had tied up counterintelligence since the Hoover-Donovan days, revealed that the overseers were at some distance from the problems they oversaw. CIA was to adopt a policy that "all relevant information" should be disclosed to federal authorities, "unless there is a legal basis to withhold information." But that *already was* the Agency's policy, even before Iraq-Gate. Unanswered was the question of what constituted a legal basis for withholding, which had been the problem in BNL. The IG also recommended that Gates form "a task force . . . for establishing Agency relationships with law enforcement personnel." The IG apparently did not realize that Gates had already created just such a task force, after the BCCI flap, fully a year before.

A report by the Senate Select Committee on Intelligence was somewhat more probing. After raising and then carefully stepping around the idea that CIA had wanted to protect "operational" information connected to BNL-Matrix, the report focused on themes of FBI-CIA conflict. Liaison between foreign intelligence and domestic security was marred by "numerous and significant 'disconnects.' " Unlike CIA's own inspector general, the senators at least knew of CIA's task force, but they doubted it would solve the problem. Needed was a more comprehensive review by the attorney general and the DCI, "in conjunction with the congressional oversight committees." Congress, in other words, did not want to be left out of any reform process. The committee report urged that CIA and FBI "address the desirability of new mechanisms . . . to ensure that appropriate coordination actually takes place," and suggested that officers at the operational level of each agency receive special training to make them sensitive to document-disclosure regulations. There might even be cause for "statutory change" to ensure that regulations for interface were obeyed and understood. Alas, like CIA's inspector general, the Senate authors were unable, or unwilling, to specify just what those regulations should be.

Gates publicly backed the Senate report, and ordered the CIA to develop guidelines for possible collection, outside U.S. territory, of "information relating to potential or ongoing federal criminal investigations and prosecutions." But that was to be one of his last acts as CIA director. Although any DCI was theoretically supposed to be apolitical, and Gates probably could have served a Democratic administration, his stewardship had been marred by a bitter and unusually public dispute with Justice and the FBI. The resulting turmoil had made it politically impossible for the new administration to keep him, and two days after Bush lost the election, Gates announced plans to retire.

He had been DCI in a difficult twilight time, during which journalists wrote tauntingly of "the last days of CIA," and policy wonks proposed abolishing the Agency as its reward for helping counter the apparently retreating Soviet threat. During his brief tenure, Gates had tried to adapt to this unexpectedly hostile climate by redefining the nation's intelligence needs, by studying ways to improve links with law enforcement, and by "opening up" the intelligence community to people like Congressman Gonzalez. But if Gates, like any good spy, was a chameleon who survived by blending in, he and many others at CIA had found it impossible to change to the shade required for public openness. CIA's inspector general, and the Senate Select Committee, saw the need for a different hue, but failed to pick it out. Perhaps what was needed, in the end, was a complete shedding of the skin.

CHAPTER TWENTY

THE KEYS TO THE KINGDOM

As GATES LEFT LANGLEY in January 1993, there had seemed to be at least the prospect that an Iraq-Gate inquiry might address long-standing interagency gaps. "This is what happened after the Watergate and Church committees—reforms were their true legacy," former House Judiciary counsel James H. Rowe told a *Harper's*-magazine colloquium on the BNL affair. "The most important thing that can come out of this . . . would be a mandate to create legislation to remedy these interbranch problems." The hoped-for hearings never materialized, but the general climate still seemed to favor reform. Clinton's transition team declaimed against turf battles, and it was a true measure of their liberalism that they believed intelligence infighting, like human nature, or government itself, could be overcome, or improved, if only certain "infrastructures" were "reinvented." Even though foreign policy was not high on the presidential agenda, and even though most members of the new team had previously served in government, especially during the disillusioning Carter years, there was an unmistakable fix-it optimism among Clinton's national-security "brain trust."

A key member of that brain-trust was R. James Woolsey, a balding man with Spock-like ears, who became the new director of CIA. Woolsey was a lawyer and a former Rhodes scholar, but he had also been a consumer of intelligence in four earlier government jobs, including undersecretary of the Navy for President Carter, and as a U.S. arms negotiator in Geneva. A few days before Christmas 1992, after Admiral William J. Crowe turned down offers to run CIA, Woolsey got a call from secretary of state–designate Warren Christopher, whom he'd known for a long time, asking him down to Little Rock to meet the governor. Woolsey caught the next plane out of Washington, and that evening the president-elect offered him the DCI job. So Woolsey went to work at Langley, whence he soon saw the post–Cold War world as "a jungle filled with a bewildering variety of poisonous snakes."

But Woolsey began by trying to hack through the bureaucratic jungles of Washington, where red tape had always grown like bromeliads along the path of least resistance. An "early item of business," as Woolsey promised Congress, was "restructing the Intelligence Community" to assure that agencies with competing imperatives could cooperate. Although some momentum was lost while Woolsey waited four months for the confirmation of an attorney general, he consulted senior Justice Department and FBI officials, including Sessions, on how "to make changes in the way we look at support to law enforcement." After all, Woolsey pointed out, "both the BCCI and the BNL scandals are evidence that we are still not to the point where we can do this properly and correctly."

In February 1993, Woolsey announced changes under which federal prosecutors could task CIA with collecting intelligence on suspected criminals. By year's end, his spies had been tasked against the Sicilian Mafia, which was trying to obtain nuclear weapons, and against the Cali cocaine cartel, which was seeking to buy a secure communications satellite. CIA officers even brokered some rather New Age help for the Bureau during the disastrous ATF-FBI siege against cultist David Koresh and his followers in Waco, Texas. On March 17, CIA and FBI officials met in suburban Virginia with Dr. Igor Smirnov of the Moscow Medical Academy, who had been working on a computerized acoustic device designed to plant thoughts in a person's mind. The Agency had been curious about Smirnov since the mid-1980s, when they learned that the Soviet army's Special Forces were experimenting with psychotechnologies in the Afghan war. Although FBI interest cooled when Smirnov couldn't guarantee a risk-free situation at Waco, the American agencies still wanted, according to a memo of the proceedings, to "determine whether psycho-correction technologies represent a present or future threat to U.S. national security in situations where inaudible commands might be used to alter behavior."

In these and other cases, under Woolsey's new rules, the Agency could be ordered outright to share more fully any relevant data in its files. Yet the more Woolsey learned about recruiting and running spies, the more he sympathized with his men for sometimes not wanting to share things. Whatever CIA's image problems with the Congress and the press, a lot of people around the world, especially idealists disgusted by totalitarian regimes, were still willing to take great risks to help the United States—to become CIA assets, agents, spies. Of course there were cases, especially involving drug cartels and terrorists, where the motives people had were not so benign, but the risks—often to the recruiting officer as much as the recruit—made care and caution no less crucial. When the stakes were so high, CIA had a duty to let an agent stay in place, to watch and wait and listen. But the FBI, as always, had an equal duty to probe and pounce and prosecute, and each agency naturally thought its interests trumped the other's. "What's involved here is two very useful and I would say extremely important sub-cultures," Woolsey said, "and they do not mesh together easily."

It was imperative that they nevertheless be made to mesh, for in 1993 Woolsey's In box brimmed with threats demanding teamwork. Economic espionage cases soared from ten to five hundred in the nine months ending in April 1993, and traditional spying was troublesome as ever. On tips from CIA, FBI agents flew in March to Liberia and found that secret data about U.S. operations in Somalia had been faxed from Washington; eventually they arrested Dominic Ntube, a Cameroonian émigré, for stealing thousands of classified documents from the State Department and CIA. A martial-arts instructor, Joseph Garfield Brown, was arrested by the FBI for passing classified CIA documents to the Philippine government. Stevan Lalas, a CIA communications officer at the U.S. Embassy in Athens, confessed to passing more than 240 secret documents to Greek military intelligence. Thomas Gerard, a former San Francisco policeman and CIA contract agent, was charged with selling secrets to South Africa. And by early 1993, CIC had isolated a single suspect in its hunt for the high-placed mole at Langley.

IT WAS RICK AMES. By most accounts, he was pinpointed by a new Russian defector. According to other reports, Ames himself raised suspicions by lavish spending, or by repeatedly asking to see intelligence beyond his "compartment" at the CNC. In any case, Ames' entire life was now assessed through a dark prism of doubt.

In some ways, he seemed fated to be a spy. He was born on May 26, 1941, just as Ian Fleming was flying to America to help found Central Intelligence. In June 1962—as the Golitsyn-driven molehunt was in full cry, as Lee Harvey Oswald returned to the U.S. from Russia, and as Yuri Nosenko made his first contact with American intelligence—Ames' CIA father helped him land a job in Langley, with a Top Secret clearance, before he had even graduated from college. In 1969 he was posted to Ankara, Turkey; in 1976, he worked with the FBI to recruit Soviets in Manhattan; by 1981, he was trying to turn Soviet agents in Mexico City. Here, it seemed, was where things had begun to go wrong.

In April 1983, Ames recruited a Colombian woman, Maria del Rosario Casas, who was serving in Mexico City as a "cultural affairs" attaché. She became a paid CIA source. Later that year, when Ames was summoned back to Langley as CI officer for the Soviet Europe Division, Maria followed him. That should have attracted suspicion, because the KGB had scored before by dangling women in front of CIA officers in Latin America; Angleton thought that was how they had recruited Philip Agee. But in Ames' case no one raised objections. Having divorced his first wife, he married Maria on August 10, 1985, just when the Yurchenko-Howard affair was boiling up. The divorce proved costly, and left Ames badly in need of cash. Conveniently enough, the first of what would be many large, unexplained deposits in his Virginia bank account occurred on May 18, 1985—only two months before CIA mole Adolf Tolkachev was arrested in Moscow. Ames had known about Tolkachev, and about most of the other sources that were rolled up. He had also shown a definite "bump" on his 1991 polygraph.

Despite these suggestive patterns, and despite the 1991 agreement to work together in the molehunt, an indecent interval still passed before the Ames case was passed to the FBI. Even the Bureau's permanent CIC representative, appointed in 1991 to head the Center's Soviet and East European counterintelligence group, was kept in the dark for several months. Not until May 12, 1993, was the FBI able to open a formal investigation of Ames.

When the Ames serial was finally shared, Wiser and other agents at the Washington Field Office were aghast. The Agency had clearly violated the 1988 Sessions-Webster Memo of Understanding, which mandated that CIA suspicions be disseminated in a timely fashion. Especially distressing was the refusal to pool Ames' 1991 polygraph results, for the Bureau now judged that Ames had clearly failed that test. CIA's secretiveness had meant at least a two-year delay in investigating Ames—and delays could mean blown cases, as the agents well knew from Howard and Bloch.

Woolsey called Sessions and tried to assure him that there wasn't anything untoward in CIA's withholding of the polygraph results. The Agency had not been trying to hide anything from the Bureau, but had merely wanted to wait for something more solid before sharing the highly personal lie-detection data, which included questions about finances and sexuality. CIA had many unresolved internal concerns about the reliability of its polygraphs—not only because bogus foreign agents passed them, but because many loyal Agency people were failing them. A dramatic expansion of polygraph use in the Turner and Casey years had required hiring many young and inexperienced examiners, who obtained an almost 50 percent initial failure rate for veteran officers. Most of the failures came on questions about sex or money and were corrected in retesting, and Ames's lower second-round responses fit that pattern. CIA had thus been hesitant to tar Ames' reputation by making his polygraph results available to outsiders, particularly at the FBI.

Sessions' deputies doubted that explanation, and the Bureau made clear that it expected CIA to cooperate fully with two special agents now assigned to work exclusively on the Ames case at CIC. The Agency obliged by letting the Bureau search Ames' office at Langley. On June 23, 1993, while Ames was away on official business, Wiser and several other FBI agents, escorted by armed guards from CIA's Office of Security, entered the "G" level basement at Agency headquarters. They proceeded to Room GVO6, which CIA's security people unlocked with a duplicate key. The small private office was beige with gray trim, a dropped white ceiling, a computer workstation, and a safe. In the safe were found 144 classified documents, including some Top Secret Codeword materials pertaining to the USSR and Russia. One was a CIA document detailing U.S. knowledge of Soviet nuclear submarines' anti-tracking abilities. Also found was a top-secret paper, "What Angleton Thought," along with two volumes of a "Nosenko/AE Sawdust Study." Checking with CIA officials, Wiser learned that these papers had no relationship to Ames' work as counternarcotics officer for the Black Sea region. From his experience in CI, Wiser knew that spies, especially those motivated by financial gain, often retained copies of documents they had transferred to the other side—in essence, keeping the espionage equivalent of a résumé. This could be especially useful in negotiating for more money with a new handler, who might not be fully briefed on what the spy had provided in the past. That was just what Wiser figured had probably occurred after the KGB was transformed into the SVR.

Wiser now got permission from his superiors to launch a massive operation, code-named "Nightmover," against Ames and his wife. Their phones were tapped, their mail was opened, and FBI agents descended on their affluent neighborhood in Arlington, Virginia. Surveillance devices were concealed behind the wooden stockade-style fence that partially bordered the back yard of their brick home. Whenever Ames or his wife left the house in their 1992 Jaguar, their movements were reported by hidden watchers to a fleet of radio-equipped FBI cars. Since Ames, as a professional intelligence officer, was trained to spot surveillance, Wiser thought it unwise to follow him physically during the day, but a homing device was affixed to the underside of his Jaguar. And at night, FBI cars followed him through the shadows.

WHILE THE BUREAU kept CIA up to date on the Ames case, Woolsey was momentarily more concerned with another threat demanding FBI-CIA teamwork. On New Year's Day 1993, a collection of Islamic figures, both secular and fundamentalist—including Muammar Qaddafi, Saddam Hussein, and clerics from Iran, Egypt, Algeria, the Sudan, and Afghanistan—had jointly announced a new holy crusade against Christian nations. In the first few months of the year, dozens of American-owned oil pipelines in Latin America were demolished by bombers believed to have been backed by Iran. In Egypt, scores of Coptic Christians were brutally murdered, busloads of Western tourists were shot up, and archaeological museums were bombed. In Turkey, a prominent leftist critic of fundamentalism was blown to oblivion when four Iranians booby-trapped his car. A gunman on a motor scooter killed the top Iranian opposition figure in Italy. In Kuwait, eleven Iraqis were arrested for allegedly attempting to assassinate former President Bush during an April visit. In Washington, an Islamic Pakistani immigrant, Mir Amail Kansi, shot to death two CIA officers during morning rush hour outside CIA headquarters, then escaped to Afghanistan. And in New York City, on February 26, Islamic militants bombed the second-tallest building in the world.

Overseas angles to the World Trade Center case had been developing since roughly 1990, when the victory of CIA-backed guerrillas in Afghanistan posed a "disposal problem" similar to the one created by the defeat of Cuban exiles at Bay of Pigs. Ayatollah Khomeini had predicted that communism's decline meant the next war was between Christianity and Islam, and guerrilla bases near the Pakistani city of Peshawar, at the Afghan border, offered a convenient staging ground for those who would blow off the hands that once had fed them. When threatened by police, terrorists could disperse by camel tracks and footpaths used by smugglers, and an easy sanctuary was provided in the autonomous Khyber Agency, a tribal territory where police were not allowed. At camps in the Peshawar region, recruits were given Sudanese passports by Iranian agents and transported, usually via Germany, to the Sudan, which had created training bases in a joint venture with Iran. The program was overseen by Mostafa Mir Salim, a former student at Moscow's Patrice Lumumba University, who had attended Soviet terrorist-training camps in South Yemen, and by Mousavi Khoeniah, another Lumumba graduate, who in the 1970s had carried nearly $400,000 in KGB funds to the Ayatollah to help finance Iran's revolution. After being tutored by the former KGB terror experts, Islamic Rambos would return to Pakistan and thence, on false documentation, proceed to Egypt, Algeria, or even the United States.

FBI and CIA had been trying to coordinate in denying visas to some of these would-be terrorists since September 1986, when the agencies joined an Alien Border Control Committee (ABCC). CIA was especially well positioned to assist domestic authorities in immigration matters, because green young officers on their inaugural foreign tours typically served under cover as U.S. consuls, whose duties included issuing visas. But after Agency tips led the Bureau to arrest eight suspected Palestinian terrorists in Los Angeles in early 1987, civil-liberties activists pressured the ABCC to drop a plan to systematize use of CIA intelligence in processing visa requests. Congressman Barney Frank then led a successful movement to amend the Immigration and Nationality Act, so that membership in terrorist groups would no longer be sufficient grounds for the denial of visas. Instead, the government would have to show that suspects had actually committed terrorism or other illegal acts. The United States therefore had no obvious grounds for refusing visas to radicals such as Kansi, who had associated with Iranian terrorists in Peshawar, or to blind cleric Sheikh Omar Abdel Rahman, leader of the Egyptian Jihad, a group which in 1981 assassinated Egyptian President Anwar Sadat.

Rahman still might have been denied a visa under a loophole in U.S. immigration law, which allowed the FBI to blackball persons with suspected foreign-intelligence links. In most cases, the Bureau relied on CIA for identification of such connections. As it happened, CIA knew that the sheikh had been on the Iranian intelligence payroll since 1981. Rahman also had at least some indirect connections with CIA—his mosques helped recruit the Agency's anti-Soviet rebels in Afghanistan—and there would later be rumors, denied by both CIA and Rahman, that the Agency deliberately eased Rahman's immigration because he was one of their agents. In any event, the CIA officer who processed Rahman's visa request at Khartoum never warned the FBI. "In the case of Rahman, none of this [exchange of data] really occurred," Webster recounted. "His name wasn't given to the FBI or wasn't recognized by the FBI, and so no objection was posed, and no vigilance was exercised."

Rahman entered the U.S. in May 1990 and founded mosques in Brooklyn and New Jersey. He denounced local Muslim grocers for selling beer, demanded the overthrow of Egypt's secular government, and issued fatwas, or religious edicts, that called for the murder of persons who stood in the way of Islam. After New York police arrested one of Rahman's followers, El Sayyid Nosair, in connection with the killing of right-wing Israeli leader Rabbi Meir Kahane in November 1990, the FBI was intrigued to learn that Nosair's legal bills were paid and his family supported by Rahman, and that Nosair was regularly visited in prison by one of Rahman's followers, Mohammed Salameh. A CIA name check, requested by Campbell, disclosed that Rahman was on the Agency's international terrorist list—a fact the Agency had not previously made known to the FBI.

While the Bureau began investigating Rahman and his followers, Egyptian intelligence repeatedly warned CIA officers in Cairo about a growing Islamic fundamentalist network in the United States, concentrated especially around Rahman's mosques. Egyptian authorities were confused and upset when the Agency told them it could not monitor the men, since counterterrorism in the U.S. was the province of the FBI. The best that could be managed was a visit to Cairo by several FBI agents on February 6–11, 1993. When the Egyptians repeated their warnings, the FBI agents promised to take action, but cautioned their hosts that because of America's unique geographic split in CI/CT duties, Rahman's followers in the U.S. had to be investigated from a law-enforcement standpoint. The Bureau did recruit an agent in Rahman's entourage—former Egyptian army officer Emad Salem—but his access was limited. Legally, there was little else the FBI could do. Whereas CIA, working overseas, could open mail and tap phones, the FBI had to show that suspects were breaking the law before conducting surveillance. The Egyptians marveled at the absurdity of this, since without surveillance the evidence was unlikely to surface. FBI agents grew testy, saying, "What are we supposed to do: round up all the Islamic fundamentalists in New Jersey?" The Egyptians countered by openly criticizing the U.S. system, which seemed to give suspected terrorists a free hand simply because they crossed from CIA into FBI jurisdiction—a policy which could only encourage such deadly immigration.

In fact, two more Rahman followers, Mahmad Muhammad Ajaj and Ramzi Ahmed Yousef, had already come to the U.S. from Peshawar in September 1992, with suitcases full of Islamic texts and books on building bombs. Following the World Trade Center bombing, for which both men were indicted, the Bureau realized that some important background information on Ajaj, Youssef, and other Rahman followers had been provided by Egypt well beforehand and was simply sitting in CIA databases.

IN THE CRISIS ATMOSPHERE after the World Trade Center explosion, American officials suddenly became more enthusiastic about sharing intelligence. The Bureau set up a "hotline" to CIA, and tasked the Agency— under Woolsey's new rules—with finding out all it could to build a prosecutable case. Langley fed a steady stream of data to the Bureau through Campbell, FBI agents accessed Agency sources in Egypt and Israel, a legal attaché worked with CIA officers to track down the "money trail" in Germany, and Woolsey later said that the two agencies' post-bombing work was "fully integrated." But it was duly noted by columnist William Safire that the FBI was only "playing catch-up . . . utilizing CIA connections in meeting what is belatedly seen as a domestic threat."

As in the aftermath of Pearl Harbor, there was a lingering sense that a great tragedy could have been averted if information had been properly centralized. Egyptian President Hosni Mubarak played the role of Dusko Popov, saying that vital information was "exchanged with American intelligence" and that the attack "could have been prevented if you listened to our advice." Fingers were pointed at the FBI for its alleged failure to pursue hints, including a January 1993 warning from German intelligence, that a terrorist operation was under way. The Bureau took public umbrage at this "Monday morning quarterbacking," insisting that neither Germany nor Egypt had offered names or documents. Any specific warnings had, rather, gone to CIA—which had not only issued Rahman his visa but seemed to have missed a chain of significances. In January 1993, after Saddam, Qaddafi, et al. declared their new holy war, Egypt had advised CIA that Islamic radicals were not merely blustering, and would soon strike against U.S. interests, both abroad and at home. The Agency took the threat seriously enough to warn all U.S. embassies—but not so seriously, it seemed, as to tip the FBI in New York.

The Agency's defenders meanwhile faulted the Bureau for failing to analyze evidence seized more than two years before the bombing. Former CTC officer Cannistraro pointed out that some of the same cast of characters implicated in the World Trade Center case had initially come to FBI attention in the Kahane murder probe. Indeed, while searching Nosair's apartment in 1990, the FBI had obtained evidence that five of the seven extremists later indicted for the bombing were gathering information on bomb design, plotting terrorist acts, and collecting photographs of the

World Trade Center. When FBI agents and linguists finally got around to examining and translating Nosair's papers in March 1993, they were able to thwart a pending plot to blow up New York bridges, bomb the UN, and assassinate U.S. government leaders. But CIA officials believed the documents also should have helped head off the Trade Center attack. "This material described major conspiracies and provided a road map to the bombing of the World Trade Center," said one Bureau critic who saw the evidence. The FBI had apparently viewed the matter as a murder inquiry alone, and showed little interest in pursuing a wider, foreign-backed conspiracy. The photographs of potential targets were interpreted as tourist snapshots, and other evidence was considered too fragmentary or inconclusive to constitute a warning. The bomb-making manuals, for instance, were explained away when CIA admitted that some of the booklets had originated at Langley, which had provided them to Rahman's rebels during the Afghan war.

According to Egyptian authorities, who dealt daily with both agencies after the bombing, Langley's alleged links to Rahman were soon causing "rifts concerning him [Rahman] between the intelligence service (CIA) and the FBI." Although the Agency denied it, Mubarak and other Egyptian officials insisted that Rahman had helped CIA channel money, men, and guns to the Afghan guerrilla groups even *after* entering the U.S. in May 1990. But once the FBI linked Rahman to a planned second wave of terror attacks in April 1993, which was to have included blowing up New York bridges, CIA "had to react quickly to protect its man and its agent . . . [who] had become a source of embarrassment for those who had used him." The Agency's alleged attempt to protect its "man" seemed to Egyptian authorities the only possible explanation of why supremely competent U.S. agencies had failed for so long to find or arrest Rahman after the World Trade Center explosion. Egyptians believed very much in the efficacy of "the American cowboy, who shoots one bullet from his gun and kills 10 people, blinks his right eye and 10 women swoon, and blinks his left eye and scores of beauties fall in love with him," as one Cairo editorialist wrote. "We will not believe the United States, which, with all its powerful equipment can detect the footsteps of an ant, penetrate walls and roofs, and use audio and video to learn everything that goes on even in underground bedrooms and offices . . . [did not know] where Shaykh 'Umar 'Abd-al-Rahman was." Instead, "What happened [in the matter of Rahman's detainment] is probably a new chapter in the conflict between the Federal Bureau of Investigation (FBI) and the Central Intelligence Agency (CIA)," Egypt's government-run press agency contended. "One party wants to arrest Shaykh 'Umar and the other party doesn't."

WEDGE

. . .

AMIDST ALL THE REPORTS of interagency bungling in the World Trade Center case, congressional critics were demanding that the fractious "intelligence community" get its collective act together. Representative Charles Schumer of New York called for a new mechanism to ensure closer links between FBI agents and CIA officers in foreign capitals. Senator Joseph Biden wanted to know why Woolsey had not done more in terms of "organizationally changing the way in which we coordinate our counterterrorism activities." Senator Orrin Hatch said angrily, "I want coordinated law enforcement and interdiction efforts, and I want to make sure that they are coordinated in a way that makes sense. And right now, they're not." Although the agencies had managed to solve the Trade Center and Pan Am 103 cases after they happened, congressmen asked for better "cooperation and diligence in the often unglamorous work that can prevent these acts . . . in the first place." Buck Revell, who had overseen FBI counterterrorism during most of the 1980s, testified that, "unless we find absolute evidence of a conspiracy to commit an illegal act, law enforcement will end up reacting to terrorist acts after the event. Unless we get a handle ultimately on how to stop illegal immigration . . . the problem is going to get worse." But Rahman and most of his followers had *not* entered the country illegally—that was the whole point. Why hadn't Rahman been denied a visa? "Everything that could have gone wrong did, and it happened over a significant period of time," admitted Undersecretary of State Tim Wirth, who now oversaw the visa process. "We have a tendency in our government to neglect the basic bricks and mortar, to neglect the basic foundation, to neglect the processes that make government work."

Even William Webster, on whose watch interagency CT had seemed to work so well, pronounced that CIA's Counterterrorism Center was not a sufficient guarantor of liaison, and proposed creating a CT czar. "I do have the uneasy feeling that it may not be enough to say we cooperate and we coordinate with each other," he said. "It might very well be helpful to have . . . a means of designating the premier terrorist-counterterrorist organization in the country, to have the responsibility for calling the shots." The former DCI also suggested that the nub of the difficulty in the Trade Center case might have been the so-called "third agency rule, in which a foreign intelligence service will tell—say the CIA—something, but CIA is not privileged then to share it outside its own agency without the permission of the other liaison." Adherence to this rule protected CIA sources when the Agency helped out friends in foreign intelligence services, but the inability to pass hot tips to the FBI "gave everyone a lot of angst." It had caused Langley to hold back much in Iraq-Gate, and might similarly have caused CIA to sit on some Rahman-related data received from Egyptian intelligence, instead of passing the information to the Bureau.

Others believed the real problem lay not in getting the Bureau more intelligence, but in making the Bureau more intelligent. Terrorism expert Yonah Alexander assailed the "conceptual bankruptcy" of FBI counterterrorism, echoing Scotty Miler's lament that post-Angleton decentralization of CI had wrecked the Bureau's ability to assess foreign-backed terrorism "contextually." Such views only seemed confirmed in July 1993, when senior FBI analysts declined to analyze CIA claims that two Sudanese intelligence officers, under cover as UN diplomats, had been directing the activities of Rahman's followers. "We try not to get into the business about motivation," a senior FBI intelligence official said. "When we do, given the nature of the evidence, it tends to make us look stupid."

BY JULY 19, 1993, a perception of stupidity at the top levels of the FBI was among the factors that led President Clinton to fire its director. The sniping campaign about William Sessions' "lackluster" leadership had become a steady crossfire during Iraq-Gate, but it actually dated back to fall 1989, when Sessions reshuffled the Bureau's Intelligence Division in the wake of the Bloch affair. The changes had been seen as an attempt to rein in the Bureau's counterspies, whom some thought too aggressive; as Sessions put it, "it's very important that the work that they [Division 5] undertake be well within the mainstream of the FBI." Sessions had received uniformly good press until the CI purges began, but soon anonymous G-men began pointing to numerous alleged bumblings. Special agents had been aghast when, during an appearance on the television show *America's Most Wanted*, Sessions took the dais and obliviously reread the introduction of himself that had just been given by the show's host. At press conferences he admitted that he did not know what an "indices check" was, didn't know the FBI was subcontracting out background investigations, and was ignorant about new rules for extracting terrorists overseas. After the World Trade Center explosion, he had seemed distracted, confused about the FBI's counterterrorism jurisdiction—and stubbornly, stolidly insistent that "there is a very careful and close coordination . . . with our counterparts in the United States intelligence," even though Woolsey, Webster, and everyone else admitted there was not.

But the kicker had been Sessions' 1992 move to transfer thirteen hundred G-men out of the Intelligence Division and into more "mainstream" work. The division had been warning Sessions since September 1991 that

KGB "reform" was really a sham, that Russian spying was actually on the rise, but Sessions went ahead with the cutbacks. At the time, some FBI counterintelligence officials had been talking to journalist Ron Kessler, who was writing an FBI-sanctioned book about the Bureau. Kessler received detailed allegations about Sessions' alleged misuse of federal funds for personal purposes, which became the basis for the Justice Department investigation of the director during Iraq-Gate.

The CI Club meanwhile apparently launched its own investigation into the boss, whose cutbacks were viewed by Bureau hardliners as near-treasonous. Sessions' wife, Alice, later claimed that the Bureau had bugged their bedroom, and that she found FBI agent Ron McCall in their room fiddling with the mike. Sessions' meeting with a top KGB official at a performance of the Bolshoi Ballet in Atlantic City, in December 1992, was not exactly smiled upon, and the whole issue of Sessions' alleged financial improprieties may have been merely a screen for darker doubts. As one intelligence official observed, "counterintelligence investigations always begin with the painstaking study of financial vouchers . . . aimed at determining whether an agent has received large, unexplained payments or lived an unusually high lifestyle."

Clinton officials had been impressed by the way Sessions stood up to CIA in Iraq-Gate, and thought some of the ethics charges against him were probably bogus. But they did not want a director whose own deputies considered him "incompetent" at best, and at worst a security risk. After leaving a meeting with Attorney General Reno on July 17, in which he was told flat out that Clinton would fire him in two days if he did not resign, Sessions tripped on a curb outside the Justice Department, in full view of TV cameras, and broke his elbow. When Clinton did terminate him as promised, Sessions' son, Lewis, intimated that his father had been "targeted" by "CIA officials who were determined to get even with him" for probing the Agency in Iraq-Gate.

SESSIONS' SUCCESSOR, federal judge Louis J. Freeh, was a short, boyish former FBI agent and assistant U.S. attorney who knew firsthand about turf battles, and had a reputation for solving them. As he grew up in a working-class neighborhood in Hudson County, New Jersey, it had been Freeh's dream to work for the FBI. He had joined in 1975 and worked organized crime in Manhattan. He left the Bureau in 1981 to join the Justice Department in New York, where he prosecuted the infamous "pizza-connection" case, which at the time was the largest international heroin-trafficking Mafia ring ever broken up by the government. Such cases had taught Freeh the importance of penetrations and intelligence in police work, and during his Senate confirmation hearings he pledged to "improv[e] our [the FBI's] intelligence capabilities." His experience had also taught him that bureaucratic infighting was "a great problem." As a special prosecutor in the investigation of Walter Leroy Moody, Jr., convicted for the 1989 pipe-bomb killing of Alabama federal judge Robert Vance, Freeh had to coordinate more than a dozen federal agencies with overlapping jurisdictions, but did so successfully. As FBI director he would face such overlaps on a daily basis, but vowed to make all the players "work harmoniously towards common objectives."

Freeh got a chance to show his stuff just nine days after he succeeded Sessions, when CTC sprang a joint operation to snatch a convicted Palestinian terrorist. A Maltese court had found Omar Mohammed Ali Rezaq guilty in the 1985 hijacking of an Egyptian airliner, in which Americans and Jews were segregated from the other passengers and shot, but Maltese authorities had released Rezaq under pressure from Libya. When CIA sources learned that he was headed for Ghana, Woolsey asked Ghanaian officials to detain him. Extradition plans went awry, however, and on July 26, 1993, Rezaq was put on a flight to Nigeria. But while CIA operatives watched the wanted man quietly from the back of the plane, Freeh got Nigerian permission for an FBI team to nab him in Lagos. When Rezaq landed there he was shoved aboard a Gulfstream-4 jet leased by the Bureau, and the next day he was in a Washington courtroom, wearing a pumpkin-orange federal prison jumpsuit. After so many failures earlier in the year, interagency CT seemed on track again.

Things were trickier in the case of Rick Ames, however.

AFTER A SHORT PERIOD of sharing in May, CIA had shut off the spigot. Freeh knew that CIA was sensitive about outside investigations of its own people, and that Woolsey worried about exposure of secrets in court, but the Agency was taking things too far. So stingy had they become with CI data that, in late 1993, Freeh closed down the Bureau's office at CIC in protest, and withdrew the FBI agent heading the Center's Soviet and East European counterintelligence group. A later review by the Senate Intelligence Committee concluded that the FBI, being denied access to vital documents, justifiably "pulled out because they didn't have anything to do." Campbell arranged a December 1993 "peace conference" at Quantico, but the two sides reached no agreement on the sharing of intelligence in criminal cases, and the session broke up testily.

Surveillance was also a sensitive matter. Too much of it might spook Ames, which was Woolsey's main fear. Yet too little might leave the FBI without a conclusive case. Freeh was familiar with such problems from his work against the Mafia, and tried to strike a balance by stressing nonintrusive methods of monitoring. One was electronic financial sleuthing, which soon established that Ames had received almost $2.5 million in undeclared, unexplained income since CIA's operations started going sour in 1985. Another technique was to plant "trapdoor" bugs in Ames' home and office computers, allowing the FBI to covertly download all data. When such a bug was installed in Ames' home computer on October 9, one of the files retrieved was an unaddressed letter, dated December 17, 1990, which read, in part: "I did learn that Gtprologue is the cryptonym for the S.C.D. officer I provided you information about earlier." Wiser shared this item with CIA officials, who told him that Ames had been on the dissemination list for a memo mentioning GT/PROLOGUE just three days before the letter was written. Other files, and tapped telephone conversations, suggested that Ames was still in touch with SVR agents through unreported travel to South America, and that they were still paying him.

When Freeh discussed the situation with Woolsey in early 1994, it was agreed that the FBI would make a big push to catch Ames in the act of transferring secrets to Yeltsin's agents. But the closest the FBI came to this was seeing Ames drive by "signal sites," which typically allowed a spy to communicate with his handlers without personal contact. On the way home from a parents' night at their young son's school, for instance, Ames and his wife detoured into Georgetown, turned slowly and dramatically through a cul-de-sac, then drove straight back to Virginia. Wiser believed that Ames was trying to verify, by checking for such a signal as an upended soda can, that a "dead drop" he had filled had been unloaded by the Russians.

Freeh pressed Wiser for more damning proof of Ames' treason, but the Agency was sure they had their man. To Ted Price, the important task now was not to arrest Ames or convict him, but to figure out just how much damage he had done.

Clearly, he could have done a lot. As Soviet Europe Division CI officer from March 1984 to July 1986, he could have thrown CIA off the scent of some Soviet spies, while warning others, like Howard, that they were under suspicion. As a vetter of Soviet sources, he could have recommended giving bona fides to many bogus agents, including perhaps Yurchenko, while sending as many as ten genuine agents to face firing squads. As a debriefer of Yurchenko, he could have loaded the KGB man with CIA secrets and tipped him to "redefect." And as a Courtship officer, authorized to meet with KGB officials in Washington, he would have had an easy means of sending secrets to Moscow.

While posted in Rome, from August 1986 to mid-1989, Ames would have been able to do less damage, but trouble had still followed him like rain. He was believed to have compromised an East German official, code-named GT/MOTORBOAT, who met with him and provided classified documents on Eastern European security. At one point, as the official was about to return to Berlin, he promised to meet again with Ames, but he never surfaced, and CIA's many attempts to recontact him failed. Furthermore, although this might have been just coincidence, it had been Rome Station, on Ames' watch, that implicated CIA in Iraq-Gate, by withholding documents from Justice and the FBI. Curiously, Ames himself had a BNL-Rome bank account, which between October 1987 and December 1990 received thirteen unexplained infusions, totaling almost $111,000, from a Swiss bank. In this connection, a little-noticed facet of Representative Gonzalez's Iraq-Gate inquiry—what the Congressman had termed BNL's "highly intricate, meshed relationship with the Soviet Union"—suddenly seemed more relevant. From electronic intercepts, CIA knew that the Soviets had disbursed $100 million through unreported BNL transactions. Some of this, it seemed, had been used to obtain U.S. technology through third countries, such as Iraq. The possibility arose that Ames had not only received KGB money through the Rome bank, but helped the Soviets illegally obtain Western defense technology.

After returning to CIA headquarters in 1989, Ames had again had direct access to raw intelligence from human sources in Moscow. As Czech desk chief in the Soviet Europe Division, he knew about GT/PROLOGUE and had access to important details of U.S. negotiating positions. He also controlled CIA's knowledge about some of the dramatic events in Eastern Europe, just as Golitsyn's predictions were coming to pass. In that role, Ames could have given the Soviets feedback on how disinformation was being interpreted at CIA, allowing the KGB to tailor it to Agency preconceptions. Just as Ames was leaving Rome in 1989, in fact, the KGB had sent him a nine-page letter asking for feedback on agents supposedly working for CIA, but actually controlled by Moscow. Indeed, since all of CIA's Moscow sources since 1985 had apparently been known to the Soviets, it was likely that these sources had been used to channel disinformation. Because of this, officials told *The New York Times*, all reporting from Moscow since 1985—in essence, all CIA intelligence on the USSR since Gorbachev came to power—would have to be considered suspect.

Nor had the potential damage ended with Ames' 1991 transfer to the Black Sea desk at CNC. Because CNC was a "brain center," Ames could access documents from all other departments at CIA, and, for that matter, all other parts of government. He appeared to have exploited this privilege to obtain secrets that had nothing to do with his real work. As a chain smoker who worked in the basement of CIA's smoke-free headquarters, he also probably picked up secrets by talking to other smokers during cigarette breaks in a sunlit courtyard. Moreover, Ames still had access to classified cable traffic, and could have compromised communications by giving the Russians plain-text copies, for comparison against the coded versions Moscow received automatically through intercepts. Finally, it might have been significant that Ames' Black Sea watch included the newly independent Georgian Republic, where CIA station chief Freddie R. Woodruff was assassinated on August 8, 1993. Woodruff had been riding in a car with the chief of the Georgian secret service, whom CIA was tutoring in counterterrorism and counternarcotics. The killers were not caught, but were suspected to have been contracted by Russian military intelligence. Ames had known Woodruff's cover identity and travel plans, and had visited Tbilisi the week before he was killed. It was just one more disaster for CIA in an area under Ames' purview.

In sum, the Ames affair seemed to be the most serious spy case in American history. But the FBI had still not caught him in the act of passing secrets, and Ames appeared increasingly nervous about being found out. He had not visited any suspected signal sites since October. Had Ames noticed the FBI surveillance? Or had he been tipped by still another mole in CIA? Woolsey would have liked to play the case out until such questions could be answered. But in January 1994, when Yeltsin's secret police arrested two Russians who had offered to sell secrets about Moscow's advanced T-82 tank, Woolsey came under pressure to stanch the losses. And the next month, when Ames scheduled a business-related trip to Russia, the FBI worried that he would take the chance to bolt. On February 21, one day before he was due to fly to Moscow, Ames and his wife were arrested in Arlington.

When the Ameses were arraigned, the case was presented both as a catastrophe for national security and as a triumph of FBI-CIA cooperation. Freeh said he had enjoyed "CIA's unwavering assistance every step of the way." Woolsey said that the arrests showed "how our [CIA] counter-intelligence officers and the FBI cooperated over an extended period." Three out of four sentences in a press release by Attorney General Reno praised the agencies for working together so well on the case. The line was echoed by Wolf Blitzer on CNN, and at a news conference by President Clinton.

This was just a facade. Within two weeks, intelligence officials on both sides were telling reporters that tensions had persisted after the joint hunt was launched in 1991. The biggest arguments, of course, had been over how to build a criminal case without compromising secret sources. The expulsion of Ames' Russian handler in Washington, a step recommended to President Clinton by the FBI, also did not please CIA, because it resulted in the retaliatory expulsion of CIA's Moscow station chief, James L. Morris. And there were suggestions that the Bureau had not shared information which might have implicated Ames much earlier.

For instance, the FBI had learned through its surveillance of the Soviet Embassy that Ames had scheduled a meeting with a Soviet official on February 14, 1986. Standard procedure was for the FBI to inform CIA of any contact between its officials and any foreign diplomats, so that the Agency could be sure each contact was authorized. After checking with Langley on perhaps hundreds of occasions over two years, however, and finding Ames' contacts authorized, in each case, through Courtship, the Bureau became slack in checking up on him. As a result, according to CBS News, the Bureau never told CIA about Ames' February 1986 meeting with the KGB. If they had, they would have found out that Ames had never reported the meeting to his superiors, as he was required to do. Ames might then have been routed out after only one year of apparent treason, instead of nine. The implication was that if the FBI had done its job, CIA could have preserved a whole trove of secrets, and the lives of perhaps a half-dozen spies could have been saved.

But the Bureau did not think it CIA's place to make any complaints about liaison. In early March 1994, Bob Bryant, recently promoted from WFQ SAC to director of the FBI's Intelligence Division, told the Senate Intelligence Committee that CIA had failed to cooperate in nearly a dozen cases since 1991. Some of the incidents were minor, but others—including the failure to disseminate Ames' damning polygraph results, and the refusal to feed files to the FBI's man at CIC—symptomized a lack of cooperation in CI generally. Because of the mutual distrust, Bryant said he seriously doubted that many tantalizing leads from the East German Stasi files would ever be turned into espionage prosecutions. Later that month William Sessions, who while in power had always insisted that relations were fine, also conceded that despite agreements reached with three successive DCIs since 1988, "when you got below that top level, the mistrust remained." And in April, senators received a "snitch fax," apparently from an anonymous senior official in CIA's Operations Directorate, alleging that the Agency was "even now verbally telling its officers not to tell the FBI everything it knows . . . to even lie to the FBI if necessary to protect CIA's reputation."

Woolsey assured a closed-door Senate hearing that the Agency hadn't been holding anything back. If the FBI had not seen Ames' polygraph results early enough, it was their own fault for not asking to see them sooner. Woolsey even denied that Ames had failed those polygraphs, insisting that the Bureau eventually reviewed them and found nothing wrong. He blamed the FBI for whatever friction there was, and cited, among other episodes, the Bureau's decision to remove its agent from CIC.

There was one FBI charge, however, to which Woolsey had no reply. The Agency's poor security, as manifest in the Ames case, had deeply damaged the Bureau's own ability to conduct counterintelligence. Ames had compromised five Soviet intelligence officers originally recruited by the FBI in Washington, including Martynov and Motorin. Nor was the destruction limited to past operations and agents. Ames had revealed not only what the FBI knew, but how it knew, how it gathered and used counterespionage data, how it tracked foreign intelligence officials in the United States. The FBI's entire M.O. might now have to be reconceived. That was the FBI's reward for sharing its cases with CIA, in Courtship. And that was the main reason why, as one congressional staffer said after being briefed by the Bureau, "The FBI is bitter about this case."

Woolsey's people were reportedly "enraged" that the Bureau had made its feelings publicly known, but many FBI agents thought CIA deserved to be held up to ridicule. Perhaps that was the only way to avoid another Ames case—and to force action against other moles who the Bureau suspected still lurked in CIA. Because Ames had easily obtained documents he wasn't cleared to possess, Bryant and others at the FBI believed that he had probably been assisted by other traitors. As FBI agents began reviewing the old polygraph exams of Ames' possible helpers, they found anomalies that the Agency should have picked up. The trail led to Helsinki station, and to Steve Weber, a former CIA officer on a shortlist of twenty mole suspects previously developed by CIA, who died of an apparent heart attack while in bed with a woman in February 1993 in Budapest. Weber was a naturalized Czech who had defected to the U.S. in 1957 in Greece and eventually become the number-three man in CIA's Soviet Europe Division; he had perhaps been a dispatched agent from the start. Two of Weber's and Ames' former supervisors in the Operations Directorate, Milton Bearden and Thomas Twetten, had taken early retirement. The April "snitch fax" claimed that Bearden had tipped Ames in 1989 that he was under suspicion, and that CIA counterintelligence had been hurting ever since Angleton's firing in 1974, when CI "was decentralized, subordinated, and was deliberately designed to cover up and protect double agents and moles." Because of FBI fears that the Agency was insecure, Freeh even persuaded Attorney General Reno to bar CIA from a direct role in Ames' interrogation.

After reaching a plea bargain with the government, Ames told the FBI that he had given the Soviets and Russians "the keys to the kingdom"—the names of all CIA sources known to him. Among the agents he admitted to blowing was Vladimir Potachov, a researcher at Moscow's Institute for the USA and Canada. In 1986, after he was blown, the KGB had tried to pressure Potachov into a major disinformation operation against the U.S. nuclear arms-control team in Geneva. Orthodox tradecraft taught that the Soviets would only dispatch a controlled agent into an area where they had a mole to give them feedback. Concerned parties therefore drew up a list of persons who had been on the U.S. arms control team at the time. One of the names that turned up on the list was James Woolsey.

What Philip Parker had termed in 1985 a "healthy paranoia about CIA personnel security, a natural concern, especially where sensitive information and sources had to be shared," now deepened into an unhealthy distrust. In this respect, interagency relations were back to the ground zero of summer 1941, when Hoover's security worries had caused the FBI to withhold Dusko Popov's questionnaire about Pearl Harbor.

IN MARCH 1994, Security Adviser Anthony Lake asked the National Security Council to review FBI-CIA problems, in the Ames affair and other cases, and determine how to avoid such butterfingering in the future. To perform their survey, NSC staffers had to sift through contradictory stories by FBI and CIA officials over the mismanagement of past CI operations. One participant remarked that the two agencies were "acting like two teenagers and raising incidents that go way back into past history."

The NSC eventually sided with the Bureau, concluding that things had broken down mostly because of CIA's hesitance to fork over facts. By late April the Clinton Administration was therefore weighing an NSC plan to "force" the Agency to alert the FBI in cases of suspected espionage. The plan called for creation of a new National Counterintelligence Center, headed by a senior FBI man but reporting directly to the NSC. The Agency would still conduct its own routine personnel security, and would retain foreign CI. Woolsey would also keep control over the CIC. But CIC's office in charge of investigating individual spy cases would be run by an FBI agent.

The NSC plan would mean some real change for the Agency, but Woolsey supported it. That seemed the only way to head off Senate legislation, which he saw as likely to cede virtually all CIA counterintelligence duties to the FBI.

The Senate Intelligence Committee had begun reviewing FBI-CIA bungling about the same time as the NSC, and by late March had reached the same conclusion. Ames and his wife might have been caught years earlier if CIA had fully complied with the 1988 Sessions-Webster Memo of Understanding, which had set down procedures for keeping the FBI briefed on security problems at Langley. Senator Dennis DeConcini (D-

Arizona), who had replaced Boren as committee chairman, was especially galled by CIA's withholding of Ames' 1991 polygraph. After reviewing that test, DeConcini's investigators concluded that Ames had indeed failed it, and that the results should have been shared, as Bureau leakers had alleged.

"To me, the FBI had the right, the absolute right, to see that [polygraph], not at the discretion of the CIA handing it to them in 1993 but in 1991," the senator said. "You've got a guy that's not doing very good [*sic*] in '91, and he's one of the suspects, and you're losing agents like crazy over in the Soviet Union, and the Cold War is just ending and people are dying over there and you're paying them money and you can't figure it out. I think you'd say, 'Now, unless this guy gets an easy 100 percent, just clean, we're going to take a look at him.'"

Because of his "mortal horror" at the results of bad liaison in the Ames case, Senator DeConcini drafted the Counterintelligence and Security Enhancements Act of 1994. A key clause stipulated that "The Director of the Federal Bureau of Investigation shall have overall responsibility for the conduct of counterintelligence . . . investigations involving persons in critical intelligence positions." That meant that the FBI would handle all CIA internal security cases and would have the run of Agency files. CIA would be required to notify FBI about the leak of secrets even before any suspects had emerged. The failure to share vital data would be made a federal felony.

Woolsey was "unalterably opposed" to the bill. He went directly to Capitol Hill and engaged DeConcini in a shouting match.

"What you want to do, Senator, is go back to J. Edgar Hoover wanting to control CIA!"

DeConcini countered that Woolsey was merely jealous of his turf. If he wouldn't yield it for the greater good of the country, maybe the President should "get some new people" in Langley.

That comment hit Woolsey hard, for he was already under fire by anonymous administration officials for his "impossibly tepid" response to the Ames case. Sensing his position eroding, he tried a direct appeal to the public. Lest his opposition to DeConcini's bill be misinterpreted as softness against spies, he declared forthrightly on "The Today Show" that CIA had a lot of good live counterespionage leads and was running them through close work with the FBI. "People should not have the impression that the Ames case is the only major counterintelligence case that they're going to see," Woolsey told television audiences on April 19. "They're going to see a number of these over the years to come. And I think all of us are sad."

This remark put Woolsey in a world of trouble. Like Bedell Smith's 1952 admission that there were probably communist spies in CIA, it created a lot of "buzz," especially at the Bureau. FBI officials were furious at Woolsey's "overstatement," which appeared to usurp their power to decide when leads added up to a case. "The Bureau went nuts," DeConcini told reporters. "They didn't know he was going to do this."

DeConcini himself turned Woolsey's words into a rallying point. The next day he hastily called a breakfast meeting with the press, and was a guest on CNN's "Crossfire." Counterintelligence probes, he said, should be conducted in total secrecy; it didn't do any good to give the impression that the government was honeycombed with spies. He called Woolsey's comments "a diversion to divert attention from his failure to cooperate with the FBI."

Matters came to a head on Tuesday, May 3, when Woolsey and Freeh testified jointly at a special public session of DeConcini's committee. Both men had been up until late the previous night, working with Lake and NSC staffers on the language of an executive order to improve FBI-CIA coordination. Owing to continuing tension between the two agencies, final details of the order were not worked out until near dawn, and President Clinton signed the order only minutes before the start of the Senate hearing.

Presidential Decision Directive 24, as it was officially known, marked a dramatic victory for the Bureau. "The Chief of the CIA's Counterintelligence Center Counterespionage Group will be permanently staffed by a senior executive from the FBI," PDD-24 stated. The FBI executive would have full access to CIA's most sensitive counterintelligence data, and would thus be in a position to "fully coordinate the joint efforts of both organizations." The directive also mandated creation of a new CIA National Counterintelligence Center, to be led by "a senior FBI executive with CI operational and management experience." Theoretically, CIA's Counterintelligence Center would still "coordinate all U.S. counterintelligence activities overseas." But in practice, the FBI would displace the CIA as the lead counterspy agency. The directive was a devastating blow to Woolsey, and a Waterloo in the fortunes of the CIA.

Both directors, however, put up a united front for the senators, who grilled them for almost eight hours. Both contended that the executive order would go a long way toward preventing future Ames cases, but also warned that DeConcini's legislation would go too far. Freeh said that "to give the FBI a total counterintelligence responsibility, as outlined in that [bill], would perhaps tip the balance too far away from what I think are the most efficient missions of both agencies." The FBI, he warned, was not really equipped or trained to conduct CI overseas. Woolsey put more of a point on this by saying that the bill would impede CIA's traditional intelligence-gathering efforts.

Echoing OSS/X-2 chief James Murphy's 1946 views about the insepara-bility of spying and counterspying, Woolsey noted that "intelligence collec-tion and counterintelligence collection are not only very closely related, often they are the same thing, the same reports." Since most leads in domestic security cases were developed overseas, from defectors or pene-trations, giving the FBI "overall responsibility" for "critical" CI investiga-tions would necessarily involve the Bureau in overseas intelligence collection, which had always been CIA's bailiwick. In short, the bill "would establish an overseas rivalry between the FBI and the CIA that now, on the whole, does not exist and existed back in the late forties and early fifties. It would take us back to some of the strife of that time." For that reason, DeConcini's legislation was "badly drafted" and "unwise."

Those remarks came toward the end of the session, when stomachs were rumbling, necks tired, throats dry, fuses short. DeConcini half-rose in his chair, leaned forward, and began literally to quake in an effort to keep his voice controlled.

"Those kinds of statements are just the exact posturing that does noth-ing constructive here! Our investigative agencies seem to be more con-cerned with protecting their own bureaucratic turf than getting down to the business of catching spies! The nation cannot afford to let this situation continue!"

DeConcini then adjourned the session. Freeh hung around for a few minutes afterward, and Senator John Warner, co-sponsor of the DeCon-cini bill, patted him affectionately about the shoulders. Woolsey packed up his attaché case and strode briskly from the room, frowning.

TO A CERTAIN DEGREE, DeConcini was himself posturing, both on the matter of Woolsey's "careless" remarks about live spy leads and on the deeper issue of his willingness to consider FBI-CIA reform. Woolsey's statement about pending espionage cases was actually somewhat vague and mild—especially compared with DeConcini's own public disclosure, two days later, that CIA had undertaken "a review of all counterespionage employees that were employed in the Eastern European area." Nor were Woolsey's remarks any worse than those of then–FBI CI chief Doug Gow, who in 1990 had caused no controversy by saying that many American traitors were going to be uncovered by the Stasi files. And although Woolsey did oppose DeConcini's particular prescriptions for FBI-CIA reform, he still had shown more willingness to cooperate with law enforcement than any previous DCI.

Even before the Ames case broke, according to one official familiar with his efforts, Woolsey had been searching for ways to ease FBI-CIA tensions, "the number one issue" in the intelligence community. Just how difficult a task it was could perhaps be measured by the delays in the issuance of a CIA–Justice Department report on methods of improving interagency cooperation, which Gates had ordered after Iraq-Gate. By May 1994, the report had been through at least eleven drafts, and was eleven months overdue. Nonetheless, while Ames was under surveillance, Woolsey had been working closely with DeConcini himself to attempt some reforms. The core change had been to task CIA in criminal cases, which even DeConcini had admitted was a great leap forward. When Woolsey thus assured Congress in 1993 that he'd "strengthened" the Intelligence Community Management staff, "to help me assess needs and plan resources on an interagency basis," DeConcini had expressed full approval. At the same time, Woolsey himself had been the first to admit that "we need to do better in the future." Just before Christmas 1993, for instance, both agencies were embarrassed by a Justice Department investigation into whether CIA had improperly used the FBI to cover up its connections to a computer-training cult called Finders, which had been accused but acquitted of child abuse.

But if the Agency was faulted for freezing out law enforcement, in the Finders probe as in the Ames affair, Woolsey was also attacked, especially from the political right, for his proposal to task CIA in criminal cases. Conservatives had not objected when Casey tried to give CIA domestic leeway against communism, but they suddenly became civil libertarians once a Democratic administration wanted to do the same against terrorism and narcotics. In both cases the press was predictably partisan. The Washington *Post*, which had helped kill the Reagan-era plan with scare headlines about spying on Americans, backed similar measures by the Clintonites (for whom a "victory party" had been held in the home of the *Post*'s publisher, Katherine Graham). Conversely, the Washington *Times*, which had always given flattering coverage to Reaganite CI superagency ideas, warned that the Democratic DCI was building, in effect, an American Gestapo. "Without amending the CIA charter, the contemplated partnerships in domestic law enforcement would be illegal," the *Times* sermonized. Woolsey was even attacked, on civil-liberties grounds, for supporting a post-Ames proposal that would allow the Bureau to look into the finances of CIA employees without their consent.

With the conservative attacks on Woolsey's reforms, things had effectively come full circle. A wedge had been driven between CIA and FBI on the day William Donovan's CIA plan was leaked to the right-wing press in February 1945; forty-eight years later, small-government Republicans were still the major obstacle to removing that wedge. Woolsey had to be constantly on guard against the conservatives' ire. Hence, in one session with Congressmen, he said that "restructuring the Intelligence Community" was his primary goal, yet quickly qualified: "I don't believe that reorganization in any major sense is what we need." How the intelligence community could be restructured without being reorganized, he did not say. Publicly, he disavowed the view "that the intelligence community . . . should regard itself simply as an arm of law enforcement." Privately, he felt frustrated by what seemed a Catch-22 situation: CIA could be blamed both for cooperating poorly with the FBI and for cooperating too much. Woolsey thus had to admit that DeConcini probably gave the right reply when Pat Buchanan asked him, on "Crossfire," "Why haven't these problems of lack of coordination between the FBI and CIA been solved?"

"You've asked the question that nobody has an answer to," the senator said.

EPILOGUE

ON NOVEMBER 11, 1994, two weeks after the first edition of this book was published, I visited CIA headquarters in Langley, Virginia. On my way to the Counterintelligence Center, where I was to discuss my findings with the CI staff, I became lost in the beige maze of corridors and wandered, for a long while, unescorted—even though my "Executive Escorted Visitor" badge stated that I must be escorted at all times. I thought about how Aldrich Ames had sometimes been seen in CIA offices where he had no reason to be. I was somewhat surprised, too, that when I left Langley my briefcase was not examined: the sign above the armed guards' post announced that all bags must be thoroughly searched. I thought about how Ames had walked out with seven pounds of secret documents.

During my talk with the CI staff, I heard little about spying or counterspying, defectors or double agents, disinformation or deception. Instead, I heard about the Agency's new focus on "global crime." Money laundering, alien smuggling, drug running, toxic-waste dumping, computer hacking—these were "the new threats." I knew that CIA was looking for work, searching for a new vision. But five years after the breach of the Berlin Wall, I had expected some recrudescence of traditional national-security concerns. The shift in focus, the lack of focus, seemed of a piece with the lax security. There might as well have been a billboard above CIA headquarters: "Relax, there's nothing to worry about."

I wondered what was going on at Langley. But not until after September 11, 2001, would I have a working hypothesis. To be plain—to risk overstatement, but vouchsafe clarity—this is what I now believe happened. After Ames, the Agency was, in a sense, put out of business. It officially existed, but ran only on federal inertia, like an Amtrak train stopping at a station where there was no longer a town. Its key divisions had been stripped and plundered in a hostile takeover. It no longer *had* any big secrets to steal. Counterintelligence and counterterrorism, in the conventional senses, no longer existed. The Agency's work in those areas was merely an adjunct to law enforcement. J. Edgar Hoover's wraith had finally vanquished Wild Bill Donovan's. The FBI had won the CIA-FBI war.

The Molehunt (I)

When I visited Langley, a CIA-FBI team was still "walking back the cat," attempting to assess the damage Ames had done. But after more than two hundred hours of prison interviews with him, the team could not determine how many sources Ames had burned or how many operations he had blown. Ames himself claimed that he could not recall what he gave the Russians, because he was always drunk when he met them; yet he was hardly a credible source, having failed almost every lie-detector test he was given. By fall 1995, the team's report had been delayed several times, and CIA officials conceded they would probably never "get to the bottom of the case." More troubling still, a report by CIA's inspector general questioned the Agency's ability "to prevent and deter activities such as those engaged in by Ames."

Since CIA could not be trusted to reform itself, the task fell to the Bureau. Presidential Decision Directive 24, which made the FBI lead agency for counterespionage, now assumed a fateful importance. For, even as Freeh publicly celebrated Ames' capture, invoking it as proof of his agents' competence, he worried that more spies were at work. Surveillance operations in New York had been compromised. Double agents in Europe were disappearing. The Russians had uncovered a tunnel under their embassy in Washington. Ames had not known about any of those operations; nor had he known about the Felix Bloch case, the compromise of which remained a mystery. One of the FBI's few extant sources in Russian intelligence spoke cryptically of a spy nicknamed "Diamonds," then went silent. Desperate to stanch the bleeding, Freeh huddled with four of his deputies. They all agreed that there must be another Ames in CIA. They would spend the next seven years hunting him.

FBI agent Edward J. Curran, chief of the counterespionage group at the CIA Counterintelligence Center, became "The Executioner." He combed a classified database of old CIA polygraph exams, looking for irregularities. Eventually he isolated three hundred suspects (an "A to Z list"). By all accounts, the inquiry soon devolved into inquisition. Curran later conceded that his agents treated CIA officers "like criminals." One highly decorated station chief was interrogated six hours a day for five days ("By then, you even react to your own name"). It was a vicious and indiscriminate probe—and though conducted by persons viscerally hostile to Angleton's ideas, it surpassed by magnitudes of indecency the discreetly focused "witch-hunt" Angleton had led.

CIA officer Robert Baer, who survived the FBI purge and later wrote of it, considered it "almost as destructive to the agency as Ames." Promising careers were paralyzed; "polygraph limbo" meant no promotions, no overseas missions, no clearances. Seasoned officers were shunted into dead-end jobs, were forced out, or simply quit. The exodus put monolingual novices in vital foreign posts, and sucked the motivation from veterans who remained in the ranks. By 1995, Baer would recall, "The [headquarters] cafeteria was filling up with people who might as well have been marked with scarlet 'A's,' all of them eating alone." These innocent but uncleared suspects were known, in the halls of Langley, as "ghosts."

Woolsey's successor, John C. Deutch, found the Agency "a defeated force— like the United States Army after the fall of Saigon." Senator Warner mused darkly that it if a bill to abolish CIA made the floor, it would receive "not one, not two, but many" votes. For the foreseeable future, even if it survived, the Agency would not be a viable player in the policy arena. And so, as Baer would write, "[t]o appease everyone and atone for our sins," policymakers "turned the CIA over to its worst enemy in Washington—the FBI."

The Coup De Bureau

Between 1994 and 2001, President Clinton issued a slew of directives that expanded the Bureau's powers and contracted CIA's. The Ames case accelerated this power shift, and was a partial cause of it. But the FBI's role broadened also because a decision was made at the policy level, even before the Ames case, to give law enforcement precedence over espionage.

The shift occurred without public debate; its genesis cannot be definitively traced. Yet the change was afoot by January 1992, when the George H. W. Bush White House asked all security agencies to reassess their "post-Soviet" priorities. At that fateful juncture, the chief of the National Security Threat List Unit, in the FBI's Intelligence Division, suggested a radical shift in focus. Instead of neutralizing organized secret warfare by states, the counterintelligence community should target criminal acts by "loose networks" of "transnational rogue actors." The collapse of the Soviet Union, it was foreseen, meant also the loss of the authoritarianism that had "suppressed to a certain level the corruption and lawlessness in that country and its Eastern Bloc neighbors." These changes, as well as technological revolutions in the transfer of information, goods, and money, would provide a fertile operational field for the "transnational criminal." The threat list was revised accordingly: three hundred FBI agents were pulled from spycatching and assigned to international crime.

The FBI agent who revised the threat list, Robert Phillip Hanssen, would later confess to being a Soviet and Russian agent. But by then the new notions about national security had become dogma. In May 1994, taking up the Hanssen Doctrine, Freeh told Congress that Russian organized crime was a major threat to American national security, and that "criminal cartels are now richer and stronger than many nations." The next year, *The New York Times* echoed that judgment: "The threats [today] are less nations than gangs. The harm they can do the United States is . . . a law-enforcement problem."

To counter global crime instead of Soviet subversion, the national-security community itself would have to be reinvented. During the Cold War, when the greatest perceived threat was a military one, the Pentagon had been seen as the agency that could best defend America. Now, during globalization, when the nascent danger seemed of a criminal nature, the FBI would be the new Pentagon. Much as the Pentagon had absorbed the Army, Navy, Air Force, Marines, National Security Agency, and satellite reconnaissance, so now the Bureau became a bureaucratic Pac-Man, gobbling up national-security functions. PDD-24 was just the start. Presidential Decision Directive 39 (June 21, 1995) made the FBI the "lead" agency for countering terrorism. Freeh was an effective lobbyist for this increasingly ambitious FBI future: Congress rained money on him. Attorney General Janet Reno backed the expansion at the Cabinet level—and in Washington, Cabinet membership was the coin of the realm. Step by step, the Bureau would assume an increasingly dominant position in the national-intelligence empire.

When Clinton signed PDD-24, the White House claimed the measure would "improve our ability to counter threats to the nation's security." Even as the 9/11 hijackers were entering the country on student visas, Reno said: "No ocean is too wide, no distance too far, no time period too long and no effort too great to make those who kill or injure Americans immune from the U.S. justice system." In fact, the ocean between intelligence and law enforcement was too wide, the distance between FBI and CIA headquarters too far, the lag between the Bureau's takeover and the Agency's resurgence too long, the joint effort needed to fuse facts too great, to thwart Al Qaeda.

The Missing Files

At 10:30 p.m. on January 6, 1995, a fire led Philippine police to Flat 603 in the Dona Josefa Apartments in Manila. They were on alert for the imminent arrival of Pope John Paul II, and the apartment was located just two hundred yards from the Papal Nunciature. Inside the burning rooms police found a pipe bomb and timer; a demolitions manual, handwritten in Arabic; ecclesiastical robes; a map of the pope's route; a mixture of crystalline chemicals in the bathroom sink (an attempt to mix explosives had apparently gone wrong); and a Toshiba laptop computer belonging to Ramzi Yousef, the suspected mastermind of the 1993 World Trade Center bombing.

The computer files and hard drive were copied by Filipino authorities and turned over to the CIA station chief in Manila. In March, officers at the agency's Counterterrorism Center passed the disks to the FBI's New York Field Office, which was still investigating the World Trade Center attack. The CIA also provided the Bureau with a summary of the disk contents, detailing one of the most brazen terrorist conspiracies of recent times: a three-pronged plot to assassinate the pope in Manila, crash a plane into CIA headquarters, and blow up a dozen American airliners, killing as many as four thousand people. Highlighted by CIA was that one of Youssef's associates—Abdul Hakim Murad—was an airline pilot who had attended flight schools in the United States.

Though FBI agents were at first appreciative of the information, they soon noticed something strange about the material. The disks and the hard drive were partially blank. Cyberforensics showed that three separate deletion programs had been used to erase data. CIA officers contended the information was destroyed while Filipino authorities had it. But FBI agents concluded that the files were, in fact, pruned while in custody of CIA. The Bureau demanded a criminal inquiry. The U.S. Attorney's Office in Manhattan found no evidence of wrongdoing. But FBI agents continued to suspect that CIA had intentionally destroyed evidence. They speculated that the Agency might have had a prior relationship with Yousef, who had fought with the CIA-financed Mujaheddin in Afghanistan in the 1980s. "Someone went to a lot of trouble to destroy that evidence and put a lot of innocent people's lives at risk in the process," a senior agent in the FBI's New York Field Office griped to *Newsday*. "You don't do that, and you don't break the law, unless there's something in those files that you desperately want to hide."

Yet CIA did not hide clues that led to Yousef. The Agency's summary memo had stressed that the files contained detailed information about his co-conspirators in the United States and overseas, including their names, addresses, and in some cases even their phone numbers. Though Yousef had disappeared minutes before the raid on his Manila apartment, he was traced to Islamabad, Pakistan, and arrested there on February 7 by FBI agents and Pakistani soldiers. The next day, he was flown Stateside and indicted for his role in the World Trade Center bombing.

As the Bureau learned more about Yousef and his associates, it became clear that they were obsessed with hijackings and with spectacular attacks against vulnerable targets. During the long flight across the Atlantic, Yousef had bragged about plans for a kamikaze attack on CIA headquarters, using a light aircraft packed with explosives. By midyear, the Bureau had obtained corroborating details from the Philippine police interrogation report of Murad, Yousef's Manila partner. A secret 1995 FBI intelligence analysis, based on the interrogation report, noted that Murad admitted discussing with Yousef "possibly flying a plane filled with explosives into the CIA building." In that operation, Murad said, he had hoped to use the training he received at flight schools in the United States.

The memo made its way to FBI headquarters, where it was filed and forgotten. There was no prospect of prosecution: the plane plots had never materialized, the core of the Yousef cell had been arrested. Both Freeh and Reno were declaring publicly that, under the aggressive leadership of President Clinton, the threat from Islamic terrorism had been neutralized (in 1995, Freeh assured Congress that the country was not "under siege by enemies, domestic or foreign"). The Bureau made no further effort to penetrate Yousef's circle of unindicted contacts. Not until later would it seem significant that those contacts included a Saudi exile, Osama bin Laden, who had taken care of Yousef financially while he was on the run.

The Gang of Eight

On May 10, 1995, John C. Deutch, a fifty-seven-year-old physical-chemistry professor from the Massachusetts Institute of Technology, became CIA's third chief in as many years. During the Kennedy administration, Deutch had been one of Defense Secretary Robert McNamara's whiz kids; at MIT, he had solved a famous problem in laser physics. Initially, publicly, Deutch vowed to "blast through the cultural and bureaucratic barriers between the CIA and the FBI," to terminate "this tussle [that] goes back to the time of Allen Dulles and J. Edgar Hoover." But eventually, privately, Deutch would conclude that the interagency problems were "probably insoluble."

Vowing to build an "entirely new relationship" between the agencies, Deutch launched regular meetings between senior management on both sides. This "Gang of Eight," four deputies from each agency, displaced the "arm's-length attitude" with a kind of fusion. The fusion, however, occurred almost entirely on the Bureau's terms. The Agency was still on the defensive, because of the Ames case; and a scandal that spring over CIA's contacts with a Guatemalan officer, implicated in the killing of an American innkeeper, further eroded the Agency's position. Deutch had little bureaucratic choice but to sign off on a Gang of Eight plan to change the thinking and the behavior of American spies.

The idea was to make CIA "more accountable" to law enforcement—or, as Deutch put it, more consistent with "American interests and American values." The Justice Department's Office of Intelligence Policy Review began to audit CIA's work, making legal rulings on matters such as the appropriateness of maintaining certain agents. Hundreds of sources were stricken from the payroll. Case officers and station chiefs received new guidelines, forbidding the recruitment of "bad actors." Where the agency had worked for sixty years in a kind of moral twilight, it would now, as CIA general counsel Jeffrey H. Smith put it, "draw on the experience of the Federal Bureau of Investigation Administration in dealing with informants."

But the Bureau had no experience running informants in the "Kalashnikov cultures" of Islamic Eurasia. Penetration of terrorist groups was *ipso facto* likely to involve a case officer with dubious characters. At the practical ultimate, agents in terror groups sometimes had to be complicit in terrorism themselves, if simply to establish or to keep their covers. To case officers who framed cases in terms of national security, not law, the FBI's do-good approach went against all best practice. "It was like a cardiologist in California deciding whether a surgeon in New York City could cut a chest open," one former officer recalled. What was more, CIA personnel felt they were being judged by a double standard. The Bureau, after all, had a long record of protecting murderers who testified against Mafia bosses.

The Deutch guidelines shattered whatever motivation remained in the Operations Directorate. By 1996, dozens of agent-handlers, tarnished by Ames and uncleared by Curran, had retired early or resigned. The veteran case officers who remained began to steer clear of sources or operations—especially against high-risk targets like terrorists—rather than hazard FBI probes which could land them in Justice proceedings. American spying became ever more cautious, even namby-pamby. "People weren't just scared to meet foreigners on their vacations; they were scared to do it in their jobs," Baer reflected. After the "human-rights violators" were cashiered, Baer looked for reports on Iranian intelligence, the Pasdaran, and found "nothing—not a single report. . . . We had voluntarily deafened ourselves and gouged our eyes."

As CIA's reporting on terrorism evaporated, Freeh moved the FBI into the void. On November 1, 1995, he teletyped new Guidelines on Domestic Security/Terrorism Investigations to the field offices around the country. Preliminary terrorism inquiries could now include the "development and operation of new sources or informants," even "the planting of undercover agents in the [suspected] organization." His agents, Freeh said, "should now feel comfortable in being more aggressive." In Phoenix, where the hot, dry climate had long attracted immigrants from the Middle East, a SWAT officer–turned–special agent, Kenneth Williams, used the new rules to recruit contacts who might travel abroad and work their way into terror cells.

This was an invasion of Agency turf—but not a violation of it. On June 21, 1995, the Bureau had scored a second decisive victory over CIA. President Clinton had given the FBI the lead role not just in hunting down spies but in thwarting terrorists.

Terrorism for Dummies

The express purpose of Presidential Decision Directive 39, "U.S. Policy on Counterterrorism," was to "integrate the roles of all pertinent federal agencies in a comprehensive, pro-active counterterrorism program." Clinton named the FBI as the "lead" agency in that program—and lest the importance of that distinction be questioned, he specified: "Lead agencies are those that have *the most direct role in and responsibility for implementation of U.S. policy* [emphasis added]."

This marked a radical change. Previously, law-enforcement agencies had been relegated to observer status at the National Security Council and in its working groups. Now the FBI and the Justice Department would play major policy roles. Congress would direct the *attorney general*—not the director of Central Intelligence, or even the national-security adviser—to develop a five-year plan to coordinate "national policy" *and* "operational capabilities" to combat terrorism. Freeh would even form a new Counterterrorism Center, patterned on CIA's, to "coordinate the efforts of various components of the U.S. intelligence community"—a function previously reserved to the director of Central In-telligence. In 1996, the Bureau would add a Threat Assessment and Warning Unit, to assess "domestic *and international* terrorist threats" [emphasis added].

But though the FBI was the best police force in the world, it was not geared to the assessment of international jihad. Asking veterans of bank robbery and child-porn cases to become scholars of comparative religion, to forecast trends in a clash of civilizations, was a form of magical thinking. Bruce Watson, FBI deputy at CIA's Counterterrorism Center, found himself trying to teach field agents the rudiments of Islamic fundamentalism and Middle Eastern geography, in sessions that became known among some attendees as "Terrorism for Dummies." Freeh's own public statements on terrorism would have a *Sesame-Street* quality: "One of the national security crimes that has become more. prevalent in recent years that is most frightening to all Americans is terrorism. . . . Some terrorism now comes from abroad. Some terrorism is home-grown. . . . Terrorism can be carried out by U.S. citizens or by persons from other countries. . . ."

In the end, the problem would be not so much bad analysis as the lack of it. Freeh's deputy Terry Turchie would later tell Congress: "Since 1995 [when it became the lead counterterrorism agency] the FBI has avoided issuing comprehensive assessments estimating the threat against U.S. interests. Given the range of potential threats . . . from terrorist organizations . . . such assessments would be inherently too broad-based to provide much practical value." In other words: the lead agency for counterterrorism would not analyze the terrorist threat.

Placing the FBI in charge of counterterrorism created a strategic vacuum at the heart of national-security work. The critical stage of intelligence management, the setting of collection priorities, required definition of the probable threat. Lacking any definition more coherent than "the threat of global crime," the Bureau could only work case by case. That increased, to a virtual certainty, the odds that the nation would be strategically surprised. As Richard Betts has written: "Surprise can be engendered if collectors focus on the wrong threat. Surprise can also be engendered, however, if collectors focus on all threats equally." The FBI was listening for everything, and hearing nothing.

By summer 1995, all the elements required for an intelligence failure were tumbling into place. The CIA was being asked to penetrate terror cells, but had been denied the means of penetration. The FBI was being asked to analyze the terror threat, but lacked the means to analyze. Each side distrusted the other, yet both were expected to work together. The system had achieved a kind of negative perfection. And then Osama bin Laden came on the scene.

The Riyadh Bombing

On November 13, 1995, a truck bomb exploded at the perimeter of National Guard headquarters in Riyadh, Saudi Arabia, killing five American servicemen. The FBI dispatched an Evidence Response Team. Unattuned to Islamic cultural sensitivities, the agents attempted to remove soil samples to the United States ("the land of the infidel"). The Saudis responded by refusing the agents access to four suspects arrested by security police. Circumstantial evidence— the sophistication of the timer, the force of the blast, similarities to attacks in Beirut—hinted at Iranian sponsorship. But there was, as yet, no awareness of a larger terror offensive.

Ten days after the Riyadh blast, on November 23, a suicide bomber slammed a pickup truck loaded with explosives into the gate of the Egyptian Embassy in Islamabad, Pakistan, killing fifteen people. Analysts at CIA's Counterterrorism Center began to see a pattern. They posited that Riyadh and Islamabad were the second and third strikes in a coordinated campaign, which actually began with the attempted assassination of pro-Western Egyptian President Hosni Mubarak in June. Saudi Arabia, Egypt, and Pakistan were perhaps America's three closest allies in the Islamic world, and someone was trying to send them a message: the price of cooperation with unbelievers would be paid in blood. Clues as to who that "someone" might be emerged when one of the Riyadh suspects reportedly confessed, before being beheaded, that he had been "influenced" by bin Laden.

In January 1996, a special Bin Laden Unit was formed in the CTC at Langley. But assessments of bin Laden were soon divided by rival biases. On the law-enforcement side, Bruce Watson took the line that bin Laden was a financier and little else, a kind of Gucci terrorist. On the intelligence side, CIA analysts were unearthing contacts between bin Laden and Iran. Baer, especially, suspected the hand of the Pasdaran. But it was at just this juncture that Baer, culling the Directorate of Intelligence database and finding nothing on the Pasdaran, came up against the full effects of Deutch's decision to "draw on the experience of the Federal Bureau of Investigation Administration in dealing with informants."

The consequences of the tilt toward law enforcement began to accumulate. In January 1996, when the Sudan offered to arrest bin Laden and turn him over to the U.S., Clinton was trapped by his own paradigm shift. Because the Justice Department found the evidence against bin Laden insufficient for prosecution, the White House could only decline the Sudanese offer. Bin Laden slithered to safety in Afghanistan.

Khobar Towers

On June 25, 1996, a car bomb exploded at the U.S. troop barracks in Khobar, Saudi Arabia, killing nineteen American soldiers. Once more Freeh led FBI agents into the Kingdom, and once more they clashed with the House of Saud. The Bureau's lack of linguists, its expectation that unveiled female agents should work with Saudi officers, Freeh's carping that Arab interrogation methods hampered prosecutions under U.S. law—all these factors exacerbated the intercultural tensions. Frozen out again, Freeh's agents did the best they could. They traced the explosive to Lebanese Hizballah, a creature of Iranian intelligence. But as the FBI's own Counterterrorism Center came fully online, in July, Bureau analyses lagged CIA's. When Reno ordered the first formal threat assessment of bin Laden, she judged FBI analysts unqualified to deliver it, and relied instead on Langley.

In early July, CIA received a burst of reporting on bin Laden. Communications intercepts suggested that he had known in advance of the attacks at both Riyadh and Dhahran. Around the same time, a Sudanese member of bin Laden's group, Jamal Ahmad al-Fadl, defected to the United States. The U.S. government began referring to bin Laden's group by the name Fadl used for it: Al Qaeda.

The war on Al Qaeda would be led by the FBI. Deutch formally ceded precedence to Freeh that fall, in a speech tellingly titled "Fighting Foreign Terrorism: The Integrated Efforts of the Law Enforcement Community." Yet Deutch also implied that CIA was better at counterterrorism than the Bureau. "CTC knows better than anyone else what is going on in the complex, international world of terrorism," he said. "In the fight against terrorists, we are the pointed end of the spear." The Agency's submission to the Bureau was thus given a defiant, even militant undertone. Deutch insisted that the CIA and FBI were teaming against terrorists in an "absolutely unprecedented" way. But veterans of bureaucratic Washington were not so sure. Senator Orrin Hatch asked: If the FBI was the "lead agency," and CIA was "the pointed end of the spear," then who was really in charge?

Russ Travers, a senior analyst at the Defense Intelligence Agency, was cynical to the point of doomsaying. In early 1997, he published a predictive essay, "The Coming Intelligence Failure," in CIA's in-house journal. "The year is 2001," Travers began. "Terrorism will have come increasingly to our shores." Weaving suggestively between the future and present tenses, Travers piled up dark clauses: "The data were there, but we had failed to recognize fully their significance. . . . No agency was postured to conduct truly integrated analysis. . . . We are operating on borrowed time. . . . From the vantage point of 2001, intelligence failure is inevitable."

The Molehunt (II)

By 1997, Curran's molehunt had run for three years, and the agent known as "Diamonds" had not been found at Langley. In December 1996, however, working from information provided by a Russian source, the FBI arrested one of its own counterintelligence agents, Earl Edwin Pitts, and charged him with espionage. Pitts confessed to providing the KGB with classified information from 1987 until 1992. Robert Bryant, the Bureau's deputy director, asked agent Tom Kimmel to conduct a damage assessment of the case.

Reading through the Bureau's files on Pitts, Kimmel noticed irregularities in the way the Russians had handled him. The KGB had not tasked him to search out specific secrets, but, rather, seemed content to accept whatever he turned over. That was unlike the Russians, who were usually quite aggressive and focused. The KGB had treated him so casually, Pitts himself said in his prison debriefings, that he had wondered whether he was Moscow's only mole in the FBI.

Kimmel recommended to Bryant that the Bureau conduct a full security review. None was conducted. When Kimmel sought access to Curran's files, which contained clues from Russian sources, he was rebuffed. His inquiry, he was told, might interfere with the molehunt at Langley.

The East Africa Bombings

On August 7, 1998, at approximately 10:30 a.m. local time, a truck pulled out of the driveway at 43 Runda Estates in Nairobi, Kenya, and prowled cautiously toward the diplomatic quarter of the city. In it rode a young Saudi man, Rashed Daoud al-Owhali, armed with a pistol and homemade stun grenades. At the gates of the U.S. Embassy, al-Owhali jumped out and threw a grenade at a security guard. He then reached for his pistol, intending to open fire, but discovered he had left it in the truck. He fled the scene as the truck exploded, killing 213 people, including twelve U.S. nationals, and injuring more than forty-five hundred.

Four minutes later, at the U.S. Embassy in Dar es Salaam, Tanzania, another truck detonated, killing eleven people and wounding eighty-five. The bombings occurred exactly eight years to the day that U.S. troops, in the campaign to dislodge Saddam Hussein from Kuwait, had arrived in Saudi Arabia.

Within hours, nearly five hundred FBI agents were on their way to East Africa. Freeh joined them, overseeing the largest overseas criminal probe in American history. The Bureau soon had a break: al-Owhali was seized by Kenyan police in a seedy Nairobi hotel. He confessed to being trained in camps run by Al Qaeda. He also reportedly provided the telephone number of a Qaeda "logistics center" in Yemen. While NSA monitored the line, the supremely cautious Al Qaeda made an inexplicable mistake. A cell-phone call from one of bin Laden's deputies pinpointed a Qaeda camp at Zhawar, Afghanistan.

At 10 p.m. on August 20, sixty Tomahawk cruise missiles, fired from warships in the Arabian Sea, obliterated the mud-and-stone barracks at Zhawar. At least twenty-eight people died. At the same time, another barrage of missiles flattened the al-Shifa pharmaceutical plant in Khartoum, which the Clinton administration said was linked to bin Laden and was producing ingredients for the nerve agent VX. Bin Laden himself was unhurt, apparently escaping Zhawar just minutes before the attack.

"The most powerful army and the world's most dangerous terrorist organization have declared war against each other," a Pakistani intelligence official told the international press. The White House had indeed now turned to the problem of bin Laden in earnest. After the embassy attacks, "terrorism became my number-one priority," Clinton's second-term national-security adviser, Sandy Berger, would recall. Bin Laden's dark eyes peered out from the FBI's "Most Wanted" posters. Freeh postponed an inspection tour of FBI offices in Norway, Bulgaria, Ukraine, and Georgia to help manage the international manhunt.

As the trail cooled, FBI and CIA officials insisted their respective agencies were teaming well. In October 1998, *Newsweek* even affirmed that "the CIA and FBI, once bitter bureaucratic rivals," had "collaborated to roll up bin Laden's elusive network." The two agencies purportedly had got his profile "down cold," and they had "a message for bin Laden and his fugitive followers: the United States knows who they are and where to find them."

But Bruce Watson, now chief of FBI's Counter-Terrorism Center, was worried. He had 2,646 people under him, and none of them knew where bin Laden was. In November 1999, hoping to improve collation of CT data, Watson formed a new Investigative Services Division, described officially as a "center for intelligence analysis, staffed by a core of highly qualified analysts." The division was headed by Cassandra Chandler, formerly a television news anchor in Baton Rouge. She was given the job of preparing "long-range strategic and tactical analytical products." Her analysts combed the files. In a folder, in a file, in a storage room, on the first floor of headquarters, was a 1998 report from an FBI pilot, recording his suspicions about some Middle Eastern flight students in Oklahoma City. Chandler's analysts did not consider the report in their predictive assessments. The report was not passed to Langley.

In September 1999, on the sixth floor at Langley, CIA chief George J. Tenet's analysts received a warning from the National Intelligence Council, a CIA-affiliated think tank. The council suggested that Al Qaeda might try to hijack a plane and crash it into a vital federal building in Washington. The report recounted Yousef and Murad's 1995 plot to fly a light plane into CIA headquarters. "Suicide bomber(s) belonging to al-Qaeda's Martyrdom Battalion," the council wrote, "could crash-land an aircraft packed with high explosives (C-4 and Semtex) into the Pentagon, the headquarters of the Central Intelligence Agency (CIA), or the White House." The report was not relayed to the Bureau.

The Molehunt (III)

On February 12, 1999, during a lull between terrorist attacks, Freeh turned his attention to counterespionage. Tom Kimmel, ushered into Freeh's seventh-floor conference room, was increasingly convinced someone in the FBI was spying for Russia.

Based on his review of the operations that had been compromised, Kimmel told Freeh, he did not believe that agent "Diamonds" could be a CIA officer. Though Russian sources had in fact reported that Moscow had a spy in CIA, Kimmel noted that the sources' credibility hinged on their exposure of low-level agents, who might have been deliberately burned to protect a more important asset. In other words, Kimmel thought the Russians were planting false clues for Curran to follow. Reading those clues in reverse, the trail led back once more to the Bureau.

Freeh asked supervisors in the National Security Division to evaluate Kimmel's thesis. They issued a twenty-eight-page analysis, arguing that he had failed to provide hard evidence. In June, a joint FBI-CIA study reaffirmed that "Diamonds" was within Langley. By August, the hunt narrowed to a single suspect, an Operations Directorate veteran who managed "non-official cover" agents. He was suspended with pay, and put under surveillance.

The Malaysia Meeting

Sixteen months after the East Africa bombings, in December 1999, bin Laden's deputies were still relaying messages through the logistics center in Yemen. Since Al Qaeda leaders knew that East African cell members had been privy to the number—and since some of those operatives had been captured and interrogated by the FBI—Qaeda's continued use of the line was unusual. Analysts at the CIA Counterterrorism Center had to consider that bin Laden was using the Yemen connection to disinform and mislead them. Nevertheless, NSA was still monitoring the line. When a call to the number revealed that Qaeda agents would convene in Kuala Lumpur, Malaysia, at the turn of the year, CIA asked Special Branch, Malaysia's internal-security service, to monitor the meeting.

On January 6, 2000, Special Branch set up surveillance near the condominium of Yazid Sufaat, a U.S.-educated microbiologist who supported Al Qaeda. Reviewing video of the comings and goings, CTC analysts identified Khalid Almihdhar and Nawaf Alhazmi, both of whom were listed in CIA files as suspected terrorists. Almihdhar had lived with Alhazmi in California, and both had attended flight schools in the United States.

The Bureau was briefed. On the day of the Malaysia meeting, a CTC officer e-mailed an FBI colleague in the center, alerting him that Almihdhar was in Malaysia. The FBI agent typed back that he had briefed the "applicable facts" to another agent at headquarters. Just what those applicable facts included would later become a matter of intense interagency dispute. Watson's agents would claim that CIA provided Almihdhar's Saudi passport number but failed to note that the two men had visited the United States—or that Almihdhar had a multiple-entry visa, which "could" have drawn suspicion. By other accounts, CTC analysts did point up Almihdhar's visa status. In the event, neither agency alerted immigration authorities to watch for Alhazmi or Almihdhar.

On January 15, Alhazmi flew to Los Angeles. In March, reportedly through "a routine report from foreign intelligence service," CIA learned that Alhazmi was in America. A month later, the Agency was told that Almihdhar had arrived in L.A. on the plane with Alhazmi. By the Agency's own account, it waited nineteen months, until August 2001, to inform the Bureau that the suspected Qaeda agents were in the United States. By then, they had disappeared.

The Attack on the USS *Cole*

On October 12, 2000, Al Qaeda agents detonated a boatful of explosives portside of the destroyer USS *Cole*, which was refueling in Aden, Yemen. The explosion killed seventeen American sailors and wounded forty-two. Freeh led more than one hundred FBI agents into Yemen. A senior CIA counterterrorism expert joined the team as an "access officer," plugging the Bureau into the Agency's network of local contacts. He looked on with chagrin as the agents, operating in an alien environment, offended their Yemeni hosts. The agents were adamant that they should be allowed to interrogate suspects and witnesses directly. The Yemenis took that as a cultural slight. It was Khobar Towers again.

But the Bureau did work the probe doggedly—and, at least Stateside, with great discretion. Behind the scenes, clues were leading to bin Laden. One of the bombers was identified as a member of Egyptian Islamic Jihad, whose leadership interlocked with Al Qaeda's. Analysts at CIA's Counterterrorism Center concluded that the *Cole* bombers worked out of Qatar, where bin Laden had shipped twenty tons of C-4 plastic explosive from Poland. By December, FBI agents were fixing on Attash Khallad, a fanatical one-legged Qaeda operative.

When CIA officers pulled the file on Khallad, they discovered surveillance photos of him taken at the January meeting in Malaysia. In one of the images, he stood by Khalid Almihdhar; it also seemed that he had met with Nawaf Alhazmi. But for reasons that have never become clear, the Agency failed to inform the Bureau, as the *Cole* probe progressed, that the two men were linked to Khallad—or that they had already entered the United States. "No one picked up on that," a CIA official later admitted.

The Molehunt (IV)

In November 2000, while Freeh was absorbed in the *Cole* probe, CIA officers handed Ed Curran a dossier of Russian documents and a plastic trash bag. The documents, which had come courtesy of a CIA mole in Russian intelligence, comprised a copy of the Russian case file on a mole in American intelligence. The bag, said the CIA mole, had been used to deliver top-secret FBI papers to Russian agents.

Bureau technicians examined the bag for fingerprints. They found some, ran a check, and came back to Curran with a match. When he read the name, he was stunned. The prints belonged not to a CIA officer, but to an FBI counterespionage agent.

The agent was put under surveillance. On February 18, 2001, he was arrested while placing classified documents under a footbridge in a Virginia park. On February 20, Freeh called a press conference and announced that Robert Hanssen had been arrested as a Russian spy.

Hanssen, known to colleagues as "Dr. Death" for his dark suits, sallow skin, and glowering stare, had passed secrets to Russia for twenty-one years. In exchange for two Rolex watches, and $600,000 in cash and diamonds, he had handed Moscow at least twenty-six diskettes and six thousand pages of classified information; tipped the KGB that Felix Bloch was being watched; surrendered a full roster of double-agent operations; and burned at least fifty Bureau and MI6 sources. Later it would emerge that Hanssen, while chief of the National Security Threat List Unit in January 1992, had set the FBI's delusive intelligence priorities for the rest of the decade. Freeh said of the damage: "We believe it was exceptionally grave."

At the press conference, Freeh invoked Hanssen's arrest as proof of an "unprecedented level of trust and cooperation between the CIA and FBI." Yet the Bureau's hunt for "Diamonds" had torn Langley apart. And for months after Hanssen's arrest, the attorney for the suspended CIA officer would complain that the Bureau had failed to exonerate him. Perhaps most gallingly, while CIA officers had been subjected to grueling polygraphs, neither Hanssen nor many other FBI employees had been tested. The wounds would take years to heal. As Baer would trenchantly put it: "While the FBI was tied up eviscerating the CIA, Robert Hanssen was giving away the FBI's own secrets in trash bags."

In the aftermath, Freeh moved to shore up the Bureau's security. He ordered that the FBI's "top 500 managers" be polygraphed, and hired a former CIA counterintelligence chief, Paul Redmond, to walk back the cat. The echoes of the post-Ames situation at Langley were duly noted. "The irony is that an FBI counterintelligence expert was sent to the CIA to upgrade its internal security operations after the Ames case," Walter Pincus wrote in the *Washington Post*, "while today a CIA counterintelligence officer has been dispatched to the FBI to do the same thing there."

As the Ames affair had done at Langley, so the Hanssen case raised questions about the Bureau's viability as a national-security institution. A panel headed by William Webster reported that dozens of foreign sources had to be shelved, since "[the sources] fear that information Hanssen passed will lead to their discovery and their handlers can do little to assuage these fears." Kenneth H. Senser, the FBI's new assistant director for security, told the Senate Judiciary Committee there was "substantial risk" that another Hanssen could be spying undetected. As Freeh let CIA counterintelligence officers loose in the Bureau, things effectively came full circle.

The "Hanssen effect" would soon assume a grim historical significance. Until CIA officers could be sure there was not another Hanssen in the Bureau, they would hesitate to share sensitive information. Until Redmond could determine whether the Bureau's wellsprings were poisoned by disinformation, CIA analysts were loath to integrate FBI data into their reports. At the Bureau, meanwhile, resentment would smolder among agents finally getting a taste of the polygraph medicine from their rivals. And so, in summer 2001, the wedge between CIA and FBI was widening just as it needed to close, just as the enemy was coiling to strike, just as the days dwindled down to another Pearl Harbor.

Chatter

In May, the NSA began to intercept communications between Al Qaeda operatives discussing an attack, one that could be larger than any previous operation. One message, describing the scope of the expected devastation, used the word "Hiroshima."

The intercepts prompted concern throughout the government. By June, CIA director Tenet was "nearly frantic" about the "chatter" in the system, the discrete yet unspecific indicators that Al Qaeda was up to something. Attorney General John Ashcroft began taking a privately chartered jet for security reasons. Embassies and entire military commands went on highest alert. On July 5, NSC Director for Terrorism Richard Clarke summoned CT officers from a dozen federal agencies to the White House Situation Room, and told them to cancel any vacation plans. "Something really spectacular is going to happen here, and it's going to happen soon," he said.

While Clarke was briefing the agencies, President Bush was outside, in the White House Rose Garden, introducing the new director of the Federal Bureau of Investigation. Robert Mueller III, a veteran prosecutor, was replacing Louis Freeh, who had decided to retire for a lucrative private-sector job. Freeh was bequeathing him a vast federal empire, and it would be some weeks before Mueller was ready to rule. Until the second week of September, when Mueller intended to step in, the Bureau would be in a state of transition.

The Phoenix Memo

In Phoenix, during the second week of July, special agent Larry Williams learned that Middle Eastern men were enrolling at Embry-Riddle Aeronautical University, in the nearby town of Prescott. He wrote up detailed descriptions of the students, noting that one had links to Al Qaeda. Positing that bin Laden's operatives might be trying to infiltrate the civil-aviation system, Williams proposed an FBI program to monitor "civil aviation colleges/universities around the country."

Williams' five-page memo, which mentioned bin Laden in the first sentence, was sent electronically to headquarters on July 10. It was addressed to David Frasca, chief of the Radical Fundamentalist Unit, but was automatically routed to his subordinates. They never forwarded it to Frasca, or to Mike Rolince, chief of the International Terrorism Section, or to the interagency Counterterrorism Security Group, which had a "threat subgroup" meeting three times a week. Williams' plan to monitor flight schools was not even considered.

At least two persons listed in Williams' memo had been independently identified by the CIA as having links to Al Qaeda. But the Agency did not know they were attending the Prescott flight school, because the memo was not shared with them until May 2002.

The Crawford Brief

On Monday, August 6, as the heat in Crawford, Texas, reached a hundred degrees, President Bush sat down at the desk in his ranch office and read a top-secret Daily Brief from CIA. The two page document carried the headline "BIN LADEN DETERMINED TO STRIKE IN UNITED STATES."

A few weeks before, Bush had told Tenet: "Give me a sense of what al-Qaeda can do inside the U.S." CTC had dug into its files. The August 6 brief reviewed bin Laden's past methods, citing the recent case of Ahmed Ressam, caught smuggling explosives across the Canadian border for a planned attack at Los Angeles International Airport. Referenced also was an unconfirmed 1998 MI6 report indicating that Al Qaeda planned to hijack an airliner and demand the release of Sheikh Rahman. The brief did not mention suicide attacks, but focused, rather, on "hijackings in the traditional sense."

In retrospect, the report would be notable not for what was in it, but for what it left out. It did not incorporate Williams' July 10 memo warning that Al Qaeda agents might be infiltrating flight schools. It did not cite the FBI's 1995 memo about Murad and Yousef's plans to nosedive a plane into CIA headquarters. It did not consider the 1999 report by CIA's own National Intelligence Council, which considered airborne suicide attacks at length. Nor was the FBI given the chance to add its own analyses: the brief was not shown to the Bureau.

Moussaoui

On August 15, a manager at the Pan Am International Flight Academy in Minneapolis, Minnesota, telephoned the local FBI field office and alleged that a French-African Muslim, Zacharias Moussaoui, might be planning a hijacking. During 747 flight-simulator training, he had asked an inordinate number of questions about the locks on cockpit doors.

The next day, FBI agents detained Moussaoui and held him on immigration charges. He revealed little under interrogation. The Minneapolis Field Office, in order to search Moussaoui's notebooks and his laptop computer, asked headquarters to apply for a Foreign Intelligence Surveillance Act warrant. After three weeks of back and forth, Washington declined the request.

Under the strict standards of FISA, lawyers at headquarters argued, the Bureau lacked probable cause.

Frustrated by the foot-dragging, agents in Minneapolis asked CIA for background on Moussaoui. The Agency relayed a French intelligence report, linking him to Chechnyan jihadists. FBI Minneapolis counsel Colleen Rowley argued that the report "confirmed [Moussaoui's] affiliations with radical fundamentalist Islamic groups and activities connected to Osama bin Laden." A supervisor at headquarters ruled that the report showed no direct ties between Moussaoui and any officially designated terrorist group. What was more, according to Rowley, headquarters "chastised" the agents for contacting CIA directly, instead of working through FBI-HQ. What really seemed to bother the brass, one FBI man sniped, was that "agents [might] cooperate with the CIA in ways headquarters might not be able to control."

By late August, the Minnesota office's file on Moussaoui, which had been copied to FBI headquarters, found its way to Cassandra Chandler's shop. Her threat analysts now had three pieces of the flight-school puzzle: the Moussaoui information, the Phoenix memo, and the 1998 Oklahoma City report. No connection was made among them. Neither the Oklahoma nor the Phoenix report was forwarded to the Minnesota agents, who might have used the documents in support of their FISA filing.

Later, when a FISA warrant was finally issued, Moussaoui's possessions would yield many clues. Agents would find a computer disk containing data on crop-dusting; flight-deck videos from an Ohio store where two other Middle Eastern flight students, Mohamed Atta and Nawaf Alhazmi, had purchased the same equipment; a notebook, correspondence, bank receipts, and two telephone numbers linking Moussaoui to an Al Qaeda cell in Hamburg, Germany; and stationery identifying Moussaoui as a "marketing consultant" for a Malaysian computer company owned by the microbiologist whose condo had hosted Alhazmi, Almihdhar, and the one-legged Qaeda agent suspected of bombing the *Cole*.

But during the second week of September, Moussaoui's possessions were still neatly piled in an FBI evidence room, his links to Al Qaeda still obscure, his co-conspirators Atta, Alhazmi, and Almihdhar still at large. Atta would later be identified as the pilot of American Airlines Flight 11, the first plane to hit the World Trade Center. Alhazmi's and Almihdhar's names would appear on the passenger manifest for American Airlines Flight 77, which crashed into the Pentagon.

The Molehunt (V)

On the day Moussaoui was arrested, Neil J. Gallagher, assistant director in charge of the FBI's National Security Division, composed a formal letter of apology to the CIA officer who had been wrongfully branded a Russian spy.

"I sincerely regret the adverse impact that this investigation had on you and the members of your family," Gallagher wrote. "It was not the intent of the FBI to either discredit you or to cause you or your family any embarrassment. If this has occurred, I am sorry."

Twenty-six days later, in a *Washington Post* article disclosing the molehunt, FBI officials admitted that their seven-year purge of CIA had been a mistake. None of the three hundred suspects was implicated in espionage. Curran, who had retired when CIA fingered Hanssen, admitted that the Bureau's performance was abysmal. "We just dropped the ball so many times," he said. Curran thought the roots of the failure traced back to 1992, when, based on its new threat list, the Bureau had cut back its counterespionage staff. The article did not reveal that the agent who drew up the FBI threat list was the very officer whose treason had spurred the crippling molehunt in CIA . . . or that those dual disasters, traceable to the same traitor, had ruined the national-security balance that had held since 1947. Even so, the disclosure of Gallagher's apology, and of the Bureau's incompetence in counterespionage, was damning. As a brilliant, cloudless day dawned in Washington, as the *Post* flopped down on doorsteps in Arlington and Georgetown, anyone who had a chance to read page A-5 before 8:57 a.m. on September 11, 2001, would have learned that the FBI's dominance of CIA, the triumph of Hoover's ghost over Donovan's, the seven years of sleep and drift and delusion, were never necessary at all.

AFTERWORD

Jack Welch, the former CEO of General Electric, used to tell his executives: "Don't bring me a problem unless you can bring me a solution." It's a good rule, but one that cannot be easily followed in the space that remains to this historian. Page constraints, created by the addition of new material to the Epilogue, preclude here a fully reflective discourse on reforms. Detailed recommendations may be accessed at www.secretpolicy.com, where an archive of published materials relating to FBI-CIA problems may also be found. In summary, however, the U.S. intelligence system is plagued by three interlocking disorders. These should be addressed, over the short, medium, and long term, by a three-step plan.

First, the United States must recentralize its counterintelligence. By decentralizing CI in 1973, William Colby effectively destroyed it. That CIA's counterintelligence staff should serve only an "advisory" function, no longer vetting sources and controlling access to files; that case officers should be allowed to assess the bona fides of their own agents; that, to ensure that each case officer knows "enough" to assess his recruitments, files have been decompartmentalized—all these changes have effectively turned off the spy world's equivalent of virus-protection software. The results have been catastrophic. Though no spies are known to have penetrated the CIA on Angleton's watch, our major spy agencies have since been found riddled with moles. Wholesale CI reform must be undertaken now—and it can be. Recentralization, a return to the Angleton model, could be mandated by an executive decision. The draft text of just such an order was prepared by Reagan staffers in March 1981. The White House should use it as a model.

But counterintelligence, as Angleton himself said, "is only as good as relations between the CIA and FBI." Since 1948, there have been no fewer than twelve White House initiatives to defuse the interagency conflict. All have failed, because they've been based on the bad idea of melding law enforcement and intelligence. "Intelligence and law enforcement," as Ian Fleming wrote in June 1941, "simply do not mix." The two functions proceed from opposite and irreconcilable imperatives. Intelligence takes pains to protect sources; law enforcement uses sources to convict criminals in public. Secret intelligence goes on offense to stifle nascent threats; law-enforcement agents react to crimes that have already occurred. In Britain, these dual purposes are effectively detangled: domestic intelligence (MI5) is separate from criminal investigation (Scotland Yard). But in the U.S. the functions have been smashed together, and each has been turned to purposes for which it was not designed. The bad results have filled this book.

Even after 9/11, the George W. Bush administration continued to enforce the unnatural union, demanding of cops that they be spies. The president's June 2002 Homeland Security Plan stated unequivocally: "The Department of Justice, and the FBI, will remain the lead agencies for preventing terrorist attacks." Attorney General Ashcroft gave the FBI a "new mission of preventing future terrorist activities." But a new mission does not, in itself, provide the new tools and methods necessary to fulfill the mission. To have obtained and interpreted the leads that could have helped prevent 9/11—to have searched Zacharias Moussaoui's laptop computer and connected its contents with clues from other sources—the FBI would have had to be a radically different outfit. It would have had to be a domestic spy agency, like Britain's MI5.

Terrorism is secret warfare, and it must be countered by a corps of secret warriors. Accordingly, the FBI's secret intelligence work should be severed from its public law-enforcement functions. Instead of being absorbed by the new Homeland Security Agency, all internal-intelligence officers should be spun off into a new agency with spy powers but no law-enforcement mandate. The result would be a British-style system, in which criminal investigation would be handled by the national police (FBI), foreign intelligence would be managed by a foreign-spying unit (CIA), and internal security would be done by a domestic-espionage agency (the new unit). Senator Bob Graham, chairman of the Senate Intelligence Committee, has already suggested splitting law enforcement and domestic intelligence into two agencies; so have others, including Fareed Zacharia and Newt Gingrich. The White House should get on board.

Creation of a domestic spy unit, however, would be only a medium-term fix. The third reform we should undertake—the most long-term measure of the three—is junking the distinction between domestic and foreign intelligence. As money, technology, information, and people cross borders with increasing ease, attempts to distinguish foreign- from domestic-based threats make progressively less sense. The 9/11 hijackers lived in Florida but were supported from Germany, and met contacts in the Czech Republic and Spain. Was their conspiracy, then, a domestic or a foreign phenomenon? The impossibility of coherently answering that question shows the bankruptcy of the paradigm.

We must revise our thinking about what national security is, how it is threatened, and how we must organize our defense. (Here again, the British are ahead of us: Conservative leader Iain Duncan Smith has criticized Prime Minister Tony Blair for attempting to distinguish between domestic and foreign terror threats.) In the U.S., there's an urgent need for the CIA to engage in domestic intelligence. The Agency needs a clear mandate, for instance, to cooperate with and train urban police. Though terrorism cannot be treated primarily as a criminal matter, it's vital that local law-enforcement officers be trained to contribute any intelligence byproduct of their beat work. The CIA also needs authority to stay in "hot pursuit" when overseas suspects cross into the U.S. The National Security Act should be amended to let the CIA work within our borders—in specific cases, against defined threats, under presidential findings, akin to those that provide authority and oversight for covert operations overseas.

We also have to ask: If the old, geographically based model of intelligence work is obsolete, what should replace it? Should we eventually combine the CIA and our domestic spy agency into a single unit, with one chief—and thus have no need to share information, no turf battles, no bureaucratic rivalry? Gregory F. Treverton, former vice-chairman of the National Intelligence Council and now a senior policy analyst at RAND, has proposed something along these lines. The White House should, at a minimum, appoint a commission to examine the issues involved in deprovincializing spy work.

There will be objections to the idea of domestic spying. The entire enterprise of domestic spying, it will be argued, runs counter to the American idea. Wasn't the CIA, for this very reason, denied all "internal-security" functions? Shouldn't we fear erasure of the bright boundary between the Machiavellian methods we sanction overseas, and the Madisonian scruples that must constrain surveillance at home?

To treat these questions fully would require a Lockean treatise on secret government. We do not have one. But we do have history, and our Constitution, and neither requires us to draw the lines we do. Neither our Founders nor our nineteenth-century presidents ran covert actions cartographically; nor does the experience of European democracies suggest that internal spying breeds dictatorship; nor has the Supreme Court ever ruled unconstitutional the domestic surveillance of suspected foreign agents; nor does the Constitution anywhere mandate that intelligence jurisdictions conform to the shapes of oceans, rather than to the judgments of men.

Politics does compel consideration of the popular will, and firm action will not be uncontroversial. But the popular will ought to be based, in turn, on reality. It ought not be based on the public-relations claims of the United States government, on the reassurances that for six decades have been duly proffered whenever scandal breaks. "Now we have addressed that issue," President Bush said in June 2002. "The CIA and FBI are now in close cooperation." Our response to all such statements should take the form of Churchill's rejoinder to status-quo-ers in Parliament, who claimed enough had been done against the Al Qaeda of another age. "They will say to me, 'Reform is not necessary, for all is going well.' I deny it. 'The position is satisfactory.' It is not true. 'All is proceeding according to plan.' We know what that means."

ACKNOWLEDGMENTS

Ash Green, my wise and patient editor, deserves great credit for whatever virtues this book may have. He brought to the editing a broad historical knowledge of national security, prudently trimmed some of my stylistic indulgences, and helped me condense case histories. Above all, he believed in the book when it was only an idea.

Jenny McPhee, an editor at Knopf, was a source of positive criticism and encouragement. Her comments on the chapters were invaluable, and contributed to the truncating of the back of the book. She told me where she was bored by the pile-up of too many petty bureaucratic squabbles, but also where she was engaged by the material. Whenever I felt down about the project, she picked me up.

Terry Zaroff-Evans, my copyeditor, made many excellent catches, and improved the notes section dramatically.

Melvin Rosenthal, my Knopf production editor, was a knowledgeable umpire on matters of style and diction, and was good enough to let me revise things even when it crowded the production schedule.

Gerry Hollingsworth did a diligent legal reading of the manuscript.

Jennifer Bernstein, on the Knopf editorial staff, was bright and efficient and helped see the book through production.

Sonny Mehta, my publisher, has my thanks for taking a chance.

James Hoge, now editor of *Foreign Affairs*, made some remarks to me in Gstaad, in January 1989, which turned my life irrevocably in the direction of this book.

Robin Winks, professor at Oxford and Yale, pointed out in 1987 that there was an important book to be written on the role of the liaison figures.

Acknowledgments

I came up with the idea of a book on FBI-CIA relations independently, but Winks' judgment encouraged me to back my hunch.

Edward Jay Epstein counseled me on how to talk to sources, and his skepticism forced me to shove some of my half-baked theories back in the oven. His seminal research on the defectors controversy awakened me to the interagency aspects of that dispute.

William Safire put me in touch with my most important source on Iraq-Gate.

Gerry Brovey, at the FBI Headquarters Reading Room, helped me find important files.

Kevin J. O'Brien, Freedom of Information coordinator at the FBI, released to me valuable documents.

John H. Wright, FOIA director at CIA, was quick in processing my many requests for memoranda.

John Taylor, overseer of OSS records at the National Archives, helped me find most of the primary materials for Book One.

Aaron "Eggy" Haspel, critic-at-large, did an outstanding close-read of the galleys.

Michael Krantz, screenwriter and journalist, encouraged me to write history, and reminded me of an important professional opportunity.

Casey Fahy, a.k.a. Aeolus, helped load the dreams in the machine.

Neil Peart gave me breaks from the headlong race, and helped me remove the wedge between wishes and fact.

Sam Vaughan, a great editor and a great man, taught me about the making of books.

Lew Grimes, literary agent, is the angel on my shoulder.

Many others helped along the way. For counsel, support, encouragement, or friendship I am grateful to Mike Hicks, Paul Covey, Larry Mone, William Hammett, Michael Limber, Robert Loomis, Chuck Osburn, Alex Gartner, Gerald Klocek, Mary Walsten, Barbara Piper, Margaret Hamilton, Lou Vail, Janice Vessey, Marilyn Colyar, Sadie Koblin, Joni Evans, Peter Osnos, Jason Epstein, Owen Lock, Michael and Judy Berliner, Jake Haspel, Ashby Manson, Burke Shelley, Gregg Eller, Steve Woodruff, Hayden Peake, and James Stevens Valliant.

The Charles and Betty Halter family deserve a special thanks for years of heartening friendship.

Robert Riebling, my father, helped track down documents in Washington, read critically the manuscript and galleys, and let me stay up late that one night, when I was six, to watch *Bridge on the River Kwai*.

Joyce Riebling, my mother, supported me always.

Kelly Rogers proved that Hume was wrong about the sun not having to come up every morning.

NOTES

Notes for the Epilogue and Afterword are posted at secretpolicy.com/wedge/epilogue

ABBREVIATIONS USED IN NOTES

AFIO President, Association of Former Intelligence Officers, who spoke to author in Vienna, Virginia, 2/7/92, on condition of anonymity.

AG United States Attorney General.

Aldhizer interview Author interviews with John T. "Jay" Aldhizer, Fairfax, Virginia, 2/6/92, and by telephone 1/93 and 1/94.

Angleton testimony Sworn testimony of James Angleton, 9/24/75, at U.S. Congress, Senate Select Committee to Study Government Operations with Respect to Intelligence [Church Committee], *Hearings, Vol. II: The Huston Plan.*

AP Associated Press.

BG Boston *Globe.*

BSC British Security Coordinator.

CCH-IV U.S. Congress, Senate Select Committee to Study Government Operations with Respect to Intelligence [Church Committee], *Hearings, Vol. IV: Mail Opening.*

CIA/YIN CIA subject file, Yuri Ivanovich Nosenko, FOIA.

Colby interview Author interview with William E. Colby, Washington, D.C., 2/5/92.

CR/BNL United States Congressional Record, House of Representatives, *Statements by Rep. Henry B. Gonzalez Regarding Banca Nazionale del Lavoro (BNL).*

CSM *Christian Science Monitor.*

CT Chicago *Tribune.*

DCI Director of Central Intelligence.

DeLoach correspondence Letter, Cartha "Deke" DeLoach to author, 1/31/92.

DT *Daily Telegraph* (London).

ECH United States Congress, Senate, Select Committee on Presidential Campaign Activities [Ervin Committee], *Hearings.*

FBI/AKP FBI subject file, Adrian "Kim" Philby, FOIA #100-374183.

FBI/CISPES FBI subject file, Committee in Solidarity with the People of El Salvador, FBI/RR.

FBI/DMP   FBI subject file, Dusko M. Popov, FOIA #65-36994, and operational file (#65-80987), available for review at the National Archives.

FBI/EB   FBI subject file, Elizabeth Bentley, FOIA #65-56402.

FBI/FGP   FBI subject file, Francis Gary Powers, FOIA #105-87346.

FBI/RR   Reading Room files, FBI Headquarters, Washington, D.C.

FBI/TR   FBI subject file, Thomas Riha, FOIA #105-78256.

FBI/WBS   FBI subject file, Walter Bedell Smith, FOIA #94-42836.

FBI/WCS   FBI subject file, William Cornelius Sullivan, FOIA #65-207182.

FBI/WJD   FBI subject file, William Joseph Donovan, FOIA #94-44672.

FBI/WKH   FBI subject file, William King Harvey, FOIA #67-168897.

FBI/YIN   FBI subject file, Yuri Ivanovich Nosenko, FOIA #65-68530.

FNS   Federal News Service.

FOIA   Freedom of Information Act.

FR-I   U.S. Congress, Senate Select Committee to Study Government Operations with Respect to Intelligence [Church Committee], *Final Report, Vol. I: Foreign and Military Intelligence.*

FR-II   Senate Select Committee to Study Government Operations with Respect to Intelligence [Church Committee], *Final Report, Vol. II: Intelligence Activities and the Rights of Americans.*

FR-III   Senate Select Committee to Study Government Operations with Respect to Intelligence [Church Committee], *Final Report, Vol. III: Supplementary Detailed Staff Reports on Intelligence and the Rights of Americans.*

FR-V   Senate Select Committee to Study Government Operations with Respect to Intelligence [Church Committee], *Final Report, Vol. V: The Investigation of President Kennedy—Performance of the Intelligence Agencies.*

GE   *Government Executive.*

GNS   Gannett News Service.

Gonzalez statement   Rep. Henry B. Gonzalez, *The President & the Rostow Gang, CIA Report on BNL . . .* , etc., 7/7/92.

Gray testimony   Sworn testimony of L. Patrick Gray, United States Congress, Senate Select Committee on Presidential Campaign Activities [Ervin Committee], *Hearings,* 8/3/73.

HAH   U.S. Congress, House Select Committee on Assassinations, *Investigation of the Assassination of President John F. Kennedy, Hearings,* 1979.

HAH-II   House Select Committee on Assassinations, *Investigation of the Assassination of President John F. Kennedy, Hearings.* Vol. II.

HAH-IV   House Select Committee on Assassinations, *Investigation of the Assassination of President John F. Kennedy, Hearings.* Vol. IV.

HAH-V   House Select Committee on Assassinations, *Investigation of the Assassination of President John F. Kennedy, Hearings.* Vol. V.

HAH-XII   House Select Committee on Assassinations, *Investigation of the Assassination of President John F. Kennedy, Hearings.* Vol. XII: "Oswald in the Soviet Union: An Investigation of Yuri Nosenko."

HC   Houston *Chronicle.*

Helms interview   Author interview with Richard M. Helms, Washington, D.C., 2/4/92.

HIR   U.S. Congress, House, *Investigation into the Death of Rep. Leo Ryan.*

Houston interview   Author interview with Lawrence R. Houston, Washington, D.C., 2/4/92.

Huston testimony   Sworn testimony of Tom Charles Huston, 9/23/75, at U.S. Congress, Senate Select Committee to Study Government Operations with Respect to Intelligence [Church Committee], *Hearings, Vol. II: The Huston Plan*.

ICH   U.S. Congress, *Joint Hearings Before the House Select Committee to Investigate Covert Arms Transactions with Iran and Senate Select Committee on Secret Military Assistance to Iran and the Nicaraguan Opposition*.

ICH-A   Appendix A, Documents, at U.S. Congress, *Joint Hearings Before the House Select Committee to Investigate Covert Arms Transactions with Iran and Senate Select Committee on Secret Military Assistance to Iran and the Nicaraguan Opposition*.

ICH-B   Appendix B, Depositions, at U.S. Congress, *Joint Hearings Before the House Select Committee to Investigate Covert Arms Transactions with Iran and Senate Select Committee on Secret Military Assistance to Iran and the Nicaraguan Opposition*.

ICR   U.S. Congress, *Report of the Congressional Committees Investigating the Iran-Contra Affair*, November 1987.

IG/67   CIA Inspector General Report, 4/25/67, CIA-FOIA.

IG/93   Unclassified Summary of the Final Report of the Office of Inspector General, "Investigation of CIA's Handling of BNL-Related Matters," 1/14/93.

IJIC   *International Journal of Intelligence and Counterintelligence*.

IR   U.S. Congress, Senate Select Committee to Investigate Government Operations with Respect to Intelligence, *Interim Report: Alleged Assassination Plots Involving Foreign Leaders*.

JEH/O&C   J. Edgar Hoover's Official and Confidential files, FBI/RR.

JSM   Joint Security Mission files, Public Records Office, London.

Lamphere correspondence   Letter, Robert J. Lamphere to author, 11/14/92.

LAT   Los Angeles *Times*.

LLM   Top Secret CIA internal history: Ludwell Lee Montague, "General Walter Bedell Smith as Director of Central Intelligence (1971)," CIA Historical Review Program declassification, 1992.

McWilliams interview   Author interviews with Lawrence F. McWilliams, Alexandria, Virginia, 2/5/92, and by telephone, 6/92.

Miler interview   Author interviews with Newton Scott Miler, Wilmington, North Carolina, 2/12–13/92, and 11/93.

N   *Newsday*.

NA/CD   Records on Cover and Deception, Headquarters of the Army, National Archives, Washington, D.C., Record Group 108, compiled by Bradley F. Smith, reproduced by Garland Publishing (New York, 1989).

NA/S   Central Decimal File, General Records of the Department of State, National Archives Record Group 59, compiled by Bradley F. Smith, reproduced by Garland Publishing (New York, 1989).

Nolan interview   Author interview with James Nolan, Mount Jackson, Virginia, 2/7/92.

NSAV   National Security Archive, Washington, D.C.

NYFO   New York Field Office of the FBI.

NYT   *The New York Times*.

NYTM   *The New York Times Magazine*.

OSS/FBI   OSS FBI files, National Archives, Washington, D.C., Record Group 226.

OSS/NA   General OSS files, National Archives, Record Group 226, Washington, D.C. The indexing and categorizing of these documents is idiosyncratic; the references to OSS files given, for instance, by Thomas Troy, 1981, are not recognized by John Taylor, who oversees OSS records at the Archives. Taylor can, however, help any researcher triangulate to locate individual documents identified by subject, sender/recipient, and date.

OSS/X-2 OSS X-2 files on FBI matters, National Archives, Washington, D.C., Record Group 226.

Papich interview Author interviews with Samuel J. Papich, Albuquerque, New Mexico, 2/12–14/91, and by telephone 5/19/92 and 2/10/93.

R Reuters.

RBD CIA internal history: Arthur B. Darling, "The Central Intelligence Agency: A History to 1950 (1953)," CIA Historical Review Program declassification, November 1990.

RCR President's Commission on CIA Activities Within the United States, *Report to the President* [Rockefeller Commission Report].

Rocca interview Author's telephone interview with Raymond G. Rocca, 12/20/91.

RTR *The Reuter Transcript Report.*

S William Stevenson, *A Man Called Intrepid.*

SDUT San Diego *Union-Tribune.*

SPT St. Petersburg *Times.*

SSCI Senate Select Committee on Intelligence.

SSCI/BNL U.S. Congress, Senate Select Committee on Intelligence, staff report, *The Intelligence Community's Involvement in the Banca Nazionale del Lavoro Affair,* 2/93.

SSCI/JP U.S. Congress, Senate Select Committee on Intelligence, *Hearings on S. 2726 to Improve U.S. Counterintelligence Measures* [Jacobs Panel].

T *Time.*

TI *The Independent* (London).

TNJ *The National Journal.*

TNR *The New Republic.*

TSCS FBI Correlation Summary, William J. Donovan, 11/11/55, in FBI/WJD.

TT Thomas F. Troy, *Donovan and the CIA*, an official CIA history declassified and published in 1981 (see Bibliography).

Turner interview Author interview with Stansfield Turner, Maclean, Virginia, 2/5/92.

UPI United Press International.

USAT *USA Today.*

USNWR *U.S. News & World Report.*

Walters testimony Sworn testimony of Vernon Walters, United States Congress, Senate Select Committee on Presidential Campaign Activities [Ervin Committee], *Hearings*, 8/3/73.

Webster interview Author interview with William H. Webster, Washington, D.C., 2/6/92.

WFO Washington Field Office of the FBI.

WP Washington *Post.*

WSJ *The Wall Street Journal.*

WT Washington *Times.*

In what follows, I have tried to provide enough information to allow other researchers to look up each source. It will be noticed, however, that there is not total uniformity in the manner of citation. Some declassified documents, for instance, are identitifed only by file abbreviation; others simply by their FOIA numbers; others simply as unnumbered FOIA releases, or as available at NSAV or NA. The basic reason for this has been the varied condition of the documents themselves, as they have come into my possession. On some the FOIA numbers are illegible; on others, especially those originating with CIA, there are no FOIA numbers at all. But in each case I have provided all the relevant data I have.

There is also some inevitable fluctuation in citing articles from newspapers, magazines, and wire services. Some articles are identified by author and page numbers in the periodicals in which they appear; others are denoted simply as, e.g., "UPI, 2/5/92." This, too, is due to variegation in "hard copy," but also to the fact that periodicals increasingly exist, for the researcher, only in the "hyperspace" of online data. Indeed, much of the research for the last four chapters of this book was done by online computer database, in which page numbers are sometimes available, sometimes not. Those that are available are only for the page on which the article begins; after the first few paragraphs, one has no way of knowing on what page of "hard copy" a given bit of electronic text actually appears. To avoid guessing at such citations and getting them wrong, I have left them out entirely, except when the "hard copy" is actually in front of me. But all periodical citations not identified by page number are searchable on NEXIS or COMPU-SERVE, simply by keying, as subject: "FBI and CIA and [date]."

When citing secondary works or government reports, I have tried to list also the source cited by the author for that particular assertion. Citing only a secondary source, after all, provides no indication of whether the data are "hard"—e.g., from a document or another researcher's interview—or "soft"—e.g., the product of hearsay or speculation. Moreover, by identifying specific documents and depositions cited in government reports (especially, e.g., FR-III), I hope to allow future researchers to file FOIA requests without having to obtain the "hard copies" of those reports. It seems to me, indeed, that the release of much primary source material, from the Church Committee in particular, is long overdue (and I have been waiting for some of it, under the FOIA, for more than three years).

Like most historians, I have been put on to much of my story by documents originally uncovered by others. In such cases the traditional rule has been to cite the historian in question, unless one has a copy of the document in one's own possession. In some cases I have gone beyond this, however, choosing to cite the historian who originally made me aware of a particular document, even when I have ended up chasing down a copy myself, so as to properly reflect the importance of that historian's research in my account.

In any book on secret intelligence, especially one of this length, some assertions are inevitably unattributed. Like intelligence officers, historians of espionage have their own sources-and-methods problems. In most cases it is a matter of protecting a source who does not want his or her identity disclosed. Powers, in his book on Helms (1979), covers this contingency by saying that "I have generally refrained from stating directly who told me what." But I have generally attempted to attribute each assertion, and except in a few cases (such as the former AFIO president), I have not relied on anonymous sources. I believe that this broader sourcing has its value, but I know that, compared with the Powers method, it creates more bother in the breach. I have personally been frustrated by such books as Dunlop (1982), which source a lot of things, but also leave empty space where important claims could have been undergirded. Much of this is a matter of expectations, and meeting them, and my great fear is that a diligent researcher may, on occasion, be frustrated in trying to follow me up. This will mostly have been due, I think, to error in my execution rather than in my intent. In a few cases, however, where facts are fairly well known (e.g., in the Castro assassination plots, or the Nosenko case) I have sometimes not felt it necessary to source every detail. In any event, I invite curious parties to write me in care of the publisher, so that sourcing may perhaps be supplied in a subsequent edition, or curiosity at least satisfied. In this age of faxes, E-mail, and file-sharing, I should hope that such matters could be handled fairly expeditiously.

Finally, when "triggering" direct quotations, I have avoided literalistically inserting ellipses [. . .] every time a quotation is cited in fragementary form. For instance, a quotation in the main text might read: "the closest possible marriage between the FBI and British Intelligence," and be represented in a note, by relevant page number, simply as: "closest possible marriage." In such cases, it seems to me, the usual [. . .] at either end of the phrase may be read as implied.

PROLOGUE: FOR SPECIAL SERVICES

3 On Fleming's mission, I have utilized extensively a Godfrey-Fleming memo (7/7/41, JSM), which Bradley F. Smith recently discovered in the British archives. I have also relied on TT, pp. 59, 81–83; S, pp. 163–64; Dunlop, pp. 281–82; and Pearson, p. 97.

For British perspectives on Hoover and Donovan, I have guardedly utilized the account of William Stevenson (S). Most of the BSC documents cited by Stevenson are not publicly available, and this has led some scholars, such as Thomas Troy, to doubt the veracity of his account. But Stevenson's reliability is confirmed in some respects by recently declassified memoranda, and his access to the British intelligence papers is in fact proved by Stevenson's accurate quotations from the Godfrey-Fleming memo (S, p. 162), fully a decade before that memo was unearthed in the British archives by Smith.

Though I disagree with Troy on the veracity of Stevenson, I have found Troy's book on Donovan (TT), originally a secret study for CIA, to be invaluable. Unfortunately, many of Troy's primary sources—like Stevenson's—are not available to other researchers; even those that have been declassified and released to the National Archives are cited by Troy in a way that is incommensurate with the Archives' own indexing system. Other documents cited by Troy have been released to the Archives but were pulled in 1987 by CIA.

A lot has been written on Donovan, but much of it is hagiography. I have tried to balance the adulatory treatments of Ford, 1970, Dunlop, and Brown, 1982, with the more straightforward TT and the sometimes quite negative TSCS.

sandbag: Quirk, whose veracity has been questioned by some.

"report on": Godfrey-Fleming memo, 7/7/41, JSM. Although the document bears Godfrey's signature, it seems to me that Fleming's authorship may be presumed. It was (and is) common practice for assistants to draft their superiors' memoranda; Fleming, moreover, had previously been a journalist and had been assigned to Godfrey specifically to write reports and correspondence; his later role in writing up recommendations for Donovan is well documented. There is no doubt, however, that Godfrey's own ideas, if not his words, must have made a great and perhaps the major contribution to the summary of the trip.

Stephenson, etc.: DT, 2/3/89.

4   "twilight-zone," etc.: Henry Stimson, "Notes After Cabinet Meeting," 4/4/41, TT, p. 46.

British trained FBI: Papich interview.

Hoover prosecution vs. secrecy: Ewen Montagu interviewed at S, p. 249; BSC Papers cited at ibid., p. 269. This complaint was not unique to the British. "Put it this way," recalled Sam Papich, an FBI agent for nearly 30 years, most of them in counterintelligence. "If he saw the potential for prosecution, Hoover's line of thinking would be, 'Go for it.' " (Papich interview.)

5   "fundamental to any understanding": BSC Papers, S, p. 162.

On Hoover's early life and career, the most valuable source is probably R. G. Powers, pp. 4–35, although it has been pointed out that Powers makes a bit much of Hoover's growing up in white, middle-class America (so did most government bureaucrats, after all).

On Hoover's appearance and character, see especially Bill Howard interviewed at Demaris, pp. 3–26; James E. Crawford interviewed at ibid., p. 34; Felt, pp. 43–44; probate records at Demaris, p. 394.

JEH/Tolson routine: Helms interview.

Hoover provincialism, "never trusted any foreigners": McWilliams interview. The former FBI agent added: "Hoover's refusal to leave the United States is even more baffling because in his position he could have traveled all over the world and *bands* would have been playing for him. In fact, I'll always remember, when we thought Hoover was getting close to retirement—the British have a tradition of a tour around the world for their security chiefs, say goodbye to all their friends, and stuff like that, a lot of countries do that, but one of our legal attachés in England said, 'Oh, my God, don't have a world tour!' Because if he was going to England, he would want the royal guard for him, you know what I mean? There'd be devastation from one end of the world to the other."

5–6   "singleness of purpose," "pride and his vanity": S, p. 162.

6   FBI headquarters: Wright, p. 101.

7   "If we didn't have Mr. Hoover": letter to *Life*, 4/30/71, at Donner, p. 82.

Hoover's turf-jealousy: DeLoach correspondence.

"closest possible marriage": BSC Papers, S, p. 80.

8   FBI refusal to analyze: Raymond Wannall testimony, 1/21/76, FR-I, p. 171.

"flanked with teams": Fleming-Godfrey memo, 7/7/41, JSM.

"prima donna"; Stimson Diary, 10/14/40, TT, p. 46.

"childish, petulant": Stimson Diary, 2/13/41, TT, p. 47.

"less strict": BSC Papers, S, p. 163.

"impressions made by Special Agents": *Bureau Bulletin*, no. 1, 1st ser., 1/2/40 (FBI FOIA #66-03-288). Bureau circulars denied that the director wanted "in any way to infringe upon . . . personal liberties" (FBI-SAC letter no. 38, 5/8/24, FBI-FOIA), but the real dangers may have been less personal than professional. Clarence Kelley, one of Hoover's successors as FBI director, conducted a study of the investigative climate under the legendary leader, and concluded that FBI agents routinely "sugarcoated" the truth for fear of upsetting Hoover. When asked about this remark, former FBI agent Sam Papich denied that he, personally, ever felt he had to sugarcoat anything for the top brass, but perhaps this was just the point, for he himself was forced out of the Bureau in 1970 for speaking his mind.

9   Foxworth: Popov, pp. 157ff.

      "small and uncoordinated," etc.: Fleming-Godfrey memo, 7/7/41, JSM.

      "not well understood": ibid.

10   "chunky enigmatic": Pearson, p. 114.

      "expressed himself": ibid.

      "Someone ought to," etc.: Fleming interviewed at S, p. 129.

      "covered with corns": Fleming, 1954, p. 18.

      "shattering roar": Fleming quoted at Pearson, p. 114.

11   For Donovan's young life and early career, see especially Ford, pp. 11–18; Brown, 1982, pp. 11–101. His father was a railroad yardmaster. One press report of the day described him as "a square-faced Irishman with China blue eyes, who looks oddly out of place behind a desk. . . . Calculating, ambitious, he has a temperamental love for intrigue." (TSCS clipping 4/6/41.) Some historians (e.g., Ranelagh) would later find it symbolic that Donovan had gone to Columbia, Hoover to the more accessible George Washington University, but to stress the contrast was to miss the fact that Columbia, during the time Donovan attended, was no longer a "preserve of the ruling class." It may have been so twenty years before, but by the 1910s it was increasingly second-generation-immigrant, increasingly Jewish, and the older money preferred to send its children to Harvard and Princeton and Yale. Franklin Roosevelt had been at Columbia with Wild Bill, but only at the Law School, and it was an undergraduate class that really conferred status. Morningside Heights was still a place where lower- or middle-class kids could go to make good, and in that sense it was appropriate that Donovan, a scholarship student from the Irish side of the tracks in Buffalo, would gain his access to higher society via Columbia, but graduating from the Ivy League hardly made him an automatic member of the "American elite." For Donovan's character generally I have drawn on Houston and Colby interviews; Cline, p. 76; Downes, p. 151; and Hyde, p. 34.

    "My secret legs," Donovan's travels: Houston interview.

    Donovan in Britain: S, pp. 8off. A later FBI memo noted: "Donovan conferred with [FBI agent] Clegg at which time reference was made to their previous meeting which was a breakfast on Christmas Day 1940 in Col. Donovan's suite at the Claridge Hotel in London. Col. Donovan commended the FBI for the approach which the FBI mission made in connection with their survey. Col. Donovan stated that he had told the President that if he accomplished nothing else of value to his Gov't during World War II, one thing which could be placed to his credit was helping to pave the way in England for FBI representatives to obtain valuable information concerning most confidential matters." Hoover noted in blue ink: "If I recall correctly I think we were there before the Colonel arrived. H." (Memo for the Director, 11/29/41, TSCS.)

    WJD-Stephenson: TSCS, 3/11/42.

    "I have been attempting": BSC cable, Stephenson to Churchill, n.d. [c. 5/19/41], S, p. 249.

    Far East informant-sharing: for Hoover-Donovan cooperation on this and other minor matters, see TSCS: [informant] to FBI, 4/18/40; Hoover to Foxworth, 4/23/40; Hoover to Donovan, 10/4/40, 10/9/40; Donovan to Hoover, 10/16/40.

12   Donovan and Hoover at Justice: FBI memos, Hoover to Donovan, 10/18/24 (at Cummings and McFarland, pp. 430–31) and 4/18/28 (at Whitehead, p. 332). For unsourced rumors of clashes, see also Corson, p. 69; Ford, pp. 19–20; Gentry, pp. 74, 135–36, 142; Donner, pp. 46–47; Lowenthal, p. 299; Theoharis and Cox, p. 216; Casey, p. 37; Dunlop, pp. 153, 162; Brown, 1982, pp. 95–97.

For rumors about the less attractive aspects of Donovan's personality, see, e.g., at FBI/WJD, Buffalo memo, n.d., [7/53]; FBI New York report, 8/19/41; FBI New York report, 6/30/53. Even so, FBI files note that Donovan, while United States attorney, had sanctioned a raid upon the Saturn Club in Buffalo, of which he himself was then a member. A number of members were charged with violation of the Federal Prohibition Act, and as a consequence Donovan lost the friendship of many wealthy and influential members of the club, who felt he had betrayed them in a public-relations scheme. But the act was widely applauded by the Buffalo citizens (FBI Buffalo memo, n.d., [7/53], TSCS).

"persuade," "personal interest": Fleming-Godfrey memo, 7/7/41, JSM.

12–13 "security of intelligence," "details as to how," etc.: ibid.

13   "trained powers," etc.: ibid.

"should be under the protection," "strategic mentality": Fleming to Donovan, 6/27/41, TT, p. 81. In 5/87, this document, available for years at the National Archives, was inexplicably withdrawn at the request of CIA. Fragments of it, however, are quoted by Troy, who was apparently the only scholar to see it before its removal. In the early 1960s, Fleming bragged to his biographer, John Pearson, that he had produced a "memorandum to Bill [Donovan] on how to create an American secret service," and the withdrawn memo does contain a suggestive "See my previous memo," but the "previous" memo has never been found. Troy quotes Fleming's 6/27 memo as saying that intelligence officers must have "trained powers of observation, analysis, and evaluation, absolute discretion, sobriety, devotion to duty, languages and wide experience and be aged about forty to fifty." Additionally, Donovan's agency "should be under the protection of a strong government department and should be insured by every means possible against political interference or control."

Donovan's proposal: Donovan to Roosevelt, 6/10/41, TT, pp. 419–20.

"discussed with the President direct": Godfrey-Fleming memo, 7/7/41, JSM.

14   "not in any way interfere": Tamm to Hoover, 6/11/41, TSCS. Donovan indeed made some pro-forma effort to play by the rules. When J. William Dooley, an experienced private detective from Troy, New York, offered to run down German-American subversives, Donovan put him off. "Unfortunately, our work does not call for the use of investigators [domestically]. . . . I would suggest, therefore, that you might submit your application to the FBI." (Donovan to Dooley, n.d. [c. 8/41], OSS/FBI.)

"neither necessary nor desirable": Tamm to Hoover, 6/11/41, TSCS.

"a loose football": Houston interview.

"calamitous," etc.: report by Hoover, Miles, and Kirk, 5/29/41, TT, p. 51.

"reduced the twilight zone": Miles to Gen. George C. Marshall, 4/8/41, TT, p. 51.

COI created: FDR executive order, 7/11/41, TT, p. 423.

"You can imagine": BSC cable, Stephenson to Churchill, 7/2/41, S, p. 249.

15   "cutting a man down the middle": Helms deposition, 4/24/75, p. 22, FR-
III, p. 710.
      "Roosevelt's Folly": Dunlop, p. 289.
      Fleming counsel: memo to Donovan, 6/27/41, TT, p. 81.
      "allay any fears," etc.: Tamm to Hoover, 6/27/41, TSCS.
      "For Special Services:" Pearson, p. 118.

1. THE TRICYCLE TRUST

The Popov/Pearl Harbor connection was revealed just after Hoover's death
by former British counterintelligence officer Sir John Masterman, who printed
a copy of the Abwehr questionnaire and alleged that American intelligence
had failed to appreciate its significance. Masterman's account was embellished
considerably in a book by Popov himself, who alleged that he had met personally
with Hoover in New York in September 1941; that the FBI persecuted him
for his "playboy" lifestyle; and that he had warned the U.S. explicitly about an
attack on Pearl Harbor before the end of the year. Popov's version was endorsed
by Ewen Montagu, a British counterintelligence official who worked with him
in both England and the United States, and was then uncritically recited by
historians such as John Toland and Anthony Cave Brown, who claimed that
Hoover "sat" on the questionnaire instead of distributing it to other government
agencies. Former CIA officials such as William Hood and William Casey have
also accepted Popov's account as gospel. Most recently, Anthony Summers has
quoted numerous former British intelligence officials as confirming that Popov
did warn of an attack on Pearl Harbor.

But Thomas Troy, in an outstanding analysis of the case, has attacked the
idea that Popov ever explicitly tipped the FBI about Pearl Harbor. And after
Popov's 1974 account received some public attention, the FBI announced that
a review of its "instant file" on Popov found no evidence that he ever met
Hoover or warned of a Japanese attack. "The Pearl Harbor story," wrote the
Bureau man who oversaw the review, "is a typical example of 'Monday morning
quarterbacking' in that he now plays up an explanation of the significance of
the material he furnished which our file does not show he mentioned contempo-
raneously." The Bureau also insisted that Hoover had not "buried" any information received from Popov.

The public release of a portion of the FBI's Dusko Popov file in 1982,
while conclusively showing that Popov's microdots *did* contain the Pearl Harbor
questionnaire, and that the FBI had the Pearl questions translated by September 3, 1941, also gave some weight to the FBI's defense. These documents
showed that Hoover had routed paraphrased versions of the questionnaire to
naval and military intelligence and even to the White House, and had not
simply "sat" on the information. Troy reviewed the documents and noted that
their declassified portions contained "no hint of an attack warning" by Popov.
Troy also argued that the British might have had good reason to treat the
questionnaire with some caution if they suspected Popov's bona fides; that the
questions did not neccesarily indicate an air attack, as opposed to sabotage;
and that if Hoover failed to appreciate the importance of the questions, the
same criticism might be made of Hoover's British attackers, who (by their own
account) had a copy of the questions. In Troy's view, then, "the accusation

against J. Edgar Hoover on his alleged responsibility for the Pearl Harbor disaster is not the truth but a canard."

But the conclusion that declassified FBI documents vindicate Hoover and refute Popov is based on a false premise—namely, the idea that if something is not reported to the public in heavily censored FBI documents, it did not happen. This kind of thinking is evident throughout Troy's work on the problem.

Alternatively, Troy posits that most of the FBI's redactions pertain to British intelligence, since there is a "total absence of any mention of" the British in the FBI files as we have them. This inference seems to me equally unsound. By Troy's logic, one might just as easily conclude that most of the redactions pertain to Popov's Pearl Harbor warning, since there is also a "total absence" of it, too, in the redacted files.

Even if Popov did not give an explicit warning, however, the point remains that the FBI did not treat the Pearl Harbor queries as strategic intelligence, did not pass them to COI, and did not handle Popov expertly—as even Troy is willing to concede.

19 secret agent entered the United States: Popov arrived by clipper on 8/12/41, according to FBI memo, Foxworth to Hoover, 8/26/41, FBI/DMP. Brown, 1975, p. 61, incorrectly gives the date as 8/24, as does Breuer.

Popov's physical appearance: Foxworth to Hoover, 8/26/41, FBI/DMP.

Estoril casino scene: Popov, pp. 125–27; Fleming, 1953, pp. 7–8.

Popov as model for Bond: It is true that Popov's recollection of the casino episode appeared twenty years after Fleming's fictional account, and it is possible that Popov modeled his memories after Fleming's fiction. But Popov's role as model for Bond is upheld, rather than disputed, by British intelligence officers (e.g., Montagu) who knew both Fleming and Popov, and Popov's daring, arrogant, prodigal nature certainly made an impression on all who came in contact with him, including, of course, the FBI. Popov's account of secret life in Lisbon, moreover, is correct in independently verifiable details. For instance, the Hotel Palacio, where Popov says he stayed, was indeed a haunt of spies during World War II. In 3/41, Donovan met there with Averell Harriman (in a room checked carefully for listening devices) before continuing across the Atlantic to report to FDR on his mission to the Balkans and the Mideast. Pinto, the concierge, later said: "All the Allied agents stayed at the Palacio. The Axis agents stayed at the Hotel De Parque, which is just across the gardens." That was just as Popov had it. See Dunlop, p. 238.

Popov's espionage gear: FBI memo for Ladd, 10/16/41; FBI New York memo, 9/17/41; FBI Personal and Confidential memo, Connelley to Hoover, 8/19/41; SAC to Hoover, 8/25/41; all at FBI/DMP. See also Popov, pp. 128–29.

19–20 His first evening in New York is described in Popov, pp. 155–56.

20 Popov surveilled: FBI New York memo, 9/17/41. One of the surveilling agents was Sam Papich, who later became liaison to CIA (Papich interview).

Popov's initial meeting with the FBI is reconstructed from FBI New York memo, 9/17/41; Tamm to Hoover, 8/6/41: addenda, 8/18/41; FBI Personal and Confidential memos, Connelley to Hoover, 8/19/41, 8/25/41; FBI blind memo, 12/19/41; FBI memo to Foxworth, 8/21/41; all at FBI/DMP.

That Popov explained his allegiance and intelligence mission to the FBI is evident from Foxworth to Hoover, 8/26/41, and Tamm to Hoover, 8/16/41. Popov (pp. 168–71) claims that he personally met with Hoover in New York concerning a Pearl Harbor attack, an allegation repeated uncritically by Hood (pp. 214–15) and other Hoover detractors. Summers (p. 128) alleges that Hoover's office records show him visiting New York in late 9/41, when Popov was there, sourcing this claim rather opaquely to "Hoover phone logs." FBI officials (Kelley to Dunn, 10/1/73) have denied that Hoover ever met Popov.

21   Pearl Harbor warning: Popov, pp. 158–59.
22   "a general picture": COI minutes, 9/10/41, Dunlop, pp. 323–24.
Landon's perspective is from his interview at ibid., pp. 301–2.
"Good morning, sir": ibid.
Jimmy Roosevelt: see Roosevelt, passim.
"anything and everything": Hoover memo for the record, 8/19/41, FBI/ WJD.
23   "much useful information": Donovan to Hoover, 8/20/41, OSS/FBI.
23–4 "Exact details," etc.: Hoover to New York Field Office, 9/17/41, FBI/DMP. The full translation of Popov's questionnaire was first made public by Masterman, pp. 196–98.
24   "to our yellow allies": testimony at espionage trial of Kurt Ludwig, New York City, 2/42, cited at Breuer, p. 199.
"results": Popov, p. 170.
25   Brazil: ibid., pp. 146–50; FBI memo, 12/22/41, FBI/DMP.
abridged questionnaire: Hoover to Watson, 9/3/41, FBI/DMP.
"the reliability of which": FBI memo, R. G. Fletcher to D. M. Ladd, 10/20/ 41, FBI/DMP.
"monkeys on the payroll," "Jewish scribblers": James Murphy interviewed at Dunlop, p. 308.
26   "to instruct my Special Agents": Hoover to Donovan, 9/15/41, OSS/FBI.
"during which many were hurt": Hoover to Donovan, 10/16/41, OSS/FBI.
"Pacific situation": Donovan to Hoover 10/22/4, OSS/FBI.
luncheon: TSCS, 12/2/41.
returning Japanese missionary: Hoover to Donovan, 12/3/41, TSCS.
Mowrer's mission: manuscript, "Final Report of Edgar Ansel Mowrer to Colonel Donovan Concerning a Mission to the Far East in the Autumn of 1941," 12/4/41, in Allen Dulles Papers, Princeton University Library.
Thurston and Foxworth as liaison points: Bruce to Donovan, 7/24/42, OSS/ FBI.
27   "upset the applecart": Mayer interviewed at Dunlop, p. 330.
28   "Donovan is taking it very easy": Memo for Hoover, 7/31/41, TSCS. The report apparently came from Henry Grunewald, a Washington lobbyist and Hoover friend.
"would be appointed," etc.: ibid.
"would be very receptive": TSCS, 11/11/41.
"Certain faux pas": FBI New York letter, 10/22/41, with 11/20/41 report, TSCS.
"Donovan knows everything": *Collier's*, 11/21/41, clipped at TSCS.
"the Bureau does not possess": Hoover to Donovan, 11/24/41, OSS/FBI.
Donovan's motorcar: FBI telegram, Washington to Police Chiefs, 4/10/28, TSCS. Brown's well-written biography of Donovan (1982, p. 222) gets wrong

both the date of the first entry in the FBI's Donovan file (1928, not 1924) and the nature of intelligence therein. The file does not consist merely of "gossip," but contains the "raw," or unanalyzed, reports that are the basis of all intelligence. Many of Hoover's sources were highly placed in government, as assistants to men such as Navy Secretary Frank Knox—the kinds of individuals who would be valued recruits for a foreign-intelligence service, not to mention as informants for Hoover's domestic network.

Donovan would have Hoover "fired": FBI letter, 7/17/36, TSCS. According to the correlation summary, this is "a letter from E. J. Connelley [he of the later Dusko Popov episode] in St. Paul, Minnesota . . . relating that former Bureau Agent O. G. Hall told of Grady L. Boatwright making the statement to him that William J. Donovan was going to have Hoover fired. . . . Boatwright went on to say that 'Wild Bill' Donovan, 'Cotton Ed' Smith, and Joe Robinson,' were in league with 'Senator MacKellar.' "

29   "from time to time": memo for Hoover, 1/5/42, FBI/WJD.
"undisciplined atmosphere": ibid.
Atherton Richards: TSCS, 7/19/41.
"totally unfit temperamentally": TSCS, 6/8/43.
Sofia nightclub: That the FBI knew about this incident is clear from TSCS, 2/5/42. In 3/45, Gestapo agents in Sofia were charged with "theft of briefcase, passport and private papers" belonging to Donovan ("Gestapo Chastens 'Wild Bill,' " Washington *Daily News*, 3/20/45, TSCS).
"drove his security chiefs": Lovell, p. 217. It is perhaps worth noting that, in the loose-goose atmosphere which favored action over security, Donovan's men relied on alcohol for the forging of close personal relations among agents and principals, who might not otherwise be inclined to trust each other. Such occupational drunkenness tended to increase as Donovan's men spent more time with members of British intelligence. Hoover, whose own agents would be fired for boozing on the job, knew that drinking-and-talking was not the best way to keep a country's secrets safe.
"claimed he had something": FBI New York letter, 9/29/41, TSCS.
"a very good friend of," "a German spy": FBI memo, 11/9/41, FBI/WJD.
"Donovan was believed": FBI memos, 12/17/41, 2/5/42, FBI/WJD.
30   "key positions": Office of War Information memo, 12/8/43, FBI/WJD.
"*anybody* in their right mind": McWilliams interview.
"consistently denied": Peters to Pfaff, 6/3/44, OSS/X-2. COI was clearly concerned, during the three weeks before Pearl Harbor, as to whether it was getting from the FBI as much intelligence as it was giving. On 11/17/41, Colonel Ned Buxton, who ran COI's New York Oral Intelligence Unit at 270 Madison Avenue, had reason to send Donovan a memo titled "Cooperation with the FBI," itemizing what Oral Intelligence had turned over to the Bureau since its inception. The disseminations included "names of half a dozen individuals whose further investigation by the FBI was deemed advisable," such as "Maria Markan, Opera Star," and "Herman von Griemeien, former German agent who is now in Bermuda, on his way to this country" (Buxton to Donovan, 11/17/41, OSS/FBI).
Although the Magic intercepts had been withheld from Donovan, the intercepts did reveal on 12/3 that an attack was imminent, and on 12/6 that the Japanese Embassy in the U.S. had been instructed to burn secret documents.

From COI's frantic actions on the eve of the bombing, it seems likely that Donovan did receive some sanitized briefing about the possibility of imminent hostilities, but code-breaking alone could not have prevented disaster, because Japan never sent any message saying, "We shall attack Pearl Harbor." Not even the ships of the strike force knew the target was Hawaii. Other intelligence— such as Popov's questionnaire—would be required to piece together a best guess about where the Japanese might strike. For an interesting round-up of the evidence from recent studies, see Mitgang.

British hid the Popov case from Donovan: Troy, 1989, rightly observes that, if Hoover is to be censured for burying or misreading Popov's Pearl Harbor queries, British intelligence deserves an equal share of the blame, for they either failed to grasp the queries' import or, if they did understand, failed to warn U.S. intelligence officials (either at FBI or COI). On the other hand, two former British intelligence officers, James Rusbridger and Eric Nave, have recently alleged that Churchill plotted to draw the U.S. into the war, in order to save his own besieged country from the Nazis. If so, perhaps that was why the British did not convey a more explicit warning to the U.S. about Popov's questionnaire. It seems a project too callous to imagine of such a heroic man, but Churchill's own account of his emotions, on hearing of the greatest disaster in U.S. naval history, has always echoed oddly. His mood (Churchill, 1960, p. 61) was one of "the greatest joy," for "at this very moment I knew that the United States was in the war, up to the neck and to the death. So we had won after all! . . . England would live. . . . No doubt it would take a long time [but] . . . united [with the U.S.] we could subdue everybody else in the world. Many disasters, immeasurable cost and tribulation lay ahead, but there was no doubt about the end."

2. NO-MAN'S-LAND

31 "They caught our ships": Donovan interviewed at Dunlop, pp. 333–34.
"That corner of Washington": Ford and MacBain, pp. 3–4.

32 "Some of his ideas": Houston interview.
"frightening, demoralizing," etc.: FDR to Donovan, 2/9/42, Smith, 1983, p. 159. The great bat scheme came to be called Project X-Ray, to mislead the Japanese in case they heard of it. Tales of vast bat colonies in Texas caused OSS officials to hire a local guano miner, who led two of Donovan's men into a cave containing about thirty million Mexican free-tailed bats; a number of captured samples were taken to a blimp hangar at Moffett Field on San Francisco Bay. After it was learned that the Japanese did not fear bats, it was decided to try attaching fifteen-gram delayed-action incendiary bombs to the specimens. Harvard chemist Louis F. Fieser, who was then pioneering the use of napalm, believed that the bats could be dropped in five-foot-long sheet-metal payloads holding 1,040 bats each; at four thousand feet above the ground, an altimeter would trigger a parachute and the bomb would blow apart, disbursing the bats and pulling the pins on their time fuses. The bats would go to roost in Japan's attics, roofs, and lofts; the napalm bombs would detonate; whole Japanese cities, being built almost entirely of wood, would be turned to ash. Tests in New Mexico showed that the idea could actually work, but the plug was abruptly pulled on the project in early 1944, apparently because U.S. planners decided to rely on a more decisive technology—namely, the atom bomb. Jack Couffer,

who helped OSS on the great bat scheme, recalls it in his book. See also Ferrell; Smith, 1983, p. 159, citing Donovan to FDR, 2/28/42, and David Bruce to NYT, 2/9/59.

33   "on numerous occasions": TSCS.

"fired by the afternoon": McWilliams interview.

"I always had the feeling": Lamphere, p. 15.

"lieutenant with guts enough": Peter Karlow interviewed at Ranelagh, p. 65.

"Identikit," "the same mold": Helms interview.

"not at all as parochial": Houston interview.

"arrogant amateurs": Maurice Isserman at Robins, p. 191.

"Ivy League dilettantes": Papich interview.

34   "appallingly low": Downes Papers, Winks, p. 179.

"a few youthful mistakes": Cuneo interviewed at Gentry, p. 268.

"Communist elements": FBI blind memo, 1/5/42, TSCS.

"the obvious remark": Malcolm Cowley Private Papers, n.d., Robins, p. 221.

35   "sort of in fun but not entirely": Lamphere correspondence.

"I have no authority": notation on Tamm to Hoover, 12/19/41, TSCS. Donovan did not in every case keep personnel over Hoover's objections. In spring 1942, an FBI background check on novelist Josephine Herbst, who worked on COI's German Desk, revealed that Herbst and her husband were Communist Party members, and that Mrs. Herbst had been a courier for the party in 1934. On 5/20/42, Donovan wrote Hoover acknowledging "adequate" reasons for terminating her employment "as of noon today." As she returned from lunch, uniformed security guards seized Herbst, padlocked her desk and locker, searched her handbag, and marched her off the premises (Hoover to Donovan, 5/20/42, FBI Herbst file, Robins, pp. 229–30).

"midwife": Philby, p. 84.

"strangle": Bruce, p. 63.

36   "a delicate case": Ernest Cuneo, quoted at Winks, p. 155.

"a fraud, a liar": Winks, p. 214.

"ideals as weapons": ibid., p. 159.

"FBI on my tail": Downes, p. 87.

37   "like blotting paper": Winks, p. 168.

"We want to read their cables": Downes, pp. 88–89.

"straighten out this whole program": FDR to AG et al., 12/30/41, FBI/WJD.

"on special occasions," "with a specific mission": "Notes on Meeting in Attorney General's Office, January 6, 1942," TT, p. 119.

"seemed considerably put out": Hoover to AG, 12/31/41, TSCS.

In the two-and-a-half-hour conference in the office of AG Francis Biddle on 1/6/42, according to FBI records, "the conclusion was reached that Col. Donovan intended to initiate operations in the Western Hemisphere. These operations would consist of sending a representative to Central or South America for the purpose of gathering information concerning general conditions as well as special matters. . . . It was felt [by some] that it would be better for Col. Donovan to take over the work of the FBI in the SIS field since he was going to embark into certain phases in that field." (Hoover to AG, 1/6/42, FBI/WJD.)

Four days after accepting the 1/6 agreement, which ceded Western Hemisphere primacy to the FBI, Donovan was working to destroy it. He griped that the agreement was based on a false premise—namely, the FBI director's worry that COI was out to steal his turf. Donovan claimed that he had "constantly refrained from going into South America," that he had turned down an offer from Hoover to take over the FBI's Latin America network because he "thought it unwise to do so," that he had no desire "to take over [JEH's] organization or set up one of my own in South America." He did, however, have the duty of coordinating strategic information, and the FBI had not been helping out. (Donovan to Biddle, 1/10/42, OSS/FBI.) Hoover, happy to have his way, moved to meet Donovan's complaint that the FBI's Latin American take was not being furnished to COI, and the floodgates were soon opened for a slush of untargeted and essentially valueless FBI intelligence, prompting an overwhelmed COI professor, Preston James, to propose for Donovan's signature a letter to Hoover, "indicating our appreciation of his numerous memoranda and letters, and suggesting a line of investigation which he apparently has not undertaken but one which is of great importance." That draft letter has not been preserved, and its suggested "line of investigation" is unknown, but the tenor of James' frustration with the FBI's "non-geographers" was apparently too much even for Donovan, who reprimanded James: "If Hoover isn't looking for this material he should, but I don't like this letter." (Notation on Hoover to Donovan, 2/3/42; notation on James to Donovan 3/9/42, OSS/FBI.) Donovan had meanwhile recommended to Hoover that COI assume responsibility for all intelligence in Mexico, and that the FBI be responsible for the continental U.S. and its territories. Hoover declined to accept this restructuring, and Donovan took the matter to FDR, who told him to "work this out yourself" (FDR to Donovan, 1/27/42, OSS/FBI). In short, Donovan had lost the fight. But COI had its needs for Latin American intelligence, and if quality product could not be culled from FBI memos, Donovan had other sources—such as Wallace Phillips and Donald Downes.

"arbitrary geographical limitations": Downes, p. 93.

38   Mexico City: Downes, pp. 102, 109; Welles to Roosevelt, 4/29/42, TT, p. 142.

"about 20 civilian agents," etc.: Phillips to Donovan, 3/11/42, OSS/FBI.

staffers nervous: Phillips to Donovan, 2/4/42; Williamson to Bruce, 2/19/42; Phillips to Donovan, 3/11/42; Phillips to Donovan, 2/25/42; all at OSS/FBI.

39   "Donald Downs" [*sic*]: Hoover to Donovan, n.d. [c. 4/2/42], Brown, 1982, p. 222. If this memo was ever in the National Archives or in the FBI's file on Donovan, it has been pulled. Brown apparently found it in Donovan's private papers.

"some ninety agents": Welles to Donovan, 3/25/42; Donovan to Welles, 3/26/42; both at OSS/FBI.

get-well wishes: FDR to Donovan, 4/14/42, OSS/FBI.

"dirty and contemptible lie": Donovan to Roosevelt, 4/27/42, OSS/FBI.

evidence: Berle to Welles, 4/29/42; Welles to FDR, 4/29/42, TT, p. 142.

"humpty-dumpties": Kimbel to Donovan, 5/23/42; OSS cable to Phillips, n.d.; both at OSS/FBI.

"for reasons of his own": Phillips to Donovan, 5/20/42, OSS/FBI.

"Donovan would attempt to take over": FBI memo for Hoover, 6/15/42, TSCS.

embassy operation: Downes, pp. 88–97.

40   "very much against the law": Winks, p. 173.

"betrayal by someone high enough": Downes, p. 93.

"only the FBI checking": ibid., p. 94.

"penetrating," "annoyed": ibid.

"no man's land": ibid., p. 87.

41   "location of any representatives": Hoover to Donovan, 10/22/42, OSS/FBI. Gentry (p. 295) incorrectly dates this episode to 4/42.

"a member of the Gestapo": this and other OSS leads to FBI are set out in OSS internal survey memo, 7/24/42, OSS/FBI.

42   "penetration of the totalitarian": Hoover to Donovan, 2/3/42, OSS/FBI.

"These charts": Preston James note on ibid.

"the Abwehr gets better treatment": quoted at Mosley, p. 129.

"properly was the Bureau's business": Houston interview.

"a Mr. Brown," "The personnel": Downes, p. 97.

"no matter to what part of the globe": ibid., p. 93

43   Bedeaux: ibid., pp. 83ff.

Naples: Downes, pp. 151–54.

3. DOUBLE CROSS

44   "vitally important:" memo to Ladd, 12/16/41, FBI/DMP.

"butterfly trays": FBI report, 12/15/41; memo for Ladd, 12/16/41; memo for Tracy, 12/23/41; all at FBI/DMP. I have also drawn on Papich interview.

45   "In the USA": memo, 12/24/41, FBI/DMP.

"was not even taken": Hyde, pp. 221–22.

"had not uncovered": memo, 11/29/41, FBI/DMP.

FBI dumped Popov: memo, 10/1/73, FBI/DMP.

46   "Double-Cross": The most valuable treatment remains that of Sir John Masterman, who helped the British plan many deceptions, including those preceding Overlord (Masterman, pp. 144–62). An excellent summary of basic principles may be found at "Informal Report by Special Plans Branch to Joint Security Control," 5/29/45, NA/CD.

Allied deceptions for Overlord: Masterman, p. 147.

Operation Cockade: U.S. Army Special Plans Branch, "Cover and Deception, ETO: Synopsis and History," 9/8/44, NA/CD.

"increasing numbers of [FBI] double agents": Hyde, p. 220.

"a useful part": ibid., p. 223.

47   "glass balls": ibid., p. 58.

"instruments for catching other spies": ibid.

Von Werthern, Ritter: Hoover to Donovan, 12/16/42, OSS/FBI.

"'submerged' themselves in their communities": Hinsley, vol. IV, p. 730.

"The FBI continued to regard": ibid., p. 229.

fifty-seven spies, White House conference: Hyde, pp. 219–20.

48   "The trouble at this stage": Montagu, p. 80.

"any meeting of the minds": Hinsley, vol. IV, p. 229.

"hail-fellow-well-met": Philby, pp. 85–86.

"knives out of [Donovan's] back": Murphy interviewed at Dunlop, p. 296.

"biographical data": Peters to Harding, "Rough Drafts," n.d. [c. 3/44], OSS/X-2.

49   Peters' assistance to FBI: Peters to Sharrar, 4/27/44, OSS/X-2.

pornographic pictures: Ladd to Hoover, 6/26/44, FBI FOIA #62-116758.

"to express appreciation": Murphy to Hoover, 4/1/44, OSS/X-2.

"hollow soles and heels": Hoover to Berle, May 25, 1943, NA/S.

"no fixed policy": Dunn to McDonough, 2/15/44.

50   "so that we might study": ibid.

"legitimate need": memo, n.d., X-2/FBI.

Viking Fund/Fejos: Gately to Sharrar, 12/18/44, OSS/X-2.

Arvad: Donovan to Hoover, 1/24/42, FBI FOIA #65-39058, Inga Arvad file. The Hoover-Donovan correspondence about Wenner-Gren is missing from OSS/FBI but is in FBI FOIA #65-8857, FBI Wenner-Gren file.

Arvad-JFK: their affair is duly chronicled in the FBI's Arvad file, FOIA.

"Mr. Hoover, my father": Nichols interviewed at Summers, p. 139.

51   "unsatisfactory and mysterious": Peters to Murphy, 10/22/43, OSS/X-2.

Lisbon film-flap: Peters to Murphy, 10/17/44, OSS/X-2.

"a known German agent": Peters to Murphy, 4/8/44, OSS/X-2.

"the unusual nature": ibid.

"According to information": Peters to Murphy, 10/23/43, OSS/X-2.

52   "With your permission": ibid.

The landings and capture of Kopff and Baarn are described in detail at NA/S. See especially Hoover's confidential memoranda to Berle, 8/20/43 and 9/11/43 (the latter contains a ten-page report from FBI legats in Brazil on their debriefings of Kopff and Baarn); also, Brazilian court documents, such as the depositions of Kopff, Baarn, and the policemen who apprehended them, summarized at Hilton, pp. 289ff. Hoover's decision to employ Kopff and Baarn as double agents is expressed in his 8/16/43 memo to Berle. The FBI's refusal to share documentation on the Kopff-Baarn case is evidenced by Hoover's routing scribbles on FBI copies of his correspondence with Berle; see, e.g., 9/19/43.

"Difficulties arose": Hyde, p. 220.

53   White House conference: ibid., pp. 219–20.

"The lie must be consistent": SHAEF, "Cover and Deception, Definition and Procedure," 9/8/44, NA/CD.

"directed from a central point": ibid.

"definitely suffered thereby": Informal Report by Special Plans Branch to Joint Security Control, 5/25/45, NA/CD.

Nazis paralyzed at D-Day: Special Plans Branch, "Cover and Deception, ETO: Synopsis and History," 9/8/44, NA/CD.

54   Donovan at beach landings: Houston interview.

"for the establishment and maintenance": SHAEF memo by Walter Bedell Smith, "Cover and Deception," 8/31/44, NA/CD.

"laying plans for post-hostility": Murphy memo, 12/24/44, OSS/X-2.

"transfer of enemy funds": ibid.

"observe Communist activities": Paris to Doering, 1/2/45, OSS/X-2.

"renegade Americans": ibid.

"steps initiated in Washington": ibid.

Dewavrin to receive Cross: Donovan to Eisenhower, 9/15/44, FBI/WJD.

55   "necessary for us to lay": Donovan to Bruce, 10/20/44, OSS/FBI.

"ruthless forces": Hoover to Biddle, 12/15/44, FBI/WJD.

"function strictly in a liaison capacity": Murphy to Donovan, 5/7/45, OSS/FBI.

"1). This is simply": Murphy to Donovan, 11/22/44, OSS/FBI.

4. AMERICAN GESTAPO?

56   "This is the greatest": Sullivan, p. 21.

57   Comintern: FBI report, "The Soviet Peace Offensive," 12/25/81, FBI/RR.
"The American Century": see Felix [McCarger], p. 36.
"The mood": ibid., p. 21.
clandestine operator's perspective: Miler interview.

58   "for an intelligence service": FDR to Donovan, 10/31/44, OSS/NA.
"Donovan recommended": Donovan to Roosevelt, 11/18/44, OSS/NA. The
name "Central Intelligence Agency" was not formally attached to the proposed
organization until 12/9/44, when an interservice committee drafted a version
of Donovan's plan.
"its objectionable features": Tamm to Hoover, 12/22/44, TSCS.
"at a series of conferences": Doering to Donovan, 2/13/45, OSS/FBI.
"such harsh things were said": ibid.
"perhaps the most modern and efficient": Ford and MacBain, pp. 5–6,
215–16.
"re-hashes of British intelligence": TSCS, 10/7/43.
" 'any damned British' ": N. Joseph Lynch, Legal Attaché, London, to Hoover, via U.S. Army couriers service, 7/12/45, FBI/WJD.

59   "a constant cause of embarrassment": E. C. Conroy, SAC NY, to Hoover,
4/13/44, FBI/WJD.
"Donovan's past sins": FBI memo for Hoover, 1/15/43, TSCS.
"an evaluation and analysis unit," etc.: Hoover to AG, 12/13/44, FBI/WJD.
"practically impossible": Tamm to Hoover, 12/22/44, TSCS.
"tied up with": Rosenbaum to Donovan, 10/7/44, OSS/FBI.

60   "a national crime detective agency": Magruder to Mayer, 7/20/45, OSS/FBI.
"Donovan Proposes Super Spy System": Washington *Times-Herald*, 2/9/45.
Similar articles appeared on the same date in CT and the New York *Daily News*.
"pry into the lives," etc.: Trohan, 2/9/45; TT, pp. 254–55.
"Ole, I want you": Dunlop, p. 464.
"personally handed": Doering interviewed at Braden, p. 6.
"marked" copies of the memo: William Duffy interviewed at Summers, p.
443; New York *Post*, 10/11/59.
"this breach of security": LLM, p. 21, note a. But see II, pp. 281–82.
"An extensive search": notation on Hoover to AG, 3/10/45, FBI/WJD.
"any superduper Gestapo," etc.: Trohan, 2/10/45.

61   "shove the entire thing under the rug": Houston interview.
Donovan revived plan: Hoover to AG, 4/13/45, TSCS.
Donovan reaction to FDR death: Mary Bancroft interviewed 6/16/80 at
Brown, 1982, p. 737; Ned Buxton interviewed at Braden, p. 7; Otto C. Doering,
Jr., interviewed 10/6/69 and 10/8/69 at TT, p. 265.
"Truman didn't like Donovan": Murphy interviewed at Brown, p. 791.
"Truman considered him": Colby interview.
"tug of war": entry for 4/26/45, "Conferences with President Truman, 1945,"
Smith Papers, TT, p. 266.

62   "weakness in and objections to": Hoover to AG, 4/13/45, TSCS.
Biddle's May 1 conference: Hoover to Clark, 8/19/45, FBI/WJD.
"OSS belongs to a nation at war": Donovan interviewed at Dunlop, p. 468.
"Capital Ax Falling": Chicago *Daily News*, 9/4/45, TT, p. 292.

"4000 stranded fliers": WP, 9/14/45, ibid.

OSS parachutists glamorized: Braden, p. 7.

purple hyperbole: Ford and MacBain, pp. 5–6, 215–16.

63   "vainglorious publicity": Ford, 1970, p. 313.

"on Donovan's payroll": Hoover scrawl on clipping, 9/7/45, TSCS.

"little Gremlins": TSCS, 6/11/45.

"I wish to return to civilian life": Donovan to Smith, 8/25/45, at Ford, 1970, p. 313.

"fatal concession": ibid.

"the beginning of a development": Truman to Donovan, 9/20/45, ibid., p. 343.

"a kind of stoic grace": Donald Stone interviewed at Dunlop, p. 473.

64   "Of course we have to kill the Nazis": Roy Cohn interviewed 4/29/86 at Robins, p. 191.

65   FBI plan on Truman's desk: Stone interviewed at Corson, p. 258.

rewritten by Smith: United States Bureau of the Budget, "Report: Intelligence and Security Activities of the Government," 9/20/45, TT, pp. 308–9.

"riddled with communists," etc.: Quinn interviewed at Dunlop, p. 485.

"a tough, open-faced man": Braden, p. 8.

"the Donovan spirit": ibid.

Quinn's meeting with Hoover is reconstructed from three interviews, and the dialogue has been interwoven freely from among them: Quinn interviewed 6/8/87, at Hersh, 1992, p. 184; Quinn interviewed at Dunlop, p. 485; McWilliams interview.

66   communists in OSS: Edwards to Hoover, 5/20/55, TSCS, refers to six communists, apparently meaning the six who were still in SSU when the FBI probed. The "seventh" may have been Josephine Herbst, purged in 1942, but, considering all the former Lincoln brigadiers and other antifascist assets utilized by officers like Downes, the actual number of communists to have worked in OSS was certainly much higher than the seven detected by the FBI in late 1945. It is unclear whether or to what extent these communists overlapped with the seven pinpointed by Elizabeth Bentley (see ch. 5).

"very sparingly": DeLoach interviewed at Robins, p. 912.

"postwar proportions," etc.: entry for 7/6/45, "Conferences with President Truman, 1945," Smith Papers, TT, p. 272.

67   "sex life of Washington bureaucrats": ibid.

State Department complaints: Sullivan, p. 40.

"unsuccessfully attempted": Harriman to FDR, 3/30/44, NA/S.

68   "highly dangerous and most undesirable": Hoover to Hopkins, 2/10/44; Hoover to Biddle, 2/14/44; both at NA/S.

Joint Chiefs debate: minutes, 2/6/44, 2/15/44, 2/17/44, NA/S.

"personally protested": Hoover note on Nichols to Tolson, 3/15/52, FBI/WJD.

"an entirely different solution"; memo for Hoover, n.d., FBI/WJD.

69   Hoover's revised "Plan": Tom Clark, "Memorandum for the President: A Plan for U.S. Secret Worldwide Intelligence Coverage," 10/22/45, FBI/WJD.

"it is not possible": ibid.

"Foreign and domestic intelligence": ibid.

70   interagency board: minutes, 11/14/45, TT, p. 322.
      Truman impatience: Houston interview.
      "I want someone": ibid.
      "If we had some central repository": Clifford interviewed at Braden, p. 9.
Donovan naturally was quick to cite the 1945–46 Pearl Harbor investigation
in arguing for a CIA. See Donovan.
      "out of bounds": General Harry Vaughan interviewed at Demaris, pp. 107–8.
      "collect, coordinate": Presidential Directive, 1/22/46, TT, pp. 464–65.
71   "The authority over the money": Houston interview.
      "I want to go home": Braden, p. 10.
      Hoover appointed to IAB: CIG Top Secret Directive #3, 3/21/46, RBD.
      "Get out of this thing now": McWilliams interview.
      "a separation": CIG memo, [deleted] to Quinn, 4/22/46, NA/X-2. Others,
like X-2 chief Murphy, questioned whether positive- and counterintelligence
could be split at all. "Information derived from counterintelligence sources in
the field is frequently of high positive intelligence value.... Contrariwise,
sources developed principally for positive intelligence are often in a position
to provide information vital to counterintelligence operations." Usually it was
difficult to determine in advance whether a given source was positive- or counterintelligence; some targets were irreducibly both. The communist movement
as a political party was primarily the concern of a positive intelligence service;
the use of its members and sympathizers as controlled double agents was the
concern of a counterintelligence agency. The same "lines of penetration" would
frequently produce information invaluable to both functions, and therefore
counterintelligence was best done in a context of "concentration on broad
strategic problems as required by the changing international situation." The
only way that the FBI would be able to conduct foreign CI, in other words,
was to become a global spy agency. But Murphy doubted "the ultimate political
wisdom of any step which goes against democratic principles by placing the
executive authority of arrest in the hands of an intelligence agency" (Murphy
to Quinn, 4/23/46, NA/X-2). The old Gestapo argument again.
72   Wisner quit over bicycles: Braden, p. 9.
      "like shit through a goose": Henry Hyde interviewed 11/8/85 at Hersh, 1992,
p. 187.
      "a good debating society": Donovan at Overseas Press Club, 3/1/46, TSCS.
      Souers budget request refused: Braden, p. 10.
      Vandenberg back story: ibid.
      "did not measure up to his standards": RBD, ch. 12, quoted at TT, p. 361.
73   "vital responsibilities," etc.: Vandenberg memo, 6/20/46, RBD.
      "all organized Federal espionage": Vandenberg to R. B. Darling, 3/17/52,
RBD.
      "confusion, duplication of effort": Hoover to W. D. Leahy, 8/23/46.
      Vandenberg to Hoover re Latin America: Vandenberg to Darling, 3/17/52,
RBD.
      "That was a damn good setup": Papich interview.
      "Hoover fought it quite hard": Houston interview.
74   "a stream of admirals, generals": Sullivan, p. 40.
      complied with a vengeance: RBD, ch. 4.

"a scorched earth policy": Helms interviewed at Summers, p. 155.

Hoover against CIG employment of FBI men: minutes of NIA meetings #5 and #7, 8/7/46 and 9/25/46, RBD.

"made by the FBI": Smith, 1976, pp. 331–32.

"My life was the Bureau": Papich interview.

75 "arrived in the morning": Phillips, p. 1.

"crummy and cold": Papich interview.

76 "pay for the duplication": Sullivan, p. 40.

"never going to forgive": Phillips, p. 1. Hoover's apparent resentment was also described to author in Helms interview.

CIG technically illegal: Houston interview.

77 Busbey against "going into the records": *Congressional Record*, vol. 93, pt. 7, p. 8299, TT, p. 396.

"J. Edgar Hoover's activities and work": Judd quoted at Braden, p. 11.

"destroy their effectiveness": *Congressional Record*, vol. 93, pt. 7, pp. 9447–48, TT, p. 399.

"state our case": quoted at Powers, 1979, p. 28.

"world's greatest power": Donovan.

"My, my, Col. Bill": Hoover note on Ladd to Hoover, 10/2/46, TSCS.

pruned by two provisos: LLM, p. 254. Text of CIA's original charter is reprinted at TT, pp. 469–70.

"a concession to J. Edgar Hoover's independence": Cline, p. 96.

78 "no established ground rules": Breckinridge, pp. 26–27.

"unanticipated circumstances": ibid., p. 27.

79 DCI's executive powers and "banana-peel clause": ibid.

5. SHAKEDOWN CRUISE

83 Defoe: Dulles, pp. 199, 201.

"rarely exist in real life," etc.: ibid., pp. 199, 201.

84 "The James Bond syndrome": Kirkpatrick, p. 5.

"3 × 5 cards and a typewriter": Phillips, p. 147.

"E. Phillips Oppenheim": Ford and MacBain, p. 8.

"the mystique was there": Cline, p. 119.

Dulles and Goldfinger: Wise & Ross 1967, p. 269.

85 Fleming's fans at CIA: Helms liked Fleming and Hunt novels, according to his interview at Powers, 1979, p. 53.

Helms hated Le Carré novels: Dennis Helms interviewed at ibid.

"little man with the heavy suitcase": Fleming, 1955, p. 184.

86 "When a soldier": Sullivan deposition, 11/1/75, pp. 95–96, FR-III, pp. 968–69.

87 Harvey character and appearance: composite from Wright, pp. 147, 152; Paul Garbler interviewed at Wise, 1992, p. 49; Lamphere, p. 61; Houston interview.

88 Harvey in New York: Papich interview.

Bentley's allegations may be found in her book, *Out of Bondage* (originally published in 1951), passim, and in FBI documents, especially Bentley's 113-page statement, 11/30/45, FBI/EB. In addition to Lee and Julius Joseph, Bentley named Joseph's wife, Bella, who worked in the OSS Publicity Division; Louis Adamic, an OSS expert on Yugoslavia; Leonard Mins, a Russian interpreter;

Maurice Halperin, in Donovan's Latin American branch, who allegedly furnished the Soviets with secret OSS and State cables; and Mary Tenney, in the OSS Spanish Division, who Bentley said had turned over "a considerable quantity of written data reflecting the activities of OSS personnel in virtually all sections and countries of the world." Natalie Robins says (p. 232) that Bentley also implicated former COI German Desk staffer Josephine Herbst, but the FBI's Bentley files do not corroborate this. In any case, since Bentley formally accused at least seven individuals in OSS, but CIA and FBI concluded that only six were Soviet moles (Edwards to Hoover, 5/20/55, TSCS), evidence against one and possibly more of the Bentley suspects must have been judged inconclusive. Indeed, since a number of other OSS employees *not* named by Bentley also fell under suspicion, it may be that the final "CIA six" included none of Bentley's suspects.

"Soviet espionage agents": Hoover to Truman, 11/8/45, FBI/EB.

"Most significant": Hoover notation, ibid.

89   "reactivating the Informant": FBI memo, n.d., FBI/EB, Martin, p. 32.

FBI's poor handling of Bentley case: Secret Service official Stephen Springarn interviewed at Demaris, pp. 118–19.

Harvey's transfer of Gregg and Lamphere: Lamphere, p. 61.

"FBI had to become more aggressive": ibid., p. 41.

"the statement of the GREGORY woman": memo, n.d. [1946?], FBI/EB.

90   Harvey's lost night, resignation: permanent brief, 2/13/62, FBI/WKH.

"That was too bad": Lamphere, p. 67.

91   drinking at lunch: Life in the CIA's "tempo" buildings, and lunch routine, etc., have been described by many former officers of CIA, including Phillips, Rositzke, etc. I have drawn also on AFIO.

DeLoach backstory: Ungar, pp. 279–80.

92   "CIA was very new": Lamphere correspondence.

Buckley recruited by both FBI and CIA: Buckley interviewed at Robins, pp. 171–72.

"If Hoover had an agent": Papich interview.

93   "To Hoover": Lamphere interviewed at Newton, p. 305.

"Harvey was definitely": Lamphere correspondence.

"I can't talk much now": DeLoach interviewed at Martin, p. 41.

"was somewhat upset over the fact": DeLoach correspondence.

"on a number of occasions": ibid.

defectors: Houston interview.

"Arguments went on": ibid.

"CIA was critical of the FBI": Lamphere correspondence.

The defector fistfight has been described by two retired intelligence officers: Felix [McCargar], p. 35 and Breckinridge, p. 27. Sam Papich, who succeeded DeLoach as FBI liaison to CIA, identified the disputed defector as Ansimov, but did not recall the affair's being a CIA-FBI clash. "I doubt very much that the FBI was involved in it, because I would have heard about it. When I came in, the first thing I did was read all the liaison files; and even if I hadn't read about the incident, it would have been a great embarrassment to the Bureau, and I would probably have known." Papich thought the episode was a conflict between CIA and Immigration, but acknowledged that there were flaps with CIA that he never put down on paper while serving as liaison, and that DeLoach might have acted similarly in the defector case (Papich interview). DeLoach declined to comment on the incident.

94 "not at all": Houston interview.
press coverage of feud: Baldwin, 7/20/48; Baldwin, 7/22/48.
"a 'Charley McCarthy' ": Ladd to Hoover, 1/14/47, TSCS.

95 "lackluster leader": Braden, p. 10.
"close" relations: Hillenkoetter to the Eberstadt Committee, 9/10/48, RBD. See also Eberstadt Report, n.d. [late 1948], pp. 33–35, 57; Hillenkoetter to Darling, 11/24/52, 12/2/52; all at RBD, pp. 288–89.
Dulles Report on FBI-CIA: Dulles Report, pp. 63–64, 58, 69–70, cited at RBD. CIA has received many FOIA requests for this document over the years, and in 1994 was still refusing to release it.
Hoover countered: Souers to Darling, 11/6/52; Action no. 202, 37th Meeting of the National Security Council, 4/7/49; NSC 17, "Report on the Internal Security of the United States," 6/28/48; Souers to Darling, 11/6/52; Souers/Darling interview; all at RBD.
"the low point": Lamphere correspondence.
"sit below the DCI": LLM.
"shooting war": clipping, 12/2/49, TSCS.

96 "war-time expediency": Emerson P. Schmidt, HUAC testimony, 3/26/47, in WFO memo, 7/3/53, TSCS.
"a Communist plotter": clipping, 9/9/47, TSCS.
"completely discredit": Ladd to Keay, 12/15/48, TSCS.
"well known hostility": Hoover to AG, 12/23/48, TSCS.
AIII: FBI memo, 9/10/46.

97 "used his high position," etc.: FBI memo, n.d. [1946], TSCS.
"botanical drugs in bulk": Dunlop, p. 490.
"Our French friends": Donovan to Forrestal, 8/14/47, Forrestal Papers, Mudd Library, Princeton University.
"various remnants of OSS personnel": FBI memo 5/25/48, TSCS. The report apparently came to CIA from an ONI source. That Katz's activities in Paris might have been the genesis of the report seems likely, because (1) he was a former naval lieutenant before joining OSS, and thus might have hinted about his activities to a former naval colleague in ONI; (2) he had spent the war in London, which would have put him in a position to work for British intelligence afterward, as the FBI memo says the former OSS agents in Paris were doing.

98 Hunt in Paris under Marshall Plan cover: Szulc, 1973, p. 61. Hunt's memoirs also confirm that he began working for CIA in Paris during 1948.
Katz brought Casey to Paris under Marshall Plan: Casey interviewed at Persico, pp. 88ff. It may be significant that even CIA Director Hillenkoetter had come into the Agency from the position of naval attaché in Paris. It seems to me that a valuable study could be done on the birth of CIA covert action in Paris during this period; in particular, Donovan's likely connection to Bloodstone would seem to bear further investigation.
"mysterious supply of uranium," etc.: Colby, p. 73. Wisner was an acting member for State on SANACC, and was point man on the effort, whose working committee included John Earman of CIA.
"suspected Rumanian spy": FBI New York letter, 7/15/48, TSCS. The Donovan associate who offered to penetrate the FBI was Walter Thayer. According

to the FBI letter, "It was believed that the close association between Thayer and Col. Donovan was the basis for Thayer's reputed claim of being able to get information."

Wisner and SANACC: See the outstanding spadework by Simpson (pp. 96ff), working from declassified State Department records such as a SANACC memo of 4/26/48. Hersh, 1992 (pp. 224ff.), fleshes out Simpson's work, drawing attention to the "remittances to Europe, Inc. payroll deductions."

99   Hillenkoetter-Wisner controversy: Memo, n.d., TSCS. In some way this episode was apparently connected to the fact that Wisner had recommended CIA employ Louise Page Morris, who was considered to have been a Donovan "informant" since 1944.

OPC intellectuals and projects: Hunt, 1974, pp. 69, 70, 77.

"ten million headaches": Papich interview.

"Guys, you can't *do* that": ibid.

100   Paperclip: Bernard Geehan interviewed at Hunt, 1991, p. 184.

"They ran all around the country": Papich interview.

FBI-CIA delimitation agreement: Wisner, memorandum for the record, "Cooperation and Liaison Between Federal Bureau of Investigation and Office of Policy Coordination, CIA," draft, 9/22/48, at Ranelagh, p. 770.

Hunt a writer of paperbacks: Hunt, 1974, p. 69.

101   OPC in Mexico: Phillips, pp. 42, 145, 154; Hunt, 1974, pp. 68, 70, 76, 85–86.

102   "hard-core stuff": Papich interview.

"When I started": Lamphere correspondence.

"The Homer investigation": ibid.

odds-on favorite: Papich interview.

103   "In the years": Lamphere interviewed 12/10/85 at Newton, p. 246.

"It personally did not take me long": Lamphere correspondence. For his London briefing on the FBI-CIA feud, see Philby, pp. 153–54.

Philby on Harvey: ibid., p. 158.

"Generally, at the party": Lamphere, pp. 229–30. The party is also recalled by Philby, interviewed 5/88 at Knightley, 1989, pp. 167–68.

104   Burgess and Maclean: Hoover to DCI, Attention [redacted], Office of Special Operations, 6/27/51, 6/28/51; FBI blind memos to CIA, 8/21/51; FBI teletype, Madrid to Hoover, 11/7/51; Hoover to [deleted], CIA, 11/20/51; FBI memo, Nichols to Tolson, 6/30/51; all at FBI/AKP.

105   FBI's failure to suspect Philby, Harvey's case against Philby, CIA's ass-covering: Lamphere, pp. 131, 231, 238–39.

106   "fairly far to the left": Hoover to DCI, 6/28/51, FBI/AKP.

"a major spy": Lamphere, p. 239.

"never forgave me totally": Lamphere correspondence. Some writers (e.g., Martin, pp. 44ff.) seem to imply that FBI gave Harvey some Venona materials, which Harvey later used to build a case against Philby, but Lamphere strenuously denies it. "I never gave Harvey officially or unofficially any information on this, and I am sure [David] Martin had it wrong in his book on Harvey writing a key memo on Philby" (ibid.).

Fallout from Philby affair: Papich interview; McWilliams interview.

6. A POISONED CHALICE

107 "bad but plentiful food": Fleming, 1954, p. 21.

"just gums": Fleming, 1957, p. 142.

"always angry": Cline, p. 108.

Smith background/character: report, 4/6/53, FBI/WBS.

108 "a cold, fishy eye": Philby, p. 185.

Smith in Moscow: Keay to Belmont, 2/5/51; SAC Philadelphia to Hoover, 9/17/48; both at FBI/WBS.

Hillenkoetter replaced: Keay to Belmont, 9/29/50, FBI/WBS.

"a poisoned chalice": Scheidt to Hoover, 8/18/50, FBI/WBS.

Smith and FBI-CIA: Houston interview; Keay to Belmont, 9/1/50, FBI/WBS; Houston to Smith, 8/29/50, RBD, pp. 505–6.

Hoover unavailable: Ladd to Hoover, 10/4/50, FBI/WBS.

109 DeLoach report on meeting Smith: Ladd to Hoover, 10/11/50, FBI/WBS.

"Whether you, Mr. Hoover, like me or not," etc.: Sullivan, p. 40.

110 "to go fuck himself": DeLoach interviewed at Martin, p. 54. DeLoach is not explicitly identified as Martin's source, but, inasmuch as DeLoach was liaison officer at the time, he would have been the one to confront Smith. DeLoach later declined to comment on the episode (DeLoach correspondence).

luncheon scheduled: Hoover to Tolson, Ladd, Nichols, 10/13/50, FBI/WBS.

Hoover-Smith luncheon: Kirkpatrick, pp. 101, 117–18; DeLoach interviewed at Martin, p. 55.

Kinsey's book: Ladd to Hoover, 10/19/50, FBI/WBS.

"pretty busy": Hoover to Tolson, Ladd, Nichols, 2/3/51, FBI/WBS.

111 "hung up": memcon, 8/6/51, FBI/WBS.

"Files reflect limited contacts": notation on Hoover to Smith, 7/19/51, FBI/WBS.

IIC refused to "perform estimates": LLM, p. 249.

no special collection effort: CIA minutes, DCI's meeting, 5/7/51, LLM, p. 250,

Improve personal relationships: CIA memo by Kirkpatrick, 11/7/51, LLM, p. 251.

November luncheon: LLM, pp. 254–66. At the meeting, Smith handed Hoover a staff study on some subject that remains classified.

Hoover adamant: CIA memo by Kirkpatrick, 11/7/51, LLM, p. 255.

"up against an immovable object" LLM, p. 256.

"As time went on": Lamphere correspondence.

"driving a wedge": Sullivan, p. 62. Sullivan and DeLoach were later bitter enemies, according to Papich and other former agents, because they differed over how to conduct FBI intelligence operations, and because, in the 1960s, both were angling to succeed Hoover. In his memoirs, Sullivan can never resist a chance to level cheap shots at his rival. "DeLoach once acted as liaison between the CIA and me when I was asked to give a speech to fifteen hundred or so CIA employees," Sullivan recalled. "Accompanied by three men from the CIA, DeLoach himself drove me to the building opposite the Lincoln Memorial where the CIA held many of its meetings. When we arrived at 6:30, no one was there. The speech was scheduled for 7:00. By 6:45, when not one other person had shown up, I began to get very nervous. DeLoach told me to calm down, that the CIA was so disorganized that everyone else was probably late.

At five minutes to seven, when we were still alone at the hall, DeLoach went to use the phone. He came back cursing the CIA, insisting that they had given him the wrong information—I actually had been scheduled to speak in [another] auditorium ... where a full house was waiting for the speaker to arrive. The CIA men and I were full of apologies when we finally arrived at the right place at 7:15, but not DeLoach: 'Couldn't help being late,' he told the anxious CIA delegation who met us at the door. 'It couldn't be avoided. We were working on an important espionage case.' " (Sullivan, p. 63.)

112   "at times similar to walking a tightrope": DeLoach correspondence.
    Leiter: See Fleming, 1954, pp. 17ff.
113   Charles Bates as interim liaison: Papich interview, 5/19/92.
114   "Reading those files": Papich interview.
    "You go back down to Ninth Street," etc.: ibid.
    Houston on Papich: Houston interview.
115   "Things improved when Sam took over," etc.: Lamphere correspondence.
    "red flag": Papich interviewed by Senate staffers, 9/22/75, FR-I, p. 172.
116   "Make an example": Fleming to Donovan, 6/27/41; reclassified by CIA, 5/87; quoted, in part, at TT, p. 82.
    "a very grave problem": Angleton testimony, p. 56.
    "an ongoing housecleaning": Papich interview.
    at least fourteen Soviet penetrations: Wright, p. 182. Since by 1955 only six of these moles had been positively identified (Edwards to Hoover, 5/20/55, TSCS, apparently discounting one who had already retired by 1945), it is possible that as many as seven or eight Soviet spies survived the Quinn purges in late 1945 and early 1946 and joined CIA.
    "coloration and biases": Ladd to Hoover, 10/2/46, TSCS.
    "a breeding ground for Commies": TSCS, 1/6/48.
    "The FBI knew": Lamphere correspondence.
117   Alsop went to CIA and FBI: Robins, p. 133, citing a "former high government official." Wise, 1992, p. 76, quotes former CIA officer George Kisevalter as saying that the Soviet intelligence defector Yuri Nosenko alleged that the KGB had compromised Alsop, who by then was a close friend to President Kennedy. If Alsop was indeed compromised by the Soviets, it may have been through his association with Guy Burgess. CIA's James Angleton noted in one memo that a drunken Burgess had referred once to having had "an interesting binge the night before at Joe Alsop's house" (Angleton memo, 6/18/51, Martin, p. 55).
    Offie investigated: FBI field report, 2/8/50; FBI memo to Hoover from Special Agent Guy Hottel, 7/21/50; both at Hersh, 1992, p. 443.
    Harvey on FBI/Offie: Mark Wyatt interviewed at Hersh, 1992, p. 448.
    McCarthyist prosecution of Offie: *Congressional Record*, 4/25/50.
    CIA against Offie prosecution: Keay to Belmont, 7/18/52, at Hersh, 1992, p. 448.
    "The usual 'brush off' ": Belmont to Keay, 8/7/50, at Hersh, 1992, p. 444.
118   AFL: Tracey to Hoover, 6/13/51, Hersh, 1992, p. 444.
    "Communists in my own organization": Smith deposition in Civil Action 1335-52, *Senator Joseph R. McCarthy* v. *Senator William Benton*, 9/29/52, Washington, D.C., quoted at Smith testimony, 10/13/52, p. 4285, FBI/WBS.
    CIA personnel security measures, FBI advantages: Smith testimony, 10/13/52, p. 4287, FBI/WBS.

119 "rumors that Smith might be leaving": Keay to Belmont, 12/2/52, FBI/WBS. "make a change": ibid.

Smith phoned Hoover: memo, 1/23/53, FBI/WBS.

120 "a great man," etc.: Papich interview.

"secret communist leanings": Mosley, p. 131.

"didn't have much of a personal relationship": Papich interview.

"Blame it on the CIA": Sullivan, pp. 184, 192–3.

CIA used as lever to advance FBI career: Lamphere, pp. 267, 269.

"never given me a winner yet": Philby, p. 168.

Hoover hesitance about McCarthy: memo for Hoover, 10/2/50, FBI McCarthy file, Robins, p. 241.

FBI assistance to McCarthy: DeLoach interviewed 9/16/87 at Robins, p. 274.

121 The Cord Meyer episode is reconstructed from his own account, pp. 67–70, 74, 80–83. Meyer includes a note from his diary entry, 9/7/51, and quotes the FBI's 9/4/51 memo to him.

122 Amory: Summers, p. 445.

Rockefeller: FBI San Francisco teletype for Director, 9/12/74, FBI/WBS.

123 crank letter about WBS: Anon. to Federal Bureau of Narcotics, 1/13/51; Bureau of Narcotics memo, Cunningham to Hoover, 1/21/51; both at FBI/WBS.

agency check of Smith begun: Nichols to Tolson, 1/13/53; Urgent FBI teletype, Hoover to SAC Baltimore, Washington Field Office, 1/13/53; both at FBI/WBS.

Eisenhower as reference: Personnel Security Questionnaire, 6/30/49, FBI/WBS.

124 to pacify McCarthy: Rosen to Ladd, 5/5/53, FBI/WBS.

"critical of . . . the spread of communism": Keay to Belmont, 10/6/52, FBI/WBS.

facts were not flattering: see especially Keay to Belmont, 10/6/52; HUAC Testimony of William Mandel, n.d. [1953]; FBI New York SAC to Headquarters, 1/15/46; FBI New Haven memo, 11/16/50; all at FBI/WBS.

"Stalin once told me": LLM, p. 256.

"realized fully," "conspirational designs": Keay to Belmont, 10/6/52, FBI/WBS.

"the leopard might have changed its spots," etc.: ibid.

"a higher cultural standing": quoted at HUAC Testimony of William Mandel, n.d. [1953], FBI/WBS.

"leading Soviet sympathizers," etc.: Confidential memo, SAC New York to Headquarters, 1/15/46, FBI/WBS.

Davies: LLM, p. 258.

Not very long after WBS's final refusal: ibid., p. 259.

125 "no derogatory information": summary memo to Army, 7/11/56, FBI/WBS.

expanded internationally: FBI teletype, 5/27/53, FBI/WBS.

Lamphere knew "nothing": Lamphere correspondence.

banquet speech: Keay to Belmont, 6/8/53, FBI/WBS.

"a most peculiar sense of humor": ibid.

"a juicy target," etc.: Nichols to Tolson, 8/3/53, FBI/WBS. Papich confirmed to the author that a G-man who applied to CIA had, in fact, been determined to be a homosexual. "I remember one time that one of our men went over to work at CIA but they polygraphed him and found out he was a homo. That was *true*." (Papich interview.)

126   " 'stinker' ": Keay to Belmont, 8/13/53, FBI/WBS.
"health reasons": Frohbose to Belmont, 10/27/59, FBI/WBS.
documents found: Washington Capitol News Service text, n.d., FBI/WBS.

127   "thirty-six–page chapter deleted": LLM, p. 260.
"a marvelous telegraph operator": Lovell, p. 176.
"damaging personal information": Corson, p. 69.
"We must certainly follow": Keay to Belmont, 2/20/53, FBI/WJD.
"for espionage purposes": T-6 report, 7/10/50, TSCS.
"in Italy on an undercover assignment": memo, 9/24/51, TSCS.
"Arabia": FBI memo, 5/28/5i, TSCS.

128   "rather patronizing": Houston interviewed at LLM, p. 61.
"fed up with Gen. D.": Hoover notation, memo, 11/1/50, FBI/WJD.
"ONI has been endeavoring": Keay to Belmont, 8/26/52, TSCS.
"Donovan wanted to set up": memo, 3/11/5, TSCS.
"an entering wedge": memo, 3/17/53, TSCS.
Dulles requested a check: J. F. Dulles to Hoover, 6/12/53, TSCS.
special inquiry: teletype, Hoover to SACs Buffalo, etc., 6/15/53, TSCS.
"soft and mushy," etc.: teletype, New York to Hoover, 6/30/53, TSCS.
"running out and documenting": Rosen to Ladd, 7/17/53, TSCS.
"all existing lists": teletype, New York to Hoover, 7/18/53, TSCS; TSCS, 6/18/53.
"take no action": NYFO (Boardman), urgent teletype to Hoover,
"one of the main contacts": Atlanta report, 12/4/53, TSCS.
Halperin: WFO memo, 8/20/51; WFO letter, 12/11/45; WFO tel, 2/7/47; all at TSCS.
Donovan attacked Bentley: FBI memos 12/16/48, 10/30/50, TSCS.
"seek a pattern": Donovan to Black, 12/8/48, TSCS.

130   tolerance of communism was noted: Hoover to J. F. Dulles, 7/14/53, TSCS.
"not to be construed as a clearance": memo, 7/10/56, TSCS.
"classified information," etc.: memo, 5/5/54, TSCS.
"correlation search": memo, 11/15/55, FBI/WJD.
"did not trust his old mentor": Dunlop, p. 502.

131   "Women's Club luncheon": Ford, 1970, p. 324.
"a very skillful game": Helms interviewed at Summers, p. 202.
"The last thing Wild Bill would have done": Houston interview.
"that Edgar had tried": Summers, p. 245.

132   Hoover wrote the widow: Hoover to Ruth Donovan, 2/9/56, FBI/WJD.
"kind expression of sympathy": Ruth R. Donovan to Hoover, 2/25/59, FBI/WJD.
"Because of his colorful career": Roach to Belmont, 2/13/59, FBI/WJD.
medal, portrait: Houston interview.

7. THE GRAY GHOST

133   Bullivant: Buchan, *The Thirty-Nine Steps*, pp. 56–61; *Greenmantle*, p. 84; both in Buchan.
"the white-collar boys," etc.: Fleming, 1953, p. 144.
"the art of angling": Dulles, p. 201.

134 wrong kind of investigative help, CIA-FBI agreement: Houston interview; CIA memo, Houston to Deputy AG, 3/1/54, SSCI files.
135 security was *everything*: Helms interview.
 "Goddamn it, we don't want counterintelligence": Miler interview.
 Additional pressures: anon. letter to George Sokolsky, 7/22/54, FBI Sokolsky file, Robins, pp. 192–93.
136 a "more ruthless" approach: Doolittle Report, 7/51, NSAV.
 "intensification of CIA's counterintelligence": ibid.
 Kennedy/Doolittle: SAC Boston to Hoover, 7/2/54; Hoover to Tolson, et al., 2/16/56; both at Theoharis, ed., p. 319.
 "As you know": Belmont to Keay, 11/17/53. The identity of the CIA employee has been excised from documents as released, but the person's last name clearly contains six letters, like Harvey's, and the memo would appear to anticipate Harvey's transfer to Berlin only a few months later.
 Angleton's office described: Phillips, pp. 242, 308, 316.
 The fullest treatment of Angleton's life before becoming Chief/CI is that of Winks, pp. 322–409. Professor Winks (p. 409) believes that "The story of James Angleton as chief of Counterintelligence cannot be told now, at least not well, and perhaps not ever. It falls into that 5 percent of information that the intelligence communities of the world are dedicated to protecting successfully." Tom Mangold has nevertheless chronicled much of Angleton's time as CI chief, relying especially on a bitter Angleton enemy (ex–CIA officer Leonard McCoy) and presenting a picture so anti-Angleton that even some of Angleton's detractors have risen up in indignation (see Carver; letter to the editor by Paul Garbler, CIRA, vol. XVII, no. 1 [Spring 1992], p. 32). More balanced but still negative is David Wise, 1992, relying quite heavily on an Angleton molehunt suspect, Peter Karlow. Also sharply critical is David Martin, relying extensively on Clare Petty, who served only briefly on Angleton's staff. Capitalizing on unique access to a retired Angleton, and highly sympathetic to his viewpoint, are two books by Edward Jay Epstein, which cover especially the war of the defectors during the 1960s. Aside from Winks, what little Tom Powers, 1979, says about Angleton seems to me to strike the most balanced tone; e.g., "If Angleton has gone out on a conjectural limb . . . there is no question intelligence services habitually look for concealed connections and hidden identities, and that they sometimes find them" (p. 317).
137 clashed with DeLoach, "a real fight," etc.: Papich interview.
138 "When the enemy is united, divide him": Sun Tzu, p. 67.
 "Drive a wedge": Ibid. This latter quote is from the ancient Chinese commentator Chang Yu, which has become part of the work-proper in the Oxford and other translations.
139 "only as good as": Angleton testimony, p. 84.
 Katz: Papich interview; Lamphere, pp. 279–82.
140 spheres of FBI-CIA cooperation: Rositzke, pp. 215–17.
 "black bag" jobs: Angleton testimony, p. 69.
141 "there weren't more than": ibid., p. 8.
 Maclean dated CIA girls: Hoover to Dulles, 10/3/55, JEH/O&C.
 "We . . . planted stories": Sullivan, p. 84.
 Hoover leak to Winchell: Hoover to Boardman, n.d., JEH/O&C.

JEH/Kennedy: Hoover to Tolson, Boardman, Belmont, Nichols, 2/16/56, Theoharis, ed., p. 320.

"instead of CIA": Hoover to Tolson, Belmont, 7/28/58, JEH/O&C.
142   CODIB: AFIO.

FBI refused to conform: DCI Directive no. 11/2, "Control and Dissemination and Use of Intelligence and Intelligence Information," 11/15/54, NSAV.
143   "a weirdo": Papich interview.

"It's clearly a case," etc.: Sullivan, pp. 180–81.

"I'm on my way," etc.: Papich interview.
144   Hayhannen's story stood up: Dulles, p. 122.

Angleton's role in bringing Hayhannen to U.S.: Papich interview.
145   Hayhannen-McWilliams: ibid.; McWilliams interview.
146   Abel: Bernikow, passim; McWilliams interview. Microfilm in wood block is from Papich interview.
147   "The Abel case was the watershed": McWilliams interview.

"a great example of cooperation": Papich interview.

"confidential inquiries": Belmont to Boardman, 1/2/58, FR-III, p. 625.
148   HT/LINGUAL origins: Angleton memo, n.d., CCH-II, p. 191.

utility: Angleton testimony, p. 45; IR, p. 576; Angleton to Schlesinger, 2/15/73, FR-III, p. 576.

morality: J. Edward Day to SSCI, 10/24/75, FR-III, p. 606.

"A strict observance of the written law": quoted at Felt, p. 315.
149   HT/LINGUAL daily procedures: Angleton memo, n.d., CCH-II, p. 191.

"watch list": Angleton testimony, p. 62; SSCI summary, 9/5/75, FR-III, p. 574.

"flaps-and-seals" course: CIA officer testimony, 9/30/75, p. 40, FR-III, p. 572.

Kirkpatrick's assessment: Helms testimony, 10/22/75, CCH-IV, p. 110.
150   "and to the FBI": Edwards to Allen Dulles, 1/4/54, FR-III, p. 570.

"pretty spotty": Angleton deposition, 9/17/75, p. 27, FR-III, p. 570.

Stephens informed Angleton: CIA memo, 5/19/71, CCH-IV, p. 206.

Angleton met Papich: Angleton memo, n.d., CCH-IV, p. 191.

Hoover response: Papich testimony, 9/22/75, p. 67, FR-III, p. 627; Papich interview.

"The question": Belmont to Boardman, 1/22/58, FR-III, p. 627.
151   "point out," etc.: Belmont to Boardman, 2/6/58; Papich testimony, 9/22/75, p. 37; ibid.

Angleton conditions: CIA blind memo, 2/14/73, FR-III, p. 602.

Hunter Project: Angleton to Hoover, 2/6/58, FR-III, p. 628.

fifty-seven thousand reports: Branigan to Belmont, 12/5/60, FR-III, p. 633.

"major benefit": IG survey, n.d., CCH-IV, p. 175.

"junk": Branigan interviewed by Senate staff, 9/11/75, FR-III, p. 579.

FBI mail-openings: FBI to SSCI, 9/8/75; Heinrich to Belmont, 9/7/51; both at FR-III, p. 561.
152   FBI mail-opening take: Wannall, 10/22/75, FR-III, p. 652; Lamphere, pp. 279–82.

FBI's method quicker: FBI Special Agent 1 statement, 9/10/75, FR-III, p. 646. Senate investigators later noted: "FBI mail openings were much more tightly controlled and rigidly administered than the CIA programs. All but one (which resulted in a reprimand from the Director) received prior approval at least annually. Several of them—unlike the CIA's New York project—were discontinued on the basis of unfavorable internal evaluations. The high degree of central control clearly mirrored the organizational differences between the FBI and the CIA, and is not limited to mail opening operations alone." (FR-III, p. 637.)

did not disclose to CIA: Moore, 10/1/75, FR-III, p. 666; Branigan, 10/9/75, FR-III, p. 627.

Hoover demurred: Hoover to SAC-NYC, 7/11/60, FR-III, p. 651.

153   Hoover finally saw: Moore, 10/1/75, p. 55, FR-III, p. 651.

"Another inroad": Moore to Belmont, 3/10/61, FR-III, p. 635.

Harvey-Popov: Hood, pp. 211ff.; Kissevalter interviewed at Martin, pp. 93ff.

Pytor Popov's data: Rositzke, pp. 68–69. Rositzke does not identify Popov as the agent, but Popov is the only GRU source known to have been working for the U.S. at the time.

154   "Oh Shit, Oh Damn!": Martin, p. 93.

Tairovs surveilled: Hood, pp. 214–26, 235–37; Papich interview; McWilliams interview.

Popov undone: Hood, pp. 241, 246–47.

"partly Hoover's fault": Nolan interview.

Angleton did not complain: Papich interview.

155   U-2 leak: Hood, p. 234.

Powers' downing: testimony at KGB trial, 8/17/60, vol. 2, p. 2; vol. 4, pp. 25–27; KGB document, A. Shelepin, "The Indictment in the Case of Francis Gary Powers, Accused of a Crime Covered by Article 2 of the Law of the Union of Soviet Socialist Republics 'On Criminal Responsibility for State Crimes,' " 7/7/60; all at FBI/FGP.

"might tend to lend approval": Worrell to DeLoach, 5/10/60, FBI/FGP.

security lapses: Beschloss, 1986, p. 358.

156   "a report sent," etc.: monograph, n.d. [8/60], FBI/FGP.

157   "pretty well destroyed": Beschloss, 1986, p. 404.

"turn the FBI loose": [deleted] to Eisenhower, 5/13/60, FBI/FGP.

"most peculiar": memo, 5/11/60, FBI/FGP.

"utterly impossible": Phillip Livingstone by King Features Syndicate, 8/24/60, FBI/FGP.

Oliver Powers admitted son not shot down: L'Allier to Belmont, 9/27/60, FBI/FGP.

"Soviet agent in Georgia": Bartlett to L'Allier, 5/12/60, FBI/FGP.

suspected Powers had defected: Houston interviewed 1/17/83 at Beschloss, 1986, p. 356. The CIA director who suspected Powers' loyalty was John McCone, who replaced Dulles as DCI on 11/29/61, while the Powers-Abel exchange was being negotiated with the Soviets. McCone, of course, would have had full access to the 2/62 debriefings of Powers by Angleton's staff.

158   Powers might stay in Russia: FBI memo, 8/4/60, FBI/FGP.

CIA leads to FBI: Hoover to Dulles, 10/12/60, FBI/FGP.

files moved: Branigan to Sullivan, 2/19/62, FBI/FGP.

"any fingerprints are received": Bowles to Trotter, 7/21/60, FBI/FGP.

Hoover opposed Abel swap: Branigan to Sullivan, 1/3/61; Hoover to AG, 6/13/63; Hoover to AG, 11/9/61; L'Allier to Sullivan, 1/10/62; Brennan to Sullivan, 1/30/62; all at FBI/FGP.

159 "he refused to come home": Hoover to AG, 11/9/61, FBI/FGP.

"They may get their 'fingers burned' ": Hoover notation on Brennan to Sullivan, 2/8/62, FBI/FGP.

Hoover sent another letter: Hoover to Tolson, Belmont, Sullivan, DeLoach, 2/9/62, FBI/FGP.

Powers secreted in U.S.: DeLoach to Mohr, 2/10/62, FBI/FGP.

Powers' interrogation: Sullivan to Brennan, 2/16/62, FBI/FGP.

marital problems: Brennan to Sullivan, 4/23/62, FBI/FGP.

anti-CIA book by Powers' wife: Brennan to Sullivan, 8/1/63, FBI/FGP.

Wise-Ross book: Brennan to Sullivan, 6/7/62, FBI/FGP.

"I never did any such thing": Hoover scrawl on Evans, at FBI/FGP.

Goldwater suspicions: Goldwater, p. 79.

RFK against Powers: Powers, 1970, pp. 311–12.

Nilsen's allegations: Nilsen interviewed in the television documentary *Counterpoint*, Villon Films, 1975, at Beschloss, 1986, pp. 358–59.

160 Wilson U-2 security work: Maas, pp. 20–21.

8. LICENSED TO KILL

161 "the most extraordinary collection of talent": T, 5/11/62, p. 18.

"Easter egghead hunt": ibid.

"uncork the touchdown play": Lansdale memo to RFK, 1/27/62, IR, p. 142.

Fleming-JFK: Pearson, pp. 297–98, 300–301.

162 urged twice: Bissell testimony, 6/11/75, p. 51, IR, p. 184.

Harvey-JFK: Lansdale interviewed at Martin, p. 129.

Harvey tasked with killing Castro: Bissell, 6/11/75, pp. 19, 47; Harvey, 6/25/75, p. 86; both at IR, p. 188.

Executive Action: Bissell, 7/25/75, p. 32, IR, p. 121; Harvey 6/25/75, p. 37, IR, p. 184; Helms to Harvey, 2/19/62, IG/67, p. ??.

"incredibly naive about communism": Nixon to Eisenhower, 4/21/59, Wyden, p. 28.

Maheu's role: Maheu, pp. 135–40, 148–49, 153–62.

163 In October: Rosselli testimony, p. 15; Maheu testimony, p. 1; O'Connell testimony, 5/30/75, p. 116; all at IR, p. 80.

Sam Giancana had stated: Hoover to DCI, 10/18/60, IR, p. 79.

"Keystone Cops," etc.: Maheu testimony, p. 36, IR, p. 77; O'Connell testimony, p. 68, IR, p. 77; 3/23/63, IR, p. 125.

164 "on behalf of the CIA": Miami SAC to Hoover, 4/20/61, IR, p. 126.

"Sam, we got problems": Papich interview.

"in connection with": Hoover to RFK, 5/22/61, IR, p. 127.

"Of course, all hell broke loose": Papich interview.

CIA vs. FBI in Havana: Thayer Waldo, quoted at Felix [McCarger], p. 107.

"like a duck": Papich interview.

Hoover-RFK: ibid.

Hoover tattled to RFK: Hoover to RFK, 5/10/62, IR, p. 78.

165 "It was just further proof": Maheu, p. 147.

Harvey consulted Wright: Wright, pp. 159–60.

Harvey met Rosselli: Harvey testimony, 7/11/75, p. 18; Edwards memo, 5/14/62; both at IR, p. 83.

166   "any prosecution": Edwards memo, 2/2/62, IR, p. 131.

Houston and Edwards briefed RFK: Houston interview.

"You're not going to win": Papich interview.

"a very pregnant possibility": Harvey testimony, 6/25/75, pp. 67–68, IR, p. 102.

167   Missile Crisis: Harvey, 7/11/75, pp. 80–81; Belmont to Sullivan, 10/29/62; both at IR, p. 148.

Harvey "out of control": Elder, 8/13/75, pp. 34–35, IR, p. 148.

February meeting: CIA report, "What Could Castro have Known?," FOIA.

"drinking a bit too much," etc.: Helms interview.

FBI found Harvey out: Angleton interviewed at Martin, pp. 145–46; Papich to Belmont, 6/20/63, FR-V, p. 100.

Harvey consulted DDP: IG/67, p. 54.

168   wetsuit plot: CIA Task Force W Assistant testimony, 9/18/75, p. 28, IR, p. 85; Helms testimony, 6/13/75, p. 135, IR, pp. 85–86; Colby testimony, 5/21/75, pp. 38–39, IR, p. 85.

"AM/LASH": CIA Case Officer testimony, 8/1/75, pp. 29, 43; CIA contact report; CIA contact plan, n.d. [fall 1963]; IG/67, p. 90; all at IR, pp. 86–88.

169   "all be targets" Richard Goodwin testimony, 7/18/75, pp. 4, 11, IR, p. 139.

"Castro would retaliate": Harvey notes, 1/26/61, IR, p. 183.

"We knew more": Castro interviewed at Szulc, 1987, p. 586.

Bender motel-room incident: Phillips, pp. 116–17.

170   "capabilities of Castro's security apparata": Harvey testimony, 7/11/75, IR.

"a Cuban official": FBI memo, Miami to HQ, 10/10/63, FR-V, p. 100.

"intelligence of Cuban 'colonies' ": "FBI-CIA Cooperation re Cuban Community," Top Secret memo, Brig. Gen Lansdale for Special Group (Augmented), 3/13/62, Cuban Missile Crisis collection, NSAV.

Fair Play for Cuba: Helms to Hoover, Attention: Papich, 11/5/62, Cuban Missile Crisis collection, NSAV.

171   Aleman's account of dealings with FBI is from Aleman interview by Andy Purdy, 3/10/77, HAH-V, p. 317; Aleman testimony, 9/27/78, HAH-V, pp. 305–15; Crile, 5/16/76.

"He's a reliable individual": Crile, 5/16/76.

Trafficante in Cuba: Trafficante testimony, 9/28/78, HAH-V, p. 355.

"outlet for illegal contraband": Federal Bureau of Narcotics memo, n.t., 7/21/61, cited at Crile, 5/16/76.

172   CIA's meeting with Cubela on 11/22: CIA AM/LASH file entry, n.d. [1965], IR, p. 89; CIA Case Officer testimony, 8/17/75, p. 92, IR, p. 85; CIA Case Officer 2 testimony, 8/17/75, p. 112, IR, p. 89.

"telescopic scope," etc.: CIA AM/LASH file entry, n.d. [1965], IR, p. 89.

"something more sophisticated": IG/67, p. 93a.

"At the very moment President Kennedy was shot": IG/67, p. 94, CIA-FOIA.

173   "they themselves will not be safe": Castro interviewed by Daniel Harker, New Orleans *Times-Picayune*, 9/19/63.

173   FBI-CIA exchanging Oswald data: CIA blind memos, 11/2/59, 11/4/59, CIA-

FOIA #592-252B; CIA memo, 9/18/75, CIA-FOIA #1187-436; CIA Out Message no. 74673, 10/10/63, 0800 hours, CIA-FOIA #622-258.

"a person of great interest to us": AP, 8/24/93.

"On 1 October 1963": CIA memo to FBI, 10/10/63, CIA/YIN.

174 "said his name was Lee Oswald": WP, 5/14/92.

My account of the Kostikov affair is based on FBI Director Clarence Kelley's review of FBI files, as described in his book, pp. 268–70, 296ff., and on CIA documents, including some on Johnston, 9/27/92, and released to the National Archives in 8/93. See also notes to ch. 10, below, where the story continues. The Kostikov case is apparently still considered so sensitive that all former intelligence officers interviewed for this book refused comment on it.

"functioning overtly as consul": CIA memo, n.d., CIA/YIN. See also "with the 13th Department" in an 11/27/63 memo, FOIA #1525–1099, CIA/YIN; and WP, 8/22/93, quoting an 11/23/63 CIA memo identifying Kostikov as "responsible for sabotage and assassination." It seems unlikely that CIA reached this conclusion within hours of the assassination; more likely, as Kelley and Johnston contend, they had known for some time. Epstein (1978, p. 16) has the FBI learning about Kostikov's Department 13 connections from a double agent, and CIA apparently learning about such connections, in turn, from the FBI. But CIA documents, including some released in 8/93, show the flow of information going the other way—i.e., from the Agency to the Bureau. Documents at CIA/YIN make clear that the Bureau did not have independent corroboration of Kostikov's Department 13 status in the days immediately after the assassination, or pretended it did not, for CIA was challenged to prove Kostikov's identity through more than mere "analysis." The FBI's apparent ignorance calls into question Clarence Kelley's contention (Kelley, pp. 293ff.) that William Sullivan would have known immediately who Kostikov was. Blame for the Kostikov bungle, if such it was, would thus fall squarely on CIA. See transcript of conversation between O'Neal and Papich in ch. 10.

"reluctance-to-share": Kelley, p. 296.

175 "There's no question": Hosty interviewed at Kelley, p. 296.

"Kostikov was the officer-in-charge": ibid., p. 268.

9. A MIND OF WINTER

179 Events of 12/15/61 are from NYT, 12/16/61.

Details of Golitsyn's defection: Friberg interviewed 6/13/89 at Mangold, pp. 71–74, and Wise, 1992, pp. 3–5. Epstein has Golitsyn defecting on 12/22/61 (1989, p. 66).

180 The move to Langley is described by Phillips, pp. 47, 73, 177.

The change from bold Easterners to prudent professionals was first noted by Alsop, pp. 213ff. Former CIA Office of Security man Tom Tripodi blames that sea-change partly on the prevalence of ex–FBI agents in CIA's personnel-screening jobs. "The prevailing attitude of the OS was that it carried the awesome responsibility of ensuring that the CIA conformed in all ways to Hoover's philosophy of morality and judicial propriety—or, as they were more likely to put it, their job was 'to ride herd on the cowboys.' More often than not, the perceived 'cowboys' were the former OSS . . . guys working covert operations in the DDP [Department of Plans]. The men of action who had distinguished themselves during World War II found themselves being restricted by the Hooveresque, bureaucratic mind-set of former FBI agents. As age and attrition took their toll on the OSS vets, younger agents took their place, agents who had been cleared for admittance to the CIA by the OS and who therefore reflected OS- [and FBI-] approved attitudes." (Tripodi, p. 83.)

181 "Ring the gong": Rocca interview.

182 The disinformation document is quoted at Bagley testimony, HAH-XII. Real and fake papers: Miler interview.

Assassinations warning: See Epstein, 1989, p. 81. Although some have alleged that Golitysn did not warn of assassinations until he returned from England in 1963, Epstein, apparently working from an Angleton interview, says that "Golitsyn had explicitly told his debriefer in 1962 that the KGB was in the process of organizing special actions, including untraceable assassinations." Former Angleton staffer Scotty Miler has backed this version (Miler interview).

Karlow was first named as a molehunt suspect by Tom Morganthau (NWK, 8/11/80); the case has been recounted in Mangold and in Wise, 1992. Morganthau alleged that Karlow was pinpointed during "a search for suspected traitors that began with defection of Soviet spy Anatoli Golitsin [sic] in 1961." Wise, Mangold, and others followed this line. But according to Miler, Karlow was under suspicion before Golitysn arrived (Miler interview). Another ex-Angleton hand, William Hood, has stated flatly: "The notion that the so-called 'mole hunt' began when Major Golitsyn opted out of the KGB is manifestly false" (Hood et al., 1994, p. 12).

183 Karlow serial formally passed to FBI: CIA memo for the record, 1/13/75, cited at Wise, 1992, p. 83.

"a discreet investigation": Hoover to McCone, 3/6/62, FBI Karlow file, cited at ibid.

set up listening equipment: Karlow interviewed at ibid.; FBI Headquarters memo, 1/15/62, cited at ibid. Wise dates the FBI visit to Karlow's home to late 1962, but finds the FBI's 1/15/62 memo ("installation of [deleted] coverage on the Subject") a "clear reference to the wiretaps on Karlow" (p. 83n).

Papich-Edwards meeting re Karlow: CIA Memo to File, 2/14/62, ibid.

Karlow in Philadelphia: FBI surveillance report, n.d., Wise, ibid., p. 85. Karlow later claimed that he had gone to the store to be fitted for a new leg, and that his old, dismembered one was in the box.

Hoover updated McCone re Karlow: Hoover to McCone, 3/6/62, ibid.

184 Karlow summoned to FBI: Karlow interviewed at ibid., pp. 125ff.

"I wish to help the FBI": Karlow to Helms, 2/21/63, ibid.

"Allegations were coming in," etc.: Houston interview.

185 "accepted procedure": Meyer, p. 378.

"Now, assuming an agent of ours": Angleton testimony, p. 78. Scotty Miler would later expand on his chief's reasoning: "At some stage, you usually had to give the FBI access to a defector. In many instances, the defector wasn't happy with this. He would say, 'Why can't you just ask me the questions, I'll answer them, and then you give them to them?' The niceties of bureaucratic infighting were somewhat lost on the defector. He's not used to that. If you had an American defector to the Soviet Union, the KGB would alone debrief him; they weren't about to let some Army or Air Force officer horn in. So, coming into our system of sharing defectors between agencies, he couldn't understand—'Why do I have to see thirty-two people?' " According to Miler, other previous defectors had not been shared with the FBI, either, until Hoover found out independently. Hoover raised a fuss in such cases, but Miler thought it was a sort of pro-forma fuss, because "Hoover really didn't want the headaches" that came from having to care for defectors (Miler interview).

186 "By the early sixties": Papich interview.

FBI officers met Golitsyn at Mayflower Hotel: Papich interview. Golitsyn's reasoning on the Abel case has been described by Don Moore to Mangold and to Wise. Moore later met Golitsyn at a CIA facility on 23rd Street, a meeting which Papich did not attend, and it is possible that the Abel case was discussed by Golitsyn at this meeting, rather than the earlier one at the Mayflower. Papich said: "There's one story that he considered Rudolf Abel a plant, and so on. That's in Mangold's book. I never heard that. But we'd never buy it. Hell, he never broke—we never got anything out of Abel himself." (Papich interview.)

187 "Frankly, that Golitsyn": Moore interviewed at Mangold, pp. 83–84.

23rd Street: Poptanich interviewed 2/14/89 at ibid., pp. 87–88; Branigan interviewed 11/29/88 at ibid.

Moore on Angleton: Moore interviewed at Wise, 1992, p. 34.

188 "We didn't have a single agent": Papich interview.

Poptanich's Performance Rating: FBI Office of Hoover to House Select Committee on Assassinations, 1/8/79, FBI/YIN.

189 "The FBI was not happy": Mangold, p. 83.

Nosenko's contact with CIA in Geneva: Bagley testimony, HAH-XII, p. 624.

"conclusively proven": CIA cable, Bagley to Headquarters, 6/11/62, quoted at Hart testimony, 9/15/78, HAH-II, p. 493.

Angleton on meeting with Bagley: Angleton interviewed by Hart, HAH-II, p. 494.

190 Golitsyn impatient, went to Britain: Papich interview. Golitsyn's handlers in CIA's Soviet Bloc Division were tiring of the difficult defector, even if their superiors esteemed his "product." One SBD officer would recall Golitsyn as a "very suspicious, very withdrawn, very difficult man" who "had a lot of problems getting along with people." Another was aghast when Golitsyn broke off one session by saying that the CIA man "did not begin to understand" the KGB. Peer de Silva, Soviet Bloc Division operations chief, spoke for many of his colleagues when he called Golitsyn "a total son of a bitch." There was another side to the problem, of course: "Golitsyn became impatient with stupid and repetitive questions," Scotty Miler recalled. "Joe comes in, he asks a question. Two days later, Frank comes in, he asks the same question. So Golitsyn began to say, 'Why won't you oxen get together?' Too often, Soviet Division guys, for instance, wouldn't even bother to read summaries of previous debriefings, or would scan the material, and miss details. The other thing is, people would come in to talk to him about the KGB, and they don't know much about the KGB. And if they hadn't even mastered the *overt* information on the subject, Golitsyn became pretty damned irritated. Why was he wasting his time? Some of the Soviet Division guys were better than he thought, but I think Golitsyn had legitimate cause for complaint." (Miler interview.)

Philby: See Winks, pp. 405–6, apparently working from Angleton interviews; Wright, pp. 193ff. Philby's own account, given years later to Philip Knightly, is not very illuminating. Concerning the typewriter ribbon, an FBI memo notes: "The typewriter ribbons, Q1 and Q2, were examined and it was determined that no intelligible information could be developed. The ribbon from Kim Philby's typewriter had been used repeatedly and, although impressions were present, no words or letter combinations could be developed. RECOMMENDATION: That this memorandum be forwarded to Liaison in order that the attached ribbons and the results of the Laboratory examination can be furnished to the Central Intelligence Agency." (6/10/63, FBI memo, W. D. Griffith to Conrad, 7/10/63, FBI/AKP.)

After smoking out Philby, Golitsyn was treated royally by Arthur Martin, head of the Soviet Section of MI5. Hearing Golitsyn talk about General Rodin and his KGB assassination plot against an "opposition leader" in Northern Europe, Martin wondered whether British Labour Party leader Hugh Gaitskell, who died from a mysterious illness in January, might have been poisoned by the KGB to clear the way for his successor, Harold Wilson, whose friends and business partners traveled with unusual frequency to Moscow. It turned out that Gaitskell had visited the Soviet Embassy in London on December 13, 1962, and consumed tea and crumpets there, just one day before being fatally stricken with systemic lupus erythematosus, a complaint almost unique to prepubescent females in the tropics. MI5's research soon discovered that the Soviets had published three scientific papers in 1956 describing a new drug which could cause systemic lupus. It also turned out that General Rodin had been stationed at the embassy during Gaitskell's visit. See Epstein, 1989, pp. 80–82; Wright, pp. 362–63.

191 Papich met with Golitsyn privately at Angleton's: Papich interview.
 "I'm going to be gone for a while," etc: ibid.
192 "I listened with great interest": ibid.
193 "controversial" and "irritating": ibid.
 "Monster Plot": Mangold, p. 115.
 "too speculative": Papich interview.
 "We need confirmation": Miler interview.
 "An attack on any employee": Rocca interview.
 FBI withheld files from CIA: Papich interview, Nolan interview.
194 Kulak: Wise, 1992, pp. 149ff.
 Polyakov: Mangold: pp. 227ff.
 "a source of unknown reliability": Sullivan interviewed at Epstein, 1978, p. 20.
 "They checked with us": Miler interview.
195 "They gave us cases": Papich interview.
 "no evidence had been found": Wright, pp. 270–71.
 "I got turned off": Papich interview.
196 "I've been working with the FBI": Garbler interviewed at Wise, 1992, pp. 50–51.
 watch for Penkovskiy: Helms interviewed 12/8/90 at Schecter and Deriabin, p. 305.
 "Go to the Washington monument": Joseph J. Bulik interviewed 7/27–28 at ibid.
 Hunter Vince: Papich to Brennan, 12/13/62, FR-III, p. 631.
 French Embassy burglary: Petty interviewed 5/17/89 at Mangold, p. 29; Papich interview. The liaison officer claimed not to remember the details of

the episode, and seemed surprised that Mangold had attributed such information not only to Petty, Angleton's onetime staffer, but to Angleton's wife, Cicely.

197 "Before assuming responsibility": Phillips, pp. 163–64.

"pink carnations": Felix [McCargar], pp. 101–2.

198 "There are": Dulles, pp. 198–99.

10. SINISTER IMPLICATIONS

198 KGB defector in Geneva: Bagley testimony, HAH-XII; various reports at FBI/YIN and CIA/YIN; *Yuri Nosenko, KGB*, by Stephen Taylor, an HBO/BBC documentary drama, 1988.

199 "CIA feared that the Cubans": Schorr.

200 "Removed from Hosty's in-box": Kelley, pp. 293–94.

"The withholding of that [Kostikov] information": ibid: , pp. 293–96.

RFK believed his brother killed by Castro: Powers, 10/29/89, p. M-1.

"speculation about Oswald's motivation": Katzenbach to Moyers, 11/25/63, at Epstein, 1978, p. 253.

"The President told me," etc.: Warren Commission internal memo by Melvin Eisenberg, 2/17/64, quoted at Kelley, pp. 293ff.

"will it mean World War III?": USNWR, 8/17/92.

commission bias against FBI, toward CIA: ibid.

201 "an identified KGB officer": WP, 8/22/93.

"responsible for sabotage and assassination": CIA document [n.d.] cited at ibid.

"We do not participate": CIA document, n.d., cited at CT, 8/30/93.

"Mr. George Bush": This story first appeared in the Inter Press Service during the height of Bush's election campaign, on 8/11/88. Conservatives have all but accused the Inter Press Service of being a communist front (Powell, pp. 138–42); it is affiliated with the Institute for Policy Studies. The Bush story was picked up and carried for a while by *The Nation*.

DeMohrenschildt: CIA memo, Att: Acting Chief, Contact Division (Direct), Support, Dallas Resident Agency, 5/1/64.

202 "They [CIA] knew that Oswald had once defected": Johnston, 9/27/92, p. C-5.

CIA welcomed playing second fiddle: ibid.

"jurisdiction in getting investigative results abroad": FBI memo to A. Belmont, 11/27/63.

Oswald at party: CIA report, "Review of Selected Items in the Lee Harvey Oswald File Regarding Allegations of Castro Cuban Involvement in the John F. Kennedy Assassination," 5/30/75, CIA-FOIA.

203 "mystery passenger": blind memo, 12/2/63, CIA-FOIA #1384-491-B.

Gilberto Lopez: FBI memo, Tampa Field Office to Headquarters, 6/3/64, FR-V, p. 62; CIA cable from Mexico Station to Headquarters. 12/3/63, FR-V, p. 61. Although referred to in the Church Committee's Final Report summaries of CIA and FBI documents simply as a "Cuban-American," this individual was later identified in a House Select Committee on Assassinations report as Gilberto Lopez. See also CIA cable and buckslip, Mexico Station to Hoover, 3/20/64; FBI memo, Mexico Field Office to Headquarters, 12/5/63, FR-V, p. 62; FBI memo, Tampa Field Office to Headquarters, 10/26/64, FR-V, p. 62.

"had through the years the responsibility": Helms testimony, 9/22/78, HAH-IV, p. 10.

"(1) Q. Was Oswald": Sullivan to Belmont, 5/13/64. FR-V, p. 49.

"on the basis of an analysis," etc.: "Last part of conversation between Mr. Papich and [O'Neal] 27 Nov 63 at 10," attachment to blind memo, 11/27/63, CIA-FOIA #1525-1099.

204 "impression": [Anderson] testimony, 2/4/76, FR-V, p. 40.

"that every bit": FBI supervisor testimony, 4/8/76, p. FR-V, p. 42.

Solo: Hoover to Rankin by special courier, 7/17/64, FBI/YIN; Kelley, p. 269; *All Things Considered* (National Public Radio), November 15, 1993; Kessler, 1993, p. 23.

"An exhaustive FBI report": Washington *Star*, 12/3/63. When informed of this report, Hoover wrote, "I thought no one knew this outside the FBI." According to Sullivan, however, Hoover himself ordered the report leaked.

"Information developed": "Relations with the CIA," n.d. [12/63], FBI Drew Pearson file, Robins, pp. 147–48.

205 "I know the importance": CIA transcript, McCone-Hoover telephone conversation, 12/16/63, quoted at Hart testimony, 8/15/78, HAH-II, pp. 505–6.

"sinister implications": quoted at Epstein, 1978, p. 249.

Cubana unidentified passenger: CIA to SSCI, n.d. [1976], FR-V, p. 61.

Kostikov had remained in Mexico City: WP, 8/22/93.

Lopez: see note for p. 203.

206 "money," "Dorticos again asked," etc.: ibid.

207 "tradecraft": SDUT, 8/14/93.

"using theaters for meeting places" Deriabin memo, n.d., at Agence France Presse, 8/23/93. Hayhannen, for instance, had reported in 1957 that he met Soviet spies at the Symphony theater on the Upper West Side of Manhattan.

"This would have been a good method": SDUT, 8/14/93.

CIA analysts speculated: Johnston, 9/27/92.

208 "would automatically ease up," etc.: Deriabin memo to CIA, 11/27/63, BG, 8/25/93.

"pure power": Angleton interviewed at Epstein, 1989, p. 281.

"In my conversations": Papich interview.

209 Bagley-Nosenko contact procedure: George Kissevalter interviewed at Wise, 1992, p. 131.

"I'm not going home," etc.: Bagley testimony, HAH-XII, pp. 627ff.

"the KGB was frightened of Oswald," etc.: Angleton to Hoover, 4/28/64, FBI/YIN.

"a plant": memo by Murphy, 2/17/64, CIA/YIN.

told Angleton doubts about Oswald story: Bagley testimony at HAH-XII, pp. 575, 590–91, 596, 609, 624, 626.

210 "a pool of pirahnas": HAH-XII, p. 591.

Bagley's doubts: HAH-XII, pp. 578, 582, 641, 637.

"Do we know anything": Branigan to Sullivan, 2/11/64, FBI/YIN.

"The defection to the United States": "Victory for CIA," Ogden, Utah, *Standard-Examiner*, 2/12/64, FBI/YIN.

"We are closely following": Branigan to Sullivan, 2/11/64, FBI/YIN.

"Keep after it": Brennan to Sullivan, 2/5/64, FBI/YIN.

"We must press CIA": Branigan to Sullivan, 2/28/64, FBI/YIN.

211 "Source was at ease": airtel, SAC, WFO to Hoover, 2/27/64, FBI/YIN.
"son of a bitch": Papich interview.
"for as long as they wanted": Bagley testimony, HAH-XII, p. 605.
"I accepted it at face value": Poptanich deposition, 7/27/78, HAH-XII, p. 540.
"The FBI does not perceive": FBI letter, Office of the Director to House Select Committee on Assassinations, 1/8/79. The letter described the FBI's views on Nosenko from 1964 to 1968.
212 "It wasn't just tension": McWilliams interview.
"I don't know if I ever trusted": ibid.
one "Krupnov": Nosenko testimony, 6/20/78, HAH-XII, p. 523.
213 "Bagley was a bright guy": McWilliams interview.
"There was a concern": Miler interview.
"The KGB is more compartmented," etc.: McWilliams interview.
214 "many important questions": CIA memorandum for the record, 5/28/64, CIA-YIN.
"no confidence": CIA memo for the record, 3/9/64, CIA/YIN.
"operational potential": Bagley memo for FBI, 3/3/64, CIA/YIN.
"stupid and not educated," etc.: ibid.
"We passed [those questions]": Bagley testimony, HAH-XII, p. 605.
"would not be asked," etc.: CIA memo for the record, 3/9/64, CIA/YIN.
"I indicated": ibid.
215 "none of our questions," etc.: Bagley testimony, HAH-XII, p. 605.
"Any bureaucracy has vested interests": Miler interview.
Hoover wasn't out in the field: Papich interview.
"How long": Sullivan to Belmont, 3/31/64, FBI/YIN.
Hoover a know-it-all: Lamphere, p. 73.
"In the event you desire": Hoover to J. Lee Rankin, 3/6/64, FBI/YIN.
216 "a report from": Rankin to Helms, 3/6/64, CIA/YIN.
"await further developments": memo, 3/12/64, CIA/YIN.
"the inability of any": memo, 3/12/64, CIA-FOIA #1053-947N.
"the FBI's investigation on this point": ibid.
"limited in its possibility," etc.: memo, 3/12/64, CIA-FOIA #603-256.
"final answer": Warren Commision memorandum, 6/24/64, CIA/YIN.
"Director McCone asked me": Helms interview.
217 "Nosenko is a KGB plant": CIA memcon, 7/28/64, CIA/YIN.
"undesirable to include": ibid.
"some irritation in the Bureau": Helms interview.
Helms pondered the options: Helms testimony, 9/22/78, HAH-IV, pp. 20–22, 30–22.
218 "Spartan": ibid., p. 29.
"hostile interrogation," "break": Murphy to Helms, 2/17/64, CIA/YIN.
"play": Papich interview.
"The transcript must be wrong," etc.: Bagley testimony, HAH-XII, p. 626.
Nosenko at Camp Peary: Houston interview.

11. MOLEHUNT
219 "should have left a wider window": CIA memo, 5/30/75, CIA/YIN.
220 "The whole idea": Miler interview.

"and really destroy him": ibid.

"the FBI wasn't doing its job": ibid.

221 The targets: Papich interview.

222 "We'd like to search," etc.: Eleanor Orlov interviewed at Wise, 1992, pp. 191–93.

"Guess what?": Igor Orlov interviewed at Hurt, pp. 141ff.

223 Hoover at retirement age: Brennan, 9/25/75, Hearings, p. 97.

"clearly and directly": ibid., p. 118.

"Hoover wasn't going to do": Papich interview.

"When Al Belmont left": ibid.

Long hearings: DeLoach to Tolson, 1/21/66, FR-II, p. 110.

224 "I would have no hesitance": Belmont to Tolson, 2/27/65, FR-III, p. 670.

joint molehunt terminated: Miler interview; Branigan interviewed at Mangold, pp. 262–63.

"a provocateur": CIA memorandum, n.d. [c. 9/67], quoted at Hart testimony, 9/15/78, HAH-II, p. 504.

"Nick Nack": Leonard McCoy interviewed at Mangold, pp, 340–44. McCoy and Mangold claim that Angleton buried Nick Nack's leads, refusing to pass them on to foreign intelligence services, but Miler insists this is "a bunch of crap. They all were followed up. I know the guy who did it." Mangold's criticism also seems to me inconsistent. He says that "it was the CIA's and Angleton's role to pass along his [Nick Nack's] leads to the relevant foreign services. If he didn't do it, it simply wasn't done." (Ibid., p. 342.) Yet Mangold also says that "the FBI maintained direct contact with MI5 (without CIA intermediaries) . . . [and] passed [Nick Nack's] leads to MI5 in London through Charles Bates, the FBI liaison officer in the British capital" (ibid., pp. 341–42). In fact, the FBI maintained independent liaison with French intelligence as well, and with the counterspy services of most NATO nations, according to Larry McWilliams. If leads were not forwarded to the relevant services, it was not because Angleton had a stranglehold on Bureau liaison with those organizations, but because the chief of the FBI's intelligence division, William Sullivan, had begun to doubt the veracity of Nick Nack and other FBI sources. Of course, it is possible to blame Angleton for that; but that is really blaming a man for making his case too well.

"Shamrock": Confidential interview with former CIA official, 12/93. The former official said that this third source was not Nick Nack and was not Vadim Isakov, a Soviet UN staffer who, according to William Sullivan, led the FBI "on a merry chase of arms dealers" during the 1960s, trying to buy rocket accelerometers (Sullivan interview, 1976, at Epstein, 1989, p. 169).

Hoover did not want to buttress Golitsyn: Epstein, 1989, pp. 95–96.

225 "We haven't proved anything": Miler interview.

"It's a waste of time": McWilliams interview.

226 "Coverage at that time": Papich interview.

Angleton understood Hoover's need: Angleton testimony, p. 69.

"Thousands of man-hours": Angleton interview, 7/10/76, FR-III, p. 947.

"clumsy bureaucratic actions": Angleton interviewed at David Binder, NYT, 4/10/87.

"go to the mat": Miler interview.

"Dave, meet our new Director": Phillips, pp. 189–91.

227 "Oligarchy": Ranelagh, pp. 423–24.
"Hoover and the Admiral": Phillips, p. 199.
ibid., pp. 192–93, 199–200, 205–6, 218–22, 237–38; Felt, p. 85.
"wanted to be able to explain": Phillips, p. 193.
"It made a great story": Sullivan, p. 70.
228 "Get along with the FBI": Phillips, p. 199.
"They didn't even have": ibid., p. 192.
"Here I am": ibid., p. 205.
229 "like hand in glove": Sullivan, p. 71.
secret communists: Phillips, p. 221.
"Mr. Phillips": ibid, pp. 221–22.
"I want to thank you": ibid., p. 238.
"At the time I was not aware": ibid., pp. 199–200.
230 "I think everyone realized": Miler interview.
"seek concurrence": Papich testimony, 9/22/75, FR-I, p. 172.
"foreign intelligence purposes": ibid., p. 173.
"internal security factors": ibid.
training courses: Helms to Hoover, 3/20/70, CCH-II, p. 355.
231 "too damn many": AFIO.
"eye to eye," etc.: Papich interview.
"come to visit": Helms interview.
"a very long span of time": Hart testimony, 9/15/78, HAH-II, p. 507.
"essentially as a rival": Helms interview.
Helms pressed Hoover: Sullivan interviewed by SSCI staff, 6/10/75, FR-III,
p. 947; Helms deposition, 9/10/75, p. 3, FR-III, p. 931.
232 "Kittyhawk": Miler interview; Hurt, pp. 131ff. Hurt gets Kittyhawk's name
slightly wrong, but in other respects his account seems to owe much to interviews with Angleton.
    CIA failed to brief FBI on Kittyhawk suspicions: Miler interview. Angleton's
secretiveness extended to CIA's purportedly porous Soviet Division, where the
molehunt was still suffering from a lack of FBI support. "We didn't want the
KGB to get playback on Kittyhawk," Miler explained. The objective of this
denial was not only defensive, but could serve a positive psychological-warfare
function—in effect, "psyching out" the enemy, and perhaps driving him to
desperate measures. "If they send Kittyhawk, and there's no playback, they
begin to wonder: What the hell is going on? Because there's no knowledge of
Kittyhawk that hits their source. That's compartment. They start to think,
Good God, we've lost! What's going on in CIA? They're compartmenting here,
they're compartmenting there. Do we have to send another one? It's the basic
reason for security, compartmentation, need to know. It's part of the game,
and part of controlling what could be very damaging penetration." (Miler
interview.)
233 "my mother's address": Wise, 1992, p. 193.
"Have you cracked the [Orlov] case?": ibid.
"It's a bunch of nonsense," etc.: Miler interview.
"There was a CIA request": McWilliams interview.
    Garbler: Morganthau and Martin, p. 33; Wise, 1992, passim; Mangold, pp.
259ff.
234 "particularly critical": CIA memo to FBI, 65/12/03, Mangold, p. 144.

Murphy: Martin, pp. 195–96; Wise, 1992, pp. 219–22; Mangold, pp. 298–99; Epstein, 1989, p. 87.

Kapusta called Papich: Wise, 1992, pp. 219–20.

235 "believed four or five guys": Sullivan interviewed at Hersh, 12/22/74.

"refused on the grounds": Sullivan, p. 194.

"It was a brush-off": Hersh, 12/22/74.

"I think where Jim": Papich interview.

236 "These individuals": Helms interview.

12. WEDGE

237 "the illegality": memo, n.d. [c. 5/7/73], CIA/YIN.

Dirksen query: Papich to Brennan, 2/11/65. FBI/YIN.

Wise discovery: CIA [Helms] Secret memorandum for the President, 3/22/68, CIA/YIN.

"Liquidate the man": Bagley notes, n.d. [c. 9/66], quoted at Hart testimony, 8/15/78, p. 525. TK

Taylor's role in Nosenko rehab: Epstein, 1978. p. 265.

238 Trafficante-Cubela connections: FBI New York Field Office to Headquarters, 7/2/65, FR-V, p. 78; IG-67 p. 103; FBI Headquarters to New York Field Office, 7/2/65, FR-V, p. 78.

"had been an insecure operation": Joseph H. Langosch [cryptonym] affidavit, 9/14/78; Chief, SAS/CI to Chief WHD, n.d. [6/65]; cable, Headquarters to JMWAVE and European Stations, 6/23/65, AMWHIP File; CIA Cable from European station to Headquarters, 3/18/65; all at FR-V, p.78.

239 Rosselli's allegations: Osborn to Hoover, 5/27/66, IR, p. 85.

FBI investigation of Rosselli's allegations: Deloach to Tolson, 3/17/67, FR-V, pp. 82–83; FBI Agent I testimony, 3/5/76, pp. 24, 25; FBI Agent II testimony, 4/13/76, pp. 18, 16, FR-V, pp. 83–84.

"FBI has not been told": IG/67, pp. 130–31.

"over a barrel": ibid., p. 131.

"ghost[ed]": Epstein, 1989, p. 284.

"taking dope": WT, 4/18/94.

"the influence or the orders of Castro": Lyndon Johnson interviewed by Marianne Means, King Features Syndicate, 4/24/75.

"something that will rock you": quoted at Summers, 1988, p. 410.

"the belief that there was Soviet," etc.: "Review of Selected Items in the Lee Harvey Oswald File Regarding Allegations of Castro Cuban Involvement in the John F. Kennedy Assassination," 5/30/75, CIA-FOIA.

"reflected the concern": Helms testimony, 9/22/78, HAH-IV, p. 12.

241 attacks on Warren Commission: CIA memo for DDCI, 6/10/66; CIA memorandum for DCI, 8/25/66, CIA/YIN. The agencies were perhaps most worried about the work of Edward Jay Epstein. According to one memo by Helms, "The FBI has advised . . . that a report furnished to the Bureau by the State Department indicates that an Edward Jay Epstein, born in 1935, traveled to the USSR as a tourist in 1958. It is believed that Epstein is probably identical with the author of *Inquest.* . . . The FBI reports that in 1959, Edward Jay Epstein, while a student at Cornell, complained to the FBI that his rights were being violated because other students were bugging or taping statements he

was making in the course of a student election at Cornell. The Justice Department found no cause for action. . . . Mr. Papich of the FBI informed [deleted] that shortly before Allen Dulles left on his recent trip to Europe, he called Mr. Papich to say that he had received a call from the journalist and author, Fletcher Knebel (Cowles Publications and *Seven Days in May*). Mr. Knebel allegedly told Mr. Dulles that he had collaborated with Epstein in preparation of the latter's book, *Inquest*. Knebel reminded Mr. Dulles of the latter's interview with Epstein some months before and sought Mr. Dulles' reaction (to what was uncertain, but it may be that Dulles saw an advance of the book). There is no indication in *Inquest* of any collaboration by Knebel. However, Knebel may not have wished to use his name openly on a book of this type. Knebel's possible collaboration on this book would explain its readability which goes beyond the usual capabilities of a student-author of an expanded master's thesis." (CIA memo for Deputy Director of Central Intelligence, Subject: New Book, *Inquest* by Edward Jay Epstein, 6/10/66, CIA-FOIA #1024-954B.)

Nosenko resettled: Osborn to DCI, 10/5/72, CIA/YIN.

Solie believed Nosenko: Osborn to Helms, 10/5/72, CIA/YIN.

January 1968 debates on Nosenko: Miler interview.

"There is no question in my mind": quoted at Epstein, 1978, pp. 263–64.

242   an easy "fit": Branigan interview, Mangold, p. 195.

"An analysis of this case": CIA memo to file, 1/5/68, CIA-FOIA #1354-495.

Jaffe: FBI teletype, 12/17/75, FBI/YIN.

"whitewash": Miler at Epstein, 1978, p. 269.

"To give him merit badges": Miler interview. Angleton's staff also felt that the new debriefings of Nosenko were based on a false methodology. According to Miler, Solie and the FBI agents had actually ladled out hints: "Well now, you said this—didn't you?" "Yep, yep." And then on to the next question. Or, "What do you think of this? Is this what you meant?" And Nosenko would say, "Sounds right." Proceeding in that fashion was a cardinal mistake, in the minds of Miler and his boss, because it "dirtied" the information. "Jim's attitude was, You play Nosenko from his own information. You don't feed him information, because then you couldn't judge what you were getting." (Ibid.)

"no conflict," never compared them: Solie deposition, 6/1/78, HAH-XII, p. 528.

"never had any reason": ibid.

243   "I do not consider": ibid., p. 530.

"As far as our office was concerned": ibid., p. 528.

"significant confirmatory information": Top Secret FBI working paper with enclosures, 10/1/68, FBI/YIN.

"The FBI summary notes": Taylor to Helms, 10/4/68, CIA/YIN.

244   "from a defector whose bona fides," "truthful and honest": Miler interview.

"the FBI just might level criticism," etc.: CIA memo, Deputy Director Rufus Taylor to Director Richard Helms, 10/4/68, CIA/YIN.

"proper characterization to be used": Hoover to SAC, New York, 4/28/69, FBI/YIN.

245   KK/MOUNTAIN: Hersh, 1991, p. 5.

Shapiro memos: ibid., pp. 250–51.

246   Scope, Eitan-Lakam: Schweizer, pp. 218ff.

247 Iraq a Soviet client: Golitsyn, 1984, p. 337.

Tuwaitha reactor: Jed. C. Snyder, "The Road to Osiraq: Baghdad's Quest for the Bomb," *Middle East Journal*, Autumn 1983.

something bad going to happen: Papich interview.

248 Lyalin flap: Wright, p. 346.

"There's no question about it": Papich interview.

"Sam routinely took on Hoover": McWilliams interview.

249 "fitting into the picture," etc.: Papich interview.

"bouncing among all those wheels": ibid.

Papich retirement letter: Felt, p. 79; Sullivan interviewed by Robert M. Smith, n.d. [10/7/71], at "FBI Is Said to Have Cut Direct Liaison With CIA," NYT, 10/9/71, p. A-1.

"never faced the kind of sophisticated": Papich to Hoover, 2/15/70, in Robert Mardian Papers, Hoover Institution, Palo Alto, Calif.

250 "taking off on the whole subject": Papich interview.

"might more easily smooth over": Papich to Hoover, 2/15/70.

"really shook up J. Edgar": Papich interview.

"drafted by the CIA": Felt, p. 79.

"I want to abolish": ibid.

Boulder: Denver Colorado, 1/22/70, FBI/TR.

251 Riha's disappearance: SAC Chicago to Hoover, 9/15/69; [deleted] to Wannall, 4/8/75; both at FBI/TR.

252 Riha's background story: FBI 302, Thomas Riha, Cambridge, Mass., 8/19/60; Report, SAC Boston, 8/31/60; SAC Denver to Hoover, 4/16/69; SAC, Chicago, to Hoover, 2/12/63; SSAC Chicago to Hoover, 9/15/69; all at FBI/TR.

"whether there was an STB," etc.: Miler interview.

"without foundation": FBI memo, [deleted] to W. R. Wannall, 4/8/75, FBI/TR.

"not utilizing subject": ibid.

"unfavorable relations": SAC Denver to Hoover, 1/28/70, FBI/TR.

253 Werner-Todorovich: SAC Denver to Hoover, 2/20/70, FBI/TR.

"I still want name of our agent": ibid.

"Papich vigorously protested": ibid.

"interviewed in detail," etc.: ibid.

"Dear Mr. Hoover": Helms to Hoover, 2/26/70, FBI/TR.

255 "drive a wedge": Sullivan interviewed at Robert M. Smith, n.d. [10/7/71], at "FBI Is Said to Have Cut Direct Liaison with CIA," NYT, 10/9/71, p. A-1.

"I was very strongly denouncing": Papich interview.

"I hope that you will share my alarm": Papich to Hoover, 3/2/70.

"IMMEDIATELY DISCONTINUE": Secret Coded Urgent FBI teletype, Hoover FBI to SAC Denver, 3/2/70, FBI/TR.

"superficial and insignificant mistakes": Kirkpatrick, p. 100.

256 deeper causes of break: Helms interview, 2/5/92; staff summary of [CIA intelligence officer], 2/9/76, FR-III, p. 933; former CIA-CI officers interviewed by Senate staff, FR-I, p. 173.

"The straw that broke the camel's back": Angleton testimony, pp. 83–84, FR-III, p. 933.

"I left under a cloud": Papich interview.

"Sam was a jewel": McWilliams interview.
"Well, I disagree with the man": Papich interview.

13. THE HYDRA PROJECT

259 events of 2/26/70: NYT, 2/27/70.
260 "You know, we just don't need": AFIO.
 Hoover's home: Anthony Calomaris interviewed at Demaris, p. 47; James
 E. Crawford interviewed op. cit., p. 34.
 communication by courier pouch: Papich interview.
 Helms' nonchalance: Helms interview.
261 break injured CIA-CI: Miler testimony, 3/19/75, p. 938, FR-I, p. 173.
 "very definitely" believed: Brennan testimony, 9/22/75, CCH-II, p. 124.
 "You may not know it": Huston testimony, p. 26.
 "we were not trained to do that": Papich interview.
262 "violence invests character": Fanon, p. 73.
 "Communist propaganda mill," etc.: Tower at Brennan testimony, 9/22/75,
 CCH-II, p. 109.
263 "so clearly right," etc.: Califano testimony, 1/27/76, p. 70, FR-II, p. 98.
 Hoover rejection of warrantless coverage: Brennan testimony, 9/25/75, p.
 99; Tordella (staff summary), 6/16/75; Sullivan to DeLoach, 3/7/70; staff summary of [FBI intelligence officer], 8/20/75; all at FR-III, p. 931.
 Johnson's push for coverage: Brennan testimony, 9/22/75, CCH-II, pp. 104,
 107, 135, FR-III, p. 928.
 "credit card revolutionaries": Brennan testimony, 9/25/75, CCH-II, p. 134.
264 McCone's 1963 directive: CIA blind memo, 2/11/63, NSAV.
 Hoover reluctant to approve leak probes: RCR, p. 56.
 1959, 1963 taps: "CIA Report on Inquiry into CIA-Related Electronic Surveillance Activities," n.d. [c. 1976], NSAV.
 "constant bureaucratic bickering": Marchetti and Marks, p. 228.
265 "SOG": Ober testimony, 10/28/75, FR-III, p. 690.
 "a new desk has been created": n.d. [8/67], quoted at Belin, p. 144.
 "definite domestic counterintelligence aspects": Karamessines to Angleton,
 8/15/67, FR-II, p. 100.
266 Suslov: FBI report, "The Soviet Peace Offensive," 12/25/81, p. 206, FBI/
 CISPES.
 Rubin: A. C. Faberge, statement on family history, in Official Report to the
 Special Committee on Un-American Activities, 1936 General Election, New
 York City, at Powell, p. 15.
267 "a very staunch stand": Angleton deposition, CCH-V, p. 81. Miler recalled:
 "There was a big controversy, for example, with respect to the Venceremos
 Brigade, in Cuba. Most people at the time said, 'They're just going down to
 cut cane.' Those of us that were concerned about it were saying, 'It's got to be
 more than that.' The naysayers said, 'Prove it.' It was some three years before
 you began to get disillusioned Venceremos Brigade people, who said, 'Yeah,
 we went down there, and we were trained. They trained us. That's why we
 went. The real brains people were isolated off and given guerrilla, sabotage,
 intelligence training. Of course, we took a lot of useful idiots along, to cut the
 cane!' " (Miler interview.)

"coordinated," etc.: Helms to LBJ, 11/15/67, p. 1, FR-III, p. 696.

"to place stops": 1960 FBI Manual, sect. 87, p. 33, FR-I, p. 519.

268   Ober would cross-index: James Eatinger [Ober deputy alias] testimony, 10/14/75, pp. 10, 12–13, FR-III, p. 694.

CIA keeping files on American activists: Ober testimony, 10/28/75, FR-III, p. 985; Karamessines testimony, FR-III, p. 716.

special reporting cryptonym: FR-III, p. 691.

"Hoover would have had": Huston testimony.

"I never knew": Aldhizer interview.

269   "pretty fairly": Miler interview.

"some information on either end": Ober testimony, 10/28/75, FR-III, p. 709.

Mexico City: Smith, 1983, pp. 403–4.

Ober believed: Papich to D. J. Brennan, 1/16/69, FR-III, p. 574.

270   Hoover-Nixon: William P. Rogers interviewed at Demaris, p. 21; Helms interview, 2/5/92.

"aided and abetted": Haldeman, p. 105.

"better information than the CIA," etc.: Sullivan, p. 241.

271   "putting our men in more embassies": Papich interview.

"furious": Sullivan, p. 241.

G-men for Phoenix: William Colby interview, 2/6/92.

"I don't think the boss ever knew": McWilliams interview.

"We were making a lot of people angry": Sullivan, pp. 200–201.

272   "keeping an eye": Helms testimony, 10/22/75, CCH-IV, p. 87.

"too timid": Helms interview.

"on a variety of problems": Helms testimony, 10/22/75, CCH-IV, p. 87.

"intensely interested": ibid.

Merrimac: Osborn testimony, 2/17/75, FR-III, p. 725.

"sources and methods": FR-III, pp. 729–30.

"foreign collection": memorandum from Director, DCS, to Field Offices, 3/23/91, FR-III, p. 703.

"How can we do a better job?": Helms deposition, 4/24/75, p. 223, FR, II, p. 101.

"A very limited amount": Cushman to Huston, 6/30/69, FR-III, p. 700.

MK/SOURDOUGH: CIA memo, Acting Chief, FE/DTA to Chief, Far East Division, 9/13/71, FR-III, p. 615; CIA MK/SOURDOUGH officer blind notes, 4/4/70, FR-III, p. 613.

273   "fully tasked," etc.: memo, 12/19/69, FR-III, pp. 701–2.

New York Review of Books: Robert Silvers at Robins, p. 367.

"reddening": FBI agent Cril Payne, quoted at Lee and Shalin, p. 223.

Chaos agents' debriefings: Chaos Agent Files, FR-III, p. 703; Ober testimony, 10/30/75, FR-III, p. 712. Probably the development of penetration agents was under consideration as early as 6/69, when DDCI Cushman noted that "new sources are being sought . . . with the assistance of . . . the Federal Bureau of Investigation" (Cushman to Huston, 6/30/69, FR-III, p. 700).

G-men impressed: Ober testimony, 10/30/75, FR-III, p. 713.

"did not wish to deal with the FBI": memo, 10/21/70, FR-III, p. 714.

274   "Wargasm": Collier and Horowitz, pp. 95ff.

FBI pursuit of Weather Underground: Felt, pp. 315ff.

14. THE SULLIVAN PLOT

275   "This agent does not always present": permanent brief, FBI/WCS.

"more on the side of CIA": Strictly Confidential memo, For the Director's Personal Files, 6/18/71, FBI/WCS.

276   "Everyone was uninhibited," etc.: Sullivan, pp. 191–93.

"After I left": Papich interview.

"more from being persuaded by Angleton": McWilliams interview.

"Some smart newspaperman": Sullivan, p. 190.

"Bill, I'm with you," etc.: ibid., p. 208.

"Relationships with Central Intelligence": Sullivan to Deloach, 3/6/70, CCH-II, p. 346.

"CIA criticism": ibid.

277   "Dear Mr. Hoover": Helms to Hoover, 3/20/70, CCH-II, p. 349.

"certain technical equipment": Hoover to Helms, 3/31/70, CCH-II, p. 354.

278   Huston's backstory: see FR-III, p. 928.

"President Nixon has designated me," etc.: Sullivan, p. 207.

279   "because of either inadequate": Huston to DDCI, 6/20/69, FR-III, p. 699.

"I do not think": Huston testimony, p. 17.

"a [U.S.] police state": Ibid., p. 32. Those who knew both men swear this is vintage Sullivan.

"preemptively resisted": Huston testimony.

"neither the manpower nor the minds": Huston testimony, CCH-II.

"quality of data on domestic radicals": Huston deposition, 5/23/75, FR-III, p. 930.

"hundreds of occasions," etc.: Sullivan interviewed at T, 1/6/75, p. 45.

280   "meetings between": Hoover to Helms, 3/31/70, CCH-II, p. 354.

"hot foot": Haldeman, p. 108.

"fertile soil," etc.: ibid.

"liaison with FBI and CIA": ibid.

"became even more important": Huston testimony, p. 26.

"Kent state . . . marked a turning point": Haldeman, p. 107.

281   "The President chewed our butts": Bennett staff summary, 6/5/75, FR-III, p. 937.

"A new and grave crisis": talking paper prepared for President Nixon, 6/5/70.

"Are you people," etc.: Huston deposition, 5/23/75, FR-III, p. 937.

"a historical study": Sullivan, p. 210.

282   "hippie intellectual": Sullivan interview, FR-III, p. 939.

"enormous respect," etc.: Angleton testimony, p. 58.

283   "I thought, since the president": Helms interview.

"the most important recommendation": Huston deposition, 5/23/75, FR-III, p. 941.

"This report has already been approved": Angleton testimony, p. 53.

"problems involved for the Bureau": Sullivan memo, 6/19/70, FR-III, pp. 965–66.

284   "That hippie": Sullivan deposition, 11/1/75, pp. 124–25, FR-III, p. 943.

"enough damned coordination": Sullivan, p. 212.

why not add footnotes: Sullivan deposition, 11/1/75, pp. 124–25, FR-III, p. 943.

"We hope this is not characteristic": Sullivan, p. 213.

"We couldn't believe": ibid., p. 214.

285 Gayler and Bennett objected to footnotes: FR-III, p. 945.

"special burdens of the FBI": ibid.

Hoover ended the meeting: Sullivan, pp. 213–14.

"bullheaded as hell": Huston to Haldeman, 7/70, CCH-II, exhibit 2.

286 "what a hot potato": Stilwell interview, 5/21/75, FR-III, p. 956.

"stroking session": Huston to Haldeman, 7/70, FR-III, p. 952.

"went through the ceiling": Sullivan interview, 6/10/75, FR-III, p. 956.

Hoover restated his objections: Hoover to Mitchell, 7/25/70, FR-III, p. 957.

"in toto": Mitchell testimony, 10/24/75, FRI-III, p. 957.

"revoke," "reconsider": Huston deposition, 5/23/75, FR-III, p. 960.

"In terms of lack of any coordination": Huston testimony, p. 19.

287 "improved," etc.: Huston to Haldeman, 9/10/70, FR-III, p. 961.

"The boss was just surrounded": McWilliams interview.

"really wanted to get rid": Helms interview.

"As far as [President Nixon] was concerned": Haldeman, p. 107.

"Those guys spend all their time": ibid.

"what would be the best way," etc.: DeLoach interviewed 9/16/87 at Robins, pp. 328–29.

288 "I wanted to see you": Felt, p. 204.

"go around the back door": Senator Schweiker at Angleton testimony, p. 71.

"He seemed to exude": B. Willard interview, 5/16/75, FR-III, p. 944.

"You've got to be kidding," etc.: Dean interview, 8/7/75, FR-III, p. 974.

"possibility of improved": Mardian interview, 1/13/76, FR-III, p. 976.

289 "to increase formal liaison": ibid.

IEC staff makeup: Angleton memo, n.d., CCH-IV, p. 289.

CI men disillusioned: Mardian memo, 12/4/70: FR-III, p. 975.

"intelligence calendars": staff summary of Col. Werner E. Michael interview, 5/12/75, FR-III, p. 976.

IEC liaising almost daily: Angleton testimony, pp. 67–68.

"not provide personnel": Hoover to Mardian, 1/3/71, FR-III, p. 977.

"to warrant continuing": ibid.

"doing nothing," etc.: Papich interview.

290 When asked by Rogers: Hoover to Tolson et al., 11/20/70, FBI Tolson file.

"Sullivan apparently does not realize": Beaver to Hoover, 6/8/71, FBI/WCS.

"The arguments advanced": Felt, pp. 131–32.

"more on the side of CIA": memo, 6/18/71, FBI/WCS.

"a Bill Sullivan thing": Nolan interview.

"more than possible that Hoover": Felt, p. 130.

"falsely accused me": Sullivan to Hoover, 10/6/71, at Sullivan, p. 277.

"would be the new Director": Felt, p. 130.

291 "I never wrote": Sullivan to Hoover, 10/6/71, p. 277.

"Breaking liaison with CIA was not rational": ibid., p. 270.

liaison break revealed: Smith, 10/9/71, passim. The article described Sullivan's "retirement," characterizing him in quite positive terms as an "expert on domestic intelligence," a "scholarly researcher on Communist philosophy," and "a moderating force in the FBI," but cited only "authoritative sources" as the basis for its account.

292   Fedora and Pentagon Papers: Rocca interview; memo by David Young, 7/21/71, at House Committee on the Judiciary, *Information Submitted on Behalf of President Nixon*, pp. 104–7.

"from a source who has proved reliable": Rocca interview.
"Henry had a problem": Haldeman, p. 112.
"the USIB unanimously requested," etc.: Sullivan, p. 193.

293   "failure to implement the Huston Plan": Haldeman, p. 112.
"a bit of a romantic": Helms testimony, 8/2/73, ECH, p. 3250.
"American James Bond": Hunt, 1974, pp. 133–34.
"The most incredible thing": Haldeman, p. 123.
"to bring Hoover into line": Sullivan, p. 217.
Special Investigations Unit: Hoover to Sullivan, 7/21/71.

294   Plumbers' schemes: Liddy, p. 262.
"The most incredible": White House transcripts.
from the kid with a bomb, etc.: Huston testimony, p. 45.

15. SMOKING GUN

295   The basic narrative of this chapter is reconstructed primarily from the Watergate testimony of Vernon Walters, Patrick Gray, and Richard Helms. For White House machinations after the burglary, I have relied especially on Haldeman, pp. 25–32.

Hoover's funeral procession: Felt, p. 181.
"That's our next job," etc.: Hunt, 1974, pp. 212–13.

296   "Those bastards in Langley": Haldeman, p. 26.
"to turn that document": ibid.
"I am now to *forget*": ibid.

297   Hunt decided to "improve" cables: Haldeman, pp. 161–62.
On search for data on anti-Castro plots as motive for Watergate burglary, see Rappleye and Becker, p. 307.

298   I am going to name you": Gray testimony, p. 3488.
"Frankly, most of us were hoping": Felt, p. 186.
"He was a dynamic guy": Aldhizer interview.

299   "At approximately 2:30," etc.: Felt, p. 246.

300   "big news": Helms testimony, 8/2/73, ECH, p. 3237.
"You'd better watch out": Helms at Meyer, pp. 148–49.
"a unanimous expression": ibid., p. 149.
"Stay cool": Colby interview, 2/6/92.
"coordinate the Agency's efforts": Colby, pp. 320–23.

For clues to Deep Throat's identity, see Woodward and Bernstein, esp. pp. 71–73, 76–77, 268–71. That he may have been a CIA officer has been argued, persuasively I think, by Jim Hougan, who considers and eliminates several candidates for Deep Throat honors, and ends by concluding that "Deep Throat is probably a spook—someone in the intelligence community." Hougan specifically considers only one CIA officer—John Arthur Paisley—but Paisley is dead, and Woodward says that Throat is (at the time of writing) still alive, and I believe him (the whole enterprise of speculating on Deep Throat's identity hinges upon an acceptance of Woodward's veracity; otherwise there is no reason for believing Throat to have existed at all).

Although I spoke with both Colby and Meyer in the course of writing this book, I have chosen not to ask either man if he was in fact Deep Throat. My reasons are twofold. (1) Woodward says that Throat has "made representations to people" that he is not Deep Throat—i.e., he is not going to tell the truth to some writer calling him up and asking him point-blank. The same principle applies, it seems to me, to asking Woodward who Throat is. Given that he is sworn to protect Throat's identity until Throat's death, he cannot be trusted to tell the truth when asked straight out about Throat's identity. (2) If I were Deep Throat, would I want some writer calling me up and asking me whether I were? Wouldn't I rather be left alone? And given that I have performed a very valuable service to the country, haven't I the right to be?

301   For Woodward's "concern" about being "used" by the intelligence community, see *PR Newswire*, 12/29/88.

Parking-garage rumors: interview with former CIA secretary, Vienna, Virginia, 8/91. The secretary indicated that she saw Colby meet another individual in the underground parking structure of a suburban Virginia shopping mall, at some time after Colby's retirement in 1975.

"the public must be informed": Colby, p. 460.

Meyer's dislike of Nixon, and other personal data, are from an interview with one of his former administrative assistants, 1/91.

302   "cool it": CIA cable, 3/27/72, quoted at Hougan, p. 110.

"The immediate problem": Colby, p. 321.

"neither Helms nor I": ibid., p. 322.

303   "In short": CIA memo, Helms to Walters, 6/28/72.

"less than cooperative": Felt, p. 255.

Miami Airport: Appendix to Senate Select Committee on Presidential Campaign Activities, *Final Report*, p. 149. An admirable summary is given also at Hougan, pp. 270–71.

Ritchie: Hougan, p. 264.

"Mr. Pennington": testimony by Pennington and other CIA officers, House Armed Services Committee, Special Committee on Intelligence, Nedzi Report, pp. 940–1039.

"to keep publicity away from CIA": Felt, p. 255.

304   "retainer of $100 per month": Osborne to Gray, 6/20/72, CIA-FOIA.

"keeping a string," etc.: Helms testimony, 8/2/73, ECH.

305   "Tell Ehrlichman this whole group": Haldeman, p. 25.

"Our brothers at Langley?": Haldeman, p. 25.

"the FBI is not under control," etc.: transcript of "smoking gun" tape, submitted as evidence in *U.S. v. John Mitchell, et al.*, CR-74-110, Nixon Presidential Materials.

306   "Guess what," etc.: Haldeman, p. 34.

Walters' character and back story: Phillips, pp. 315–16.

Helms and Walters and White House: Haldeman, pp. 34–38.

"creating a lot of noise," etc.: Walters testimony, p. 3404.

307   "We're *not* connected": Haldeman, pp. 34ff.

"Nevertheless": Walters testimony, p. 3405.

"The President asked me": Haldeman, pp. 34ff.

"dead cat": Helms testimony, 8/2/73, ECH, p. 3275.

"I'm just following my instructions": Haldeman, pp. 34ff.

"All right": ibid.

"What is the purpose": Helms testimony, 8/2/73, ECH.

"General Walters should get down": ibid, p. 3239.

308 "in all of those Nixon references": Haldeman, pp. 39–40.

"reminding Helms, not so gently": ibid.

309 "I think you should put this": Helms testimony, 2/7/73, Senate Foreign Relations Committee, *Hearing on Nomination of Richard Helms*, p. 89.

"south of the border," etc.: Walters memo, ECH, p. 3815.

"scrupulously," etc.: ibid.

310 "work around this problem," etc.: Gray testimony, p. 3453.

"Under no circumstances": ibid., p. 3455.

"We have done everything": ibid., p. 3500.

"these kids": ibid., p. 3458.

311 "electorally mortal": Walters testimony, p. 3414.

"You should call the President" Gray testimony, p. 3458.

"No matter·how high?": CIA memo for the record, Vernon A. Walters, 7/13/72, ECH, p. 3821.

312 "By refusing to participate": Meyer, pp. 154–55.

Schlesinger accession: Ranelagh, pp. 539ff.

"a very sensible study": Cline, p. 219.

"absolutely no problem at all": Helms testimony, 2/7/73, Senate Foreign Relations Committee, *Hearing on Nomination of Richard Helms*, p. 35.

"simply new in history": ibid.

313 "a full-court press": Gray testimony, 2/28/73, Woodward and Bernstein, p. 272.

"In the service of my country": Gray testimony, p. 3488.

"When Gray got in trouble": Aldhizer interview.

314 "arrived at Langley running": Colby, p. 329.

315 "like a string of exploding firecrackers": Meyer, p. 148.

16. BLOWBACK

315 In chronicling FBI-CIA conflicts after 1974, it is difficult to assemble a rich or reliable history. Only in two post-Watergate cases, both of them national scandals, have relevant documents been declassified, and only in these cases may facts be historically grounded. Otherwise, the years 1974–1994 must be chronicled and reconstructed from the oral testimony of participants—some of it anonymous, most of it fragmentary and subjective—and from press reports. The closer one gets to the present, naturally enough, the less is known. Still, lessons can be drawn from what has emerged.

Colby appearance: cf. Foote, p. 137.

316 "It all changed": AFIO.

"a man's kind of guy": Ungar.

"Look, I don't care": Colby interview.

317 Colby ceded Chaos primacy to FBI: memo, 8/29/73 FR-III, p. 707.

"Bill really was": interview of former FBI agent, McLean, Virginia, 2/92.

"Cregar had a high profile": Aldhizer interview.

318 "Hoover put us out of business": FBI counterintelligence expert [Cregar], staff summary, 8/20/75.

"Cregar liked CIA": Aldhizer interview.

"Under Bill Cregar": Nolan interview.

seven CIA officers training at Quantico: CIA memo for DDO, "Items for Use in Briefing the DCI," n.d., CIA/YIN.

FBI CIA training course: McWilliams interview.

"CIA officers in that class": ibid.

319 "This big difference in philosophy": ibid.

"a gruff old man," Kelley-Colby relations: Colby interview.

"the highest respect, etc.": ibid.

320 "I just thought CI": Colby interview.

Angleton lost liaison: Colby interview, 2/6/92; Colby interviewed at Wise, 1992, p. 239; Angleton interview, Epstein, 1989, p. 96.

321 "You must be crazy": Burleson.

322 Jennifer Project: Burleson, especially pp. 148–57, where the FBI memo-recovery episode is discussed.

323 "Jesus, Jim," etc.: Moore interviewed at Mangold, p. 317.

324 "Oh, my God!" NYT, 12/22/74.

325 "unchecked independent initiative": NYT, Op-Ed, 12/23/74.

"Internal security tasks": RCR, pp. 149–50.

Rockefeller recommendations on FBI-CIA liaison: RCR, pp. 23, 24, 232, 240, 169, 26, 13, 39.

Kelley assured the commission: Kelley to Rockefeller, 4/18/75, FBI/TR.

"an albatross": Helms deposition, 4/24/75, FR-III, p. 730.

"There is no impropriety": RCR, p. 240.

"or otherwise engage in activities": ibid., p. 169.

"a detailed agreement": ibid., p. 39.

326 Church Committee on FBI-CIA liaison: FR-I, pp. 72–73, 177; FR-III, pp. 63, 986–87, 654, 717.

"These agencies are fiefdoms": Church at Huston testimony, p. 46.

"CIA should not infiltrate groups": RCR, p. 26.

"setting restraints": FR-III, p. 717.

"shall not engage in": Executive Order 11905, 2/18/76, NSAV.

National Foreign Intelligence Board: DCI Directive no. 1/8, 5/6/76, NSAV.

"coordination of national intelligence": ibid.

"maintenance of effective interface": ibid.

327 For the coming of McCoy and his impact on FBI-CIA relations, I have relied on McWilliams and Nolan interviews.

328 "McCoy is a horse's ass": McWilliams interview.

McCoy's support for Nosenko: Hurt, pp. 211–212, 292, 294.

McCoy's purge of files: Miler interview.

"False picture": Miler, 1979, p. 52.

FBI threatened Golitsyn about files: Petersen interviewed 2/17/89 at Mangold, p. 337; Gmirkin interviewed 6/2/88 at ibid.

McCoy and Kittyhawk: James Wooten interviewed 3/23/88, Branigan interviewed 1/27/88, at Corson et al., p. 230; Hurt, p. 215; Miler interview.

The story of Shadrin's disappearance is reconstructed primarily from interviews with Ewa Shadrin at Hurt, et al., pp. 209, 212–13, 218, and at Corson et al., pp. 230ff.

329 Surveillance botch: Neil Sullivan interviewed at ibid.

CIA-FBI reactions to Shadrin's disappearance: Hurt, pp. 17–18, 255–56, 271, 286.

"sort of the boundary line": Wilson interviewed at Hurt, p. 254.

"Clearly it did fall": Colby interview.

330 "was to have the substance": Ford, 1970, p. 315.

"very much from outside": Bagley testimony, HAH-XII, p. 623

"all these old fuds": Turner interview.

331 "I never looked down my nose": ibid.

"I would get frustrated," etc.: ibid.

332 "In the old days": Nolan interview.

"A number of former senior": "Discussion," Miler, 1983, p. 47.

"that no one is responsible": Godson, ed., 1980, p. 49.

Truong: Allen and Polmar, p. 192; Tully, 1980, pp. 55–57.

333 "no more contact with Krall": Bell.

"About once every eight weeks": Turner, 19??, p. 158.

334 "deep down in the system": Webster interview.

"filtered down": Aldhizer interview.

"I signed something": Turner interview.

"It wasn't a simple thing," etc.: Webster interview.

"the War of the Granting of Visas": ibid.

335 "start a spy war," etc.: Turner interview.

"spy war": T, 6/26/78, p. 29; Allen and Polmar, p. 210.

Kampiles: Tully, 1987, pp. 39–42.

336 "The case was embarrassing to CIA": Nolan interview.

"U.S. person": Executive Order 12036, 1/1/78, NSAV.

"Only when there are suspicions": Turner, 19??, p. 68.

Jones: interviews by House investigators, 12/78, HIR, pp. 3–21.

"the dual reincarnation": ibid.

337 warrants for all surveillance: "Discussion," Miler, 1979. p. 62.

"In order to convince": ibid., pp. 62–63.

"McCarthyist witch-hunt": Lane to Ryan, 11/6/78, HIR, p. 3.

"No violation of the Federal kidnapping statute": HIR, p. 21.

"We didn't commit suicide": Jones audiotape, broadcast on A&E documentary, *American Justice*, 7/92.

338 "I do remember": Turner interview.

"The Bureau did a lot of investigation": Webster interview.

"In the case of the People's Temple": "Discussion," Miler, 1979, p. 63.

339 "That was a big drawback": Aldhizer interview.

"knocked out": Turner, 1991, p. 29.

Vesco: T, 11/10/80, 9/19/83.

340 Noriega: Dinges, pp. 106ff.

341 "no control (and often no knowledge)": WP, 3/20/88.

"to assure that no Soviet agent profits": Rositzke, p. 263.

"an act of Congress": Colby, pp. 456–57.

"on a functional not geographic basis," etc.: Miler, 1979, pp. 57–58.

"a rotting root system": "Discussion," at Miler, 1979, p. 49.

Courtship: Kessler, 1992, pp. 17ff.

342 Courtship methods: Yuri Shvets interviewed at Dobbs and Smith.

"Ever since the Donovan days": AFIO.

17. THE LAST BUCCANEERS

345 "William Casey": Clair George testimony, 8/6/87, ICH, p. 268.
"to walk off with a slice": Casey, p. 10.
"an inordinate amount of time": ibid., p. 5.
Casey on Popov and Pearl Harbor: ibid., p. 10; Mure, pp. 174, 182.
Dewavrin: Casey, p. 129.

346 Debategate: Persico, pp. 325–32.
New Zealand: Webster interview.
"Ed won't talk to me": Aldhizer interview.

347 Inman centerfold: ibid.
"That was not the way": ibid.
Meese made the case: Inman interviewed at Woodward, pp. 92–93.
"Intelligence Groups Seek Power": NYT, 3/10/81.
"conduct counterintelligence," etc.: Executive Order 12333, 12/4/81, NSAV.

348 "resolve interagency differences": ibid.
to request the FBI: NSDD-22, 1/29/82, NSAV.
"to use [U.S.] athletic": DCI Directive, 9/9/82, NSAV.
Nicaraguan tourists: UPI, 12/10/87.
polygraphs: WP, 3/4/87.
reduce number of Soviet diplomats: T, 7/10/89.
"classified documents": WP, 3/3/89. See also Kessler, 1988, pp. 64–62.
Osborne and Thomas: Kessler, 1988, p. 104.
Haro: CT, 12/27/88; WP, 1/7/89, 7/16/90.
superagency idea: John Bross interviewed at Woodward, p. 60.

349 "all agencies and departments": Executive Order 12333.
Orwellian fears: CSM, 8/29/88.
"task force": Webster interview, LAT, 10/26/87.
background investigations: TNJ, 9/9/89.
Martynov and Motorin: Yuri Shvets interviewed at Dobbs and Smith; cf. Kessler, 1992, pp. 22–24.

350 Ames: My basic source has been the affidavit in support of his arrest, filed 2/22/94 by Leslie Wiser, Jr. Available from the Department of Justice, Office of Media Relations, Washington, D.C.
Ames' father: WT, 2/23/94.

351 embassy probes: USNWR, 5/18/87.

352 Koecher: see esp. Kessler, 1988, pp. 42–3, 135–43.

353 Tolkachev arrest: KGB videotape, at "CIA: The Secret Files," A & E's *Time Machine*, 11/92.

354 "It was like the beginning": Woodward, p. 425.
Yurchenko: CIA report, "Vitaly Sergeyevich Yurchenko," n.d., declassified 11/2/85, CIA-FOIA; Kessler, 1991, pp. 52–9. In general, my treatment of the Yurchenko-Howard affair owes much to Wise, 1988, and Kessler, 1991, but I have also consulted Epstein, 1989. Wise and Kessler believe that Yurchenko was genuine, Epstein that he was bogus; some of the facts are still disputed. I have also drawn on interviews with Nolan, Parker, and Aldhizer.

355 "Robert": Thompson interviewed at Epstein, 1989, pp. 202–3.
"As a kid": Howard interviewed at *ABC News* 20/20, 10/25/90.
"We'd like you to resign": ibid.

CIA's Howard cover-up: Aldhizer interview; Wise, 1988, pp. 20, 90–3, 141–3, 163–72, 185–8.

356 "In any case": Executive Order 12333.
"CIA has a problem": Parker interviewed at Wise, 1988, p. 166.
"from the moment": Parker interviewed at ibid., p. 169.
"Maybe it took that long": ibid., p. 170.

357 "That was the low point": Aldhizer interview.
Bosch: Wise, 1988, pp. 196, 247–8.
Howard's escape: Howard interviewed by Wise, 1988, pp. 170–92.
Yurchenko's handling/redefection: Thompson and Rochford interviewed at Kessler, 1991, pp. 122–30, 144–5, 149–50; Epstein, 1989, pp. 208–9, working from Thompson interview.

359 "I was forcibly abducted": NYT, 11/3/85.

360 FBI agents told journalists: Kessler, 1991, p. 158.
"That is when he began": NYT, 11/13/85.
"I think if I were asked": quoted at Kessler, 1988, p. 17.
"never been anything": Yurchenko interviewed at ibid., p. 133.

361 "a massive propaganda assault": Murphy memo, 2/17/64, CIA/YIN. Emphasis added.

362 four more agents burned: CT, 2/23/94.
third FBI source: NYT, 2/24/94.

363 Chin: SSCI report, "Meeting the Espionage Challenge," p. 15; WT, 6/4/92.
Pollard: USNWR, 6/1/87.
"Mr X": WP, 2/19/88
Lonetree: Kessler, 1988, p. 207.
Stoll: WT, 10/24/89; CSM, 10/13/89; NYT, 10/19/89.
"constant risk of fragmentation," etc.: SSCI report, "Meeting the Espionage Challenge," pp. 39, 51.
"a memorandum of understanding": Webster interview.
"The department and geographic CI boundaries": Kalaris and McCoy, "Counterintelligence," in Godson, 1989, pp. 131–32.

364 separate molehunts languishing: WP, 3/6/94.
blocked independent FBI scrutiny: ibid.
eighty Soviet officials: USNWR, 6/1/87.
Senate's ninety-five recommendations: TNR, 10/3/88.
"drumbeaters": NYT, 4/18/87.
"the bureaucratics involved": DeGraffenreid testimony, SSCI/JP, p. 180.
"a healthy paranoia": Parker telephone interview, 2/7/92.

365 "ripe for problems": Aldhizer interview. All quotes from Aldhizer in this chapter are from that interview. My accounts of the Beirut-embassy affair, and CT generally on Casey's watch, owe much to Aldhizer's memory. He was careful to steer clear of operational details, however.
"roll back": HC, 1/24/93.
Buckley's background: NYT, 12/28/91.

366 "Man alive": Aldhizer interview.
"You had our agents out": ibid.
"extremely sensitive": ibid.

367 Clarridge: LAT, 7/18/87.

"on a case-by-case basis": Revell testimony, SSCI, *Inquiry into FBI Investigation of CISPES*, 9/14/88, p. 42.

Perot-Buckley scheme: T, 6/8/87; WP, 11/25/87.

Mugniyeh: UPI, 5/25/88.

368 "You can't have them": Aldhizer interview.

a new counterterror strategy: Emerson and Rothschild.

possibility of failure and embarrassment: WP, 2/26/88.

Reagan's finding allowed CIA to seize terrorists: Emerson and Rothschild.

Congress authorized the Bureau: FBI FNS, 11/27/89.

369 "That is something": House Committee on the Judiciary, *Terrorism*, p. 121.

"MJ/HOLIDAY": Perry, p. 41.

"We were told," etc.: FNS, 7/15/91.

"There is never an excuse": FNS, 3/15/93.

370 "unable to get the CIA": USNWR, 10/31/88.

"intelligence-fusion center": ibid.

Buckley's death: UPI, 5/25/88.

"The thing that would go off-track": Aldhizer interview.

"circumstances [that] helped create": Webster interview, USAT, 1/12/89.

371 North and Casey: North testimony, ICH, p. 245. See also North, p. 179.

Cuban "advisers": Christian, p. 159.

"the potential for dissident action": Casey, p. xiv.

"The Soviets are turning Nicaragua": CIA memo by Robert Gates, cited at his confirmation hearings, 11/91.

372 "body and soul": North testimony, ICH, pp. 74, 265.

logistics of anticommunist network: CIA cable, D. Clarridge, 4/5/84, ICH-A; ICR, pp. 38–39.

Owen's work with Caribs: ICR, p. 41; Owen testimony, ICH, pp. 327, 236–42.

airdrop logistics: Castillo testimony, ICH, pp. 40ff.

373 Doubts about Pastora: CIA memo, "The Disruptive Actions of Eden Pastora," n.d. [c. 8/85 or later], FOIA; Curtin S. Winsor, "Eden Pastora: A Critical Reappraisal," unpublished monograph in possession of author; interviews with Winsor, Robert W. Owen, John Hull, Tom Green, Bruce Jones, Eden Pastora, Arturo Cruz, Jr., Carol Prado; Elliot Abrams testimony, ICH.

"disinformation experts": Owen to North, 4/7/86, ICH, exhibit RWO-15.

"The biggest concern": Owen to North, 8/25/85, ICH-A.

"buffer," "the other side of the line": Fiers testimony, SSCI, 9/19/91; NYT, 9/20/91.

374 "wealthy American rancher": Currier deposition, 5/5/87, pp. 6–7, ICH-B.

"who says he is CIA": FBI memo, 3/25/86; FBI teletype, n.d. [c. 7/12/86]; both at NSAV.

"CIA contract man": FBI memo, 7/18/86, NSAV.

Terrell and Honey's article: Feldman deposition, 4/30/87, pp. 37–38, ICH-B.

"attract the attention": Terrell, p. 314.

375 "employees had direct access": ibid., p. 351.

"given a list of 40 names": ibid., p. 338.

information checked out: Currier deposition, 5/5/87, pp. 12–18; Kiszynski deposition, 5/5/87, pp. 11–12; both at ICH-B.

"Get Fernandez in here," etc.: Feldman deposition, 4/30/87, pp. 56ff., ICH-
B. All quotes on the subject are from this source until otherwise indicated.

376   "We all thought we were on to something": NYT, 2/18/88.

377   "no connection": Revell deposition, 7/15/87, ICH-B.

Fernandez briefed North: North notebook, ICH-A.

"active measures": FBI teletype, 5/16/86, NSAV.

"unable to resolve": FBI teletype, 6/11/86, NSAV.

joint investigation into Terrell: Revell deposition, 6/11/87, pp. 25–28,
ICH-B.

378   Terrell traveled to Miami: FBI report, 7/28/86, NSAV.

"concocted" the story: Terrell, p. 316.

"another file existed," etc.: UPI, 9/12/87.

"fishy": Currier deposition, ICH-B.

379   resuming of airdrop and poor opsec: Dutton testimony, ICH, pp. 215, 218,
234.

"really something there": Feldman deposition.

FBI investigated Southern Air: Revell deposition, 6/11/87, pp. 60–61.

"kicking dollars": Fiers testimony.

"Presidentially authorized": Revell deposition, 6/11/87, ICH-B.

"put in the kicker": Fiers testimony.

380   "most likely trip over": NSC computer-system note, 10/17/86, ICH-A.

"right information": Revell deposition, 6/11/87, ICH-B.

"ethical questions": NYT, 5/10/87.

North and Hall hid CIA documents from FBI: LAT, 6/9/87, 8/5/87.

FBI found CIA disk: WP, 9/6/87.

North asked CIA to inflate TOW prices: UPI, 12/9/88.

"CIA will provide the advice": UPI, 4/20/89.

381   FBI found George's fingerprints: CT, 8/7/92.

18. HERE COMES THE JUDGE

382   Tower Commission pressure: CT, 3/4/87.

Tower declined: NWK, 3/16/87.

Baker declined: CT, 3/4/87.

pending nomination leaked: ibid.

383   "totally honest," etc.: USAT, 8/1/89.

only two vices: WP, 3/9/89.

"He doesn't cut your head off": NWK, 3/16/87.

Webster's sting: WP, 3/4/87.

"No one, not his harshest critics": TNJ, 12/16/89.

"unique position": Webster interview.

"choosing the editor": Kessler, 1992, p. 178.

"CIA would rather be run": LAT, 11/27/88.

384   "The Agency would never stand": Aldhizer interview.

analysts worried: Butterfield.

operations officers feared: NWK, 10/12/87.

Turner friendship raised specter: USNWR, 5/25/87.

thirty-five FBI agents investigating CIA: NYT, 10/25/87.

pledging not to hurry: LAT, 7/18/87; Gates interviewed at LAT, 10/26/87.

stonewalling Congress: WT, 10/30/89.

"Lack of mission": Representative Charles E. Schumer (D–New York) at Webster Confirmation Hearings, 2/25/87, p. 97.

385 Webster's new routine: see TNJ, 12/16/89; Kessler, 1992, pp. xxi–ii, 204–7.
CIA security detail: Baker interviewed at Kessler, 12/12/90, p. 190.
bodyguards courtside: LAT, 11/26/89.

386 "wooden security guards"; "just gotten off the boat": Baker interviewed at Perry, p. 93.
the four "C's": Rosenthal.
Langley tourist plans: Baker interviewed at Kessler, 12/12/90, p. 235.
Younis: Emerson and Rothschild; R, 9/18/87.

387 symbolic statement: WP, 8/6/89; NYT, 3/5/89.
courts questioned Younis' seizure: WP, 2/24/88.

388 "hello tour": WP, 11/16/88.
leaning on Gates: USAT, 8/1/89.
too many perks: NYT, 9/8/87.
being too detached: USNWR, 8/24/87.
slave to Congress: LAT, 12/7/88.
"aides" problem: WP, 10/22/89.
Redrawing operational rules: BG, 12/8/88.
Hotis-McGregor: NWK, 10/12/87.

389 undercover agents comparison: WP, 6/5/88.
"they actually sit down": NWK, 10/12/87.
"The Judge simply asks": LAT, 12/7/88.
"not a cowboy": BG, 12/8/88.
Iran-contra purges: LAT, 10/26/87.
Stolz: TNJ, 12/12/87.
"the new watchword": WP, 6/5/88.
misprinted stamps: CSM, 9/10/87.

390 McGregor background/perspective: interviewed 7/15/91 at Kessler, pp. 194ff.

391 day-care center: CT, 11/14/89; NWK, 11/27/89.

392 "double switch": Aldhizer interview.
Peter: Aldhizer interview.
"dial twirlers," "They check to see": CT, 4/6/87.
"basis to ask": USNWR, 6/1/87.
Varelli: Paul K. Minor, FBI polygrapher, interviewed at Kessler, 1993, p. 151.

393 "czar": CT, 4/6/87.
opposed to radical changes: USNWR, 2/15/88.
"cohesive": UPI, 11/13/87.
CIC: Rosenthal; Gertz, 4/16/90.
"in each other's offices": FNS, 3/15/93.
"trying to do analysis": SSCI, *Nomination of Kerr*, 2/28/89, p. 66.
Nancy Reagan's astrologer: Anderson, N, 5/20/88.
AWOL analysts seeking Antichrist: GNS, 7/19/90.

394 "CIA does not want," "turf consciousness": WP, 11/1/88.
Conrad: Gerth, 8/24/88.
"There were hints": NWK, 9/5/88.
paid $100,000 by CIA: LAT, 3/11/89.

395   a "memorandum of understanding": Pound and Duffy.

Consortium's report: LAT, 11/17/88.

Machines Bull: Pierre Marion interviewed at Schweizer (3/14/92), pp. 109–11; Wines, 11/18/90, p. 20; WSJ, 5/18/90, p. A-8.

"buried the hatchet": TI, 5/11/93.

Another of CIC's first priorities had been to resolve interagency molehunt problems that went back to Angleton's era. Former CIA employee Peter Karlow, the original suspect in the search for "Sasha," had been fired in 1963 when Hoover refused to clear him. Now he wanted CIA to compensate him for his ruined career. Webster brought in a group of aides from the FBI to reconsider the case. The Bureau declared that it had been wrong about Karlow. The price of that FBI error was $500,000, disbursed to Karlow by Congress under a so-called "Mole-Relief Act." (Wise, 1992, p. 290).

There was also one last attempt to answer a riddle that linked the mysterious defector Vitaliy Yurchenko with an earlier intelligence émigré, Igor "Sasha" Orlov. Angleton had believed that Orlov, the Alexandria picture-framer who had worked with Dave Murphy in Berlin, was a Soviet mole, but that the case had been bungled by the FBI's "clumsy bureaucratic actions." New attention had been drawn to the case in 1985, when Yurchenko told the FBI and CIA that Orlov was not only a false defector, as Angleton had claimed, but that Orlov had recruited his own two sons as Soviet agents. Yurchenko had then skipped back to Moscow, casting doubt as to whether his Orlov accusations were true, and the Bureau had declined to interrogate until CIA asked them to. When the FBI finally returned to the Alexandria picture-frame gallery in 1988, Orlov was dead, but special agents polygraphed his sons. Both were cleared. Apparently Yurchenko had lied, which only deepened CIA suspicion that he himself had been bogus. The FBI, however, stuck to their original belief that Yurchenko was bona fide, and that he had not been sent to deflect suspicion from any mole. See Wise, 1992, pp. 275–81.

continuing pattern of losses: LAT, 4/11/87.

Bracy; codes not compromised: See David Wise, "Once More into the Embassy," NYT, 3/19/89, section 7, p. 12.

396   "Was it communications . . . ?": NYT, 3/8/94.

memorandum of understanding: LAT, 3/11/94.

FBI suspected CIA still holding back: WP, 3/6/94.

"other things to do": ibid.

"wrapped up and disposed of": LAT, 4/11/87.

397   CIA's Vienna apparat: WP, 8/27/89.

Bloch: WT, 10/29/90; Wise, 5/13/90.

Bloch's access to secrets: WP, 8/27/89, 7/24/89; WT, 8/4/89.

soft line on trade: WP, 8/27/89.

Bloch's "M.O.": WP, 7/30/89.

398   Gikman telephoned Bloch: WP, 8/1/89.

wondered how KGB tipped Bloch: *Economist*, 7/29/89.

whether leaks originated at Langley: T, 9/11/89.

"dozens of FBI agents": T, ibid.

"least intrusive mode": WP, 6/23/89.

into public restrooms: *Fortune*, 10/9/89.

399   "fell between the cracks": LAT, 10/25/89.

"failed": CT, 7/27/89.
"bureaucratic infighting": WT, 7/31/89.
"That's one of the problems": WT, 7/31/89.
"We did not examine the need": SSCI/JP, p. 8.
"time for a hammer": DeGraffenreid testimony, ibid., p. 183.
Campbell named liaison officer: Aldhizer interview.

400 "offbeat areas": ibid.
"Ah! Gotcha!": AFIO.
Hathaway retired: WP, 3/2/90.
Price: Kessler, 1992, p. 206.
Penrith: LAT, 10/25/89.
Geer had improved cooperation: ibid.

401 "at a time of debate": NYT, 10/25/89.
"If this provision": WT, 10/31/89.
"the most expertise": WT, 7/31/89.
Captain Will Rogers: N, 3/14/89; UPI, 3/14/89.

402 plot to assassinate President Bush: R, 9/15/89.
CIA officers on Pan Am 103: FNS, 2/2/89.
tip not passed to FBI: *Aviation Daily*, 1/9/89; States News Service, 3/14/89;
Daily Telegraph, 12/23/88; R, 12/19/89.
"The bureau believes": T, 1/9/89.
Transportation Subcommittee: *Travel Weekly*, 12/11/89.
Airport Operators Council: *Aviation Daily*, 11/20/89.
National Business Travel Association: *Travel Weekly*, 12/11/89.
"chaotic mess": WP, 5/11/89.
"The CIA believe": LAT, 5/12/89.
"like essays from grade school": *Sunday Telegraph*, 4/2/89.
"Tremendous cooperation": Webster interview.

403 Solution of Pan Am 103 case: Cannistraro interviewed at Perry, p. 155;
Webster interview; WT, 11/21/90; TI, 12/14/90; Wines, 3/31/92; AP, 4/4/92.
Jaaka: Duffy.
"interchangeable parts": WP, 3/3/91.
"paper tiger with nerf teeth": FNS, 8/7/89.
assassinate terrorist leaders: NWK, 8/21/89.
Cannistraro resigned: R, 1/1/91.

404 CTC on full alert: WP, 3/3/91.
Iraqi embassies: GE, 9/91.
disrupt lines of communication: WP, 3/3/91.
"When you're at war": Webster interview.
Strategic Petroleum Reserves: WP, 1/18/91.
Mormon churches: LAT, 1/25/91.
Wariat: FNS, 7/15/91.
suspected Palestinan terrorists: N, 1/16/91.
Hamid Al-Amri: GE, 9/91.
"very close coordination": FNS, 1/18/91.

405 Woolworth's: WP, 1/18/91.
Chile: WP, 1/19/91.
"the really heavy hitters": Webster interview.

19. THE FALL OF BABYLON

405   precise targeting: USAT, 5/9/91.
"The war might have been avoided": Lacayo.
warning was conveyed: USAT, 5/9/91.
better policy knowledge: LAT, 10/17/89.
"It is not our role": WP, 10/22/89.
Panamanian coup warning: LAT, 10/13/89.

406   "facts-and-only-the-facts": WP, 10/22/89.
"behind events" TNJ, 12/16/89.
Gorbachev surveilled: UPI, 12/10/87.
"wrong in virtually every prediction": Fukuyama, NYT, 2/9/92.
"the black mourning frame": Medvedev, pp. 3–4.

407   "Who would have thought": Gates testimony, 9/19/91, FNS.
"We're here to help": SSCI, *Nomination of Richard J. Kerr*, 2/28/89, p. 62.
"Crystal ball prediction": Broder, *The Los Angeles Times Magazine*, 4/19/92.
"Our business": ibid.
"a younger man," etc.: see Golitsyn, pp. 327–54.

408   "with several grains of salt," etc.: An ample file of articles on Golitsyn and
the public reception of his thesis is maintained by Charles S. Via of the Center
for Defense Studies, Alexandria, Virginia.
"not withstand": *Library Journal*, 4/1/84, p. 725.
"As a crystal-ball gazer": Mangold, p. 355.
"Unfortunate is the only term," etc.: *Studies in Intelligence*, n.d. [1984], p.
115. CIA-FOIA.

409   "we tend to disbelieve": James, p. 194.

410   "tantamount": Gorbachev, p. 127.
"we are going to": Blumenthal, 1990, p. 5.
"whirled in fractured atoms": T. S. Eliot, "Gerontion."
"Mild Bill": USAT, 4/25/91.
Afghan rebels: R, 10/16/89.

411   "krytons": Webster testimony, Senate Governmental Affairs Committee, *Nuclear Proliferation Hearings*, 5/18/89, FNS.
Jordanian agents compromised: Wines, 3/12/90.
Webster resigned: for a general retrospective on his term as DCI, see Webster interviewed 5/91 at Johnson, IJIC, p. 288.
"fusion centers": TNJ, 12/16/89; FNS, 7/15/91.
"interesting times": WT, 5/10/91.
Gates backstory: testimony, 9/19/91, FNS.

412   "green menaces": SPT, 10/14/91.
"hazardous waste disposal": WT, 10/24/90.
"a very rough neighborhood": Gates testimony, 9/19/91, FNS.

413   "the KGB was abolished": Afanasiev at Wines, 1/18/92.
"KGB Network Grinds to Halt": LAT, 8/30/91.
"Gorbachev strips KGB of duties": USAT, 8/29/91.
"Closing Down the KGB": NYT, 11/24/91.
seven defectors: WT, 11/5/92.
Ochenko: Nandy.
fifty Russian spies: T, 6/29/92.

Italy, Germany, Belgium: ibid.
Defector's tip: NYT, 2/24/94: LAT, 2/24/94.
Stasi files: USAT, 11/27/90.
414　"I would think": WT, 10/29/90.
"There was infighting": WP, 3/6/94.
CDs or diskettes: NYT, 8/4/91.
East German operations blown: USNWR, 4/12/93. At the time of writing, there was some dispute about just when the East German files had played their catalytic role in the molehunt. According to WP, 3/6/94, "East German intelligence files [about compromise of CIA agents] *prompted* the creation of a 1991 joint CIA-FBI investigative effort." But NYT, 3/7/94, contended that "The [key East German counterespionage] information was provided to the United States *sometime after* a joint inquiry was begun in 1991 by the C.I.A. and the Federal Bureau of Investigation." [Emphases added.] It is possible, of course, that the Stasi files are sort of a red herring, and that the story of their importance in the molehunt has been floated by U.S. officials to camouflage (and protect) the real source of suspicions against Ames.
Joint FBI-CIA molehunt launched: WP, 3/6/94.
GT/PROLOGUE: Wiser affidavit, 2/21/94. Available from the Department of Justice, Office of Media Relations, Washington, D.C.
415　Cuban networks: USNWR, 2/15/88; WT, 3/6/90.
416　Japanese espionage: Herbert Meyer interviewed at Schweizer, p. 18.
"business ventures": WT, 11/17/92.
"no friendly services": Rocca deposition, 11/25/75, at FR-I, p. 170.
"nearly twenty governments": FNS, 4/29/92.
"We know that they rifle briefcases": R, 9/17/91.
417　"They're suspicious": FNS, 4/29/92.
Boren proposal: FNS, 2/5/92.
"Senator's Plan": Gertz, 2/5/92.
"compelled to cooperate": WP, 2/6/92.
Levchenko: quoted at Gertz, 2/5/92.
Stasi files: NYT, 8/4/91.
under the desk: WP, 7/22/92.
visa for Russian UN employee: *Maclean's*, 4/10/89.
worth the tradeoff: NWK 8/21/89.
418　"not what I would call": USNWR, 6/3/91.
"hampered by its foreign-targets mind-set": Nolan interview.
"an enormous coverup": Blum interviewed at Tolchin. Questions were also being raised, in the wake of the great savings-and-loan crisis, about possible CIA relationships with other failed financial institutions. Pete Brewton, a stubborn reporter for the Houston *Post*, claimed to have found CIA-Mafia links to at least twenty-two failed thrifts, including sixteen in Texas. Experts had wondered how so many billions of dollars could just vanish from the thrift industry without a trace; Brewton believed it was because CIA fraudulently obtained some of this S&L money to fund some of its covert operations, including support for the Nicaraguan contras. Brewton additionally alleged that a Justice Department prosecutor investigating a bank failure in 1985 was warned off by FBI agents because one of his targets had CIA ties, and that, "even when there

are neon signs pointing toward the crooks, the FBI seems to get lost." Sessions denied this, saying that any FBI inability to follow up specific leads came from the fact that there were more bank-fraud cases floating around the Justice Department—some estimates went as high as twenty-one thousand—than there were FBI agents to investigate them. But any widespread trouble in the financial industry was likely to have an impact, to some extent, on Agency interests; CIA had to pay employees and fund operations through banks, yet hide the Agency's own role as bursar, so there had always been a vexing need to "shelter" CIA money through "shell" accounts at various U.S. banks. Possibly the FBI had investigated the disappearance of funds at a few Texas S&Ls and found that CIA had pulled strings to get its money out, to protect "methods and sources." This would have been beyond the FBI's charter to stop, but it pointed up the same lesson as the BCCI affair, which was that problems could develop in the world of high finance because of conflicts between cops and spies. See Sherrill; Zolgin, p. 43.

Gates' task force: Adams; Meddis.

419 Operation Babylon: this was the official Israeli code name for the operation, but it appears to have been used by U.S. officers as well, and has come to stand generically for Western efforts to thwart Saddam's nuclear quest (Ivri, pp. 31–35).

Babylon would help Iraq buy: "That was the whole philosophy of CI, to let it run out, to handle double agents, rather than to nip it off. To know your enemy. So, sure, to thwart those helping Saddam, and to find out how much they might be learning from the U.S.—we wanted to get in there." (Miler interview.)

"You can't get in among black hats": ibid.

CIA satellite intelligence: Casey interviewed at Persico, p. 254.

Bombing of Osirak: Weinraub and Gadot; Ivri, pp. 31–35.

Agency had little intelligence: Webster testimony, Senate Governmental Affairs Committee, *Nuclear Proliferation Hearings*, 5/18/89, FNS.

NCD: Aldhizer interview, 1/5/93. It is also described in a recent book authorized by CIA and written with their cooperation (Kessler, 1992, p. 18), and rather extensively discussed at Perry, pp. 194ff.

NCD files on Saddam's projects: Perry, p. 352.

"as hairy as it gets": USNWR, 6/3/91.

London BCCI and nuclear smuggling: *Moneyclips*, 1/18/92.

false customs declarations: Senator John Kerry at Senate Committee on Foreign Relations, *BCCI Hearings*, pt. I, 8/8/81, p. 537.

420 BNL's communications intercepted: CIA memo, 9/4/89, CR/BNL, p. H6340.

Iraqi entities/BNL: State Department memo, Kelly to Bartholemew, 9/22/89, CR/BNL, p. H6345. Webster alluded to CIA's knowledge of the front companies in testimony to the Senate Governmental Affairs Committee, *Nuclear Proliferation Hearings*, on 5/18/89: "We have found that nuclear technology is acquired illicitly and clandestinely through front companies, all-export documents, and multiple transshipment points. We're finding that regulations are being circumvented by ordering equipment or material in quantities that fall just below the export control guidelines, but which, in the aggregate, would be subject to controls. . . . Recently, we've begun to find that once a nation establishes a procurement network in one field—missiles, for example—that network is used as a conduit for procurement in other fields, such as nuclear . . . weapons."

Hussein Kamil: CIA memo, 9/4/89, CR/BNL, p. H6341; CIA dissemination to Gonzalez, 11/12/91, CR/BNL, p. H2548; cf. Barr to Gonzalez, 5/15/92, CR/BNL, p. H3372.

"shopping lists": CIA State Department briefing, 11/20/89, CR/BNL, pp. H6339–40.

Iraq purchased Matrix: CR/BNL, 7/21/92, p. H6340.

Matrix officials' purchases: Matrix-Churchill documents (Gordon Cooper to Al Arabi Trading Company, etc., 5/15/88) and congressional interviews of Matrix-Churchill employees, Cleveland, Ohio, cited by Gonzalez, 8/10/92, p. H7874.

MI6 learned: CIA dissemination to Rep. Henry Gonzalez, n.d. [1/92]; *Congressional Record*, 4/25/92, p. H2552; cf. Barr to Gonzalez, 5/15/92, at p. H3372.

"grand-slam": Dobson and O'Dwyer-Russell, p. 13.

double agents in Matrix: The British government formally admitted in 11/92 that Cooper, Henderson, and Gutteridge were double agents. See, e.g., numerous stories in TI, 11/4–14/92.

Henderson's handling: TI, 11/4/92.

CIA received "raw" reports: SSCI/BNL, p. 15.

CIA played lead role: Double agent Henderson was told by British Trade Minister Alan Clark in 1/88 that British policy on the matter of sensitive exports to Iraq was dependent on U.S. policy toward Iraq, and had no doubt that the information he and his colleagues were providing was shared with CIA and available to the White House in formulating Western policy toward Saddam (statement issued by Irwin Mitchell, solicitors, in the defense of Paul Henderson, London, 11/9/92; text at TI, 11/10/92).

421   Agency did worry: CIA report, 6/89, p. H7873.

fraud working groups: testimony of Charles E. Schumer, House Committee on the Judiciary, Subcommittee on Criminal Justice, *Hearings*, 3/22/89, p. 5.

but not to CIA: Timmerman, p. 352.

doubt among criminal agents: Aldhizer interview, 1/5/93.

FBI raid on BNL-Atlanta: Atlanta *Constitution-Journal*, 8/5–11/89; Timmerman, p. 354.

BNL illegally loaned: Gonzalez testimony, 2/4/92, CR/BNL, p. H847.

raid revealed Iraq-BNL links: ibid., 9/28/92, p. H9991.

FBI kept Foreign CI desk advised: Justice Department memo, 11/2/89, CR/BNL, p. H9595.

422   "stumbling blocks": Justice Department memo, 7/3/90, CR/BNL, p. H9593.

CIA had still not replied: Justice Department memo, 12/10/90, CR/BNL.

faulty filing system: IG/93, p. 6: "In order to maintain internal compartmentation, records have been intentionally fragmented. The result is a system that was never designed to facilitate external requests that depend upon complete divulgence of all information in the Agency's possession regarding individuals or entities . . . making it impossible at this time for searchers to say with complete certainty that all information on a given subject has been found."

"Adults need not linger": Powers, 10/18/92.

"CIA was uncomfortable": testimony of FBI Official #1, transcript, p. 13, SSCI/BNL, p. 161.

FBI's two top men in Rome: LAT, 10/18/92. Although the FBI men in Rome may seem to have also been covering up by not going to Bureau headquarters with what CIA knew, it has not been established whether either man saw all the relevant CIA cables. It would, moreover, have been a departure from usual practice for the men to have sent cables of their own to FBI headquarters. Instead, the normal practice for handling data that originated with CIA was to allow the CIA's Rome Station to cable the material to Langley, which then would send it across the Potomac River, via Barbara Campbell, to FBI headquarters. (FNS, 10/27/92.)

"This information is discoverable": testimony of FBI Official #2, transcript, pp. 27, 32–33, SSCI/BNL, p. 161.

423   "it's just as well": CIA Reports Officer, deposition conducted by the House Permanent Select Committee on Intelligence, 11/21/92, pp. 10–13, 33, SSCI/ BNL.

The prospect of secrets being exposed: IG/93.

double agents at risk: The concern for double agents in Matrix-Churchill is well documented in British papers released during 11/92 (see TI, 11/4–13/ 92). There was also some concern that Iraqi bank officials had already been executed by Saddam before they could give evidence to U.S. investigators. (State Department memo, 10/11/89, CR/BNL, p. H866; Justice Department memo, 7/3/90, at CR/BNL, p. H9593.

"The Agency cannot afford": IG/93, p. 8. Cf. a vital need, in the BNL case, to "protect DO operational information" (ibid., p. 4). And: "The Agency has a general bias against disclosing all relevant information in response to legitimate requests from . . . other Federal agencies. This was particularly evident in the DO responses to particular requests for information pertaining to certain individuals and firms." (Ibid., p. 7.)

Unless he gained new revenue soon: Gonzalez testimony, CR/BNL, 4/25/ 92, p. H2548.

CIA's Oval Office briefing: Perry, p. 370. Perry interviewed Webster and other CIA officials.

424   NCD debriefed businessmen: ibid., pp. 370–71; Kessler, 1992, p. 127.

Matrix's Cleveland office: CR/BNL, Congressional Record, 7/21/92, p. H6340.

"a sensitive case": Thornburgh to Gonzalez, 9/26/90, CR/BNL.

"serious damage": Sessions to Gonzalez, 10/5/90, CR/BNL, p. H3372.

"embarrassment level": U.S. Treasury Department notes, 11/7/89, cited at Gonzalez statement.

bombing of Baghdad: "Secrets of the Stealth," *Nova*, PBS broadcast, 2/93.

CIA targeting intelligence: Perry, pp. 370–72; USNWR, 6/3/91.

"vital project": Gonzalez testimony, 9/9/92, CR/BNL, p. H8182.

"a secret operation": interview with House Banking Committee investigator Dennis Kane, 1/5/93.

"coddle, powder, and diaper Saddam": Gonzalez statement.

425   Gates released to Gonzalez: Stanley M. Moscowitz, director of congressional affairs, to Rep. Gonzalez, 11/12/91, CR/BNL, p. H8354.

"unfettered": RTR, 10/13/92.

"You'd better protect yourself": *Washingtonian*, 3/93.

"coverup bigger than Watergate": R, 10/15/92.

426 Democrats seemed strangely silent: Lewis, 1/25/93, p. B-6.

CIA's image badly battered: Sciolino, 10/17/92.

Gates did not say anything of the sort: Although Henderson's spy work was admitted by the British government on 11/4/92—election day in the U.S.—this obviously came too late for CIA to undo Iraq-Gate by 'fessing up to its real reasons for witholding data on BNL. Moreover, public disclosure of the Matrix deception had already caused Saddam's secret police to zero in on Iraqis who had worked most closely with Matrix in the construction of uranium-enrichment equipment, on the premise that those Iraqis might have been recruited by British intelligence. One nuclear physicist who fell under suspicion, Moayyad Hassan al-Janabi, escaped to Amman, Jordan, but on December 7, 1992, was shot to death by two men in front of his wife and children. Six Iraqis traveling on diplomatic passports were arrested in connection with Janabi's killing, which was apparently intended to deter other nuclear scientists from defecting. (See Ibrahim, NYT, 12/13/92.)

Iraqi nuclear equipment remained hidden: Gates testimony, House Armed Services Committee, n.d. [3/92], at CR/BNL, p. H2429.

Zaafraynia attack: NYT, 1/18–20/93.

inspector general's prescriptions: IG/93.

427 "operational," etc.: SSCI/BNL, pp. 34–5.

"information relating to": WP, 2/10/93.

"evaluating and possibly expanding": ibid.

428 Gates' retirement: Sciolino, 11/7/92.

20. THE KEYS TO THE KINGDOM

428 "This is what happened": "Iraqgate: The Making of an Investigation," *Harper's*, 1/93, pp. 59ff.

Clintonites against turf battles: Arizona *Republic*, 5/23/93; FNS, 7/13/93.

429 Woolsey background: RTR, 3/3/93; T, 7/5/93.

Crowe: WP, 7/16/93.

Little Rock: Woolsey interviewed on *Larry King Live*, 11/30/93.

"poisonous snakes": T, 7/5/93.

"early item of business": WP, 2/10/93.

"restructuring the Intelligence Community": FNS, 3/9/93.

"both the BCCI and the BNL scandals": RTR, 3/9/93.

prosecutors could task CIA: WP, 2/10/93.

Mafia, Cali cartel: NWK, 12/13/93.

CIA officers detailed to FBI-CT: WP, 11/7/93.

430 "determine whether psycho-correction": *Defense Electronics*, 7/93.

a lot of people willing to help CIA: Woolsey interview, "Larry King Live," 11/30/93.

"What's involved here": RTR, 3/9/93.

ten to five hundred economic-espionage cases: LAT, 4/30/93.

Ntube: WP, 8/5/93; CT, 8/5/93.

Brown: Bradsher.

Lalas: NYT, 5/6/93.

Gerard: UPI 4/14/93; SDUT, 4/29/93; *Guardian* (London), 5/10/93; NYT, 5/9/93.

431   Ames: Again, my basic source is Wiser's affidavit.
May 12: AP Online, 3/10/94, 16:28 Eastern Time.
beyond his "compartment": WT, 2/23/94.
divorce: WT, 2/23/94.
Delay in passing Ames serial: Pound and Duffy.

432   Failure to pool polygraph results: Pincus and Thomas.
CIA hesitance on polygraphs: Ibid.
Two agents at CIC: Smith and Thomas.
submarine tracking: WT, 3/4/94.
"What Angleton Thought": ibid.

433   "Nightmover": WP, 3/6/94.
American-owned pipelines demolished: Jehl, 3/18/93.
Iraqi plot against Bush: Jehl, 5/8/93; WP, 3/3/91.
Langley shootings: Ayres; Lewis, 2/10/93.
Peshawar: Ibrahim, 3/6/93.

434   Salim/Khoeniah: statement of Nathan T. Adams, Senate Committee on Foreign Relations, *International Terrorism Hearings*, 5/15/85, pp. 40–42.
Alien Border Control Committee: LAT, 2/7/87.
eight suspected Palestinian terrorists: ibid.
Barney Frank's bill: FNS, 7/13/93, 8/7/89.
Rahman: Hedges; Gargan.
Rahman on Iranian intelligence payroll: Vincent Cannistraro interview, ABC News, 3/18/93.
Rahman a CIA agent?: Agence France Presse, 7/4/93; N, 6/27/93; *Gazette* (Montreal), 5/29/93; BG, 7/3/93.

435   fatwas: Emerson, 6/27/93.
Egyptian intelligence warned CIA: Jehl, 4/6/93.
Emad Salem: WP, 7/16/93.

436   sharing intelligence after bombing: Reuter Library Report, 3/1/93; T, 3/8/93.
"money trail": USNWR, 3/22/93.
"fully integrated": FNS, 3/9/93.
"playing catch-up": Safire, 5/3/93.
a lingering sense: NYT, Op-Ed, 3/11/93.
Mubarak: Sciolino, 4/5/93, p. A-1.
failure to pursue hints: BG, 7/3/93.
warning from German intelligence: Emerson, 6/27/93.
"Monday morning quarterbacking": LAT, 6/30/93.
no names or documents: USNWR, 4/19/93.
Egypt had advised CIA: WP, 7/16/93.
warn all U.S. embassies: *Mednews*, 3/22/93.
same cast of characters: Cannistraro interview, ABC News, 6/28/93.
searching Nosair's apartment: N, 6/25/93; NYT, 7/4/93.

437   "This material described": ibid.
bomb-making manuals: ibid.
"rifts concerning him": Agence France Presse, 5/27/93.
Agency denied it: GNS, 7/1/93.

"had to react quickly": Agence France Presse, 7/4/93.

"We, the naive Egyptians": *Middle East Intelligence Report*, 7/4/93.

"What happened": UPI, 7/3/93.

"One party": *Middle East Intelligence Report*, 7/4/93.

438   Schumer: "Keep Terrorism Foreign," NYT, Op-Ed, n.d. [3/93].

"I want coordinated": FNS, 4/21/93.

"cooperation and diligence": ibid.

"Everything that could have gone wrong": FNS, 7/13/93.

"I do have the uneasy feeling": FNS, 3/15/93.

"It might very well be": ibid.

"third agency rule": ibid.

"gave everyone a lot of angst": ibid.

439   "conceptual bankruptcy": GNS, 8/3/93.

"We try not to get into": USNWR, 7/5/93.

"lackluster": *Legal Times*, 9/25/89.

too aggressive: WT, 11/8/89.

"well within the mainstream": Sessions news conference, FNS, 11/7/89.

America's Most Wanted: *Legal Times*, 9/25/89.

Barr testimony: Sessions news conference, FNS, 11/7/89.

"indices check": ibid.

subcontracting: WP, 6/23/89.

extracting terrorists: WT, 11/8/89.

confused about CT jurisdiction: FNS, 4/21/93.

"there is a very careful": ibid.

the kicker: *Washingtonian*, 3/93.

440   Kessler: ibid.

Ron McCall: ibid.

a top KGB official: ibid.

"counterintelligence investigations": UPI, 12/14/87.

"incompetent": *Washingtonian*, 3/93.

"targeted": CNN transcripts, 7/20/93.

441   "improv[e] our": FNS, 7/29/93.

"a great problem": ibid.

Robert Vance: Kessler, 1993, p. 435.

"work harmoniously": FNS, 7/29/93.

law-enforcement superagency: FNS, 4/8/92, 4/21/93.

"unnecessary overlap": NYT, 11/17/93.

"to help me assess": FNS, 3/9/93.

illegal immigration: *The San Francisco Chronicle*, 6/5/93.

CIA officers detailed to FBI CT: WP, 11/7/93.

Rezaq: NWK, 7/26/93; NYT, 7/17/93.

Ames case: again, see Wiser affidavit, 2/21/94.

"pulled out": Gertz, 4/22/94.

broke up testily: NWK, 12/13/93.

442   ten agents executed: NYT, 2/24/94.

443   GT/MOTORBOAT: AP Online, 3/1/94, 14:04 Eastern Time.

"highly intricate"; $100 million: CR, H-2934ff.

Ames and western technology: Reuters, 2/22/94.

nine-page letter: WT, 3/7/94.

Moscow intelligence suspect: NYT, 4/20/94.

negotiating positions: CNN, 2/23/94, 05:00 Eastern Time, Transcript #684–5.

chain smoker: WT, 3/4/94.

444   plain-texts: LAT, 2/23/94.

Woodruff: WP, 8/11/93; *The Reuter European Business Report*, 8/13/93; WT, 8/21/93.

Increasingly nervous: NYT, 2/23/94, p. A-13.

T-82: ibid.

scheduled Turkey/Russia trip: USAT, 2/28/94.

"CIA's unwavering assistance": Department of Justice press release, 2/22/94.

"how our [CIA] counterintelligence": ibid.

tensions persisted: NYT, 3/8/94; WP, 3/6/94.

CIA ignored tip about Ames spending: WP, 3/6/94.

polygraphs: NYT, 3/8/94.

445   Feb. 1986 meeting: Wiser affidavit, 2/21/94.

FBI didn't inform CIA about Ames: David Martin, CBS Evening News, 2/23/94; Reuters, 2/23/94; UPI, 2/23/94.

Bryant testimony: Fenyvesi.

pessimistic about leads: NYT, 4/20/94.

"when you got below": Pincus and Thomas.

"even now verbally": WP, 4/20/94.

CIA on Ames polygraph: T, 3/21/94.

Woolsey in closed-door session: Fenyvesi.

446   5 FBI recruitments lost: Powers, 3/27/94.

"The FBI is bitter about this case": NYT, 2/24/94.

"enraged": NYT, 3/8/94.

FBI suspected other moles in CIA: WP, 3/6/94.

FBI reviewing old CIA polygraphs: Reno press conference, FNS, 3/31/94.

anomalies: NWK, 3/21/94.

Helsinki: USNWR, 4/18/94.

Bearden, Twetten: NYT, WT, 4/14/94.

"was decentralized": WP, 4/20/94.

CIA barred from Ames debriefing: Kilian.

447   Potachov: interview with retired CIA counterintelligence official.

Lake asked NSC: Pincus and Thomas.

"acting like two teenagers": Smith and Thomas.

Details of NSC plan: ibid.

"To me, the FBI had the right": Gertz, 4/22/94.

"The Director of the Federal Bureau of Investigation": Draft legislation, Counterintelligence and Security Enhancements Act of 1994, released by Senator DeConcini's office 4/94.

"What you want to do, Senator": AP Online, 4/21/94.

"impossibly tepid": USNWR, 4/18/94.

"People should not have the impression": FNS, 4/22/94.

"overstatement": CT, 4/21/94.

"The Bureau went nuts": NYT, 4/20/94.

"a diversion": ibid.

PDD-24: The document remained classified at the time of publication. Details of the directive are given in two statements by the White House Press Secretary—"Statement by the Press Secretary on U.S. Counterintelligence Effectiveness," and "Fact Sheet: U.S. Counterintelligence Effectiveness"—both dated May 3, 1994.
Freeh-Woolsey testimony, DeConcini remarks: FNS, 5/3/94.

450   "a review": Gertz, 4/22/94.

451   "the number one issue": NYT, 3/8/94.
CIA-Justice report overdue: ibid.
"Finders Corp.": WT, 12/17/93.
"admitted to owning": ibid.
"Without amending": WT, 2/24/93.
allow the Bureau to look: WT, 3/16/94.
"that the intelligence community": RTR, 3/9/93.

452   "restructuring the Intelligence Community": FNS, 3/9/93.
"I don't believe": RTR, 3/9/93.
"Why haven't these problems": *Crossfire* (CNN), 4/19/94.

SOURCES

Sources for the Epilogue and Afterword are posted at secretpolicy.com/wedge/epilogue

Adams, James. "Help Wanted: Bring Cloak, Dagger." Washington *Post*, February 9, 1992, p. B-2.

Allen, Thomas B., and Norman Polmar. *Merchants of Treason: America's Secrets for Sale*. Dell, 1989.

Alsop, Stewart. *The Center: People and Power in Washington*. New York: Harper and Row, 1968.

Alsop, Stewart, and Thomas Braden. *Sub Rosa; The OSS and American Espionage*. Harcourt, Brace, and World, 1964.

Anderson, Dave. "The Infamous Day That Colonel Donovan Was Paged." *New York Times*, December 1, 1991.

Anderson, Jack. "Behind John F. Kennedy's Murder." Washington *Post*, September 7, 1976, p. C-19.

Anderson, Jack. "Did Moscow Tap Nancy's Calls to Her Astrologer?" *Newsday*, May 20, 1988.

Angleton, James. "Golitsyn—'Indispensable Reading.'" *AFIO Persicope*, Spring 1984.

Ayres, B. Drummond, Jr. "Gunman Kills 2 near CIA Entrance." *New York Times*, January 26, 1993.

Bailey, Geoffrey [Prince Vasilyichkov]. *The Conspirators*. Harper and Brothers, 1961.

Baker, Russ W. "Iraqgate: The Big One That (Almost) Got Away." *Columbia Journalism Review*, March 1993, pp. 52ff.

Baldwin, Hanson W. "Intelligence I: One of Weakest Links in Our Security, Survey Shows—Omissions, Duplications." *New York Times*, July 22, 1948.

Baldwin, Hanson W. "Intelligence II: Older Agencies Resent a Successor and Try to Restrict Scope of Action." *New York Times*, July 20, 1948.

Barzun, Jacques. "Meditations on the Literature of Spying." *American Scholar*, Spring 1965.

Belin, David. *Final Disclosure: The Full Truth About the Assassination of President Kennedy*. Scribner's, 1988.

Bell, Griffin B., with Ronald J. Ostrow. *Taking Care of the Law*. William Morrow, 1982.

Bentley, Elizabeth. *Out of Bondage*. Ballantine, 1988.

Bernikow, Louise. *Abel*. Ballantine, 1982.

Beschloss, Michael R. "Fools or Traitors?" *New York Times Book Review*, March 15, 1992.

Beschloss, Michael R. *Mayday: Eisenhower, Khrushchev and the U-2 Affair*. Harper and Row, 1986.

Black, Bob, and Adam Parfrey. *Rants & Incendiary Tracts: Voices of Desperate Illumination 1558 to Present*. Amok Press/Loompanics, 1989.

Blumenthal, Ralph. "$100,000 from Abroad Linked to Trade Center Suspects." *New York Times*, April 25, 1993.

Blumenthal, Sidney. *Pledging Allegiance*. HarperCollins, 1990.

Bohlen, Celeste. "Russia Orders American Reporter Questioned in State-Secrets Case." *New York Times*, April 8, 1993.

Braden, Tom. "The Birth of the CIA." *American Heritage*, vol. XXVII (February 1977), pp. 4–13.

Bradsher, Keith. "American Is Accused of Passing Secrets to Philippine Government." *New York Times*, December 29, 1992.

Bratzel, John, and Leslie Rout. "Once Again: "Pearl Harbor, Microdots, and J. Edgar Hoover." *American Historical Review*, vol. 88, no. 4 (October 1983), pp. 953–60.

Bratzel, John, and Leslie Rout. "Pearl Harbor, Microdots, and J. Edgar Hoover." *American Historical Review*, vol. 87, no. 5 (December 1982), pp. 1342–49.

Breckinridge, Scott. *The CIA and the U.S. Intelligence System*. Boulder, Col.: Westview, 1986.

Breuer, William. *Nazi Spies in America: Hitler's Undercover War*. St. Martin's, 1990.

Broder, John C. "Secrets and Mysteries." Los Angeles *Times Magazine*, April 19, 1992.

Brown, Anthony Cave. *Bodyguard of Lies*. Harper and Row, 1975.

Brown, Anthony Cave. *The Last Hero: Wild Bill Donovan* ... Times Books, 1982.

Bruce, David. "The National Intelligence Authority." *Virginia Quarterly*, July 1946, pp. 355–69.

Buchan, John. *The Four Adventures of Richard Hannay*. Introductory essay by Robin Winks. Boston: David R. Godine, 1988.

Burleson, Clyde W. *The Jennifer Project*. Sphere Books, 1987.

Butterfield, Fox. "Long Feud Nears End: Move to Heal Split in FBI and CIA." *New York Times*, March 4, 1987.

Carver, George. "The Prosecution's Case." *CIRA* [Central Intelligence Retirees Association] *Newsletter*, vol. XVI, no. 4 (Winter 1991–92).

Casey, William. *The Secret War Against Hitler*. London: Simon and Schuster, 1988.

Center for the Study of Intelligence [Central Intelligence Agency]. *Of Moles and Molehunters: A Review of Counterintelligence Literature, 1977–92—An In-*

telligence Monograph. Springfield, Virginia: National Technical Information Service, October 1993.

Central Intelligence Agency. "Unclassified Summary of the Final Report of the Office of Inspector General—Investigation of CIA's Handling of BNL-Related Matters." CIA Office of Media Affairs, Washington, D.C., January 14, 1993.

Christian, Shirley. *Nicaragua: Revolution in the Family.* Random House, 1985.

Churchill, Winston S. *A History of the English Speaking Peoples, vol. I: The Birth of Britain.* Cassell, London, 1971.

Churchill, Winston S. *The Second World War.* Abridged ed. Time-Life, 1960.

Cline, Ray. *Secrets, Spies, and Scholars.* Washington, D.C.: Acropolis, 1976.

Cohen, Roger. "Case of the Adaptable Spy: Agent for Soviets and Russia, Too." *New York Times,* May 12, 1992, p. A-11.

Colby, William. *Honorable Men: My Life in the CIA.* Simon & Schuster, 1978.

Collier, Peter, and David Horowitz. *Destructive Generation: Second Thoughts About the Sixties.* Summit, 1990.

Coon, Carleton S. *A North Africa Story: The Anthropologist as OSS Agent.* Ipswich, Mass.: Gambit, 1980.

Corn, David. "Still in the Cold." *Nation,* March 22, 1990, p. 336.

Corson, William. *The Armies of Ignorance.* Dial, 1977.

Corson, William, Susan B. Trento, and Joseph J. Trento, *Widows: Four American Spies, the Wives They Left Behind, and the KGB's Crippling of American Intelligence.* Crown, 1989.

Couffer, Jack. *Bat Bomb: World War II's Other Secret Weapon.* University of Texas Press, 1992.

Crile, George. "The Mafia, the CIA, and Castro." Washington *Post,* May 16, 1976, p. C-1.

Crile, George. "The Riddle of AM LASH." Washington *Post,* May 2, 1976, p. C-1.

Crozier, Brian, Drew Middleton, and Jeremy Murray-Brown. *This War Called Peace.* Universe Books, 1985.

Cruz, Arturo, Jr. *Memoirs of a Counter-Revolutionary.* Doubleday, 1989.

Cummings, Homer S., and Carl McFarland. *Federal Justice: Chapters in the History of Justice in the Federal Executive.* Macmillan, 1937.

Darling, Arthur B. *The Central Intelligence Agency: A History to 1950.* 1953. Central Intelligence Agency Historical Review Program, declassification November 1990. National Archives, Record Group 226. Published at University Park, Pa.: Pennsylvania State University Press, 1990.

Davis, David Brion, ed. *The Fear of Conspiracy: Images of Un-American Subversion from the Revolution to the Present.* Ithaca, N.Y.: Cornell University Press, 1971.

Demaris, Ovid. *The Director: An Oral Biography of J. Edgar Hoover.* Harper's Magazine Press, 1975.

Deriabin, Peter, and Frank Gibney. *The Secret World.* Doubleday, 1959.

Dickey, Christopher. *With the Contras.* Simon and Schuster, 1984.

Dinges, John. *Our Man in Panama.* Random House, 1990.

Dobbs, Michael, and Jeffrey Smith. "80s Brought Decline to KGB's Prime Post." Washington *Post,* February 19, 1993.

Dobson, Christopher, and Simon O'Dwyer-Russell. "The Undercover Nuclear War." *Sunday Telegraph*, April 1, 1990, p. 13.

Donner, Frank. *The Age of Surveillance.* Alfred A. Knopf, 1980.

Donovan, William. "Intelligence: The Key to Defense." *Life*, September 30, 1946.

Downes, Donald. *The Scarlet Thread: Adventures in Wartime Espionage.* Derek Verschoyle, 1953.

Duffy, Brian. "The Prosecution's Prize Witness." *U.S. News & World Report*, December 20, 1993.

Dulles, Allen W. *The Craft of Intelligence.* Harper and Row, 1963.

Dunlop, Richard. *Donovan: America's Master Spy.* Rand McNally, 1982.

Eco, Umberto. "Narrative Structures in Fleming." In Eco, *The Role of the Reader: Explorations in the Semiotics of Texts.* Indiana University Press, 1984. Pp. 144–72.

Emerson, Ralph Waldo. "Literary Ethics: An Address to the Literary Societies in Dartmouth College." July 27, 1838. In Emerson's collected *Essays and Lectures.* The Library of America, 1983.

Emerson, Steven. "A New Terrorism: Islamic Fundamentalism's Terrible Threat to the West." San Diego *Union-Tribune*, June 27, 1993.

Emerson, Steven, "A Terrorist Network in America?" *New York Times*, April 7, 1993.

Emerson, Steven, and Richard Rothschild. "Taking On Terrorists." *U.S. News & World Report*, September 12, 1988.

Engelberg, Stephen. "U.S. Is Criticized on Spy Deterrence." *New York Times*, July 27, 1990.

Epstein, Edward Jay. *Deception.* Simon and Schuster, 1989.

Epstein, Edward Jay. *Legend: The Secret World of Lee Harvey Oswald.* Reader's Digest Press/McGraw-Hill, 1978.

Epstein, Edward Jay. "On the Team." *The New Republic*, March 28, 1994.

Evans, Rowland. "68,000 feet? Senate Wants the Full U-2 Story." New York *Herald-Tribune*, February 16, 1962.

Fain, Tyrus G. *The Intelligence Community: History, Organization, and Issues.* R. R. Bowker, 1977.

Fanon, Franz. *The Wretched of the Earth.* Grove, 1965.

Farago, Ladislas. *The Game of the Foxes.* McKay, 1971.

Felix, Christopher [James McCargar]. *A Short Course in the Secret War.* Dutton, 1963.

Felt, Mark. *The FBI Pyramid.* Putnam's, 1979.

Fenyvesi, Charles. "Ames Fallout further strains FBI-CIA relations." *U.S. News & World Report*, March 21, 1994, p. 27.

Ferrell, Tom. "Bats Away!" *New York Times Book Review*, September 30, 1992.

Fleming, Ian. *Casino Royale.* Macmillan, 1953.

Fleming, Ian. *From Russia with Love.* Macmillan, 1957.

Fleming, Ian. *Live and Let Die.* Macmillan, 1954.

Fleming, Ian. *Moonraker.* Macmillan, 1955.

Fleming, Ian. *You Only Live Twice.* Signet, 1965.

Foote, Alexander. *Handbook for Spies*. Museum Press, 1953.

Ford, Corey. *Donovan of OSS*. Boston: Little, Brown, 1970.

Ford, Corey, and Alistair MacBain. *Cloak and Dagger: The Secret Story of OSS*. Foreword by William J. Donovan. Collier's, 1945.

Ford, Gerald R. *A Time to Heal*. Berkley, 1980.

Friedman, Alan. *Spider's Web: The Secret History of How the White House Illegally Armed Iraq*. Bantam, 1993.

Fukuyama, Francis. "Rest Easy. It's Not 1914 Anymore." *New York Times*, February 9, 1992, p. A-17.

Gargan, Edward A. "Radical Arabs Use Pakistan as Base for Holy War." *New York Times*, April 8, 1993.

Gentry, Curt. *J. Edgar Hoover: The Man and the Secrets*. W. W. Norton, 1991.

Gerth, Jeff. "The C.I.A. and the Drug War, a Special Report: C.I.A. Shedding Its Reluctance to Aid in Fight Against Drugs." *New York Times*, March 25, 1990.

Gerth, Jeff. "U.S. and Europeans Reportedly Break a Major Spy Ring." *New York Times*, August 24, 1988.

Gertz, Bill. "CIA suspected Ames in '91 but didn't tell FBI." The Washington *Times*, April 22, 1994, p. A1.

Gertz, Bill. "Report Urges Single U.S. Counterspy Agency." Washington *Times*, April 16, 1990.

Gertz, Bill. "Senator's Plan Calls for 'Intelligence Czar.' " Washington *Times*, February 5, 1992.

Godson Roy, ed. *Intelligence Requirements for the 1980s: Elements of Intelligence*. National Strategy Information Center, 1979.

Godson, Roy, ed. *Intelligence Requirements for the 1980s: Counterintelligence*. National Strategy Information Center, 1980.

Godson, Roy, ed. *Intelligence Requirements for the 1980s: Elements of Intelligence*. National Strategy Information Center, 1983.

Godson, Roy, ed. *Intelligence Requirements for the 1990s: Collection, Counterintelligence, and Covert Action*. Lexington Books, 1989.

Goldwater, Barry. *With No Apologies*. William A. Morrow, 1979.

Golitsyn, Anatoliy. "The Long-Range Strategy and 'Convergence.' " *Soviet Analyst*, vol. 21, nos. 1–2 (December 1991), pp. 11–16.

Golitsyn, Anatoliy. *New Lies for Old*. Bodley Head, 1984.

Gonzalez, the Hon. Henry B. *The President & the Rostow Gang, CIA Report on BNL . . .* , July 7, 1992. Distributed by Office of Rep. Gonzalez, Washington, D.C.

Gorbachev, Mikhail. *Perestroika*. Harper & Row, 1987.

Haldeman, H. R. *The Ends of Power*. Times Books, 1978.

Halpern, Samuel, and Hayden Peake. "Did Angleton Jail Nosenko?" *International Journal of Intelligence and Counterintelligence*, vol. 3, no. 4 (Winter 1989).

Hedges, Chris. "A Cry of Islamic Fury, Taped in Brooklyn for Cairo." *New York Times*, January 7, 1993.

Hersh, Burton. *The Old Boys: The American Elite and the Origins of CIA*. Scribner's, 1992.

Hersh, Seymour. "Huge C.I.A. Operation Reported in U.S. Against Antiwar

Forces and Other Dissidents in Nixon Years." *New York Times*, December 22, 1974, p. A-1.

Hersh, Seymour. *The Samson Option*. Random House, 1991.

Hilton, Stanley E. *Hitler's Secret War in South America, 1939–1945: German Military Espionage and Allied Counterespionage in Brazil*. Baton Rouge: Louisiana State University Press, 1981.

Hinsley, F. H., et al. *British Intelligence in the Second World War*. Five volumes. Her Majesty's Stationery Office, 1979.

Hofstadter, Richard. *The Paranoid Style in American Politics and Other Essays*. Alfred A. Knopf, 1964.

Hood, William. *Mole*. Ballantine, 1983.

Hood, William, James Nolan and Samuel Halpern. *Myths Surrounding James Angleton: Lessons for American Counterintelligence*. Washington: Consortium for the Study of Intelligence, 1994.

Hoover, J. Edgar. "The Enemy's Masterpiece of Espionage." *Reader's Digest*, September 1946.

Hougan, Jim. *Secret Agenda: Watergate, Deep Throat, and the CIA*. Random House, 1984.

Hunt, E. Howard. *Undercover*. Berkley-Putnam's, 1974.

Hunt, Linda. *Secret Agenda: The United States Government and Project Paperclip, 1945 to 1990*. St. Martin's, 1991.

"The Hunt for Saddam's Secret Weapons." *Nova*. Public Broadcasting Service, January 12, 1993.

Hurt, Henry. *Shadrin: The Spy Who Never Came Back*. Berkley, 1983.

Hyde, H. Montgomery. *Room 3603*. Farrar, Straus, 1962.

Ibrahim, Youssef M. "Jordanians Think Iraqi Agents Killed Scientist." *New York Times*, December 13, 1992.

Ibrahim, Youssef M. "Throughout Arab World, 20 Years of Growth of Islamic Terror Groups," *New York Times*, March 6, 1993.

Ivanidze, Vladimir. "The Spy Year in Russia." *Russian Press Digest*, March 18, 1994.

Ivri, Maj. Gen. David. "The Attack on the Iraqi Nuclear Reactor: June 1981." In *The War Against Terror*. Tel Aviv: Revivim, 1988. Pp. 31–35.

James, William. "The Will to Believe." In James' *Pragmatism and Other Essays*. Washington Square Press, 1963.

Jehl, Douglas. "Iran-Backed Terrorists Are Growing More Aggressive, U.S. Warns." *New York Times*, March 18, 1993.

Jehl, Douglas. "Man Sought in Killings in CIA May Have Vanished in Pakistan." *New York Times*, February 12, 1993.

Jehl, Douglas, "U.S. Confirms FBI Alerted by Egyptians." *New York Times*, April 6, 1993.

Jehl, Douglas. "U.S. Convinced Iraqi Saboteurs Plotted to Kill Bush." *New York Times*, May 8, 1993.

Johnson, Loch K. "DCI Webster's Legacy: The Judge's Self-Assessment." *International Journal of Intelligence and Counterintelligence*, vol. 5, no. 3 (Fall 1991).

Johnston, James. "The CIA's JFK Secret: The Classified Files Will Show the

Agency Believed in a Conspiracy." Washington *Post*, September 27, 1992, p. C-5.

Johnston, James, "Did Cuba Murder JFK?" Washington *Post*, November 19, 1989.

Kalaris, George, and Leonard McCoy. "Counterintelligence." In Godson, ed., 1989.

Keating, Susan Katz. "Peering Through a Glasnost Darkly." *Insight*, July 3, 1990, pp. 60–61.

Kelley, Clarence E. *Kelley: The Story of an FBI Director*. Kansas City, Kans.: Andrews, McMeel, and Parker, 1987.

Kessler, Ronald. *Escape from the CIA: How the CIA Won and Lost the Most Important KGB Spy Ever to Defect to the U.S.* Pocket Books, 1991.

Kessler, Ronald. *Inside the CIA: Revealing the Secrets of the World's Most Powerful Spy Agency*. Pocket Books, 1992.

Kessler, Ronald. *Inside the FBI*. Pocket Books, 1993.

Kessler, Ronald. *Spy vs. Spy: Stalking Soviet Spies in America*. Scribner's, 1988.

Kilian, Michael. "Spy Case Puts Spotlight on CIA-FBI Turf Battle." Chicago *Tribune*, April 30, 1994.

Kirkpatrick, Lyman B., Jr. *The Real CIA*. Macmillan, 1968.

Kurland, Michael. *The Spymaster's Handbook*. Facts on File, 1988.

Lacayo, Richard. "Crisis in Spookville." *Time*, September 23, 1991, pp. 16ff.

LaFraniere, Sharon. "Sessions: FBI's Leader or Cheerleader?" Washington *Post*, December 15, 1991, p. A-1.

Lamphere, Robert. *The FBI-KGB War: A Special Agent's Story*. Random House, 1986.

Laqueur, Walter. *Second World War: Essays in Military and Political History*. Beverly Hills: Sage, 1982.

Leary, Timothy. *Flashbacks*. Los Angeles: J. P. Tarcher, 1983.

Leary, William M., ed. *The Central Intelligence Agency: History and Documents*. University, Ala.: University of Alabama Press, 1988.

Ledeen, Michael. *Perilous Statecraft: An Insider's Account of the Iran-Contra Affair*. Scribner's, 1988.

Lee, Martin A., and Bruce Shalin. *Acid Dreams: The CIA, LSD, and the Sixties Rebellion*. Grove, 1985.

Lester, Julius. *Look Out Whitey! Black Power's Gonna Get Your Mama!* Vintage Books, 1969.

Lewis, Neil A. "Many Legislators Reluctant to Hold Iraq Loans Inquiry." *New York Times*, January 25, 1993, p. B-6.

Lewis, Neil A. "Pakistani Sought in CIA Shootings." *New York Times*, February 10, 1993.

Liddy, G. Gordon. *Will*. Dell/St. Martin's, 1980.

Lockhart, Robin Bruce. *Reilly: Ace of Spies*. Penguin, 1987.

Lovell, Stanley P. *Of Spies & Stratagems*. Prentice-Hall, 1963.

Lowenthal, Max. *The Federal Bureau of Investigation*. William Sloane, 1950.

Lyubimov, Vitaly. "Yurchenko and the Aldrich Ames Case." Los Angeles *Times*, March 7, 1994.

Maas, Peter. *Manhunt.* Random House, 1986.

Maheu, Robert. *Next to Hughes.* Harper, 1991.

Mangold, Tom. *Cold Warrior: James Jesus Angleton, The CIA's Master Spy Hunter.* Simon and Schuster, 1991.

Marchetti, Victor, and John D. Marks. *The CIA and the Cult of Intelligence.* Alfred A. Knopf, 1974.

Marks, John. *The Search for the Manchurian Candidate: The CIA and Mind Control.* Times Books, 1979.

Martin, David C. *Wilderness of Mirrors.* Ballantine, 1981.

Masterman, J. C. *The Double Cross System in the War of 1939 to 1945.* Ballantine, 1982.

McLachlan, Donald. *Room 39.* Atheneum, 1968.

McMillan, Penelope. "A James Bond Affair." New York *Daily News*, May 16, 1974.

Meddis, Sam Vincent. "Gates to Unveil Overhaul for CIA." *USA Today*, April 1, 1992.

Medvedev, Zhores A. *Gorbachev.* W. W. Norton, 1986.

Meyer, Cord. *Facing Reality: From World Federalism to the CIA.* Harper and Row, 1980.

Miler, Newton S. "Counterintelligence." In Godson, ed., 1979. pp. 49–63.

Miler, Newton S. "Counterintelligence at the Crossroads." In Godson, ed., 1983. pp. 45ff.

Miler, Newton S. "Discussion." In Godson, ed., 1980. Pp. 40–44.

Mitchell, Alison. "The CIA's Old Friends Come Around, Menacingly." *New York Times*, April 15, 1993.

Mitgang, Herbert. "Commemorating Pearl Harbor." *New York Times*, November 30, 1991.

Montagu, Ewen. *Beyond Top Secret Ultra.* Coward, McCann, 1978.

Montague, Ludwell Lee. *Walter Bedell Smith as Director of Central Intelligence.* Philadelphia: University of Pennsylvania Press, 1992.

Morganthau, Tom, with David C. Martin. "An Epilogue to the Mole Hunt." *Newsweek*, August 11, 1980, pp. 32–33.

Mosley, Leonard. *Dulles: A Biography of Eleanor, Allen, and John Foster Dulles and Their Family Network.* Dial, 1978.

Mure, David. *Master of Deception: Tangled Webs in London and the Middle East.* Kimber, 1980.

Nandy, Julian. "France Smashes Spy Ring." *Independent* (London), November 3, 1992.

Nechiporenko, Col. Oleg Maximovich. *Passport to Assassination: The Never-Before Told Story of Lee Harvey Oswald by the KGB Colonel Who Knew Him.* Birch Lane Press, 1993.

Newton, Verne W. *The Cambridge Spies: The Untold Story of Maclean, Philby and Burgess in America.* Lanham, Md.: Madison Books, 1991.

North, Oliver. *Under Fire: An American Story.* HarperCollins, 1991.

Pearson, John. *The Life of Ian Fleming.* McGraw-Hill, 1966.

Persico, Joseph. *Casey: The Lives and Secrets of William J. Casey: From the OSS to the CIA.* Viking, 1990.

Philby, Kim. *My Silent War*. Ballantine, 1983.

Phillips, David Atlee. *The Night Watch*. Ballantine, 1984.

Pincus, Walter, and Pierre Thomas. "CIA, FBI at Odds Over Ames Polygraph; Agency Reportedly Held Alleged Spy's Failed Test From Bureau." Washington *Post*, March 29, 1994.

Popov, Dusko. *Spy/Counterspy*. Grosset and Dunlap, 1974.

Pound, Edward T., and Brian Duffy. "Wilderness of Mirrors." *U.S. News & World Report*, March 14, 1994, p. 22.

Powell, S. Steven. *Covert Cadre: Inside the Institute for Policy Studies*. Introduction by David Horowitz. Ottawa, Ill.: Green Hill, 1987.

Powers, Francis Gary. *Operation Overflight*. Holt, Rinehart, and Winston, 1970.

Powers, Richard Gid. *Secrecy and Power: The Life of J. Edgar Hoover*. Free Press, 1988.

Powers, Thomas. "Ames Affair Blurs the Circles Within Circles of Intelligence." Los Angeles *Times*, March 27, 1994, Part M; Page 2.

Powers, Thomas. "CIA: A Case of Domestic Intrigue." Los Angeles *Times*, November 27, 1988, pt. 5, p. 1.

Powers, Thomas. *Heisenberg's War: The Secret History of the German Bomb*. Alfred A. Knopf, 1993.

Powers, Thomas. "In the Know." Los Angeles *Times*, October 18, 1992.

Powers, Thomas. *The Man Who Kept the Secrets: Richard Helms and the CIA*. Alfred A. Knopf, 1979.

Powers, Thomas. "The Perils of Covert Policy." Los Angeles *Times*, October 29, 1989, p. M-1.

President's Commission on CIA Activities Within the United States. *Report to the President* [Rockefeller Commission Report]. Washington, D.C.: Government Printing Office, June 1975.

Quirk, John Patrick, et al. *The Central Intelligence Agency: A Photographic History*. Guilford, Conn.: Foreign Intelligence Press, 1987.

Ranelagh, John. *The Agency: The Rise and Decline of the CIA*. Simon and Schuster, 1987.

Rappleye, Charles, and Ed Becker. *All American Mafioso: The Johnny Rosselli Story*. Doubleday, 1991.

Raviv, Dan, and Yosi Melman. *Every Spy a Prince*. Boston: Houghton Mifflin, 1990.

Riebling, Mark. "Counterintelligent System." *New York Times*, March 22, 1994, p. A-19.

Riebling, Mark. "Fearsome Failures When Spooks Are at Odds." *The Guardian* (London), March 25, 1994, p. 16.

Riebling, Mark. "Tinker, Tailor, Stoner, Spy." *Grand Royal* (Los Angeles), Spring–Summer 1994.

Robins, Natalie. *Alien Ink: The FBI's War on Freedom of Expression*. William Morrow, 1992.

Roosevelt, James. *My Parents: A Differing View*. Chicago: Playboy Press, 1976.

Roosevelt, Kermit, ed. [and Peter Karlow]. *OSS War Report*. Walker, 1976.

Rosenthal, Andrew. "Webster Leaving as CIA Director; Ex-Deputy in Line." *New York Times*, May 9, 1992, p. A-1.

Rositzke, Harry. *The CIA's Secret Operations: Espionage, Counterespionage, and Covert Action*. Reader's Digest Press/Thomas Y. Crowell, 1977.

Russbridger, James, and Eric Nave. *Betrayal at Pearl Harbor: How Churchill Lured Roosevelt into World War II*. Summit, 1991.

Safire, William. "The April Surprise." *New York Times*, January 13, 1992.

Safire, William. "A Cat Named Gourmand." *New York Times*, July 29, 1991, p. A-15.

Safire, William. "Islam Under Siege." *New York Times*, May 3, 1993.

Schecter, Jerold L., and Peter S. Deriabin. *The Spy Who Saved the World: How a Soviet Colonel Changed the Course of the Cold War*. Scribner's, 1992.

Schmemann, Serge. "KGB's Successor Charges Scientist." *New York Times*, November 1, 1992.

Schmidt, William E. "A Philosopher Is Called a Spy for the Queen." *New York Times*, August 31, 1991.

Schorr, Daniel. "The Assassins." *New York Review of Books*, October 13, 1977.

Schweizer, Peter. *Friendly Spies: How America's Allies Are Using Economic Espionage to Steal Our Secrets*. Boston: Atlantic Monthly Press, 1993.

Sciolino, Elaine. "Attorney General Names Prosecutor in Iraq-Loans Case." *New York Times*, October 17, 1992.

Sciolino, Elaine. "Egypt Warned U.S. of Terror, Mubarak Says." *New York Times*, April 5, 1993, p. A-1.

Sciolino, Elaine. "Gates Announces He Will Retire as Director of Central Intelligence Early Next Year." *New York Times*, November 7, 1992.

Sciolino, Elaine. "Iraq Case Reveals 3-Way Tug-of-War." *New York Times*, October 21, 1992.

Seth, Ronald. *Unmasked! The Story of Soviet Espionage*. Hawthorn, 1965.

Sherrill, Robert. "The Looting Decade: S&Ls, Big Banks and Other Triumphs of Capitalism," *Nation*, November 19, 1990.

Sherwood, Robert E., ed. *The White House Papers of Harry L. Hopkins*. London: Eyre & Spottsiwoode, 1948.

Shils, Edward A. *The Torment of Secrecy: The Background and Consequences of American Security Policies*. Free Press, 1956.

Simpson, Christopher. *Blowback: The First Full Account of America's Recruitment of Nazis, and Its Disastrous Effect on Our Domestic and Security Policy*. Collier Books, 1989.

Sloterdjik, Peter. *Critique of Cynical Reason*. University of Minnesota Press, 1987.

Smith, Bradley F. *The Shadow Warriors: OSS and the Origins of the CIA*. Basic Books, 1983.

Smith, Joseph Burkholder. *Portrait of a Cold Warrior*. Putnam's, 1976.

Smith, R. Jeffrey, and Pierre Thomas. "Plan Shifts CIA Tasks to FBI Staff; Changes Intended To Speed Detection of Foreign Spies." *The Washington Post*, April 26, 1994. p. A1.

Smith, Robert M. "FBI Is Said to Have Cut Direct Liaison with CIA." *New York Times*, October 9, 1971, p. A-1.

Somoza, Anastasio Debayle. *Nicaragua Betrayed*. Western Islands Press, 1980.

Stafford, David. *Camp X: OSS, 'Intrepid,' and the Allies' North American Training Camp for Secret Agents, 1941–1945*. Dodd, Mead, 1986.

Stevenson, William. *A Man Called Intrepid*. Harcourt Brace Jovanovich, 1976.

Sullivan, William C. *The Bureau: My Thirty Years in Hoover's FBI*. W. W. Norton, 1979.

Summers, Anthony. *Official and Confidential: The Secret Life of J. Edgar Hoover*. Putnam's, 1993.

Sun Tzu. *The Art of War*. Trans. Samuel B. Griffith. Oxford University Press, 1963.

Szulc, Tad. *Compulsive Spy: The Strange Career of E. Howard Hunt*. Viking, 1973.

Szulc, Tad. *Fidel: A Critical Portrait*. Avon, 1987.

Terrell, Jack. *Disposable Patriot: Revelations of a Soldier in America's Secret Wars*. National Books Press, 1992.

Theoharis, Athan, ed. *From the SECRET Files of J. Edgar Hoover*. Chicago: Ivan R. Dee, 1991.

Theoharis, Athan G., and John Stuart Cox. *The Boss: J. Edgar Hoover and the Great American Inquisition*. Bantam, 1990.

Thomas, Pierre. "Interagency FBI-CIA Tensions Defy Decades of Efforts to Resolve Them." Washington *Post*, May 3, 1994.

Thucydides. *The Peloponnesian War*. Trans. Rex Warner. Penguin, 1982.

Timmerman, Kenneth R. *The Death Lobby: How the West Armed Iraq*. Boston: Houghton Mifflin, 1991.

Toland, John. *Infamy: Pearl Harbor and Its Aftermath*. Doubleday, 1982.

Tolchin, Martin. "Bank's Worldwide 'Black Network' Reported." *New York Times*, July 21, 1991.

Tripodi, Tom. *Crusade: Undercover Against the Mafia and KGB*. Brassey's, 1993.

Trohan, Walter. "Donovan Proposes Super Spy System." Washington *Times-Herald*, February 9, 1945.

Trohan, Walter. "Postwar Spy Plan Assailed by Senators." Chicago *Tribune*, February 10, 1945.

Troy, Thomas F. "The British Assault on J. Edgar Hoover: The Tricycle Case." *International Journal of Intelligence and Counterintelligence*, vol. 3, no. 2 (Summer 1989).

Troy, Thomas F. *Donovan and the CIA: A History of the Establishment of the Central Intelligence Agency*. Washington, D.C.: University Publications of America, 1981.

Troy, Thomas F. "Tricycle Never Mentioned Pearl Harbor Attack, Says FBI Review of His File." *Foreign Intelligence Literary Scene*, vol. 3, no. 2 (April 1984).

Tully, Andrew. *CIA: The Inside Story*. William Morrow, 1961.

Tully, Andrew. *Inside the FBI*. Dell, 1987.

Turner, Stansfield. *Secrecy and Democracy: The CIA in Transition*. Boston: Houghton Mifflin, 1985.

Turner, Stansfield. *Terrorism and Democracy*. Boston: Houghton Mifflin, 1991.

U.S. Congress. House. *Committee on Foreign Affairs. Investigation into the Death of Rep. Leo Ryan*. Washington, D.C.: Government Printing Office, 1979.

Ungar, Sanford J. *FBI*. Boston: Atlantic Monthly Press/Little, Brown, 1976.

United States Congress. House. Armed Services Committee. Special Committee on Intelligence. *Inquiry into the Alleged Involvement of the Central Intelli-*

gence Agency in the Watergate and Ellsberg Matters [Nedzi Report]. 94th Cong., 1st sess., May 1973–July 1974. Washington, D.C.: Government Printing Office, 1974.

United States Congress. House Committee on the Judiciary. *FBI Oversight and Authorization Request for Fiscal 1989: Hearings*. 100th Cong., 2d sess. Washington, D.C.: Government Printing Office, 1988.

United States Congress. House. Committee on the Judiciary. *Statement of Information Submitted on Behalf of President Nixon: Hearings Before the Committee on the Judiciary*, 93d Cong., 2d sess., bk. IV. Washington, D.C.: Government Printing Office, 1974.

United States Congress. House. Committee on the Judiciary. *Terrorism: Oversight Hearings Before the Subcommittee on Civil and Constitutional Rights*. 99th Cong., 1st and 2d sess. Washington, D.C.: Government Printing Office, 1987.

United States Congress. House. Select Committee on Assassinations. *Investigation of the Assassination of President John F. Kennedy: Hearings*. Vols. II, IV, XII. Washington, D.C.: Government Printing Office, 1979.

United States Congress. *Joint Hearings Before the House Select Committee to Investigate Covert Arms Transactions with Iran and Senate Select Committee on Secret Military Assistance to Iran and the Nicaraguan Opposition*. Multiple volumes. 100th Cong., 1st sess. Washington, D.C.: Government Printing Office, 1987.

United States Congress. *Report of the Congressional Committees Investigating the Iran-Contra Affair*. Washington, D.C.: Government Printing Office, 1987.

United States Congress. Senate. Committee on Foreign Relations. *Drugs, Law Enforcement and Foreign Policy*. Washington, D.C.: Government Printing Office, 1989.

United States Congress. Senate. Committee on Foreign Relations. *International Terrorism, Insurgency, and Drug Trafficking: Present Trends in Terrorist Activity: Joint Hearings*. 99th Cong., 1st sess. Washington, D.C.: Government Printing Office, 1986.

United States Congress. Senate. Committee on Foreign Relations. *Hearing on the Nomination of Richard Helms as Ambassador to Iran*. Washington, D.C.: Government Printing Office, 1974.

United States Congress. Senate. Committee on Foreign Relations. *The BCCI Affair: Hearings*. 100th Cong., 1st sess. Washington, D.C.: Government Printing Office, 1992.

United States Congress. Senate. Select Committee on Intelligence, *Hearings on S. 2726 to Improve U.S. Counterintelligence Measures* [Jacobs Panel], May 23, 1990, and July 12, 1990. Washington, D.C.: Government Printing Office, 1990.

United States Congress. Senate. Select Committee on Intelligence. *Inquiry into the FBI Investigation of the Committee in Solidarity with the People of El Salvador (CISPES)*. 100th Cong., 2d sess. Washington, D.C.: Government Printing Office, 1989.

United States Congress. Senate. Select Committee on Intelligence. *Meeting the*

Espionage Challenge: A Review of United States Counterintelligence and Security Programs. 99th Cong., 2d sess. Washington, D.C.: Government Printing Office, 1986.

United States Congress. Senate. Select Committee on Intelligence. *Nomination of Richard J. Kerr.* Washington, D.C.: Government Printing Office, 1989.

United States Congress. Senate. Select Committee on Intelligence. *The Intelligence Community's Involvement in the Banca Nazionale del Lavoro Affair.* Staff report distributed by Senate Select Committee on Intelligence, Office of Media Relations, 103d Cong., 1st sess., February 1993.

United States Congress. Senate. Select Committee on Presidential Campaign Activities [Ervin Committee]. *Hearings.* 93d Cong., 1st sess. Washington, D.C.: Government Printing Office, 1973.

United States Congress. Senate. Select Committee to Investigate Government Operations with Respect to Intelligence [Church Committee]. *Interim Report: Alleged Assassination Plots Involving Foreign Leaders.* W. W. Norton, 1976.

United States Congress. Senate. Select Committee to Study Government Operations with Respect to Intelligence [Church Committee], *Hearings: (Vol. II) The Huston Plan; (Vol. IV) Mail Opening.*

United States Congress. Senate. Select Committee to Study Government Operations with Respect to Intelligence [Church Committee]. *Final Report: (Vol. I) Foreign and Military Intelligence; (Vol. II) Intelligence Activities and the Rights of Americans; (Vol. III) Supplementary Detailed Staff Reports on Intelligence and the Rights of Americans; (Vol. V) The Investigation of President Kennedy—Performance of the Intelligence Agencies.* Washington, D.C.: Government Printing Office, 1975–76.

United States Congressional Record. House of Representatives. *Statements by Rep. Henry B. Gonzalez Regarding Banca Nazionale del Lavoro (BNL), February 4, 1991 to September 28, 1992.* Selected and distributed by Office of Rep. Gonzalez, Washington, D.C., January 1993.

Weinraub, Yehuda, and Tony Gadot. "Long-Range Operations in the Israeli Air Force." *Israel Defense Forces Journal,* Spring 1986.

Whitehead, Don. *The FBI Story: A Report to the People.* Random House, 1956.

Wilford, John Noble. "Ruins Yield Tales of Ancient Wars and Spies." *New York Times,* January 5, 1988.

Williams, Robert Chadwell. *Klaus Fuchs, Atom Spy.* Cambridge, Mass.: Harvard University Press, 1987.

Wines, Michael. "The FBI and Russian Agency Thwart a Kidnapping." *New York Times,* January 18, 1992.

Wines, Michael. "French Said to Spy on U.S. Computer Companies." *New York Times,* November 18, 1990, p. 20.

Wines, Michael. "It Was Libya, U.S. Insists." *New York Times,* March 31, 1992.

Wines, Michael. "Jordan Link Reported for Spies Slain in Syria." *New York Times,* March 12, 1990.

Winks, Robin W. *Cloak and Gown: Scholars and the Secret War 1939–1961.* William Morrow, 1987.

Sources

Wise, David. *The American Police State*. Random House, 1974.

Wise, David. "The Felix Bloch Affair." *New York Times Magazine*, May 13, 1990.

Wise, David. *Molehunt*. Random House, 1992.

Wise, David. *The Spy Who Got Away: The Inside Story of Edward Lee Howard, the CIA Agent Who Betrayed His Country's Secrets and Escaped to Moscow*. Random House, 1988.

Wise, David, and Thomas B. Ross. *The Espionage Establishment*. Random House, 1967.

Woodward, Bob. *Veil: The Secret Wars of the CIA 1981–1987*. Simon and Schuster, 1987.

Wright, Peter. *Spycatcher*. Viking, 1987.

Wyden, Peter. *Bay of Pigs: The Untold Story*. Simon and Schuster, 1979.

Zolgin, Richard. "Spooky S&L Stories." *Time*, December 3, 1990, p. 43.

INDEX

ABOUT THE AUTHOR

MARK RIEBLING is editorial director at the Manhattan Institute for Policy Research. He also edits secretpolicy.com, a site devoted to national-security issues. Formerly he was an editor at Random House. He was educated at Dartmouth, Berkeley, and Columbia universities. His writing has appeared in *The New York Times, The Guardian* (London), *The Wall Street Journal,* and *National Review.* He lives in New York City.